RED TAPE

C000145143

Red Tape tells the sometimes astonishing story of the making of laws, both good and bad, the recent explosion in rule making and the failure of repeated attempts to rationalise the statute books – even governments themselves are concerned about the increasing number and complexity of our laws. Society requires the rule of law, but the rule of too much law means that the general public faces frustrating excesses created by overzealous regulators and lawmakers. Robin Ellison reveals the failure of repeated attempts to limit the number and complexity of new laws, and the expansion of regulators. He challenges the legislature to introduce fewer yet better laws and regulators by encouraging lawmakers to adopt practices that improve the efficiency of the law and the lives of everyone. Too much law leads to frustration for all – *Red Tape* is a long overdue exposé of our legal system for practitioners and consumers alike.

ROBIN ELLISON is a solicitor, a consultant with an international law firm, Pinsent Masons, where he specialises in the development of pensions and related financial services products for insurers and other providers, and is the Cass Business School Professor of Pensions Law and Economics, City, University of London. He acts for a number of governments and government agencies and has been an adviser to the House of Commons Select Committee on Work and Pensions.

RED TAPE

Managing Excess in Law, Regulation and the Courts

ROBIN ELLISON

Cass Business School, City, University of London

Pinsent Masons, London

CAMBRIDGE
UNIVERSITY PRESS

CAMBRIDGE
UNIVERSITY PRESS

University Printing House, Cambridge CB2 8BS, United Kingdom

One Liberty Plaza, 20th Floor, New York, NY 10006, USA

477 Williamstown Road, Port Melbourne, VIC 3207, Australia

314–321, 3rd Floor, Plot 3, Splendor Forum, Jasola District Centre, New Delhi - 110025, India

79 Anson Road, #06-04/06, Singapore 079906

Cambridge University Press is part of the University of Cambridge.

It furthers the University's mission by disseminating knowledge in the pursuit of education, learning, and research at the highest international levels of excellence.

www.cambridge.org
Information on this title: www.cambridge.org/9781108426954

DOI: 10.1017/9781108618748

First published 2018

Printed and bound in Great Britain by Clays Ltd, Elcograf S.p.A.

A catalogue record for this publication is available from the British Library

ISBN 978-1-108-42695-4 Hardback
ISBN 978-1-108-44692-1 Paperback

Cambridge University Press has no responsibility for the persistence or accuracy of URLs for external or third-party internet websites referred to in this publication and does not guarantee that any content on such websites is, or will remain, accurate or appropriate.

CONTENTS

FIGURES

TABLES

PREFACE

Between 1989 and 2009, parliament approved over 100 Criminal Justice Bills and more than 4,000 criminal offences were added to the statute book … From an historical context, the figure is more startling: Halsbury's Statutes of England and Wales has five volumes devoted to criminal laws that (however old they may be) are still currently in force.

Volume One covers the law created in the 637 years between 1351 and 1988, and is 1,249 pages long. Volumes Two to Five cover the laws created in the 24 years between 1989 and 2013 and are no less than 4,921 pages long. The 2013 Supplement adds a further 200 pages.

So more than four times as many pages were needed in Halsbury's Statutes to cover laws created in the 24 years between 1989 and 2013 than were needed to cover the laws created in the 637 years prior to that.[1]

This book has been written because, over the years I spent in practice and in academic life as a lawyer working in the UK in the field of company pension plans, my colleagues and I watched in amazement and despair as what was once the most successful system in the world for workplace provision for retirement in sickness and old age was inexorably destroyed mostly (though not solely) through the explosion of well-meaning but counter-productive law and regulation and over-zealous regulators.

When I started as a lawyer in the field in the early 1970s, there were about (depending on how you counted) 100 pages of UK pensions legislation; today, there are close on 160,000 pages, many of which are virtually incomprehensible.[2] One of the regulators' budgets rose eight-fold in 12 years. Legal practitioners in other areas of legal activity – health and

---

[1] The Rt Hon Sir Brian Leveson, *Review of efficiency in criminal proceedings*, Judiciary of England and Wales, January 2015, para. 13.

[2] *Pensions and chocolate: the state of pensions regulation 2017*, Perspective, Pinsent Masons and the Pensions Institute, London, 2017.

safety, employment, crime, tax – and in other jurisdictions make similar observations: all complain about the growth in legislation and the cost and difficulty of complying with it, and its unintended and frequently harmful consequences.

Many of us (in the pensions field at least) did not accept the changes passively; we tried to explain to legislators why not every wrong required a remedy, that regulators could create more problems than they solve and that the best should not be enemy of the good. Nonetheless, a holy combination of the system, the press, the politicians and the times combined to create an oppressive legal framework for pensions which operated tragically to deprive many millions of the possibility of a decent income in retirement.

Through years of negotiating (rather badly) with civil servants and politicians on behalf of the pensions movement, it became clear that the UK in particular and many other countries in general had a pernicious system for the making of law. The question began to be insistently asked about how Western economies managed to get themselves into this destructive mode, when they had mostly a functioning democracy, an honest and trained civil service and a free press.

My experience is not of course unique. Colleagues and friends around the world confirm that regulatory excess is an international problem. This book not unnaturally derives many examples from my own jurisdiction, but its ideas suitably adjusted to suit local circumstances hopefully may well be applied wherever in the world there is a democratic surplus.

It is also important to place the problem into perspective: however dreadful our emancipated systems may be in the production of rules and regulations (and they are), our adherence to the rule of law makes them infinitely preferable to the Russian, Zimbabwean or Afghani systems.

In the meantime, the concerns are difficult to resolve without an analysis of where we are and how we got here. And we need to consider why many of the existing remedies so often fail, and whether there are alternative solutions available. In that analysis it is important to maintain a sense of proportion and balance, to be dispassionate and to allow for example that contrary to popular opinion some things actually work rather well.[3]

---

[3] There are many passionate excoriations of the excesses of the English legal system; see e.g. Proclamations of James 1, 24 September 1610 (see Chapter 6); Charles Dickens, *Bleak House*, 1853; and more recently Richard Deacon, *The truth twisters: disinformation: the making and spreading of official distortions, half truths and lies*, Macdonald, 1986; Simon

But the structures as a whole are often deeply flawed, and whilst politicians and civil servants seem resigned to work within the existing arrangements, the public are increasingly less attracted to the status quo. In due course, if we do not get the balance right – and it is a question of balance – there will be a reduced respect for the law, people will find expensive ways round many of the complexities, politicians and civil servants will find that their jobs become all but impossible and we, the man and woman on the Clapham, Auckland or Vancouver omnibus, will find our lives much diminished.

This is not a pessimistic book. The rule of law is better understood than it used to be (although tarnished in recent years in the UK). And it is encouraging that governments around the world understand that the rule of law includes the rule of not too much law. Few, if any, have managed thus far to find a way in which to curb their own regulatory enthusiasm, but they do occasionally attempt initiatives which have so far been of modest effect. This book explores some lateral ideas which might be adopted to mitigate the impact of regulation and even roll back some of it. The remedies involve less the passing of new laws to stop more laws and more a change of mindset,[4] rather along the lines of the change of mindset in undergraduate binge drinking, or tobacco smoking or drunk driving. The addiction of rule makers to making rules can be treated. But they just need to want to get better.

Hills, *Strictly no! How we're being overrun by the nanny state*, Mainstream, 2006. In the USA, similar frustrations are frequently expressed; see e.g. Philip K. Howard, *The death of common sense*, Time Warner, 1996. Howard subsequently established a specialised think tank and pressure group; see http://commonsense.org.

[4] As the Canadians have done, see e.g. the Red Tape Reduction Act 2015 (*Loi sur la réduction de la paperasse*); Canadian laws are of course inevitably double the length of those of other countries.

ACKNOWLEDGEMENTS

Much of this book is based on a synthesis of the work of others, including academics and the unacknowledged authors of government papers. I have wherever possible given credit to those upon whose work I have relied. To those whom I have failed to acknowledge, my apologies, and, if they let me know, I will make good my negligence in any future edition. I would like to thank in particular my colleagues at Pinsent Masons, who have supported me in this effort; my family, who have missed many holidays because of it; my long-suffering agent, Micheline Steinberg; and for thoughts, comments, notes and advice, Julia Black, David Blake, Chris Cummings, Jay Elwes, Simon Freeman, Philippa Ingram, Nina Jaglom, Daniel Johnson, Con Keating, John Plender, Joshua Rozenberg, Simon Tyler and many others. The team at Cambridge University Press have been brave, supportive and merciful. Errors and omissions are mine alone.

TABLE OF CASES

TABLE OF LEGISLATION

United Kingdom

European Union

International

TABLE OF STATUTORY INSTRUMENTS

ABBREVIATIONS

We need to tackle regulation with vigour to free businesses to compete and create jobs, and give people greater freedom and personal responsibility ... I want us to be the first Government in modern history to leave office having reduced the overall burden of regulation, rather than increasing it.[1]

ABME	Administrative burden measurement exercise
ACUS	Administrative Conference of the United States (US federal agency)
ADR	Alternative Dispute Resolution
AFMA	Australian Fisheries Management Authority (Aus)
AKA	Also known as
ALB	Arm's length bodies
All ER	All England Law Reports
AMLD IV	Anti-Money Laundering Directive IV
AMS	Agricultural Marketing Service (AUS)
APFA	Association of Professional Financial Advisers
API	Application programming interfaces
ARI	Accountability for Regulator Impact
ATE	After-the-event insurance
BBC	British Broadcasting Corporation
BIS	Department for Business Innovation and Skills
BIT	Business impact target
BRDO	Better Regulation Delivery Office (UK)
BRE	Better Regulation Executive (UK)
BRG	Bureaucracy Reduction Group (UK); BRG Bureaucracy Review Group (UK)
BRRD	Regulation Bank Recovery and Resolution Directive
BRTF	Better Regulation Task Force (UK)
BRU	Better Regulation Unit (UK)

[1] David Cameron, UK Prime Minister, letter to all Cabinet Ministers, 6 April 2011, cited in *Better regulation framework manual: practical guidance for UK government officials*, March 2015.

BTE	Before-the-event insurance
BTF	Bureaucracy Task Force (UK)
CAA	Civil Aviation Authority; Clean Air Act
CAPEX	Capital costs
CBA	Cost-benefit analysis
CCA	Cumulative cost assessments
CCD	Common commencement Date
CEA	Cost-effectiveness analysis
CFA	Conditional fee agreements
CGE	Computable general equilibrium
COFEMER	National Regulatory Improvement Commission (Mexico)
CORE	Centre of Regulatory Expertise
CPR	Civil Procedure Rules
CQC	Care Quality Commission
CRD IV/CRR	Capital Requirements Directive IV/Capital Requirements Regulation (EU)
CSDR	Central Securities Depositories Regulation (EU)
DBA	Damages-based agreement
DC	Direct costs; defined contribution
DSGE	Dynamic stochastic general equilibrium models
EANCB	Equivalent annual net cost to business
EC	Enforcement costs
EDS	Economic and Domestic Secretariat (UK)
EFER	Economics for Effective Regulation (FCA) (UK)
ELTIF	Long-Term Investment Funds Regulation
EMIR	European Market Infrastructure Regulation Omnibus II
EU	European Union
EWHC	England and Wales High Court
FCA	Financial Conduct Authority
FOREX	Foreign exchange
FSA	(1) Financial Services Authority (2) Food Standards Authority
FT	*Financial Times*
FTSE	Financial Times Stock Exchange
GAAR	General Anti-Avoidance Rule
GIGO	Garbage in, garbage out
HBOS	Halifax Bank of Scotland
HC	House of Commons
HL	House of Lords (see also Supreme Court, UK)
HMRC	Her Majesty's Revenue and Customs
IA	Impact assessment
IC	Indirect [regulatory] costs
ICA	International Compliance Association

IMD II	Insurance Mediation Directive II
IMPA	Impact assessment
IORP	Institutions for Occupational Retirement Provisions Directive
IPRR	Independent Panel for Regulation and Risk
ITMA	Institute of Trade Mark Attorneys
LIBOR	London inter-bank offered rate
LIP	Litigant in person
LRO	Legislative Reform Order (UK)
LSB	Legal Services Board
MAR	Market Abuse Regulation
MiFID2/MiFIR	Markets in Financial Instruments Directive II /Markets in Financial Instruments Regulation
MMF	Regulation on Money Market Funds
MP	Member of Parliament
NAO	National Audit Office
NDPB	Non-departmental public bodies
NHS LA	National Health Service Litigation Authority
NHS	National Health Service
NICE	National Institute for Health and Care Excellence (UK)
NPRM	Notice of proposed rule making
NPV	Net present value
NY	New York
ODR	Online Dispute Resolution (EU)
OECD	Organisation for Economic Co-operation and Development
Ofcom	Office of Communications (UK)
OFDOGS	Collective name for UK economic regulatory agencies
OFT	Office of Fair Trading (dissolved 2014)
Ofwat	Water Services Regulation Authority
OIOO	One in, one out
OIRA	Office of Information and Regulatory Affairs (US)
OITO	One in, two out (one in, three out) (UK)
OMB	Office of Management and Budget (US)
PAD	Payment Accounts Directive (EU)
PBLR	Pensions Benefits Law Reports
PIAB	Personal Injuries Assessment Board
PIR	Post-implementation review
PLS	Post-legislative scrutiny
PPI	Payment Protection Insurance; Pensions Policy Institute
PRA	Prudential Regulation Authority
PRIIPS	Packaged retail and insurance-based investment products (EU)
PSDII	Payment Services Directive II (EU)

PSPO	Public Spaces Protection Order (UK)
PV	Present value
QC	Queen's Counsel
RCM	Regulatory cost model
REFIT	Regulatory fitness and performance programme (EU)
RIA	Regulatory impact assessment
RIPA	Regulation of Investigatory Powers Act 2000
RIS	Regulatory impact statement
RIU	Regulatory impact unit
ROB	Regulatory oversight bodies
RPC	Regulatory Policy Committee (UK)
RRC	Reducing Regulation Sub-Committee (UK)
RRO	Regulatory Reform Orders (UK) (Regulatory Reform Act 2001)
RSPCA	Royal Society for the Prevention of Cruelty to Animals
RTA	Red Tape Assessment; Regulatory Triage Assessment
RTAW	Red Tape Awareness Week (Canadian Federation of Independent Business)
RTC	Red Tape Challenge
RTRT	Red Tape Reduction Taskforce (Manitoba, Canada)
RTS	Red Tape Scoreboard
SaMBA	Small and micro-business assessment
SCM	Standard cost model (European equivalent of UK RIA)
SEC	Securities and Exchange Commission
SEPA	Single Euro Payments Area
SI	Statutory instrument
SIP	State implementation plan
SLIM	Simpler legislation for the internal market (EU)
SNR	Statement of New Regulation (UK)
SRA	Solicitors Regulation Authority
SRO	Self-regulatory organisation
St Tr	State Trials [law reports]
STC	Simon's Tax Cases
TPO	The Pensions Ombudsman
TPPF	The Pensions Protection Fund
TPR	The Pensions Regulator
UCITS V	Undertakings for Collective Investment in Transferable Securities Directive
UK	United Kingdom
UKSC	United Kingdom Supreme Court
UN	United Nations
UOC	Ultimate outcome of concern

US	United States
WKB	Unit for the quality of regulatory policy (Netherlands)
WLR	Weekly Law Reports
ZNC	Zero net cost

1

Introduction

Laws are like cobwebs, which may catch small flies but let wasps and hornets break through.[1]

1.1 The Challenge of Balance

We all want laws and rules. If we play football, we need the rules of the game. If we drive a car or ride a bike, it can be life-saving to have a High-way Code. If we live in a flat, it is critical to have building regulations to ensure that the risk of the block being engulfed in flame is minimal. We of course need rules and conventions to oil the wheels of social intercourse, to protect the weak against the strong and to limit the need to inquire about everything. In general we can expect that our packaged food does not poison us, or that people do not drive on the road who whilst drunk might kill us or that the washing machine does not electrocute us the first time we load it. Laws (and regulators, a modern form of policeman) can not only protect us but also make our lives easier and save us time and effort.[2] The existence of the rules and of the policemen does not provide a guarantee that we are protected, but it improves our chances of a com-fortable life.[3] We need laws and policemen.

---

[1] Jonathan Swift, *A critical essay upon the faculties of the mind*, 1707 (contributed by John Boyd).

[2] As explored in William Goldman's novel *The lord of the flies*, Faber, 1954.

[3] For a balanced articulation of the dilemmas of regulation, see e.g. speech by Nick Clegg, then UK Deputy Prime Minister, *DPM announces plans to cut red tape for small business*, 25 October 2011, on the DPM website. And for a more dispiriting analysis of regulation, see John Seddon, *The Whitehall effect*, Triarchy Press, 2014, Chapter 14: *Regulation is a disease*, which considers in particular how the vision of the Camphill Village Trust dedicated to supporting people with mental health disabilities was destroyed by well-meaning regu-lation. For an amusing and mostly sensible rant, see Ross Clark, *How to label a goat: the silly rules and regulations that are strangling Britain*, Harrisman House, 2006. A more academic review is Martin Lodge and Kai Wegrich, *Managing regulation: regulatory analysis, politics and policy*, Palgrave Macmillan, 2012.

In modern times we can see very clearly what happens where there are few or inadequate rules. For example, one of the first requirements for the newly liberated Russian state in the 1990s was the introduction of a system of commercial law that would make it easier for trade and industry to prosper. Understandably, Western companies were reluctant to engage in trade with and establish businesses in, and provide capital to, the new Russia unless their interests were protected. There needed to be honest courts where rights could be enforced and a general benchmark of commercial standards under which businesses could trade. All societies need a system of law, and sometimes, as social and economic affairs become more complex and sophisticated, they need a more complex and sophisticated system of law.[4] And in countries, such as Zimbabwe, where the rule of law has all but evaporated, the population dreams of more and better law – or more probably at least a just and effective application of the existing law. The rule of law is a mark of a civilised society.[5]

The question this book attempts to deal with is whether we can have too much of a good thing. Trying to comply with the employment laws (whether employer or employee), or trying to understand the rules for tax relief on pension contributions or trying to organise a school trip whilst complying with the safeguarding and health and safety rules can sometimes feel overwhelming. And there is no doubt that there are many more rules than there used to be, affecting much more of what we do. Few, apart from anarchists, hermits and fundamentalist libertarians, think we can manage without at least some rules, but there seems to be a general consensus that we may have overdone it a touch in recent years. Even the least grumpiest amongst us regale each other with stories about legislative and regulatory excess, some of which may perhaps be urban myth (or *Daily Mail*/Fox News myth) but many of which seem grounded in reality and experience.

---

[4] Navroz Dubash and Bronwen Morgan, *The rise of the regulatory state of the south*, Oxford University Press, 2013, discusses economic regulation in developing countries, two aspects of regulation not covered by this book. For economic regulation generally, there is a vast literature, but see Christopher Decker, *Modern economic regulation*, Cambridge University Press, 2015.

[5] The UK has one of the more robust systems, but see e.g. Tom Bingham, *The rule of law*, Allen Lane, 2010, for a jaundiced analysis of where the state of England and Wales currently is in relation to the rule of law. Lord Bingham was Lord Chief Justice and one of the most admired justices of modern times; the book is both one of the most penetrating analyses of the situation and one of the most readable. It won the 2011 Orwell Prize for literature.

Are we indeed over-regulated? To try to answer this question, it might be sensible to ask some basic questions:[6]

- whether there is in fact an *excess* of regulation, and how we might decide that is the case, and in particular
- whether we need the *quantity* of the rules and regulations that affect us on a daily basis,
- whether the *quality* of the rules that we do need is satisfactory,
- whether the rules sometimes do us *more harm than good*,

and, if rule making is badly implemented,

- whether there is anything that can be done about it, and if so
- what should be done?

While the questions may be simple, the answers are not always easy to find, largely because any legal system depends on balancing the rights and obligations of the individual and society. Getting that balance right is an art, and it is inevitable that sometimes we will get it wrong. The issue is not whether we are in fact getting it wrong but whether we are getting it more wrong than we should.

There are obvious dilemmas (and unintended consequences) in the operation and design of laws and regulations. In some cases what may be bad or unnecessary law to one may be critical to the existence of another. It is not always clear whether law is good or bad, and rather messily, the truth may sometimes lie in the mud of no-man's land.[7]

1.1.1   Good Law

New laws can do an astonishing amount of good, albeit not necessarily always the good intended.[8] For example the UK Protection from

---

[6] Complaints about the legal system are explored in more depth in Chapter 2. And see Jason Hazeley and Joel Morris, *The Ladybird book of red tape*, Michael Joseph, 2016, and Josie Appleton, *Officious: rise of the busybody state*, Zero Books, 2016.

[7] See e.g. the debate in the US in January 2011 about the alleged need to protect copyright which led to a one-day 'strike' by Wikipedia in relation to proposed US legislation SOPA (Stop Online Piracy Act) and PIPA (Protect Intellectual Property Act) (20 January 2012). And see *Over-regulated America: the home of laissez-faire is being suffocated by excessive and badly written regulation*, The Economist, 18 February 2012: 'Every hour spent treating a patient in America creates at least 30 minutes of paperwork, and often a whole hour. Next year the number of federally mandated categories of illness and injury for which hospitals may claim reimbursement will rise from 18,000 to 140,000. There are nine codes relating to injuries caused by parrots, and three relating to burns from flaming water-skis.'

[8] Rory Sutherland, *How good laws change our ways*, Spectator, 19 July 2014: 'Good laws can make a habit easier to adopt by making it universal (the Greek word for "law" – nomis – also

Harassment Act 1997 was introduced to protect women (mostly) from sexual harassment in circumstances where the existing legal protections seemed insufficient. And it seemed to be a useful law for that purpose.

Its use was soon expanded in practice to protect employees in the workplace against bullying – and later to prevent individuals being hassled for money by large corporations whose computers were unable to accept that no money was owed. This later extension was largely the work of one woman, Lisa Ferguson, who ran a small business and who decided to change her gas supplier from British Gas to nPower. She paid her final account with British Gas, but between August 2006 and February 2007, British Gas sent Ms Ferguson bill after bill and threatening letter after threatening letter.

Nothing she could do would stop them. There were three threats: to cut off her gas supply, to start legal proceedings and, a matter most important to her as a businesswoman, to report her to credit-rating agencies. She had written frequently to British Gas, pointing out that she had no account with British Gas, and she had also made numerous fruitless phone calls (with the usual difficulty of getting through). Mainly her letters received no response, although sometimes she received apologies and assurances that the matter would be dealt with.

Meanwhile the bills and threats continued. So she tried other means. She complained to Energy Watch, an official consumer protection body. She wrote to the chairman of British Gas, twice, with no response. Even when her solicitor wrote on her behalf about an unjustified bill in January 2008, no response was received. There seemed little she could do. Then she or her legal advisers had a brainwave.

She issued proceedings in her local court to claim that British Gas's course of conduct amounted to unlawful harassment contrary to the Protection from Harassment Act 1997. She was open about her reason for bringing the proceedings. It was mainly not to claim damages for herself – she said she would give a substantial proportion of any sum awarded to charity.

British Gas were worried; they asked the local judge, before he decided on the merits of the case, to refer the matter to the Court of Appeal to

means "custom" or "social norm").' See also David Colander and Roland Kupers, *Complexity and the art of public policy, solving society's problems from the bottom up*, Princeton University Press, 2014, which explores the case of the German *Reissverschlussverfahren* (traffic zipping), which directs traffic merging where there is a constriction, which is adopted by German drivers but has proved impossible to enforce in the Netherlands, perhaps because of cultural norms.

decide whether the local judge could in fact use the act for this purpose. She succeeded beyond all expectations despite having to face British Gas's impressive legal arsenal and their fragile defence that it was all the fault of the computer.

Of course, the reason that British Gas fought back so strenuously was not only that they would have to expensively upgrade their staff and their computer software to provide a more humane service if she succeeded – and maybe compensate many other similarly aggrieved customers or former customers – but that if they failed to rebut Ms Ferguson's charges, the main board of directors would be vulnerable to criminal convictions for harassment. Harassment under the act is both a civil and criminal offence. If British Gas were convicted of harassment, its directors could face fines, they would be prohibited from travel to the US – and they might even serve short terms of imprisonment.

It is possible that the three judges of the Court of Appeal who allowed Ms Ferguson to pursue her claim had also in their time suffered at the hands of large corporations; Lord Jacobs in one of those Denning-like orations that are nowadays rare in judgments held,

> It is one of the glories of this country that every now and then one of its citizens is prepared to take a stand against the big battalions of government or industry. Such a person is Lisa Ferguson, the claimant in this case. Because she funds the claim out of her personal resources, she does so at considerable risk: were she ultimately to lose she would probably have to pay British Gas's considerable costs.[9]

The Court of Appeal in the end decided that the local judge could indeed use the act to protect Ms Ferguson – but very sensibly, British Gas settled out of court before he had the chance to send the directors to prison. Those who had initially promoted the introduction of the act could never have dreamt that their efforts would be applied in employment cases or to control the practice of major corporations using their disproportionate powers against an individual; indeed, had they anticipated it, it is likely that the act would have been amended to restrict it to non-commercial areas of activity. It is a prime example of the almost inexorable

---

[9] Lord Jacobs in *Ferguson v British Gas Trading Ltd* [2009] EWCA Civ 46, 10 February 2009, para. [1]. The Protection from Harassment Act 1997 was reviewed by the Home Office in 2000 to explore how often it was used – but did not anticipate its use, as in the *Ferguson* case (*An evaluation of the use and effectiveness of the Protection from Harassment Act 1997*, Home Office Research Study 203, 2000).

application of the law of unintended consequences with a (not to British Gas) beneficial ending.

1.1.2 Bad Law

While there are many examples of laws helping people, and righting wrongs or fixing problems, there are also examples of laws which are less successful. Anecdotally (there are few academic studies on the point), many examples of new legislation involve unintended consequences with malign or certainly counter-productive endings.[10] There is any number of serious examples of such legislation. One minor though equally illustrative example is that of government policy on the provision of garages in homes; it partly depends for its impact on an understanding that cars, unlike computers, have added weight over the years. A current MINI is much larger than an original Mini.

In 1999 the government required housebuilders to discourage car ownership by making it difficult to park and in particular by providing undersized garages, not by law but by fiat, a guidance equivalent to law in many respects. In 2009, however, a study by Essex County Council found that 78 per cent of garages were not being used to store vehicles, largely because a trend towards larger cars and 4×4s meant that many did not fit comfortably inside the space. Rather than reducing car usage, the policy turned modern housing developments into obstacle courses for pedestrians and cyclists, who routinely found pavements and cycle paths occupied by cars with nowhere else to park.

In 2009 Essex rejected government requirements and issued its own guidelines that required larger garages and driveways, more parking spaces per dwelling, bigger on-street bays and at least 25 extra spaces for visitors for every 100 homes. The new parking standards were treated as a minimum rather than, as before, a maximum, and developers were made free to offer as many spaces as they believed their customers sought. The minimum was increased to seven metres by three metres (23 feet by 10 feet), as opposed to the former guidance of five metres by two and a half metres – and any home with two or more bedrooms required at least two spaces.

---

[10] See e.g. in relation to the otherwise much-lauded Companies Act 2006 Arad Reisberg, *Corporate law in the UK after recent reforms: the good, the bad and the ugly,* in *Current legal problems,* Oxford University Press, 2011; and Nick Gould, *Common sense – the dark matter of business law,* paper given at University College London, Centre for Commercial Law, February 2011.

The council found that planning guidance issued between 1998 and 2001 had created a severe shortage of spaces in many developments. Families had responded not by giving up their second car but by parking on narrow residential roads, blocking access for emergency services and refuse collection lorries. There were more than one and a half cars per home in 35 per cent of council wards in Essex; nationally, there were more homes with two or more cars than there were homes without a car. Indeed, the proportion of carless households fell from 45 per cent in 1976 to 24 per cent in 2006, while over the same period, the proportion of homes with two or more cars rose from 11 per cent to 32 per cent.

Essex council's then 'Cabinet member for transport', Norman Hume, articulated the dilemma for lawmakers in political-speak: 'This new parking guidance is a radical break from the past failed approach which has seen local communities blighted by parked cars. We are effectively asking people whether we should continue living in neighbourhoods that often have the appearance of disorganised car parks or if instead we should look much more closely at how we accommodate the car to allow a better quality of life for our residents.'[11] The law had been used, in other words, to try to change social behaviour and had failed to respond to the way in which people had worked round it to achieve their own aspirations. The frustration of lawmakers in trying, often hopelessly, to use law to create rather than reflect change is a recurrent theme in many of the recent political memoirs.[12]

---

[11] Ben Webster, *Limit on garage size reversed to bring drivers back off the streets*, The Times, 17 March 2009. Department of Environment, Transport and Regions, *A new deal for transport: better for everyone, 1988*; cf. Essex County Council, *Regional planning guidance 9 and planning policy guidance 13*, March 2001. There was as ever a different view. The Campaign for Better Transport, which promotes alternatives to cars, said that Essex was undermining a decade of work to help people to become less car dependent. Its director, Stephen Joseph, said, 'Essex will create a new generation of car-dominated estates, causing congestion and pollution. In the guise of offering freedom, people will be locked into car dependency. Homes will be too spread out to make good public transport feasible.' He said that Essex should have adopted the approach elsewhere (e.g. in Cambridge and Kent Thameside) where clusters of new homes were being built close to dedicated bus lanes offering fast, regular services. The then 'Cabinet member for planning' in Essex said, 'Whether you like it or not, you have to live with the car. Rationing parking spaces doesn't stop people owning cars, it just means they park where it is most inconvenient for everyone else.' He later explained that Essex was considering reducing the number of people commuting by car by other means, including imposing a charge on workplace parking spaces. Cf. Essex County Council, *Parking standards: design and good practice, Consultation draft*, March 2009.

[12] See e.g. Chris Mullen, *A view from the foothills*, Profile Books, 2009. Sir Michael Barber, an adviser to Tony Blair, operated a theory of deliverology, later much criticised as making

1.1.3   Three Strands of Lawmaking

Assuming that in fact we do have too much law,[13] and assuming too much law can be damaging,[14] it seems helpful to explore first how we make our law. It is handy to look at three main strands of lawmaking, the legislators, the courts and the regulators, and explore the strengths and weaknesses of each of them in separate chapters.

As Bismarck is famously said to have remarked, 'Laws are like sausages. It is better not to see them being made.' But looking at how dysfunctional our system really is may help to explain why long, complex and inappropriate legislation seems to be the norm. In a post-Bismarckian world, it might perhaps be said that law, like chocolate, can be a delight, but too much can make you sick. Indeed, the system is now such that the legal-sugar overload is causing obesity and ill health throughout the legal body politic – and that lawmaking, like sugar, is addictive.

The book treats law and regulation as separate items, and the later individual chapters on both law and regulation seek to explain some differences between the two and the reasons why regulation seems to have expanded even faster than law. So far as the citizen is concerned, there may seem to be little difference, but to the policy maker, it is sometimes easier and less confrontational to have a regulator impose controls than to employ the machinery of central government. In theory, there are also useful philosophical benefits; a regulator can in theory use discretion, rather than black-letter law, to impose more practical and less heavy-handed controls than a prescriptive legal system needs to do. As we shall see, although the theory seems fine, the reality may be somewhat different.

From time to time it is suggested that concerns about excessive rule making are overdone and that, in a complex society, it is inevitable that we will require sophisticated legal structures. This is self-evident, but even establishment bodies are concerned about excess; the 2015 UK Conservative government introduced a Cabinet sub-committee

---

things worse by the management thinker John Seddon; see Barber, *Instruction to deliver: Tony Blair, the public services and the challenge of delivery*, Politico, 2007. It explained that while a Prime Minister could attempt to operate a lever for change, policy would not necessarily respond on the ground.

[13] See Chapter 6 on unregulation, where the assumption is illustrated by a description of government initiatives.

[14] See e.g. Bruce Bartlett, *How excessive government killed ancient Rome* [1994] 14(2) Cato Journal 287; Christine Parker, *The 'compliance' trap: the moral message in responsive regulatory enforcement*, [2006] 40(3) Law & Society Review 591.

dedicated to deregulation, and the UK Law Commission some years ago commented:[15]

> Each year over 10,000 pages of new legislation are introduced either by Acts of Parliament or by orders made under Acts of Parliament. If European directives and regulation are added, the figure is doubled. There is a need to take stock and reflect on the effects of new laws to see if they are working as intended, and if they are not, to discover why. Parliament should be able to address how any problems can be remedied cost-effectively and to learn lessons for the future on the best methods of regulation.

We also need to consider whether the dysfunctionality is fixable, or is merely a necessary evil of a democratic and pluralistic system – and explore some initiatives which may contribute to reform. There is no room for naivety; the inertia of the system, reflected in the difficulty in reforming for example the House of Lords (if it needed reform) shows how difficult it is to achieve reform in such a regulatory culture. Too many political parties either have an interest in the status quo – or are concerned not to expend too much political capital in trying to achieve reform. One possible engine of change is the growing public perception and anger at the

[15] Sir Terence Etherton, Chairman of the Law Commission, *Speech*, 25 October 2006; see also Law Commission, *Post-legislative scrutiny*, Law Com 302, 25 October 2006, Cm 6945, Consultation paper no 178;. cf. Richard Cracknell and Rob Clements, *Acts and statutory instruments: the volume of UK legislation 1950 to 2014*, House of Commons Library, 19 March 2014. And even the judiciary have become exasperated, see e.g. 'Can we possibly have less legislation, particularly in the field of criminal justice. The overwhelming bulk is suffocating. May I take as an example the year 2003. In that year we had criminal statutes with the following titles: Crime (International Co-operation) Act; Anti-Social Behaviour Act; Courts Act; Extradition Act; Sexual Offences Act; Criminal Justice Act. The Crime (International Co-Operation) Act had 96 sections and 6 schedules containing 124 paragraphs. The Anti-Social Behaviour Act had no fewer than 97 sections and 3 schedules containing 8 paragraphs. 97 sections in an Act which is merely making provisions "in connection with anti-social behaviour". The Courts Act contains 112 sections and 10 schedules with 547 paragraphs. The Extradition Act has 227 sections and 4 schedules containing 82 paragraphs. The Sexual Offences Act has 143 sections and 7 schedules with 338 paragraphs. But finally, the great Daddy of them all, the Criminal Justice Act has 339 sections and 38 schedules with a total of 1169 paragraphs. This analysis excludes schedule 37, which sets out no fewer than 20 pages of statutory repeals – and that's not the end of it. No fewer than 21 Commencement and Transitional Savings Orders have been made under this Act – the first in 2003, and the last in 2008. Plenty of provisions have not been brought into force. Many will not be, or so we are told. They will go into some sort of statutory limbo. But this year the Criminal Justice Act 2003 (Commencement No 8) and Transitional and Savings Provisions (Amendment) order of 2009/616 was made, amending the eighth Commencement Order. Each of these orders produced different starting dates for different statutory provisions. All for a single Act.' Lord Judge (formerly Lord Chief Justice) *The Safest Shield*, Bloomsbury, 2015, p. 97.

current arrangements, which may grow to such a stage that the political system will have to recognise it. That time might not be too far away.

There have been innumerable attempts to roll back the regulatory tide, and they have failed. We also need to review some proposals which might over time be adopted by lawmakers to improve the system. The proposals may probably stand little chance of success of early adoption, if at all; but if they influence the debate in some small way, or prompt one or two regulators and legislators to re-think the occasionally absurd pronouncement, or give food for thought to an irritated citizen, they may have achieved their limited purpose. Some of the suggestions may seem facile, flippant, facetious or simply absurd, but they are seriously made.

Finally, there are a few appendices; one sets out a syllabus for a diploma in legislation and regulation which lawmakers and regulators may want to complete before they make decisions that affect the lives of us all.

1.1.4   Balance and Proportionality

Running as a theme throughout the book is the dilemma of achieving balance and proportionality in rule making: easy to agree to as a matter of public policy, but not quite so easy to achieve in practice. Coupled with that rather theoretical or philosophical notion there is another one, its more pragmatic counterpart, and that is the principle of the law of unintended consequences. Many of the laws that are introduced are done so with good intent and by good people but may actually make a problem worse than it already was.[16]

It is of course not simply a British concern; but the issue does seem to affect Anglo-Saxon legal systems such as those of the US, Canada and Australia more than other, more codified, systems. This book looks at a number of trends that affect these societies in particular, but also at the developing countries, who might be thought to be able to avoid the worst excesses of our system. Other countries' experience is brought into account wherever possible (sometimes they do it rather better elsewhere). The discussion however mostly looks at the UK, although there is no doubt that the problem if anything is worse in the US. Whether there is a structural reason that means that the Anglo-Saxon rule making system is afflicted more badly than the Continental system is not clear. When exploring the growth in law, the book looks not just at (in the UK) the

---

[16]   Plato, *Laws*, Penguin 2005.

statutes made by Parliament, but also the subsidiary rules, laws, conventions, guidance notes, regulatory requirements, the impact of interference by regulators and compliance officers, and the influence of not only national bodies but EU and international bodies contributing to international agreements and conventions.

Regardless of whether there is too much, too little or just enough it seemed constructive to first explore why lawmaking is now almost an industry in its own right, and whether this is in some ways a corrupting mechanism, imposing costs and burdens which will allow the fleeter-footed around the world to take advantage of us.

1.1.5 The Scope of the Book: What the Book Covers

In coming disingenuously to its maybe inevitable conclusion the book attempts to be balanced, to avoid polemics, to disentangle urban myth from truth and to distinguish press reports from reality. The reader will judge the success of that ambition. At the same time no discussion of the topic can stay above the fray when it comes to incidental issues, for example the issue of whether the law should reflect morality, or whether the principle underlying a particular law is right or wrong. This book cannot ignore these debates, but it leaves it to others to explore them in depth – there are many distinguished studies on these and other allied concerns.[17] This book concentrates on whether there may be better or less destructive ways of applying public policy than by passing more and longer laws and hiring more regulators.

This book therefore tries to explore how we have arrived at a position where the rules frequently seem to be (or even are) so complicated that few ordinary non-professionals can understand them,[18] so confusing that even expert professionals struggle to interpret them, where the growth seems unending and incessant, where the quantity of change

---

[17] Abortion and homosexuality, and more recently assisted suicide, are issues which have concerned and which involve issues of morality or public acceptability rather than protection of the individual, see e.g. Assisted Dying Bill (HL) 2014 and the debates on its Second Reading in the House of Lords 18 July 2014.

[18] Andy Haldane, Chief Economist, Bank of England, has said: 'To give a personal example, I consider myself moderately financially literate. Yet I confess to not being able to make the remotest sense of pensions. Conversations with countless experts and independent financial advisors have confirmed for me only one thing – that they have no clue either. That is a desperately poor basis for sound financial planning.' *The Great Divide*, speech to the New City Agenda Annual Dinner, 18 May 2016.

seems exhausting, and where the costs of compliance seems overwhelming. Whether we are teachers, health and safety professionals, independent financial advisers, smokers, hunters or child minders, we all have stories to tell. At the same time, we are all consumers who have been badly affected by a malfunctioning product, or cyclists knocked off bicycles by careless drivers, or readers of the *Daily Mail* outraged by most things, and we need a redress. And as consumers or cyclists of course we may feel we need more not fewer rules.

1.1.6   What the Book Does Not Cover

'Regulation' is used in a number of ways by governments and academics. The way it is used in this book is in relation to law, legislation and the activities of regulators and the courts. It does not cover the other sense of regulation, namely the administration of industries so as to ensure for example effective competition in the supply of goods and services, or consumer protection. In some cases the areas overlap in some form of Venn diagram, and are not always necessarily mutually exclusive, but the thrust of the discussion excludes for the most part the economic regulation of particular sectors.[19]

1.1.7   Over-Regulation and Under-Regulation

Before becoming over-indignant at the growth of regulation, it may be useful to try to understand some of the factors that may be leading to the phenomenon. The possible causes mentioned below are not exhaustive, but many involve the perception of loss of control both by individuals and government to world events.

1.1.8   Failures in Society

The usual example of a deep failure in society is war. But no one suggests (apart from international law adherents) that rules can avoid war. The more immediate major failure event has been the Great Recession, and this is touched on below.

More prosaically there are profound concerns expressed in the popular newspapers in slightly less critical yet important matters about which the

---

[19] See e.g. Journal of Regulatory Economics, Journal of Regulation and Governance, Journal of Governance and Regulation etc.

individual has been disempowered. Understandably this feeling of help-lessness is provoked for example by the virtually unconstrained behaviour (and expense) of certificated bailiffs who mostly operated as licensed or unlicensed thugs;[20] or the virtual impossibility of overturning the enforcement of parking tickets by a court in Northampton when the dispute is 100 miles away in Westminster. These are simply the most egregious, notorious and obvious examples.[21] And the behaviour of the billing departments of large companies has already been dealt with above. These are cases in which there are few rules, or the rules that do exist are unenforceable by an individual. For these, or myriad other cases (often involving the imbalance of power between the individual and the state) it is clear that more, or more effective, rules would be welcome if not essential.

1.1.9 Never Again: Financial Services Failures and the Great Recession

The mantra that 'it must never happen again' is one which commonly drives the call for rules. But most experienced regulators and politicians are all too aware, as they utter the cliché, that it absolutely will happen again, whatever they do, although hopefully not on their watch;[22] and they know in their hearts that new rules are not a practical answer, though they may offer short-term political relief.

The recent challenges of the Great Recession, including the behaviour of financial institutions in a chain of failures or perceived failures including the LIBOR scandal, the FOREX scandal, the PPI scandal, the banking collapses of RBS, Lloyds, HBOS, Northern Rock and others, the corporate excesses involving the increasing disparity in pay between senior executives and junior employees, have provoked argument for more intervention rather than less. Meanwhile government grandstanding on tax avoidance/evasion, personal accident claims and earlier instances of

---

[20] There is supposed to be a government register of bailiffs on the Ministry of Justice/government website, so that individuals can check whether someone who says he is a bailiff is one. At the time of writing it is not operative even if it does exist.

[21] See e.g. Zacchaeus 2000 Trust, www.z2k.org. Zacchaeus is involved in remedying the causes of poverty and in particular helps people living on benefit or low incomes gain to access justice when they face claims for debt or fines, one of the great injustices of the present civil, and civil fines, debt system with, in effect, unregulated debt collecting. See also www.manifestoclub.com. Hastings Council was required to pay £1,000 for failing to call off bailiffs enforcing a rescinded £30 parking ticket, David Millward, *Motorist in parking fine blunder wins £1,000 for stress*, Daily Telegraph, 21 May 2009.

[22] See e.g. the proceedings of the House of Commons Public Accounts Committee under the chairmanship of Margaret Hodge in the 2000–2015 Parliament.

personal pensions mis-selling, the Equitable Life collapse, the failures of Merrill Lynch, Lehman Brothers, ABN-Amro and other financial institutions, and the pensions scams many of which emerged following the introduction of 'pension freedoms', i.e. the ability to take pension in cash rather than annuity form,[23] has argued that failures lie partly at the feet of deregulation or light-touch regulation.[24]

These experiences have understandably led to calls for heavier regulation, not lighter. And governments have responded; they have detonated an explosion of European regulation most notably in financial services (around 60,000 pages) and in the equivalent Dodds Frank legislation in the US (around 32,000 pages) intended to avoid future failures.[25]

---

[23] See www.thepensionsregulator.gov.uk/pension-scams.aspx and www.gov.uk/government /consultations/pension-scams/pensions-scams-consultation with virtually unworkable protections.

[24] By March 2015 the European Union as a consequence largely of the Great Recession had promoted regulation of financial services in Solvency II (insurance companies), Single Euro Payments Area (SEPA), European Market Infrastructure Regulation (EMIR), Omnibus II, Alternative Dispute Resolution Directive / Online Dispute Resolution regulation, Mortgage Credit Directive (CARRP), Capital Requirements Directive IV / Regulation (CRD IV/CRR), Transparency Directive II, Accounting Directive, Markets in Financial Instruments Directive II and Regulation (MiFID2/MiFIR), Market Abuse Regulation (MAR), Credit Ratings Agencies Regulation, Audit Regulation and Directive, Venture Capital Funds and Social Entrepreneurship Funds Audit Regulation and Directive, Revised Data Protection Directive and Regulation, Ventral Securities Depositories Regulation (CSDR), Bank Recovery and Resolution Directive (BRRD), Packaged Retail and Insurance-based Investment Products (PRIIPS), Insurance Mediation Directive II (IMD II), Undertakings for Collective Investment in Transferable Securities Directive (UCITS V), Anti-Money Laundering Directive IV (AMLD IV), Wire Transfer Regulation, Payment Accounts Directive (PAD), Regulation on Interchange Fees, Long term Investment Funds Regulation (ELTIF), Payment Services Directive II (PSD II), Regulation on Money Market Funds (MMF), EU Benchmarks Regulation, Bank Structural Reform Regulation, reporting and Transparency of Securities Financing Transactions Regulation, Institutions for Occupational Retirement Provisions Directive (IORP), Revised Shareholders Rights Directive, Review of the Prospectus Directive. See Timothy Edmonds, *Financial Services: European aspects*, House of Commons Library, Briefing Paper 07435, 17 December 2015. It was reported that MiFID II alone involved 1.4M paragraphs at launch, with more expected, Hannah Murphy and Madison Marriage, *Fund managers face $1M bills for research: At least 1.4m paragraphs of rules and more on the way*, Financial Times, 25 July 2017.

[25] Andy Haldane, *The dog and the Frisbee*, Bank of England, 31 August 2012. There is a history of failed financial services regulation (dating back to the Bubble Act 1720, which lasted for 105 years until the then Attorney General said its meaning and effect were altogether unintelligible) in New City Agenda, *Cultural change in the FCA, PRA and Bank of England: practicing what they preach*, 2016.

1.1.10   An International Issue

As will be seen Chapter 6 on the attempts at deregulation, the concern about over-regulation is a worldwide one:

> While most Italians might remain unaffected by crime and corruption, few were able to circumvent the obstacles set up by a slow, cumbersome and extremely inefficient bureaucracy. Even a minister for the civil service once admitted that Italians wasted between fifteen and twenty days a year simply trying to cope with the problems it caused. The tax system was so compli-cated and confusing that citizens often found it difficult to calculate even roughly how much they might have to pay. Nor was it easy to navigate the nation's legal system because, according to different reckonings, Italy had between five and twelve times as many laws as France or Germany. The law was perhaps the most frustrating of all aspects of Italian life. In the late 1990s it was estimated there were 2 million criminal cases and 3 mil-lion civil cases pending, and the figure had apparently risen to a total of 9 million early in the next century. It is not surprising, then, that most civil cases are abandoned, four out of five crimes have gone unpunished and, even when a guilty verdict has been returned, the convicted in non-violent cases could spend an average of eight years at liberty before being in danger of going to prison.[26]

1.2   Why Is There So Much Law?

1.2.1   Introduction

There seems little doubt therefore that the common perception, that there has been an absolute growth in the quantity of law (including regulation and other analogues) over the last few decades, is correct. Before we exam-ine whether that growth has been proportionate or justified, it might be worth exploring first some of the possible drivers of that growth.

There seem to be several factors. These perhaps include:

- the use of law as a solution in place of other solutions
- the use of law as a placebo
- the rise of consumerism
- the change in role of legislators
- the influence of the press
- the cultural move away from trust to regulation

---

[26] David Gilmour, *The pursuit of Italy*, Penguin, 2012.

No doubt there may be other causes, but these may do as a starting point.

1.2.2   Using Law as a Social Instrument

Mark Twain and others have had attributed to them the observation that to a man with a hammer, every problem is a nail. To legislators it does sometimes appear that every social problem requires a specific piece of legislation to manage it, even if common sense would suggest that there may be other and better methods of social engineering, or that there indeed might be existing laws (which are not being applied for some reason) to cope with the problem. The next few pages explore whether law is the solution to the problem in many cases – and why despite adverse experience to the contrary it is so often used instead as an alternative remedy.

On the other hand, many of us would still like the law to fix problems which immediately concern them (my vote would be the immediate destruction of any domestic animal that fouled the footpath, which would affect the lifestyle of a famous polemical playwright neighbour of mine).[27]

We all want some things, and reject others, sometimes at the same time; or we have a nimby approach (I want a high speed train from London to the north [or from the north to London], but not if it passes my backyard). A useful game might be to tick some of the items in the following list to establish how interventionist you are (Table 1.1).

It may be therefore that we are using law where other solutions to social problems may be available. Libertarians (not all of whom are as extreme as the Tea Party in the US) consider that the use of the law should be as minimal as possible; other political views (which can curiously be on the right, witness Michael Heseltine a former Conservative politician who famously promised to intervene before breakfast if he thought it wise to do so) suggest that only the state or regulation can solve a particular social problem.

Law can be (and is) used therefore to make a statement (as in equal treatment or race relations or dangerous dogs) or as an economic tool, rather than simply to enforce rights, or remedy a wrong. The clearest examples are those used to enforce prohibition, most famously of alcohol consumption in the US from 1917 onwards until 1933, and in other areas most notably of narcotics since 1909.[28] Such examples had had a mixed

---

[27] Sir David Hare walks his dog daily past my house, against whose wall it regularly micturates.

[28] The astonishing pointlessness and counter-productiveness of prohibition in several areas has been explored in numberless books and studies, with little political effect; see e.g.

Table 1.1 *Am I a secret nanny?*

Do I believe in . . .

Public health interventions
- disease surveillance
- quarantines
- mandatory or government-subsidised vaccination
- food labelling regulations
- school lunch programmes
- sugar controls

Consumer protectionism that enforces (or discourages) certain behaviours
- Bicycle and motorcycle helmet laws
- Anti-smoking laws
- Speed limits on roads
- Bans on texting and other laws seen by some as interfering in personal choices and/or personal privacy

Creation and enforcement of laws that prohibit victimless crimes
- Gun control
- Building codes
- Prohibitions on drug use and dealing, gambling and prostitution

National economic and social policies (regulation and intervention)
- International trade policies

Moral, ethical or religious issues
- Adultery (e.g. whether it should affect the distribution of assets on divorce)
- Abortion
- Assisted suicide/euthanasia

---

outcome, with most independent observers concluding that on balance they do more harm than good, despite the benign intentions of the promoters. There seems little information on whether legislation that 'sends a signal' might achieve some benefit without a concomitant adverse consequence, for example in matters involving behaviour to others, and it seems probable that some other areas of prohibition, such as possession of firearms, does indeed have beneficial effect, but the evidence is even there mixed, and may have more to do with cultural issues than with legislation. In firearms control for example there is no doubt that deaths from

Christopher Snowdon, *The art of suppression: pleasure, panic and prohibition since 1800*, Little Dice, 2011 and David Nutt, *Drugs - Without the Hot Air: Minimising the Harms of Legal and Illegal Drugs*, UIT Cambridge, 2012. See also notes 53 and 67.

firearms are high in the US where control is weak, and low in the UK where controls are strict – but they are equally low in Switzerland where guns are endemic.[29] Some observers consider the UK is one of the more regulated states, using an index of the best and worst places in the EU to drink, eat, smoke and vape; it puts Britain at the number three spot as 'the most meddling country' in the EU, just behind Finland and Sweden.[30] The survey suggested that although paternalistic laws are often said to be justified on health grounds, analysis of the figures found no link between nanny state regulation and longer life expectancy. It reported that countries with heavy regulation of alcohol do not have lower rates of drinking, and countries with heavy regulation of tobacco do not have lower rates of smoking (Table 1.2).

1.2.3   The Rise of Consumerism

For you and me (for want of a better word, now usefully described as consumers) daily life is incontrovertibly more complicated than it used to be in say Dickens' time. For example, in times where villagers popped into the local market on a Thursday to buy some fruit or vegetables they could feel, prod and smell the product. They could argue with the vendor, who might also have been the grower. If they had a bad deal, the next week they could visit another supplier. And because word of mouth was quicker in a small community, the pressure of peer groups or buyers to improve quality or ensure safety was more effective.[31]

---

[29] Cf John Lott, *More Guns, Less Crime*, University of Chicago Press; 3rd rev. edn (24 May 2010), ISBN-13: 978-0226493664 which attempts to show that free availability of guns reduces crime; a more balanced study is David Kopel, *International Perspectives on Gun Control*, [1995] 15 NYL Sch. J Int'l & Comp L 247.

[30] Institute of Economic Affairs, *2016 Nanny State Index*, IEA and European Policy Information Centre, 30 March 2016. The study gave every EU country a score out of 100 according to how it regulated private lifestyle choices: 'Finland is the EU's number one nanny state thanks to its taxes on chocolate, soft drinks, alcohol and tobacco. Finland also has an outright ban on e-cigarettes, a ban on happy hours and heavy restrictions on advertising. The UK has the highest rates of tax on wine and cigarettes in the EU. Its beer duty is second only to Finland and its smoking ban is more draconian than any other member state. In total, it ranks first for tobacco, fourth for alcohol and seventh for food and soft drinks. Britain takes a more liberal approach to e-cigarettes, however, giving it a final ranking of third. See Christopher Snowdon, *various works*, Institute of Economic Affairs and see nannystateindex.org; cf. US site www.nannystate.com.

[31] Although the internet may now have re-invented the community or enhanced consumer protection.

Table 1.2 *The Freedom Index 2016*

	Country	E-Cigs	Tobacco	Food	Alcohol	Total
1	Finland	8.3	10.7	5.7	29.0	53.7
2	Sweden	8.3	6.0	1.0	25.3	40.6
3	UK	0	15.0	2.0	18.0	35.0
4	Ireland	0	11.8	2.3	20.3	34.4
5	Hungary	8.3	10.2	8.7	6.0	33.2
6	Greece	12.2	11.0	1.3	7.0	31.5
7	Lithuania	9.8	8.2	2.3	10.7	31.0
8	Malta	7.3	8.2	0	11.3	26.8
9	France	0	10.7	3.3	12.7	26.7
10	Belgium	11.8	8.2	2.0	4.3	26.3
11	Latvia	3.8	10.0	0	12.3	26.1
12	Denmark	8.3	6.8	2.7	7.0	24.8
13	Estonia	4.0	7.7	0	11.3	23.0
14	Croatia	4.3	10.2	0	7.7	22.2
15	Poland	0	8.7	0.7	11.3	20.7
16	Slovenia	0	8.3	1.3	10.3	19.9
17	Italy	1.7	7.3	0.7	7.3	17.0
18	Cyprus	0	9.3	0	6.7	16.0
19	Romania	0	9.0	0	7.0	16.0
20	Portugal	4.8	6.5	0.7	4.0	16.0
21	Spain	4.3	8.7	0	2.7	15.7
22	Bulgaria	0	9.8	0	4.7	14.5
23	Austria	0	5.5	0.7	8.0	14.2
24	Slovakia	1.7	7.5	0	4.3	13.5
25	Netherlands	1.7	6.8	0	4.7	13.2
26	Luxembourg	0	5.3	0	5.3	10.6
27	Germany	0	5.3	0	3.7	9.0
28	Czech Republic	0	4.5	0	4.3	8.8

Shading key: Dark grey, least free; mid-grey, less free; light grey, freer; white, freest.

But as we begin to live in larger communities, it becomes more difficult. One example is the increasing power of the supermarkets over our
lives. They now supply over 80 per cent of groceries in the UK for example and there are only around five such groups. In theory, if they grew too
powerful, they could agree, or might find it easier to agree, to have less
competition, or to squeeze suppliers unfairly or to exploit their monopoly
power against the consumer. It might be increasingly difficult for fresh

competition to arise; the incumbents do not face in the same way for example the planning restrictions which make it difficult to open new supermarkets. And marketing and advertising costs make it difficult for new entrants, as does predatory pricing (reducing prices just long enough to drive new companies out of business).

In 2003 for example there was a bid for the Safeway supermarket chain, by a number of competitors, and at a time when there were relatively few supermarket groups in the UK. But deciding whether one chain can buy another can involve drawing delicate balances. The decision was made in the UK by the Competition Commission (now Competition and Markets Authority) which needed to ensure that, with adequate competition, prices could be consumer-friendly. But even the Commission faced dilemmas in deciding what was fair. The Competition Commission defined a supermarket as a one-stop grocery store of 1400 sq m or more – so should it have ignored other products such as clothing, electrical goods or petrol?[32] It was supposed to look at local competition which it regarded as within a 10 minute drive in urban areas and 15 minutes in other areas. But with poorer public transport and changing populations was that still right? Excessive market share is not a problem only for consumers – but excessive dominance can wreak havoc on producers, as farmers continually complain. If there are only three or four major customers for milk, a dairy farmer has little bargaining power with his customers. Supermarkets are a concern for regulators – but whether regulation is the right way to manage competition is not a settled matter – and raises as many problems as it is supposed to solve. Should competition be managed on a local, regional, national, European or global scale? And how should it respond to changes in patterns of shopping (for instance I bought my new printer memory from America at 10 per cent of the cost of buying it from a UK retailer, where any protection I may have had would in practice be only through my credit card company)? Control of competition is essential in a capitalist economy. But deciding what the rules should be can be challenging.

1.2.4   The Rise of Consumer Expectations

In the meantime the expectations of the consumer have also risen. Consumers in Western societies are less prepared to accept the cavalier

---

[32] Competition Commission, *Safeway plc and ASDA Group Limited (owned by Wal-Mart Stores Inc); Wm Morrison Supermarkets PLC; J. Sainsbury plc; and Tesco plc: A report on the mergers in contemplation*, 2003, www.competitioncommission.org.uk/rep_pub/reports/2003/481safeway.htm#full

behaviour of large companies such as BA or Heathrow Airport, or the lengthy waiting periods to speak to a major bank on the phone, and where the call centre operatives are unempowered to resolve issues, or uncaring civil servants in the DWP or HMRC, or where regulators such as the Financial Conduct Authority or the Pensions Regulator do not put direct contact details of their senior officials on their website.[33]

These changed expectations mean that if things go wrong, there is pressure for someone to establish an organisation to ensure that it can never happen again. This is explored later on in the discussion of the role of the media and politicians, but there is a common belief that a regulator or a politician or a government can and will prevent unacceptable behaviour. Western cultures understandably expect higher standards of behaviour by firms and governments, there is less acceptance of a fatalistic approach (things do *not* just happen), and the public and the press has a poor understanding of risk.[34] Some blame this on what has been called the growth of the 'nanny state'.[35] When politicians and the press deliver calls that all forms of affliction should be remedied, they may eventually wish to bear in mind that lawyers have long been taught that not every wrong has (or should have) a remedy.[36]

Proportionality: Not Always the Regulators' Fault

As you are aware our new computer system rounds to four decimal places, rather than two. In some circumstances this can give rise to a difference of 1p, or exceptionally 2p.[37]

We recognise that the result of the calculations, depending on whether one rounds to two decimal places or to four, will often be the same and will never be more than a few pence...In the context however, that difference matters...It has long been taken by administrators to be a fundamental requirement that Guaranteed Minimum Pension calculations reconcile to the penny with the amounts calculated by your systems. So, by the time you received a limited number of queries about differences of a few pence,

---

[33] Or even EasyJet; tried flying from Luton Airport on an early morning flight recently?

[34] See e.g. Barry Glassner, *The culture of fear: why Americans are afraid of the wrong things: crime, drugs, minorities, teen moms, killer kids, mutant microbes, plane crashes, roads rages and so much more*, Basic Books, 2009. Cf Mary Douglas and Aaron Wildavsky, *Risk and Culture*, University of California, 1983.

[35] The term 'nanny state' has many claimed parents; it was probably coined by the Conservative MP Iain Macleod who referred to 'what I like to call the nanny state' in his column 'Quoodle' in the December 31, 1965, edition of The Spectator.

[36] There is a principle of law that where there is a right, there is a remedy (*ubi jus, ibi remedium*). But courts will not listen to complaints about trivial matters or immoral acts.

[37] Letter from Inland Revenue to Society of Pension Consultants, 10 October 2002.

> hugely disproportionate expense would have been incurred by those who
> contacted you in trying to reconcile slightly differing amounts they had
> calculated, in the belief that you were still rounding to two decimal places.[38]

Some individuals feel that there need to be laws to protect them against the use or abuse of discretions (for example by doctors and nurses and families in the case of assisted deaths). In fact it may be for the best that some things are left to the discretion of the authorities; it is not always possible to reduce to writing the circumstances in which assisted death is appropriate in another country and so far in the UK the authorities have where appropriate turned a blind eye. The use of the blind eye (or the use of the disapproving eyebrow, as in the control of UK banks until 1997 by the Governor of the Bank of England, mentioned below) has been much misunderstood because of the fear of misuse or abuse. The question again is whether the abuse of legalism is better or worse than the abuse of discretion,[39] or whether the wider use of eyebrows would be preferable.[40]

1.2.5   The Need for External Protection

As mentioned, products and services are now complicated and an ordinary person could not be expected to know whether a car is safe to drive, an electrical product is safe to use or a can of beans is fit to eat. The purity of the *caveat emptor* principle (i.e. 'let the buyer beware') has been diminished in the UK since the late nineteenth century, when it was argued that the balance of power between consumer and producer was unfairly to the benefit of the producer in an industrialised economy.[41]

The difficulty is trying to find the balance between protection and the anarchy of the Wild West. If someone buys a car which is fine for a single man or woman, but not for a family, should the car salesman be blamed for not explaining that the car will not hold more than one passenger? In some cases the consumer will need to be assumed to know something about life – or be able to use the internet or the press to find out about the suitability of products or services. In other cases proportionality must

---

[38] Letter from Society of Pension Consultants to Inland Revenue, 5 December 2002.

[39] Matthew Parris, *The Governor's eyebrow should trump the law*, The Times, 21 March 2009.

[40] See e.g. Sir Keir Starmer, then Director for Public Prosecutions, *Policy for Prosecutors in Respect of Cases of Encouraging or Assisting Suicide*, Crown Prosecution Service, February 2010, updated October 2014.

[41] See e.g. Sale of Goods Act 1893; and later extended in every law student's favourite case of the 'snail in the ginger beer bottle', *Donoghue v Stevenson*, [1932] UKHL 100 where the court developed the concept of product liability.

come in; if a film is boring is there a right to sue for waste of time and a return of the ticket price? We all draw the line somewhere. But regulators find that hard to do,[42] although the judiciary seem recently to have insisted on an increasing duty of care by consumers.[43]

1.2.6   The Decline of Trust and Discretion

Allied to the perceived need by governments to reduce discretion and increase rules is the destruction of trust in society. One of the reasons for the growth of prescription has been a distrust by government of, for example, self-regulation by the professions (e.g. the actuaries or the solicitors)[44] or even by the doctors. Whenever there is a failure of the exercise of trust, and the nature of trust predicates there will be occasional failures, there is a call for regulation to prevent it happening again;[45] whether it will, or at a reasonable cost in resources, is not always clear. In practice, whatever the strength of legal protection, we none of us have a choice but to place trust

---

[42] LCB Gower, *Review of Investor Protection*, Report Part 1, Cmnd 9125, January 1984, para 1.16 suggested that consumers should remain liable for their own foolishness, but should not be misled or stolen from. That recommendation has not been adopted by modern regulators such as the Financial Conduct Authority, which has disbanded the concept of caveat emptor to levels not anticipated or recommended by Professor Gower, upon whose report current UK financial services legislation is based.

[43] Compare for example the US case on hot coffee injuries (*Liebeck v McDonald's Restaurants*, 18 August 1994, Bernalillio County NM Dist Ct, 1995 WL 360309) where the court awarded $640,000 damages on appeal, with the English approach to hot tea injuries (*Bogle v McDonald's Restaurants* [2002] EWHC 490), where the action was dismissed. And see the dismissed complaints in *Worsley v Tambrands Limited* [1999] EWHC 273 QB (toxic shock from a tampon), *Richardson v LRC Products Limited* [2000] 59 BMLR 185 (split condom), *Foster v Biosil* [2001] 59 BMLR 178 (ruptured breast implant), *XYZ v Schering Health Care* [2002] EWHC 1420 (contraceptive pill side effects), *TESCO Stores v Pollock* [2006] EWCA Civ 393 (child resistant bottle not child proof).

[44] See e.g. *Morris Review of the Actuarial Profession*, HM Treasury, 16 March 2005, ISBN 1-84532-089-1; and see Sir David Clementi, *Review of the regulatory framework for legal services in England and Wales*, December 2004.

[45] See e.g. Dame Janet Smith DBE, *Shipman, The Final Report*, 27 January 2005, www.the-shipman-inquiry.org.uk. Although Dame Janet seems to refrain from using the phrase 'never again' the temptation was too great for politicians (see e.g. Chris McCafferty, Labour MP for Calder Valley, Hansard, Commons, 21 June 2007, Column 522WH). Harold Shipman was a doctor who probably killed around 250 of his patients and became almost certainly the greatest mass murderer in English history. See also R. Baker, *Harold Shipman: The Aftermath, Implications of Harold Shipman for general practice*, [2004] 80 Postgraduate Medical Journal 303–306. The unintended consequences were described in a tragic story in the *Times* (Sam Lister, *How one petty complaint put GP in disciplinary agony for seven years*, The Times, 17 April 2009 and Dr Mark Porter, *Pendulum has swung too far after Shipman*, ibid).

somewhere, whether in our local doctor, or our lawyer or our neighbours or family. Day-to-day life is simply impractical unless we trust others to do their job properly and exercise their judgment in a sensible and proportionate way. From time to time we will be let down; individuals will fail to deliver to the standards required or machines will fail, but we have no choice if we need to carry on our daily life. The risks are usually quite small, but there are risks. The alternative however seems to involve a great deal more rules and prescription, and later chapters explore the balance between trust and law, and suggests that we may have no alternative but to leave certain issues to trust.[46]

A similar argument is put forward to encourage a reduction in prescription and a growth in the exercise of discretion by those who should know. In the UK this applied (it is said) when banks found themselves slightly stretched; the Governor of the Bank of England would have a cup of tea with the errant bank and change its direction with a gentle raising of the eyebrow. There is probably some truth to this, and it made for an orderly market (usually), and a low-key solution out of the public eye. There are downsides to such an approach; more junior officials would or could adopt a jobsworth response to initiatives or novel products or services, and it is this fear, that the official would be officious, that has led the rulemakers to suggest that a more formal legal structure would be preferable. And as one who has suffered from rather graceless and self-interested regulation and regulators, I am rather sympathetic to this view. For it to work well it needs respected and sensible officials, and they are not always available, and indigenous peer pressure is less operative in a globalised market. But, in any event, even prescriptive law inevitably eventually involves the use of discretion; the question seems to be at what level it is exercised. Systems which use discretion benefit from it being used at a senior level, reducing the need for the involvement of more junior, inexperienced and hesitant officials. Lawyers find it harder to game the system but need to understand how regulators think.[47] Its use of course requires an acceptance of

---

[46] Onora O'Neill, *A question of trust*, BBC Radio 4, Reith lectures 2002 (www.bbc.co.uk/radio4/reith2002), lecture 4 ('*Trust and transparency*') published by Cambridge University Press, 2002; cf. Michael Power, *The audit society: rituals of verification*, Oxford University Press, 1999; Marek Kohn, *Trust: self-interest and the common good*, Oxford University Press, 2008. See also Phillip Blond et al., *In professions we trust: fostering virtuous practitioners in teaching, law and medicine*, ResPublica, July 2015.

[47] See e.g. the work of Graham Aaronson, in HMRC, *General Anti-Abuse Rule (GAAR) Advisory Panel, terms of reference*, May 2013; the (virtually) unaccountable GAAR panel is a creature of HMRC and decides whether transactions which are designed to mitigate tax

deference, a quality which may be in less supply than before, especially where national and social boundaries are less effective than they used to be, and where regulators have abused the use of their discretion.[48]

1.2.7 The Role of the Press

Press and media attention can in many cases hound dangerous plumbers and electricians out of business. But often they fixate on some wrong (often a genuine wrong) and impose pressure on regulators and government to do something, even if it is not quite clear what. There are many such pointless calls which have produced small government disasters; the Child Support Agency (and its successors) is one well-known example, but there are many others. The life expectancy of a quango designed to fix a particular ill is rather short.[49]

The press of course does not have to pay for the creation of a new law and its enforcement – and they do not carry out a risk/reward assessment. Balance is not part of the news agenda even in the broadsheets. While the press complain about over-regulation, especially of themselves,[50] they show little shame about calling for more of it, despite evidence suggesting that the regulation might be ineffective, disproportionate, excessively costly or even counter-productive.[51] The role of the printed media in

are effective and acceptable. And see attempts at tort law reform in the United States which have been generally regarded as having failed (see *Halliburton* decision in the US Supreme Court, 2014 573 US ___ (2014) (23 June 2014).

[48] Especially notable in financial services, see the extensive debate on cross-border financial regulation since 2008. There are international standards on regulation, but the impact of the application of their principles is uncertain, see e.g. *OECD framework for regulatory policy evaluation*, OECD, Paris, 2014.

[49] Look for example at the history of the Child Support Agency, below.

[50] See e.g. *Say no to state regulation of the press*, Leader, The Times, 23 October 2016; cf. Independent Press Standards Organisation (www.ipso.co.uk/) and Press Recognition Panel (http://pressrecognitionpanel.org.uk/) in the UK, and Crime and Courts Act s40 (not implemented).

[51] See e.g. *Daily Mail* seriatim; The Child Maintenance and Enforcement Commission took responsibility for the Child Support Agency in November 2008 following its widely reported failure, see e.g. Andrew Woodcock, *Child Support Agency chief quits as criticism mounts*, Independent, 17 November 2004: 'The chief executive of the Child Support Agency has resigned following widespread criticism of the organisation's record in getting cash to single mothers, it was revealed today. Work and Pensions Secretary Alan Johnson announced Doug Smith's resignation as he gave evidence to the House Of Commons Work and Pensions Committee this morning. The committee's chairman Sir Archy Kirkwood was highly critical of the agency's performance, which he said has caused unnecessary suffering to many single parents, particularly because of long-running problems with

public excoriation will diminish in future years, as circulations decline; the lynch-mob views expressed through the social media seems in practice to be much less effective.

1.2.8   The Aspirations and Role of Politicians

There is little doubt that part of the pressure to expand the statute book is driven by the ambitions of politicians. Some see little honour in being a glorified social worker, and seek to make their mark on the world by changing things for what they see as the better. One study of the political animal pointed out:[52]

> Where did they all come from, this extraordinary breed? Once upon a time they must have been normal. Can they really have sprung from their mother's wombs full of doctrinaire certainties? Confronted by their mother with a plate of mashed banana at the age of two, did they exclaim, 'I congratulate the honourable lady on her choice of acceptable food for an infant. She will no doubt be aware of the vital importance of the banana trade to many member states of the Commonwealth. And will she join with me in protesting at the American government's attempt to force the World Trade Organisation to capitulate to the interests of the American banana growers who provide such enormous donations to the Republican presidential campaign.' From some political memoirs, you might think they did.
>
> In a strict sense, politicians are not like the rest of us. Whether they have been driven into political careers by a simple desire to represent their community in Parliament or, like Margaret Thatcher, from a conviction that they alone could save their country, wielding power is essential. Mercifully, the proportion of people in any society who wish to tell everyone else what to do is limited. If it were not so, the country would be ungovernable.

The drive by politicians to add to the statute book is perhaps inevitable; they need to make a mark on society rather like a dog on a tree. Politicians are approached by pressure groups, by governments and by civil servants who suggest that if they tweaked the law here or redrafted it there, life for the rest of us could be immeasurably improved. But they know

its computer system. Mr Johnson told the committee: "Doug has decided that now is the time to stand aside. He believes we have reached a natural breakpoint at which to hand over the reins".'

[52] Jeremy Paxman, *The political animal: an anatomy*, Penguin, 2003, ISBN 978-0-140-28847-6, p1; a famous interview where a Home Secretary refused 19 times to answer a question posed by Jeremy Paxman is at www.youtube.com/watch?v=BkIT7Qy071s. Jeremy Paxman is a British television current affairs journalist and presenter whose interviewing technique in relation to politicians is reported as 'I ask myself, Why is this lying bastard lying to me?'. Cynicism is a significant driver of increased regulation, but not further explored categorically in this book.

intellectually if not emotionally that actually there may be unexpected consequences to any new law, and that what may often be needed is less a law to fix the problem than a change in the conduct of society (e.g. a reduction in binge drinking) – and which a law, even if it simply 'sends a signal', often cannot achieve or even influence. Law may indeed send a signal, as for example in equal treatment or non-discrimination, but experience suggests it is usually a blunt instrument which may have a different result from that intended. Some of the anti-gender-discrimination legislation intended to improve conditions for women has for example had the perverse consequence of improving conditions for men.[53]

And, as mentioned, politicians also often feel that things need to be put into legislation rather than be left to the discretion of others. This is a permanent tension between the adherents of the use of discretion and the adherents of prescription.[54] For example, there is continuing angst about whether there should be dedicated legislation to deal with the issue of assisted suicide, or whether the prosecuting authorities should be given the discretion to make decisions which are hard to reduce to a code of rules, as to whether to prosecute individuals who assist other to commit suicide to inherit money or to reduce the suffering of their spouse.[55] The book later looks at a series of suggestions on how to curb politicians' enthusiasm for reform through law.

1.2.9   Laws of Taste, Fashion and Morality

Most laws and rules protect the person or protect property. Other laws relating to matters of taste, fashion or morality fall uneasily into the study

---

[53] For example, the equal treatment provisions of the Treaty of Rome Article 119, which were intended to provide equal pay for women, have in fact been used to gain improved pensions for men, see e.g. *Barber v Guardian Royal Exchange* [1991] 1 QB 344; [1990] 06 PBLR 49; [1990] 1 ECR 1889; [1990] 2 CMLR 513; [1990] 2 All ER 660; [1990] ICR 616; [1991] 1 WLR 721; ECJ Case C-262/88.

[54] This is an ancient debate, sometimes held to be at the heart of the establishment of Christianity for example, see e.g. St Paul, *Letter to the Galatians*; see also for example the application of *ex aequo et bono* in Roman law jurisprudence; and see e.g. Shakespeare's discussion in the *Merchant of Venice* of whether the letter of the law should be applied, or whether discretionary mercy should be applied on top of it 'It must appear / That malice bears down truth. And I beseech you, / Wrest once the law to your authority. / To do a great right, do a little wrong' (IV.i.211–14). And of course the courts of equity in England (using judicial discretion) were established to resolve the inadequacies of the mainstream courts and law based on 'black-letter' law.

[55] *The Queen on the application of Debbie Purdy v Director of Public Prosecutions and Omar Puente and Society for the Protection of Unborn Children* [2009] EWCA Civ 92, 19 February 2009.

of regulation. Such laws are designed to reflect the mores of a society (e.g. blasphemy or sedition) or the fears or distaste of a society (drugs, prostitution or homosexuality) although sometimes addressed in the form of a desire to protect the individual (e.g. the Taliban's concerns over the education of women or the US right's approach to abortion).[56] It is not the place of this review to explore the pros and cons of such laws, except to say that they vary over time and can become disproportionately important to the thinking of legislators and others. It does make it difficult to draft such laws without expressing the policy objective, so as to give a guide to the citizen and the judge how such a law is to be applied. As many studies have shown, such laws are hard to apply in practice, and may also lead to a disrespect for the law generally.

1.3   Is There Too Much Law?

Nonetheless, despite the individual successes that the legislator can point to, there seems to be something in the air that has drawn most people to conclude that regulation has gone too far.[57] The newspapers write grumpy-old-man articles about it,[58] people in the pub consume endless pints whilst railing against it,[59] and there are internet sites and groups that are devoted to interminable complaining against the excesses of

---

[56] Hugh Tomlinson, *Woman given royal pardon for driving may still be flogged*, The Times, 15 November 2011: 'A report this week by Kamal Subhi, a former professor at King Fahd University, warned that allowing women to drive would provoke a surge in prostitution, pornography, homosexuality and divorce. Within ten years of the ban being lifted, it warned, there would be 'no more virgins' in the kingdom'.

[57] This is nothing new. There is an old Jewish joke based on the Biblical commandment that it is forbidden to seethe a kid in its mother's milk (Ex. 23:19; Ex. 34:26; Deut. 14:21) a rule around which many of the Jewish dietary laws have been built. Moses seeks interpretation of the law, and asks God whether it should be read to mean the Jews should never eat milk and meat together. God replies that no, what He was saying was that you should never cook a calf in its mother's milk. Moses presses and asks whether He is are really saying is that the Jews should wait six hours after eating meat to eat milk so the two are not in their stomachs together. God replies that what He was saying was never cook a calf in its mother's milk. Moses asks a third time, does that mean that Jews should have a separate set of dishes for dairy meals and a separate set for meat and if we make a mistake we have to bury that dish outside. In the end God loses patience and responds wearily 'Do whatever you want.'

[58] See e.g. Andrew Lilico, *We need more risk and less regulation*, Daily Telegraph, 16 March 2009, Gary Duncan, *Biting reality of too much regulation*, The Times, 27 January 2003 and many thousands of other similar articles. See also e.g. Ian Vince, *The Little Black Book of Red Tape: Great British Bureaucracy*, Orion, 2008.

[59] There is no scientific observation to support this; this is purely empirical.

government regulation.[60] In itself all this may mean little; there are always people who will complain about anything. But even the Law Commission, the UK semi-government law reform body, and hardly a hot-bed of grumpiness, suggests that there may be too much of a good thing.[61] And of course there are innumerable government initiatives dedicated to rule reduction.[62]

There are probably two separate issues that need disentangling. Firstly whether the role of law is expanding beyond its proper remit;[63] this is discussed later. And secondly, whether there has been an absolute increase in the volume of law and regulation in recent years. The numbers look rather depressing, and are probably worse than the standard statistics indicate since they by and large ignore the less formal laws (which nonetheless often carry sanctions and costs). These quasi-laws include substantial rulebooks, guidance notes, official and unofficial controls and case law; in addition there are laws outside any individual jurisdiction also affect nationals, including those from the European Commission, international institutions such as the United Nations, the OECD and the Council of Europe and international conventions such as agreements between the UK and the US on tax or extradition, or the Geneva Conventions on for example the status of the International Committee of the Red Cross.

The quasi-law poses particular concerns: for example, although the UK tax law on pensions is contained in around 200 pages of statute and another 200 pages of statutory instrument, there are another 3200 pages of HMRC guidance notes which in practice have the effect of law. By way of contrast most other countries have around two to five pages of pensions tax law.[64]

---

[60] See e.g. the mostly (but not exclusively) right-inclined and libertarian-inclined organisations, Adam Smith Institute, Centre for Policy Studies, Taxpayers Alliance, CBI, British Chambers of Commerce. They often produce outstanding research, much of which has been appropriated in this book, but are generally written in polemic and partisan form, see e.g. Tim Ambler and Keith Boyfield, *Route map to reform: deregulation*, Adam Smith Institute, 2005, 40pp.

[61] Law Commission: see below at n16; see also Better Regulation Executive, *Citizens perceptions on regulation*, January 2007, 65pp; and see also Cabinet Office, June 2007, 15pp; and see Legislative and Regulatory Reform Act 2006 (together with explanatory notes), the former Regulatory Reform Act 2001 and the Deregulation Act 2014.

[62] Described in detail in Chapter 6.

[63] The question of whether law is exceeding its remit is discussed below, see Chapter 2.

[64] Pensions law used to be around 200 pages at the end of the 1970s; it is now around the 160,000 page mark (see e.g. *Perspective*, the pensions industry regulatory service, www .pendragon.co.uk). Much of the excess is an outcome of quasi-law.

There do therefore seem to be several growth areas in regulation, which are related but separate. It may be convenient to classify them as

- law,
- regulation and
- case law (or law made by judges).

There are dedicated chapters on these issues later in the book; at this stage it may be helpful just to summarise some of the issues in each area.

1.3.1 Law

There does seem to be a view abroad that there is more law than there used to be. Is that view just a figment of the excitable imagination of the middle-brow newspapers, or is it true? In 2006 the Law Commission published a consultation paper on the potential for developing a more formal system of reviewing laws ('post-legislative scrutiny') and encouraging better regulation; it thought that this could ultimately improve the accountability of governments for the legislation they pass and lead to better and more effective law.[65] It also incidentally took a rough count of the growth of law. It produced a table (Table 1.3) to demonstrate the number of pages of legislation that had been produced. The number had increased by over 250 per cent in less than 40 years. In addition to the increase in the number of pages of legislation produced each year, the size of the page had also increased by 11 per cent.

---

[65] Law Commission, *The need for post-legislative scrutiny*, Article Number 21, 31 January 2006; Law Commission, *Post-legislative scrutiny, a consultation paper*, No 178, 31 January 2006; www.lawcom.gov.uk/post_leg_scrutiny.htm. Some overseas commentators believe that the UK is ahead of many (see e.g. Senator Charles E. Schumer and Michael R. Bloomberg (Mayor of New York), *Sustaining New York's and the US Global Financial Services Leadership*, 2007 cited (out of context) in Cabinet Office, *A better regulation strategy for the public sector*, 2007: 'The UK is preferred across many regulatory dimensions but is most distinguished in cost and simplicity of regulations.'). De-regulation is a perverse industry in itself, see e.g. *The Lifting the Burdens Task Force*, July 2006, Secretary of State for Communities and Local Government and innumerable simplification plans issued by departments and regulators. See also Patrick Vollmer and Lara Badger, *Volume of legislation*, House of Lords Library Note, 10 May 2013 LLN 2013/008. It shows (these are selective statistics) that in 1938 there were 3 Acts of Parliament totalling 15 pages; in 1986 there were 60 acts with over 2000 pages. In more recent years there are signs of a reduction both in numbers of acts and pagination. The position is actually worse than the figures indicate; later pages are A4 in size whereas earlier pages were A5. It is also not a new complaint, see e.g. JPW Mallalieu, *Passed to you please: Britain's Red Tape Machine at War*, Left Book Club, 1942.

Table 1.3 *Pages of UK legislation between 1965 and 2003*

	1965	2003
New laws	83	45
Pages	1817	4030
Consolidation acts*	14	None
Pages	683	–
Statutory instruments	2201	3354
Pages	6322	11,977
EU legislation	None	–
EU directives	–	122
EU regulations	–	2348
Total EU pages	–	11,000
Total pages	7500	26,400

* Acts which draw together acts on similar subjects in order to make the law more intelligible.

These statistics of course do not include the number of pages of quasi-legislation produced by regulators, for which few figures seem to be available. It is not an unreasonable guesstimate to suggest that the multiple is around 10. And the statistics do not assess the increase in the complexity of expression; modern laws can be much more complicated than older laws.[66]

1.3.2 Quasi-Domestic Law: The Role of the European Union

Many countries in customs unions have semi-supranational laws. There are dissenting views for example in the UK on whether the EU has been a prime driver of excess regulation.[67] The advocates of the reasonableness

---

[66] See e.g. Companies Act 1948 as against the length of the Companies Act 2006; see also the Building Regulations or the notorious FCA Handbook. For periodic reviews of the quantity of legislation, see e.g. House of Lords Library, *Volume of legislation*, 10 May 2013, LLN 2013/008. An unfair analysis shows that in 1938 there were three Acts of Parliament with an average of 5 pages each (i.e. 15 pages a year; in 2008 there were 27 acts with an average of 114 pages each (i.e. 3088 pages a year).

[67] See e.g. Mats Persson, *Out of control? Measuring a decade of EU regulation*, Open Europe, 2009 (www.openeurope.org.uk): 'of the cumulative cost of regulations introduced over the past decade, £106.6 billion, or 71.9%, had its origin in the EU' and Sarah Gaskell and Mats Persson, *Still out of control? Measuring eleven years of EU regulation*, Open Europe, 2010; or by way of contrast, Denis MacShane, *It is a myth that UK laws emanate from Europe,*

Table 1.4 *EU legislation produced annually from 1958 to 2003*

Year	Regulations	Directives	Decisions	Total
1958	20	0	23	43
1963	96	8	266	370
1968	443	37	182	662
1973	1110	57	254	1421
1978	1329	116	615	2060
1983	1454	84	514	2052
1988	1801	133	546	2480
1993	1566	166	707	2439
1998	3008	158	735	3901
2001	2769	136	820	3725
2002	2537	120	896	3553
2003	2461	153	804	3418

Note: For a history of foreign jurisdictions imposing laws on Britain, see Peter Jones, *Henry III v EU law*, Spectator, 30 April 2016.
Source: Taken from Ambler and Boyfield, *Route map to reform: deregulation*, Adam Smith Institute, 2005, based on information extracted from CELEX by Chanyeon Hwang, Manchester Business School.

of the EU argue that much of the regulation would have had to have been introduced domestically in any event, and that the rules are merely harmonising (and reducing) the amount of regulation that cross-border activity would otherwise have demanded. The advocates of the view that there has been an intrusive explosion of EU legislation simply point to Table 1.4. Both sides complain about 'gold-plating' (i.e. that the way the UK has implemented the otherwise limited requirements of the EU rules has added to those requirements):

Financial Times, 29 November 2014: 'According to the most recent study by the House of Commons Library 'from 1997 to 2009 6.8 per cent of primary legislation and 14.1 per cent of secondary legislation' emanated from Europe'. And see Vaughne Miller, *EU obligations: UK implementing legislation since 1993*, House of Commons Library, SN/1A/7092, 29 January 2015 which indicated that out of 34,000 acts and statutory instruments around 1.4 per cent of acts and 12.9 per cent of statutory instruments exclusively dealt with EU obligations. Patrick Vollmer and Lara Badger, *Volume of legislation*, House of Lords Library Note, 10 May 2013. For EU attempts to deregulate, see Chapter 6. On the effect of leaving the EU, see *Yes, we have no straight bananas*, The Economist, 28 May 2016.

Table 1.5 *The cabbage story*

Document	Words
Pythagorean theorem	24
Lord's prayer	66
Archimedes' principle	67
10 Commandments	179
Gettysburg Address (US)	286
Declaration of Independence (US)	1300
Constitution with all 27 amendments (US)	7818
EU regulations on the sale of cabbage	26,911

Whatever the truth of the matter, there is little doubt that EU legislation is an issue and was one of the political drivers of Brexit. It is important of course to disentangle myth and reality; Table 1.5 is sometimes cited as a demonstration of the legislative incontinence of the European Union.

The cabbage story has an ancient heritage, first being used in relation to US law, and only later being adopted for EU purposes. It is untrue, although its mythic status has not prevented it being widely employed.[68] And within the EU there is recognition that there have been excesses, and steps, rather like those in the UK, have tentatively been taken to redress the problem.[69]

---

[68] For the history of the making of the story, see *Of cabbages and kings*, 9 April 2012, Snopes .com; Jan Harold Brunvand, *Too good to be true*, 1999, New York, W. W. Norton, pp283–284; Tim Harford, *The great EU Cabbage myth*, BBC Radio 4 Programme, April 2016.

[69] European Commission, *Regulatory Fitness and Performance programme (REFIT)*, December 2013, European Commission, Strasbourg, 12.12.2012, COM(2012) 746 final, Communication from the Commission to the European Parliament, The Council, The European Economic and Social Committee and the Committee of the Regions, *EU Regulatory Fitness*, SWD(2012) 422 final, SWD(2012) 423 final; European Commission, Communication from the Commission to the European Parliament, The Council, The European Economic and Social Committee and the Committee of the Regions, *Regulatory Fitness and Performance (REFIT): Results and Next Steps*, Brussels, 2.10.2013, COM(2013) 685 final. Curiously there are motes and beams; much EU effort has gone on deregulation of other economies, see e.g. *Deregulation is Essential for Economic Recovery, Says the European Commission* EU Press release 1998/11/04 EU NEWS 26/98, 'Today, the European Commission held a high level meeting on deregulation with Japanese Ministries. At the meeting, which was co-chaired by Mr Gérard Depayre, Deputy Director-General for External Relations in the European Commission, and Mr Shotaro Oshima, Director-General, Economic Affairs Bureau, Ministry of Foreign Affairs, the Commission urged Japan to accelerate its deregulation process.'

1.3.3   Regulation

There has been something of an astonishing growth not only in laws, but also in the number of regulators, bodies and individuals charged with enforcing those laws – and frequently making laws of their own. The amount they spend is now also significant; the Financial Conduct Authority alone spent £500M in 2008/09[70] and the list of regulators is now legion.[71] The general rule of thumb is that the cost to the regulatee is roughly five times the cost of the regulator, although there is little substantive evidence on the number (experience in my own industry suggests the multiple is greater).[72]

---

[70] Financial Services Authority, Business Plan 2009/10 (www.fsa.gov.uk/pubs/plan/pb2009_10.pdf)]; now the Financial Conduct Authority and the Prudential Regulatory Authority. A study paper in 2016 outlined the Herculean challenges of deciding whether regulation was cost-effective, or even effective at all, see Zanna Iscenko et al., *Economics for effective regulation*, FCA Occasional paper in financial regulation No 13, March 2016; cf. C. R. Sunstein, *Financial regulation and cost benefit analysis*, Yale Law Journal Forum, 2015, which is an unintended powerful argument for leaving well alone (and mentioning the horrific fact that there are 650,000 rapes a year in US prisons, and that it would be worth spending $500B a year to reduce the number of rapes by 1700 a year).

[71] See *Quango reform: full list*, Daily Telegraph, 14 October 2010.

[72] See e.g. Deloitte, *The cost of regulation*, 2006, 72pp (www.fsa.gov.uk/pubs/plan/pb2009_10.pdf); see also '*Estimation of FSA Administrative Burdens*' conducted for the FSA by Real Assurance Risk Management. It concluded (with results that were 'indicative rather than statistically representative') that the costs of financial services regulation amounted to some £600 million, which equates to approximately 0.5 per cent of this industry's total costs (highly improbable, given that the FSA's declared costs the following year were just shy of £500M). It suggested that the most significant costs arose in relation to anti-money laundering rules and some general reporting rules; see also '*The Benefits of Regulation – what to measure and how*', a study, conducted for the FSA by Oxera Consulting, attempted to set out a framework for identifying and measuring the benefits of regulation, with a best practice methodology for this, building on the FSA's existing cost-benefit analysis tools. It was intended to enable a better analysis to be made of the benefits of individual rules or clusters of rules and support the comparison of such benefits to compare with the level of incremental cost imposed by such rules; John Tiner, the then FSA CEO, said, presumably as an aspiration rather than a declaration of fact, 'We are determined to strike the right balance between discharging our statutory duties and avoiding unjustified costs. We can do this only with a sound understanding of both the benefits and the costs of regulatory action. The three studies published today underpin that understanding and the update on the Better Regulation Action Plan shows the progress made in the last six months.' In fact, it is virtually impossible to gauge the real costs of regulation on the regulated, except to say that most academic studies underestimate it (they ignore training and defensive habits and behaviour for example). The then Department for Trade and Industry had promised in 2004 to reduce the regulatory burdens on business from DTI regulations by more than

For a variety of reasons there has been a strong growth in the number of regulators over the last 20 years. Some have been designed to control inherent monopolies, such as utility suppliers. Some have been to enforce initiatives in social policy, such as the former Child Support Agency or CAFCAS (Children and Family Court Advisory and Support Service). And others have involved the regulatorisation of self-governing bodies which had previously operated without external regulation, such as the Solicitors Regulation Authority (instead of the Law Society), the Actuarial Professional Oversight Board (instead of the Institute of Actuaries), the Financial Accounting Standards Board (instead of the Institute of Accountants of England and Wales) and others.

Not all of the regulators were new; some of them simply assumed the roles of the previous self-governing bodies. The SRA for example assumed the former role of the Law Society of regulating the solicitors' profession, and allowed the Law Society to revert to its primary role of lawyers' trade union, a role which it is also struggling to perform effectively – but the budget inevitably expanded significantly.

The change from self-regulation to external regulation, understandable though it might be in certain circumstances, inexorably involves significant additional costs. And perversely regulators bring with them not only additional costs and a larger bureaucracy but also regulations and rules of their own.

The reasons that governments encourage regulators rather than assume responsibility themselves through the main administrative organs such

---

£1B by 2009 (see DTI, *Five year work programme: creating wealth from knowledge*, November 2004, p31). There does not appear to have been any way to measure whether the target was met. See also Peter Andrews, *Did life and pensions 'disclosure' work as expected?*, Financial Services Authority, April 2009 (FSA Occasional papers in financial regulation). Regulations introduced under the Financial Services Act 1986 required that consumers be given standardised information about the price of life and pensions investment products. This was deemed by the Office of Fair Trading to be anti-competitive, and new regulations required product-specific information to be disclosed from 1995. The paper concluded that the regulations had a benefit to consumers, but was unable to produce a useful cost-benefit analysis – or of course explore the difference that new technology (e.g. comparison websites) would have had, not to mention the offerings of financial journals. UK government estimates suggest that regulation costs about 10 per cent of GDP, around £120B a year, see, *Regulation – Less Is More: Reducing Burdens, Improving Outcomes: a BRTF Report to the Prime Minister*, Better Regulation Task Force, 2005; and Allister Heath and David B. Smith, *At a price! The true cost of public spending*, Politeia, 2006, p4.

as departments are several. One is the belief that dedicated regulators know about the industry they are regulating better than a central administration. One is that it is more efficient (in theory) to have a focussed organisation specialising in just one sector (the FCA for example has declined to oversee the allied but distinct occupational pensions sector – for which the sector is truly grateful). One is that they can exercise a different form of discretion than the usual organs, such as government departments, local authorities or the police. It may be that they need skills such as an understanding of economics or science that the usual authorities cannot hope to acquire. And one is the belief that self-regulation is ineffective.[73]

But however well-justified, and however well-meaning and efficient, the establishment of a regulator inevitably involves creating an overhead – and carries with it the risk of injury as well as therapy. This is not a discussion of the need or otherwise for a general extension of government – the introduction of the Disclosure and Barring Service (formerly Criminal Records Bureau), the Crown Prosecution Service, the creation of children's registers, each of which individually may have a justification, others of which probably need greater examination, has continued to raise concerns. Collectively they have all imposed immeasurable benefits, unquantifiable costs and possibly incalculable disbenefits on society. One test however of the need for or efficiency of a regulator is what would have happened if they did not exist – or what happened before they existed.

Some of these organisations are not supposed to be rule makers like the Financial Conduct Authority, but have more specific powers with ancillary regulatory interests. This book covers such non-governmental organisations in so far as they have incidental rule-making powers or some control over the community, such as the Human Fertilization and Embryology Authority. In addition there are semi-government organisations which do not actually make rules, but simply for example express consumer irritation (e.g. the Rail Users Consultative Committees); usually they do not make rules that affect the lives of others, but may on occasion affect the way rules are made elsewhere.

---

[73] Susan Dudley and Melinda Warren, *Regulators' budget from Eisenhower to Obama, Regulatory Studies Center*, Washington DC, 17 May 2016, p8 sets out a graph of the increase in the volume of federal regulations and its budgetary costs.

1.3.4   Cases in the Courts

Included amongst the complaints about excess regulation is a complaint about the impact of the judiciary. Some complain that for example additional rules are being introduced under the guise of human rights law;[74] others complain that the judges are too soft on criminals,[75] and others that the judges interfere where it is the remit of Parliament to hold sway.[76] The courts have for centuries held an ambivalent attitude to their role in lawmaking. On the one hand they have claimed that equity was designed to overcome the gaps of the common law where clear injustices were involved; on the other hand they have claimed that they are simply servants of Parliament, although free to observe that some of its legislative drafting was absurd. A separate chapter explores some of the concerns (and myths) about judge-made law.

1.4   The Consequences and Unintended Consequences of Hyper-Legislation and Regulation

While legislation has clear benefits in offering protection to individuals and businesses, the converse can have serious side effects. It will always be debated whether law is necessary or excessive, as was seen above in the debate over garage doors, or below about the extent of financial services regulation, but where there is broad consensus that it is indeed excessive, its costs can be significant, and not always readily apparent, or maybe not apparent for many years in the future. The costs therefore can be both direct and indirect.

---

[74] Even governments themselves sometimes complain about excessive legal intervention, but of course by others; see e.g. Theresa May, Home Secretary, *speech to the Conservative Party Conference 2011*, in relation to the impact of human rights law on the powers of the Home Secretary.

[75] See e.g. Daily Mail, virtually any edition; Prof. Ken Pease (Manchester Business School) *Prison, Community Sentencing and Crime*, Civitas, August 26, 2010.

[76] Tom Bingham, *The Rule of Law*, Allen Lane, 2010; Jonathan Sumption QC, *Judicial and political decision-making: The uncertain boundary*, The FA Mann Lecture, 2011; judicial activism was given greater support in a response to the Sumption lecture by Sir Stephen Sedley in the London Review of Books, 2011, see Francis FitzGibbon *Judicial Activism*, 6 September 2013, www.lrb.co.uk/blog/2013/09/06/francisf/judicial-activism. More recently see James Slack, *Enemies of the people: Fury over 'out of touch' judges who have 'declared war on democracy' by defying 17.4m Brexit voters and who could trigger constitutional crisis*, Daily Mail, 3 November 2016.

1.4.1   Direct Costs

Direct costs are normally readily identifiable.[77] Many regulators publish their own budgets[78] and by law[79] most legislation is nowadays supposed to have a Regulatory Impact Assessment attached to it to indicate the cost to the public of its introduction; usually it substantially underestimates the real costs, since rather like the Channel Tunnel or the London Olympics, if the true cost had been revealed they would never have been introduced.[80]

Governments regulate in many areas to protect the public: in the management of the labour markets, in product markets through the competition policy and through taxation. Sometimes regulation looks worse than it is. In the labour market for example controls have proliferated. For example it was illegal (by the end of 2003) to discriminate in membership of pension schemes against homosexuals, heterosexuals and bisexuals – but permissible to discriminate against sado-masochists or

---

[77] The cost of regulation in the UK has been estimated at 10 per cent of GDP, see Allistair Heath and David B. Smith, *At a price! The true cost of public spending*, Politeia, 2006 p4, and Better Regulation Task Force, *Regulation: less is more*, March 2005 at www.regulation.org .uk/library/2005_less_is_more.pdf. The UK spends about 2 per cent of GDP on defence.

[78] It is rare that budgets diminish, even in times of austerity. The Pensions Regulator (whose original budget when established was expected to run at £10M pa) spent in its first full year of operation £31.9M, and this rose to £48.8M by 2013, with forecast expenditure of over £80M by 2017. These budgets do not include the on-cost to the consumer, which as mentioned seem to be around 10 to 1. More critically, it is virtually impossible to determine whether it is value for money; se OECD, *Better regulation in the United Kingdom*, 2010, part of a study on better regulation in Europe. Attempts to measure regulatory overheads can result in absurd outcomes. The cost of introducing auto-enrolment in pension plans was estimated as costing around £9.2B pa, with benefits estimated at £9.2B. The estimates attached to regulatory impact assessments (see footnote below) seem little more than fingers in the air.

[79] A reformed process of regulatory impact assessments has been introduced in the UK since 2007 through prime ministerial fiat rather than law; its effect seems largely to add to the work of the civil service rather than diminish the quantity, and its impact as a reality check seems to have been minimal, see National Audit Office, *Better Regulation: Making good use of regulatory impact assessments, report by the Comptroller and Auditor General*, HC 329, 15 November 2001. The absurdity of the attempt is illustrated by the example of the cost and benefits of introducing the auto-enrolment pension scheme in the UK, see *The total benefit/cost ratio of new regulations 2008/2009*, 21 October 2009, Better Regulation Executive, Department for Business Innovation and Skills, p4. It showed the annual cost was £9.95B a year, with a benefit of … £9.95B, i.e. a ratio of costs to benefits of 1. The normal target is around 3.

[80] The Channel Tunnel between England and France was budgeted at 1985 prices as £2.6B; actual costs were £4.65B, an 80 per cent overrun. Financing costs were 140 per cent higher than forecast. Similarly the bid for the UK hosting of the Olympic Games in 2012 was £2.4B; it cost eventually £8.92B, an overspend of £6.52B.

paedophiles.[81] Few UK pension schemes operate overtly such policies so for most of them it is business as usual (although there will always be peripheral breaches at the edges) – but the compliance paperwork can be irritating and hardly productive for the economy. I recall being a non-executive compliance director of a Jewish social housing project subsidised by the government for the benefit of frail elderly (mostly) women. I was interrogated by the then Housing Corporation, a quango, about whether our tenancy application forms inquired as to the sexual orientation of the proposed tenants. I was less than inclined to pursue whether our 85-year-old frail elderly tenants had a lesbian inclination, and declined to place the question on the tenant application form, although the reason for the inquiry was a benign one, i.e. to check we did not discriminate against homosexual women.

There are few reliable figures on what the direct costs of regulation can be, although there are academic and official studies which are rather broad in their conclusions. A useful rule of thumb however suggests that where there is a regulator, the cost to the industry regulated is around ten-times that (see below) in responding to the regulation.[82]

1.4.2   Indirect Costs

Indirect costs are even harder to calculate in financial terms, and are often exaggerated by one side or minimised by the other. The truth is in

---

[81] See Department for Employment guidance (www.nidirect.gov.uk/index/information-and-services/employment/discrimination-at-work/sexual-orientation-discrimination.htm) which explained that 'sexual orientation is defined as being an orientation towards persons of the same sex (this covers gay men and lesbians); the opposite sex (this covers straight men and women); or both sexes (this covers bisexual men and women). It does not extend to sexual practices and preferences (e.g. sado-masochism and paedophilia)'; see also the way in which the provisions of the Regulation of Investigatory Powers Act 2000 have been misused; the Act was intended to give powers to the authorities to pursue terrorist concerns. In fact they were used variously to engage in surveillance in such matters as seeking miscreants involved in dog fouling, seeking school entry for children not within local authority boundaries, littering, and paperboy permits (Richard Ford, *Trivial pursuits that turned the town hall snoopers into tyrants*, The Times, 17 April 2009). The Investigatory Powers Tribunal seemed ineffective to control misuse of the Act (Dr Murakami Wood, *A very British tendency must not be ruled by public outcry*, The Times, 17 April 2009).

[82] See National Audit Office, *Regulating financial services: the Financial Conduct Authority and the Prudential Regulation Authority*, HC 1072, 25 March 2014 which suggests costs of £664M for 2013–2014, showing an increase of £127M on the earlier year. The report indicates that actual costs are considerably more than this because of outsourced costs paid direct by the industry.

practice rarely calculable, and it may involve not merely financial obligations but also other implications which may have a more important relevance. Some of them are set out below. Costs of tax collection in the UK are
considered to be around £15–£20B a year for example, with the costs of tax
collection bearing about 16 times more heavily on the smallest business
than on the largest. The UK tax system is notorious for failing the Adam
Smith tests of convenience and efficiency; the average Finance Act in the
2000s was around three times (about 460 pages) as long as a Finance Act
in the 1980s.[83] National insurance (social security) collection and administrative costs in the UK (which bear no marketing or distribution obligations) are around 5 per cent, compared with limits on private pension
systems of costs of around 0.75 per cent.[84]

1.4.3   Changes in Behaviour

There is little doubt, though there are few studies on the point, that legislation intended to drive behaviour in one direction may have an unintended
consequence. One example has been pointed out above, the way in which
people responded to a directive to reduce their car use by reducing the size
of garages. But there are similar examples elsewhere; one much-debated
issue was the prohibition on alcohol in the US in the 1920s and similar prohibitions today on drug use. Consumers of alcohol responded in the US
by adjusting the way in which they consumed, and drug users do the same
in the UK today. Sometimes regulation can have the opposite effect to that
intended, so that for example an attempt to control gambling by regulation and in particular taxing it simply resulted in gambling arrangements
being made outside the jurisdiction so that it became even less regulated
than before. In the end the law had to be withdrawn.[85] Behavioural regulation is not a widely studied topic, but it is well understood by those who
are subject to regulation they are unhappy with. The financial collapse in

---

[83] Francis Chittenden, Hilary Foster and Brian Sloan, *Taxation and Red Tape*, Institute of
Economic Affairs, 2010.

[84] *National Insurance Fund Account, 2015–15*, HC 485. There was about £1.2B uncollected;
allocated costs on top are only around 1 per cent, but there are substantial unallocated costs;
Occupational Pension Schemes (Charges and Governance) Regulations 2015, SI 2015 No
0879.

[85] There are any number of studies on the pointlessness of most prohibition exercises, see
e.g. Daniel Okrent, *Last Call: The Rise and Fall of Prohibition*, Scribner, 2011; and John
Meadowcroft, ed, *Prohibitions*, Institute of Economic Affairs, 2008; it is hard to find any on
the effectiveness of it as a control mechanism for the improvement of society (maybe guns
excepted). See also Notes 26 and 67.

2008 following a substantial credit expansion was followed by a spate of regulation (in the EU known as Basel III) intended to constrain future such expansions; the regulators however normally fight the last war. In respect of Basel III a member of the Financial Stability Board's enhanced disclosure task force wrote:[86]

> Bankers are not stupid... For decades banks have shaped their businesses to maximise profits, given the regulatory rules that exist at the time. And when the rules change, smart bankers change what they do... New rules being introduced for European banks make huge swaths of traditional bank lending unprofitable... If European banks responded by reshaping their business to resemble their US rivals' then bank lending in Europe would collapse, from €45tn to €15tn... it would dwarf the €1tn... of quantitative easing... coming from the European Central Bank... Bankers usually prove adept at adjusting to new rules. In the past, the result was a massive credit expansion. This time around it could be a frightening contraction.

1.4.4   Impact on Entrepreneurship

Similarly excessive regulation can make it difficult for new business to become established or to flourish. The UK has a reasonable reputation in this respect, but the capital requirements for investment managers, insurance companies and banks for example make for a tough barrier to entry and many successful businesses today could not have been established had such rules been in force when they started. Regulation favours the large and well-funded, and already established, enterprises; others may have to find alternative ways round the constraints. For example controls on broadcasting mean that it is hard for a new entrant to establish a TV or radio station – although once broadband was invented and became widespread, the main point of regulation (i.e. limited frequencies) disappeared. It is rare however for regulators to declare that their function is no longer necessary; their argument is that they are a creature of statute and it is for others to say whether they should stay or go.

1.4.5   Growth of Defensive Practices

If we pop in to see our doctor about a minor indisposition, we will often find that he or she recommends a range of tests, x-rays and other inquiries, not so much because he knows we only have a cold, but because he needs

---

[86] Simon Samuels, *Withering regulations will make for shrivelled banks*, Financial Times, 31 January 2015.

to practice defensive medicine, so that if there were to be a rare disease or infection, he could not be accused of negligence.

The cost of not being able to rely on the judgment of a clinician is high, but hard to calculate. And it is not only doctors; lawyers write reams of advice which is not read, not because the client needs to know the legal position, but to make sure that he cannot come back years later and suggest that he was not informed of the position, and he would have taken another route if he had known.[87] Financial services is a special category; the Financial Conduct Authority for example is known for requiring independent financial advisers to send key features documents to buyers of insurance policies which are virtually unreadable, and mostly unread, as a prophylactic. And anyone who listens to UK commercial radio and hears adverts for mortgages, which recite in a gabble at the end some warnings which no one can understand, but which formally comply, will know the pointlessness of it.[88] In some cases the requirements are disproportionate or counterproductive.[89]

It is not known what are the costs of defensive law or compliance, but in my own field, for example, the costs of pensions compliance multiplied to such an extent that it became common practice (as in the US) to have lawyers present at many meetings, and the paperwork probably multiplied ten-fold, less to manage the scheme than to provide a paper trail for any future regulatory inspection. In itself that may not be a bad thing, but it does involve a cost in paper, time, resource and advice which is not regarded as a cost by the regulator. Regulatory arbitrage is now a feature

---

[87] Instances of defensive medicine, their reasons and consequences, is explored in Gerd Gigerenzer, *Risk Savvy*, Allen Lane, 2014, Chapters 9 and 10. It is particularly instructive on the adverse outcomes that emerge from physicians' imperfect understandings of risk.

[88] See e.g. Financial Conduct Authority, *Consultation paper CP13/10, Detailed proposals for the FCA regime for consumer credit*, 3 October 2013; RadioCentre, *Response to FCA Consultation*, December 2013. Only 3 per cent of listeners can recall the meaning of the warnings.

[89] 'Key features' documents, letters which advisers have to send to clients which advising on pensions or financial products, are notorious for their unreadability; they are produced more to protect the regulator and adviser than for the benefit of the consumer. An extraordinary example of consumer protection is in the 2014 draft of the IORPS Directive (European Directive on occupational pensions) which required substantial information to be given on no more than two sides of A4, in a readable size font – which was impossible, see *Proposal for a Directive of the European Parliament and of the Council on the activities and supervision of institutions for occupational retirement provision*, EU 2014/0091 (COD), Article 38(2) and following.

of pension scheme design[90] as a consequence and the unintended adverse consequences of regulation elsewhere are now legion.[91]

1.4.6   Reduction of International Competitiveness

Excessive regulation can have an impact on international competitiveness or the ability of a country to compete in world markets. For example the UK requirements on animal husbandry make it hard for UK pig-farmers to compete against Danish or Dutch pig producers because of the space requirements for pigs. It is hard to balance the need for humane practices for animals against the commercial realities of life, but the impact on the ability of the country to produce its own pig-meat was not an issue that was discussed when the regulations were introduced.[92]

1.4.7   Exploitation of Regulatory Arbitrage

The story of lawmaking is littered with examples of well-intentioned initiatives having a contrary effect. One major example is the destruction of defined benefit pension arrangements for about half the workforce in the UK. Some ascribe the decline to the costs of increasing longevity, falling investment returns, declining annuity yields and changing employment patterns, and there is no doubt that these factors had an impact. But all these factors were in force in the mid 1970s, when stagflation, the combination of inflation and falling stock markets, in principle all but destroyed

[90] The UK unintentionally became a haven for pension arrangements because in 2014/15 it removed the requirement for pension funds to pay benefits in annual form, contrary to the rules of almost all other EU member states. It was expected that residents of other member states would transfer their rights to UK schemes to take advantage of the new freedom, much to the discomfort of the regulatory authorities of the rest of the EU.

[91] See e.g. Philip Aldrick, *Regular guys?*, The Times, 25 January 2014, which details the impact on 100,000 Somali refugees who were unable to send remittances back to their families following the decision by Barclays Bank to cut off Dahabshiill, the Somali money transfers service, on the grounds that the regulatory environment (designed to reduce money laundering) made such service impracticable. The article concluded that 'The higher cost of banking since the [financial] crisis has made lending to the poor more uneconomic than ever. Stricter capital demands and costly money laundering regulations have – inadvertently – proved effective deterrents.' The article suggests that it also ironically led to the 'pawnbroker virus' of payday lenders and extremely high interest rates for the very poor. The Barclays decision was suspended by a court decision in November 2013, pending a full court review.

[92] See e.g. John Henley, *'Welfare doesn't come into it'*, The Guardian, 6 January 2009 (pig farming in Europe).

the finances of pension schemes (and indeed companies) – yet schemes continued to be maintained. There were however, odd though it might seem to modern observers, at that time no funding requirements for pension schemes, so the fact that they were nominally insolvent did not affect them. Indeed, just under a decade later, their biggest problem was surpluses.

The sea-change that followed (after a scandal involving a well-known entrepreneur, Robert Maxwell) was the introduction of well-meaning funding requirements and accounting rules introduced to protect plan members but which over time that made it all but impossible for employers to continue such schemes. Schemes were better (more) regulated, and were required to have more funds to back the expected pensions and other benefits payable. The bad news was that employers consequently felt compelled to withdraw the schemes, and replace them if at all with defined contribution schemes, with much lower levels of expected benefits. The legislation in practice drove out the existence of schemes, rather than supporting the legitimate expectations of members.[93] Similar rules all but wiped out 30 per cent of policyholders' values in insurance companies when well-meaning but destructive solvency rules compelled insurance companies at the worst time in the economic cycle to move many of their assets into government bonds (when they were expensive) from shares (when they were cheap). This is probably a bigger destruction of value than the actual collapse of any life insurer, yet because it was imposed by the regulator attracted little comment.[94]

1.4.8   Change in Behaviour

Legislation can also have a perverse impact on behaviour, contrary perhaps to that intended. This can happen when it becomes hard to understand the balance between outcomes. In childcare for example the outburst of public concern following the death of several children led to

---

[93] Debbie Harrison et al., *Pyrrhic victory?: the unintended consequences of the Pensions Act 2004*, The Pensions Institute, Cass Business School, October 2005.

[94] See e.g. Financial Services Authority, *Report of the Financial Services Authority on the review of the regulation of the Equitable Life Assurance Society from 1 January 1999 to 8 December 2000 which Her Majesty's Government is submitting as evidence to the inquiry conducted by Lord Penrose*, 16 October 2001, para 1.6.2, where the blame is avoided by expressing the problem in the passive voice. Similarly unnecessary (for the consumer) costs were imposed on other insurers following the credit crunch in 2008.

the requirement for registration of childcare workers, which became expensive and time consuming (and insulting) and disproportionate to the risk to children.[95] And non-regulatory, but politically correct or defensive behaviour can have an absurd outcome as set out below:

> Her primary school had a purpose-built padded cell. Yes, padded, the whole caboodle, the works, just like in mental hospitals – for disruptive children . . . It's called the Calming Down Room. If a child becomes uncontrollable, she may not touch him but must put in an urgent request for a specially designated member of staff (called a 'positive handler'). If a PH is unavailable, she must lead all the other children out of the classroom away from the disruptive child to a place of safety. The rules . . . state . . . that:
> After the restraint, staff must ensure that:
>
> * SMT [senior management team] with responsibility for Health and Safety are informed
> * A first-aid form is completed
> * A Sleuth [computerised incident system] form is completed
> * A suitable person makes contact with the young person's family
> * The Head of Year ensures that a Personal Handling Plan is drawn up for that person which includes identification of specific strategies and triggers.[96]

Similarly, the Competition Commission was responsible in January 2003 for reducing high charges for calls between mobile phone users. It ordered mobile operators to cut the fees that they charge each other and other telecoms companies for access to their networks – with the intention that the rates would fall over the following three years. But the consequence was that mobile operators then tried to recover lost income by increasing charges to consumers – which the Competition Commission had no jurisdiction to control. Ironically the biggest operator, BT, benefitted most by paying £2B a year less for calls that ended up with competing companies.[97]

---

[95] See e.g. Hannah Kuchler, *UK regulator to tighten childcare rules*, Financial Times, 19 April 2013; at just about the time another part of government pledged to deregulate, see Elizabeth Truss, *More Great Childcare*, speech to Policy Exchange, 29 January 2013 and www.gov.uk/government/speeches/elizabeth-truss-speaks-about-childcare-reform-2 and www.bizzymumsblog.com/2012/03/dear-mr-cameron-open-letter-regarding.html where a mother describes why more regulation may mean less care.

[96] Matthew Parris, *My week*, The Times, 9 April 2009.

[97] See e.g. decision of the Court of Appeal in *British Telecommunications plc v Office of Communications* [2012] EWCA Civ 1051.

1.4.9   Reduction in Respect for Law

Where there is too much law, there can be a disregard for its importance by those it is expected to govern; familiarity may breed contempt. This has been a concern for many years in relation to moving traffic offences or drug use. Where more than a small proportion of the population is criminalised, there is less fear by even the bourgeois of being made a criminal. At one time, there was a new Criminal Justice Act around every 25 years, dealing with minor reforms to the definition of theft or murder. Since 1997 there has been a new act every year, with over 3000 new offences, and the situation has become so complex that magistrates in practice find the application of the law very confusing.[98]

A somewhat peripheral example is that of the Hunting Act 2004 which outlawed hunting with dogs (particularly fox hunting, but also the hunting of deer, hares and mink and organised hare coursing) in England and Wales. The pursuit of foxes with hounds was banned in Scotland two years earlier – but remains legal in Northern Ireland.

There is probably general acceptance that cruelty to animals is wrong. In fact it had been illegal for many years.[99] Attempts to ban hunting as a form of animal cruelty had been made over many years, but it was far from clear that cruelty was involved in hunting. An early report[100] investigated all forms of hunting and concluded that 'Fox hunting makes a very important contribution to the control of foxes, and involves less cruelty than most other methods of controlling them. It should therefore be allowed to continue.' After prolonged campaigning by interest groups, in 1997 the Labour Party manifesto provided 'We will ensure greater protection for wildlife. We have advocated new measures to promote animal welfare, including a free vote in Parliament on whether hunting with hounds should be banned.'

A later inquiry concluded that hunting 'seriously compromised the welfare of the fox',[101] but did not draw any conclusion on whether hunting should be banned or should continue; the inquiry chairman, Lord Burns

---

[98] Since 1997 50 new criminal justice bills were introduced; with 3055 new criminal offences and 115,000 pages of legislation. By contrast there were six acts between 1925 and 1985, *Society matters*, Open University, No 11, 2008/09.

[99] For at least 100 years, see Protection of Animals Act 1911.

[100] *Report of the Committee on Cruelty to Wild Animals*, Scott Henderson, Chairman, Cmd 8266, 31 Dec 1951.

[101] Lord Burns, Chairman, Final Report, *Committee of inquiry into hunting with dogs*, Home Office, 9 June 2000.

later said that 'Naturally, people ask whether we were implying that hunting is cruel ... The short answer to that question is no. There was not sufficient verifiable evidence or data safely to reach views about cruelty. It is a complex area.' Following the Burns inquiry, and a General Election the re-elected government introduced a bill which would have allowed some licensed hunting. In the end the Hunting Act 2004 was passed when the Speaker of the House of Commons invoked the Parliament Acts 1911 and 1949, the Bill not having received the approval of the House of Lords.

The issue for lawmakers was not whether hunting is right or wrong, or whether it is cruel or humane. The issue was whether a law can actually constrain the activity proscribed. If a law is widely disregarded or not enforced, it carries with it the possible stain of carrying with it a growing disrespect for the existence of the law. Hunting activists continue to hunt, and police forces have said that enforcement of the Hunting Act was a low priority for them, although they would enforce the law, most notably by investigating evidence of illegal hunting. Despite claims that the Hunting Act was unworkable, convictions under the Act rose from eight in 2005–2006 to 48 in 2007.

Meanwhile the meaning of the Hunting Act remained a matter of public dispute, and hunting in one form or another continued. Supporters of hunting maintained that 'the Act made it an offence to hunt a mouse with a dog but not a rat, and to legally hunt a rabbit but not a hare'. It was legal to flush a fox to guns with two dogs but illegal if three dogs were involved. It remained legal to flush a fox to a bird of prey with unlimited numbers of dogs.[102]

How did such confusion arise? The Hunting Act bans activities that Parliament believed to be cruel sports and permitted activities that it believed to be necessary for land managers. Parliament accepted the view that, where rats and rabbits were pests, hunting them was legitimate. MPs did not believe that there was any necessity to use dogs to hunt mice and believed that hare hunting was cruel, which is why these activities were not exempted from the Act.

The introduction of the statute flushed out an impressive inventory of complexities. The two exemptions did not make it possible for 'traditional' hunting to continue. Rabbits tend to stay close to their warrens and go underground at the sight of dogs, thus not providing the chase that hunts seek. Traditionally, in some upland areas, foxes were flushed by packs of

---

[102] Johnny Scott, *The repeal of the Hunting Act*, The Field, 1 May 2010.

dogs to be shot (this activity is still permitted in Scotland).[103] However MPs, in making law for England and Wales, decided that this activity did result in unnecessary suffering, not least because it is more difficult to control a large number of hounds in dense woodland where this activity used to take place. This exemption was claimed by one stag hound pack in the Exmoor area. In an appeal judgement following the conviction of two stag hunt officials, the judge said that such hunting conducted primarily for recreation was illegal. Many traditional hunts have bought birds of prey and say that they are using hounds to flush foxes so that the bird of prey can hunt them. The Act requires that the intention must be 'for the purpose of enabling a bird of prey to hunt the wild mammal.' Many experts, such as the Hawk Board, denied that any bird of prey could reasonably be used in the British countryside to kill a fox which has been flushed by (and is being chased by) a pack of hounds. If they were right, then it is unlikely that any use of dogs undertaken in this manner was legal. The limits on flushing foxes to guns seemed to become advisory on courts considering cases of the flushing of foxes to birds of prey. Hunting below ground takes place with terriers; the Act outlawed hunting with terriers (also known as terrier work of fox baiting) with a narrowly drawn exemption, described as existing 'for gamekeepers'; it required that any hunting below ground must comply with a number of conditions. In practice despite this, many fox hunts continued to use terriers on a regular basis. The Hunting Act did not stop, and was not intended to stop, 'drag hunting' where hounds are trained to follow an artificial scent, because no animal is chased. According to the High Court, hunting 'does not include the mere searching for an unidentified wild mammal for the purpose of stalking or flushing it.' While the equivalent law in Scotland similarly made it illegal to chase or deliberately kill mammals with dogs, there are a number of differences between the two Acts. The Scottish Act did not place a two-dog limit on the flushing of a mammal to guns in order to shoot it; with respect to flushing foxes above ground to guns to shoot them, only the Scottish Act permits this to be done to protect game birds. With respect to flushing foxes below ground to guns to shoot them, only the Scottish Act permitted this to be done to protect livestock; the Scottish Act allowed someone convicted to be sentenced for up to six months in prison, while there is no such power in the Hunting Act. In itself, the complexity in practice created a cavalier attitude to the law both for the ordinary citizen and those charged with enforcing it and applying sanctions.

[103] Protection of Wild Mammals (Scotland) Act 2002.

Foxhunting, however is considered by many people to be unacceptable for reasons other than possible cruelty. But even those who have managed to read the previous paragraphs, and struggled to understand what can and cannot be done under the law, will realise that the key issue of course was cruelty to animals. And there were many laws already in force which limited cruelty to animals.[104]

1.4.10   Abuse of the System by Consumers

There is no doubt that whilst individuals indubitably need protection from over-mighty corporations and government, they can also be over-demanding. Groups such as the Consumers' Association and other organisations need at some time to justify their existence, and sometimes convert what may be minor problems into major issues. These groups have made individuals more aware of their rights, although oddly in employment matters the trade unions have not been as active as they might or should have been. Consumer demand can create rights without obligations, as has been seen many times in the financial services industry, where individuals can select against the provider, complaining where they have lost out but keeping silent where they have gained by the unpredictable outcome of investment life. One of the debates that continues throughout this book is whether those intended to be protected by the law should also have obligations; in former times we believed much more strongly in 'caveat emptor', the ancient Roman legal principle that it was up to the buyer to take care, and not of the seller to disclose everything. The pendulum may however have swung too far the other way for a reversion to the norm to be sustainable in the long term.[105]

---

[104] See e.g. Scott Henderson, *Report of the Committee on Cruelty to Wild Animals*, 1951; *The Final Report of the Committee of Inquiry into Hunting with Dogs in England and Wales*, HMSO   www.defra.gov.uk/rural/hunting/inquiry/mainsections/huntingreport .htm; T. Burns, 12 March 2001, '*Official Report, Lords*'. House of Lords www.publications .parliament.uk/pa/ld200001/ldhansrd/vo010312/text/10312-06.htm#10312-06_para26. Ninety-four per cent of eventual hunting convictions related to poaching rather than formal hunting, Ministry of Justice statistics 2005–2014.

[105] Parliamentary Ombudsman, *Equitable Life: a decade of regulatory failure*, 4th Report, Session 2007–2008, Presented to Parliament pursuant to Section 10(4) of the Parliamentary Commission Act 1967, 16 July 2008, HC 815i (Session 2007–2008). The (second) report although hailed by consumer interests did nothing to enhance the reputation of the office of the Parliamentary Ombudsman in analysing causes of failure, merely repeating the allegations of aggrieved policyholders without further investigation whilst ignoring the issues of systemic regulatory failure or merely ill-fortune (if the House of Lords had upheld the decision of the High Court there would have been no failure). Nor did she explore the

Mrs Woolf was one such determined consumer.[106] In 1996, a leap year, she went into her local post office and bought £100,000 of National Savings pensioner's bonds, which at that time paid interest of 7 per cent a year. The prospectus governing the bond granted interest at a rate fixed for five years at a time, and earned interest for each day the bond was held. It was calculated at 1/365 of the annual interest for each a day (and 1/366 for each day in a leap year). The question which Mrs Woolf raised before an adjudicator and subsequently the high court was whether a leap year meant a calendar year or an investment year. The court agreed it should be an investment year – and her persistence earned her an extra £3.17. Whilst it is an unusual individual who goes to so much trouble for so little reward, it appears that are now many more of them.

Much of the consumerist pressure is brought about by pressure groups. Such groups are in practice essential in a democracy where the conventional voting system restricts the power of the individual to express their views; at the same time the power of pressure groups can be disproportionate, affecting the resolve of government to rebuild the infrastructure (e.g. a third runaway at Heathrow airport or a new motorway or a high speed rail track), even if it is for the benefit of many others. Pressure groups are not interested in balance, they are interested in their own concerns. Legislators can on occasion be disproportionately concerned with pressure groups, although pressure groups might contend they were not concerned enough.

I have to confess a certain minor personal hypocrisy in relation to pressure groups. One of my sons has the Asperger Syndrome condition, a condition on the autism spectrum of conditions. In 2009 the National Autistic Society promoted the Autism Bill[107] to try to ensure that proper care and management arrangements were available for those with the condition, even though it might be at the expense of others with perhaps more deserving conditions. I supported the proposal. The difficulty is that in trying to gain more community resource, changing the law seemed easier than changing the attitude of those who manage the health service and

---

real damage to policyholders caused by the requirement of the regulator for the insurer to change its investment allocations towards gilts from equities at the worst time in the economic cycle, thus guaranteeing that policyholders would lose around 30 per cent of their benefits to meet counter-productive regulatory requirements to assuage the discomfort of the regulatory community. The report was a lesson in how not to do these things (in five volumes).

[106] *Director of Savings v Woolf* (1997) Times 9 July.   [107] Autism Act 2010.

other social services. But the better way of reform was not necessarily to have a new law.

Finally there is a change in societal culture that involves an increasing unwillingness to exercise personal responsibility or to take a reasonable and calculated risk, however small. Around 400 people in the UK, for example, have travelled overseas to carry out their assisted death with such organisations as Dignitas. Technically anyone assisting them, such as a spouse or child is guilty of a criminal offence under the English law of assisting suicide.[108] In practice the authorities have avoided the prosecutions that a strict approach would involve, and used their discretion to prosecute only those assisting suicides where there is a suspicion that the assistance was tinged by an element of self-interest (as is the law in Switzerland). Nonetheless legal proceedings were initiated in the UK by a wife of an individual seeking clearance or immunity from prosecution despite being aware of the discretionary and liberal practices of the Director of Public Prosecutions. Understandably in some ways, the spouse sought absolute dispensation rather than rely on the DPP discretion. Law however is not easy to draft to provide for that approach; reducing it to legal principles may cause more sclerosis than is intended by the parties. The introduction of a new law in that case was probably not the answer – but without formal protection vulnerable spouses seemed not prepared to take the risk of helping. This reluctance to carry risk may in the end introduce legalisms which would do the cause of assisted suicide more harm than good, which was not the intention.[109]

We can all think of instances where rules have affected our lives and which have turned us into grumpy old men and women. Many rules, it is true, we can live with, some we can ignore, some do not really affect us, and

---

[108] Suicide Act 1961, which is admirably short, and with only three sections. Dignitas, www.dignitas.ch; Patricia Hewitt; *Coroner's Bill*, Times, 23 March 2009]; Coroners and Justice Act 2009. The statute is a hodge-podge of unrelated provisions, including deregulation by abolishing the offences of sedition, seditious defamation and obscene libel.

[109] Keir Starmer (Director of Public Prosecutions) *Policy for Prosecutors in respect of cases encouraging or assisting suicide*, Crown Prosecution Service, 25 February 2010. Cf the attitude of John Denham, then Secretary of State for Innovation, in relation to giving criminal records to people who sold in imperial measures, contrary to metrication legislation, 'It is hard to see how it is in the public interest, or in the interests of consumers, to prosecute small traders who have committed what are essentially minor offences. I would like to see an end to this kind of prosecution, which is why I have asked for new guidance to be introduced.' (cited in *The Yardstick*, Journal of the British Weights and Measures Association, January 2009, p1). For later responses, post Brexit, see Ysenda Maxtone Graham, *Imperial ambitions*, The Spectator, 9 July 2016: 'You can legislate for how things must be described, but it's almost impossible to legislate for how people think'.

some we do not like but we understand the reason for. But increasingly we can think of rules for which we can see no point, or which are so complicated that few can comply with them, or where the cost of compliance is disproportionate to the benefit, or where the effect is counter-productive, or where the sanction is excessive.

That there has been an expansion is indisputable; but there is less certainty as to the why. One major influence, however, is the failure of one or more elements of our life; it could be, for example, increasing gun crime, increasing obesity or insufficient equality. More recently the presumed collapse (hopefully temporary if so) of the capitalist system at the end of 2007 and financial losses that were incurred by individuals and their pension plans fuelled just the latest of such demands for regulation,[110] with the prospect of a further explosion in controls on financial services. The banking collapse in particular posed governments an unenviable but familiar dilemma; they needed to meet at least a presumption that such a collapse could never happen again. At the same time, if they developed too tight a corset of regulation, there might indeed never be such a similar collapse – but there equally might not be a recovery either, and new, improved entrants to the markets might find it hard to develop solutions to new financial problems.

1.5   Solutions

Because of the consensus view that regulation, or over-regulation, has been destructive, there have been several initiatives, both in the UK and in Europe, to manage the growth – or even reverse it. Regulation in recent years has also become a political issue, with both major parties considering political capital can be made of the increase in regulation – and suggesting solutions to the problem. The EU, long considered a cause of much of the problem, has also turned its attention to cleansing its own stables.

---

[110] See e.g. Martin Friel, *Sants: FSA's tough new stance should be feared*, Insurance Age, April 2009, p1; it describes a change of approach from principles-based regulation to outcomes-based regulation. This is a further move from prescriptive regulation. The third change in approach as many years might have provoked a discussion by the Chief Executive of the FSA of the limits to regulation, but it did not. Jiang Jianqing, chairman of the Industrial and Commercial Bank of China, warning of rejecting innovation in financial services merely because it bears some risk: 'Derivatives weren't the straw that broke the camel's back ... In China, we say: you can't stop eating just because you're afraid of choking on your food' (Financial News, 6 April 2009).

1.5.1 Attempts at Cutting Back

Some of the attempts by government have already been discussed above.[111] The political parties have also from time to time adopted deregulation as a policy (in theory at least). The Conservative Party, for example,[112] suggested that business is affected by an average of 15 new sets of regulations each working day, and an increase of 50 per cent in regulation since the Labour Government took office in 1997. It pledged that if it came to power it would reduce the regulatory burden by introducing sunset clauses in new regulations and exempting small business from red tape. The Labour Party, in government, established and dismantled a series of committees until establishing a full department with the words 'regulatory reform' in its title.

---

[111] See e.g. John Meadowcroft, ed, *Prohibitions*, Institute of Economic Affairs, 2008, ISBN 978-0-255-365857; the book discusses (and argues strongly against on pragmatic grounds) controls on recreational drugs, boxing, firearms, advertising, pornography, medical drugs and devices, prostitution, gambling, human body parts for transplantation and alcohol. It cites the famous English constitutional theorist Dicey: 'The beneficial effect of State intervention, especially in the form of legislation, is direct, immediate, and, so to speak, visible, whilst its evil effects are gradual and indirect, and lie out of sight ... Hence the majority of mankind must also of necessity look with undue favour upon government intervention. This natural bias can be counteracted only by the existence ... of a presumption or prejudice in favour of individual liberty – that is, of laissez faire.' AV Dicey, *Lectures on the relation between the law and public opinion in England during the nineteenth century*, 1914, New York. For regulation of prostitution and the sex industry, see Catherine Hakim, *Supply and desire: sexuality and the sex industry in the 21st century*, Institute of Economic Affairs, August 2015, which was not without dissent when it was published, especially in its conclusion that: 'The commercial sex industry is impervious to prohibitions and cannot be eliminated.'

[112] The cost of such regulations appears to increase; the Institute of Directors for example suggested the cumulative cost for new regulations introduced since 1997 as £5.92 billion per year by 2002. The Peninsula Group, which specialises in employment law, conducted a survey of 3,000 businesses in January 2003 and found that the amount of time spent dealing with government regulation by the average employer increased from 3 hours in 1997 to 9 hours in 2003. The average financial cost per business had increased by 50 per cent to £26,762 in 2002. A survey by the Institute of Directors quoted in 'The Red Tape Menace' by Richard Bacon found that 84 per cent of respondents felt that 'payroll red tape' had become 'worse' or 'much worse' since 1997 and that 93 per cent felt that 'employment regulation' had become 'worse' or 'much worse' since 1997. In 2001 Gallup surveyed several thousand businesses across the European Union on the subject of regulation on behalf of the European Commission with regard to regulation. They asked all firms with relevant knowledge to rate the complexity of other Member States' regulatory environment when trading. The UK came bottom and was judged as having the most complex regulatory environment of all 15 member states. There are other studies that place the UK somewhat higher in the table.

A later chapter examines some of these efforts, both in the UK and in Europe, to dismantle or simplify the legislative infrastructure, and a final chapter makes some suggestions as to practical reforms, seeing that most of the attempts so far have struggled to make much progress. But the failure to reform has not been for want of trying; for example the Better Regulation Task Force 2003 announced a programme of research intended, amongst other things, to explore the question that permeates this book – the question of balance. As David Arculus, the Chairman of the Task Force, explained,[113]

> It is important that people are able to enforce their rights and to be protected, but has it become too difficult for all of us [sic]. Fear of litigation can make businesses and public sector organisations improve their performance, but it can also put a huge drain on resources – both in time and money – and result in over-cautiousness. There are also the emotional costs of litigation, which can be very stressful.

The European Union similarly announced an initiative to simplify the system of EU rules, which have become in themselves a major issue.[114] But as will be seen, however, few if any of these initiatives, whilst involving recognition by governments that the regulatory framework has become excessive and counter-productive, have made much, if any, progress. A later chapter examines both the efforts that have been made and suggests some reasons for their apparent failure. A separate chapter also looks at a side issue, though nonetheless important, that of the role of the courts and the judges in creating or expanding law. There is a perception that court decisions make life difficult for all of us by, for example, expanding the definition of negligence, so that cafes are responsible for paying thousands of pounds in damages to foolish customers who spill hot tea on

---

[113] David Arculus, Better Regulation Task Force, *Press release*, 17 July 2003. See also Brian Griffiths (Lord Griffiths of Fforestfach), *Markets can't be improved by rules. Only by personal example*, The Times, 9 April 2009. Lord Griffiths was head of the Prime Minister's Policy Unit 1985–90 and served on the Economic Affairs Select Committee in the House of Lords; Tim Ambler and Keith Boyfield, *Route map to reform: deregulation*, Adam Smith Institute, 2005. [Conservative Party] Cathy Newman, *Businesses ensnared in Labour red tape, says Howard*, Financial Times, 17 April 2004.

[114] For Europe, see John Tate and Greg Clark, *Reversing the drivers of regulation: The European Union*, Conservative Research Department, Policy Unit, August 2004. See also http://ec.europa.eu/governance/better_regulation/simplification_en.htm; European Commission, *Third annual report on simplifying the regulatory environment*, Brussels, 28.1.2009, COM(2009) 17 final; EU Commission, *Subsidiarity and Proportionality, 18th Annual report on Better lawmaking*, Brussels 10.06.2011 COM(2011) 344 final. For other countries: United States: see e.g. http://commongood.org.

themselves. The chapter looks at whether such complaints are valid – and again, if so, what might be done to improve matters. Lord Woolf's reforms (followed by those of Lord Justice Jackson) in reforming the litigation system was intended not so much to improve the law as to make the system more efficient, and has also had its critics.[115]

1.6 Conclusions

It is fairly evident that there is a consensus view shared by academics, parliamentarians and elements of the civil service, that there is an excess of government in the UK and in much of the developed world.

This is shown by statements of the judiciary, senior members of government and the establishment of numerous government bodies to attempt to cut back regulations. In the UK for example the government in 2007 changed the name of one of its government departments from 'Trade and Industry' to 'Business, Enterprise and Regulatory Reform'.[116]

Now that it is accepted that there is over-regulation, and that it is harmful, it is time to turn to how it operates in the three main areas of lawmaking – and then explore what can be done about it, other than utter curses in the manner of Richard Wilsons or of 'Disgusted, Tunbridge Wells'.[117]

---

[115] In the Andrew Mitchell case a former government minister who had been falsely accused by a police officer of inappropriate use of language was engaged in litigation to recover his reputation when his lawyers failed to file a costs order by a few hours, with a loss of several hundreds of thousands of pounds, because of a strict application of the court procedural rules. It resulted in lawyers thereafter being unwilling to be helpful to those on the other side – thus driving up costs as a whole (*Mitchell MP v News Group Newspapers* [2013] EWCA Civ 1537). The decision was ameliorated by later courts. Attempts to reform court procedure are examined in Chapter 5.

[116] The Department for Business, Enterprise & Regulatory Reform, www.berr.gov.uk; it took over its deregulatory role from the Better Regulation Commission in 2008 which itself took over from the Better Regulation Task Force in 2006; see e.g. BERR, *25 ideas for simplifying EU law*, 22 July 2008, 36pp; and see also Cabinet Office, Better Regulation Executive, *A bill for better regulation: consultation document*, July 2005, 49pp; ibid, *Administrative burdens: routes to reduction*, 18pp, September 2006. See also Philip Hampton (former Chairman, Sainsbury's), *Reducing administrative burdens: effective inspection and enforcement*, HM Treasury, December 2004.

[117] See e.g. '*One foot in the grave*' a BBC sitcom series broadcast from 1990 to 2000, featuring the misanthropic character Victor Meldrew, played by Richard Wilson, mostly railing about the current condition.

2

The Law Will Fix It

He who seeks to regulate everything by law is more likely to arouse vices than to reform them. It is best to grant what cannot be abolished, even though it be in itself harmful. How many evils spring from luxury, envy, avarice, drunkenness and the like, yet these are tolerated because they cannot be prevented by legal enactments.[1]

There has never been a 'war on drugs'! In our history we can only see an ongoing conflict amongst various drug users – and producers. In ancient Mexico the use of alcohol was punishable by death, while the ritualistic use of mescaline was highly worshipped. In 17th century Russia, tobacco smokers were threatened with mutilation or decapitation; alcohol was legal. In Prussia, coffee drinking was prohibited to the lower classes; the use of tobacco and alcohol was legal.[2]

2.1 Introduction

This chapter explores in more detail one of the possible main reasons given for the growth in law and regulation, mentioned in the earlier chapter, namely the belief that law or rules are an answer, or even the answer, to a problem of society. In particular, it traces some of the development away from the belief in *caveat emptor*, the duty of the buyer to check before he buys, towards a duty of the producer to make sure the goods or services are fit for their purpose, and looks at the history of the extended use of law and the growth of regulation.

It covers a number of areas looking at the background to the belief that law can fix problems, including

- the role of trust and religion,
- the balance between rights and expectations,

[1] Baruch Spinoza, *Theologico-Political Treatise*, Chapter 22, (1670) Dover Philosophical Classics, 2013.
[2] Sebastian Marincolo, *High: Insights on marijuana*, Dog Ear, 2010.

- the balance between rights and responsibilities,
- whether there is a blame culture,
- whether there is a compensation culture,
- the development of the theory of negligence and
- the reluctance to trust the use of executive and judicial discretion,

and then explores the limitations to the use of law in practice, including

- what law can (and cannot) do,
- the limits to laws and rules,
- the use and misuse of law as a political response,
- the exaggerated or misplaced belief in the use of law and
- whether controls on lawmaking are sufficient.

The overall theme therefore considers the complementary issues of belief, of blame and of compensation – and the expectation that regulation will work where the conventional legal process does not give a sufficient remedy. And there are no prizes for guessing that it concludes, on the evidence, firstly that the belief in the usefulness of law to fix things is often unwarranted, and can even be counter-productive, and secondly and counter-intuitively that it might be better to return to the conventional legal process (i.e. the courts), with all its flaws, than enhance the role of regulators. The pressures on legislators however are considerable; they include

- changes in society, particularly the declining influence of the single indigenous religion and social norms, and the changing expectations in relation to rights and responsibilities, as well as the decline in respect for conventional authority;
- the perhaps temporary role of the press and other expressions of public opinion;
- the changing nature and professionalisation of politics and politicians;
- the changing expectations of the public; and
- the litigation process: one of the major complaints about the Anglo-Saxon legal system is the way in which it is thought that it encourages litigation. The costs of litigation to an economy are difficult to measure, but it is clear that for example the Americans spend just under 2 per cent of their GDP in tort costs. The general consensus (of the American Bar Association at least) is that that is money well-spent.

2.1.1   Changes in Society

There have been astonishing advances in English society over the last 50 years, so great that we sometimes forget how far we have come, especially when we criticise less advanced societies, such as that of Saudi Arabia, for their homophobia or attitudes to women's rights. Not only is it bad form to be homophobic today it is also illegal – a direct reversal of the English criminal law in force until the late 1960s.[3] Similarly other areas of behaviour have become unacceptable which were formerly the norm.[4]

But with the change for the better some argue that there has been also a relaxation in public norms in other areas. The change in respect for women, or for the military, or for the elderly, or for the church has meant that certain behaviours, which had been unacceptable without any need for prescription have become nearly the norm: public displays (and more) of affection, the general availability of pornography through the internet, the relative cheapness of alcohol, the ready availability of drugs, the prevalence of cheating in sport, the corruption through professionalisation of sport, or the abuse by politicians of their expense accounts. At one time such breaches of good taste or decent behaviour were constrained by peer pressure. The change in family structures, the reduction in the influence of the church, and the abolition of compulsory military service may have minimised such peer pressures – and led to the feeling that laws may be needed in their place.

2.1.2   Religion, Respect, Trust and Deference

Complex law has been around for centuries, even millennia.[5] And, whether simple or complex, whatever the law may provide it invariably needs to be accompanied by sanctions, whether internally imposed or not. In some cases the law is enforced by the King; in others by the state or by religion – or by heaven in times to come. But sanctions need to have public

---

[3] Homosexuality is still illegal in over 60 countries today; it was illegal in the UK until the Sexual Offences Act 1967 (see e.g. Buggery Act 1533; Offences Against the Person Act 1861 and Criminal Law Amendment Act 1885 s11 [the Oscar Wilde clause]).

[4] E.g. the television series Mad Men indicated how changed are the relations between men and women, and what is no longer acceptable.

[5] E.g. the *Code of* Ur-Nammu, the oldest known law code surviving today, from Mesopotamia, written in c. 2100–2050 BC. It established financial compensation for many torts, rather than lex talionis ('an eye for an eye').

acceptance; whatever the law provides, they need to be accepted by those whom it affects, or at least a majority of them, or they are unenforceable (see e.g. the recent laws on prohibition or on narcotics), and that in turn depends on the extent of the trust in their rulers by the ruled.

As communications improved, firstly with print, and later with the internet, it was inevitable that, with increased familiarity, respect for rulers – and their laws – was likely to diminish.[6] Previous cultures of deference if they ever existed are certainly now much reduced and, after that of estate agent, journalist and lawyer, amongst the least trusted occupation is that of politician or lawmaker. Because trust in politicians is low, the public has for example been reluctant to give discretionary powers to political individuals. Few have trust in such individuals not to abuse such powers as they have. The only establishment group that has so far preserved its reputation is that of the judges (at least in the UK), who as we shall see in a later chapter may have challenges of their own, especially following the appointments of non-legally qualified Ministers of Justice (Lord Chancellors).

But the other institutions in which the community reposed its trust have also fallen into disfavour – the church, the professions or the military. So the law is now expected to fill some of the holes left by the diminishing influence of these trusted groups or persons. And it can struggle to do that.[7]

---

[6] See e.g. the discussions about whether the Home Secretary could be trusted with a discretion to authorise the security forces to search private emails: the Investigatory Powers Bill 2015. Or see Philip Johnston, *Give us our lives back: a frenzy of unnecessary law-making is seriously damaging our freedom and it's no surprise we're angry*, Daily Telegraph, 25 May 2009, which pointed out that in the UK it was made illegal to sell a grey squirrel but remained legal to kill one. And see the analysis by Camilla Cavendish, later ennobled, discussing whether the complex rules about child protection are appropriate or relevant: *Children are safer with their natural families*, The Times, 8 May 2009.

[7] The debate in the USA and the UK on whether corporations should not make use of cross-border or other tax reliefs but should pay an appropriate level of taxation suggests that governments are already discussing whether to rely more on trust than on legislation; see e.g. Jane Frecknall Hughes et al., *An empirical analysis of the ethical reasoning process of tax practitioners*, Open University [2013] 114(2) Journal of Business Ethics 325–339; and see the remarks of the former Chairman of the Public Accounts Committee (Margaret Hodge) in the proceedings of the Committee with criticism of companies such as Amazon, Starbucks, Ikea and Google, and their advisers, of their moral duty to pay more tax than the law obliged them to. Session 2012–13, 12 November 2012, Public Accounts Committee, *Minutes of Evidence*, HC 716. Lady Hodge owned significant holdings in a family company that paid low rates of tax, see e.g. Helia Ebrahami, *Margaret Hodges's family company pays just 0.01pc tax on £2.1bn of business generated in the UK*, Daily Telegraph, 9 November 2012.

2.1.3   Public Understanding of Rights, Duties and Responsibilities

Allied to the issues of trust are concerns about the proper balance between rights and responsibilities. Many laws quite properly impose or introduce rights for individuals: rights to human rights, to social security benefits, to consumer protection. Less common is the imposition of a duty or responsibility on those who enjoy rights, other than penalties for breaches. It is the counter-party of the reduction in trust; the government does not trust its governed to do the right thing, and the governed see no reason to have moral duties to the state – e.g. by not claiming benefits they do not need, or by assuming responsibilities which the state also is involved in, such as family care. For a personal example, I was advised by a very capable social worker not to financially support my disabled son, and allow him to claim state benefits as part of a move to give him independence.

Politicians from time to time make efforts to improve the balance, most recently in attempts to introduce a 'big society' or 'shared society'.[8] But without a categorical statement of the balance between rights and responsibilities, and some intelligent commentary by lobby groups and the media, it is hard for politicians. One obvious example is whether old people (of whom I am one) should be entitled to expensive medical treatment at the expense of the state (for which read everyone else) or simply dignified care if we cannot afford to pay for it ourselves.

2.1.4   Public Understanding of Risk and Cost

It is part of the function of the press and broadcast media to entertain and frighten us. But they are imperfect vectors of common sense, and in particular of risk appreciation. For example, the popular press calls for

---

[8] The Big Society was a project of a former UK Prime Minister, David Cameron, involving citizen obligations as well as rights; it was succeeded by proposals for a 'shared society' by his successor, Theresa May (*The shared society*, Prime Minister's speech at the Charity Commission annual meeting, 9 January 2017, at the Royal Society, London). For a utopian manifesto, see Tony Wright MP (Labour), who once believed that structure and law were all that mattered but came to see that 'culture' was more decisive than either: 'We can do politics differently if we choose to . . . Politicians could play it straight. Journalists could play it fair. Parties could resist the rise of a political class. Ministers could make sure that cabinet government works. MPs could decide that Parliament matters (and clean up their expenses!). Interest groups could say who would have less if they are to have more. Civil servants could tell truth to power. Government could promise less and perform more. Intellectuals could abandon their 'mechanical snigger' as Orwell called it. Social scientists could write plain English. The blogosphere could exchange rant for reason. Electors could become critical citizens', *Doing Politics Differently*, [2009] 80(3) The Political Quarterly 319.

controls on immigration, even where even though statistically the numbers seem manageable or even beneficial, or for new criminal laws to prevent a particular kind of murder, despite the fact that such violence is already unlawful, or that certain anti-cancer drugs should be compulsorily available despite the imperfect understanding of cost-effectiveness. Nor is it a newspaper's job to worry about whether the cost is worth it. Interviewers on the Today current affairs daily programme on BBC Radio 4 will typically allow Mrs Trellis to complain that she is not being given access to a particular cancer drug, but neglect to quiz her on what amount the public should be expected to pay for any extra few months of life. Is it £4000, £40,000, £400,000 or is perhaps no limit at all? It is not a question for the popular media to inquire whether a medicine is value for money, or seek answers to complex questions of what value the rest of us should put on a human life. Easy populism can make for flawed lawmaking.

The risks of introducing a measure, compared with the call for its need, struggle to reach the public consciousness – and politicians and civil servants are usually ill-equipped to articulate whether making legal provision for a new road or a law against dangerous dogs is cost-effective.[9] So explaining that travelling by bike or walking down the street is riskier than travelling by plane, or that not wearing a cycling helmet might actually save lives (passing drivers who cause most injuries give a wider berth to cyclists who look amateur) is hard to explain – as is the fact that doing nothing may be better than doing something. Table 2.1 indicates the risks involved by individuals in moving about using various forms of transport, not always appreciated by travellers.[10]

The lifetime risk of dying in a transport accident, for example, is remarkably high – with most of the risk coming from road traffic

---

[9] David Spieghalter is the Winton Professor of the Public Understanding of Risk at Cambridge University: 'He played a leading role in the public inquiries into children's heart surgery at the Bristol Royal Infirmary and the murders by Harold Shipman. He promotes concepts such as the micromort (a one in a million chance of death) and microlife (a 30-minute reduction of life expectancy). He specialises in the media reporting of statistics, risk and probability and the wider conception of uncertainty as going beyond what is measured to model uncertainty, the unknown and the unmeasurable'. For one example of a competing university's misunderstanding of risk, see *After 400 years, stepladders are banned from Oxford's library*, Daily Mail, 9 May 2009, which meant that Oxford students had to travel to London to see copies of books the originals of which were in the Bodleian Library.

[10] www.bandolier.org.uk/booth/Risk/trasnsportpop.html; and for relative pedestrian injuries in the US see www.pedbikeinfo.org/data/factsheet_crash.cfm. The results are shown in terms of annual risk and lifetime risk. These risks are calculated on a population basis, not miles or kilometres travelled, or journeys taken; the numbers change when those other calculations are made.

Table 2.1 *Risk of dying in a transportation accident on a population basis*

Country	Year	Deaths	Population	Crude rate per 100,000 population	Annual odds (1 in)	Lifetime odds (1 in)
All transport accidents						
USA	2004	47,385	293,656,842	16.14	6197	80
UK	2004	3555	59,834,312	5.94	16,831	229
EU	2004	–	–	–	–	127
France	2004	5389	60,643,308	8.89	11,253	151
Germany	2004	6087	82,501,272	7.38	13,554	185
Spain	2004	5287	42,691,752	12.38	8075	115
Ukraine	2004	9427	47,271,272	19.94	5014	69
Motor vehicle accidents						
USA	2005	43,443	281,421,906	15.44	6478	82
UK	2004	3389	59,834,312	5.66	17,655	240
France	2004	5171	60,643,308	8.53	11,728	158
EU	2004	–	–	–	–	137
Ukraine	2004	7939	47,271,272	16.79	5958	82
Pedestrians killed in road traffic accidents						
USA	2005	4881	281,421,906	1.73	57,657	730
UK	2006	675	58,858,000	1.15	87,197	1104
Cyclists killed in road traffic accidents						
USA	2005	784	281,421,906	0.28	358,957	4544
UK	2006	146	58,858,000	0.25	403,137	5103
Motorcyclists killed in road traffic accidents						
USA	2005	4398	281,421,906	1.56	63,989	810
UK	2006	599	58,858,000	1.02	98,260	1244
Car users killed in road traffic accidents						
USA	2005	18,440	281,421,906	6.55	15,261	193
UK	2006	1612	58,858,000	2.74	36,512	462
Passenger airline deaths						
USA	2003	66	290,809,777	0.02	4,406,209	55,078
UK	2006	17	60,023,858	0.03	3,530,815	44,135
World-wide	2006	755	6,548,696,975	0.01	8,673,771	108,422
		755	704,000,000	0.11	932,450	11,656
Passenger train deaths						
USA	2006	2	299,398,484	0.0007	149,699,242	1,871,241
UK	2005	10	58,858,000	0.02	5,885,800	73,573

Table 2.2 *Relative annual and lifetime transport risk in UK, based on relative traffic and kilometres travelled*

Cause of death	Deaths	Relative traffic per 100 million vehicle kilometres	Crude rate per 100 million vehicle kilometres	Odds of dying in average year (1 in)	Lifetime odds (75 years) (1 in)
All transport	3555	7970	0.45	19,327	258
Motor vehicle	3389	7320	0.46	30,967	413
Car	1612	6780	0.24	73,198	976
Motorcyclist	599	60	9.98	286,191	3816
Cyclist	146	40	3.65	761,191	10,147
Airline	25	99	0.25	4,082,474	54,433
Train	10	520	0.019	9,848,485	131,313

Note: The table shows the data in terms of an annual risk of dying, and in terms of a lifetime risk assuming a 75 year life expectancy. Road is much more risky than train or plane; the table shows the lifetime risk of various sorts of travel.
Source: www.bandolier.org.uk/booth/Risk/transporttrav.html.

accidents. While the risk of dying in a road accident in any year in the UK approaches 1 in 20,000, the lifetime risk is 1 in 240. In the Ukraine on the other hand it is 1 in 80.

But that is a general comparison; the different risks of travelling on different means of transport disclose road travel is much riskier than other forms, despite public perception of the converse (Table 2.2).

Public policy might suggest we should all travel by air or rail wherever possible, even to school. But the figures make it clear that the UK has low transport risks and that further measures to reduce them further may not be worthwhile – other than requiring cars to proceed with a red flag in front of them.[11] Whatever the numbers it is evident that not all lawmaking

---

[11] There are continual calls for reduction in speed limits to save lives, but the evidence is mixed, see Hayley Birch, *Do 20 mph speed limits actually work?*, The Guardian, 29 May 2015. See also Locomotives Act 1865 (Red Flag Act); speed was limited to 2 mph in urban areas, with all vehicles to have a crew of three; it and some others were eventually repealed by the Locomotives on Highways Act 1896:

> To-day a new and important Act of Parliament will come into operation – the Loco-motives on Highways Act, which removes many vexatious restrictions upon the use of horseless vehicles on ordinary roads. Hitherto, the law has been such that a light motor

is evidence-based – and even where it nominally is, the evidence may not be clear.

Risk theatre may also have a place in the pantheon of risk reduction, but it can be costly – and ineffective. The checks on airline passengers have become irritating for most passengers – and they and the authorities both know they are pointless and costly. None of the security measures imposed following 9/11, for example, would have stopped 9/11, although they might have stopped the odd shoe-bomber. And there are no similar checks on underground passengers, although experience suggests that bombing an underground train can be more catastrophic. The difficulty is always, as has been pointed out, that it is difficult for regulators and politicians to argue for a relaxation of safety and security rules; the risk to the

car, propelled by steam, electricity or oil, has had to conform to regulations originally framed to meet the case of the heavy traction engine, one of these rules being that the locomotive must be driven at a very slow rate, and must be preceded by a man on foot carrying a red flag. During the last few years the construction of the motor-car has been carried to a high degree of perfection on the Continent, where its use has become increasingly common. In this country, however, the employment of these vehicles, which the French term auto-mobiles, has been completely handicapped by the now antiquated laws which a British Parliament once deemed necessary for the protection of the lives and limbs of lieges traversing the highways of the United Kingdom. By the passing last session of the new Act referred to, however, the difficulties formerly experienced by English inventors and owners of motor-cars, with respect to their rights to country roads and city streets, will disappear. The statute, which comes into force today (Saturday), concedes practically all that has been claimed by the advocates of horseless carriages; and the code of regulations issued by the Local Government Board this week, and relating to the use on the Queen's highway of what are officially described as 'light locomotives' seem likely to satisfy both local authorities and the drivers of these engines, the maximum speed of which has been fixed at twelve miles an hour.

Horseless vehicles, Grantham Journal, 14 November 1896. Three months earlier had seen the first road accident death: Bridget Driscoll was a 44-year-old mother with two children who had come to London with her teenage daughter and a friend to watch a dancing display. On 17 August 1896 the crash occurred on a terrace in the grounds of Crystal Palace in London, and while the driver was reported to be doing 4 mph, witnesses described her at being hit by a car travelling at 'tremendous speed'. She died minutes later of head injuries. The car was owned by the Anglo-French Motor Car (Roger-Benz) Company who were offering demonstration rides to the public. At the time of the crash, the car was being driven by Arthur Edsell, an employee of the company. He had had been driving for only three weeks (no driving tests or licenses existed at that time). He had apparently tampered with the belt, causing the car to go at twice the intended speed and was also said to have been talking to the young lady passenger beside him. After a six-hour inquest, the jury returned a verdict of 'Accidental Death'. No prosecution was proposed or brought against the driver or the company. The Coroner at the enquiry is reported to have remarked: 'I trust that this sort of nonsense will never happen again'.

politician is asymmetric. No one will lose their job for being over-cautious, and the cost is mostly borne by someone else – whereas the penalty for laxity is severe, even if the menace changes or disappears.[12]

2.2   Belief in Law as an Instrument of Public Policy

Many legislators seem to have a belief that the primary way to fix a perceived ill is to legislate against it. The US Bill of Rights (which amounted to the first 10 amendments to the US Constitution, one of which amendments remains unratified to this day) is a well-known example. The intention was categorically to limit the power of the federal government (and indeed all government) to make law. The attempt signally failed, but the ramifications of the objective could later be seen during the years of the Obama administration where the intentions of President and the Congress were frequently frustrated by the checks and balances so that the business of government was impeded. This was not so much a fault of the system as an in-built element of its design. There are much lower barriers in other states, especially where there are bicameral legislatures, but the UK system has all but emasculated its second chamber. The impediments to lawmaking in most constitutions are limited.

2.2.1   Market Failure

Market failure is sometimes used as the basis for introducing consumer protection where there is an imbalance of power between an individual and an institution for example. But it can work both ways. Following the Black Death in England in the middle of the fourteenth century, around a half of the population died – and there was a consequent dearth of labour, which promptly realised its market value. After pressure from the nobles, Edward III passed the Statute of Labourers 1351, to make sure that wages stayed at the same level as before:

> Whereas lately it was ordained by our lord king and by the assent of the prelates, earls, barons, and others of his council, against the malice of servants who were idle and not willing to serve after the pestilence without excessive wages, that such manner of servants, men as well as women, should be bound to serve, receiving the customary salary and wages in the

---

[12] Michael Hanlon, *Flying scared*, The Spectator, 12 July 2014; but see the public response to a tragic fire in June 2017 in the Grenfell Tower, London and the call for more regulation, probably on the basis of insufficient information.

places where they are bound to serve in the twentieth year of the reign
[1347] of the king that now is, or five or six years before, and that the same
servants refusing to serve in such a manner should be punished by imprisonment of their bodies, as is more plainly contained in the said statute.
Whereupon commissions were made to diverse people in every county to
enquire and punish all those who offend against the same. And now for
as much as it is given to the king to understand in the present parliament
by the petition of the commons that the servants having no regard to the
ordinance but to their ease and singular covetousness, do withdraw themselves from serving great men and others, unless they have livery and wages
double or treble of what they were wont to take in the twentieth year and
earlier, to the great damage of the great men and impoverishment of all
the commonality; whereof the commonality prays remedy. Wherefore in
the parliament by the assent of the prelates, earls, barons, and those of the
commonality assembled there, in order to refrain the malice of the servants, there are ordained and established the underwritten articles.

The legislation reflected the views of the equivalent of Canute's advisers;
it failed to work and eventually wages doubled between 1350 and 1450.[13]

In fact 'market failure' is often used as an excuse to intervene even where
it is hard to demonstrate such failure, which normally occurs where there
is an oligopoly, where the competition authorities should intervene, or
where it is not unreasonable, e.g. where a producer has a monopoly by
patent.

One well-known market failure was the production of meat in the US
in the nineteenth century. A novel by Upton Sinclair described in gut-
wrenching detail the production of sausages made of horse-meat, dog-
meat, sawdust, fillers and formaldehyde. As a consequence the US passed
the Federal Meat Inspection Act and the Pure Food and Drug Act; but
stores as a consequence also competed on the quality of their products,
which in some ways made the legislation otiose.[14]

2.2.2   Sending a Message

The Criminal Justice and Courts Act 2015 s33 makes it illegal to publish what has become known as revenge porn, i.e. sexually explicit images
involving a former partner with intent to cause distress. The section,

---

[13] Gregory Clark, *The long march of history: Farm wages, population, and economic growth,
England 1209–1869*, [2007] 60(1) Economic History Review 97–135.

[14] Upton Sinclair, *The Jungle*, Doubleday, 1906; Lloyd Handwerker and Gil Reavill, *Famous
Nathan: A Family Saga of Coney Island, the American Dream, and the Search for the Perfect
Hot Dog*, Flatiron Books, 2016.

which is well-written in simple and understandable English, was published in a portfolio bill of criminal changes. Publishing revenge porn can cause immense distress, and there seems to be a public consensus that it needs to be controlled either by the criminal law or the civil law or both. The civil law might have been more useful, since it would enable the offended individual to cause distress back, i.e. by making the perpetrator pay money. It is of course hard to issue civil proceedings, but it might be argued that that is the difficulty of access to a remedy, i.e. the courts, that needs to be fixed, not the introduction of a new criminal offence, which may or may not be prosecuted, and where the burden of proof is higher.

In any event, no such new offence needed to be created. Prosecutions were (and still are) available under the Malicious Communications Act 1988 s1 which deals with the sending of electronic communications which are indecent, grossly offensive, threatening or false, provided there is an intention to cause distress or anxiety to the recipient, or under the Communications Act 2003 s127 which makes it an offence to send or cause to be sent through a 'public electronic communications network' a message that is 'grossly offensive' or of an 'indecent, obscene or menacing character'. Where there is more than one incident, or the incident forms part of a course of conduct directed towards an individual, a charge of harassment could be considered under the Protection from Harassment Act 1997. And where the images may have been taken when the victim was under 18, prosecutors could consider offences under the Protection of Children Act 1978. Finally, in more serious cases, where intimate images are used to coerce victims into further sexual activity, there are offences available to be prosecuted under the Sexual Offences Act 2003.

s33 was unnecessary to resolve the problem of new technology. It did however send a message, and it may have made it easier to prosecute where there is a dedicated section for a prosecutor to lean on. But new law confuses prosecutors and perpetrators, especially where, enacted out of context as it was, it exposes individuals to multiple offences for a single act, and it may make prosecution harder, since any new and untested law offers fresh legal arguments to be presented by the defence.[15]

Another area which has had unintended consequences involves the money laundering rules. It is understandable that countries should try and

---

[15] Criminal Justice and Courts Act 2015, s33; *Crown Prosecution Service offers clear guidance for prosecutors on 'revenge pornography'*, CPS, 6 October 2014. And it was also considered that in itself it was insufficient for example to cover activities and nuisances such as upskirting.

control the money made from crime; but the rules against criminals create offences by otherwise legally compliant citizens. In 2012 the US imposed a $1.9B fine on HSBC, a British bank, for poor controls on money laundering. And similar fines were imposed on Barclays, ING and Standard Chartered. BNP Parisbas faced a fine of $10B in the States in 2014. The effect of these fines are that banks move away from countries and businesses where there is even the slightest risk of a regulatory breach, so that innocent consumers are unable to find banking services. US regulations require banks to know not only who their customers are and what they are doing with their cash, but also the identities and intentions of their customers' customers. As a consequence the number of correspondent-banking relationships fell. Around a third of such relationships closed in recent years, with a serious consequential effect for individuals in poor countries. Money transfers into Somalia by Barclays Bank for example were cut, causing severe personal hardship for thousands of indigent people who were being supported by foreign remittances. It is evident that such money laundering rules are not normally effective to restrict the flows – and they make it harder for the police to track terrorists once the cash flows cease. The public may be being misled by governments and international organisations who claim that criminals and terrorists are ceasing their activities because of the controls. But there is little political capital in changing the policy and the law to make it so that the system attacks the criminals, rather than those caught up in the flows of criminal money. The system criminalises ordinary businesses and citizens without obviously damaging the real criminals.[16]

2.2.3   Information Asymmetry

Financial services regulation is often justified on the fact that there is an unbridgeable asymmetry of information between the consumer and the producer. It reflects in some ways the move from the principle of *caveat emptor* to the Sale of Goods Act which imposed new duties on the manufacturer and seller. There is however no limit on the degree of intervention that seems to be required to prevent consumers being foolish, and the balance has been all but impossible to achieve.

---

[16] See *Hitting at terrorists, hurting business: forcing banks to police the financial system is causing nasty side effects*, The Economist, 14 June 2014. See also real hardships imposed on people who are unable to open accounts at all, Tony Hetherington, *Why are banks allowed to play judge and jury on their customers*, Mail on Sunday, 21 August 2016. The fact that banks are not permitted to say why they have closed an account makes it impossible for a customer to explain that he may have been confused with another – or even complain.

The argument against a 'TripAdvisor'-style consumer protection policy for financial services for example is that unlike hotels or flights, the purchase of a financial product is infrequent and major. Similarly, there might be a need for restaurant hygiene inspections, even with the existence of a TripAdvisor, on general public health grounds. On the other hand a careful consumer can now always find out much more about a service provider, including the experience of other consumers, than they ever could before. If a regulator were indeed to seek lower cost regulation, it might do worse than invent a TripAdvisor for its own sector. Information asymmetry continues, but is much less material nowadays with the improvement of access to information by the public.

2.2.4   Local Rule Making: Checks and Balances

Sometimes there are problems that need to be fixed. In 2014 the UK passed the Anti-Social Behaviour, Crime and Policing Act 2014; the idea was amongst other things to give local authorities the power to control anti-social behaviour, which can frighten local citizens. It was part of a decentralisation agenda so that local people could decide local issues. The legislation however depended on the good behaviour of the local councils. The Act introduced 'Public Spaces Protection Orders'; such orders could be made by a single council official, after a brief consultation with the police, in a matter of days. In some cases such orders have proved useful and popular (with the law-abiding citizens). By 2016 around 79 authorities had made 130 PSPOs. They created new criminal laws, with what seemed to be minimal checks and balances, and a low burden of proof. The orders that were eventually made however now appear absurd: it is an offence to carry a golf bag in North East Derbyshire, to use noisy remote controlled vehicles in Hillingdon, to cover the face in Sefton, Halton and Birmingham, to engage in pavement art in Swindon or to occupy a camping vehicle in Luton or Wolverhampton. Whilst they seem to be merely a variety of the otherwise mostly harmless bye-laws that councils still have (and the Act codified three other orders which used to exist: Gating Orders, Designated Public Place Orders and Dog Control Orders), the Act in fact extended criminal liability and for example criminalised young people in trouble-free areas and could criminalise an elderly person feeding a pigeon.[17] By way of contrast with bye-laws, which are enforced through the magistrates

---

[17] See Josie Appleton, *PSPOS: a busybodies charter*, Manifesto Club, 2016; Home Office, *Anti-social Behaviour, Crime and Policing Act 2014: reform of anti-social behaviour powers: statutory guidance for frontline professionals*, July 2014.

courts, PSPOs are punishable by on-the-spot fines of up to £100 by police officers and local authority officials. The way in which this can be abused is demonstrated by what happened in Cambridge for example in an attempt to control who can establish a punt company:[18]

> The PSPO is related to the council's new not-for-profit Destination Man-agement Organisation (DMO) which seeks to be self funding in three years time. It will do this by making money from commission via punting sales to one major operator and its own walking tours. This PSPO will mean that the 6% of the punts currently held by independents will be out of business. No rival tours will be permitted to compete with the council's own by tout-ing or advertising their services in the city centre. 65% of river frontage is already leased at below market rental by the council to one dominant com-pany. This company owns 60% of the punts on the river. Both the council via its DMO and this company stand to reap several hundred thousand pounds per annum from this order being passed. This financial benefit has been completely omitted from the consultation. 100 young people stand to lose their jobs from this order and four independent companies stand to go out of business.

2.3 Implementing Policy through Law and Regulation

2.3.1 Law as a Solution of Choice

Whether or not there is an actual problem to be fixed, or whether there might be alternative solutions, it does look as though law has become the solution of choice for policymakers in fixing societal problems. Indeed law and regulation have increasingly reflected not only basic principles of morality and social equity, but also broader matters of public pol-icy. A law for example can 'send a message' even if it may not be the best way of implementing policy and civil servants have long complained that politicians insist on designing policy and that they are simply left to implement it inevitably through law.[19] The self-confidence (or arro-gance) of politicians, i.e. that they decide policy and then leave it to oth-ers to implement the reforms, can be addictive, and the convention that ministerial decisions are personal rather than collective or collegiate is

---

[18] Josie Appleton, *PSPOS: a busybodies charter*, Manifesto Club, 2016. The report lists drafting and other absurdities, and points out several accidental criminalisation of lawful activities. There are also no requirements on publication of the Orders, so that the public does not know what the rules are.

[19] See e.g. Richard Mottram, *Civil service reform: hidden dangers*, Better Government Initia-tive, 2013.

frequently expressed in political interviews ('I have decided...', not 'we have decided').[20] Nonetheless because tenure in political office is often limited, and civil servants move from job to job as well, accountability does not often travel in company with the decisions.[21]

Since ministerial responsibilities shift frequently, as do political headwinds, in practice it also inevitable that this can lead to inconsistencies in policy making – and in particular to the announcement of sound-bite or short-term policies. This was noted by a group of retired civil servants which established a small think tank to deal with just this issue.[22] It made some rather obvious recommendations, expressed in mandarinese, including the advice that government should

- base policy on evidence and front-line experience;
- reduce involvement of central government (code for 'the Treasury') in department operations to absolute minimum;
- minimise and justify changes in machinery of government, delivery structures and appointments;
- ensure proposals for legislation meet required standards;
- limit legislative programme to a size that Parliament can cope with;
- set standards for preparation of bills and other major proposals;
- ensure parliamentary compliance with the standards; and
- implement a 'professional skills for government programme'.

The conclusions reflected partly a call for a restoration of the power and influence of senior civil servants, and it had some modest justification. It had been the reluctance (or perceived reluctance) of civil servants to engage in ministerial proposals for reform that had original driven the civil service to be given an implementive rather than a policy role. But in

---

[20] Norman Fowler, *Ministers decide, a personal memoir of the Thatcher years*, Chapmans, 1992.

[21] See in relation to EU regulation, former EU Industry Commissioner Gunther Verheugen: 'There are 27 commissioners, which means 27 directorate-generals. And 27 directorate-generals means that everyone needs to prove that they are needed by constantly producing new directives, strategies or projects. In any case, the rule is: More and more, more and more, all the time.' Spiegel, 9 February 2010, *The EU has no vision of where we are heading*, www.spiegel.de/international/europe/former-european-commissioner-guenter-verheugen-the-eu-has-no-vision-of-where-we-are-heading-a-676784.html.

[22] Better Government Initiative, *Good government: reforming parliament and the executive*, 56pp mimeo, January 2010 (www.bettergovernmentinitiative.co.uk). A similar rubric was issued some years later by The Constitution Society, with about as much impact: Jack Simson Caird, Robert Hazell and Dawn Oliver, *The constitutional standards of the House of Lords Select Committee on the Constitution*, The Constitution Society, January 2014 (www.consoc.org.uk/wp-content/uploads/2014/02/Screen-Shot-2014-02-11-at-15.42.03.png).

practice the balance had probably swung too far, to a situation where the stream of political initiatives had become impossible for the machinery to deliver.[23] The complaint of MPs is that they have been diverted to spending more time on constituency business than on parliamentary business,[24] and when they do become ministers they on average have no more than three years on the front benches.[25] During a previous UK Labour administration for example the average life expectancy for a pensions minister was around nine months, whilst pension strategy normally involves a 50-year outlook. Policy changes are therefore rapid (while the minister makes his mark, or inherits a previous minister's mark that the new minister is uncomfortable with) and unstable. The issues raised by the ad hoc think tank included

- the impact of perverse incentives and unintended consequences of targets and performance indicators;
- the difficulty of speaking truth unto power;
- the confusion and loss of expertise resulting from frequent changes of policy or organisation and movement of staff to meet new demands;
- the loss of direction as one initiative is laid on top of another, or 'trialled' and 'rolled out' distracting attention from ordinary business;
- the excessive bureaucracy in prescribing new systems or procedures, often in unnecessary detail; and
- a 'tick box' culture in which complying with the rules replaces responsible judgment and individual discretion.

Many of the government changes seem to involve change for the sake of change, perhaps for presentational rather than administrative purposes.[26] There is no obvious solution to the problem, but the motherhood and

---

[23] Michael Barber, *Instruction to Deliver: Tony Blair, the Public Services and the Challenge of Delivery*, 320pp, Politicos, 2008. Michael Barber operated a 'delivery unit' for the then Prime Minister, Tony Blair, who had become frustrated with the barriers that the Civil Service erected to his ideas for reform. Mrs Thatcher had had a similar frustration. Michael Barber's function was to manage the civil service so as to achieve the reforms.

[24] Sir David Omand, Professor Ken Starkey and Lord Victor Adebowale, *Engagement and aspiration: reconnecting policy making with front line professionals*, Cabinet Office, London, 2009.

[25] For a sobering review of how ill-equipped new ministers are when they enter office, see Nicola Hughes, *How to be an effective minister: What ministers do and how to do it well*, Institute for Government, Analysis Paper, March 2017.

[26] House of Commons Public Administration Committee, *Machinery of government changes*, Seventh report of Session 2006–07, HC672; ibid, *Further report on the machinery of government*, Seventh Report of Session 2008–09.

apple pie nostrums mentioned above have clearly not worked. Alternative or additional solutions might include

- a change of prime ministerial mindset avoiding frequent reshuffles;
- a change of civil service practice requiring civil servants to retain responsibility for previous decisions; and
- a change of ministerial mindset so that the objective should be improved administration rather than policy reform. Such a change is hard to develop because there are inevitable failures of the machine, and slow-but-sure is less exciting and often incompatible with the nature of political ambition.

As a later chapter explores, none of these suggested improvements could take place without a change of mindset; it is that which may lie at the heart of improved public administration. And helping people move towards that new mindset might need amongst other things the formal adoption of a set of principles when appointed, rather like an oath of loyalty to the Crown, as well as training or qualification for ministers, involving the development of both hard and soft skills.

2.3.2   Pressures for Change: Lobbyists and Interest Groups

> Because half-a-dozen grasshoppers under a fern make the field ring with their importunate chink, whilst thousands of great cattle, reposed beneath the shadow of the British oak, chew the cud and are silent, pray do not imagine that those who make the noise are the only inhabitants of the field; that of course they are many in number; or that, after all, they are other than the little shrivelled, meagre, hopping, though loud and troublesome insects of the hour.[27]

The earlier chapter explored some of the drivers for regulatory expansion; one of them was that the lobbying system can on occasion provoke increased regulation. Legislators need lobbyists to help them explore the wider effects of the proposals they are making, and often lobbyists argue for new or changed legislation to meet their particular objectives, as much as they object to new laws. A study of the US system suggests that there is a lobbying excess (it might be less of an issue in the UK):[28]

> Washington DC is home to almost 12,000 lobbyists (more than 20 for every member of Congress) who cost their clients $2.4 billion in 2012.

---

[27] Edmund Burke, *Reflections on the Revolution in France* (1790).
[28] John Micklethwait and Adrian Wooldridge, *The Fourth Revolution*, Allen Lane, 2014, p257.

> These lobbyists are not only responsible for obvious sins like getting sweet-heart deals for their clients. They also add to the complexity of legislation. The more convoluted a law is, the easier it is to smuggle in special privileges.

In the UK there is now some rather superficial regulation of lobbying, again contained in a portmanteau Act, dealing also with non-party campaigning and trade union administration, requiring the registration of professional lobbyists.[29] Lobbying is a necessary part of the legislative process so that legislators can develop a better understanding of issues than their more closed world would normally allow. But it can also have a malign effect, pushing for legislation which is not strictly necessary to achieve the desired objective, simply because it looks good to clients and others to have achieved some minor change in the legislation. In September 2015 the HM Inspector of Constabulary, not of course a lobbyist in the general understood sense, but with lobbying inclinations, reported that he thought that the system for firearms licensing needed urgent change: 'Britain faces new gun massacres unless the chaotic firearms licensing regime is overhauled . . . ' His conclusions were severely criticised by a former Inspector who concluded: 'It is unfortunate that the report is short on risk-managed solutions and makes easy calls for more bureaucracy. The Law Commission is already considering whether or not it should seek to amalgamate the existing 34 pieces of firearms legislation.'[30] A code of practice for lobbyists as well as legislators, might be one modest tool to help them refrain from grandstanding.[31]

---

[29] Transparency of Lobbying, Non-Party Campaigning and Trade Union Administration Act 2014.

[30] *Targeting the risk: an inspection of the efficiency and effectiveness of firearms licensing in police forces in England and Wales*, Her Majesty's Inspectorate of Constabulary, September 2015; Geoffrey Dear (Lord Dear), *Monitoring of firearms holders needs to be continuous and more effective*, The Times, Letter, 17 September 2015. *The administration of firearms licencing*, HMIC, 1993; Law Commission, *Firearms Law: a scoping consultation paper*, Law Commission Consultation Paper No 224, July 2015.

[31] Transparency of Lobbying, Non-Party Campaigning and Trade Union Administration Act 2014; see for the supposed ill-effect of the Act on the activities of charities, Richard Harries, *Impact of the Lobbying Act on civil society and democratic engagement*, Commission on Civil Society and Democratic Engagement, September 2014 (Interim Report). There are lobbyists' codes in Australia and Canada, and in the European Union Communication from the Commission, *European Transparency Initiative, A framework for relations with interest representatives (Register and Code of Conduct)* SEC(2008) 1926, Brussels, 27 May 2008 (COM(2008)323 final). And see http://ec.europa.eu/transparencyregister/public/homePage.do.

2.3.3   Risk and Public Safety

Law can perform a useful task by limiting the public to exposure to risk. The default situation is that people are allowed to adopt their own level of risk; for example, they are allowed to sky-dive without a parachute.[32] On the other hand in the UK homeowners are not allowed to fix an electrical socket in their own kitchen.[33]

Many of the risk-control restrictions are imposed by professionals or quasi-professional pressures, even where such controls seem hard to justify objectively. The regulations to license hair braiders in the US vary from requiring six hours training to 2100 hours, in theory to protect the public. Some states require no qualifications at all. One measure of the need for regulation is whether there are complaints about a service provider. Of the 103 complaints made in the US about hair braiding from 2006 to 2012, one was made by a consumer, 77 were filed by cosmetology boards and 24 by other licensees or competitors.[34] Similarly a report by the White House looked at licensing for a wide range of occupations in the US, with large material differences between the requirements in the individual states. Michigan required three years of education to become a security guard, with most other states requiring fewer than 11 days. The downsides to requirements included impediments to immigrants being able to find work, to petty criminals being able to resume employment, and to military spouses who moved from state to state being able to practise their skills. The costs of licensing were high, which meant higher costs for consumers.[35]

In the UK the charges of lawyers, which needed to cover as well as the usual office overheads, the costs of compliance, training and professional liability insurance, had risen to such a level that many litigants and defendants could not afford representation in the absence of legal aid. As a consequence there emerged an unqualified and uninsured group of practitioners, known as 'McKenzie Friends' – lay people, sometimes

---

[32] Luke Aikins was the first, see David Millward, *Skydiver becomes first to jump 25,000 feet without a parachute*, Daily Telegraph, 31 July 2016; curiously the Screen Actors Guild originally insisted on him wearing a parachute, although that would have been more dangerous when he landed in a net.

[33] See e.g. UK Building Regulations, Part P, 1 January 2005.

[34] Angela C. Erickson, *Barriers to Braiding: how job-killing licensing laws tangle natural hair care in needless red tape*, Institute for Justice, July 2016, Arlington, Virginia.

[35] The White House, *Occupational licensing: a framework for policymakers*, a report prepared by the Department of the Treasury Office of Economic Policy, the Council of Economic Advisers and the Department of Labor, July 2015.

remunerated, who helped litigants-in-person. The rise of course led in turn to calls for their qualification and professional liability insurance, to avoid delays in the court process and to protect the consumer, leading in turn to an increase in their charges.[36] Getting the balance right seems to be intractable.

2.3.4   Distrust of the Exercise of Discretion

In the US following the introduction of Medicare, with substantial sums flowing into the medical industry, proper accounting was considered necessary to control costs. In 2015 Medicare introduced 150,000 codes, including nine different ones for injuries caused by turkeys (was the victim struck or pecked? once or more often? did she suffer negative side effects?). There are around half a million appeals against wrong coding and the system deters doctors from taking on Medicaid patients – around 80 per cent of doctors refuse to take on such patients.[37]

2.3.5   Other Engines of Change (Nudge)

The nudge principle in lawmaking has enjoyed a sustained period of fashion, most notably in UK second-tier pension provision.[38] The UK has a social security pension provided through the tax system; but membership of workplace pension arrangements had been falling for 30 years. Membership of a workplace pension was made compulsory – but with a right to opt-out to avoid complaints of additional taxation. In practice because of the bureaucracy involved, and the initial low sums deducted, few have opted-out. It was regulation by nudge, to encourage good behaviour by default decision-making. It is too early to determine whether it is working well, and there are indications of unintended consequences, e.g. people

---

[36] See e.g. Practice *Guidance: McKenzie Friends (Civil and Family Courts)*, 12 July 2010 (English Courts); *Reforming the courts' approach to McKenzie Friends, A Consultation*, Lord Chief Justice of England and Wales, February 2016.

[37] *The 140,000-code question: how complex are health regulations?* The Economist, 31 May 2014.

[38] See Richard H. Thaler and Cass R. Sunstein, *Nudge: Improving Decisions about Health, Wealth, and Happiness*, 2008. UK Cabinet Office, Behavioural Insights Team, *Annual Report 2016* at http://38r8om2xjhhl25mw24492dir.wpengine.netdna-cdn.com/wp-content/uploads/2016/09/BIT_Update_Report_2015-16-.pdf

considering they have adequate pensions when they do not.[39] So far, there are few other successful instances.[40]

2.3.6   Foreigners and Devolution

It has been observed that the growth of globalisation inevitably adds cross-border agreements, and treaties to the legislative mix. There are cross-border insolvency treaties, double taxation agreements, inheritance arrangements and harmonisation of patent law. Clients increasingly require advice on issues that straddle the law in several jurisdictions, and on the impact of international treaties of the Council of Europe and the United Nations and the World Trade Organisation.

In the UK, the impact of devolution means that where there was once one body of law, there may now be separate English, Irish, Welsh and Scottish law all applying within a couple of hundred miles of each other; as the UK withdraws from the European Union, and the influence of a separate corpus of law diminishes, additional levels of legislation are likely to increase internally.

2.3.7   Is There a Problem to Be Fixed Anyway?

Many problems are invented problems. One example has been long-standing controls on the ability of lawyers to advertise. Anyone who watched Breaking Bad might have reservations about the huckstering of legal services, but rules against advertising involved more matters of good taste and restraints of trade than of a need to protect the consumer:

> I recently came across a file dating back to 1975 when my firm moved offices. Among the papers is correspondence with both the Law Society and Yorkshire Law Society, seeking approval for plinth mounted signage outside the new office. No fewer than nine letters passed between the parties with concerns expressed by the local law society (in committee) that the proposed 5' by 2' 6" sign was 'perhaps on the large side'. Only when

---

[39] Pensions Act 2008.

[40] The UK Behavioural Inights Team wrote a letter to general medical practitioners using a Thaler/Sunstein derived piece of advice, saying that other doctors in their area prescribed fewer antibiotics. Those written to reduced prescriptions by 3 per cent, UK Cabinet Office, Behavioural Insights Team, *Annual Report 2016* at http://38r8om2xjhhl25mw24492dir .wpengine.netdna-cdn.com/wp-content/uploads/2016/09/BIT_Update_Report_2015-16- .pdf.

drawings had been supplied and the signage reduced in size to 3′ by 18″ did both societies express themselves satisfied.

Guidance was also sought as to how many times we were permitted to insert a notice in the local paper advising of our change of address; what wording was permitted; and what size the notice could be.[41]

2.4 Negligence, the Blame Culture and Compensation

One of the reasons that there is so much law is that it is relatively easy to make, especially by way of regulation. Another is the belief amongst legislators that by changing the law a problem may be solved. This belief in the efficacy of law as a remedy for society's ills is not totally naïve. It is not unreasonable that if there is a problem in society, the legislators should strive to fix it. But while in some cases the fixing may resolve the mischief, in other cases it may make an already difficult situation worse, or involve an unanticipated expense. And despite protestations to the contrary, it is not only legislators and regulators who make the rules – the courts are also involved.

2.4.1 The Compensation Culture

The most obvious development of legal obligations by the courts lies in the law of torts – civil wrongs. Part of the court system was indeed developed to solve the problem of 'black-letter' law, the fact that the law of the land as laid down in statute or the common law was imperfect, and only the judges, using their judgment and their application of what they thought was right, could resolve a legislative injustice. Such developments continue today in most areas of law, such as those of equity and chancery, or the scope of judicial review, or the application of human rights, and of course in relation to the definition of negligence.[42]

The classic case study in negligence involves the way in which the courts have treated beverage burns over the years. The two standard cases, reversing the usual stereotype, involved McDonalds in England, where hot coffee was involved, and Starbucks in the States, where tea was involved. In England Sam Bogle, for example, was 15 months old when he was taken by

---

[41] Charles Broomer, *Letter*, Law Society's Gazette, 29 September 2014.

[42] This is explored further in Chapter 5, where the struggle between the executive and the judiciary has turned into a binary form ('who is the master') and the judges have been encouraged to be apprehensive of making new law.

his child-minder to McDonald's in Hinckley Town Centre. It was alleged that Sam went to drink a cup of hot coffee which had been left on the table with its lid removed and in doing so spilled it onto himself, with distressing injuries to face, neck, chest shoulders and back.[43] It is hardly surprising that his parents sought to try to blame someone for these unpleasant injuries to their child; the big question however was whether it was McDonald's fault. They complained that McDonald's had a duty to avoid serving drinks so hot that the cups were inherently unsafe and that the lids did not fit properly. They complained that McDonald's should have warned its customers that they might be scalded by hot drinks. And they claimed under the then Consumer Protection Act 1987 that the drinks were 'defective'.

The current version of that Act, the Consumer Rights Act,[44] is just one of a vast library of consumer protection legislation; setting aside much of the considerable volume of material emanating from the European Union, the consolidating legislation includes the terms of much of what had been the Sale of Goods Act 1979, Trading Schemes Act 1996, Trade Descriptions Act 1968, Price Marking Order 1999, Consumer Credit Act 1974, Consumer Credit (Advertisements) Regulations 1989, Property Misdescriptions Act 1991, Timeshare Act 1992, Trade Marks Act 1994, Copyright Designs and Patents Act 1988, Data Protection Act 1988, British Codes of Advertising and Sales Promotion, Distance Selling Regulations, Unfair Contract Terms Act 1977, Unfair Terms in Consumer Contracts Regulations 1999 and a host of supporting regulations. All of these counter the *caveat emptor* principle, and are designed to protect individuals against a fraudulently calibrated pump failing to dispense a full litre when buying fuel at a petrol station, and against estate agents misleadingly describing properties they are keen to sell.

---

[43] *Bogle v McDonald's Restaurants* [2002] EWHC 490 (QB) (27 March 2002). That case declined to follow the US practice (and a US case, not cited in the English case, when an 81-year-old woman also bought a coffee from McDonalds, spilt it over herself and was badly burned (*Stella Liebeck v McDonald's*, State Court, Albuquerque, 1 September 1994). The jury award of $2.9M was subsequently settled for a reported $300,000. For illustrations of abuse of the tort system in the US see e.g. www.palawwatch.org/sbtpast.htm: people have sued in the United States when baseball players chuck the ball into the grounds after the game as a souvenir for children, for being misled into seeing a film by made-up film reviews, for maligning Italian lawyers in the Sopranos TV series, and for making peanut butter and jelly sandwiches contrary to a US patent.

[44] Consumer Rights Act 2015 see e.g. Consumer Protection (Distance Selling) Regulations 2000 SI 2000 No 2334.

In the *Bogle* case the Consumer Protection Act 1987 provided that a manufacturer is liable for damage caused by a defect in a product, and there is a defect if the safety of the product is not such as persons generally are entitled to expect. And Sam Bogle (together with 35 other claimants, 16 of them under 4) failed in his claim. But McDonald's had to do some homework to prove they had not been negligent. They always knew there was a risk that someone might be scalded; that was hardly at issue. The big question was whether they had been 'negligent'.

The evidence provided an intriguing insight into the technology of coffee production. The specialised coffee machines had to produce coffee between 86.66C to 90C brewing temperature and 86.66C to 90C holding temperature. Tea was served even hotter. But, said the judge, what would have happened if the drinks had been served cooler? Customers would have objected; they want hot drinks – and they know there are risks in handling hot drinks. In any event, if the drinks had been cooler, the scalds would have been not much less serious – and the coffee a lot less drinkable. Then was there was an extended debate about the (then Styrofoam) cups.[45] Their manufacturing specification was detailed: the cup must not leak, must not have any off-odours or impart any off-flavours, must be free of defects that would detract from their appearance or affect their performance, must resist leaking or tipping, must be rigid enough for use without a lid, be of a density at least 50 per cent above the industry standard and subject to rigidity tests, vacuum tests, weep tests, a lid fit test, a shake test, a tilt test, a tipping test and several lid tests. One complaint was that the cups were too good: their insulation was so effective that it did not give a sensory indication to the customer of how hot the liquid was.

Not only was this claim dismissed – but also the claim that there was a duty to warn the customers of the risk of scalding from hot drinks. Later cups did have a legend that said 'Caution: Hot', but for many years the cups were free from the warnings. The judge was temperate in his conclusion, but it was clear where his sympathies lay: 'I accordingly find that that there was no duty on McDonald's to warn their customers about the risk posed by the temperatures at which tea and coffee were served, notwithstanding the warnings they gave to their employees and the fact that from 1995 a warning has been printed on the cups.' It was evident that McDonald's had not been negligent.

---

[45] *Dart v Dart* [1996] EWCA Civ 1343 was a case dealing with the financial implications of the divorce of a husband who held a McDonald's supply contract, which illustrates the profits to be made from Styrofoam products.

And the position is not much different, despite popular belief, in the US. In the *Moltner* case,[46] Rachel Moltner was 76 in 2008 when she spilled tea on her left leg and foot when she tried to remove the lid from a venti-sized cup of tea she bought from Starbucks. She claimed $3 million. She had burns so severe that she required a skin graft. Her hospital stay later resulted in other injuries, including bed sores as well as herniated discs caused by a fall out of bed. Mrs Moltner accused Starbucks of serving tea that was too hot in a double cup – one cup placed inside another – that was defectively designed. She also said Starbucks should have warned her the tea could spill. The appeals court rejected her case, saying 'double-cupping is a method well known in the industry as a way of preventing a cup of hot tea from burning one's hand.' Her lawyer thought she might have won if the court had read the Starbucks directive to employees that you should not double cup because it changed the centre of gravity and could cause the cup to tip over, but looking at the trend of cases, it seems improbable.[47]

The story of hot drinks indicates that however developed a code of law, there will always be cases which had not been thought of by legislators. The tort of negligence is an ancient tort (a civil wrong) deriving back before the Bible and the Code of Hammurabi.[48] It was no doubt expressed in the very first legal codes. The civil wrong of damaging another's interests has been remedied by the law and the courts for thousands of years. In

---

[46] *Moltner v Starbucks*, 2010 (November 2), US Second Circuit Court of Appeals, upholding a decision of the district court.

[47] See e.g. *Kennedy v Cordia (Services) LLP* [2014] CSIH 76 (Scotland, Extra Division, Inner House, Court of Session) where the Scottish court of appeal held (against the decision of the court below) that 'No employer is under a duty at common law to address, ameliorate or eliminate every risk which an employee may encounter in the course of the working day'. Tracey Kennedy was a carer who slipped and injured her wrist whilst visiting a patient. She sued on the grounds that the employer had not provided a safe system of work. On the other hand, in Australia, the High Court held that a civil servant sent to a regional office in New South Wales, and who engaged in sexual intercourse with an acquaintance whilst staying at a local motel could claim compensation against her employer for her injuries under domestic health and safety legislation since 'In that process, the glass light fitting above the bed was pulled from its mount by either the respondent or her acquaintance [during intercourse] and it struck the respondent on her nose and mouth. As a result, the respondent suffered physical injuries and a subsequent psychological injury'. *Comcare v PVYW* [2013] HCA 41.

[48] Cf Deuteronomy 22:8: 'When you build a new house, make a parapet around your roof so that you may not bring the guilt of bloodshed on your house if someone falls from the roof.' See Alan Webber, *Building regulation in the land of Israel in the Talmudic period* [1996] 27(3) Journal for the Study of Judaism 263–288.

Anglo-Saxon law it developed into a sophisticated legal system by the end of the nineteenth century to cope with the needs of the industrialisation of the economy. In particular it recognised that the usual protective mechanisms were inadequate to cope with the fact that fewer individuals could cope with the increasing impact of technology; while any competent housewife could decide whether a fish was tainted before she bought it in the marketplace from the fishmonger's slab, it was unreasonable if not impossible for her to judge the quality of sardines in a tin. Similarly it was unreasonable to expect a layman to understand whether a piece of mechanical engineering would work or was safe to use; few of us today can determine whether a washing machine or a toaster is safe or useable without danger to ourselves or our family. The usual principle of *caveat emptor*, let the buyer beware, was radically amended over the nineteenth century, and changed the principles of contract law to involve what we now know as consumer protection.

There are some grounds for believing that consumer protection in contract law may have gone too far; the previous requirement for the consumer to exercise normal prudence and caution of a consumer no longer seems to be imposed by regulators or expected by legislators. In practice it appears to many that there is no longer much need for a consumer to take care at all or to exercise any form of judgment, since there is a belief that the law should protect him in all events. As has been seen elsewhere the cost of that protection however may be disproportionate; and a similar sense of disproportion seems also to be emerging in that parallel area of consumer protection law, that of negligence.

But looking at the case law, this view, whilst probably correct amongst regulators, seems not to be so when looked at by the courts. Mountaineering is one sport where the risks of injury and death are high; but the courts accept that, and with some rare exceptions will not allow claims just because there has been an accident:

> The question of whether a person has acted negligently is not answered simply by analysing what he did or did not do in the circumstances that prevailed at the time in question and then testing it against an objective standard of 'reasonable behaviour'. Before holding that a person's standard of care has fallen below the objective standard expected and so finding that he acted negligently, the court must be satisfied that a reasonable person in the position of the defendant (i.e. the person who caused the incident) would contemplate that injury is likely to follow from his acts or omissions. Nor is the remote possibility of injury enough; there must be a sufficient

probability of injury to lead a reasonable person (in the position of the defendant) to anticipate it.[49]

Add to that the statement by Lord Hoffman, one of the greatest of the Supreme Court judges in recent years:

> The question of what amounts to 'such care as in all the circumstances of the case is reasonable' depends on assessing, as in the case of common law negligence, not only the likelihood that someone may be injured and the seriousness of the jury which may occur, but also the social value of the activity which gives rise to the risk, and the cost of preventative measures. These factors have to be balanced against each other.[50]

and it is clear that the judiciary take a pragmatic view of the extent of negligence.[51] The contrast between a fundamentalist and a pragmatic view is illustrated by the different conclusions of the court of first instance and the court of appeal in the case of the bouncy castle party. Mr and Mrs Harris were celebrating the tenth birthday party of their triplets, and hired a bouncy castle. A neighbour asked whether his somewhat older child could join in, and despite the instructions for the use of the castle explaining that children of different ages should not be mixed, and that all children should be monitored at all times, and the failure to follow the instructions and following a serious injury to the one of the guest children, the first court ordered payment of £2M damages. The Court of Appeal, reversing the decision said:

> Children play by themselves or with other children in a wide variety of circumstances. There is a dearth of case precedent that deals with the duty of care owed by parents to their own or other children when they are playing together. It is impossible to preclude all risk that, when playing together, children may injure themselves or each other, and minor injuries must be commonplace. It is quite impractical for parents to keep children under constant surveillance or even supervision and it would not be in the public interest for the law to impose a duty upon them to do so. Some circumstances or activities may, however, involve an unacceptable risk to children

---

[49] *Whippy v Jones* [2009] EWCA Civ 452 (the foreseeability of the possibility of injury when letting a dog off the lead in a park is insufficient to establish breach of duty when the dog was not known to jump up a people); cf. *MacIntyre v Ministry of Defence* [2011] EWHC 690 (QB) – there's nothing wrong with instructors being at the edge of their competence.

[50] *Tomlinson v Congleton Borough Council* [2004] 1 AC 46 para 34.

[51] For a review of the court's approach to sports injuries generally see Richard Caddell, *The referee's liability for catastrophic sports injuries – a UK perspective*, [2005] 15(2) Marquette Sports Law Review 415.

unless they are subject to supervision, or even constant surveillance. Adults who expose children to such circumstances or activities are likely to be held responsible for ensuring that they are subject to such supervision or surveillance as they know, or ought to know, is necessary to restrict the risk to an acceptable level.[52]

There are less optimistic views as to the impact of the role of the tort of negligence; one study looked particularly at the health and safety issues, and while understanding the good that regulation can do in defining negligence, suggested that most of it was excessive.[53]

A similar dilemma is faced for example in pensions regulation. Following a series of pensions scandals in the UK, including that involving Robert Maxwell in the early 1990s, pensions regulation was expanded considerably; it is not established that members have in fact been better protected as a consequence, but it does seem clear that such protection has proved expensive and encouraged employers to withdraw from defined benefit schemes as a consequence. One of the drivers for regulation has been to reduce risk for members but possibly at the cost of reduced provision. One policy issue is how much intervention was needed to allow adults to judge the risk of pensions for themselves; unintended consequences have included restricting pension funds and insurer from investing in unquoted securities, making it difficult to invest in the funding of infrastructure funds, and requiring members to have information about their scheme on no more than two pages, at a minimum type size, which proved an impossibility given the amount of information obliged to be included. Making pension funds safe against all eventualities is almost impossible, and the price of trying is high.[54]

This raises the debate about the balance to be struck between security and protection for the consumer, and the counter-productive impact of excessive security. Similar debates have taken place for years about the

---

[52] *Harris v Perry* [2008] EWHC 990 (QB) reversed on appeal at *Perry v Harris* [[2008] EWCA Civ 907; see also Matthew White, *Climbing accidents – the duty and standard of care*, St John's Chambers, September 2011 and *Harrison v Jagged Globe* [2012] EWCA Civ 835 (Sir Ralph Fiennes' stunt accident).

[53] Tracey Brown and Michael Hanlon, *In the interests of safety: the absurd rules that blight our lives and how we can change them*, Sphere, 2014.

[54] Giving guarantees on pensions may make the price of the pension two or three times higher than without or, looked at another way, result in pensions half or a third the size for the same contributions. See European Insurance and Occupational Pensions Authority, *Report on issues leading to detriment of occupational pension scheme members and beneficiaries and potential scope of action for EIOPA*, EIOPA-BoS-14/071, 27 June 2014, para 2.3.3 and Article 54 of the IORP II Directive.

safety of drivers and pedestrians on the roads: on the one hand we require seat belts to be worn and strong drink to be denied. Those rules save lives. On the other hand 3500 people a year still die each year on the roads because we do not insist on a 5mph speed limit. One of the reasons we accept this is that adults (and rather fewer teenagers) appreciate the risks. If they do not like them, they can stay at home (where they may become scalded by a cup of tea), or take the train, where the risks are lower, or the plane, lower still. If they walk, they may not however appreciate the risks are higher.

The question we might need to ask ourselves is whether adults (not so much teenagers) are aware of the risks – and rewards – of salary-related pension schemes. If the risks of such schemes were increased, by reducing protection (for example by mitigating the effect of accounting and funding rules) and explained the degrees of risk to the consumer, on the basis that more people would gain more protection for their old age by doing so, how much risk might they accept? One of the keys is trying to devise a measure of risk; another is that of accepting that people are adult enough to understand it. The understandable reaction of government and regulators is to minimise risk, almost at any cost, because failures reflect badly on them, and the press is merciless on failure. Sadly it was not a question that was explored by a committee into the reform of pensions law; the timing was not right to mention that perhaps a few failures (or more commonly simply a reduction in benefit) were an acceptable price to pay for the greater good.[55]

The approach of the courts to risk seems more sensible, as the *McDonald's* case shows. The paradox is that only when our regulators accept that risk is a good thing (in moderation, like red wine), when rare and occasional pension scheme failure (like the rare and occasional scalding when drinking tea) is accepted as a reasonable price to pay for the ready availability of pension accruals (like the ready availability of hot tea) will we see a reversal of the current trend away from defined benefit systems. In theory the financial services regulators already have a statutory obligation to accept risk; the Financial Services and Markets Act 2000 s2 provides specifically that in operating its functions the Financial Conduct Authority must be proportionate, encourage innovation and be aware that competition is a good thing. The Pensions Regulator's statutory framework contains no such exhortations to risk-balancing. Gazing over some of the

---

[55] *Pension Law Reform: Report of the Pensions Law Review Committee* (The Goode Committee), HMSO, 1993.

smoking embers of what regulation has done to pension scheme design, it may be that legislators need to be trained, as clearly the English judiciary already have, in the language of risk.

2.4.2   The Costs of the 'New Negligence'

Despite the fact that UK compensation culture may be more myth than reality, there are still excesses. A study[56] of the 'compensation culture' suggested that the cost of the system is around £10B a year in the UK; in itself that sounds relatively modest (even though increasing at about 15 per cent pa) being about 1 per cent of GDP. In the UK criminal injuries compensation (around £341M was paid to 750,000 victims in 2000) was higher than that paid in all other member states of the EU combined; the claims against the public authorities caused particular concern: the police, the health service (around £4.4B alone), local authorities, the cost of the mad cow epidemic and industrial injuries. But despite the concerns, the direct sums are relatively modest.[57]

More importantly are the non-immediate financial costs of the so-called compensation culture. Defensive procedures ultimately cost a great deal in resources and time. Anyone who visits a doctor or hospital knows that much of the treatment is 'defensive' – in other words an X-ray is requested, which might cost say £100, even though the doctor knows in his judgment it is probably not necessary but who requires it for the file and to protect against any future claim. The cost of financial advice has increased so as to exclude most ordinary mortals because of the cost of the required investigation to be taken by an independent financial adviser.

How has this situation arisen? Mostly it is because the definition of 'negligence' by the courts has expanded in recent years – and because there is a greater awareness of the right to claim by the public, accompanied by an expansion in 'ambulance chasing', i.e. firms that specialise in promoting claims.

This is not necessarily a bad thing. The fact that people will and can claim is likely, all other things being equal, to ensure that manufacturers, doctors, lawyers and others will provide a proper product or service; what (apart from the loss to their trade) is to compel them to give a proper

---

[56] Julian Lowe et al., *The cost of compensation culture*, UK Institute of Actuaries, December 2002.

[57] *Annual Report and Accounts 2015–2016*, Criminal Injuries Compensation Authority, HC 470, July 2016; payments had fallen to around £175M pa.

service – or what is to prevent the public being passed off with shoddy goods or services if it were not for the law?

That question is the one that runs as a theme throughout this book: the issue of balance. It is clear that the public need to be protected, especially where they cannot protect themselves. But it is also clear, as Professor Gower made clear in his report in 1984 leading to the UK's Financial Services Act 1986, that no amount of law could or should protect little old ladies from their own foolishness; his advice was rejected in principle by a government white paper which was issued before he had concluded his review.[58] It has been argued that since there are protective mechanisms in place the failure of those mechanisms is itself actionable, and gives rise to a claim, a point made by class action lawyers to the House of Commons Select Committee examining the fall of the UK insurer Equitable Life in 2002.[59]

However there is a tandem move in public policy on consumer protection. One, already explored elsewhere in this book, is the drive of the legislators and regulators to legislate and regulate – even though they know they must ultimately fail. The other is the attitude of the courts.

2.4.3   The Attitude of the Courts and the Expansion of Negligence

The 'Bolam' test in medical negligence was for many years the test by which the courts were supposed to judge whether a doctor had been negligent.[60] Provided there was a body of medical opinion that would have supported the treatment rendered, there was no claim against the doctor. The doctor also had to apply the question of the appropriate risks and benefits to reach a defensible conclusion. None of the court decisions discuss the issues of the costs of defensive medicine and whether doctors should practice their profession with the judge at their shoulder. I remember vividly discussing a delicate and revolutionary life-saving operation with a surgeon about to operate on my own newborn son. The surgeon froze when he learned of my profession of lawyer. A surgeon worried by the threat of litigation may be more careful but less creative and inspired than one unworried. It is not the threat of litigation for negligence that

---

[58] *Review of Investor Protection, Report Part I* (Chairman Professor LCB Gower), London, HMSO, January 1984, Cmnd 9125.

[59] *Equitable Life and the Life Assurance Industry: an Interim Report, Minutes of Evidence*, HC 449-II, ISBN 0 10 235201 1, Tenth Report, 30 March 2001, Volume II – Minutes of Evidence and Appendices, HC 272-II, ISBN 0 10 222801 9.

[60] *Bolam v Friern Hospital Management Committee* [1957 1 WLR 582].

inspires a concert pianist to perform at his best, or a footballer to score a goal. Yet there must be some clubs who have paid a high price for a football star who persistently fails to score goals who must dream of contemplating an action for breach of contract or negligence.

In practice of course the judges make it clear (usually) that they take the balancing act very seriously; and of course there are judges who make bad decisions – they are only human. Incidentally those very beings who are involved in the expansion of the definition of negligence (judges, lawmakers, journalists) are themselves immune from any such allegations. The fact they enjoy some form of sovereign immunity does not make them careless of their obligations.

It has been argued, on thin evidence, that the cost may put companies, and their employees, out of business – or make the cost of for example obstetric services, beyond the reach of the ordinary citizen. In late 2002 the premiums for employers liability insurance, which is compulsory, tripled because of the increase in claims. Some suggest that the existence of such cover encouraged the judiciary to be generous at the expense of the insurers when claims are made.[61]

2.4.4   The Law of Unintended Consequences

Saying sorry

Q: I was humiliated by the manager of my local Choice (a chain that sells discounted Next products). I asked for a refund on a nail-care kit. He refused, saying I had moved nail varnish from it. In fact, he was confusing my set with another bigger set and, to prove it, I showed him both sets on sale in his shop. He became so distressing that other customers urged me to take action. I wrote to the company which just thanked me for my letter. The Trading Standards office and my solicitor could do nothing. All I want is an apology. (Mrs M G London).

A: Unfortunately, many organisations no longer say sorry; they say it opens the way to compensation claims in court. However, Choice's managing director has spoken firmly to the shop manager. Choice has sent you £50 in vouchers and £10 for postage as a goodwill gesture. It

---

[61] John Hyde, *Mishcon's £1m ID fraud bill sounds alarm bells*, Law Society's Gazette, 30 January 2017; *Review of employers' liability compulsory insurance*, Second Stage Report, Department of Work and Pensions, 4 December 2003.

is worth adding that you don't have a legal right to a refund on goods bought in a shop unless they are faulty.[62]

There has been discussion elsewhere about the fact that the excessive protection of pension schemes has all but lead to their destruction. A similar episode arises in relation to the protection of bats. Most bat species are not rare or declining. Nonetheless and for understandable reasons, there are laws protecting them and their roosting spaces. One government body, Natural England, is responsible for enforcing a directive that churches may not disturb bat roosts, even if they erect alternative sleeping accommodation. Another government body, English Heritage, enforces EU directives to preserve cultural heritage. Sometimes these bodies come into conflict; in particular the urine of bats has been causing the destruction of brasses in English churches. It may be an example of bad law, or bad application of law. Those enforcing it are unable often to take a pragmatic approach or operate some form of compromise or liaise with other bodies.[63]

Similarly the legislation which encouraged drivers to use diesel fuel instead of petrol as a anti-pollution measure has been found many years later to have been counter-productive. The pollutants in diesel have been found to be worse than the petrol ones: 'The boom in "dirty diesel" cars, vans and taxis on Britain's roads was the last Labour Government's biggest green blunder, the party's environment spokesman has admitted'.[64] This is not to say that legal controls on pollution are foolish; the Clean Air Acts in the 1950s and 1960s were spectacularly successful in abolishing smog, the modern equivalent of which currently afflicts South East Asia.

However there probably remain too many instances of unintended consequences. One example is that of payday lenders, what used to be called usurers or moneylenders. Because of the imbalance of power between borrower and lender there have been rules controlling what is a fair rate of interest for thousands of years. In England there used to be the Moneylenders Act which was effective (mostly) for many decades, imposing a maximum interest rate of 49 per cent pa; when it was replaced by the Consumer Credit Act 1974 interest rates were unconstrained but supposedly limited by market forces through the requirement for transparency on true rates, the APR, the annual percentage rate. It took some years for an

---

[62] Daily Telegraph, 4 January 2003; Scotland now has a 'say sorry Act', Apologies (Scotland) Act 2016.

[63] Matt Ridley, *Human intervention ruins wildlife everywhere*, The Times, 26 January 2015.

[64] Jonathan Leake, *Labour admits tax blunder on deadly diesel*, Sunday Times, 15 January 2015.

understanding of new abuses to emerge. Companies with brands to maintain would be expected to have a greater interest in fair treatment than back street lenders. Political pressures eventually led to the Financial Conduct Authority introducing interest rate rules that were expected to lead to a reduction in the number of lenders to around three, with unfortunate economic and competition consequences. The evidence suggested that however unattractive payday lenders' behaviour seemed to policymakers and the press, the alternative (driving borrowers to resort to unregulated lenders) was likely to be even worse.[65]

Also causing concerns have long been the propensity of lawmakers to make it easier for them to enforce their provisions. In criminal matters for example law students have long been taught that to be guilty of a crime there must not only be a criminal act (*actus reus*) but also an intent (*mens rea*). But proving intent can be slow and expensive, so the tendency has been more recently to make offences 'absolute', i.e. without the need to show an intent. And that can result in injustice or absurdity. One example in England involves breaking the rules on yellow box junctions where it is forbidden to wait, so as to enable crossing traffic not to be impeded. Such junctions can result in fines being imposed which are out of all proportion to the offence. For example one box junction in Hackney London raises £1M a year in fines. This shows that drivers in practice find it all but impossible to avoid being caught in a junction – particularly since such junctions have no prior signposting. Rather like the spider and the fly, by the time the driver has found out there is a box junction it is too late.[66] Similarly:

> Bobby Unser, a former car racer, was snowmobiling with a friend in Colorado when a blizzard sent them off course. After their vehicles broke down the two men spent a night in the wilderness, nearly freezing to death. They survived, but two weeks later the Forest Service charged Mr Unser with operating a motorised vehicle inside a protected area, a federal crime.[67]

To avoid this kind of injustice some jurisdictions insist on greater precision in the drafting of criminal legislation. Ohio's state legislature now provides that any new crime introduced must specify a threshold level of intent – or be declared void. Any absolute offences must be stated to be

---

[65] James Quinn, *FCA reforms pay day lending, but loan sharks will still be out there*, Daily Telegraph, 5 January 2015. *The future of illegal lending*, Policis, 17 December 2014.

[66] Joshua Surtees and David Churchill, *The box junction outside a fire station in East London that rakes in almost £1m each year*, Evening Standard, 19 January 2015.

[67] *Mens rea: What were you thinking?*, The Economist, 24 January 2015, p39.

specifically in the law itself. In the absence of categorical provision the default threshold is 'reckless behaviour'. It is thought that around two-thirds of US nonviolent crimes lack an intent requirement.[68]

2.4.5   Justifiable Negligence and Legal Oppression

In August 1999 Tony Martin shot Fred Barras and killed him. He also shot Brendon Fearon in the legs and groin.[69] Tony Martin was a farmer who had been burgled innumerable times, in his remote farmhouse (Bleak House) at Emneth Hungate in Norfolk, and had decided that the next time he found intruders on his property he would deal with them in his own way. Mr Barras and Mr Fearon were the next to attempt burglary, Mr Martin, in fear and confusion let off his shotgun in the dark and, he said, shot them by accident. Tony Martin was sentenced to five years imprisonment, and served two-thirds of it, longer than normal, because he showed no remorse. There was considerable discussion at the time of the case whether Mr Martin should have received such a sentence as a vigilante, or whether he had a right to defend himself against crime bearing in mind the fact that the police service were unable to protect his property over many years. Much of the popular press criticised the judicial process. The case was heard on appeal, and the appeal court confirmed the sentence.

While the case itself raised issues of whether and to what extent an individual may defend his property, much of the debate circled around what happened next. Brendon Fearon obtained legal aid to sue Tony Martin for £100,000 for his injuries, complaining that his sex life had been affected.

Some of the commentary discussed both whether he should be allowed to sue in the first place, and also whether the state should fund such a claim. Mr Fearon was not a prepossessing case; he had a long and undistinguished record for offences against both persons and property. The main issue however is whether he was exceptional in thinking that he had a claim in such circumstances.

---

[68] See ibid: 'Lisa Synder, who was accused of running illegal day care after watching over her neighbours' children as they waited for the school bus'. And see Harvey Silverglate, *Three felonies a day*, Encounter Books, 2011 (US). See Brian W. Walsh and Tiffany M. Joslyn, *Without Intent: How Congress Is Eroding the Criminal Intent Requirement in Federal Law*, Heritage Foundation Special Report No. 77 (May 5, 2010); John Malcolm, *The pressing need for mens rea reform*, The Heritage Foundation, 1 September 2015.

[69] See e.g. *A victim, not a hero: Tony Martin needs protection and help*, Leader article, The Guardian, 29 July 2003.

There is even today, despite changes to legislation and incessant court decisions to the contrary, a belief that there is an inveterate compensation culture in Britain. Lord Levene, who amongst other careers was chairman of Lloyds of London, the insurer, claimed that 'Britain's spiralling compensation culture costs more than £10billion a year and is the greatest external threat to the insurance industry'.[70] He also criticised the industry for 'suicidal behaviour' in chasing business, but he was even then worried mostly about the issues in the US. A year or so earlier he had said in a speech in Los Angeles that America's compensation culture was 'pernicious, cancerous and ruinous' and that Britain was 'falling into the same abyss of the blame culture ... the tort crisis is not just an insurance industry problem but a national economic problem; the cost of the tort system is like a 5pc payroll tax; it's a tax without representation at the most basic level and it's growing ... there is strong evidence that the compensation culture is starting to plunder the UK economy.'

He cited the case of a Wolverhampton postman who was taking legal action against a university lecturer for posting too many letters after pulling a muscle. 'This culture is costing UK plc about £10billion a year and rising at 15pc per annum. The average cost of an employers' liability claim has increased by over 100pc over the last five years. Clinical negligence, which cost the NHS £6m in 1975, cost nearly half a billion pounds by 2002 ... Compensation and legal costs have soared to £100m in the Ministry of Defence and there is concern now too that this blight is spreading to the rest of Europe, where until recently the practice of suing company directors and officers was unheard of. Politicians in Whitehall and in Brussels need to wake up to this problem, and they need to wake up now ... Ignoring it and hoping it will go away is not an option. If they need any proof, they need just look across the Atlantic.'

2.4.6   Blaming and Not Blaming

The understandable urge to control bad behaviour and minimise harm to those less well able to protect themselves manifests itself in many areas. One example has been the dilemma emerging in child protection. Lord Laming identified a dozen occasions when Victoria Climbié, who died in a notorious case of child abuse, could have been saved by social workers, police or the NHS. He proposed the establishment of a Child

---

[70] Andrew Cave, *Blame culture 'is road to suicide'*, Daily Telegraph, 3 February 2004.

Commissioner to prevent such incidents of failure from being repeated.[71] Observers argued that it would merely generate a bureaucratic support structure, that would justify its existence by issuing directives, gathering information and seeking statistics, overstretching professionals and putting children further at risk.[72]

The General Medical Council also became involved in attempting to control child abuse; on the other hand several paediatricians in 2004 had been investigated for 'over-diagnosis of child abuse'. To complicate matters, the Children's Act 2004, which resulted from the Climbié case, in its draft form proposed that professionals would be held liable for missing the diagnosis and created a 'ContactPoint' database, later decommissioned. The challenge in practice was that diagnosis of child abuse was not always easy, there was no reliable test or investigation process, and diagnosis usually depends on a subjective view of small indications. Unless there was overdiagnosis, cases would be missed and it seemed harsh to criticise professional who were encouraged to overdiagnose to protect themselves yet find themselves subject to criticism from the professional body when they do.

2.4.7   Criticism of Judges

Despite complaints in the *Daily Mail* about lenient, interfering and out-of-touch judges, evidence suggests that modern judges, even in the US, are sensible of the concerns that expanding the definition of negligence has unacceptable consequences. Robert Uren was a senior aircraftman in the RAF and took part in a form of 'It's a Knockout' game organised as part of a health and fitness day by the RAF. In one game he had to run up to an inflatable pool, grab a piece of plastic fruit, and put it in a bucket. When he entered the pool, he knew it was shallow, so he launched himself in a continuous movement head first with arms outstretched ahead of him. Tragically he hit his head on the bottom of the pool, broke his neck and became a tetraplegic confined to a wheelchair. He sued the Ministry of Defence for damages for personal injury, alleging a breach of the common law duty of care by the MoD. There was no argument that the MoD owed Mr Uren a common law duty to take reasonable care to ensure that he was

---

[71] The Victoria Climbie Inquiry (Lord Laming), *Report*, January 2003, CM 5730.
[72] Michael Cavanagh-Pack, *Letter*, Times, 10 March 2004.

safe in taking part in the game. The issue was what was reasonable. The judge was sympathetic but firm:[73]

> Does the existence of a very small risk of serious injury mean that the defendants were in breach of the common law duty of care they each owed to Mr Uren? In my judgment it does not. Enjoyable competitive activities are an important and beneficial part of the life of the very many people who are fit enough to participate in them. This is especially true in the case of fit service personnel...such activities are almost never risk-free. This means that a balance has to be struck between the level of risk involved and the benefits the activity confers on the participants and thereby on society generally. The pool game was an enjoyable game, in part because of the physical challenges it posed to contestants. The risk of serious injury was small. In my judgement...[neither the MoD nor the provider of the pool] was obliged to neuter the game of much of its enjoyable challenge by prohibiting head-first entry.

There are of course, judgments which are less understanding of risk, but the majority of judges in the majority of cases seem in practice prepared, contrary to public perception, to take a pragmatic approach, in particular to avoid what they perceive as the law of unintended consequences. It helps that unlike in the US, where many of the extreme awards are reported, there is in the UK a national health service, so that the need to pay for medical care is less of a problem.

2.4.8   The Reluctance to Use Discretion

Sometimes judges are reluctant to take brave decisions, despite the fact that they are guardians of the common law, in a continual state of development. But they are not alone; even council officials struggle sometimes to use common sense (Figure 2.1).

---

[73] *Uren v Corporate Leisure (UK) Ltd* [2010] EWHC 46 (QB), para 59; cf. Provision and Use of Work Equipment Regulations 1998 regs 4(1),(2),(3) and Management of Health and Safety at Work regulations 1999 regs 3, 10. The Compensation Act 2006 provides that 'a court considering a claim in negligence or breach of statutory duty may, in determining whether the defendant should have taken particular steps to meet a standard of care (whether by taking precautions against a risk or otherwise) have regard to whether a requirement to take those steps might (a) prevent a desirable activity from being undertaken at all, to a particular extent or in a particular way, or (b) discourage persons from undertaking functions with a desirable activity'.

Figure 2.1   Merton Council, in south-west London, said, 'The sign was put up to remind motorists that it is illegal to park on the footway'

2.5   Legal Design: When Law Does Not Work

Schlimmbesserung: an improvement that makes things worse (possibly should be 'Verschlimmbesserung').

2.5.1   Introduction

Law is often the first weapon that policy makers turn to when faced with a policy objective. It is an imperfect solution, and can in many cases make a problem even worse. Set out below are some instances where law has been later found to be an inappropriate response.

2.5.2   Penalties Even Where There Is No Law

It is understandable that where events lead to a scandal or market abuse, there should be calls for reform, involving increased protection. But the fact there has been a failure does not necessarily mean that either a change in the existing law is required, or that there has been a breach. At the end of 2002 it was discovered that several US investment banks had advised their clients to buy shares that they knew were unattractive. It led to an agreed $1.4B fine on 10 leading banks including such names as Credit Suisse First Boston and Merrill Lynch. The settlement, however, did not make it clear that whatever these financial groups had done was not in violation of existing laws or regulations.[74] Observers suggested that the fine was disproportionate to the damage – or that if the banks had indeed

---

[74] See e.g. Roy Smith, Professor of Finance at the Stern School of Economics, New York, *Attacking Wall Street with a blunt instrument*, Financial Times, 7 January 2003: 'We do

committed fraud they should have been prosecuted in the normal way and been subject to civil litigation for losses that were incurred by their clients.[75] There have been objections that the reforms to the markets that this episode led to has added yet further layers of cost and regulations, when the existing remedial systems would have been sufficient.

Similar concerns have also been expressed about the disproportionate impact of regulation on smaller business, which lack the infrastructure sometimes to cope with complex regulation. In a survey in January 2003 Ernst & Young reported that in the UK 90 per cent of business owners expressed disillusionment with Whitehall. Many blamed a series of employment reforms, including the introduction of flexible working practices for additional bureaucracy and escalating costs. Surveys like this are sometimes self-fulfilling; there are few surprises that business would like less regulation, so the validity of the survey itself is probably limited. But it remains probable that smaller businesses are disproportionately affected and that the legislation imposing regulatory obligations could be simpler and shorter.[76]

Sanctions have now become bewildering in their frequency and application; regulators feel they need to flex muscles, to send a message, to justify their existence by pointing to the imposition of fines.[77] The expansion

not want reforms to damage the efficient flow of information or to ignore the cost of additional regulation to the users of the market. Group settlements for the sake of establishing scapegoats are not the way to regulate a complex, sophisticated global securities industry.'

[75] *Jail bait: the lock-'em up mentality for white-collar crime is misguided*, Schumpeter, The Economist, 29 October 2016. Cf Eugene Soltes, *Why they do it: inside the mind of the white collar criminal*, PublicAffairs, United States, 27 October 2016 and Samuel Buell, *Capital offenses: business crime and punishment in America's corporate age*, WW Norton & Company, United States, 14 September 2016.

[76] Elizabeth Judge, *Small businesses rage at Whitehall*, Times, 6 January 2003.

[77] Jonathan Macey, *The Death of Corporate Reputation*, Yale University Press, 2013: 'The SEC appears to have a mission. Unfortunately, its mission appears to be that of advancing its own agenda, including its own budget and power, along with the careers of its most highly placed executives. New SEC Commissioners focus more on trying to improve the Commission's status in Washington instead of trying to improve the Commission itself... Other Commissioners spend more time explaining the SEC's failings and in suing small firms and new entrants than they do on the important issues of the day. Worst of all, the SEC has played an active role in undermining the ability of firms to maintain their reputations and in destroying the incentives of firms to build reputations in the first place. Certainly, having a great reputation was a never a way to impress the SEC because the SEC sues all market participants with equal fervor.' Cf. 'a vast profusion of laws, regulations and direct government interventions has provided a substitute for reputation, albeit a toxic and inadequate one... requirements for ratings and audits, for instance, are now set by regulation, not the market, and an entirely new Federal agency, the Consumer Financial Protection Agency,

of sanctions to involve transportation did little to reduce sheep stealing in the eighteenth century, and moral philosophers today suggest that the use of sanctions should be kept to a minimum for effectiveness.[78]

2.5.3 Traffic Speeds and Management

Speeding traffic can cause deaths and injuries, and intimidate pedestrians and cyclists. It is unsurprising therefore that public policy should seek to reduce vehicle speeds on roads. In 2009 the UK government announced plans to reduce speed limits; the default maximum speed on A-class roads was to be reduced from 60 mph to 50 mph, with the intent of reducing road fatalities from 3000 a year to 2000 a year. Deaths had already fallen a third in the previous 10 years, and pedestrians hit by lower speed vehicles certainly have a greater chance of surviving. It is not however established that changing speed limits in itself is a sensible or cost-effective way of reducing injuries and deaths. One issue, for example, is whether the provision of additional signing actually changes behaviour. Even at slow speeds[79] drivers may be competitive, anxious and intimidating to pedestrians.

Hans Monderman, a Dutch traffic engineer famously concluded[80] that if you treat people like idiots they will behave like them. His solution was to deregulate the traffic management, to force drivers to work out appropriate rules for themselves. Instead of traffic calming methods such as humps which were expensive and destructive, he removed all signing and road markings and pavements. Accidents fell markedly – as did speeds. Such deregulation may not apply universally, but a rule that said even on motorways (one of the safest forms of road) that there would be no limits, but that if there were an accident at a speed of over (say) 70 mph would be presumed to be the fault of the speeder even if not, or that high speeds would

---

has been created to expand this approach in retail finance . . . there is [now] little need for financial intermediaries to invest in their reputations. It is, however, important for them to invest in regulators, whose own career prospects are increasingly tied to their ability to advance rules that are both vague and highly technical, as this increases their value both within government and to potential private employers. The system is now fundamentally flawed. Those who propose even more regulations will only ensure more damage.' *Broken: recollections of a bygone era when the market enforced good behaviour*, The Economist, 13 July 2013.

[78] Samuel Bowles, *The Moral Economy: why good incentives are no substitute for good citizens*, Yale University Press, 2016, Chapter 6.

[79] See Will Self, Evening Standard, 22 April 2009.

[80] See Tom Vanderbilt, *Traffic: why we drive the way we do (and what it says about us)*, Allen Lane, 2008.

be treated as not driving carefully might help. For example, the real problem in driving, tailgating, probably causes more issues than most forms of driving but is rarely if ever prosecuted.

Monderman who died in 2008, had developed a concept of 'shared space' in relation to traffic management. His theory was that if road traffic controls in urban spaces were removed, drivers and pedestrians would find a modus vivendi to manage their safety instinctively. The idea was that if the message went out that the roads belonged to everyone, motorists would learn to slow down and navigate their way safely through other road users: pedestrians, cyclists and others. There were objections, reasonably justifiable, to the removal of fences and road signs, with the suggestion that there would be increased accidents especially for blind people and children. And his ideas did not decry the value of design; the roadways and pathways had to be designed to meet their purpose. Where his designs were implemented (most notably in Drachten in the Netherlands, and more recently in Kensington, London [eventually]) the accident rate declined. The intention was to create a space for people not for traffic; it would have been inappropriate for motorways for example. And a town with fewer signs is more attractive, especially where the signs are replaced by trees.[81]

The introduction of a self-responsibility policy requires, of course, the adoption of self-reliance and self-responsibility by citizens. The purity of the idea can be hard to apply in practice; there can be an almost irresistible demand for controls to be imposed (if there were an accident for example), or because people feel it is dangerous to walk the streets.[82] But it does increase the sense of responsibility – provided the street design tells the right message.[83]

2.5.4   Financial Services

One of the consuming debates, especially following the financial collapses in 2008, was whether regulation, or increased regulation, would have

---

[81] And could save money, see e.g. Martin Cassini and Richard Wellings, *Seeing Red: traffic controls and the economy*, IEA Discussion paper No 68, January 2016, which suggests wholesale removal of traffic signals and controls; K. Todd, *Traffic control: an exercise in self-defeat*, [2004] (Fall) Regulation 10–12.

[82] See e.g. the debate about autonomous cars following a fatal accident, even though the figures show conclusively they are safer than driven cars. Alice Klein, *Tesla driver dies in first fatal autonomous car crash in US*, New Scientist, 1 July 2016.

[83] Matthew Engel, *Dispatch*, FT.COM Magazine, 7 November 2009.

mitigated the issues. The problem was at least anticipated in 1986 when the City of London was radically reformed in the 'Big Bang', which was part of the raft of changes that brought the City's financial services into the twentieth century, and in particular dismantled many of the restrictive trade practices. But the identified worry was that whilst the old-boy network was broken-up and the market was opened to international competition (which in fact created the City of London as a major international centre and generator of taxable profits for the UK), the usual checks and balances which operated in a closed community to prevent bad behaviour would disappear. David Willetts, then a member of the No 10 Policy Unit, and later a Cabinet minister, noted that it was inevitable that there would be failures, as the City became more competitive, and that the temptation to commit fraud or engage in unethical behaviour would increase (although he saw the new system as a showpiece for the government's policies on deregulation and increased competition). His colleague, John Redwood, and his senior, took a different view; he, by way of contrast, considered new principles of fair dealing, new duties of skill, care and diligence and a new duty of disclosure would emerge. Neither discussed the issue that the immediate globalisation of London's operations would mean that the peer pressures of colleagues and the central bank would no longer apply, and it was these, rather than rules, which had hitherto controlled behaviour. David Willetts could be forgiven for a modest gloat for his prescience, but it will be noted that City behaviour before the Big Bang was, by modern standards, corrupt.[84]

2.5.5 Child Protection

The case of Victoria Climbié has already been noted above. In February 2000 Victoria Climbié, an eight-year-old girl from the Ivory Coast was killed by her great aunt after months of neglect and abuse. Following the conviction for murder, and immense press interest, there were several government inquiries into the events surrounding her killing, in order to find out whether or not it was time to look again at the statutory framework for child protection. First, a group of joint chief inspectors published a report

---

[84] Jim Pickard and Barney Thompson, *Fierce debate over pros and cons of City's big ban*, Financial Times, 30 December 2014.

Safeguarding Children in October 2002.[85] And then in January 2003 Lord Laming published a graphic report.[86] It concluded:

> 1.21 Having considered the response to Victoria from each of the agencies, I am forced to conclude that the principal failure to protect her was the result of widespread organisational malaise.

There had been no shortage of resource, systems or law, and after the tragedy no shortage of inquiries. It was just that the protection arrangements were poorly implemented; government, under pressure to be seen to do something, however felt that something had to be seen to be done. In due course a cabinet post was established, with a Minister for Children. A ministry, the Department for Children, Schools and Families (abolished in 2010 following widespread criticism) was given lead responsibility in Whitehall for policy on children. Later the Independent Safeguarding Authority was established, and it developed further codes of conduct and rules for child minders and others, with controlled and regulated activities set down in ways not always easy for a child-minder to understand. These were relatively new rules (from 2010) but they and their similarly equivalent predecessor rules would have made no difference to the outcome of the later Baby P case.

The Baby P case, involving similar facts, was a tragedy which occurred under the watch of a host of suitably qualified officials and experts. It is

---

[85] Joint Inspectors, *Safeguarding Children*, October 2002, Department of Health. Its joint authors were the Chief Inspector of Social Services, The Director for Health Improvement, Commission for Health Improvement, Her Majesty's Chief Inspector of Constabulary, Her Majesty's Chief Inspector of the Crown Prosecution Service, Her Majesty's Chief Inspector of the Magistrates' Courts Service, Her Majesty's Chief Inspector of Schools, Her Majesty's Chief Inspector of Prisons and Her Majesty's Chief Inspector of Probation; www.dh.gov.uk/prod_consum_dh/groups/dh_digitalassets/@dh/@en/documents/digitalasset/dh_4060833.pdf. There was a similar report, *The Bichard Report*, in 2004, following a notorious couple of child murders by Ian Huntley at Soham in the UK, which concentrated on vetting people who work with children. If its recommendations had been in force at the time, they would not have prevented the Soham murders. The unintended consequence of the implementation of the report was that it became increasingly difficult to find people to work with children in Scout groups for example. There were other reports, see e.g. the Singleton review (*Drawing the Line*, 2009) and the Munro review (2011), with similar outcomes.

[86] www.victoria-climbie-inquiry.org.uk http://www.victoria-climbie-inquiry.org.uk/finreport/introduction.htm/: Lord Laming, *The Protection of Children in England: A Progress Report*, HC 330, London, The Stationery Office, 12 March 2009. The Independent Safeguarding Authority was established in 2007 to remove those who posed a known risk to children; it was closed in 2012, when its operations were merged with the Criminal Records Bureau, now known as the Disclosure and Barring Service.

possible to argue in fact that the changes and controls actually led to Baby P's death, because everyone thought that the system (applied by someone else) worked to protect such children, so led to the dependence on other people's actions. It was perhaps the lack of responsibility as a consequence of the increase in controls that led to a repetition of the tragedy. In the Baby P case the child had been examined over 60 times by various authorities before he was eventually murdered by his parents in a sickening story of neglect and deliberate violence.[87]

One other child murder case had also provoked public outrage; the murder of two schoolgirls in Soham in 2002. A school caretaker was eventually convicted of their murder – but he worked at a different school to that which the girls attended, and could just as easily have been for example a security guard at a factory. The girls met him because his girlfriend was a teaching assistant. Had the Independent Safeguarding Authority, with its eventual register of 11.3 million who might in the course of their work come into contact with children or vulnerable adults, existed at the time, it would not have necessarily picked up Huntley as a potential threat. The later expansion of the record keeping obligations to show not only general convictions (Huntley had a record for driving a motorbike whilst uninsured), but also suspicions, has in itself has led to further injustices. For example John Pinnington had had unwarranted allegations made against him of sexual abuse (which can include for example trivial incidents whilst a teenager). He was a highly regarded deputy head of a college for autistic children in Oxfordshire but was required to resign as a consequence of his being outed. Similarly in East Renfrewshire a father whose son suffered from Asperger's syndrome was told he could not get on the school bus to do up the boy's seat belt without a disclosure check;[88] no parents were allowed on school buses. And even keeping child molesters out of schools and scout groups does not necessarily help; the massacre of 16 children at Dunblane was committed by Thomas Hamilton, who had already been asked to leave a scout group because of inappropriate behaviour, and his crime would not have been prevented by the new systems. Not only is it broadly ineffective, the new system is expensive. It charges parents and others around £36 a head and the clearance needs to be repeated for each activity the individual is involved in; and the

---

[87] The Baby P case is explored further at p. 365, where the political interventions in particular by the then Minister Ed Balls, later deeply criticised by the High Court, are explored.

[88] Camilla Cavendish, *We are all suspects in the new inquisition's eyes*, The Times, 1 May 2009.

institutional establishment costs were around £84M for the original ISA (about five times the original estimate).[89]

The question for policymakers is whether the system of vetting and supervision was saving many children from abuse, how many it saved, what was the cost per reduction – and whether, as in the story of counter-productivity, perversely it could make the situation of children less safe. The dilemma is whether legislation should be introduced on the basis that the vast majority of parents and others are a danger to children. The impact of the Act and the checking service suggests that even if many of the stories are something along the lines of urban myths, there were genuine concerns that, for example, scouting was badly affected by the inability to recruit sufficient Brown Owls. It is hard scientifically to connect cause and effect, but it is not unreasonable to suspect that the one is connected to the other. And it is possible that millions of children were even more neglected because of the spread of checks, perhaps because of the reluctance of parents to undertake the bureaucratic checking process.[90]

As mentioned, none of the new systems and controls would necessarily have led to the avoidance of future Victoria Climbié or Baby P episodes; the offences were carried out by immediate family not strangers. There has been no proposal that parents, who have close relationships with their children, should be licensed to either bear and/or look after children.[91] Secondly none of the controls later introduced for licensing those who

---

[89] See *Checking the checks: restoring trust*, http://manifestoclub.info/checking-the-checks-restoring-trust. Margaret Matthews in Bisley, Woking was recently asked for a criminal records check to volunteer to help elderly people at the local lunch club: 'My husband and I wanted to volunteer to be involved with a lunch club in the village hall in the next village. We would go back in the minibus with the elderly people and help them into their house. All we would do is walk the elderly person from the vehicle to their front door. I was asked to do a DBS check, and I felt a bit pressured by the request for documents – as if I was a stranger in that area. We've lived in the same house for 50 years. I feel there is such a lack of commonsense nowadays. I went to do the check, but they wanted a passport or picture driving licence, neither of which I had. They wouldn't accept utility bills as proof of address, and wanted me to return with my marriage certificate – which did make me feel that I was something other than someone wanting to give a little of my spare time! I said that I would leave it for now. It's a shame because they are lovely old people and I think they would appreciate someone new to talk to. There is a lovely lady running the club – she said she was so sorry, and that volunteers had been put off before. It's a terrible nuisance and unnecessary.'

[90] Dame Elisabeth Hoodless, Executive Director, Community Service Volunteers, *Criminal checks must not discourage volunteers from giving time*, Guardian, 7 February 2009.

[91] Although Scotland has the named person legislation, which does just that, under the Children and Young People Scotland) Act 2014; its provisions were heavily criticised by the Supreme Court in *The Christian Institute v The Lord Advocate* [2016] UKSC 51. Libby

come into contact with children would have prevented the Soham tragedy. And thirdly there are repeated instances of profound injustices to third parties through the protection system itself,[92] as well as less tragic but nonetheless damaging effects, by making it hard, for example, for authors to read their works in front of schoolchildren.[93]

2.5.6 Signage, Labelling and Disclaimers

Regulation on signage can often be seen to be absurd, even more so in the absence of simple signs, such as city and suburban signs indicating road names. In the Lake District outside William Wordsworth's house, there are no-smoking signs inside, outside on the terrace and incised into the railings 'lest some opium deranged fan dream of sparking up'.[94] Excess signage has a dedicated study group; the Manifesto Club, a single issue deregulation group, has specialised in recent years on showing the excesses involved in some signage. Many signs are required by law, others by people thinking that the law requires it, so as to limit liability under public works legislation or the Occupiers Liability Act.[95]

The anecdotes are legion, and some are actually true. The Marks and Spencer label on a pack of Tiramisu (an Italian dessert, the word meaning 'pick me up', and idiomatically 'upside down pudding') has a label, on its base, stating 'do not turn upside down'. Much food labelling states the product may contain nuts, whether they do or not; bottles of water are sometimes labelled 'suitable for vegetarians'. Much of this labelling is helpful, setting out the lists of ingredients, so that a vegetarian can remain so, or so that those trying to manage their diet can reduce consumptions of sugars and fats, or avoid consumption of hydrogenated fats. But the campaigns against lemon cheese because they are misleading (since they do not contain cheese), or on cups of coffee which are too hot are possibly steps too far. Some electrical goods such as computers find themselves partly disfigured by safety labelling, and excessive highway signage can be

---

Brookes, *Scottish plan for every child to have 'named person' breaches rights*, Guardian, 28 July 2016.

[92] Camilla Cavendish, *Two men are incarcerated by the State, when they should be the stability in two children's lives*, Times March 13 2008; ibid, *We are all suspects in the new inquisition's eyes*, Times, 1 May 2009; Independent Safeguarding Authority, www.isa-gov.org.uk.

[93] Miller H. Caldwell, *Authors and Children*, letter to the *Times*, 18 July 2009.

[94] Will Self, *Fewer rules on our roads will make us better drivers*, Evening Standard, 22 April 2009.

[95] *Attention Please*, Manifesto Club, 2 July 2009, ISBN: 978-0-9561247-15.

confusing to drivers.[96] In financial services the disclaimers in mortgage advertisements on the radio are notoriously pointless, but insisted upon by regulators who find it hard to apply common sense.[97]

2.5.7 Policing

Policing governance is an area of regulation which has swung over the years between extremes. Many officers are frustrated by the regulatory framework which attaches to the management of crime, intended to keep them straight, but which can be overbearing. One partisan commentator has described what was needed for the arrest of a minor act of criminal damage of throwing a brick through a window by a drunk youth with a string of minor offences, witnessed by several passers-by and on CCTV, and admitted to by the youth, coupled with an explanation that it was because he wanted to get back at his girlfriend. The paperwork involved[98]

- a full handwritten pocket notebook entry detailing the incident, the grounds for the arrest and anything he said about the incident;
- a typed arrest statement containing exactly the same information, in more detail;
- a typed form requesting the release of the cctv tapes, even though they may not be viewed, to avoid defence claims that the tape would exonerate the offender, regardless of the witnesses' evidence and the confession;
- a handwritten custody search and booking-in form;
- a property sheet, listing the contents of the offender's pockets;
- a typed persistent offender form, containing the same information as the arrest warrant;
- a typed young offender form, containing the same information in another format;
- a typed or verbal update for the computer log held by the control room;
- a typed crime report, with the same information as in the notebook, arrest statement and young offender form, but with the details in different fields;

---

[96] See e.g. signs on the A3 Kingston By-Pass road, SW London; Kirsty Walker, *End of the road for signs clutter*, Daily Mail, 14 October 2011; Department for Transport, *Signing the way*, *Traffic signs policy paper*, October 2011.

[97] See e.g. Joe Zieja, *I love legal disclaimers*, YouTube, www.youtube.com/watch?v= VSiuxEXV6Nc.

[98] Inspector Gadget, *Perverting the Course of Justice*, Monday Books, 2009.

- at least two copies of guidance forms for the case file, summarising all of the above;
- witness statements;
- a check of any previous convictions;
- a witness statement from the owner of the damaged property denying permission to damage;
- an intelligence report about the incident;
- a typed domestic violence form with all the same information again, coupled with a risk assessment;
- the paperwork for the offender's fingerprinting and DNA record, running to four pages;
- the custody record, about 10 pages;
- the forms about the missile;
- a typed update on the night-time economy incident diary sheets;
- a handwritten two-page form for the licensing officer, discussing where the offender might have bought alcohol; and
- a control sample of the broken glass, with additional relevant forms.

Much of this involves poor administration, and much of the information has to be replicated on different forms because the administration has not been joined up. In part the rules have been designed to avoid abuse by the police of their powers, such as maltreatment in custody, or of fitting-up criminals, or ignoring domestic violence. But a part is also designed as a control mechanism, as a response to former breaches of trust by the police. Many of the systems have emerged as a response to some poor policing techniques or abuses in the past; but in fact abuses still occur despite the paperwork – and it is not the paperwork normally that controls bad policing – it is a culture and trust in the system. And with the prevalence of smartphone cameras now the necessity of much of this has probably diminished, but not reflected in the rules.

2.5.8   Health and Safety: Petting Farms

The 0157 strain of Escherichia coli is a virulent bacterium that in its benign form appears in most people's digestive system. Normally it does nothing more than cause a temporary indisposition, but on occasion can make people very ill, and in some cases kill them. It is often caught from infected animals, which usually show no symptoms, and it can be a couple of weeks for the symptoms to emerge, so it is not always clear where the infection arose. In autumn 2009 several petting farms, where children are encouraged to feed and stroke animals, suffered from infections, and some children became seriously ill. As a consequence farms were closed by the Health Protection Agency (too late according to some complaints) and children warned by a proliferation of notices that they should wash their hands at every stage of walking around petting farms. In practice relatively few children who are brought up on farms, and do not adopt hygiene practices, are found to die as a consequence.[99] There is clearly a need for hygiene, and farms which are badly infected should point out to visitors that there may be a problem; but the difficulty for the Agency was the political pressure from the press and elsewhere to close farms. Without such an agency in the first place it may have been that common sense should simply have applied. It hardly needed an agency to recommend the washing of hands.

2.5.9   Health Screening

It is not really a legal issue, but health screening neatly illustrates the issue of risk management, which is a concern in evidence-based legislation. The American Cancer Society in 2009 concluded that screening for breast and prostate cancer is inefficient, inaccurate and alarmist. Such programmes, designed to detect cancer early (when it is much easier to treat and recover from) do damage as well because they often detect cancers or pseudo-cancers that were never going to maim or kill.[100] The problem with screening and even early detection is that while the two elements seem to be useful, the evidence may indicate that they are not. After 25 years of screening overall cancer rates are higher, many more patients are being treated yet the absolute incidence of aggressive or later-stage disease has not been significantly decreased. The issue is whether the cost of screening, with overdiagnosis and overtreatment (and the complications of therapy at later ages) and the impact of treatments for indolent diseases (particularly prostate cancer) may in themselves do harm. Most clinicians are now rethinking the cost-benefits of screening. This is a challenge once a screening industry has been developed, especially within for example a national health service, and presenting an argument that screening may be a mistaken policy, and that the resources not required, or could be

---

[99] *A toxic mix: risk, regulation and children*, The Economist, 19 September 2009, p42.

[100] Margaret McCartney, *Second opinion: screen test*, FT.COM magazine 7 November 2009; Brian Rank, *Executive physicals: bad medicine on three counts*, [2008] (Oct 2) New England Journal of Medicine.

better employed elsewhere, pressure from press and pressure groups may be hard to resist.

Pressure groups and single issue campaigns can do a great deal of good; Florence Nightingale established her own pressure group following the Crimean War with results that are still beneficially with us (although some of her lessons were forgotten along the way). But as a seed to the growth of legislation it may be helpful were the facts and presentations of pressure groups subject to some form of independent analysis; such analysis might be best organised by the lobby group itself, despite any suggestions of conflict of interest, in compliance with an ethical code, so as to preserve the reputation of such groups and improve the quality of legislation.

2.5.10   Prostitution

Prostitution has been a cause for concern for public policy makers since the story of Tamar.[101] There were major changes to its legislative controls following (in the UK) the Wolfenden Report[102] which did its best to remove street prostitution. Sixty years later the Policing and Crime Act 2010 was introduced also with the intent of reducing kerb-crawling and in particular to protect around 5 per cent of the 80,000 sex workers who were trafficked from overseas. It incidentally also criminalised men who sought to buy sex, with the unintended consequence that they were increasingly reluctant to inform the police where they suspected trafficking as they had in the past.[103]

Similar concerns about the availability of sexual services through the internet have provoked those who wish to further impose controls. The Economist pointed out,[104] only slightly tongue in cheek:

> Street-walkers; kerb-crawlers; phone booths plastered with pictures of breasts and buttocks: the sheer seediness of prostitution is just one reason governments have long sought to outlaw it, or corral it in licensed brothels or 'tolerance zones'. NIMBYs make common cause with puritans, who

---

[101] Genesis 38.

[102] *Report of the Departmental Committee on Homosexual Offences and Prostitution*, Committee on Homosexual Offences and Prostitution, HMSO, 1957, Cm 247 (Wolfenden Report).

[103] Karen Bartlett, *Drawing attention to the sex trade*, The Times, 20 March 2010; Scott Cunningham and Manisha Shah, *Decriminalizing Indoor Prostitution: Implications for Sexual Violence and Public Health*. Working Paper No 20281, National Bureau of Economic Research, Washington, 17 July 2014.

[104] Leader, *A personal choice: the internet is making the buying and selling of sex easier and safer. Government should stop trying to ban it*, The Economist, 9 August 2014.

think that women selling sex are sinners, and do-gooders, who think they are victims. The reality is more nuanced. Some prostitutes do indeed suffer from trafficking, exploitation or violence; their abusers ought to end up in jail for their crimes. But for many, both male and female, sex work is just that: work.

This newspaper has never found it plausible that all prostitutes are victims. That fiction is becoming harder to sustain as much of the buying and selling of sex moves online. Personal websites mean prostitutes can market themselves and build their brands. Review sites bring trustworthy customer feedback to the commercial sex trade for the first time. The shift makes it look more and more like a normal service industry.

It can also be analysed like one. We have dissected data on prices, services and personal characteristics from one big international site that hosts 190,000 profiles of female prostitutes...The results show that gentlemen really do prefer blondes, who charge 11% more than brunettes. The scrawny look beloved of fashion magazines is more marketable than flab – but less so than a healthy weight. Prostitutes themselves behave like freelancers in other labour markets. They arrange tours and take bookings online, like gigging musicians. They choose which services to offer, and whether to specialise. They temp, go part-time and fit their work around child care. There is even a graduate premium that is close to that in the wider economy.

More plausibly it added:

Governments should seize the moment to rethink their policies. Prohibition, whether partial or total, has been a predictable dud. It has singularly failed to stamp out the sex trade. Although prostitution is illegal everywhere in America except Nevada, old figures put its value at $14 billion annually nationwide; surely an underestimate. More recent calculations in Britain, where prostitution is legal but pimping and brothels are not, suggest that including it would boost GDP figures by at least £5.3 billion ($8.9 billion). And prohibition has ugly results. Violence against prostitutes goes unpunished because victims who live on society's margins are unlikely to seek justice, or to get it. The problem of sex tourism plagues countries, like the Netherlands and Germany, where the legal part of the industry is both tightly circumscribed and highly visible.

The failure of prohibition is pushing governments across the rich world to try a new tack: criminalising the purchase of sex instead of its sale. Sweden was first, in 1999, followed by Norway, Iceland and France; Canada is re-writing its laws along similar lines. The European Parliament wants the 'Swedish model' to be adopted right across the EU. Campaigners in America are calling for the same approach...

This new consensus is misguided, as a matter of both principle and practice. Banning the purchase of sex is as illiberal as banning its sale. Criminalisation of clients perpetuates the idea of all prostitutes as victims forced into the trade. Some certainly are – by violent partners, people-traffickers or drug addiction. But there are already harsh laws against assault and trafficking. Addicts need treatment, not a jail sentence for their clients.

Sweden's avowed aim is to wipe out prostitution by eliminating demand. But the sex trade will always exist – and the new approach has done nothing to cut the harms associated with it. Street prostitution declined after the law was introduced but soon increased again. Prostitutes' understandable desire not to see clients arrested means they strike deals faster and do less risk assessment. Canada's planned laws would make not only the purchase of sex illegal, but its advertisement, too. That will slow down the development of review sites and identity- and health-verification apps.

The prospect of being pressed to mend their ways makes prostitutes less willing to seek care from health or social services. Men who risk arrest will not tell the police about women they fear were coerced into prostitution. When Rhode Island unintentionally decriminalised indoor prostitution between 2003 and 2009 the state saw a steep decline in reported rapes and cases of gonorrhoea...

Nonetheless the new laws remain, although their enforcement is sporadic, depending on police resources and fashions in public concern.

2.5.11   Smoking and Vaping

There is no doubt (now) that smoking tobacco is very unhealthy. Almost all governments have a public policy of discouraging tobacco smoking, part of which they sometimes achieve by making it expensive and difficult to buy cigarettes. One way it makes it difficult (or more difficult) is by banning the sale of tobacco products from vending machines. It became illegal in in the UK in October 2011.[105] The idea was in particular to reduce sales of cigarettes to the young; once non-smokers reach 25 they are non-smokers for life. However the statistics suggest that only just under 15 per cent bought cigarettes from machines; 57 per cent got them from friends, and 55 per cent from newsagents (there is double counting in the figures). It is however more than the population as a whole.

---

[105] Health Act 2009; Tobacco Advertising and Promotion Act 2002. There is a fine of up to £2500. Display in shops was also controlled from 6 April 2012. See for public policy Department of Health, *Healthy lives, healthy people: our strategy for public health in England*, 2010; Department of Health, *Consultation on the future of tobacco control*, 2008; Tobacco Advertising and Promotion (Point of Sale) regulations 2004; Tobacco Advertising and Promotion (Display of Prices) (England) Regulations 2010; *Guidance on ending tobacco sales from vending machines in England*, Local Government Regulatory Support Unit and Department of Health, 25 August 2011. See also Action on Smoking and Health, *Briefing on Tobacco Vending Machines*, September 2011.

Most EU countries also ban vending machine sales (and some never allowed them), and it is true that where youngsters find it difficult to buy from conventional sources, they turn to machines where there is little to prevent them. An alternative control might have been to have machines operated by a card available to those over 18 only (the current legal minimum). By way of comparison the minimum age in the UK for military (though not armed) service is 16 and a half.

One issue was whether the ban was proportionate to the aim. Cancer Research UK conducted a survey that concluded that 77 per cent of adults supported a complete ban on vending machines. The Court of Appeal[106] considered whether the ban was indeed proportionate to achieve the public policy aim. One issue was whether the imposition of the ban was likely to achieve the 40,000 saved lives its adherents thought possible. The debate as ever was about the balance between the interests of the state in saving lives, and the rights of individuals to smoke and take a risk to their health. There was little debate about the fact that minors are deemed not yet capable of making such decisions, nor that the state is entitled to make such decisions on their behalf. The argument was whether it is acceptable to take such steps where in practice it is the majority of adults who are inconvenienced.

Similar legislative and regulatory excesses have been applied to a cigarette replacement, the e-cigarette (vaping), mostly relying on the precautionary principle. EU regulations impose more draconian rules on the relatively harmless vaping machines than they do on cigarettes themselves,[107] despite strong evidence that such products were an effective

---

[106] In *Sinclair Collis Ltd and Nacmo v The Secretary of State for Health* [2011] EWCA Civ 437 (17 June 2011) the Court of Appeal upheld the legislation which prohibits the sale of tobacco from vending machines. It rejected appeals brought by a subsidiary of Imperial Tobacco and members of the cigarette vending machine industry who argued that the legislation was unlawful because it contravened the free movement of goods provisions of EU law (Article 34 TFEU) and property rights protected by Article 1 Protocol 1 of the ECHR. The majority of the Court of Appeal (by 2 to 1, the Master of the Rolls and Arden LJ, Laws LJ dissenting) held that the legislation fell within the broad margin of appreciation accorded in the field of public health and was proportionate.

[107] Matt Ridley, *The latest emissions scandal is the draconian and health-threatening regulation being imposed on e-cigarettes*, The Times, 28 September 2015. European Commission, *Tobacco Products Directive (Directive 2014/40/EU on the approximation of the laws, regulations and administrative provisions of the Member States concerning the manufacture, presentation and sale of tobacco and related products and repealing Directive 2001/37/EC)*, OJ L 127 29.4.2014 p1, Article 20; Department of Health, *Consultation on the implementation of the revised Tobacco Products Directive (2014/40/EU)*, July 2015; Tobacco and Related Products Regulations 2016, regs 30–41.

way of reducing tobacco smoking. One commentator observed 'It's like regulating coffee in a hard-drugs law'.[108] It imposed a six-month standstill on new products, and required testing over and above that required for the much more harmful real cigarettes. There are around 4000 different chemicals in cigarette smoke, most of which are toxic at some level, but only three are required to be tested or listed, while e-cigarettes have to list the emissions in much more detail. The evidence suggests that e-cigarettes are 20–100 times safer than real cigarettes; yet their regulation is harsher:

> When regulation goes wrong, people call for more regulation. Sometimes, though, regulation is the cause of the original problem. It is steadily becoming clear that the way the European Union does regulation is especially pernicious. It stifles innovation, often favours danger over safety, plays into the hands of vested interests and is inflexible and unaccountable.[109]

2.5.12   Prohibition and Alcohol

> '*Tis simple,' said the Man from Minn.,*
> '*To cure the world of mortal sin –*
> *Just legislate against it.'*
> *Then up spake Congress with a roar,*
> '*We never thought of that before.*
> *Let's go!'*
> *And they commenced it.*[110]

The 'Man from Minn' was Andrew Volstead, a member of the House of Representatives for Minnesota who sponsored the National Prohibition Act 1919 in the US, later repealed in 1933. The control of alcohol however remains an obsession of governments around the world, partly because taxation of alcohol produces significant revenues for the Treasury, and partly to manage the adverse consequences of excess. Management of excess continues to be a policy objective. In the UK in 2010 the government suggested for example amongst many other suggestions a fine of £20,000 for serving alcohol to under-eighteens. Later lobbying suggested imposing a minimum charge, such as 40p a unit.[111] Experience with

---

[108] Matt Ridley, *No smoke without fire in this EU nightmare*, The Times, 28 September 2015.
[109] Matt Ridley, *The latest emissions scandal is the draconian and health-threatening regulation being imposed on e-cigarettes*, The Times, 28 September 2015.
[110] Wallace Irwin, *Owed to Volstead*, 1992.
[111] Josie Appleton, *Let's call time in this flow of useless booze rules*, The Times, 13 August 2010; Christopher Snowdon, *Drinking, Fast and Slow: Ten Years of the Licensing Act*, Institute of Economic Affairs, 20 May 2015.

tobacco suggests that pricing can play a part in reducing consumption, as can licensing and other controls; but there can be unintended consequences as well, such as an increase in smuggling and an increase in consumption at home rather than in licensed premises.

2.5.13   Drugs: Psychoactives and Narcotics

Attempts to control the use of psychoactive drugs has been a relatively modern phenomenon and one which has been hard to achieve. Conventional narcotics, cannabis, heroin, and cocaine, have been subject to controls worldwide since the 1960s.[112] By and large such controls have been largely ineffective, seemingly having learned little from the USA's experience with prohibition. There has been a steady stream of studies, some from unexpected sources, suggesting that the law may be an inappropriate solution to the consumption of drugs.[113] Because of the ineffectiveness of existing legislation, the UK more recently attempted catch-all legislation, the Psychoactive Substances Act 2016, although its implementation was delayed indefinitely, largely because the police considered the law was unenforceable.[114] The government's Advisory Council on the Misuse of Drugs suggested that it 'may not achieve its aims and may produce unintended consequences'. Professor David Nutt, an authority on drugs, and a former chairman of the Council said, 'This is the worst piece of legislation since the Dangerous Dogs Act. More people will die as a result of it. The market will go underground and there will be less quality control. Government drugs policy isn't about saving lives, it's about looking tough.' Around 600 psychoactive substances had been identified in England; the legislation applied a blanket ban on all such substances (because the drafters were unable to think of an alternative solution), with liberty returned to the citizen on a case-by-case basis; but it has proved all but impossible to define 'psychoactive'. The Act bans anything which 'by stimulating or depressing the person's central nervous system ... affects the

---

[112] Christopher Snowdon, *The new ban on 'legal highs' is unworkable. The government doesn't even know what it's banning*, Spectator, 27 May 2015; Christopher Snowdon, *The Art of Suppression: Pleasure, Panic and Prohibition since 1800*, Little Dice, 2012.

[113] See e.g. David Nutt, *Drugs – without the hot air*, UIT Cambridge, 2012; Independent Scientific Committee on Drugs, www.drugscience.org.uk/; Rachel Sylvester, *This legal highs law is mind-bendingly useless*, The Times, 19 April 2016.

[114] It seemed incidentally to outlaw church incense, Alan Travis, *Incense in churches safe from new substances bill, say ministers*, Guardian, 2 October 2015.

person's mental functioning or emotional state'. There are specific exemptions for approved psychoactive substances such as alcohol, nicotine and caffeine, but involves a reversal of the usual presumption of permission unless forbidden. It also confused the scientific (chemical impact on the brain) with the spiritual (the emotional impact on the person): 'How can a court determine, objectively, what is going on – or has gone on – in somebody's mind? Is Proust's madeleine a psychoactive substance? No sooner had the warm liquid mixed with the crumbs touched my palate than a shudder ran through me and I stopped, intent upon the extraordinary thing that was happening to me . . . I had ceased now to feel mediocre, accidental, mortal. Whence could it have come to me, this all-powerful joy?'[115] Fortunately cakes are exempt, as a food (although not for VAT purposes), as are alkyl nitrites (poppers) on the grounds they have only peripheral effects on the brain.[116] A similar law in Ireland introduced in 2010 resulted in four prosecutions in five years, while the proportion of young people using the substances increased from 16 to 22 per cent.[117] The evidence overwhelmingly suggests that the criminalisation of all drugs creates more harm rather than less, although pressure for further controlling legislation continues.

2.6   Thinking That the Law Is the Answer

Alcoholism has been one of the greatest scourges as well as benefits of civilisation. And binge drinking has been a problem in the UK for many years.

---

[115] Rachel Sylvester, *This legal highs law is mind-bendingly useless*, The Times, 19 April 2016, referencing Marcel Proust, *Remembrance of Things Past*.

[116] Following an intervention by Crispin Hunt MP during the debate in Parliament, Hansard, Commons, 20 January 2016. Sarah Barber, *The Psychoactive Substances Bill 2015–2016: Report on Committee Stage*, House of Commons Library, Briefing Paper Number 7468, 15 January 2016.

[117] Originally in the Single Convention on Narcotic Drugs 1961; for current thinking see Global Commission on Drugs Policy, *War on Drugs*, June 2011, www.globalcommissionondrugs.org/reports/war-on-drugs and Advancing drug policy reform: a new approach to decriminalization, 2016 report, Global Commission on Drug Policy, 2016; cf. for the conventional approach, the United Nations Office on Drugs and Crime, www.unodc.org; see also Kofi Annan, Secretary General United Nations, 1997–2006: 'I believe that drugs have destroyed many lives, but wrong government policies have destroyed many more. We all want to protect our families from the potential harm of drugs. But if our children do develop a drug problem, surely we will want them cared for as patients in need of treatment and not branded as criminals.' *Essay*, Spiegel Online, 22 February 2016.

It is understandable that there has been pressure to seek a solution to at least part of the problem. But recent remedies have probably come too late; drinking is already diminishing, especially amongst the young, despite public perceptions to the contrary, without any regulatory intervention, and despite the fact that the prices of alcoholic drinks have reduced in recent times in real terms. Despite this there is immense pressure by doctors and other pressure groups who have to daily face the consequences of alcoholism that there should be a minimum price imposed on at least cheap alcohol.

The questions that need to be asked is whether it would work, and what might be the unintended consequences. In other words, does a legal intervention into the market produce a common good? In fact there is hardly any evidence that supports minimum pricing and the consequences could be what has happened to cigarettes, where around a third of tobacco consumption is now contraband.[118] It sounds common sense (and basic economics) that consumption falls as prices rise. In fact behavioural economics suggest that bright individuals may find a way around a problem where the price is not market-related.

And of course, from time to time there are occasions where a reduction in regulation can be shown to have marked economic advantages. Belgium has had a reputation for managing adequately without a government for long periods, and in October 2015 Spain had no operating government for nearly a year, during which period the growth rate during its first quarter without government was an annualised 2.9 per cent, more than Italy, France or Germany, and unemployment fell substantially:

> On 7 July 1948 Ludwig Erhard, the Director of Economics [in Germany] going well beyond his official authority, grabbed the power to abolish hundreds of price and production controls. He removed with a sudden yank a great blanket of government that covered the economy. He just let the market get on with it. The bureaucrats in the occupying forces were appalled. What would happen to poor Germany in the absence of their guiding hands?

---

[118] See John C. Duffy and Christopher Snowdon, *The minimal evidence for minimal pricing: the fatal flaws in the Sheffield alcohol policy model*, Adam Smith Institute, 2012. For example Denmark reduced tax on spirits by 45 per cent in 2003 without experiencing any increase in alcohol consumption (Makela et al., *Changes in volume of drinking after changes in alcohol taxes and travellers' allowances: results from a panel study*, [2008] 103(2) Addiction 181–191).

What happened was spectacular economic growth. There had been terrible shortages of everything from bricks to stockings. These were replaced with jumps in production. Production of stockings, as it happens, soared from 23 million pairs in 1949 to 152 million in 1956. Industrial output overall rose 140 per cent over the same period . . . Britain's industrial production grew by less than a quarter of the amount in Germany . . . because Britain had a government that planned, rationed and managed whole industries.[119]

2.7   Conclusions

There is self-evidently a culture of lawmaking by both legislators and regulators, even in areas of personal morality. Although the application of tort law by the judiciary is much less problematic than urban myths would have us believe, there is no doubt that there has been an expansion in the scope of the intervention of law, and a reduction in its quality. There are occasional successes in the introduction of rules, but they seem increasingly infrequent.

The consequences of these trends are disappointing. The damage to the common good has been profound. Principal concerns involve increases in the cost and availability of goods and services. In the US, for example, it was widely recognised that there was a need for additional rail tunnels under the Hudson River between New Jersey and New York City; the existing tunnels were over 100 years old. They had also been severely damaged during Superstorm Sandy in 2012. The problem had been studied since 1971, and approved after six years of environmental review. It required before work could commence reviews and permits from almost two dozen federal, state and local agencies, with no clear path to review and permit the project. It is estimated that each six year delay in gaining approvals doubles the cost of a project (it was $8.4B in 2009, and about $24B for completion in 2028).[120] The loss to the economy was estimated as including 80,000 additional train trips a day, additional 1.1M miles driven per day, 100,000 jobs during construction phase, £9B in business activity and $1.5B in federal, state and local tax revenue, and between 44,000 and 100,0000 additional permanent jobs with an increase of $4B in personal income over the 10 years following completion. Other countries, such as

---

[119] James Bartholomew, *Who needs governments? The Spanish seem to be doing better without one*, Spectator, 30 April 2016.
[120] Philip K. Howard, *Billions for Red Tape: Focusing on the approval process for the Gateway rail tunnel project*, Common Good, Brooklyn, USA, May 2016.

Germany and Canada, complete reviews and permits within one to two years.[121]

These trends are not inexorable. The next chapters look at the state of progress in each of three separate areas: legislation, regulation and the courts, and then engages in a discussion of attempts by governments to deal with the problem.

---

[121] Philip K. Howard, *Two years, not ten years: redesigning infrastructure approvals*, Common Good, Brooklyn, USA, September 2015.

3

Legislation and Legislators

Ninety percent of the politicians give the other ten per cent a bad name.[1]

They have but few laws, and such is their constitution that they need not many. They very much condemn other nations, whose laws, together with the commentaries on them, swell up to so many volumes; for they think it an unreasonable thing to oblige men to obey a body of laws that are both of such a bulk, and so dark as not to be read and understood by every one of the subjects.[2]

3.1 Introduction

3.1.1 Background

One of the reasons that there seems to be so much law, and that it seems to be so complicated, is that the machinery of lawmaking, especially the parliamentary machinery, looks to be designed to produce law almost regardless of the need for it, and law that is not coherent. This chapter examines that machinery and explores whether there is dysfunctionality in the process and, if so, what might be done about it. But whether dysfunctional or not, the process described below seems almost guaranteed to make what might have been originally a simple idea for a simple reform in a simple draft bill transformed into something rather more complicated when it emerges as an Act of Parliament ready for signature by the Queen.

3.1.2 Just How Much Law Is There?

Chapter 1 set out some preliminary indications of the scale of legislation. The volume of law can be measured in several ways, although on its own the simple counting of pages may miss or obscure some of the other issues, such as the mode of expression contained within a law. In simple page-number terms, the Law Commission reported on the growth in the

---

[1] Attributed to Henry Kissinger.   [2] Thomas More, *Utopia*, 1516.

amount of law and the number of acts that are passed each year;[3] what the Law Commission is less in a position to do is to estimate the quality of or the necessity for the new law.[4] The quality is regarded as a remit for the parliamentary draftsmen; the need, unless otherwise agreed, is reserved as a political issue. But despite or perhaps because of the buckpassing on responsibility, there is no doubt that there is public concern about both.[5]

Indeed in relation to the necessity of most of the laws that parliaments pass, a jurisdiction could probably survive, and might even flourish, without many of them. In one recent year, the legislative programme in the UK for example, that is the Acts of Parliament that were promoted, was as follows:[6]

Airport Expansion (Parliamentary Approval) Bill
Apprenticeships, Skills, Children and Learning Bill
Armenian Genocide Remembrance Day Bill
Autism Bill
Bank of England (Amendment) Bill [HL]
Bankers' Pensions (Limits) Bill
Banking Bill
Banking (No. 2) Bill [HL]
Beverley Freemen Bill [HL]
Borders, Citizenship and Immigration Bill [HL]
Bournemouth Borough Council Bill [HL]
British Museum Act 1963 (Amendment) Bill
Broadcasting (Public Service Content) Bill
Broadcasting (Television Licence Fee Abolition) Bill
Broads Authority Bill
Business Rate Supplements Bill
Canterbury City Council Bill
Children in Care (Custody) Bill
City of Westminster Bill [HL]
Climate Change (Sectoral Targets) Bill

---

[3] See Chapter 1; Law Commission, *Annual Report 2014/15*, p58 (there have been 200 consolidation acts since 1965; there have been 19 statute law repeals bills, repealing over 3,000 statutes in their entirety and the partial repeal of thousands of others).

[4] There are crude tests of readability including the ones included as part of the Microsoft Word word processing software package, the Flesch-Kincaid system.

[5] See e.g. for a United States expression of concern Michael D. Tanner, *Too many laws, Too much law*, Cato Institute, 2 March 2016: One of the complaints that the Founding Fathers levelled against King George III in the Declaration of Independence was that 'He has erected a Multitude of New Offices, and sent hither Swarms of Officers to harass our people, and eat out their Substance'.

[6] The United Kingdom 2009/10 programme.

Cohabitation (No. 2) Bill
Cohabitation Bill [HL]
Community Amateur Sports Clubs (Support) Bill [HL]
Companies' Remuneration Reports Bill [HL]
Consolidated Fund Bill
Consolidated Fund (Appropriation) Bill
Constitutional Renewal Bill [HL]
Co-operative and Community Benefit Societies and Credit Unions Bill
Coroners and Justice Bill
Corporation Tax Bill
Council Tax Rebate Bill
Crown Employment (Nationality) Bill
Damages (Asbestos-Related Conditions) Bill
Disabled Persons (Independent Living) Bill [HL]
Dog Control Bill [HL]
Driving Instruction (Suspension and Exemption Powers) Bill
Drugs (Roadside Testing) Bill
Employers' Liability Insurance Bureau Bill
Employment Opportunities Bill
Employment Retention Bill
Employment Rights Bill
Equal Pay and Flexible Working Bill [HL]
Equality and Diversity (Reform) Bill
European Union (Audit of Benefits and Costs of UK Membership) Bill
Exercise of Reasonable Discretion Bill
Food Labelling Regulations (Amendment) Bill
Forces Widows Pensions (Equality of Treatment) Bill
Fuel Poverty Bill
Geneva Conventions and United Nations Personnel (Protocols) Bill [HL]
Green Energy (Definition and Promotion) Bill
Health Bill [HL]
Holocaust (Stolen Art) Restitution Bill
Home Repossession (Protection) Bill
House of Lords (Members' Taxation Status) Bill [HL]
House of Lords Bill [HL]
Human Rights Act 1998 (Meaning of Public Authority) Bill
Illegally Logged Timber (Prohibition of Sale) Bill
Industrial Carbon Emissions (Targets) Bill
Industry and Exports (Financial Support) Bill
Land Use (Gardens Protection Etc) Bill
Law Commission Bill [HL]

Leaseholders Rights Bill
Leeds City Council Bill
Lending (Regulation) Bill
Local Democracy, Economic Development and Construction Bill [HL]
London Local Authorities Bill [HL]
London Local Authorities and Transport for London (No. 2) Bill [HL]
Manchester City Council Bill [HL]
Marine and Coastal Access Bill [HL]
Northern Ireland Bill
Nottingham City Council Bill
Online Purchasing of Goods and Services (Age Verification) Bill [HL]
Organ Donation (Presumed Consent) Bill
Palliative Care Bill
Pedlars (Amendment) Bill
Pension Credit and Personal Expense Allowance (Duty of Consultation
    and Review) Bill
Perpetuities and Accumulations Bill [HL]
Pharmaceutical Labelling (Warning of Cognitive Function Impairment)
    Bill
Policing and Crime Bill
Political Parties and Elections Bill
Postal Services Bill [HL]
Presumption of Death Bill
Protection of Children (Encrypted Material) Bill
Protection of Garden Land (Development Control) Bill
Protection of Shareholders Bill
Reading Borough Council Bill
Registration of Births and Deaths (Welsh Language) Bill
Renewable Content Obligation Bill
Royal Marriages and Succession to the Crown (Prevention of Discrimina-
    tion) Bill
Safety of Medicines (Evaluation) Bill
Saving Gateway Accounts Bill
Schools (Health Support) Bill
Scottish Banknotes (Acceptability in United Kingdom) Bill
Short Selling and Bank Accounts Bill
Small Business Rate Relief (Automatic Payment) Bill
Sovereignty of Parliament (European Communities) Bill
Special Educational Needs and Disability (Support) Bill
Sports Grounds Safety Authority Bill [HL]
Statutory Redundancy Pay (Amendment) Bill

Teaching of British History in Schools Bill
Theft from Shops (Use of Penalty Notices for Disorder) Bill
Torture (Damages) (No. 2) Bill
Torture (Damages) Bill [HL]
Transport for London (Supplemental Toll Provisions) Bill [HL]
Welfare Reform Bill
Young People Leaving Care (Accommodation) Bill

It is entirely possible to believe that the country could have survived or thrived if Parliament had failed to pass any of the bills in this list. In particular:

• Several of these acts were private bills, that is that they related to some technical powers that for example Manchester or Leeds or Newcastle councils needed to do their jobs. They were broadly non-contentious, and in many cases they were probably not uniquely necessary to achieve the needs of the councils, many or most of which could have been achieved by other means, although perhaps not so simply. The government and MPs spend little time thinking about them, and although there are debates, they are usually cursory.
• Some acts were promoted to meet the need to comply with international obligations. The Geneva Convention Bill, for example, was needed to add a new symbol to the internationally recognised Red Cross and Red Crescent symbols, used on military ambulances and on relief organisation vehicles, to give protection to the wounded. They needed ratification by the government and passing an Act of Parliament was one way of doing it. It was nominally debated, but the debate was formal and uncontentious.
• The Consolidated Fund Bill was a sister bill to the Finance Bill, as part of passing the budget of the country. It was contentious, but most other countries, while they have finance bills, do not have them of the length and complexity of those of the UK. The financial rules in most countries change but slowly, and are intended to be in place virtually indefinitely. Where there is considered to be a need for change, such change is introduced specifically rather than in an omnibus finance bill of several hundred pages. The length of the UK finance bills comes as something of a mystery to other countries who manage to raise the taxation income they need without the length, complexity and frequency of legal changes that are seen to be necessary in the UK.[7]

---

[7] Jill C. Pagan, *Increasing length and complexity of tax legislation – avoidable or inevitable?*, [1993] 14(4) *Fiscal Studies* 90–105. The UK tax code now exceeds 20,000 pages, although the

But it is clear that there is a lot of law, a high frequency of change in the law, and that not all of the law and its change is digestible. Superficially there seem to be several reasons for this torrent of lawmaking, not all of them connected, and before examining the process of lawmaking, it might be helpful to address some at least of the reasons behind the great expansion.

This chapter looks at 'pure' law, that is law made by legislators and the government; it, and the following two chapters (judge-made law, and regulation), together expand on several of the drivers behind the expansion of rule making. This chapter in particular considers

- why law is made,
- who makes it,
- how it is made, and then
- if there are indeed challenges, what might be done to improve lawmaking.[8]

3.2   Why Law Is Made

> I am opposed to the laying down of rules or conditions to be observed
> in the construction of bridges lest the progress of improvement tomorrow

effective length is debated, see e.g. Caroline Turnbull-Hall and Richard Thomas, *Reviewing the length of the UK tax code*, [2012] (1 February) Tax Journal, which suggested it is rather shorter and that ironically part of any increased length was due to part of it being drafted in accordance with the principles of simplified drafting. The authors were part of the UK Office for Tax Simplification. An alternative view is that it doubled to 10 million words between 2009 and 2016, see *UK tax code now 12 times size of King James Bible*, CCH Daily Newsletter, 9 March 2016 and see David Martin, *A new, simple, revenue neutral tax code for business*, Centre for Policy Studies, March 2016. Cf Adam Broke, *Simplification of tax, or I wouldn't start from here*, ICAEW Tax Faculty Hardman Lecture, 1999.

[8] For a graphic description of when new law does not work, see Jaqui Smith, *How not to do it*, BBC Radio 4, *Analysis*, broadcast 6 February 2016 at 20:30: 'Jacqui Smith, the former Labour home secretary, investigates why government policies fail, focusing on one of her party's most cherished reforms. Indeterminate sentences for public protection (IPPs) were devised by David Blunkett and the Home Office to reassure voters that those convicted of serious violent and sexual offences would stay in prison [after they had served their fixed sentence] until they could show by their changed behaviour that they could safely be released. But much larger numbers of offenders received the sentences than had been expected and, as the prison population rose, jails struggled to provide the facilities IPP prisoners needed to show that they had reformed. The new sentencing structure, first passed in 2003, had to be drastically changed by Labour in 2008 and finally to be repealed by the coalition four years after that. Jacqui Smith discovers the reasons why the change in sentencing was embarked upon, why its potential flaws weren't detected before its introduction and why the policy was maintained even as problems mounted. She considers the difficult legacy of IPPs – for those still in prison and for politicians devising shiny new initiatives in other fields of government.'

might be embarrassed or shackled by recording or registering as law the prejudices or errors of today.[9]

3.2.1 Background

Law is made for a variety of reasons and sometimes none. In most countries, in most circumstances, there is probably enough law to cope with most of a nation's problems for the immediate or even foreseeable future: laws against murder and theft, or to encourage driving on the correct side of the road, or requiring stopping at red traffic lights have usually been in place for a while, and even in some of those cases, law might not have actually been needed. Sometimes, of course, there is genuinely a need for a new law or a change in the existing law.

The drivers for the creation of additional and often unnecessary law have been discussed in the previous chapters; but there are two main factors in Western liberal democracies which seem to be critical.

First is simply a combination of the time available to make laws, and idle hands available to do so. Governments often complain that the parliamentary schedule is tight; nonetheless there does in fact seem plenty of time to make new laws. The UK Parliament sits for around 180 days a year, and to that extensive sitting must be added the committee hearings which take place. This seems to be maybe not long enough to create decently drafted law, but it is certainly long enough to introduce substantial quantities of poorly drafted law.[10]

In other countries, by way of comparison, the time available for making laws can be limited, and so there are relatively fewer laws. The Swiss Parliament for example only meets during the winter, and its members are supposed to devote not more than 60 per cent of their time to Parliament, so there is less time available to introduce fresh legislation; it only manages four sessions of three weeks each in which to pass laws.[11]

---

[9] Attributed to Isambard Kingdom Brunel; the verbatim citation is probably 'If the Commission is to enquire into the conditions "to be observed," it is to be presumed that they will give the result of their enquiries; or, in other words, that they will lay down, or at least suggest, "rules" and "conditions to be (hereafter) observed" in the construction of bridges, or, in other words, embarrass and shackle the progress of improvement tomorrow by recording and registering as law the prejudices or errors of to-day.' in a letter objecting to any interference by the State with the freedom of civil engineers in the conduct of their professional work, 13 March 1848 to the Royal Commission on the Application of Iron in Railway Structures, collected in *The Life of Isambard Kingdom Brunel, Civil Engineer*, 1870, at p487.

[10] James Bortholomew, *The Welfare of Nations*, Biteback, 2015, p251 et seq.: 'The public sector tends to create excessive regulations'.

[11] See e.g. www.parlament.ch/e/organe-mitglieder/bundesversammlung/Pages/default.aspx. Similarly, the Texas legislature only meets every other year, and even then for a maximum

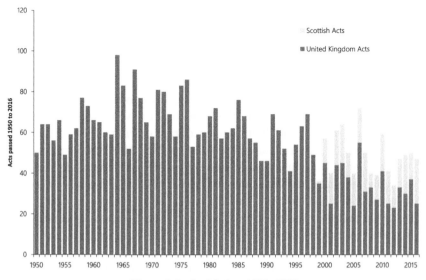

Figure 3.1   Legislation, 1951–2015

Many of the laws that the Swiss federal government needs to pass are relatively straightforward. They include for example the Finance Acts, which are less 'laws' than annual budgets that are agreed by the country. They include Acts of Parliament to compulsorily purchase land to build a road or a railway for the public good, or to agree an international treaty to allow free movement of goods and services. The Swiss example is not strictly comparable with those of other jurisdictions because the cantons have lawmaking powers as well.

3.2.2   Drive to Make Law

Second is the hunger of MPs and government to have laws passed in their name, already discussed in Chapter 1. Members of parliament are under continual pressure from constituents, from the media and from themselves to deal with a burst of drug-related crime, or youth violence, or too many gun deaths. Whatever the particular concern of the day there will invariably be an MP (or even the government) who may pick up the cause and suggest that a change in the law would be a good idea and would fix the

of 140 days; delegates earn around $7,500 a year, which encourages them to be brief. Texas is three times the size of the UK with approximately half the population. The fact that there is federal legislation in addition makes it an imperfect comparator.

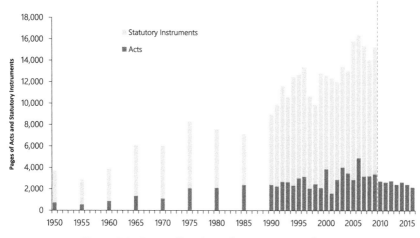

Figure 3.2   Pages of legislation between 1950 and 2015

problem. Many MPs claim on their websites that they have been instrumental in creating or fine-tuning a new law.

3.2.3   Size of the Rule Book

It has already been shown that there has been growth in the volume of law; at first glance it looks as though in fact has been more continence that popularly believed (Figure 3.1).[12]

The diagram however slightly disguises the increasing length of legislation; for example, see Figure 3.2.[13]

And their complexity (Table 3.1).[14]

In 2001 there were only 44 statutes – but with 2868 pages. With the addition of statutory instruments in recent years there have been up to 16,000 pages of rules a year (ignoring the additional rules imposed by the Welsh, Northern Ireland and Scottish assemblies); it is not possible to include recent figures because not all statutory instruments are printed. These figures do not include the explanatory memoranda which are

---

[12] Ross Turner, *Acts and statutory instruments: the volume of UK legislation 1950 to 2015*, House of Commons Library, Briefing Paper CBP 7438, 21 December 2015, p5.

[13] Ross Turner, *Acts and statutory instruments: the volume of UK legislation 1950 to 2015*, House of Commons Library, Briefing Paper CBP 7438, 21 December 2015, p10.

[14] Hansard Society, *Making the Law*, 1992, p11.

Table 3.1 *Complexity of legislation, 1901–1991*

Year	No. of public general acts	Pages	Number of sections and schedules
1901	40	247	400
1911	58	584	701
1921	67	569	783
1931	34	375	440
1941	48	448	533
1951	66	675	803
1961	65	1048	1087
1971	81	2107	1963
1981	72	2276	2026
1991	69	2222	1985

nowadays attached to statutes to enable them to be better understood, which may add another 50 per cent to the number of pages.[15]

Looking at the list of the bills in the list above, several involved political posturing. The Autism Bill, the Teaching of British History in Schools Bill, the Torture (Damages) Bill and the Bankers' Pension Bill were the result of single-issue initiatives and were intended not to be passed but to make a point. There will have been a debate in one or other of the Chambers, the debates that ensued may have influenced government thinking, or may have brought the matter to the attention of the public, and it was possible that there might have eventually been a change in administration or

---

[15] See Chapter 1; Hansard Society, *Making the Law*, 1992, p11. And see Ross Turner, *Acts and statutory instruments: the volume of legislation 1950 to 2015*, House of Commons Library CBP 7438, 21 December 2015. Whilst the number of Acts passed seems to have settled down from previous peaks, the number of statutory instruments has increased. Looking at the long-term trends, we may have reached peak legislation in Parliament at least. More concerningly, the amount of time spent debating legislation in the House of Commons seems to be on the decline, falling from the time available from 42 per cent in 1997 to 32 per cent by 2013, see Nicola Newson, *Publishing statistics on the time spent on parliamentary proceedings on each part of an act*, House of Lords, In Focus, 11 January 2017; see also Daniel Greenberg, *Dangerous Trends in Modern Legislation... and how to reverse them*, Centre for Policy Studies, April 2016. In relation to the European Union, there are around 19,000 EU legislative acts in force, including directives, regulations, decisions, external agreements, resolutions, reports, rules of procedure, guidelines, declarations, inter-institutional and internal agreements, programmes, opinions, communications, conclusions and statutes. In the UK there are around 7900 statutory instruments implementing EU legislation, see Vaughne Miller, *Legislating for Brexit: statutory instruments implementing EU law*, House of Common Library, Briefing Paper 7867, 16 January 2017.

provision of help in some way – perhaps by the reallocating of resource. But they were not intended genuinely to change the law. Their promotion involved an expenditure of parliamentary time, but ministers, civil servants and others did not spend their hours worrying about them. Whilst they consumed a certain amount of parliamentary resource, they did not add materially to the parliamentary burden.[16] Meanwhile a few of the bills had a genuinely necessary purpose, or were essential to the proper governance of the country.

Others could have been regarded as frivolous, pointless, supernumerary or even counter-productive. And some of those that did have a functional purpose merely fine-tuned reforms that might perhaps have been better achieved by improved administration and implementation of existing legislation.[17]

3.2.4   Law or Administration?

One of the reasons that governments want to see more law is that they are concerned that the usual levers of power do not work effectively, or there has been a failure of administration. Improved cleanliness on hospital wards, improved policing or improved transport rarely needs new law to bring about the necessary reforms; usually it needs merely a will to implement existing provisions by the existing officials. Improved administration is regarded as hard to implement where power is centralised, but the desire to centralise control continues – and politicians suffer criticism when there are the inevitable failures even where they have outsourced to a quasi-independent agency, as happened with the UK Border Agency and its failure to implement policy to control levels of immigration into

---

[16] Other countries have similar problems: In the United States: 'By law government departments have to publish new regulations in the Federal Register. In the 1950s the Register expanded by an average of 11,000 pages a year. In the first decade of the twenty-first century it expanded by an average of 73,000 pages a year. From 2009 to 2011 the Obama administration produced 106 major regulations, with 'major' defined as having an expected impact of $100 million a year, and thousands of minor regulations. The Obama health bill was over 2,000 pages long; the Dodd-Frank law of finance is 870 pages long and has 400 subsidiary regulations [around 32,000 pages]. The federal government requires hospitals to use 140,000 codes for the ailments they treat, including one for injuries being caused by a turtle.' John Micklethwaite and Adrian Wooldridge, *The Fourth Revolution*, Allen Lane, 2014, p117; Edward McBride, *Cheer Up*, The Economist, 16 March 2013. And see Appendix II below for a copy of the Obama administration Executive Order minimising regulation.

[17] As elsewhere discussed, law can be introduced to set a tone, rather than necessarily to create an offence, called 'non-law-bearing legislation' see David Feldman, *Legislation as aspiration: statutory expression of policy goals*, Statute Law Society, lecture, 16 March 2015. Professor Feldman refers to four forms of such legislation: promissory, declaratory, aspirational and statements of political support.

the UK. As will be seen when regulation is considered in a following chapter, one way in which government maintains control, but distances itself from responsibility, is by the establishment of an intermediary agency or regulator; in practice the strategy may not always work. Sometimes, paradoxically, the buck insists on being passed up to where it really does not and should not belong.[18] A failure by an agency can in extreme cases cost a Minister his job, despite his not being responsible for the error.

3.2.5   The Difficulty of Thinking Strategically

One issue that understandably occupies the thoughts of politicians is getting (re)elected. And in a country which requires that general elections are held at least every five years, and where there is a belief that the concerns of the electorate are short term, it is hard to persuade politicians to spend much of their time thinking longer term. Other democratic countries, admittedly with different problems, seem to manage to establish longer-term plans. For example, passengers emerging from Madrid's magnificently rebuilt Atocha railway station will face a large sign claiming it has been updated as part of Spain's 25-year transport strategy. The strategy may be poor or wrong, or badly executed, or unaffordable – but at least the Spanish public have an understanding that someone is thinking longer term about the strategy which may later need to change to meet changing circumstances. In other countries, such as the UK, or in the US, the political drivers are shorter term, and can involve a greater concern by politicians in about-turns, short-term fixes and attempts to gain media bites. All parties seem addicted to this, and consider it is effective to manage public opinion; there are few politicians who feel able to award themselves the luxury of daring to think longer term.

Politicians in power find strategic thinking even harder. They are often over-worked, often exhausted, and with scarcely time to think.[19] Part of this dysfunctional system results from the way in which they struggle to distinguish administration from policy. The cynical might explain it as a stratagem by the senior civil servants in 'Yes minister' fashion, so as to keep ministers in their place. The role of a minister is also complex; it can involve PR for the government, advice to local citizens, departmental administration, policy making and public speaking and eating. They also have to adopt a chairman's role: to meet with (and occasionally chide)

---

[18] United Kingdom Border Agency, disbanded 26 March 2013 by the Home Office; its failures threatened the position of Theresa May as Home Secretary.

[19] Tony Blair, A Journey, Hutchinson, 2010.

their civil servants, and discuss policy issues. The best of ministerial chairman, of course, mostly leave their team and their senior civil servants well alone, intervening only if there is a particular problem. There is no formal job-description for ministers, and some of the guides that do exist are misleading, so it is hard to avoid dysfunctionality.[20] Meanwhile there is little appetite amongst those thinking politicians to press for reform; there are few votes in it.[21]

3.2.6   The Nature of Politicians

As evidenced by the wave of populist voting in recent years, there seems to be a widespread cynicism about both politics and politicians, with a weary acceptance that they are a necessary evil. And indeed it is curious why, given the arduous and uncertain process of becoming a politician, the bizarre hours involved, the limited salary (for many) and the absence of any work-life balance, anyone would want the job. Many are maybe driven by a wish to help and improve society in line with their own beliefs; but most once elected find themselves compromised by the political realities of the need to survive and to play the political game, which they have no option but to be part of. The question here is whether that game necessarily involves a need to create more rules for the rest of community; telling other people how to behave is an occupational disease inherent in politics and politicians.

Two areas of continual change and interest in the UK, the control of pensions taxation and of terrorism, neatly demonstrate the dysfunction in the system. In pensions taxation, it was decided in the early part of the millennium that the existing system was too unwieldy and should be simplified and restated. This was eventually achieved rather clumsily in the Finance Act 2004, the reform being intended at the time to last for a generation. The original dream of the Treasury was to sweep away around 14 different tax regimes and around 1300 pages of rules and replace it by around 20 pages of law, at the same time removing discretions of HMRC so as to save about 100 highly skilled staff who were otherwise needed to exercise those discretions. The stability lasted around a year. The reformed taxation system was then changed in 2005, 2006, 2007, 2008, 2009, 2010 (three times), 2011, 2012, 2013, 2014 (twice) and 2015 (twice). In addition a Taxation of Pensions Act 2014 completely reversed earlier

---

[20] Gerald Kaufman, *How to be a Minister*, Faber and Faber, 1980.
[21] Although see John Gill, *David Willetts interview: 'What I did was in the interests of young people'*, Times Educational Supplement, 18 June 2015 where decisions were taken in relation to raising university fees despite adverse political consequences.

policy and complicated the system beyond normal comprehension. And following a General Election in 2015, a further drastic reform was consulted on. Meanwhile the language of the Taxation of Pensions Act 2014 is incomprehensible even to experts:

> (c) in the case of an arrangement to which section 165(3A) never applied but only if the time falls after the member's drawdown pension fund in respect of the arrangement is converted into the member's flexible access drawdown fund in respect of the arrangement of paragraph 8B or 8C of Schedule 28, 80% of the maximum amount that could have been paid in accordance with pension rule 5 in the drawdown pension year in which the conversion occurs had no conversion happened in that year by the operation of either of paragraphs 8B and 8C of Schedule 28.[22]

and the original dream of simplicity in the 2004 Act long ago disappeared down the Looking Glass burrow. The urge to fiddle with the detail, and cater for short-term expediency, overcame the need of the consumer for the consistency of a long-term strategy.

Similar confusion attended the development of legislation in the UK intended to respond to the growth of terrorism. The Terrorism Act 2000 in the UK was introduced following (mostly) Irish terrorism. Following the jihadi attacks of 9/11 in New York, the Anti-Terrorism, Crime and Security Act 2001 was passed. Government powers were extended in the Prevention of Terrorism Act 2005 (which didn't manage to prevent serious attacks in London in 2005), further extended in the Criminal Justice Act 2003, further extended in the Anti-terrorism, Crime and Security Act 2001 Order 2003, the Prevention of Terrorism Act 2005, the Terrorism Act 2006, the Counter Terrorism Act 2008, the Coroners and Justice Act 2009, and the Terrorist Asset-Freezing (Temporary Provisions) Act 2010. The Terrorism Prevention and Investigation Measures Act was passed in 2011. The Justice and Security Act was passed in 2013. In 2015 yet another counter-terrorism act was enacted.[23] If passing legislation controlled terrorism, the country would have been spared the attacks in 2017 on

---

[22] Finance Act 2014: inserting Schedule 36 paragraph 20(4)(c) of the Finance Act 2004. See also Andy Haldane, Chief Economist, Bank of England, *The Great Divide*, speech to the New City Agenda Annual Dinner, 18 May 2016: 'To give a personal example, I consider myself moderately financially literate. Yet I confess to not being able to make the remotest sense of pensions. Conversations with countless experts and independent financial advisors have confirmed for me only one thing – that they have no clue either. That is a desperately poor basis for sound financial planning.'

[23] Counter Terrorism and Security Act 2015. It marked seven acts in 14 years. See *Liberty's Second Reading briefing on the Counter-Terrorism and Security Bill in the House of Lords*, Liberty, January 2015, which details the ineffectiveness of most of the previous legislation and the unintended consequences of promoting rather than reducing radicalism.

Westminster Bridge, London Bridge and in Manchester. In fact most observers (though not all)[24] consider that the legislation reflects a 'bias to action' or 'bias to immediacy' rather than a bias to fixing a problem – and that many of the powers had a malign effect, in criminalising people who might otherwise have helped the authorities, or radicalising them because of harsh treatment and the withdrawal of normal human rights. The problem of terrorism is probably best responded to by improved intelligence, and police action, rather than new law. Politicians know this too, but prefer in practice to blame their inadequate powers rather than their inadequate administration.[25]

This activity has bred a certain cynicism in those affected. Savers, for example, have a diminished faith in a pension system that instead of promoting a necessary 60-year stability, changes several times a year. And terrorists seem unafraid by the slabs of legislation, control orders and restrictions on liberty without due process, that have been enacted. The scepticism about the use of legislation is compounded when not only resources are devoted to additional legislation where it is little needed, but resources are removed from areas where they are genuinely required, in particular in relation to access to justice. As a former Attorney General observed:[26]

> Realistically, a government's three main duties to its citizens are defence, the maintenance of order and access to justice. The lack of remedies where there is inadequate access to justice undermines public trust in politicians and fuels the alienation of growing numbers of people from the democratic process.

As we shall see in a following chapter, greater expenditure on legal aid is not necessarily the solution to grant improved access to justice, but improved judicial management – which the then Attorney General despite his best endeavours was unable to introduce – might make a difference to the ability of a citizen to enforce his rights.

---

[24] For conflicting views see John Kay, *Lessons for the politicians from the Sage of Omaha*, Financial Times, 13 January 2015; and Tim Ross, *Ex-MI5 chief [Jonathan Evans] warns spy laws 'not fit for purpose'*, Daily Telegraph, 17 January 2015.

[25] See e.g. Clive Walker, *The Anti-terrorism Legislation*, Oxford University Press, 2002 which cites the Home Affairs Committee: 'This country has more anti-terrorist legislation on its statute books than almost any other developed democracy', Home Affairs Committee, *Report on the Anti-Terrorism, Crime and Security Bill 2001*, 2001–02, HC 351 para 1. There is now even more. The list of legislation recited above excludes United Nations-linked implementation orders.

[26] Jonathan Rayner, *Dominic Grieve: Straight talker*, Interview, Law Society Gazette, 12 January 2015.

3.2.7   It's the System, Stupid

If the general consensus is that the legal factory is obsolete, and that what comes out of the factory gate is so often damaging, how and why does it work like this? The problem may be the system itself as much as the players. A former President of the Supreme Court, Lord Neuberger, has said:[27]

> The need for clearly drafted laws is obvious: unclear drafting results in uncertainty and expense: it undermines society, the economy, private interests, commercial interests, and the rule of law itself. We need a more deliberate approach to law making. As I have already emphasized, we need more considered legislation. And, I respectfully suggest that inevitably means that we need less legislation. Like Sir Thomas Gresham's adage about money, bad legislation drives out good. That is because our old friend, lack of Parliamentary time . . . And we have had a welter of legislation in the past 20 years or so, pressed on with by the Government because it wants to be seen to be dealing with the problems identified in the headlines.
>
> I have called this the Mikado delusion. You may recall the scene: Koko is explaining why, despite the Mikado's command to decapitate him, Nanki-Poo has been allowed to escape. He says:
>
> > 'It's like this: when your Majesty says, "Let a thing be done," it's as good as done, practically, it is done, because your Majesty's will is law. Your Majesty says "Kill a gentleman", and a gentleman is told off to be killed. Consequently that man is as good as dead; practically, he is dead, and if he is dead, why not say so?'
>
> And the Mikado says: 'I see. Nothing could be more satisfactory.'

Other judges have been similarly critical. Sir Brian Leveson was the judge in charge of the inquiry into the telephone hacking of well-known individuals. Shortly after that he was commissioned by the Department of Justice to see what he could do to streamline the criminal justice process. He reported:[28]

> 12 The criminal justice system is presently crowded with plans for future development. There are currently in the region of a dozen pilots, initiatives

---

[27] Lord Neuberger of Abbotsbury, *General, equal and certain: law reform today and tomorrow* [2012] 33(3) Statute Law Review 323–338 at p337.

[28] Sir Brian Leveson, *Review of efficiency in criminal proceedings*, Judiciary of England and Wales, January 2015, para 12 et seq. Footnotes omitted, but the remarks refer to figures taken from the Law Commission *Consultation Paper*, 2010, paragraph 1.17. The paper also references the Ministry of Justice's revised figures for new offences creation 2009–13; its methodology is criticised in Leverick and Chalmers, *Tracking the creation of criminal offences* [2013] Criminal Law Review 543.

and schemes operating in England and Wales. Each has been created and implemented in the desire to improve one or more aspects of the operation of the way in which criminal justice is delivered.

13 Compounding the above problem is that the landscape is subject to frequent change. Between 1989 and 2009, parliament approved over 100 Criminal Justice Bills and more than 4,000 criminal offences were added to the statute book. From an historical context, the figure is more startling. Halsbury's Statutes of England and Wales has five volumes devoted to criminal laws that (however old they may be) are still currently in force. Volume One covers the law created in the 637 years between 1351 and 1988, and is 1,249 pages long. Volumes Two to Five cover the laws created in the 24 years between 1989 and 2013 and are no less than 4,921 pages long. The 2013 supplement adds a further 200 pages. So, more than four times as many pages were needed in Halsbury's Statutes to cover laws created in the 24 years between 1989 and 2013 than were needed to cover the laws created in the 637 years prior to that.

14 It is hardly surprising then, given all the above, that the Review encountered what might best be described as 'transformation exhaustion'.

His remarks echo those of Lord Steyn, a Law Lord, who referred to there being 'an orgy of statutes' in a lecture in 2003:[29]

> My subject is the interpretation of legal texts, and particularly the interpretation of statutes, seen inevitably from an English perspective. You may think that some of my reflections exaggerate the complexities of the subject. It is true that, unlike other professionals, judges are usually able to start with a comforting feeling that they have a 50 per cent chance of getting the answer to the question right. Moreover, judges can be reassured by the fact that Lord Reid advised judges that if their average success rate drops significantly below 50 per cent they have a moral duty to spin a coin.[30]

He added:

> In his influential book *A common law for the age of statutes*,[31] Guido Calabresi described what he called the statutorification of the law. He referred to the modern phenomenon of an orgy of statute making. That description is particularly apt in the case of my country. In the last twenty years

---

[29] Johan Steyn, Lord of Appeal in Ordinary, *Dynamic interpretation amidst an orgy of statutes*, The Brian Dickson Memorial Lecture, Ottawa, 2 October 2003, 35(2) Ottawa Law Review 163.

[30] Johan Steyn, *The intractable problem of the interpretation of legal texts*, The John Lehane Memorial Lecture delivered to the University of Sydney, September 2002, [2003] 25 Sydney Law Review 1.

[31] Guido Calabresi, *A Common law for the age of statutes*, Cambridge, Harvard University Press, 1982.

there has been an orgy of legislation in Britain, particularly in the criminal justice field. Almost every year there is a huge criminal justice act. One feature of this frenzied statute-making in the criminal justice field is a legislative see-saw; measures based on half-baked ideas are adopted in haste, published with minimal consultation, and puffed up to be the ideal solution for solving problems of crime, but then abandoned very soon after and replaced by yet another solution said to be the perfect one. The complexity of each new statute defies belief. And so, to the bewilderment of the public and judges, the process continues. Year after year, the editors of our major criminal treatise have commented adversely on this phenomenon. They have said:

> 'Major criminal legislation is now an annual event; the quality of it borders on the scandalous. If testimony to this were needed, it is only necessary to look at the way in which each year's Act is extensively amended or repealed by the next. If any government really wanted to improve the quality of the criminal justice it would announce a moratorium on criminal legislation for five or seven or, even, 10 years.'[32]

There are a number of factors which have led to this dispiriting explosion of concern by the judiciary and many others. They include poor drafting – and poor instructions.[33] A former Lord Chief Justice of England and Wales made a similar point:[34]

> Law-making by secondary legislation has become habitual. Every year statutory instruments covering something like 12,000 printed pages come into force. Some extend to major issues of policy; some give ministers power to dispense with primary legislation. Virtually every page creates laws or duties, powers or prohibitions. They are by no means confined to matters of administration.
>
> The last occasion when the House of Commons rejected secondary legislation was in 1979. Since 1950 the House of Lords has done so on six occasions. When it did so recently it apparently created a constitutional problem; hence the Strathclyde Review, set up by the Prime Minister.

---

[32] Archbold, *Criminal pleading, evidence and practice*, 1995, preface.

[33] See Lord Judge, former Lord Chief Justice, 'My Lord Mayor ... last year I spent some time addressing the problem of legislative plenitude – overload – ... which I wonder of the 2,492 – yes, 2,492 laws – introduced during 2009 will still be in force 700 years from now. Presumably, whether there is a nuclear explosion or not, no one will have been charged with causing a nuclear explosion under the Nuclear Explosions (Prohibition and Inspections) Act 1998. But what if they had? After such an explosion it might be a little tricky to get a judge and jury together to try any defendant who might have survived the explosion, and been found and traced by any surviving member of the police force. That is what I call a really useful Act of Parliament!', *The Safest Shield*, Hart, 2015 p102.

[34] Lord Judge, Lord Chief Justice of England and Wales 2008–2013, *Statutory oversight*, letter to the *Times*, 7 May 2016.

There is indeed a constitutional problem, but it is not the problem identified in the review. The real problem is and remains law-making on a vast scale without adequate, indeed with virtually no, effective parliamentary scrutiny. It must be addressed, not by the executive, but by both Houses of Parliament, working together.

3.2.8   Good and Bad Drafting

Drafting of legislation is a specialist craft. The outcome is improved by clear instructions from the instructing department, with time for thinking about how best to implement those instructions, and by fewer but more thoughtful amendments by commentating MP's. Such a utopian environment is rare and as a consequence there are innumerable instances of bad drafting. Confiscation, for example, was a sensible sanction to deal with the proceeds of crime, although the funds went to the state rather than to the unfortunate citizens who had been defrauded. It was introduced by the Proceeds of Crime Act 2002. In *R v Ahmad*[35] the Supreme Court had to undertake a labyrinthine exercise in statutory construction, but struggled to do so:

> The legislation is largely impenetrable, the authorities lengthy and internally inconsistent, and the facts of individual cases complex. The net result is that most cases end up either being fudged or flawed on any proper legal analysis. Either way, one party or the other misses out, either the defendant because he is on the wrong end of a decision which has no basis in common sense or fairness, or the Crown because the legislative purposes of the scheme have not been met.[36]

And it is not as though the legislators are not aware of the problem. Lord Neuberger pointed out in relation to the drafting of the Financial Services (Banking Reform) Bill 2013:

> Lord Higgins, a Conservative, said that 'the way that the Bill is drafted . . . makes it extremely difficult for the House to work out what is happening from moment to moment on an unbelievably complex matter'. Lord Phillips of Sudbury, a Liberal Democrat, described 'the complexity of both the Bill and the amendments' as 'quite barbaric', and Lord Barnett, Labour, agreed with the view of Lord Turnbull, a cross-bencher, 'that he has never seen such a shambles presented to any house'.[37]

---

[35] *R v Ahmad, R v Fields* [2014] UKSC 36.
[36] Christopher Coltart, *Rip it up and start again*, Law Society Gazette, 30 June 2014.
[37] House of Lords Debate on the Financial Services (Banking Reform) Bill 2013, Hansard HL Deb 8 Oct 2013 Column 22, cited in Lord Neuberger, *The future of the Bar*, speech to a conference of the Bar Councils of Northern Ireland and Ireland, Belfast, 20 June 2014.

It was voted through on 18 December 2013, with over 200 pages being enacted.

3.2.9   Incessant Variation

The constant change to the system is in some ways to be applauded; it shows that there is a response to changing circumstances, and that the former sclerotic inability to reform which led to the development of chancery and equity as a response is now less needed than it was several hundred years ago. On the other hand, too much change makes it hard for the layman and even judiciary to cope. A former Lord Chief Justice acerbically pointed out:[38]

> A recent case[39] illustrates the problems to which this legislative confusion gives rise... A defendant was accused to a tobacco smuggling offence and pleaded guilty in 2007. A community sentence was imposed, and application made for a confiscation order. His liability to a confiscation order depended on his having evaded payment of duty to which he was personally liable to pay. To show he was liable, the prosecution relied on some 1992 regulations. The trial judge was satisfied that he was liable, and ordered him to pay £66,120 or serve 20 months in prison if he did not. He appealed. The appeal came before three senior judges in the Court of Appeal, who heard argument and announced they would give their judgment later in writing. They concluded that the defendant was liable to pay the duty under the 1992 regulations and circulated a draft judgment upholding the confiscation order. On the eve of formally delivering judgment, however, they learned that the 1992 regulations no longer applied to tobacco products, as a result of different regulations made in 2001. Neither the trial judge, nor the prosecutor, nor defending counsel, nor the judges in the Court of Appeal knew of these later regulations, and they were not at fault. As Lord Justice Toulson said, giving judgment allowing the appeal:
>
> > 'there is no comprehensive statute law database with hyperlinks which would enable an intelligent person, by using a search engine, to find out all the legislation on a particular topic. This means that the courts are in many cases unable to discover what the law is, or was at the date with which the court is concerned, and are entirely dependent on the parties for being able to inform them what were the relevant statutory provisions which the court has to apply. This lamentable state of affairs has been raised by responsible bodies on many occasions'...[40]
>
> Reporting and commenting on the case in the Guardian, Marcel Berlins suggested that the age-old maxim might have to be revised: ignorance of the law is no excuse, unless there is no way of finding out what the law

---

[38] Tom Bingham, *The rule of law*, Allen Lane, 2010, pp 41–42.
[39] *R v Chambers* [2008] EWCA Crim 2467, 17 October 2008.
[40] *R v Chambers* [2008] EWCA Crim 2467, 17 October 2008, at para 28.

is . . . [41] This was plainly written in jest. But in 1988 and again in 1995 the Italian Constitutional Court ruled that ignorance of the law may constitute an excuse for the citizen when the formulation of the law is such as to lead to obscure and contradictory results.[42]

3.2.10   Costs to the Economy: Unintended Consequences

The World Bank has examined whether regulation can have adverse economic consequences, in other words whether the price that is paid for some controls is worth it. It may be sensible to regulate against small boys going up chimneys, and it is a price that many would be prepared to pay (or not, if we buy clothes from certain department stores) – if we knew the human cost of a product or service. One test of over-bureaucratisation is the ease of doing business in a particular country and the evidence seems to indicate that those with easier regimes generally have healthier economies.[43] One study suggests that in the US the amount of regulation added since 1949 reduced economic growth by 2 per cent a year. The cumulative effect to 2005 was that the economy was only 28 per cent of what it would have been if the amount of regulation had stayed at 1949 levels, in other words the US would be three times richer.[44] What is not estimated is whether the quality of life would be any different; to make an excessive point, would the outcome of the Three-Mile Island nuclear power station episode have been worse without the post-1949 regulations at the time. This is the counter-factual that regulatory authorities often posit, perhaps with justification.[45]

3.3   Who Makes Law

3.3.1   Introduction

If it seems self-evident that the laws that are being made are so badly flawed, it raises the question of what might be done to improve matters, so

---

[41] Marcel Berlins, *A Kafkaesque excuse for ignorance of the law*, Guardian, 3 November 2008 p12.
[42] Ewoud Hondius, *Sense and nonsense in the law*, 28 November 2007, inaugural address when accepting the chair in European private law, University of Utrecht, Kluwer Deventer, 2007, p23, citing Joseph Kimble, *Answering the critics of plain language*, Scribes Journal of Legal Writing 5 (1994–5) pp 51–85.
[43] World Bank, *Ease of doing business*, website.
[44] John Dawson and John Seater, *Federal regulation and aggregate economic growth*, January 2013.
[45] The late Nobel Prize–winning economist Milton Freedman has many YouTube videos debating his theory of excessive regulation, and the unnecessary costs to economic activity and human well-being.

that perhaps simply with a few tweaks the outcome could be improved significantly. Some tweaks are proposed in the final chapter (although effective reforms are seldom as simple as that); in the meantime the next sections glance at not only who makes the law but how it is made. The people involved in lawmaking involve of course the usual suspects, but there are many cooks in the making of this complex broth, and some of them are dealt with now.

3.3.2   The Minister

A minister may decide (either because it was in the manifesto, or because the department has had it in mind for a while, or perhaps there had been a consultation and/or recommendation at some time) to introduce some legislation. He will ask his civil servants to prepare a bill for presentation to Parliament, and depending on the timetable and political exigencies, in the UK its journey may start in either of the two chambers of the legislature. But the actual first draft is prepared by civil servants.

3.3.3   The Civil Service and the Department

The officials will, following the ministerial request, draft instructions to the Parliamentary Counsel's Office to prepare the draft legislation. The instructions can be drafted by a senior official, with some experience or a junior officer with less. Such officials are not specifically trained in drafting such instructions

3.3.4   Parliamentary Counsel

Then a Parliamentary Counsel will draft according to these instructions; government bills are drafted by a Treasury department, that of Parliamentary Counsel. Until 1869 they were drafted by barristers in private practice, and looking at legislation of the time, such bills were admirably short and succinct. There are today around 60 draftsmen, around 10 of them seconded elsewhere. They are (or see themselves) as more than simply draftsmen; they regard themselves as 'guardians of values customarily regarded as integral to the legal order'.[46] They also consider themselves as a check on the constitutionality of legislation and will reprimand either politicians or civil servants if they feel the constitutional bounds have been pressed

---

[46] T. Daintith & E. Page, *The executive and the constitution*, 1999, p255.

too far. With some mild justification they feel themselves to be the crème de la crème of the parliamentary system. They are normally intellectually distinguished,[47] and they do not suffer from false modesty. There are two consequences of this high calibre of lawyer. First is (or was) a somewhat elevated view of their own qualities:

> One could say that they are, taking them by and large, the rudest, most arrogant, most vain and most self-satisfied group of people inside (and as far as I know, outside) the Civil Service.[48]

Today their self-regard is somewhat diminished – or it should be having regard to the quality of legislation emanating from their office. The second consequence is that while the intellectual strength of the draftsman's mind can be a formidable strength, it is also a significant weakness. It is hard for a lawyer of that distinction to understand, rather like an autistic person struggles to comprehend how a neurotypical person thinks (and vice versa), how normal people think and understand. In some ways the development of drafting standards around the world has improved much modern legislation. But much of it remains less than acceptable.[49]

What is surprising to the outsider, and both comforting and depressing, is how many changes the draft goes through before it even reaches the parliamentary process. Such continual redrafting may reflects a lack of clarity of the original objective; very often the longer and more complex the legislation the greater is evident the lack of policy preparation. Some of the complexity may be due also to a conflict between the commissioning department and the draftsman. A draftsman can often see the legal consequences of an Act and be determined because of his upbringing to confine its terms to legal matters; by contrast the department often wishes to make political capital. For example, explanatory memoranda to the UK Finance Acts dealing with the taxation of pensions state *ad nauseam* that 'because of the fiscal privileges attaching to pension' then tax will

---

[47] Sir Granville Ram, *The law making process*, [1951] NS Journal of the Society for the Public Teachers of Law 442.

[48] R. T. Oerton, *A lament for the Law Commission*, 1987 p51. But see Richard Heaton, *The Sir William Dale Memorial Lecture on legislation and good law*, 14 May 2014. Richard Heaton was a new breed of Parliamentary Counsel: young, brilliant and thoughtful. He was later translated elsewhere in government. And see Richard Heaton, *Good law*, Office of Parliamentary Counsel, 7 February 2014; Richard Heaton, *TEDx Houses of Parliament Speech*, 2014; Richard Heaton, *When laws become too complex, A review into the causes of complex legislation*, Office of Parliamentary Counsel, 16 April 2013.

[49] See e.g. the Finance Act 2009 on pensions in relation to pension contributions in relation to salaries over £150,000 or the Taxation of Pensions Act 2014.

be increased on certain pension arrangements. In fact most independent observers (OECD, EU, World Bank) consider that UK pensions taxation is or at least was fiscally neutral.[50] And (rather rarely) amendments will be made as a consequence of consultation; consultation is sometime used to flush out issues which the industry or the citizens will spot and which a legislator acting on the basis of imperfect knowledge may not. But such comments and eventual revisions will impact on the intellectual purity of the first draft.

The draftsman can face many problems in practice,[51] including the demand of his client for speed, certainty, comprehensibility, acceptability, brevity and debatability. In practice the desired parameters are rarely achieved, mostly because there is so little time to reflect on the draft. What there is however is a general consensus that the quality of drafting is below par, or in the current cliché, 'not fit for purpose'. This raises the issue of whether there is any remedy.

The Office of Parliamentary Counsel itself has sought to fix the problem, despairing of the quality of both quality of policy and therefore of its instructions. It complains somewhat bitterly but with dignity of being asked to draft legislation which is either unnecessary – or even impossible:[52]

> The digital age has made it easier for people to find the law of the land; but once they have found it, they may be baffled. The law is regarded by its users as intricate and intimidating.
>
> That experience echoes observations that have been made about statute law for many years. The volume of legislation, its piecemeal structure, the level of detail and frequent amendments, and the interaction with common law and European law, mean that even professional users can find law complex, hard to understand and difficult to comply with.
>
> Should we be concerned about any of this? After all, modern life in a developed country like the UK is complicated, and we use the law to govern many aspects of it. So it is not surprising that statutes and their subordinate regulations are complex; and it is perhaps reasonable to assume that citizens will need help or guidance in understanding the raw material of law.
>
> But in my view, we should regard the current degree of difficulty as neither inevitable nor acceptable. We should be concerned about it for

---

[50] See e.g. Edward Whitehouse, *The tax treatment of funded pensions*, OECD 1999.

[51] Francis Bennion, *Statute law obscurity and the drafting parameters*, [1978] 5 British Journal of Law and Society 235,

[52] Richard Heaton, *When laws become too complex, a review into the causes of complex legislation*, Office of the Parliamentary Counsel, Cabinet Office, March 2013, preface.

several reasons. Excessive complexity hinders economic activity, creating burdens for individuals, businesses and communities. It obstructs good government. It undermines the rule of law.

As the UK prepares to leave the EU, some have blamed EU interventions for added complexity. They may be a factor, but much of the injury seems self-inflicted. For example when domestically implementing EU legislation Germany provides one document per EU Directive, the UK produces 2.6; and in one extreme example, Directive 2002/42/EC consisting of 1167 words in the EU English text resulted in 27,000 words of implementing legislation in the UK.[53]

3.4   How Law Is Made

3.4.1   The Process of Making Law

Bismarck's remark about sausages is a theme which runs throughout this section. But it is useful to explore not just why Acts of Parliament come about – but also actually how they are made. This discussion does not cover private bills (such as those promoted by the City of Manchester for example and which invariably pass) or private members bills (such as those introduced to meet a particular MP's concern, and which usually fail to pass). A bill is a draft Act of Parliament before it is passed into law. The usual bills are called public general bills, and are usually introduced by the government. Their quality has been criticised almost since statutes were invented:[54]

> In the earliest times statutes were drafted, in Latin or Norman French, ... by a committee of judges, counsellors and officials, in response to a petition or bill which asked for a remedy but left the terms of the remedial act to the King in Council. In the 15th century the practice began of drafting bills in the form of the act desired. By the end of that century this became the established method and the earlier practice had been discontinued. After 1487, parliament appears to have handed over the drafting of the Bills (in English) ... to conveyancers, and from the laconic and often obscure terseness of our earliest statutes, especially when in Latin, we swung in

[53] Tim Ambler, Francis Chittenden and Mikhail Obodovski, *How much regulation is gold plate?*, British Chamber of Commerce, 2003; Sarah Shaefer and Edward Young, *Burdened by Brussels or the UK? Improving implementation of EU Directives*, Report for the Foreign Policy Centre, August 2006; *Comparative study on the transposition of EC law in the member states*, European Parliament, July 2007.

[54] *The Preparation of Legislation: report of a Committee appointed by the Lord President of the Council*, May 1975 (the Renton report), paras 2.4 and 2.8.

the sixteenth, seventeenth and eighteenth centuries to a verbosity which succeeded only in concealing the real matter of the law under a welter of superfluous synonyms...

As long ago as the 16th and 17th centuries there were in England many expressions of dissatisfaction with, and projects for reforming the drafting of statutes and the shape of the statute book. These early critics included Edward VI ('I would wish that ... the superfluous and tedious statutes were brought into one sum together, and made more plain and short, to the intent that men might better understand them'), Lord Keeper Sir Nicholas Bacon ('a short plan for reducing, ordering, and printing the Statutes of the realm'), James I ('divers cross and cuffing statutes... [should] be once maturely reviewed and reconciled; and... all contrarities should be scraped out of our books'), and Sir Francis Bacon, when Attorney General ('the reducing of concurrent statutes, heaped one upon another, to one clear and uniform law').

Each year the government announces its programme of legislation. This may arise because of manifesto commitments (rare) or ad hoc (e.g. the Drought Act 1976) to meet an immediate concern, or to respond to a recommendation of a report or commission, or to consolidate existing legislation. In recent years, much of it has seemed to emerge as a consequence of hyperactivity by government, not necessarily to do something, but rather to be seen to do something.[55]

Most of the books on parliamentary process set out in some detail the formal processes through both the House of Commons and the House of Lords, how they are introduced, how they are discussed in committee and how eventually they come into force.[56]

Unlike many other products designed in commercial circumstances laws (in the UK) are subject to the democratic process. And while that is a good thing, it also has its drawbacks.[57]

---

[55] See e.g. the Criminal Justice Acts 1997–2007. The best study by far, though rather disjunctive, is Michael Zander, *The law-making process*, 6th edn, Cambridge University Press, 2004, ISBN 978-0-521-60989-0]. See also House of Commons Information Office, *Parliamentary stages of a government bill*, Factsheet L1, August 2010, ISSN 0144-4689.

[56] House of Commons Information Office, *Parliamentary stages of a government bill*, Factsheet L1, August 2010, ISSN 0144-4689.

[57] Richard Heaton, *When laws become too complex, a review into the causes of complex legislation*, Office of the Parliamentary Counsel, Cabinet Office, March 2013, p25, Figure: *From policy to Bill: a summary of 'upstream causes' of excessively complex legislation*. See also papers available on the website of the Commonwealth Association of Legislative Counsel, www.opc.gov.au/calc/papers.htm.

Other countries, which are also democratic, have a much simpler system for their much simpler laws. The civil service produces a draft law, it is debated by the Parliament, and is then redrafted in the light of the comments. In the UK Parliament, each comma and sub-sub-section is debated in excruciating detail, and amended section by section by many different people, each usually with only a single issue in their mind, and without regard to the document or its effect as a whole.

There is no doubt that the work that is put in by government and opposition Members of Parliament is profound. Hours of preparation are reflected in Hansard, the report of parliamentary proceedings, and one can only stand in awe at the expertise and understanding displayed.

Nonetheless, the process also displays the drawbacks, some of them serious, to the system. MPs and others who broadly enjoy little knowledge of the subject matter of the legislation they are asked to vote on, and who and depend on lobbyists and others for their briefing, in practice are required to articulate half-formed ideas, sometimes at great length. And because of time constraints within the parliamentary process, detailed provisions, which can affect peoples' lives and standard of living, are nodded through or guillotined. The Pensions Act 2004, for example, had over 600 amendments (government amendments, indicating how ill-formed the original document was) at a stage where there was no time to debate them. That raises two questions. How was it possible to introduce a bill which needed over a thousand amendments by the government as it went through the process; did it not raise questions of whether the project was properly thought through before it was presented for approval? And secondly, did the MPs who mindlessly trooped through the chambers to vote understand what they were voting for? It suggests a slightly disreputable working of the parliamentary mind, to vote for something that is not understood. This applies particular in relation to tax bills, where few really understand what is happening. And yet pension fund trustees and others are criticised strongly for agreeing to put money into investments which they do not understand, and rely on the assurances of others. Signing blank cheques is normally regarded as bad governance, but MPs seem obliged to do it daily with only the occasional qualm.[58]

---

[58] Richard Heaton, *When laws become too complex, a review into the causes of complex legislation*, Office of the Parliamentary Counsel, Cabinet Office, March 2013, p23 Figure: *Mapping the cases of unnecessarily complex legislation*.

In looking at the way law is made (the example of the UK is particular but not broadly dissimilar from other jurisdictions) it is remarkable that legislation is not worse than it is. There are normally three tasks involved,[59] namely deciding the policy, producing the bill, and then processing the bill through Parliament. First the government has to decide it wants some legislation. That may be sometimes opportunistic or a response to populism or to the latest opinion piece in the *Daily Mail*. That is a matter of policy, and governments sometimes feel that legislation is the way to fix the problem, rather than improving the administration. There is little doubt that ministers and others would benefit from considering strongly whether major changes in policy are appropriate, and if so whether they need to be implemented by legislation. Because all ministers feel they need more legislation, there is always a demand for more legislation than is possible in the system. There is therefore a Legislative Programme Committee, a sub-committee of the Cabinet which approves the list of requests; it may also need clearance from a Cabinet sub-committee with an interest in the subject. In some cases, to defuse public objections, a Green paper (announcing tentative proposals for legislation) or a white paper (announcing firm proposals for legislation) will have been produced and there will have been a form of public consultation. Sometimes the system works: sometimes legislation is abandoned, or radically changed as a consequence. Sometimes there are minor changes.

Assuming the act really is needed, or even where it is not, the draft has to be prepared. English law drafting has been criticised for many years as outlined above, and whilst in recent years it has improved in some ways (rationalising the appropriate use of capital letters, and with consistent tabbing, shorter sentences and simpler numbering of the sections) it is still hidebound, compared for example with Australia or New Zealand, countries where great efforts have been put into making legislation understandable.

In some ways the process is admirably thorough: the government department sets up a bill team, which could be as small as four or as large as a dozen. A departmental lawyer is assigned to act as legal adviser, and while such legal advisers vary widely in experience, and most consider themselves over-worked, many struggle to offer considered advice. Meantime the time frame is tight, somewhere between three months or up to a

---

[59] See e.g. Edward Page, *The civil servant as legislator: law making in British Administration* [2003] 81 Public Administration 651; and see Stephen Laws, *Giving effect to policy in legislation: how to avoid missing the point*, [2011 32(1) Statute Law Review 1–16. Stephen Laws was then the First Parliamentary Counsel at the Office of Parliamentary Counsel.

year. That team does not of course actually prepare the law – but merely the instructions for drafting the law, in other words they 'prepare the instructions' for the parliamentary draftsman (or 'counsel').

3.4.2 Post Drafting Amendments

Following on the drafting of an act comes its consideration within the parliamentary process.

In theory that process appears rigorous and detailed. It is considered several times by two Houses of Parliament and several times in each. Sometimes special committees will examine it line by line, and word by word. There is nowadays invariably an explanatory note to the drafts. Increasingly there are drafts bills submitted for pre-legislative scrutiny, so that interest groups can comment on it. Many of the debates, especially in the House of Lords, demonstrate considerable abilities by both promoters and commentators and critics. So why is so much of it so bad?

The problem is that in practice, despite the scrutiny process (or even because of it) the document which may have made sense originally (or not – sometimes there is little time for the draftsmen to prepare a decent draft in the first place) by the time several dozen amendments (or even several hundred amendments) have been made, the original clarity of drafting and purpose may have been lost. In other jurisdictions, once the parliamentarians have criticised the drafting, the bill is taken away by the civil service and redrafted to meet the concerns of parliamentarians. Drafting in committee is thereby avoided.

And anyone who has had the misfortune to be in the House of Commons when a vote is called will bear testament to the absurdity of grown men and women rushing to pass through a lobby to vote having frequently no idea what they are voting on, and certainly no idea whether what they are voting for makes sense or is even coherent. It comes as something of a disappointment to realise that few MPs either understand what they are voting for – or understand the law they have just voted for. Sometimes the system punishes those appropriately. For example, in 2009 the UK Border Agency conducted an investigation into allegations that Baroness Scotland, then the Attorney General, a law officer, was employing an illegal immigrant. Baroness Scotland was fined £5000 for a breach of the Immigration, Asylum and Nationality Act 2006 for failing to retain photocopies of her housekeeper, Loloahi Tapui's passport. Ms Tapui was later jailed for eight months for fraud, possessing a false identity stamp, and overstaying her UK visa. The person who had introduced and supervised the passing into law of the 2006 Act was of course Baroness Scotland. But such acts of God are rare.[60]

The fact that much of the law remains old is not in itself an issue. Some of the best pieces of law are those drafted by private enterprise, such as the Partnership Act or the Sales of Goods Act. And even modern laws can be well drafted, though it is hard to think of many. But badly drafted law irritates not only those who are subject to it, but also those who have to administer it:

> Sir Nicolas Browne-Wilkinson VC sitting in this court described the [Landlord and Tenant] Act of 1987 as 'ill-drafted, complicated and confused'. The argument in this case has given new force to this understated criticism.[61]

As Lord Renton said in his review of legislative drafting:

> Legislation which cannot be understood even by experts, or which is of uncertain legal effect, brings the law into contempt and Parliament which makes it. This is a disservice to democracy. It blurs and weakens the rights of the individuals. It eases the way for wrongdoers and places honest people at the mercy of the state. We must all try to do better.[62]

His report listed over 120 proposals for reform, including a presumption against retrospection, which has signally failed to be followed, especially in tax legislation. Retrospection, passing laws to take effect before it was passed has had a bad press since the Acte for Poysonyng in 1530:

> This Act was hastily enacted after Richard Roose, cook to the Bishop of Rochester (more than 400 years before David Renton was Recorder of that City) had 'caste a certain venym or poison into a vessel replenysshed with yeste or barme stondying in the kechyn of the Reverend Father in God'. As the very lengthy recital went on to explain 'xvij persons of [his] familie which dyd eate of that porrage were mortally enfected'. The Act not merely declared that this poisoning was retrospectively 'demed high treason', for which Roose was to be 'boyled to death', without benefit of the clergy, in the very vessel in which he had prepared his poisoned porridge, but it provided that all future murders by poison should be so deemed and all future

---

[60] John Bingham and Rosa Prince, *Attorney General Baroness Scotland fined £5,000 over illegal immigrant housekeeper*, Daily Telegraph, 22 September 2009; Baroness Scotland had not retained copies of the documents she had inspected in breach of the law.

[61] *Belvedere Court Management Ltd v Frogmore Developments Ltd* [1997] QB 858, referring to a decision in *Denetower Ltd v Toop* [1991] 1 WLR 945 at 952G.

[62] Lord Renton, *The evolution of modern statute law and its future*, Inaugural Statute Law Society Lecture 1 November 1995, p3; cf. Renton Committee, *The preparation of legislation*, Cmnd 6053, 1975.

poisoners punished by being boiled to death and escheat of their property to their feudal lords. This hasty piece of legislation was effectively sidelined by a statute in 1547, but it was not finally repealed till 1863.[63]

But retrospection remains.

3.4.3 Solutions to the Poor Drafting of Law

The obvious question is whether there is anything that can be done in practice about the drafting of legislation. One might be changes in drafting styles and techniques, already discussed. Drafting has improved significantly – but it is still too often deeply opaque. But testing intelligibility is also a lot easier than it used to be, and word processing systems invariably contain systems for analysis of text. For example, a fog index application test would check whether the content was understandable.[64]

The impenetrability continues despite considerable efforts by in the UK the Office of Parliamentary Counsel to improve matters. The Office can do little to improve the parliamentary process, and can only slightly influence any improvement to drafting instructions from a Department. It can chip away however at historic precedent; numbering, indenting, scheduling, the skeleton of legislation remains a mixture of medieval and eighteenth-century inheritances, deriving from the fact that legislation was originally in manuscript, and then in letterpress. There are increasing nods to the invention of the computer and the internet, but it is not yet accepted as part of the framework, and incessant tinkering with legislation without providing clean copies makes them hard to read. Other countries (most notably Australia and New Zealand) have consciously accepted the need to legislate in simple English, and while they still have the drive to incontinence and tinkering, at least they do it comprehensively.[65]

It may be of course that it is the nature of the subject that long, complicated and incomprehensible legislation is inherent in the price we pay for a modern complex democracy. That is not the view of a former Chief

---

[63] Cited in Lord Neuburger of Abbotsbury, *General, equal and certain: law reform today and tomorrow* [2012] 33(3) Statute Law Review 323–338 at p327, also referring to Miller, *Where there's life there's lawsuits*, ECW Press, 2003.

[64] Or the Flesch-Kincaid readability index, usually free with Microsoft Word.

[65] Wim Vowermans, *Styles of legislation and their effects* [2011] 32(1) Statute Law Review 38–53. See also the European Academy for Law and Legislation (www.innovatingjustice.com); and the EU has a Directorate for Quality of Legislation in the European Commission Legal Service (a similar role has been assumed in the absence of anything similar in the UK Parliament, by the Office of Parliamentary Counsel).

Parliamentary Counsel, and despite continual, often ineffective attempts to improve matters, in many respects the position is becoming worse.[66] Techniques in themselves are only one part of the solution. In the meantime it may be possible to establish some general principles, including:

For Ministers

There may need to be a code of practice for ministers who introduce legislation.

Despite the pressure of parliamentary business, and the political drivers, ministers might uphold a code of principles which could include

- an undertaking to encourage and be prepared to be involved in a genuine policy discussion, from first principles,
- ensuring that White Papers or equivalent are honest and open about both the pros and cons of legislation,
- eschewing any urge to make government papers (Green or White) marketing documents and
- accepting that there are limitations and possible dangers involved with new legislation.[67]

For Civil Servants

The lack of accountability for legislation, where in the UK around 1200 members of the two chambers of collectively accept responsibility, which means no one does, on the basis of drafting not only by ministers but by senior civil servants, who also claim that the legislation is as a result of political rather than administrative action, is one of the prime reasons for the dysfunctionality. It would be preferable that a named someone, with a telephone number and email address, should own the draft legislation, and put their name to it rather like it is said that an Aston Martin engineer who engraves his name on, and becomes responsible for, each car.

---

[66] E.g. the UK's Tax Law Rewrite project which started in 1997 and closed in 2010 with only modest achievements to its name, largely because of its inability to cope with incessant subsequent revisions; its successor, the Office of Tax Simplification, distinguished itself by being emasculated by government and limited to advising on technical matters, see Finance Act 2016, Part 12. But the existence of the Office in itself is recognition by the government that tax law is too complicated.

[67] There is a UK *Ministerial Code* (Cabinet Office, October 2015), the latest version of which removed ministerial obligations to comply with international law. It mostly deals with travel expenses and conflicts of interest. It studiously avoids establishing overarching principles, for example of responsibility to country over party. See Diane Taylor, *No 10 Faces legal challenge over ministerial code rewrite*, Guardian, 11 February 2016.

Some of the best legislation in the past has been drafted by a single person (e.g. the Partnership Act, the Sale of Goods Act), and while this may no longer possible (although it might) the adoption of personal responsibility might be influential if not transformational. Because of the way in which most current legislation is drawn up there is a diffusion of responsibility between several civil servants in the department, the several draftsmen, the several politicians involved and the MPs who insist on changes. Every bill should therefore have someone whose name should be affixed to it – and who should take responsibility for its holistic construction.

That sign-off (rather like the rather cursory current sign-off on compliance with the Human Rights Act) might also contain a statement that the bill is understandable by any ordinarily educated citizen, and that the costs are properly estimated, and that its practical implementation will be straightforward. It is then that the select committee system could genuinely later earn its corn, provided its members were also compliant, by engaging in a subsequent post-legislative scrutiny.

For Members of Parliament

A code of practice for MPs is suggested elsewhere in Chapter 7; in relation to voting on legislation MPs might, when voting on legislation:

- undertake to vote only on legislation they can personally understand;
- undertake to have a greater duty to the country than to their party;
- affirm their honest and reasoned belief that the costs and effectiveness of any legislation they vote on is correct, that their beliefs will be subsequently assessed, and with any excess costs of failures attached to their name on a website.

Parliamentary Counsel

The job of a parliamentary draftsman is to draft the detailed form of proposed laws, in a way that will accurately reflect the intentions of the politicians who are promulgating them, without leaving loopholes or producing perverse results. This has proved to be an ambition which has been too vaulting and the pursuit of exact and watertight legislation has often resulted in obscure and convoluted language.

There have been attempts over the years to try and persuade them to reduce their ambitions (and that of their instructing departments and the government) and encourage them to use simpler language, simpler layout and shorter forms. Counsel, most of whom have astonishing intellectual acuity and increasing experience, usually respond that if their instructions were clearer, if MPs did not attempt to redraft in committee and if policy was straightforward they could perform their objectives. One objection is that if counsel were not so bright, they would not be able to construct the edifices they do; less skilled counsel might have tried to simply their output so that could understand it. Speed is also a problem; more time to draft might result in simpler drafting. Also helpful might be outsourcing; some of the longest-lived and simpler legislation such as the Sale of Goods Act or the Partnership Act have lasted over 100 years with little need for amendments over that time.

There have been continual suggestions for reform. A committee under Sir David Renton that reported in 1975 recommended drafting which was more based on principles than specific details to address every possible situation.

Draftsmen should similarly have a set of principles to which they should generally adhere. These might include the following:

- A duty to recruit colleagues with normal rather than above average intelligence and intellectual ability. This might help develop the drafting of statutes that less intelligent people can understand. In most other countries take pride in the fact that legislation is simple and understandable; others such as the UK take pride in the intellectual challenges faced by the draftsman. It would also slow down the urge of politicians to try and draft for things that by and large are not possible or even desirable. It seems rare in practice that politicians are told that their pet project cannot be simply provided for through law.
- A commitment to adopt simplicity and modern typographical design to help make the terms of the act more readily accessible. The worst excrescences of Georgian and Victorian typesetting have gone, but normal typographical conventions remain largely absent. Simple things like proper tabbing, or not mixing justifications, cost nothing and make for improved comprehension.
- Insisting to ministers that any law that requires formulae is too complicated to implement.
- A professional duty to refuse to be involved in any legislation which they consider excessively complicated.

Bill Promoters

Politicians, ministers and departments who wish to introduce a new law should be asked to rough out a draft of the legislation themselves, to see what issues emerge in trying to draft laws that have not had proper policy stress-testing. Training in drafting skills should be part of a politician's training. This would make them aware of the limitations of law and legislation. Draft laws should be tested on those intended to be subject to it, to ensure that it is understandable. It is true that *ignorantia legis neminem excusat*, but incomprehensibility or ambiguity should be an automatic defence. Complaints about the drafting of law are almost as old as drafting itself, which suggests that it is time they were resolved. Edward VI complained, for example,

> I wish that . . . the superfluous and tedious statutes were brought into one sum together, and made more plain and short, to the intent that men might better understand them.[68]

And in a famous case, Lord Justice Harman complained,

> To reach a conclusion on this matter involved the court in wading through a monstrous legislative morass, staggering from stone to stone and ignoring the marsh gas exhaling from the forest of schedules lining the way on each side. I regarded it at one time, I must confess, as a Slough of Despond through which the court would never drag its feet but have, by leaping from tussock to tussock as best I might, eventually, pale and exhausted, reached the other side.[69]

It is now over 40 years since a committee chaired by Lord Renton, a barrister and politician who passed his driving test at the age of 94, was commissioned to respond to these and other concerns. His committee suggested that there were four basic complaints:

- language was obscure and complex,
- the standard draft was over-elaborate,
- the structure was often illogical and
- the arrangement of the structure of the clauses was often confusing.

One solution, which had been suggested as far back as 1938, was that where new law changed old law, the revised law should be set out in full as

---

[68] Lord Renton, *The evolution of modern statute law and its future*, inaugural Statute Law Society Lecture, 1 November 1995, p3; Edward VI died in 1553, having been King since age nine, and see Gilbert Burnet, *The History of the Reformation of the Church of England*, Volume 2, 1680, at p73. Cf Renton Committee, *The preparation of legislation*, Cmnd 6053, 1975, and King James I, *A proclamation signifying his Majeties pleasure touching some former Proclamations; and some other things*, Proclamation, Hampton Court, 24 September 1610, which expresses a similar view, discussed in Chapter 6.

[69] *Davy v Leeds Corporation* [1964] 1 WLR 1218 at 1224.

an attachment to the new act, so that the reader could see the consolidated law so that it was easier to read. It was tried once or twice, but it proved to be too much work for the draftsmen, and added to the bulk of the printing (something which would be less of an issue these days). Lord Renton wanted more consolidating statutes, he wanted full text amendments (so that the reader did not have to work with scissors and paste), and he wanted clear English. He wanted statements of principle, rather than catalogues and he wanted the system to adopt some of innovations developed in the New World and on the continent. The New World specialised in clarity of writing; the European civil systems specialised in codes, something regarded in the UK with some suspicion. There are drawbacks even to principles-based law, and to codification; principles rather than particularity are not always the answer. In particular, much to the annoyance of the executive, no system can manage without at least some interference by the judiciary who are called upon to explain and translate the codes into practice. The courts can find that the words of a statute are ambiguous and that where there is lack of clarity, the provisions must be construed in the interests of the individual. Such judicial intervention occurs much less in the civil (European) system than in England and Wales.[70] Renton also suggested that the English problems with statutory draftsmen derive from the establishment of a specialist drafting office, and that while the office might be retained to provide consistency of style and approach it would benefit from drastic reform. That last is one of the few reforms which have emerged in practice, but the office nonetheless continues to pride itself on its ancient origins and its intellectual superiority. The style remains (less so these days) often deliberately arcane and antiquarian. They can contain a multiplicity of different commencement dates, for example, even within the same legislation – as if it really mattered to within a month or two when the laws came into force. And regardless of the problems with European codes:

> The basic difference between the drafting of the Code and that of the Act is that the draftsman of the Code clearly appears to attach paramount importance to making himself readily intelligible to the citizen whereas the British legislator is at best heedless of the user and at times even seems deliberately obscure.[71]

---

[70] Clarence Smith, *Legislative Drafting: English and Continental* [1980] Statute Law Review 14. Judicial intervention is explored in Chapter 5; see e.g. *Miller v Secretary of State for Exiting the EU*, [2017] UKSC 5.

[71] Timothy Millett, *A comparison of British and French legislative drafting* [1986] Statute Law Review 130.

There has been improvement since that was written, but complexity of policy has rendered most modernisation of drafting conventions otiose.

Lobbyists and Nimbys

Lobbyists, and even nimbys, have their useful part to play in the process; it is crucial that proposed legislation is tested in some public crucible. At the same time, partisan and one-sided presentations show lack of balance and hence a lack of authority. Lobbyists and others, who are now required to be registered in some jurisdictions, might want to adhere to some form of code of conduct which might include

- an undertaking to present both sides of the argument in a balanced way,
- an undertaking to present possible unintended consequences and
- an undertaking to present the estimated costs, and how those costs should be met.

3.4.4 Delegated Legislation

Delegated legislation is law that is made by government under the authority of a statute or Act of Parliament. It is often non-contentious, and is intended to deal with the minor details or technicalities which Parliament would not have the time or competence to deal with. In England these rules are made through 'statutory instruments'. Every year around 10,000 to 13,000 pages of statutory instruments (compared with 2000 to 5000 pages of public Acts of Parliament) are issued. These figures are roughly double the numbers for the period 1975–1985.[72]

In recent years there have been concerns about the increase in the volume of delegated legislation, about the checks and balances that apply and about possible abuses of the system. Fresh impetus was given to a review following a constitutional challenge when the UK government attempted to change the UK tax credit system in 2015.[73] The government had a majority in the House of Commons, but when it came to be considered by the House of Lords it was rejected, embarrassing the government. The constitutional convention had been since 1911 that the Lords could not decline to approve a 'money bill', usually considered to be a tax law. The statutory instrument was intended to bring in £4.4B of benefit cuts – but

---

[72] *Acts and statutory instruments: the volume of UK legislation 1950–2015*, House of Commons Library, CBP 7438 Tables 1a, 1B and 3.
[73] *Draft Tax Credits (Income Thresholds and Determination of Rates (Amendment) Regulations 2015*.

not as part of primary legislation. It was this that provoked the concern of the other part of a bicameral system. The government was dismayed, to put it politely, at the challenge to its authority and a member of the House of Lords, Lord Strathclyde, was asked to review whether there should be some kind of constitutional reform.[74]

Following his recommendations, which were not followed, a committee of the Lords themselves subsequently concluded that there were wider issues. They included the following:[75]

- the use of 'Henry VIII powers', i.e. powers contained in primary legislation which granted ministers wide discretion to change the terms of primary legislation without the usual consideration by Parliament, often with few indications as to how those powers should be used;
- the use of delegated legislation to address issues of policy and principle, rather than to manage administrative and technical changes;
- the fact that delegated legislation could not be amended in debate; it could only be accepted or rejected; and
- the absence of sufficient time available to consideration of delegated legislation compared with primary legislation, so that where governments used statutory instruments to implement policy, the usual democratic checks and balances were absent.

The committee sought proper consideration of the issue, rather than what had been proposed by government, namely a six-week review:[76]

> The balance of power between Parliament and the Executive lies at the heart of our constitution. There is a strong case for reviewing the operation of delegated legislation, but change must be careful, considered and, importantly, not undertaken in haste or for the wrong reason.

The lack of effective checks on delegated legislation means that in practice the usual reviews of both the content and manner of expression are also lacking. This form of lawmaking is easier for the executive to implement, there is less challenge, and although there are cases where drafts

---

[74] Cabinet Office, *Strathclyde Review: secondary legislation and the primacy of the House of Commons*, Cm 9177, December 2015.

[75] House of Lords, Select Committee on the Constitution, 9th Report of Session 2015–16, *Delegated legislation and Parliament: a response to the Strathclyde Review*, 23 March 2016, HL Paper 116.

[76] House of Lords, Select Committee on the Constitution, 9th Report of Session 2015–16, *Delegated legislation and Parliament: a response to the Strathclyde Review*, 23 March 2016, HL Paper 116, p2. See also Hansard Society, *The devil is in the detail, Parliament and delegated legislation*, 2014.

are submitted to the public for consultation,[77] in practice the responses are cursory.[78] In practice few statutory instruments are struck down; there are been a vote in the Lords only 150 times since 1950, and only six were defeated (out of 23,000). Similar criticisms have been expressed elsewhere:[79]

> a heavy burden of scrutiny responsibility falls on the House of Lords in large part because House of Commons procedures and the engagement of MPs is wholly inadequate.

In fact the last time the House of Commons rejected a statutory instrument was in 1979.[80] But the concern about the management of secondary legislation goes back even further; a Committee in 1932 established to provide a temperate response to an alarmist book by a Lord Chief Justice concluded:[81]

> We doubt ... whether Parliament itself has fully realised how extensive the practice of delegation has become, or the extent to which it has surrendered its own function in the process, or how easily the practice might be abused.

In particular, Henry VIII clauses have continued to cause concern amongst constitutional thinkers, although rather less so with Ministers.[82] These provisions enable a government to repeal or amend an Act after it

---

[77] Over-consultation can be as much of a curse as no consultation, it sometimes being used as a way to deflect criticism. In the pensions policy arena in the UK, for example, there can be several dozen proposals subject to consultation at any one time, making it all but impossible for the interested parties to respond since they lack sufficient resource.

[78] Cf the position of executive orders by the President of the United States, the use of which was supposed to be limited by the US Constitution to avoid the repetition of monarchical lawmaking, Todd F. Gaziano, *The use and abuse of executive orders and other presidential directives*, The Heritage Foundation, Washington, 21 February 2001.

[79] See also Hansard Society, *The devil is in the detail, Parliament and delegated legislation*, 2014.

[80] Paraffin (Maximum Retail Prices) (Revocation) Order 1979 on 24 October 1979.

[81] Committee on Ministers' Powers, *Report*, Cmd 4060, April 1932, p24 (the Donoughmore Committee). It followed the publication of a book by The Rt Hon Lord Hewart of Bury, Lord Chief Justice of England, *The New Despotism*, Ernest Benn, 1929, on the subject. Only modest reforms to the process were introduced in the following 80 years. It considered the new despotism as 'to subordinate Parliament, to evade the Courts, and to render the will, or the caprice, of the Executive unfettered and supreme' (at p17), referring to increasing quasi-judicial decision-making by the civil service and the subordination of Parliament which resulted from the growth of delegated legislation.

[82] See seriatim Richard Gordon QC, *Why Henry VIII clauses should be consigned to the dustbin of history*. And see also Lord Judge, *Speech*, Mansion House Lord Mayor's Annual Dinner for Her Majesty's Judges, 13 July 2010.

is brought into force. It allows amendment of primary legislation by secondary legislation and echoes the Henry VIII Statue of Proclamations in 1539 which gave the King's decisions the same force as an Act. The 1539 Act was repealed in 1547 immediately after Henry's death, but such provisions have emerged again in modern times, the most notorious example being that of the Banking (Special Provisions) Act 2008 which granted Treasury ministers the power to 'disapply any specified statutory provision or rule of law' – without limit for example to Treasury or fiscal matters. Similarly the Constitutional Reform and Governance Act 2010 allowed minsters to amend or repeal any prior statute dealing with the civil service, treaties or MPs expenses.[83] These powers are easy to abuse; the Legislative and Regulatory Reform Bill 2006 Clause 1 provided that a Minister by Order could make open-ended provision for 'reforming legislation'. The intention had been to streamline the Regulatory Reform Act 2001 to try and reduce red tape. The provision overstepped the mark and attracted the epithet of the 'Abolition of Parliament Bill'; in the end certain minor safeguards were introduced. Similarly the Public Bodies Act 2011 was called 'one vast Henry VIII clause'.[84]

There have been academic suggestions of guidelines for the control of such clauses:[85]

2 **Delegated powers, delegated legislation and Henry VIII clauses**
 2.1 **Defining the power**
  2.1.1 Delegations of legislative power should be framed as narrowly as possible.
  2.1.2 The policy aims of a Ministerial power should be included in the bill itself.
  2.1.3 The scope of a Henry VIII power should be limited to the minimum necessary to meet the pressing need for such an exceptional measure.
  2.1.4 The use of Henry VIII powers should only be permitted if specific purposes are provided for in the Bill.

---

[83] See also e.g. deregulation and Contracting Out Act 1994; it is reported (Lord Judge, *Speech*, Mansion House Lord Mayor's Annual Dinner for Her Majesty's Judges, 13 July 2010) that several hundred such clauses have been passed in a single Parliamentary Session despite the conclusion of the Donoughmore Committee that their use must be demonstrably essential and justified on each occasion by the Minister to the hilt.

[84] *Response to Ministry of Justice Consultation on reforms proposed in the Public Bodies Bill Reforming the public bodies of the Ministry of Justice*, Justice, September 2011. Cf. House of Lords, Constitution Committee, 6th report 2010–2011, *Public Bodies Bill*, HL51.

[85] Jack Simson Caird, Robert Hazell and Dawn Oliver, *The constitutional standards of the House of Lords Select Committee on the constitution*, University College London, Constitution Unit, January 2014, *Code of constitutional standards*.

2.1.5 Ministerial powers should be defined objectively.

2.1.6 Ministerial powers to make secondary legislation should be restricted by effective legal boundaries.

2.2 Safeguards in delegation of legislative powers

2.2.1 Laws that contain delegated powers should strike a balance between the desire for effectiveness and the safeguards needed to ensure constitutional propriety.

2.2.2 If constitutional safeguards can be added to a delegated ministerial legislative power without undermining the policy goals of a Bill then they should be included.

2.2.3 Henry VIII powers should be accompanied by adequate procedural and legal safeguards.

2.2.4 Henry VIII powers that relate to a constitutionally sensitive subject matter should use a super-affirmatory parliamentary procedure.

2.2.5 Ministers should not be able to suspend legal powers by giving directions; instead orders, which are subject to parliamentary oversight, should be used.

2.2.6 Provision should be made for Parliament to be informed promptly of all ministerial exercises of legislative power.

2.3 Appropriate uses of delegated powers

2.3.1 Henry VIII clauses should be limited so that they cannot be used to alter constitutional arrangements.

2.3.2 Laws should not permit the sub-delegation of legislative powers

2.3.3 Delegating order-making powers to Ministers to change the statute book should be avoided when there are other more constitutionally appropriate alternatives available.

2.3.4 Delegated legislation should not be used to create regulations that will have a major impact on an individual's right to respect for private life.

2.3.5 Delegated legislation should not be used to create new criminal offences.

2.3.6 Bills should identify the provisions in other enactments that require amendment, rather than using Henry VIII powers to leave the power to make amendments to the subsequent discretion of the relevant department.

2.3.7 The most important aspects of a policy should be included on the face of a bill and not left to be decided through delegated legislation.

2.3.8 Rules that are central to a bill of constitutional significance should be to the greatest extent possible on the face of the bill, so allowing full legislative amendment and debate.

2.3.9 Rights of appeal should be defined in primary legislation and not in secondary legislation.

2.3.10 Delegations of legislative authority should fit within the overall scheme of the bill.

2.4 **The parliamentary justification of delegated powers, delegated legislation and Henry VIII powers**

    2.4.1 Ministers should provide Parliament with their justifications for proposing the delegation of legislative powers.

    2.4.2 Ministerial assurances as to the purpose of order-making powers are not a substitute for legal safeguards on the face of the Bill.

    2.4.3 Widely drawn delegations of legislative authority cannot be exclusively justified by the need for speed.

    2.4.4 The justification for a Henry VIII clause should refer to the specific purpose that it is designed to serve.

    2.4.5 Where an 'incidental and consequential' Henry VIII power is likely to be used in relation to constitutional legislation, the Government should provide a clear and detailed account to Parliament of how and why it intends to exercise that power.

The guidelines have not been adopted.

3.5   Attempts to Improve the Process

A later chapter looks at attempts to reduce the quantity of legislation; this section simply looks at attempts to improve the content. Attempts in the past have largely failed, despite the fact that there are now several studies and organisations dedicated to the improvement of the statute book. One example is that of the Tax Law Rewrite project, instituted by Sir Geoffrey Howe, a former Chancellor and Home Secretary but which after some early success ran into the ground. The story of attempted improvements is explored later in the book, but there is little doubt that with a few exceptions in the UK at least the two Houses of Parliament glory in the obscurity of their processes.[86] Similarly, while the drafting process has improved, and the drafters themselves have called for simplification, the ministers and departments make their work hard. Any reforms probably need separately to look at principles and then process.

3.5.1   Principles for Improvement: The Tom Bingham Proposals

Lord Bingham, a former Lord Chief Justice of England, and one of the most highly respected judges of his generation, wrote shortly before his death a prize-winning book on the rule of law in England. Amongst other things it set out eight principles, not intended to be exhaustive, which

---

[86] Cf Sir William Dale, *The European legislative scene* [1992] 13 Statute Law Review 79.

might be applied to improving the judicial and legislative system. They are:

1 The law must be accessible and so far as possible intelligible, clear and predictable. He drew on a comment of Lord Mansfield 250 years earlier that 'The daily negotiations and property of merchants ought not to depend on subtleties and niceties; but upon rules easily learned and easily retained, because they are the dictates of common sense, drawn from the truth of the case.'[87]

2 Questions of legal right and liability should ordinarily be resolved by application of the law and not the exercise of discretion. The use of administrative discretion is handy for administrators and government, but it has been savaged by several generations of lawyers. Its abuse can be seen most recently in the invention of the GAAR system, where an unelected group can decide whether tax arrangements are abusive or not; but it was criticised around a hundred years ago and frequently since.[88]

3 The laws of the land should apply equally to all, save to the extent that objective differences justify differentiation. The most evident current breach of this principle is the treatment of citizens and non-citizens in terrorism issues.

4 Ministers and public officers at all levels must exercise the powers conferred on them in good faith, fairly, for the purpose for which the powers were conferred, without exceeding the limits of such powers and not unreasonably.

5 The law must afford adequate protection of fundamental human rights.

6 Means must be provided for resolving, without prohibitive cost or inordinate delay, bona fide civil disputes which the parties themselves are unable to resolve.

7 Adjudicative procedures provided by the state should be fair.

8 The rule of law requires compliance by the state with its obligations in international law as in national law.

The first three of these are self-evidently under pressure in current circumstances. In the meantime, some steps towards achieving these objectives have been proposed by many observers; they include (as later

---

[87] *Hamilton v Mendes* (1761) 2 Burr 1198, 1214, cited in Bingham, *The Rule of Law*, 2010; the idea has been repeated by many jurists since.

[88] See e.g. Lord Hewart, *The New Despotism*, 1929.

discussed) codification (to force legislators to think holistically), consolidation (which would help towards a code), modern English language and layout, and individual accountability, especially on later review of legislation. There have also been many reviews, including Lord Renton's which have had only minor influence. The process of nit-picking in committee, while it has immense advantages, makes for incoherent law, and proposals for prior review have made little progress.[89] Even Parliament itself is unhappy, but has done little to reform itself.[90] The prime review, and one which bears re-reading, the Renton Report, in 1975 concluded:[91]

> If our Acts of Parliament cannot be understood, even by experts, it brings not only the law into contempt, it brings Parliament in to contempt – and it is, moreover, a disservice to our democracy. It weakens the rights of the rights of the individual, it eases the way for wrongdoers and it places honest people at the mercy of the bureaucratic state.[92]

In the consequent debate on the Report in the House of Lords, Lord Airedale noted:[93]

> My Lords, I feel overawed in taking part with noble and learned Law Lords in a debate on a legal subject. I am afraid that I can offer only random thoughts that have arisen from reading this most interesting Report. I suppose that the necessity for a study of the preparation of legislation could not be better stated by implication than in the opening words of the judgment of the noble and learned Lord, Lord Edmund-Davies, in the recent case of *Daymond v South West Water Authority*, in which judgments were delivered on 3rd December. The noble and learned Lord started his judgment with these words: Section 30 of the Water Act 1973 is a deplorable piece of legislation. Those charged with the duty of applying it appear to have little inkling as to its import, for until recently they thought it has a

---

[89] Anthony Watson-Brown, *Does it work? Reviewing legislative drafts before others have a chance* [2008] 29(1) Statute Law Review 45–52.

[90] House of Commons Political and Constitutional Reform Committee, *First Report of Session 2013–2014*, 9 May 2013 HC 85; Cabinet Office, *Guide to Making Legislation*, June 2012; Treasury Solicitor, *Judge over your shoulder*, 2006; 'Good law' initiative: UK Government *Effort to make Legislation More Effective and Accessible*, 2013; *Good government: reforming Parliament and Executive*, January 2010; *When laws become too complex*, Cabinet Office, March 2013; *Good government: mid term review*, November 2012.

[91] *Report of the Renton Committee on the Preparation of Legislation* (Cmnd 6053) May 1975.

[92] Lord Renton, *Renton and the need for law reform* (6 April 1978) Statute Law Society Annual Lecture, cited in Lord Neuberger of Abbotsbury, *General, equal and certain: law reform today and tomorrow* [2012] 33(3) Statute Law Review 323–338.

[93] Hansard HL Deb 10 December 1975 vol 366 cc945–1038.

meaning completely opposite to that for which they now contend. My sympathy goes out to the draftsman responsible who has to read those words. But it seems to me that the strain on the shoulders of the draftsman would be lightened if he could feel that the attention of the court did not have to be riveted solely upon the words of the Act of Parliament, but could, in appropriate cases, extend a little beyond.

Not everyone believes that the system is broken. Some have described the process of making a law in relatively positive terms,[94] and have described the bill team, the group of civil servants within a department which includes policy administrators and lawyers who liaise with the lawyers, the parliamentary section of the department the press office and Parliamentary Counsel as working collegiately and effectively. But even then there are challenges:

It is inevitable that when what may have started as a simple policy objective is subjected to increased probing by some very fine minds, difficulties emerge and there is a trade-off between watering down the policy or, in the interests of purity, making the legislation ever more complex so that it copes with every eventuality.

But even where the bill is in early draft, there are timetabling challenges (imposed by the Cabinet Office), and the burden has increased by the need to ensure the production of explanatory notes, ECHR compatibility statements and a Regulatory Impact Assessment. There may be devolution issues, coalition issues and pre-legislative scrutiny, i.e. showing it to the opposition (and the public) to try and flush out issues that might have been overlooked.

As the bill is being prepared, or shortly thereafter, supporting regulations are programmed through the production process. In practice departments often pay less attention to that element of legislation than they might and it does not help that civil servants who were involved in the production of the Bill are frequently moved to other departments just at the time that the regulations are being prepared.[95]

---

[94] Paul Regan, *Enacting legislation – a civil servant's perspective* [2012] 34(1) Statute Law Review 32–28.

[95] This can happen to primary legislation as well; I have been involved in discussions with senior officials on what was the meaning of the Finance Act 2004 Schedules 33 and 34, which numbering is in itself testament to the incontinence of policymaking in the Treasury on overseas pension arrangements which are inscrutable without background knowledge. The only civil servant who did understand the schedules was moved almost immediately thereafter, and the schedules stand to this day, with in practice no one in HMRC having

Not everyone agrees that it is possible to make the law accessible to the public (though as seen below, a recent Parliamentary Counsel does). Frances Bennion was a talented, idiosyncratic and opinionated Parliamentary Counsel (the only one to have resigned twice, as he remarked), responsible for the drafting of a long act on consumer credit, to replace the former Moneylenders Act. Many years on it is clear that while the Moneylenders Act was imperfect it worked much better than the subsequent regulatory framework. For example, if the interest charged was more than a certain amount, the lender could not claim his money back; that was considerably simpler that the contortions that regulators had to undergo to manage the perceived (though maybe not real) excesses of modern moneylending, e.g. payday lending, in 2014. Frances Bennion later enhanced his living by writing a four-volume encyclopaedia to explain his legislation, to make it easier for others to use. One commentator remarked:[96]

> In those remarks on the Act, Bennion contemplates making legislation comprehensible not to non-lawyers, but instead only 'to the [legal] profession'. 'Non-lawyers ought', Bennion has said, 'to be able to understand the law that binds them, and in a perfect world they would. In our world they can't. Not fully, and safely. If they think they can, and act on that, they may find they have inadvertently broken the law, or taken on an unwanted obligation, or missed an entitlement, or suffered in some other way. So they had better not try. Many lawyers rail against this situation. Here is an example from the judiciary relating to an Act I drafted myself, the Consumer Credit Act 1974 ("the CCA"). The drafting was criticized by Clarke LJ, who started one of his judgments with the following: "These appeals raise a number of issues under [the CCA] which has recently provided so much work for the courts. Like others, this case demonstrates the unsatisfactory state of the law at present. Simplification of a part of the law which is intended to protect consumers is surely long overdue so as to make it comprehensible to layman and lawyer alike. At present it is certainly not comprehensible to the former and is scarcely comprehensible to the latter."[97] With his legal training and experience, Clarke LJ ought to know that he is demanding the impossible here. It simply is not practicable for legislation which is required to do the work that the CCA is required to do to be "comprehensible to the layman". It would be dangerous for lay persons to think they could extract the legal meaning of such texts without skilled help ... a

much idea about how they were supposed to work, or even what was the policy objective behind them.

[96] Ross Carter, *Statutory interpretation using legislated examples: Bennion on multiple consumer credit agreements*, [2011] 32(2) Statute Law Review 86–115 at p114.

[97] *McGinn v Grangewood Securities Ltd* [2002] EWCA Civ 522.

movement that wishes the public to read and act on raw legislation without professional guidance obviously does not truly believe law to be an expertise.'[98]

As we shall see below, those Olympian views seem to be no longer fashionable.[99]

3.5.2 The Good Law Initiative

Exasperation about the extent and complexity of legislation has frequently been expressed within government. The Better Regulation Executive was intended to implement the 2010 Coalition Government's policy on one in, one out and encourage the effectiveness of the Red Tape Challenge. The Chief Parliamentary Counsel a year or so later published an explanation of why laws were too complex, and blaming departmental instructions and poor policy thinking – and saying it was nothing new: 'I wish that the superfluous and tedious statutes were brought into one sum together, and made more plan and short,' said Edward VI (1537–1553). The House of Commons Political and Constitutional Reform Committee also rehearsed the complaints against excessive and complicated law, and made recommendations. All these were brought together in an initiative supported by a think tank, the Institute for Government in April 2013. The intention was 'to build a shared pride in the quality of our law and . . . create confidence among citizens that legislation is for them'. Nothing transpired.[100]

3.5.3 Tax Law Simplification Projects

There is no doubt that the UK tax system is one of the most complex in the world (although India and the US are worse). The wonder is that it is not more dysfunctional in practice than it is. There have been for example in

---

[98] See www.FrancesBennion.com/2009/011.

[99] Except by some ministers, see 'Legislation is not primarily for the use of people who have common sense; it is to regulate people who have not got a great deal of common sense', Andrew Stewart MP, Parliamentary Under-Secretary of State, Communities and Local Government, *debate on Co-operative housing*, HC Deb, 11 July 2012, col 145WH.

[100] www.gov.uk/government/news/join-the-good-law-conversation, Press release, 16 April 2013; *When laws become too complex*, Cabinet Office, 16 April 2013; *The Fifth Statement of New regulation*, Better Regulation Executive, December 2012; House of Commons Political and Constitutional Reform Committee, *Ensuring standards in the quality of legislation*, First Report of Session 2013–14, Volume I: Report, HC 85, 20 May 2013.

the UK five Finance Acts longer than 600 pages; three of them were products of the 2010–2015 Coalition Government. There are 1140 separate tax reliefs, and the Office of Tax Simplification has virtually in practice given up the unequal struggle to achieve its objectives, rather like the Tax Law Rewrite project before it.[101] And neither the Treasury nor HMRC itself can cope with the complexity, says the Public Accounts Committee, despite it being responsible for the complexity.[102]

Tax and VAT

The Tax Law Rewrite project avoided dealing with one kind of tax, value added tax, partly because VAT was largely derived from European Union rules. But nonetheless VAT contained its own absurdities, one of which is illustrated below, to demonstrate in part that even where legislation appears clear, there can always remain ambiguities. One involves the difference in tax treatment between biscuits (cookies) and cakes. Of course Marie Antoinette almost certainly never said 'let them eat cake'; but if she had, she would have said so, being a sensible woman, on the basis that both bread and cakes were taxed the same. If she had said 'let them eat biscuits', then the French mob may have had real cause for complaint, because in the UK at least while cakes are VAT free, biscuits face a 20 per cent tax. The logic is that food should be free of VAT, bread is a food, and cake is a relative of bread. But a biscuit is confectionery, a luxury, and therefore not a food.

There are inevitably definitional issues. A snowball is a Scottish creation, consisting of a biscuit base, a marshmallow topping and chocolate covering. The courts were required to determine its gender as it were. In a previous leading case some years previously concerning 'Jaffa cakes', a type of cake-biscuit, the UK HMRC had accepted since the introduction of VAT that Jaffa cakes were zero-rated as cakes, but always had misgivings about whether this was correct. Following a review, the department reversed its view of the liability. Jaffa cakes were then ruled to be biscuits partly covered in chocolate and standard-rated. United Biscuits (through

---

[101] *Review of Rewritten Income Tax Legislation*, Ipsos MORI on behalf of HM Revenue and Customs, research report No 104, 2011, especially para 5.4 ('Unexpected consequences of rewrites'); Antony Seely, *Tax Law Rewrite: the final Bills*, House of Commons Library, Standard Note SN5239, 21 April 2010.

[102] See e.g. *HM Revenue and Customs: dealing with the tax obligations of older people*, House of Commons Public Accounts Committee, Eleventh Report of Session 2009–2010, HC 141, 25 February 2010, para 3.

one of its subsidiaries as McVities, one of the largest manufacturers of Jaffa cakes) appealed against this decision. The Tribunal listed the factors it considered in coming to a decision; legend had it that the distinction was based on what happens if, like chewing gum, it was left on the bed-post overnight. If it went hard it was a cake, if it went soft it was a biscuit. The tribunal that examined the problem noted:[103]

- The product's name was a minor consideration.
- Ingredients: cake can be made of widely differing ingredients, but Jaffa cakes were made of an egg, flour and sugar mixture which was aerated on cooking and was the same as a traditional sponge cake. it was a thin batter rather than the thicker dough expected for a biscuit texture.
- Cake would be expected to be soft and friable; biscuit would be expected to be crisp and able to be snapped. Jaffa cakes had the texture of sponge cake.
- Size: Jaffa cakes were in size more like biscuits than cakes.
- Packaging: Jaffa cakes were sold in packages more similar to biscuits than cakes.
- Marketing: Jaffa cakes were generally displayed for sale with biscuits rather than cakes.
- Ongoing stale: a Jaffa cake goes hard like a cake rather than soft like a biscuit.
- Jaffa cakes are presented as a snack, eaten with the fingers, whereas a cake may be more often expected to be eaten with a fork. they also appeal to children, who could eat one in a few mouthfuls rather like a sweet.

---

[103] *United Biscuits* (LON/91/0160); cf. *Adams Foods Ltd* (MAN/83/0062) (on the nature of chocolate shortcake); *Marks and Spencer plc v Her Majesty's Commissioners of Customs and Excise* [2005] UKHL 53 (on the nature of chocolate-covered teacakes: 'So, a cake covered in chocolate is zero-rated, but a biscuit covered in chocolate (or chocolate substitute) is within an exception to an exception to an exception, and attracts standard-rate VAT.'); *Lees of Scotland and Thomas Tunnock Ltd v HMRC* [2014] UKFTT 630 (TC) (on the nature of snowballs); *Revenue and Customs Brief 36 (2014): VAT – liability of snowballs*, 13 October 2014; *HMRC Reference: Notice 701/14* (February 2014) par 3.4 (on the nature of gingerbread men; no VAT is charged if the figure has two chocolate spots for its eyes, but any chocolate-based additions, such as buttons or a belt, mean VAT is payable; it is cheaper to buy no-chocolate gingerbread men). *Tunnock's sales take the teacake after Commonwealth Games ceremony: confectionery firm 'bowled over' as Waitrose reports 62% sales rise after giant dancing teacakes feature in opening event*, Guardian, 25 July 2014. And cf. *United Biscuits v ASDA Stores* [1997] RPC 513 (did a Puffin biscuit made by ASDA look too much like a Penguin biscuit made by United Biscuits; the court decision contains an irresistible illustrated review of the history of the design of the chocolate penguin).

- The sponge part of a Jaffa cake is a substantial part of the product in terms of bulk and texture when eaten.

Taking all these factors into account, it was held that Jaffa cakes had characteristics of both cakes and biscuits, but the tribunal thought they had enough characteristics of cakes to be accepted as such, and they were therefore zero-rated. An earlier case which concerned Chocolate Dundees, a traditional type of shortcake with a chocolate base and individually wrapped for sale, came to the opposite conclusion. The decision contains a useful, if technical, table of comparative differences between cakes and biscuits, provided by an expert witness, and the tribunal was unable to see any factors supporting a view of the product as cake. It was ruled to be a biscuit partly covered in chocolate and accordingly standard-rated.

Some years later the UK HMRC issued a guide to the problems of snowballs. Snowballs were of national and international interest; they had been a symbol of the Commonwealth Games earlier in 2014. In a previous tribunal decision the court had found that a snowball did not have all of the characteristics of a cake but displayed 'enough of the characteristics of a cake that it should be classified as such'. The tribunal had to decide whether a Scottish snowball had the characteristics that ordinary people would consider to be a cake, including the ingredients used, its manufacture, unpackaged appearance, taste and texture, circumstances of consumption, packaging and marketing. In its written decision, the tribunal concluded that

> A snowball looks like a cake. It is not out of place on a plate full of cakes. A snowball has the mouth feel of a cake. Most people would want to enjoy a beverage of some sort whilst consuming it. It would often be eaten in a similar way to cakes; for example to celebrate a birthday in an office. We are wholly agreed that a snowball is a confection to be savoured but not whilst walking around or, for example, in the street. Most people would prefer to be sitting when eating a snowball and possibly, or preferably, depending on background, age, sex etc with a plate, a napkin or a piece of paper or even just a bare table so that the pieces of coconut which fly off do not create a great deal of mess. Although by no means everyone considers a snowball to be a cake we find that these facts, in particular, mean that a snowball has sufficient characteristics to be characterised as a cake.

There is of course no VAT on cream gateaux, but it is imposed at a rate of 20 per cent on ice cream gateaux.[104] Adding to the confusion is the

---

[104] HMRC, *VAT Notice 701/14: food*, Updated 15 December 2015. Ice cream gateaux includes arctic rolls.

variety and multiplicity of tax reliefs, the cost of which is never what they were budgeted to be.[105] Film tax relief for example was expected to cost around £30M over three years; in the end it cost £700M a year by 2006 and it took 10 years to rationalise it. Entrepreneurs tax relief similarly rose by 500 per cent since its introduction in 2008; the revenue cost in 2013/14 was £2.9B, three times greater than forecast, and around 35 per cent less than the total revenue of the tax it offered relief from. The statutory reliefs were complicated to administer and it was evident that most of the social or industrial policy objectives were either not achieved or had become distorted.

3.5.4 The Review of Efficiency in Criminal Proceedings

One example of the attempt to simplify not so much the law but the pro-cess of law was reflected in a report on efficiency in criminal proceedings, already referred to above,[106] deemed necessary following the cutbacks to the availability of legal aid. The author of the report had achieved some prominence having conducted an earlier inquiry into the abusive listen-ing in (hacking) to the personal phone calls of celebrities.[107] Although not a criminal lawyer, he was asked to re-think minor criminal proceed-ings, which had become notorious for their prolixity and delay. The con-clusions suggested reforms to the judicial process, but was accompanied by a despairing plea for statutory simplification of the criminal statutes, if only to make life easier not only for the judiciary but more impor-tantly for the magistracy who enjoy fewer resources to determine what the law is.

---

[105] See National Audit Office, *HM Revenue and Customs: Effective management of tax reliefs*, 20 November 2014.; there are 398 UK tax reliefs. Cf the cost of contracting-out rebates (relating to a now abolished state pension system: 'Ministers, he [Sir Michael Partridge, Permanent Secretary at the Department of Social Security] said, regarded the far greater take-up of the scheme – and thus its far higher cost – as a 'success', not a matter for apology. But he also disclosed that the cost of [contracting-out] rebates had been so high that min-isters had had to transfer three benefits, including statutory maternity and sick pay, out of national insurance and onto general taxation, in order to balance the National Insur-ance Fund's books. Michael Latham, Tory MP for Rutland and Melton told Sir Michael: 'Any more successes [like that] and we are all ruined', Nicholas Timmins, *The Independent*, 18 December 1990.

[106] The Rt Hon Sir Brian Leveson, *Review of efficiency in criminal proceedings*, Judiciary of England and Wales, January 2015, para 12–14. See note 24 above.

[107] The Rt Hon Sir Brian Leveson, *An Inquiry Into the Culture, Practices and Ethics of the Press*, November 2012, (*the Hacking Inquiry*).

3.5.5   Other Attempts at Management of Legislation

Later chapters explore in more detail some of the other attempts to constrain the growth of legislation. They have included

- *Regulatory impact assessment*, using inevitably crude techniques for assessing what the financial and other costs of implementation might be; they rarely if ever include an analysis of unintended consequences, what the pharmaceutical industry classifies as side effects, and which by law must be disclosed on the drug packaging.
- *Scrutiny*, whether prior- or post-implementation. In practice there is usually too little time to properly examine proposed legislation before implementation, and post-legislative scrutiny arrangements are infrequent and ad hoc.
- *Staged repeal (sunsetting)*, so that after a prescribed period, the legislation times-out. It is rare in practice in the UK. Some countries have a system that laws have to be renewed after a certain period of time (Australian legislation is limited to 10 years in many cases). In practice while the theory is good, in practice it becomes renewed semi-automatically, rather like the Finance Bill in the UK needs to be renewed since income tax was only supposed to be a short-term provision. Sadly it simply does not seem to work as a method of controlling the expansion of law.[108]

3.5.6   Statute Law Repeals

Several jurisdictions, most notably England,[109] orchestrate regular programmes of repeals of ancient and obsolete provisions. Whilst they are a useful tidying-up, in practice, since few ever refer to them, since there is no longer a 'statute book', it has little impact on day-to-day practice.

3.5.7   Unintended Consequences

Post-legislative scrutiny has so far had little effective impact on reform. But even good and well-drafted law can have unfortunate consequences, which it can be hard to remedy once black-letter law has been baked into

---

[108] See e.g. Stephen Argument, *Legislative scrutiny in Australia: wisdom to export?*, [2011] 32(2) Statute Law Review 116–148.

[109] Law Commission, *Statute Law Repeals: Consultation Paper: General repeals*, November 2014.

the system. One factor can be the misuse of law for purposes other than intended, such as the use of the Regulation of Investigatory Powers Act 2000, originally intended to control and empower public bodies carrying out surveillance and investigation, and covering the interception of communications, taking account of technological change such as the growth of the internet and strong encryption. It has since been widely misused, often by local authorities for relatively trivial matters.[110]

Similarly, in the US, John Yates, a fisherman, was charged under the US Sarbanes-Oxley Act 2002 which was passed following the Enron scandal in the States to control corporate excesses. An official in Florida found that 72 red grouper fish caught by his boat were an inch or two shy of the 20-inch minimum. Mr Yates received a citation and was ordered to bring the offending fish to shore the next day. Instead, the government claimed, he asked a crew member to toss them overboard and replace them with bigger fish. The government insisted that this breached the Act which condemns anyone who 'knowingly... destroys... or makes a false entry in any record, document, or tangible object' to impede a federal investigation. A fish is a tangible object, but fish-shredding had probably not been within the contemplation of lawmakers. Were he to have been convicted, he would have been liable to a potential 20-year jail sentence. The US is not alone in possessing prosecutors and regulators who feel able to use laws not necessarily to protect the public but to establish their own reputation, and where common sense and proportionality take second place to career advancement.[111]

---

[110] See e.g. *The Regulation of Investigatory Powers Act (RIPA)*, Briefing Note, Big Brother Watch, December 4 2014; *The Grim RIPA*, Big Brother Watch, 28 May 2010. The extent of the Act was later constrained by the Protection of Freedoms Act 2012, but extended under the Data Retention and Investigatory Powers Act 2014, which had a sunset clause of 31 December 2016. Elements of DRIPA were held illegal at first instance, see *R v Secretary of State for the Home Department ex p David Davis MP, Tom Watson MP, Peter Brice and Geoffrey Lewis* [2015] EWCA Civ 1185. Just before the sunset clause took effect, the act was replaced by the Investigatory Powers Act 2016, which allowed access to information about internet usage by several dozen public authorities (including the police but also the Welsh Ambulance Services National Health Service Trust) without a warrant.

[111] *Yates v United States*, 574 US ___ (2015) (Supreme Court). Again, nothing new here; 'Lamenting what he believed to be the state governments' innumerable blunders, Madison suggested charitably that 'these have proceeded from the heads rather than the hearts of most of the authors of them'. 'What indeed,' he added, 'are all the repealing, explaining, and amending laws, which fill and disgrace our voluminous codes, but so many monuments of deficient wisdom', *Federalist Papers 62*, 27 February 1788, cited in Anthony King and Ivor Crewe, *The Blunders of our Governments*, Oneworld, 2013, p3.

3.6 Conclusions

A combination of an antiquated parliamentary process, a disinclination for whichever government is in power to spend political capital in a reform of the system, and MPs who somewhat glory in arcane procedures (in which the system still uses Norman French, despite the fact that Henry VIII in 1485 decided to prohibit the use of Latin and Norman French)[112] means that our laws are too long, too many and too complicated. This situation continues despite innumerable reviews, and even more recommendations, many from within government itself.

There is however little will amongst parliamentarians who in some ways seem to enjoy the procedures, although they have introduced some minor changes in times for sittings. More relevantly, there remains little personal accountability, despite efforts of select committees to bring government as a whole to account. Previous well-known pieces of legislation such as the Sale of Goods Act by way of contrast bore a personal hallmark. Nor have the despairing efforts of Parliamentary Counsel's Office or the relevant select committees made much if any impression on either ministers or the civil service to encourage them to improve at least the drafting of the law, if not the making of policy.[113]

One of the contributors to change has in the past been the remarks of senior judiciary. In recent times these have become of less effect, partly because of the translation of the members of the Supreme Court out of the senior parliamentary chamber, and partly because of the tensions arising from the use of judicial review, which has made members of the judiciary less comfortable in challenging government decisions.

Consequently there might need to be a somewhat different approach to the management of the creation of legislation. They include the use of 'smart legislation', improved understanding following experience with

---

[112] And possibly as far back as 1362, see The Pleading in English Act 1362 (36 Edw. III c. 15), also known as the Statute of Pleading. The Act provided that 'all Pleas which shall be pleaded in [any] Courts whatsoever, before any of his Justices whatsoever, or in his other Places, or before any of His other Ministers whatsoever, or in the Courts and Places of any other Lords whatsoever within the Realm, shall be pleaded, shewed, defended, answered, debated, and judged in the English Tongue, and that they be entered and inrolled in Latin'. The Act was repealed in 1863. Fifty years later English became the language of official government under the Chancery Standard, during the reign of Henry V, around 1420.

[113] Cf Sir Patrick Mayhew, *Can legislation ever be simple, clear and certain?* [1990] Statute Law Review 7; Sir Patrick was not one of society's great reformers, so the answer was predictable. Other countries face similar if not greater problems; see the Canadian efforts to draft simultaneously in English and French, Serge Lortie and Robert C. Bergeron, *Legislative drafting and language in Canada*, [2007] 28(2) Statute Law Review 83–118.

European Union cross-border legislation of embracing different legal cultures, namely the civil and common law structures;[114] and making use of the recommendations made in 1992 which set out five criteria that each new legislative measure had to meet as a means of achieving legislative quality, and which remain relevant despite any future fragmentation of the European Union.[115] None of these in the past have had much if any effect, and more practical solutions are explored in Chapter 7.

---

[114] See e.g. Helen Xanthaki, *European Union Legislative quality after the Lisbon Treaty: the challenges of smart regulation* [2014] 35(1) Statute Law Review 66–80; Helen Xanthaki, *The problem of quality in EU legislation: what on earth is really wrong?* [2001] CML Rev 651–676.

[115] *The internal market after 1992: meeting the challenge*, Report to the EEC Commission by the High Level Group on the operation of the internal market, SEC (92) 2044; Supplement to European Report No 1808 of 31 October 1992 ('*The Sutherland report*'); Commission Communication to the Council and the European Parliament, *Follow up of the Sutherland Report*, COM (93) 361 final and SEC (92) 2227 fin; Opinion of the Economic and Social Committee (ESC) of 5 May 1993 On the Commission Communication on the Operation of the Community's Internal Market after 1992: Follow-up to the Sutherland Report OJ No C 201/59 of 26 July 1993; Communication from the Commission, Follow-up to the Sutherland Report: legislative consolidation to enhance the transparency of community law in the area of the internal market, 16 December 1993 COM (93) 361(fin); Communication from the Commission to the Council, the EOP and the ESC, *On the handling of urgent situations in the context of implementation of Community Rules: Follow up to the Sutherland Report*, COM(93)430 fin.

4

Regulation and Regulators

Rules are not an impediment to genius, but an inspiration to it.[1]

Progress is precisely that which the rules and regulations did not forsee.[2]

All plans of government, which suppose great reformation in the manners of mankind, are plainly imaginary.[3]

Show me the person who has actually read the 'important information' you must understand before entering the website of an institution regulated by the Financial Services Authority and I will show you a man who has difficulties with girls.[4]

Sir, There are times when measures put in to promote 'health and safety' actually end up paradoxically, by increasing isolation between staff it adversely affects the health of both the staff and our patients rather than promote it.[5]

Sir, The letter from Dr Chase reminds me of one you printed many years ago from the headmaster of primary school in Lincolnshire (I think). He said that since the introduction of compulsory primary education in the 19th century not one schoolchild had been so much as singed in a fire at school, but as soon as fire doors had been fitted, his school alone was sending to hospital a couple of children a week because their fingers had been trapped in the doors.[6]

Sir, Dr Chase omitted to mention that fire doors are by long tradition propped open with fire extinguishers.[7]

---

[1] Sir Joshua Reynolds, *Seven discourses on art*, Lecture to the Royal Academy, 2 January 1769.
[2] Ludwig von Mises, *Bureaucracy*, 1944.
[3] David Hume, *History of England*, 1752, Chapter 55.
[4] John Kay, *The $10 minibar is no basis for capitalism*, Financial Times, 6 July 2011.
[5] Dr Derek Chase, FRCGP, King's College Health Centre, *Letter to The Times*, 29 January 2014.
[6] Richard Channon, *Letter to The Times*, 31 January 2014.
[7] Nick Parmee, *Letter to The Times*, 31 January 2014.

4.1 Introduction

4.1.1 The Rise of Regulation and Regulators

The growth of regulation is one of the more remarkable developments in law over the last 50 years; compared with earlier changes in legal direction, such as the development of equity, it has been a relatively fast and unexpected phenomenon:[8]

> Twenty-five years ago, no partner in a corporate law firm in London, Paris or New York would likely have identified himself as a regulatory specialist. Commercial law was then, for the most part, about private law activity. Contrast the position now. What business lawyer today dare profess ignorance about the law and practice of regulation?
>
> ... The profile of certain regulatory bodies is such that they are known solely by acronym. They have substantial pay-rolls. They exercise powers, particularly over livelihoods, in some respect greater than senior judges. They can administer punitive and exemplary sanctions. When legally challenged (in British courts at least), those challenges more often than not fail. No surprise then that in 2007 the House of Lords Sessional Select Committee Report on UK Economic Regulators said:
>
> > 'There is a crucial need for greater parliamentary oversight ... over regulation bodies. The question of who regulates the regulators has not been answered and will not go away.'[9]

The regulators themselves of course are unlikely to go away, nor are their supporting regulations. Meanwhile the issue of their governance continue continues to pose challenges. The first question is: why has there been such a proliferation and why it has been so hard to slay the Hydra, or at least slice off one or two of its heads.[10]

---

[8] Michael Smyth, *Foreword*, in Dawn Oliver et al., *The Regulatory State: Constitutional implications*, Oxford University Press, 2010, page v.

[9] *UK Economic Regulators*, House of Lords, Select Committee on Regulators, 1st Report of Session 2006–07, Paper 189, 13 November 2007, para 1.29, in relation to economic regulators, a different group of regulators than those covered by this chapter, but faced with similar issues. In 2017 its website indicated that it was still waiting for a parliamentary debate on its conclusions. Cf *The Regulatory State: ensuring its accountability*, House of Lords Constitution Committee, 6th Report, 2003–04, HL 68.

[10] There were over 900 in 2011 in the UK: *Smaller government: Shrinking the Quango State*, House of Commons Public Administration select Committee, Fifth Report of Session 2010–11 HC 537, p7.

4.1.2   The Belief in Regulation

One of the reasons for growth has been fashion, and the fashionable belief that regulation works. This belief is sometimes compounded by self-interest of the regulated. For example, those who wish to become a hairdresser in California must spend a year studying the art of cutting and blow-drying:[11]

> For that we have to thank the California Board of Barbering in Cosmetology, whose web site boasts a picture of the bald governor Brown as well as dire warnings about 'dangerous pedicures' and encouraging encomiums to 'the safe sandal system'. California is not alone: if you want to work in the wig trade in Texas, you need to take 300 hours of classes and pass an exam; Alabama obliges manicurists to sit through 750 hours of instruction; Florida will not let you work as an industrial designer unless you complete a four-year university degree and a two-year apprenticeship and pass a two-day examination. Sidney and Beatrice [Webb] might have written a ten-volume tome on local government, but even they never imagined Leviathan saving its subjects from clashing colour schemes.

Believers in greater regulation often adopt what in European Union circles has been called the precautionary principle (to outlaw genetically modified crops, despite the fact that they might scientifically be proved harmless and beneficial – because if the science is wrong, the damage could be immense, as witness the thalidomide scandal).[12] This notion is an ancient one; in 1908 FM Corford, a Cambridge classicist, noted the rule of the Dangerous Precedent:[13]

> The Principle of the Dangerous Precedent is that you should not now do an admittedly right action for fear you, or your equally timid successors, should not have the courage to do right in some future case, which, *ex hyopthesi*, is essentially different, but superficially resembles the present one. Every public action which is not customary, either is wrong, or, if it is

---

[11] John Micklethwaite and Adrian Wooldridge, *The Fourth Revolution: the global race to reinvent the state*, Allen Lane, 2014, p116.

[12] See discussion with Milton Freedman, the economist, about the role of the Federal Drug Administration in the licensing of thalidomide, *Government regulation*, www.youtube .com/watch?v=dZL25NSLhEA. Thalidomide was an ethical drug that had been licensed in Europe, where it caused immense damage to children born of women who had taken it, but not in the United States. Milton Freedman's argument was that tort law would have been sufficient control.

[13] F. M. Cornford, *Microcosmographia Academica*, 1908, cited in John Kay, *Absurd roots of modern regulatory practice*, Financial Times, 23 December 2015; see also for the dangers of dihydrogen monoxide, www.dhmo.org.

right, is a dangerous precedent. It follows that nothing should ever be done for the first time.

And he added:

> Plainly, the more rules you can invent, the less need there will be to waste time over fruitless puzzling about right and wrong. The best set of rules are those which prohibit important, but perfectly innocent, actions ... The merit of such regulations is that, having nothing to do with right or wrong, they help to obscure these troublesome considerations in other cases, and to relieve the mind of all sense of obligation towards society.

The Dangerous Precedent in real life can be illustrated by the Food Standards Agency's imperative to avoid an e-coli problem by imposing requirements on how to cook a hamburger:[14]

> You can achieve a pinky-grey steak or burger (seared to 75 degrees), but all other meats and offal require the following:
>
> 60°C – 45 minutes
> 65°C – 10 minutes
> 70°C – 2 minutes
> 75°C – 30 seconds
> 80°C – 6 seconds.

The advice is not one which day-to-day chefs have greeted with enthusiasm:

> Are they seriously expecting a busy chef to stand over the grill with six different orders, stopwatch in hand and probe in the other? ... In the US they let the customer take the risk, though menus come with the unsavoury note on the bottom: 'Eating raw or undercooked meat can cause food poisoning'.[15]

Food poisoning is an unpleasant and sometimes fatal condition, and rules to make it less likely are clearly beneficial for restaurant customers. The dilemma for policymakers is that while there is evidently a need for hygiene in restaurants, the way in which to achieve that can look and may actually be absurd. As an alternative to regulation, or customers simply

---

[14] *The safe production of beef burgers in catering establishments: advice for food business operators and LA officers*, Food Standards Agency, May 2016, 37pp; *Report from the ad hoc group on raw, rare and low temperature (RRLT) cooked food*, FSA Advisory committee on the microbiological safety of food, April 2014, p6.

[15] Prue Leith, *No more steak tartare?: strict food rules won't make you any safer – but they could ruin many small restaurants*, Spectator, 17 August 2013.

accepting the risk coupled with a warning, restaurants could gain a reputation for cleanliness through private certification agencies, or through internet systems such as TripAdvisor.[16]

4.1.3   Why, What and Who Are Regulators and Regulation

There has not been a deliberate policy move towards moving away from legislation towards regulation; it seems merely to have followed political fashion and expediency. Regulation can be seen as a form of subcontracted legislation; the legislature may not have the time, the interest or the expertise to closely administer protection of the public through, for example, the application of rules for an industry, and instead appoints a regulator to do it on its behalf. There are also political advantages for government in distancing itself from a problem that cannot readily be solved, and to which responding properly may involve high expenditure of political capital. Such delegation can of course sometimes backfire, witness the adsorbtion in the UK of the UK Borders Agency and the Passport Office back into direct Home Office control after having been granted autonomy for a while during which it failed to assuage political pressures.[17]

Nonetheless, over the last hundred years or so, initially gently, and latterly with increasing frequency, greater numbers of ostensibly nongovernmental bodies have been established to micro-manage industries, or activities, or occupations, to provide improved service delivery or deliver independent advice. The list of regulators is long, and despite intermittent government announcements of a reduction in their number, shows every sign of growing.[18] Indeed while there seems to be little regulation of regulators (although most would deny it)[19] not only are there

---

[16] There is a large literature on the pointlessness of financial services regulation, and for a global view see e.g. *Global Regulatory Outlook 2017*, Duff & Phelps, New York, p5.

[17] *Fast and Fair?*, Parliamentary Ombudsman, 9 February 2010; *The Work of the UK Border Agency, Conclusions and Recommendations*, Home Affairs Select Committee, UK Parliament, 19 March 2013.

[18] *Smaller government: Shrinking the Quango State*, House of Commons Public Administration select Committee, Fifth Report of Session 2010–11 HC 537.

[19] *The Regulatory State: ensuring its accountability*, House of Lords Constitution Committee, 6th Report, 2003–2004, HL 68. There is now in the UK a Regulator's Code; and most regulators are supposed to have imposed on them appropriate constitutional checks and balances, which are sometimes captured by the regulators themselves. Unlike the regulations issued by regulators themselves, it is short (7 pages): *Regulators' Code*, Department for Business Innovation and Skills / Better Regulation Delivery Office, April 2014.

more of them, but there is a large increase in the number and extent of their powers.[20]

One of the other drivers is possibly the increasing realisation by both government and the public that legislation can be a flawed vehicle to perfect the national economy and the human condition. That conclusion has understandably led not so much to improved legislation, or improved administration by the government and the civil service but to both additional legislation and to the invention of an additional layer of law, that of regulation, which usually does not replace legislation but adds to it.

Legislation, perhaps simply stating that the courts will grant protection to an individual or to the public, has been perceived to be insufficient, inadequately policed or supported with slow and expensive remedies. The obvious solution, improving the law, is often considered too politically challenging. As a flanking response, therefore, government has placed increasing trust in regulators, bodies which are presumed to have the agility and expertise to manage increasingly complex matters which the central administration of justice is presumed unable to deal with. Such bodies are usually granted both delegated legislative powers and powers of sanction, and usually but not invariably a system of constraints to ensure their own powers are not abused. The regulators have in practice in many cases themselves proved to be prolific creators of rules. This chapter looks at the ways in which regulators behave, and the rules they engender.

4.1.4   The Operations of Regulators

The market economy depends on trust. Absent that, and depend instead on contracts, lawyers, regulations and supervisory authorities, and there will be yet more scandals, collapses and crashes, since the ingenuity of those who seek to sidestep the rules always exceeds those whose job it is to apply them. The only safe regulatory authority is conscience, the voice of God

---

[20] Governments of all persuasions and in many jurisdictions have attempted over the years to cull the number of administrative bodies (aka quangos (quasi-autonomous non-governmental organisations), gongos (government-organised non-governmental organisations), ALB's (arm's length bodies) and NDPB's (non-departmental public bodies)); there are also public bodies, executive agencies, non-ministerial departments and independent statutory bodies, see e.g. the UK Public Bodies Act 2011. Lucinda Maer, *Quangos*, House of Commons Library, Standard Note SN/PC/05609, 31 January 2011. 'NDPB' was invented by a senior UK civil servant (Sir Leo Pliatsky, *Report on Non Departmental Bodies*, Cabinet Office, 2000) to avoid use of the word 'quango', which had become a term of opprobrium.

within the human heart forbidding us to do what we know is wrong but think we can get away with.[21]

Lord Sachs, a former Chief Rabbi of the Commonwealth, may be right when he observes that the establishment of trust may be preferable to the imposition of rules to resolve many of our problems. But the inevitable occasional failures of trust have provoked not merely a sense of disappointment, as perhaps they should, but a growth in regulation as response and as an adjunct to legislation.[22] That growth has been so substantial that it has become over the last few decades virtually a stand-alone industry. One reason is that the regulations which emerge very often require the creation of regulators to administer them; the creation of rules, their administration and enforcement, has required the establishment of a large and expanding number of regulators and, in response, the formation of a new trade or profession, that of compliance officers since, without advisers on how to comply with the rules, businesses will all too easily commit breaches and suffer consequent fines and loss of reputation.[23] In the past the charge has cynically been that lawyers welcome new laws but there are many other groups now dependent on the flourishing of a regulatory culture, including judicial officials (judges, tribunal chairman, disciplinary bodies), compliance officers and directors, officials working within regulators, civil servants, Parliamentary Counsel, MPs (in the UK in four separate legislative chambers), and local government officials (enforcing for example parking breaches, or trading standards breaches, or animal welfare breaches or building control standards). Indeed, regulators often consider themselves members of a new occupation, and are happy to move between regulatory offices without necessarily having any knowledge or experience of those they are intending to regulate or the industry they are intent on regulating. As an example of the growth in numbers involved, in 2013 JP Morgan was reported to have recruited in that year alone an additional 3000 compliance officers.[24]

---

[21] Lord Sachs, *Devarim (5772) – Prophets and profits*, 23 July 2012 (http://rabbisacks.org/covenant-conversation-5772-devarim-profits-and-prophets/).

[22] *Regulatory policy in perspective: A reader's companion to the OECD regulatory policy outlook 2015*, OECD, 2015.

[23] See e.g. International Compliance Association, which has developed training and qualifications, but is a trading organisation (www.int-comp.org/).

[24] 'The US banking group JP Morgan Chase has employed an extra 3,000 staff in its compliance department during 2013 in its latest attempt to prepare the market for the outcome of negotiations over a $770m (£440m) settlement with regulators over the 'London Whale' trading incident . . . the chief executive, Jamie Dimon, said: 'Adjusting to the new regulatory environment will require an enormous amount of time, effort and resources. We fully

There seem to be few figures detailing the cost of all this; adding the operational costs of the regulation bodies themselves to the costs to the industries affected, and the cost of behavioural change clearly involves several billions, although it is hard to quantify scientifically. One insurer and asset manager calculated at the end of 2013 that in relation to investment management, regulation cost investors a reduction in return of around 2.3 per cent pa, a huge amount.[25] It is in the end the consumer who pays for this overhead, and it is hard for them or for government or for regulators to assess whether the expenditure represents added value.

There are other internal drawbacks to a regulatory framework. Regulators periodically feel the need to justify their existence, so as part of their remit they feel the need to collect statistics which they may need to produce to external enquirers, such as government departments. In the US it has been estimated that 2 billion forms a year (10 for each citizen, including children) need to be completed.[26] Some of these returns are useful, maybe even essential; others can be irrelevant, duplicative, contradictory or ineffective, or have survived past their useful term through inertia, or whose effect may be counter-productive. Regulators are criticised (or are keen to avoid being criticised) for being subject to regulatory capture, sometimes defined as being prisoners of those they regulate rather than the consumer. Regulatory capture can include being controlled or at least strongly influenced by major producers who welcome regulation as a way of stifling competition and limiting entry by competitors.[27] And regulation as a solution to a problem can involve a cost disproportionate to the benefit – witness in the UK for example the £6.3M pa cost of the audit office controlling the expenses of MPs compared with the previously much criticised £0.5M pa improper spend.[28]

---

intend to follow the letter and spirit of every rule and requirement.' He said that since 2012 more than 4,000 extra staff had been assigned to control areas such as risk, compliance, legal and finance and that 3,000 of those had been hired this year. An extra $1bn was being spent on controls and 500 'dedicated professionals and several thousand others' were helping the bank submit its regulatory files on capital to US regulators. Staff had undergone 750,000 hours of training on compliance issues.' Guardian, 17 September 2013.

[25] *Investors miss 2.3% of return due to regulatory costs*, Funds Europe, 7 October 2013, (Elizabeth Corley, Allianz Global Investors survey) (www.funds-europe.com/news/12084).

[26] Herbert Kaufman, *Red Tape: its origins, uses and abuses*, Brookings Institution Press, 2015, p9.

[27] Described in some detail in Herbert Kaufman, *Red Tape: its origins, uses and abuses*, Brookings Institution Press, 2015.

[28] Robert Winnett and Gordon Rayner, *No Expenses Spared*, Bantam, 2009; an alternative (and cheaper and simpler) method of control would be for the MP's to pay themselves their expenses without control – provided they were disclosed on their website, allowing the public to judge. It would have been self-policing and transparent. See Independent

4.1.5   The Regulators

There are very many regulators. It is hard to determine exactly how many there are since they are not always called that, and some bodies which have regulatory duties do not always regard themselves as such.[29] In addition, their coverage can be wide with a bewildering variety of objectives; they can separately have commercial, professional or consumer oversight obligations. There is therefore no standard taxonomy, but they are sometimes classified into the following:[30]

Executive NDPBs, established by Act of Parliament, carrying out executive, administrative, regulatory or commercial functions (e.g. in the UK, the Environment Agency). There are around 190 of them in the UK.

Advisory NDPBs, which provide independent expert advice to minsters, for example the Low Pay Commission or the Committee on Standards in Public Life. If the advice which emerges is not to the Minister's liking, the chairman or the members of the board can and will be dismissed.[31] There are around 400 of them in the UK.

Tribunal NDPBs which have jurisdiction in a specialised field of law, such as valuation tribunals, or appeal tribunals within a regulator. There are around 20 of them in the UK.

Independent monitoring boards, examining the conduct of prisons or hospitals. Their reports are sometimes trenchant and independent and similarly often not taken much notice of by government in practice. There are around 150 of them.

There are commonly agreed to be around 600–900 such bodies (depending on issues of definition) in the UK and they spend around £50B pa.[32]

Parliamentary Standards Authority, *Annual Report and Accounts for 2015–16, Presented to Parliament pursuant to Schedule 1 of the Parliamentary Standards Act 2009*, 19 July 2016.

[29] There is little agreement on an accepted taxonomy; the Institute for Government suggested there are at least 11 varieties – Institute for Government, QPD9, evidence to the Select Committee, *Smaller government: shrinking the Quango State*, House of Commons, Public Administration Select Committee, HC 537, 2011. Cabinet Office, *Public Bodies 2012*, 2012. Cabinet Office, *Next steps in the government's quango programme*, Press Release, 28 December 2012. By March 2016, following several years of deregulatory policy, there were still 463 public bodies, spending nearly £200B pa and employing 260,000 people, see *Public Bodies 2016*, Cabinet Office, January 2017.

[30] See e.g. *Information on national regulators* (http://discuss.bis.gov.uk/focusonenforcement/list-of-regulators-and-their-remit) Department of Business, 19 September 2015.

[31] Described in David Nutt, *Drugs without the hot air*, UIT Cambridge, 2012.

[32] Others suggest there are around 1200 bodies, with spending powers of £90B. See Taxpayers Alliance, *ACA to YJB: A guide to the UK's semi-autonomous Public Bodies 2007–08*, 2010.

The 2010 Conservative Party manifesto in the UK promised a bonfire of the quangos, hence the passing of the Public Bodies Act 2011 intended to give the government power to manage the number of such bodies (which it already had), as did the Coalition Manifesto following the 2010 election. Most of the reduction involved little more than window dressing, converting bodies into 'committees of experts', or merging them back into government departments.[33] Nowadays there is supposed to be a triennial review of such bodies to try and ensure that they are still required, with formal impact assessments, to look at the costs and benefits of their continued existence. Some of the bodies have been around for a considerable period: the Bank of England has been operating since 1753, and the Commissioners of Bankruptcy since 1570. But repeated inquiries and reviews have thought, as a group, there was an excess of them.[34] They include in the UK, for example:

Charities
Charity Commission for England and Wales[35]

Education
Office for Standards in Education, Children's Services and Skills[36]

Qualifications
Office of Qualifications and Examinations Regulation[37]

Environment
Environment Agency (EA)
Northern Ireland Environment Agency (NIEA)
Scottish Environment Protection Agency (SEPA)
Natural Resources Wales (NRW)

---

[33] Cabinet Office, *Public Bodies Reform – proposals for change*, 14 October 2010.
[34] See e.g. *Fulton Report on the Civil Service*, 1968; Brian Hogwood, *The Growth of quangos: evidence and expectations*, in FF Ridley and David Wilson, *The quango debate*, Oxford University Press, 1995.
[35] www.charitycommission.gov, and its analogues: Office of the Scottish Charity Regulator and the Charity Commission for Northern Ireland.
[36] 'Ofsted', and its analogues the General Teaching Councils for Scotland, Wales and Northern Ireland.
[37] 'Ofqual'.

Finance

Financial Conduct Authority
Office of the Regulator of Community Interest Companies
The Pensions Regulator

Health

Care Quality Commission (CQC)
Complementary and Natural Healthcare Council (CNHC)
General Chiropractic Council (GCC)
General Dental Council (GDC)
General Medical Council (GMC)
General Optical Council (GOC)
General Osteopathic Council (GOsC)
General Pharmaceutical Council (GPhC)
Health and Care Professions Council (HCPC)
Health and Safety Executive
Professional Standards Authority for Health and Social Care
Human Fertilisation and Embryology Authority
Medicines and Healthcare products Regulatory Agency (MHRA)
Nursing and Midwifery Council (NMC)
Pharmaceutical Society of Northern Ireland (PSNI)

Law

Discussed below

Social Care

Care Council for Wales (CCW)
General Social Care Council (GSCC)
Northern Ireland Social Care Council (NISCC)
Scottish Social Services Council (SSSC)

Transport

Civil Aviation Authority (CAA)
Office of Rail Regulation (ORR)

Utilities

Ofcom – Independent regulator and competition authority for the UK
communications industries

PhonepayPlus – regulator for phone-paid services in the UK, part of Ofcom, replaces ICSTIS

Ofgem – the Office of the Gas and Electricity Markets

Office for Nuclear Regulation (ONR)

Ofwat – the Water Services Regulation Authority

The Utility Regulator – regulating electricity, gas, water and sewerage industries in Northern Ireland

Water Industry Commissioner for Scotland

Other

Advertising Standards Authority (ASA)

British Board of Film Censors (BBFC)

Competition and Markets Authority (CMA)

Consumer Focus – the statutory consumer champion for England, Wales, Scotland and (for postal consumers) Northern Ireland

Council for Registered Gas Installers

Direct Marketing Authority

Engineering Council – the regulatory body for the Engineering profession

Equality and Human Rights Commission (EHRC)

Food Standards Agency

Forensic Science Regulator

Gaming Board for Great Britain (GBGB)

Gangmasters Licensing Authority

Independent Press Standards Organisation (IPSO)

Information Commissioner's Office

Planning Inspectorate

Police Complaints Authority

Scottish Housing Regulator (SHC)

Security Industry Authority

Mail

Postal Services Commission (Postcomm)

Aviation

Civil Aviation Authority (CAA)

Water Supply

Water Services Regulation Authority (Ofwat)

Passports

Identity and Passport Service (converted into HM Passport Office in 2013 and incorporated into the Home Office in 2014)

Not all of these organisations produce rules, but they all have an impact of some degree on personal, professional or commercial activity. Meanwhile in addition most countries need to work with international cross-border agencies (the EU and its own rule makers, the OECD, the Council of Europe, United Nations), with rules of their own, some of them with significant domestic impact. Some of the rule-making bodies seem to have broadly universal support in their rule making, often because they manage the process well, or they avoid excessive imposition of blame, a notable example being that of the Civil Aviation Authority. In that case the checks and balances seem to operate satisfactorily, since if the rules were excessive both the public and the airlines would complain about the cost of flights or the restriction on their availability – but if they are not strict enough there would be lack of public trust in the safety of air travel. The CAA has to maintain a balance between safety and commerciality, despite its (and the airlines) protestations to the contrary. Unlike perhaps some other regulators the CAA has a necessarily profound understand of risk issues, which may be one reason there are few protests against its regulatory operations.[38]

The list of regulators set out above is not complete. Just taking one section, that of lawyers, there can in fact be several additional regulators, not set out in the usual list of regulators, but which have regulatory powers, which can make it hard both for service providers and for consumers to know where to turn. In some cases, however such proliferation can have advantages in the provision of competition between regulators. In the provision of legal services alone, for example, there is no shortage of regulatory bodies:[39]

---

[38] Although the libertarian free-market economist Milton Freedman reckoned that air safety would be self-policing if there were no separate regulator. It is possible that the industry itself could have set up its own organisation, but there would probably still need to be an organisation, for the sharing of information if nothing else. Airports for example would be free to refuse landing rights to unsafe airlines, which would be effective as a method of control, as they do now.

[39] See e.g. The Bar Council; Solicitors Regulation Authority; Law Society of Northern Ireland; Law Society of Scotland; Legal Services Board; Law Society; Bar Standards Board; Chartered Institute of Legal Executives; CILEx Regulation; Council for Licensed Conveyancers; Chartered Institute for Patent Attorneys; Intellectual Property Regulation Board; Chartered Institute of Trade Mark Attorneys; Costs Lawyers Standards Board; Association of

Solicitors

The Law Society (the approved regulator)
Solicitors Regulation Authority (independent regulatory body)

Barristers

Bar Council (the approved regulator)
Bar Standards Council (independent regulatory body)

Legal Executives

Chartered Institute of Legal Executives (approved regulator)
ILEX Professional Standards Limited (independent regulatory body)

Licensed Conveyancers

Council for Licensed Conveyances (independent regulatory body);

Patent Attorneys

Chartered Institute of Patent Attorneys (approved regulator)
Intellectual Property Regulation Board (independent regulatory body)

Trade Mark Attorneys

Institute of Trade Mark Attorneys (ITMA) (approved regulator)
Intellectual Property Regulation Board (independent regulatory body)

Costs Lawyers

Association of Costs Lawyers (approved regulator)
Costs Lawyers Standards Board (independent regulatory body)

Notaries

Master of the Faculties.

The list does not include the Legal Services Board as a regulator of legal regulators, nor other regulators that can offer competing regulatory services (the Institute of Chartered Accountants in England and Wales and

Costs Lawyers; Master of the Faculties (notaries); Institute of Chartered Accountants in England and Wales (Probate Committee); Institute of Chartered Accountants of Scotland (for probate matters); Association of Chartered Certified Accountants (for probate matters); The Notaries Society; The Society of Scrivenor Notaries; The Society of Licensed Conveyancers; Legal Ombudsman.

the Bar Council both offer regulatory services to solicitors, in competition with the Solicitors Regulation Authority, and are cheaper and easier to deal with).

Nor does the list include the accounting institutes (two of them) which can offer probate services, regulated elsewhere, and other bodies which are not regulated at all: the Notaries Society, the Society of Scrivener Notaries and the Society of Licensed Conveyancers. One of the few sensible things that was proposed by a former Lord Chancellor, Chris Grayling, one of the otherwise more reviled of Lord Chancellors, was a simplification – and deregulation – of this complex regulatory system. He did not achieve his objective.[40] Meanwhile each regulator charges fees, employs administrative staff, human resources managers, public relations advisers and involves the use of many other support services. They interfere, sometimes unfairly or disproportionately, perhaps because they feel the need to show effectiveness, and because of the internal incentives to intervene.[41]

---

[40] Catherine Baksi, *Grayling not giving up on regulatory reform*, Law Society Gazette, 9 July 2014. Nor did the Solicitors Regulatory Authority which proposed regulatory reform of solicitors, but allegedly with no sense of what the SRA itself wanted to achieve nor what it intended to replace the then current arrangements with, see Desmond Hudson, *Breaking the covenant of trust*, Law Society Gazette, 30 June 2014.

[41] For example the Solicitors Regulation Authority was severely criticised for its oppressive conduct in cases in 2016 (for example a 79-year-old solicitor who was winding-up his practice was referred for prosecution because in the course of winding-up he had not made transfers he should have done to client account of £25, £100 and £636; on appeal the Solicitors Disciplinary Tribunal took mercy on him) (Nick Hilborne, *SDT questions prosecution of solicitor with almost 50 years of exemplary service*, Legal Futures, 11 January 2016). For similar cases see *SRA v Hemmings* Case No 11283–2014 and *RA v McDonald* reported by Dan Bindman, *Legal Futures*, 6 May 2016; The Disciplinary Tribunal Panel of the Institute and Faculty of Actuaries penalised one of its members because he had not properly told the Institute that he was not subject to continuing professional development obligations; it was not an easy thing for him to understand because the CPD rules changed three or four times over two years. In the end on appeal he was mostly discharged of liability but required to pay £16,000 plus VAT in regulator's costs, even though he was no longer in practice, a grotesque outcome (*The Institute and Faculty of Actuaries, v Mr Michael James Asher AFA*, Appeal Tribunal of the Institute and Faculty of Actuaries, 3 December 2015). See also Martin Donald Binns FIA, Disciplinary Tribunal Panel, 15 February 2016 (minor trivial VAT issues). For absurd requirements on the provision of toilets in cafes see *The Queen on the application of Kingston Upon Hull City Council v Secretary of State for Business Innovation and Skills and the Council of the City of Newcastle upon Tyne and Greggs PLC*, [2016] EWHC 1064 (Admin) arguing about the application of the Regulatory Enforcement and Sanctions Act 2008. The Pensions Regulator fines people for not telling it they are not subject to their requirements on auto-enrolment into pension schemes, *Automatic enrolment: Compliance and enforcement*, The Pensions Regulator, *Quarterly bulletin* 1 April – 30 June 2016.

4.1.6 Reduction in Number of Regulators

One attempt in the UK to reduce the number of quangos, which was a key plank of the UK 2010 Coalition Government manifesto, may have resulted from populist thinking but was nonetheless sincere. The policy-maker's intention was to try to reduce the degree of government, rather than the machinery of government, but the effort was criticised for lacking strategic thinking.[42] The policy was found characteristically hard to apply, especially since there was no personal accountability for its implementation; the eventual reforms under the Public Bodies Act were criticised not only by the Select Committee on Public Administration, but also by the National Audit Office.[43]

Following the UK government's 2010 initiative, on the surface there had been a reduction of around 250 public bodies;[44] but much if not most if that achievement seemed to have been either window dressing, merger of one body into another, or recapture and adsorption by a governing department. Paradoxically where a quango is reintegrated into departments the continuing regulatory obligations if any are closer to government and subject to the normal checks and balances, and increased accountability. The centralisation of control of spending on quangos within the Cabinet Office may have made it difficult in practice for quangos to manage their business efficiently because of increased bureaucracy and longer reporting lines. Confusingly the other reporting lines are non-standard: it could be the department, the Cabinet Office or Parliament direct, or sometimes, in practice, no one, although judicial review, i.e. limited court control of their activities, applies to all.

4.1.7 Competition in Regulation

One way to make regulation less oppressive might paradoxically be to increase the number of regulators, and so introduce competition in

---

[42] *Smaller government: shrinking the Quango State*, House of Commons, Public Administration Select Committee, HC 537, 2011. Cf Katherine Dommett, Matthew Flinders, Chris Skelcher and Katherine Tonkiss, *Did they read before burning? The Coalition and quangos*, [2014] (85) Political Quarterly 133–142.

[43] National Audit Office, *Progress on public bodies reform*, HC (2013–2014).

[44] National Audit Office, *Progress on public bodies reform*, HC (2013–2014). This is nothing new. A former UK Prime Minister, Mrs Thatcher, said she abolished 436 public bodies, speech December 1979, although later studies suggested that actually more bodies had been created, see Matthew Flinders, *MPs and icebergs: Parliament and delegated governance*, [2004] 57(4) Parliamentary Affairs.

regulation, or at least between regulators. There is no consensus as to whether competition in regulation is a beneficial thing. Regulators argue that having competing regulators promotes a race to the bottom by organisations anxious to attract clients, and that regulatory arbitrage is not a public good. Consumers might agree, at least in relation to having only one body to complain to. But there is also evidence that competition can promote efficiency in regulation. For example, solicitors may now register with the Bar Council, which is cheaper, quicker and simpler, rather than the Solicitors Regulation Authority. The SRA does not suggest that the Bar Council has lower standards. Similarly, until 1971, in Manchester the now disbanded Salford Hundred Court of Record maintained a High Court jurisdiction in competition with the Manchester High Court, with a rule book a few pages long compared with the 3200 pages of the high court rules, and with lower complaint (writ) fees. Its standards of justice were seemingly identical.

In any event, with or without competition, it is unclear is whether there is any accepted way in which to measure the efficiency or efficacy of regulators. Certainly the public seems unclear about the added value if any;[45] and conventional measures of efficiency seem not to work.[46]

4.1.8 Governance of Regulation and Regulators

The control of these bodies has posed difficult constitutional dilemmas, in particular the question of accountability. On the one hand, regulators are intended to be independent of government (the clue is in the title: 'non-departmental') and provide greater transparency than central government can or does offer.[47] That is why they were established. They operate as a fire-break between consumer and government and can recruit decent expertise on salaries higher than the civil service can provide. Yet it seems as hard to have off-balance-sheet government as it was for banks to have off-balance-sheet sub-prime mortgages. The reason is that when things go wrong (flooding in 2014 was the responsibility of the Environment Agency, but government ministers were nonetheless required to go walking through sewage in wellingtons; immigration in 2013 was the

---

[45] Martin Blaxall and Rob Sheldon, *Out of sight*, Utility Week, 22 February 2008.

[46] See e.g. Deloitte, *The cost of regulation study*, Financial Services Authority and Financial Services Practitioner Panel, 2006.

[47] *Who's accountable? Relationships between Government and arm's length bodies*, House of Commons, Public Administration Select Committee, First Report HC 110, 10 November 2014.

responsibility of the Border Agency until it was recalled back into the Home Office) in the end the government itself is called to account.

In theory in the UK the Cabinet Office oversees all such bodies; in practice this is challenging, especially as their governing legislation usually makes them reportable (belying their notional independence) to their creating department. They also have different constitutional establishments; as mentioned above they can operate as a ministerial department (Cabinet Office), an executive agency (Rural Payments Agency), a non-ministerial department (Ofsted, Food Standards Agency), a non-departmental public body (executive form) (Health and Safety Executive), a non-departmental public body (advisory form) (Veterinary Products Committee), a non-departmental public body (tribunal form) (The Valuation Tribunal), or a non-departmental public body (independent monitoring board) (statutory bodies attached to prisons).

Select committees opportunistically review the work of regulators when there are public concerns.

4.1.9 Regulator's Charter

In practice where regulators are established by legislation, the legislation itself will invariably contain some checks and balances, and rules of procedure may be developed by the regulator in due course. In the UK the Department for Business Innovation and Skills and the Better Regulation Delivery Office produce an outline Regulators' Code which proved a useful first start for some regulators. It sets out in a few pages some well-meaning basic principles:

1 Regulators should carry out their activities in a way that supports those they regulate to comply and grow.
2 Regulators should provide simple and straightforward ways to engage with those they regulate and hear their views.
3 Regulators should base their regulatory activities on risk.
4 Regulators should share information about compliance and risk.
5 Regulators should ensure clear information, guidance and advice is available to help those they regulate meet their responsibilities to comply.
6 Regulators should ensure that their approach to their regulatory activities is transparent.

The code seems little more than a statement of motherhood and apple pie, and in any event its implementation by regulators seems uneven. In the pensions arena for example the three regulators offer three different responses. The Pensions Regulator mentions, in a hard-to-find section of its website, that its policy is to comply with the Code. The Financial Conduct Authority ignores the Code, and publishes its own principles – in which it sets out obligations of its subjects rather than itself. The Pension Protection Fund makes no reference to any code of principles at all, and its board contains no members with any practical experience of pensions governance. Other regulators apply one law to its regulated persons and another to themselves. For example, the Financial Conduct Authority fined Deutsche Bank £163M for poor money laundering controls, whilst doing nothing to prevent fraud by criminals opening fraudulent bank accounts.[48] Similarly the Information Commissioner's Office proposed to fine 11 charities for breaching the Data Protection Act, having already fined the British Heart Foundation and the RSPCA for breaches. Charities of course do not have shareholders or make profits; they have beneficiaries, so it was dogs and heart patients (and 11 other kinds of suffering people) who were in practice paying the fines. The ICO self-reported 14 breaches, some of them serious by its own standards, committed by itself, but with no fines being imposed, and with no damning (or any) press releases being issued. Instead, without telling anyone, it ordered itself to take action to prevent further breaches.[49]

4.1.10   Governing Boards

Most regulators have boards the majority of which are non-executive, often populated with individuals of distinction, though not necessarily in the area of activity which the regulator is involved with. Their function is to provide an oversight of the organisation, perhaps appoint the officers, and add experience to encourage its better functioning. In practice the selection of the members of boards in certain sectors seem to suffer

---

[48] John Bakie, *DB fined after $10 billion seeps through money laundering controls*, Global Custodian, 31 January 2017; *Hughes v Royal London* [2016] 033 PBLR (010); [2016] EWHC 319 (Ch); [2016] PLR 069–078, where a pension provider was forced by the courts applying black-letter law to transfer pension rights of a policyholder to a scheme it suspected was fraudulent, with the FCA simply standing by.

[49] Information Commissioner's Office, *Press release*, 30 January 2017; Joe Murphy, *Data watchdog finds itself guilty of 14 breaches of confidentiality laws*, Evening Standard, 3 January 2017. See also Margaret McCartney, *Punishing individuals won't prevent mistakes happening*, [2017] (18 March) British Medical Journal 441.

from the same qualities or lack of them that members of corporate boards suffer from, i.e. that while they may be a safe pair of hands, they also are reluctant or unable to challenge executives.

4.1.11   Reporting Authorities

Different regulators have different chains of command and reporting. As well as a governing board, the Financial Conduct Authority for example in practice reports to the Treasury and thence to Parliament. In practice such supervision is intermittent and limited, so that regulators, which are intended as a matter of policy to be independent of government are left free to pursue their objectives in line with their constitution and their own views. This can make for an uneasy relationship between the governors and the governed – and with government itself. Professor David Nutt was Chairman of the UK government's Advisory Council on the Misuse of Drugs when his approach to research in the classification of harm caused by drugs was criticised by two Home Secretaries despite it being accepted that his conduct was in line with government guidelines. His dismissal was political and following his dismissal most of the members resigned to form a truly independent body, the Independent Scientific Committee on Drugs; reporting to government does not always give true independence even when it is considered one of the criteria for the establishment of the body. The Nutt affair pointed up the dilemma of bodies intended to be non-political needing to have regard to political imperatives, despite in the Nutt case, having to have regard to scientific truths. It was not quite the Galileo story, but there were resonances.[50]

Governance generally of regulators has posed challenges: *quis custos ipsos custodes?* In 2014 the Bank of England hired an eminent barrister Lord Grabiner to investigate its own conduct in connection with the manipulation of the foreign exchange market. He concluded that the Bank of England officials involved were innocent of any misconduct subject to a minor criticism of its chief forex dealer for not reporting to his superiors that there were concerns about the markets. There were press complaints that the Bank had set the terms of the inquiry too narrowly in looking only whether its staff were involved in the failures, not whether it should have

---

[50] David Nutt, *Drugs without the hot air: minimising the harms of legal and illegal drugs*, UIT Cambridge, 2012.

been more aware.[51] Similarly a failure by senior management of the Financial Conduct Authority in a press briefing which would have resulted in severe penalties if carried out by one of its regulated bodies was investigated by an independent solicitor; the report was commissioned and paid for at the request of the body that had possibly committed the breach, which some considered tarnished the independence of the conclusions, however distinguished the reporter.[52] It also creates a certain degree of cynicism when there are different sets of outcomes for regulated and regulator on broadly equivalent facts. Similarly regulators themselves produced a report into the failure of a major UK bank, HBOS, which touched only lightly on their own failures in the collapse of a bank they had been supervising for many years.[53]

4.1.12 Proportionality in Regulation

It is sometimes hard for rules or regulators to be proportionate in their response to those they regulate, having regard for example to their commercial strength, or the gravity of the offence. It can be argued that it would be unfair to treat different groups in different ways, with different costs of doing business, or different outcomes for consumers. This purity of approach is however rare in practice; the financial services industry for example has for some time had a different way of treating professional and retail customers; and electricity power supply companies charge smaller and poorer customers more than they do larger customers. Similarly, it is possible that financial institutions are excessively regulated, since even

---

[51] Jesse Norman MP, *Self-criticism is a habit the Bank of England has to learn*, Financial Times, 26 May 2015. Higher standards were adopted in three other inquiries for example: in a BBC inquiry into sexual abuses committed by a BBC presenter Jimmy Savile, the inquiry by Mr Justice Leveson into the role of the press and the Bingham Inquiry (by the Bank of England) into the failure of Bank and Credit and Commerce International.

[52] Simon Davis, *Report of the inquiry into the events of 27/28 March 2014 relating to the press briefing of information in the Financial Conduct Authority's 2014/15 Business Plan*, Clifford Chance, 20 November 2014.

[53] See e.g. John Kay, *The HBOS collapse offers a lesson on the winner's curse*, Financial Times, 25 November 2015. PRA and FCA, *The failure of HBOS plc (HBOS): a report by the Financial Conduct Authority (FCA) and the Prudential Regulation Authority (PRA)*, November 2015, especially Part 4, which lists the considerable resources devoted by regulators, and the imposition of many benchmarks and tests, in the years before the corporate failure, and fails to raise the obvious question of whether regulation can ever be effective, and if not, what should be its role.

small companies in the sector are regarded as systemically important with consequential over-intrusive levels of supervision.[54]

Nor indeed does regulation always appear to be necessary. For 40 years tattooing was outlawed in New York, which is not to say no tattooing took place; it simply took place illegally. In the 1960s a tattoo artist, Fred Grossman (aka Coney Island Freddie) sued the city for illegitimately crushing his business. (Mike Bakaty, 'the founder of Fineline Tattoo and an East Village tattoo legend', who died in 2014, told a journalist that Mr Grossman felt that the Health Department's motive was to 'clean up the city' before showing it off at the 1964 World's Fair.) Mr Grossman lost at first instance, then lost again on appeal. A state appellate judge Aron Steuer ruled that the city had the right to decide what was healthy behaviour and what was not. Furthermore, he noted, 'the decoration, so-called, of the human body by tattoo designs is, in our culture, a barbaric survival, often associated with a morbid or abnormal personality.' One of the other appeal judges, Samuel Rabin, dissented, saying that 'the testimony of the defendants' medical experts indicates that the practice of tattooing can be safe, if properly conducted in accordance with appropriate principles of asepsis. That being so, I am of the opinion that the outright prohibition of the practice of tattooing is an unwarranted extension of the police power and therefore is invalid.' This was clearly medically correct, but it was societally unacceptable. The tattoo ban was later lifted in 1997 when it had become obvious that unregulated, underground tattoo studios existed all over New York. The then mayor, Rudy Giuliani, stated, 'There has not been a single documented case of Hepatitis B in New York City transmitted by tattooing in almost 40 years since the ban was enacted.'[55]

4.1.13   Proportionality in Response

Bruce Hogan was a 54-year-old science teacher. He said following a complaint about his conduct that one day one of the school pupils aged 15 was in the canteen, but not queuing for food. He instructed the pupil to leave, indicating the main door. The pupil made a dash for another door beside him, and careered into Mr Hogan. Once Mr Hogan regained his

---

[54] See e.g. Guy Jubb, *Is there no accounting for management?*, lecture to the Chartered Institute of Management Accountants' President's Conference, 28 October 2015, commented on in Anthony Hilton, *Time to end this 'one size fits all' regulation*, Evening Standard 28 October 2015.

[55] *Grossman v Baumgartner*, 40 Misc.2d 221 (NY Misc 1963); New York Mayor's Office, *Press release*, 12 March 1997. Tattooist licensing is now in force in New York.

balance, he took hold of the pupil's coat and with one hand in the small of his back, walked him to the exit. Once outside, Mr Hogan took hold of the pupil's coat shoulders, admonished him, asked for an apology, which was grudgingly given, and sent on him on his way.

The boy's parents complained to the school, the police were called and took statements from witnesses; he was eventually arrested and charged by the Gloucestershire Constabulary Child Protection Unit, bailed and suspended on full pay by the school. At the trial, the boy complained that he had been grabbed by the throat and pinned against a wall; his friend said that he had been held by the throat for at least a minute, feet six inches above the ground. The case was dismissed. The magistrates at the hearing concluded Mr Hogan's actions were within guidelines and necessary in the circumstances. Until this episode he had had 31 years' unblemished record.[56] What upset Mr Hogan was that the incident reached the magistrates in the first place.

Mr Hogan's case was not an isolated one. The teachers' union dealt with 146 accusations against teachers in 2002, of which three-quarters turned out to be false; another teachers' union dealt with 1600 allegations over 12 years, with 64 convictions and 360 cases outstanding. The figures disclose a very low rate of prosecution, and neither an epidemic of bullying by teachers (there are over 400,000 teachers and around 9 million pupils) nor an epidemic of false accusations. But the pain and anguish to the teachers involved in trivial episodes is immense and the question arises whether there are better ways of dealing with student-teacher episodes than involving the criminal law process, especially where, in schools for example there are extensive records of teacher complaints and there has never been a complaint against a teacher before. It is the disproportionate response to minor incidents that upsets the teachers (and no doubt the pupils) and leads to a defensive teaching pattern. Students in difficult schools can sometimes feel they can control the teachers because teachers although allowed by the rules to use reasonable force in exceptional circumstances to restrain unruly pupils, most if not all teachers feel the fear of accusation of assault hanging over their heads – assaults by pupils on teachers rose from six in 1991 to 42 in 2002.

These figures need to be treated with caution; a rise in accusations does not necessarily mean an increase in bad behaviour by either side of the blackboard divide. But there is no doubt empirically that there is increasing concern by teachers about their exposure to liability; that

[56] *Evening Standard*, 8 September 2003 p3; Richard Savill, *Teacher cleared of assaulting 'lying' pupil*, Daily Telegraph, 22 August 2003.

caution may affect the way in which they manage their charges, and the constraints in their own turn affect the behaviour or lack of it by pupils.

It is always difficult to get the balance right; the question is whether the law and regulation is the right way, short of serious assault, of dealing with pupil/teacher discipline, especially where there are so many other methods of governance, including head teacher supervision, governor councils and other committees. A soft touch approach nonetheless seems hard to achieve, although it can happen in other areas.[57]

Similarly, the safeguarding of patients in NHS hospitals may be a sensible objective as a policy;[58] its implementation in practice however has had foreseeable and unpleasant consequences. Volunteer hospital visitors are now regulated following a report on patient data, but the consequences are uneven:[59]

> A neighbour broke her leg. When I arrived at the hospital, it proved impossible to see her. 'If you don't know which ward she's on we are not allowed to tell you,' said a woman on the front desk. Of course I got in by going through a side door. On the ward there wasn't a nurse in sight to stop me.
>
> This silly secrecy about patient identity or 'safeguarding' is a recent NHS obsession... a patient told me he was going to kill himself when he was discharged, with details of how he was going to do it. When I reported it, a nurse told me it was not my business.
>
> I gave a man with two broken arms a drink, which was on the tray above his bed. This was noticed by a nurse and reported. Shortly afterwards I was told by phone not to come to the hospital anymore because I had 'endangered' a patient and there had to be an inquiry. I was cleared, but warned not to do it again.
>
> ... Confidentiality is coming before care.

4.1.14 Complexity

The checks and balances that the public service need to impose has been a long-running issue. If the checks are too severe, individuals feel embarrassed and exposed; if they are too lax, the press will concentrate on the failures of the system. One area, for example, whether this

---

[57] Weatherbys Bank was established after taking deposits for over 200 years without a banking licence. After a polite inquiry to it from the Bank of England about its status, it applied for and was granted a licence, Christopher Fildes, *A new bank from a very old stable*, Spectator, 9 May 2009. The bank lends out less than half its deposits.

[58] *Report on the Review of Patient-identifiable Information*, Department of Health, December 1997 (the Caldicott Committee).

[59] Jane Kelly, *Rules for loneliness: hospitals are putting NHS data-protection policies above simple humanity*, Spectator, 4 February 2017.

dilemma is mostly sharply pointed is in the issue of means testing of public benefits. The objective of means testing is incontrovertible; it is to ensure that public funds are used to help those worst-off, and are not wasted on those who can well look after themselves.

In practice, however, means testing can involve substantial checking, anomalies and paperwork. Rita Ball wished to claim for a £7 a week reduction on her council tax charge. She needed to produce savings books, personal identification and details of a small US pension. She was required in the absence of a driving licence to produce a passport. Many individuals, especially those who are claiming, lack these basic samples of identification.[60] In due course it was expected that over half of the UK's pensioners would need to be means tested, involving substantial expense (although a later change in the state pension system should now avoid much of this). The tests can be complex; savings of over £6000 for example disqualify a claim – but mortgage payments can be taken into account, even though this is often forgotten by advisers. The Pensions Credit involves over 11 million people in means testing; in 2001 there were 23 different benefits for elderly people, 16 of which were connected to each other in 30 different ways. Besides the state pension there were 35 such benefits. Assumptions as to the value of assets are arbitrary – anyone with savings of £20,000 for example is assumed to be earning 10 per cent on the savings, involving a disincentive to save. Around 65,000 pensioners received less than £4 a week in Pension Credit – the cost of the administration of the benefit. Around 12,000 received less than £1 a week. The claim form was 12 pages long, with 16 pages of explanation. People could claim by phone, but needed to have to hand details of savings, NI number and pension information. Other benefits, most notably the Attendance Allowance which gave funds to help with nursing and attendance costs, were hard to complete.

The system needed to maintain a balance between paying benefits to older people, using a system which is simple and cheap to claim under, yet ensuring that there was no fraud on the state. An alternative social security system, universal benefits, has sought to reduce the paperwork, but is as yet untested. Social security rules have become too hard for most people to understand or apply and what has not become apparent is whether the incidence of fraud would be a cost worth paying for simpler procedures, or the closing of *de minimis* claims which involve payments worth less than the cost of administration would be unfair.

---

[60] Nina-Montagu-Smith, *Nightmare on Benefits Street leaves pensioners humiliated*, Daily Telegraph, 18 June 2004.

4.1.15   The Behaviour of Regulators

One complaint of the regulatory system frequently levelled is that there is every incentive for a regulator to increase liability, and few to minimise it. One instance of this was that experienced by an independent financial adviser regulated by the now defunct Financial Services Authority (although its soul lives on elsewhere). An IFA was subjected to an enforcement action by the FSA. As part of the process the FSA:

1 Sent confidential information relating to the case by courier which left the envelope with a neighbour.
2 The courier arrived after 10 pm, disturbing both the neighbour and the IFA's wife not used to helmeted individuals appearing at that time of night.
3 The package contained two discs containing 5000 pages of a Preliminary Investigation Report.
4 The information was not encrypted, despite the fact its publication could have damaged the reputation of the wife and the IFA husband.
5 Did not check that the IFA had access to a printer that could cope with this quantity of information.
6 Left it to the last minute to send the information. It was sent on the afternoon of 31 August, nominally giving the IFA 28 days to respond, but in practice giving two hours for the IFA to print and collate the papers.

While the FSA Complaints Commissioner reprimanded the FSA for its behaviour, there was no criticism of the sheer of material and or any suggestion that such a report should better have been written succinctly and simply, or that the time demands were impractical. The length of the submission might have been perhaps because of legal obligations, but there seems to be no obligation on a regulator to present information in a simple, timely and balanced fashion (as there might similarly be, for example, on an IFA presenting information to his client).[61]

4.1.16   Rulebooks

Rulebooks rarely reduce in size. If printed out on A4 paper, the Financial Conduct Authority handbook for example would stack over eight feet high. Its content been criticised incessantly[62] but its length and complexity

---

[61] Tony Hazell, *Making contact*, Financial Adviser, 19 May 2011
[62] Ruth Gillbe, *APFA tells FCA to streamline '8 foot' rule book*, FT Adviser, 2 September 2014. The Director-General of the Association of Professional Financial Advisers said: 'If it wants to encourage innovation, if it wants to allow people to do things [it should review it], just

seems to expand inexorably, and simplification is nowhere on the agenda. In banking the situation is similar; the Basel Accords are non-statutory arrangements for ensuring banks are properly managed; the first version dedicated to bank insurance, Basel I, was emerged as 18 pages long in the US and 13 pages in the UK. By the time it reached version III, the domestic legislation exceeded 1000 pages in both countries.[63] The response to the Great Depression was a regulatory one; the US introduced the Glass-Steagall Act in 1933 with 37 pages, most of them dedicated to better governance of financial institutions. The response to the Great Recession in the States was the Dodd-Frank Act 2010. It is 848 pages long, and at the time of writing it was expected that there would be an additional 30,000 pages of additional subsidiary rules (equivalent to statutory instruments in the UK context). By 2014 about 8500 pages had been completed; the initial rules were also continually adjusted and amended.[64] The equivalent EU regulatory blanket is expected to amount to around 60,000 pages once completed.[65]

4.1.17   Number and Size of Regulators

Previous chapters have explored the profusion of regulators – and their size and power to intervene ostensibly on behalf of the consumer. There is no point in repeating that here, except to observe that it is hard for regulators once established to diminish in size. The Pensions Regulator, for example, was expected to waste away in line with the expected demise of the defined benefit schemes it was established to recite the last rites over. In fact it expanded its role in defined contribution pension scheme systems, where regulation was not anticipated to be required because of the existing checks and balances of contract and trust law. And reductions where announced are not necessarily real reductions; in 2016 for example the Pensions Regulator announced a 17 per cent reduction in its spend over

---

in terms of streamlining it . . . I know there's a lot of European legislation requirements in there where it's gold plated . . . you shouldn't have a rule book that is eight foot high? How can anyone read that?'

[63] Andy Haldane, *The Dog and the Frisbee*, Speech, Bank of England, 31 August 2012. Even Andy Haldane would have been surprised that just one of the EU Directives, the Markets in Financial Instruments Directive, MiFID II, resulted in the production of 1.4 million paragraphs of rules, Philip Stafford, *Markets break out in sweat as new rules loom*, Financial Times, 5 July 2017.

[64] In 2017 the Financial Choice Act was passed under the Trump administration, intended to undo significant parts of Dodd-Frank.

[65] Andy Haldane, *The Dog and the Frisbee*, Speech, Bank of England, 31 August 2012.

the following five years. The actual figures in its five-year plan indicated that while the number was right, it was misleading. In summary, the gross numbers were as follows:

	2015–2016 Budget	2015–2016 Actual	2016–2017 Budget	2017–2018 Budget	2018–2019 Budget
Total costs (£)	64,174	76,081	79,527	85,379	66,898
% increase/decrease on previous year		+18.5	+24	+4.8	−20
Staff numbers	480	480	547	607	576
% increase/decrease on previous year		0	+14	+11	−7

The later years did involve a reduction, but only against an earlier increase. The baseline of the original expected cost of tPR was around £10M a year when it started in 2005.[66] It had expanded its costs eight-fold in 14 years not only in relation to defined contribution schemes, but also in relation to a new quasi-state scheme known as auto-enrolment, so there was some justification for the increase, but it came at a time when government was attempting to shrink the machinery of the state as a whole by about 30 per cent.

4.1.18 Fines

One trend in recent years has been the growth in fines imposed by regulators; around £200B of fines were paid by financial institutions for example in 2014.[67] Many of the infractions involved were significant; they involved money laundering, rate-rigging, sanctions-busting and mis-selling of subprime mortgages and bonds during the credit bubble.

The level of penalties at first sight seem not unreasonable; the institutions involved made substantial profits out of inappropriate behaviour.

---

[66] *Corporate Pensions Plan 2016–2019*, The Pensions Regulator, April 2016; One well-known economist has illustrated how figures can be presented in this way, see Tim Harford, *How politicians poisoned statistics*, Financial Times Magazine, 16 April 2016.

[67] Gillian Tett, *Regulatory revenge risks scaring investors away*, [2014] Financial Times, 29 August; Roger McCormick (London School of Economics and Political Science), CCP Foundation, Conduct Costs Project, 2013.

And there is no doubt that the institutions' behaviour was ethics-light. The fines are however in effect paid for by consumers and shareholders rather than managers and directors who were the principal beneficiaries of the infractions and the regulators, who broadly stood idly by whilst the activity was openly conducted, benefit from the imposition of fines because it elevates their own importance. It is also easier to impose regulatory penalties than impose criminal penalties, because the burden of proof is lower, and the power to cause harm to the business higher. Thirty years before, however, the authorities successfully prosecuted savings and loan officials and several hundreds went to prison. The behavioural drivers of the fining system and the counter-productive elements has been explored by Professor Macey at Yale who pointed out that US Securities and Exchange Commission normally seeks only low-hanging fruit, and has a propensity for targeting more junior employees on whom to impose sanctions:[68]

> The SEC appears to have a mission. Unfortunately, its mission appears to be that of advancing its own agenda, including its own budget and power, along with the careers of its most highly placed executives. New SEC Commissioners focus more on trying to improve the Commission's status in Washington instead of trying to improve the Commission itself...Other Commissioners spend more time explaining the SEC's failings and in suing small firms and new entrants than they do on the important issues of the day. Worst of all, the SEC has played an active role in undermining the ability of firms to maintain their reputations and in destroying the incentives of firms to build reputations in the first place. Certainly, having a great reputation was a never a way to impress the SEC because the SEC sues all market participants with equal fervor.

In a later review of the book, it was observed:[69]

> A vast profusion of laws, regulations and direct government interventions has provided a substitute for reputation, albeit a toxic and inadequate one...requirements for ratings and audits, for instance, are now set by regulation, not the market, and an entirely new Federal agency, the Consumer Financial Protection Agency, has been created to expand this approach in retail finance...there is [now] little need for financial intermediaries to invest in their reputations. It is, however, important for them to invest in regulators, whose own career prospects are increasingly tied to their ability to advance rules that are both vague and highly technical, as this increases

---

[68] Jonathan R. Macey, *The death of corporate reputation: how integrity has been destroyed on Wall Street*, Yale University Press, 2013, Chapter 11.

[69] *Broken: recollections of a bygone era when the market enforced good behaviour*, The Economist, July 13 2013.

their value both within government and to potential private employers. The system is now fundamentally flawed. Those who propose even more regulations will only ensure more damage.

The conclusion was that legal risk was beginning to replace credit risk as the key uncertainty, which raised questions about the investibility of the banks, in other words whether the legal risks are so high as to make investment in bank shares not worth the candle, and therefore reduced the availability of banking facilities. The imposition of high if not excessive penalties has had an unintended consequence.

In former times, to avoid taxpayers being landed with the bill for supporting a systemically important bank for example, good banks would be persuaded by regulators to absorb a failed bank. With globalisation, and the size of systemically important banks, this is much harder if not impossible. But fining as a control mechanism seems unhelpful and perhaps counter-productive. In August 2014 Bank of America paid $16.7bn to resolve allegations that it misled investors in its mortgage-backed securities. It seemed grotesquely unfair; the allegations related not to the activities of Bank of America but those of companies it had acquired after the crash, Merrill Lynch and Countrywide, companies which it had been persuaded to take over by the authorities. But other regulators, in this case the Department of Justice, the Securities and Exchange Commission and six state attorneys-general 'had a splendid opportunity to put all four feet in this potentially lucrative trough'.[70]

4.1.19   Competition

Banking understandably faced significant criticism following the financial collapses in 2008; the increase in regulation as a consequence has been described above. Some of the changes have however been regarded more as helping regulators rather than consumers. EU regulations, following the US reforms, affected the ability of banks to lend, reducing capacity from €45T to €15T – compared for example with the then impact of €1T of quantitative easing. Whilst the EU rules followed those of the US, so that banks should not hold assets equivalent to more than the value of the economy, the fact was that the US had long had alternative sources

---

[70] John Plender, *Financial reforms will make the next failure even messier*, Financial Times, 2 September 2014. Similarly JP Morgan Chase was penalised for the behaviour of Washington Mutual before it was absorbed in 2008.

of finance, whereas the Europeans depended on banking.[71] There seems
to be consensus that despite exhortations to the contrary, regulation can
work to the disadvantage of competition.[72]

4.1.20   Regulatory Behaviour and Over-Zealousness

Regulators understandably wish to cover every avenue, for safety's sake.
There are however dangers, appreciated by regulators themselves. Following the 2008 financial crash, European regulators understandably resolved
to ensure that such defaults could not happen again. Nearly 10 years later
it was appreciated they may have overdone it:[73]

> [We have come to] the realisation that while we want stability, we don't
> want the stability of the graveyard. That without risk there is no growth.
> And it is that which first led me to reflect that in various areas we need to
> think again . . .
>
> . . . The problem comes if a number of different regulators or supervisors
> are all taking an equally risk-averse approach. Then the cumulative impact
> of a series of micro-prudential judgments can itself become a source of
> macro-prudential risk . . . As a regulator . . . you should seek to avoid unnec-
> essary conflict between the regulator and the regulated . . . Keep it simple. A
> lot of regulation is so complicated that only a handful of people can possi-
> bly understand [it]. It's like some priesthood speaking in a special language
> that is beyond the comprehension of mere mortals. But complex legislation
> is good only for lawyers and compliance officers. It is bad for values-based
> leadership. It weakens individual responsibility. It leads people to ask 'can
> I get away with it?' rather than 'is it the right thing to do?' It eats away at
> trust in law making.
>
> Try to legislate in a way that can accommodate the rapid pace of techno-
> logical change. Most legislation is, by its nature, backward-looking, paper-
> based, related to old products and challenges.
>
> A huge number of responses . . . called for a more proportionate applica-
> tion of our rules. There's a strong sense that rules could be getting in the

---

[71] Simon Samuels, *Withering regulations will make for shrivelled banks.*, Financial Times,
13 January 2015. Conventional economic policy would have been to break up the banks
to make for improved competition, but regulators prefer larger and fewer institutions as a
client base.

[72] See e.g. Guy Jubb, *Is there no accounting for management?*, lecture to the Chartered Institute
of Management Accountants' President's Conference, 28 October 2015, commented on in
Anthony Hilton, *Time to end this 'one size fits all' regulation*, Evening Standard 28 October
2015.

[73] *Keynote speech by Commissioner Jonathan Hill at Bruegel on the Call for Evidence: 'The
impact of the EU regulatory framework for financial services'*, European Commission, Brussels, 12 July 2016.

way of diversity. That they're not attuned enough to companies' business
models, to their risk profiles and to their size . . .
     The volume of data collected and exchanged between nation authorities
and the European supervisory authorities has drastically increased. That's
clear. Less clear is whether it's all essential.

4.1.21   Scepticism in Relation to the Effect of Regulation

Whilst governments are keen to cut back on regulations, and concerns are
expressed from time to time in international organisations about the governance of regulators and their powers of enforcement, it it is rare to see
general doubts about the efficacy of regulations or the positing of alternatives to regulation.[74] It does happen occasionally but there is virtually no
evidence of any success in diminishing the role of regulation in practice;
indeed such evidence as there is suggests the opposite.

4.2   Regulatory Creep

One issue that has been concerning policymakers over the years is that of
'regulatory creep'. The term is used in practice in different ways, but it can
include a growth of regulation beyond that originally intended. Regulatory
creep seems to be one of those inexorable laws of regulation; it may include
an understanding that[75]

• once a regulator has been established it is hard to dissolve it;
• once a regulation has been issued, it is hard to repeal it;
• a regulator always finds new things to do; and
• a regulatory budget is hard to reduce.

There have been occasions when a regulator has been abolished, rarely
at its own request, but such disappearance may simply involve a merger
of one regulator into another, perhaps to form a super-regulator. Once
formed, a regulator seems adept at finding reasons for justifying its continued existence, and expanding its role, and few have sunset clauses in
their constitution. The attempt to reduce their number has already been
described above.
     One example which typifies both problems of expansion and of conti-
nuity is that of Ofcom, the UK communications regulator. Itself the merger

---

[74] *Regulatory policy in perspective: a reader's companion to the OECD regulatory policy outlook
2015*, OECD, 2015.
[75] *Avoiding Regulatory Creep*, Better Regulation Task Force, October 2004.

of five prior regulators (Broadcasting Standards Commission, Independent Television Commission, Oftel, the Radio Authority and the Radiocommunications Agency), it developed (within days of its inception) an additional bureaucratic overlay. For example, in 2004 the *Daily Telegraph*, one of Britain's major broadsheet newspapers, seemed to be for sale. Its circulation was then around 1M a day (in a population of around 60M). In January 2004 Ofcom, which was charged with ensuring the avoidance of monopoly or oligopoly in newspapers, issued documents setting out how officials proposed to review possible purchasers of the newspaper. It did not explore whether the public needed protection against concentration of ownership – or more pointedly whether an owner was a proper person to take control of an existing newspaper, given that anyone could start a new newspaper without intervention. The work that it does in managing the radio spectrum, where there is a finite resource, and the misuse of which might cause havoc, is more evident.[76]

Nonetheless even today, Ofcom and the Secretary of State for Business, Energy and Industrial Strategy have the power to intervene in media mergers if they believe it is in the public interest. The regulator made it clear in the *Daily Telegraph* case that it would seek a hitherto unprecedented amount of information from interested parties.[77] Newspaper groups looking to merge would have to give details about the number of column inches devoted to advertising, news, sport and features. Proprietors would have to detail the level of contact they have with their editors and would-be owners would have to serve notice of any plans to alter the level of contact between senior management and editorial staff. It sought to know the likely level of involvement of proprietors in editorial decisions and the track record of editorial interference as well as the political allegiance of would-be proprietors. The regulator required information about plans to alter staff numbers after an acquisition. Broadcasters who make a bid had to detail the proportion range and cost of programmes made outside an area of England surrounded by a motorway, the M25, and of any arrangements to ensure the accurate presentation of news pre-and post-merger. It sought information on reporting techniques and journalistic standards as well as evidence of complaints.

---

[76] Although see Thomas Winslow Hazlett, *The political spectrum: the tumultuous liberation of wireless technology from Herbert Hoover to the smartphone*, Yale University Press, 2017 which suggests that the need to control access to the radio spectrum is largely unnecessary.
[77] Stephen Glover, *We have never been closer to state control of the press*, Spectator, 10 January 2004.

None of this applied to cases where a newspaper starts up from scratch.[78] There is no need in most Western democracies to seek a licence to publish a newspaper. Nor is there statutory monitoring of current standards of newspapers, such as the *Sun* or *Star* or *Daily Express* or *Daily Mail*, some of whom can be considered to practice alternative truths. The question, which the regulator did not address, was why an existing newspaper, which sold copies more on the basis of its quality rather than its entertainment, should be so affected – and in so doing of course affect its value in the market. In other circumstances the requirements of the regulator would be seen as sinister or excessive. In this case it was argued by observers that it intervened because the regulator felt it had a need to justify its existence. The question for policy makers remains whether what a regulator is doing is necessary or proportionate.[79]

Ofcom's mission statement was rather different; it declares that it is intended to promote choice and competition and support the need for innovators, creators and investors. A challenge for organisations such as Ofcom is that the skills and inclinations of the people involved in applying regulations are inevitably not those which apply in business. Business people take risks, and are prepared to make mistakes. If an initiative fails – like a new kind of washing machine that people find too expensive – businesses have wasted money (often other people's), time and resource, but creative destruction is necessary for the capitalist system, and competition, to thrive. It can become excessive – through the emergence of a monopoly, for example – although even monopolies in time become self-regulating as newer products emerge which may outflank those of the monopoly. That question that was not explored, in the *Daily Telegraph* case, i.e. whether what it was considering allowed for the evolution of a product – and one which might fail. Regulators inevitably are driven to try to constrain failure in the subject of their regulation; and it informs why, for example, a press regulator concerns itself on the issue of whether an owner of a newspaper intervenes in its editorial policy. Experience suggests that some of the best newspapers in earlier times flourished under egomaniacal owners. A newspaper, or at least a news distributor, can be established nowadays especially with modern technology by almost anyone. If a paper does not

---

[78] And has not been since the end of the seventeenth century, see e.g. Licensing of the Press Act 1662.

[79] Raymond Snoddy, *Media mergers face red-tape hurdle*, The Times, 6 January 2004; www .radioauthority.org.uk; *Ofcom guidance for the public interest test for media mergers*, January 2004, www.ofcom.org.uk/codes_guidelines/ofcom_codes_guidancve/pi_test.

attract readers it will fail, but it is hard for a regulator to ensure success. Issues of public protection are broadly dealt with by defamation laws. Similar criticisms can be made of the regulation of broadcasting. When the spectrum was limited it might have been that a regulator was needed to ensure the available space was reserved for quality broadcasts. Regulation today has not stopped the proliferation of seemingly identical music radio stations, and most listeners through the internet have access to thousands of stations around the world, few of them regulated. The function of a regulator like Ofcom has increasingly become otiose,[80] but it is hard to find an Ofcom document discussing whether it has outlived its purpose.[81]

4.2.1   Creep and Guidelines

ELIZABETH TURNER: Wait! You have to take me to shore. According to the Code of the Order of the Brethren...

BARBOSSA: First, your return to shore was not part of our negotiations nor our agreement so I must do nothing. And secondly, you must be a pirate for the pirate's code to apply and you're not. And thirdly, the code is more what you'd call 'guidelines' than actual rules. Welcome aboard the *Black Pearl*, Miss Turner.[82]

Regulators (and governments) frequently issue guidelines. In some ways this is a sensible alternative to prescription; it is hard in many cases to set down hard rules for complex and varied circumstances. The downside is that it tends to reverse the burden of proof; a guideline which is not followed can in practice be used to raise a civil suit, and the defendant will need to show a paper trail that the guidance was considered and a decision taken not to follow the guidance in the particular circumstances and for particular reasons, which could be challenged by either civil litigants or regulators. In some ways it improves governance; in other ways it increases paperwork.[83]

---

[80] Incidentally once the merger of the five regulators took place, ostensibly in order to save money, the new regulator recruited an additional 300 staff. It was a quintessential example of regulatory creep, see below.

[81] See e.g. Andrew Child, *Tackling a business burden: red tape remains a serious challenge, especially for small and mid-sized companies*, Financial Times, 10 May 2011. In relation to economic regulators, see David Currie and John Cubbin, *Regulatory creep and regulatory withdrawal: why regulatory withdrawal is feasible and necessary*, City University, March 2002.

[82] Film: *Pirates of the Caribbean: The Curse of the Black Pearl* (2003).

[83] Margaret McCartney, *Crossing the guideline*, FT Weekend, 25 April 2009.

4.2.2   Creep and Gold-Plating

It is inevitable that draftsmen attempt to ensure that no one can find a way round the rules they are trying to promulgate. English judges are celebrated for attempting to constrain the interpretative skills of the courts and the layman. One area, which is a source of constant comment, is the way in which the UK, in particular, implements the rather broad prescriptions of EU law. This allegation of 'gold-plating', often strongly refuted by UK civil servants, does seem to carry an element of truth in it. The EU issues approximately 3400 regulations and directives a year, many if not most of which require transposing into UK law. One study[84] examined 88 separate EU directives and concluded 'The average UK relative elaboration ratio for all 100 directives is 334 per cent i.e. the UK adds two and one-third as much verbiage, and perhaps regulation, as it needs to.' A directive on the labelling of air conditioners, 2409 words in the original Brussels version, became 7504 words when enacted in the UK; the French version, by comparison, totalled 1061 words. And for every 10 EU directives, the UK has to issue 26 legal documents, partly a consequence of devolution.

This kind of survey is inevitably imperfect. Sometimes the opportunity is taken of the implementation of EU legislation to fine-tune the UK provisions or even consolidate them. The way in which UK legislation is expressed, nowadays sometimes including explanatory words, may tend to additional length. UK drafting techniques invariably are more formal than those of the rest of Europe. But even taking the UK cultural idiosyncrasies into account, the disparities seem large. And the way in which the money laundering controls are applied, for example, have become oppressive. Anyone who has ever tried to open a bank account will be aware of the difficulties, and feel with some justification that there is a disproportionate effort involved in what should be a simple process – all the more aggravating where the matter is a transfer from another bank for example, where the process had already been gone through.[85]

Similar creep applies in other jurisdictions; in the US when the Glass-Steagall Act was introduced in the 1930s it was around 200 pages long,

---

[84] British Chambers of Commerce, 2004: Gabriel Rozenberg, *Whitehall applies EU directives at length*, Times, 19 April 2004.

[85] *Avoiding Regulatory Creep*, Better Regulation Task Force, 2004, p30 and p33 (The Financial Services Authority's money laundering theme): 'The Financial Services Authority has this year fined the Royal Bank of Scotland £1.75m for having inadequate anti-money laundering procedures in place. Last year it fined Abbey National £2.3M. It said that these fines

and operated, mostly successfully, for around 70 years. It was dismantled piecemeal over the years and eventually repealed in 1999 (which allegedly contributed to the credit crunch of 2007). Its replacement, the Dodd-Frank Act, enacted in 2010 was 2319 pages long, with an additional 30,000 pages of regulation intended to follow. Paperwork required to support governance requirements can also be considerable:

> In a secret location in the UK there is a warehouse the size of a football pitch that climbs five stories into the sky. Under its gargantuan roof are more than 3 million boxes and in these boxes are thousands and thousands of files and innumerable documents. The warehouse uses all of the latest security systems and fireproofing to keep the unending rows of records, forms and copies of forms safe. It is a storage facility amassing all of the documents companies need to archive to prove they have complied with a range of regulations and procedures, from accident reports to disciplinary notes, from invoices to parking permits.[86]

4.2.3   Outpacing by Events

Regulations and regulators also struggle to cope with changes in markets and products, sometimes emerging as a response to earlier regulation, using perhaps regulatory arbitrage.

4.2.4   Criminal Records Checking

Following the murder of two schoolgirls, Jessica Chapman and Holly Wells, in the village of Soham in Cambridgeshire in 2002, the government commissioned the Bichard Report[87] in 2004 to consider what might be done to stop such murders ever happening again. The murder had been committed by Ian Huntley, who had by chance been working as a school

---

were for repeated and significant breaches of its money laundering rules. The fines, along-side other contributory factors, seemed to have played a part in creating what the sector refers to as the "fear factor", which in turn has contributed to the over-zealous identity checking that has taken place recently.' Cf its comments on the Proceeds of Crime Act 2002, which carries penalties for a failure to report suspicious transactions to the national Criminal Intelligence Service: 'A lack of clarity about what constitutes "reasonable ground to suspect" that someone is engaged in money laundering combined with a 5 year prison sentence for failure to report its suspicion seems to have contributed, together with other factors, to the over-zealous application of customer identity checks. It has also led to what is known as "defensive reporting" where those regulated submit reports to cover their backs, just in case, as opposed to when there is a genuine suspicion.'

[86] Polly Botsford, *Working to rule*, Law Society Gazette, 23 June 2011.
[87] *The Bichard Inquiry Report*, House of Commons, HC653, 22 June 2004.

caretaker, but at another school, not the school that the victims attended. He might as well have been working in a pub; his position of employment had no bearing on the opportunity to commit the murder. Nonetheless the Report recommended the establishment of a central registry on which could be checked the antecedents of anyone working with children or other sensitive areas.[88]

At the time the outcome seemed not unreasonable; but the implementation of the policy proved largely unworkable – and in most cases would not have operated to prevent the murders that triggered the inquiry. Its scope expanded well beyond the original expectations. The initial legislation, the Safeguarding Vulnerable Groups Act 2006, was intended to manage around 8.5M people who had interaction with children. The number affected in fact rose to 11.3M and later fell again to 9M – although the number actually affected is not known. It was not always easy to work out if an individual needed to be vetted. For 10 years the then quango the Independent Safeguarding Authority (which issued an advertisement which had to be withdrawn claiming that if the Act had been in force at the time the Soham murders would not have occurred) ran training sessions trying to explain who should and should not registered.

The policy of vetting everyone who came into contact with vulnerable people seemed sensible at the time; it was clearly wrong that people convicted of serious relevant offences should have access to children. But the cost, the complexity, the bureaucracy and the unintended consequences even now make it doubtful that the benefits outweigh the burdens. And the minutiae of the rules became absurd. For example, if an aerobics class was advertised as being 'For all ages welcome', then the course leader would have to be checked, even if a very small number of children (or indeed no children) came to the group. Even the government concluded that the vetting policy had created 'public confusion, a fearful workforce and a dysfunctional culture of mistrust between children and adults'.[89] And, it added, 'For too long child protection policy has been developed in haste and in response to individual tragedies, with the well-intentioned though misguided belief that every risk could be mitigated and every loophole closed.'

In fact, thousands of people each year lost their jobs for convictions other than child sex offences, or on the basis of unproven local police

[88] Josie Appleton, *Checking Up: how the coalition's plans to cut back on criminal records have been defeated*, Civitas, October 2014 ISBN 978-1-906837-66-2
[89] *Guidance on the meaning of supervision*, Department of Education, 2012.

information. In 2013/14 there were just short of 4M criminal records checks, around 850,000 on volunteers. Despite attempts to simplify the system, and changing one quango for another (the Disclosure and Barring Service) the cost was around £200, more than before it was simplified, there were 730 people in the service plus it required the time of hundreds of employees in police forces, 300 employees from the computer service support and 3600 bodies who submit checks. Many individuals needed to have several checks made on them, a separate one for each capacity in which they volunteered for example.

The question arose whether the spending of £200M centrally, and several times that by the persons subject to checks, was worth it. Any parent whose child is murdered by a sick or criminal individual would say that no price is too high; on the other hand society might conclude that (1) no one has shown what the benefit has been for the £200M spent and (2) whether the £200M might be spent elsewhere to save more lives, for example in hospitals.[90] It is clear that criminal records checking has not materially added to the safety of the vulnerable at a cost which is sensible, and indeed may have added to a spurious sense of security, since many people who were prepared to work with scout groups and church groups were dissuaded by the bureaucratic requirements, and dangerous individuals but with clean records could give an impression of having been vetted. Most involved in the system know in their hearts that the system needs dismantling, but no one has the political courage raise their head above the parapet and say so, for fear of being accused of being soft on crime. That is partly the fault of the populist press such as the *Daily Mail* and of politicians who find it hard to preserve their integrity and common sense when faced with public outrage, even if confected. The scope and cost of the scheme was eventually halved and the processes much simplified under a later scheme (Disclosure and Barring) but its value remains unproven.

4.2.5   Safety Curtains

London theatres in former times had mainly wooden interiors and, because of the method of stage lighting scenery and of the construction

---

[90] See e.g. Frank Furedi and Jennie Bristow, *Licensed to Hug*, Civitas, 2nd edn, 2010, which suggested that 'one of the adverse consequences was that it assumed that the default position of one human being to another is predatory rather than kindness... the basic mode is not of trust but suspicion. And that means that children who need reassurance through hugs suffer as a consequence.'

of back stage equipment, were profoundly vulnerable to fire. Theatres frequently burned down, often with the audience inside. In 1794 the Drury Lane Theatre in London introduced the first safety curtain, made of iron, which would eventually become a statutory requirement in all large theatres. It also had a large water tank on its roof – a feature that was adopted by other theatres – to extinguish fire in the stage area. The theatre also began to make its scenery more fire-resistant. Today such curtains are compulsory, to seal the audience from the stage, and very expensive. With other fire safety features in operation these days, including fire extinguishers, piped water and hose reels, and sprinklers, it is questionable whether there remains a need for safety curtains. They are expensive to install and expensive to maintain, and while they would contain fires on stage (where the staging machinery can act as a chimney with updraft) it is not clear that their use is still necessary. It is hard however for a local fire authority to dispense with their requirement; public concerns are a force even if the logic is impeccable. A former high-profile Mayor of London, Boris Johnson, reduced the number of fire stations and engines in London following a 40 per cent reduction in fires in London over the previous 10 years, partly driven by improved safety features in buildings and improved technology, yet faced immense political pressure from unions and others to maintain the status quo.[91]

4.3   The Costs of Regulation

Identifying a regulatory cost/benefit analysis process has proved hard. Working out the benefits is marginally easier: regulators will usually have the equivalent of a mission statement, dictated by the governing statute or department. But identifying the success of a regulator remains difficult because it is hard to prove a negative, and there is no double-blind testing of regulation. Even where there has been evident failure, regulators will argue that matters would have been even worse without them. In addition breaches of regulations are given as evidence that there is failure in the market, rather than the actual harm the regulator was intended to avoid. Finally, even though it is often straightforward to identify internal

---

[91] Sir Ken Knight, *Facing the future: findings from the review of efficiencies and operations in fire and rescue authorities in England*, HMSO, May 2013 ISBN 978-1-4098-3887-6. There no longer appears any legal requirement to have a safety curtain in the UK (and it is clearly impractical on non-proscenium theatres) although as a matter of custom theatres that do have them theatrically lower them during intervals.

regulatory costs, it is much more difficult to identify the on-costs, i.e. the costs to the market of responding to regulation.

Nonetheless attempts are made from time to time to explore whether the benefits justify the costs. Many of the studies are necessarily superficial and it seems that a scientific cost-benefit analysis is simply not possible. There are ad hoc studies, but they by and large lack rigour or at least involve rough and ready methodology; one study used the impact assessments attached to legislation as a model, which seems reasonable, and which suggested that the total net cost of major regulations to business approved in the UK between 1998 and 2010 was around £90B.[92] Whatever the real numbers may be, they are significant.

Semi-scientific attempts have been made at quantification. Financial services regulators have commissioned research to show that their efforts are cost-effective, when they were under criticism from failures which took place on their watch, such as pensions mis-selling, sub-prime mortgages, bank lending market, FOREX and LIBOR conspiracies and insurance guarantees. It has nevertheless been hard for the authorities to show that if it had not been for their efforts, significant failures of the system would have been even worse, and that consumers in particular have benefitted from their efforts. They also do not take account of the fact that many of the failures might well have been dealt with by conventional legal remedies, such as tort or breach of contract or breach of trust – with the injured being compensated by way of damages, rather than benefitting the state by way of fines. Benefits to business and the consumer also need to be set against the costs, and these are equally hard to identify, which is not to say they are not useful either as a political imperative or a financial protection. Business itself can sometimes benefit from regulation, allowing them to sell more services or goods where the consumer feels protected by a regulator rather than a brand. In theory regulators could allow smaller competitors to emerge who would otherwise be swamped by the consumers' reliance in larger brand names to protect them.

4.3.1   Regulatory Impact Assessments

Understandably regulators and legislators are prone to underestimate the costs and overestimate the benefits of their involvement. It has been argued that there are five counterfactuals to estimating the costs,

---

[92] *The Burdens Barometer 2010*, British Chambers of Commerce, 2010.

which make it impossible to genuinely estimate the costs and benefits of regulation.[93] They include the following:

- the cost of market innovation that does not take place because of the presence of regulation;
- the cost of self-regulation, as an alternative (which might and probably would be simpler and cheaper);
- the absence of competition in regulation where there is a monopoly regulator, which might lead to better regulation and innovation in regulatory approaches;
- the costs of distraction by service providers from providing an improved product or service by focusing on consumer needs: one example is the absurdity of money laundering rules applied by banks and building societies when attempting to open an account – and the fact that the rules make it difficult for poor people to send remittances to their families back home;[94] and
- the costs of the regulated bodies which, although the hard costs may be disclosed in their accounts, can involve soft costs which are not.

These additional and unquantified costs could be very heavy; in some cases, as in the example of the provision of occupational pensions, they can actually lead to the destruction of the thing they were intended to protect.[95]

Unintended consequences of overbearing regulation can be advantageous where regulatory arbitrage is available; London's current pre-eminent position in financial services was founded primarily on the introduction in the US of an interest equalisation tax in 1963, together with its 'Regulation Q', which limited interest rates paid on American onshore deposits. In addition foreign governments were uncomfortable in placing deposits in jurisdictions which had a habit of freezing bank accounts.[96]

---

[93] Terry Arthur & Philip Booth, *Does Britain need a financial regulator? Statutory regulation, private regulation and financial markets*, Institute of Economic Affairs, 2010, p143; cf. Europe Economics, *The cost of regulation study*, 2003 (FSA); Deloitte, *The cost of regulation study*, 2006, Financial Services Authority.

[94] *Remittances: Costly cash: Regulation is raising the cost of sending money to the world's poor. Reform it*, The Economist, 5 September 2015.

[95] See e.g. A. Byrne, D. Harrison & D. Blake, *Pyrrhic victory? The unintended consequences of the Pensions Act 2004*, [2006] 26(3) Economic Affairs 9–16, or ask any professional in the pensions movement.

[96] Michael Stern, *Balancing the ledger, Letter*, Economist, 21 January 2012.

4.3.2   Side Costs: the Case of US Infrastructure

One of the issues that is concerning the US, and on which President Trump mounted his election campaign in 2016, is its decaying infrastructure. One of the side-concerns are the regulatory impediments. Approvals for major projects, for example, can take around 10 years and the costs of delays have been estimated at around $819B in rebuilding electricity transmission systems, $760B in electricity generation, $224B in rebuilding inland waterways. The total costs of a 6-year delay in starting projects is estimated at $3.7T; $800B was allocated during the start of the Great Recession in 2009 and intended to be devoted to infrastructure had necessitated the spending of $30B by 2014, because of regulatory delays. This is not because regulation in itself is wrong; it is sensible to avoid pollution, protect wildlife and avoid danger to the public. But

> multiyear approval processes are not the price of good government; they are the enemy of good government.

In the example of a San Diego desalination plant, urgently needed at a time of water shortages in California, permits had been applied for in 2003, and construction begun in 2012 after 14 legal challenges. Similarly, raising the roadway of the Bayonne Bridge took five years to approve, with a 10,000 page environmental assessment and 10,000 pages of permits. The question is whether the harm caused by bureaucratic delay exceeded the conceivable benefits that regulation was intended to engender.[97]

4.3.3   Regulatory Creep Costs

Instances of regulators concluding that they might be able to manage on less seem to be rare; indeed where an industry is in decline, such as that of defined benefit pension schemes, the argument is that there needs to be higher expenditure to better manage their demise.

Nor is there apparent correlation between increased expenditure and success. The UK Financial Services Authority increased its overheads in the six years 2005/06–2010/11 by 115 per cent and its staff count by 51 per cent, but only after the wrongdoings of pre-2008, which were unlikely to be repeated for another economic cycle (Table 4.1).[98]

---

[97] Philip K. Howard, *Two years not ten years: redesigning infrastructure approvals*, Common Good, Brooklyn, 2015.

[98] Terry Arthur & Philip Booth, *Does Britain need a financial regulator? Statutory regulation, private regulation and financial markets*, Institute of Economic Affairs, 2010, p145

Table 4.1 *The growth of UK financial regulators*

Year	Total budget (£M)	Growth on previous year (%)	Total staff	Growth on previous year (%)
2001–2002	195.8	–	2030	–
2002–2003	194.0	−1	2095	3
2003–2004	215.4	11	2200	5
2004–2005	211.0	−2	2165	−1
2005–2006	266.0	26	2425	12
2006–2007	274.1	3	2600	7
2007–2008	300.1	9	2700	4
2008–2009	320.7	7	2740	1
2009–2010	413.8	29	2800	2
2010–2011	454.7	10	3260	16
2011–2012	462.0	1	3291	0
2012–2013	505.9	8	3596	9
2013–2014	(FCA) 469.8	–	(FCA) 2663	–
	(PRA) 202.0	32	(PRA) 1038	3
	Total 671.8	–	Total 3701	–
2014–2015	(FCA) 533.5	–	(FCA) 3188	–
	(PRA) 236.0	15	(PRA) 1107	16
	Total 769.5	–	Total 4295	–

Some solutions to cutting costs run against the times; one is a reversion to self-regulation. Self-regulation is far from perfect, and gives rise to accusations of self-interest. My own profession, that of solicitor, was at one time self-regulated, to the satisfaction of neither lawyers nor the public. But even with its several drawbacks it was astonishingly better value than the current Solicitors Regulatory Authority, which continues to cause discontent amongst lawyers and the public, but at much greater expense.[99]

and author's own additions based on FSA, FCA and PRA annual reports. The FSA split into the FCA and PRA in 2012. The figures after that date combine both budgets.

[99] There are many criticisms of the SRA which, like many regulators, lacks the kind of accountability recommended by the Better Regulation Task Force; see e.g. Stephen K. Hargreaves, *Ashamed of the profession*, Law Society Gazette, letter, 16 January 2017; David Moore, *SRA and costs*, Law Society Gazette, letter, 16 January 2017; *SRA v Hemmings*, Case No 11283–2014; *SRA v McDonald*, reported by Dan Bindman, Legal Futures, 6 May 2016. The Solicitors Regulatory Authority in its first ten years of existence issued 18 editions of

4.3.4   Estimates of Costs

Few regulators publish a cost/benefit analysis of their work. In primary legislation, some jurisdictions including that of the UK, publish what are called 'regulatory impact assessments', intended to deliver a basic cost-benefit analysis. In practice these rarely amount to little more than a finger in the air.[100]

Not even fingers in the air seem to afflict regulators. As seen above, a major international insurer, Allianz, tried to work out what the costs of financial services regulation might be; and there have been similar efforts in the European context.[101]

4.3.5   International Complexity

Whatever the costs and complexities of national regulation, those costs can increase materially where there are international ramifications. There are costs estimates, which seem modest in the totality of other costs, but they are likely to be underestimated, and are proportionately larger for smaller organisations.[102]

4.4   Conclusions

Governments have used regulators and regulation as an alternative form of government which can occasionally play a useful part in the protection of the public at a cost and convenience which is beneficial. In many

---

its rulebook. For an equivalent excess in relation to actuaries, see *The Institute and Faculty of Actuaries v Mr Michael James Asher AFA*, Appeal Tribunal of the Institute and Faculty of Actuaries, 3 December 2015.

[100] There are complex spreadsheets available (see e.g. *Business Impact Target Assessment Calculator* (Excel spreadsheet) and *Regulatory Impact Assessments: a guide for government officials*, Department for Business Energy and Industrial Strategy, 7 June 2016) but they are only as good as the numbers inserted, which are inevitably and invariably unproven (i.e. GIGO). See e.g. Claire A. Dunlop and Claudio M. Radaelli, *Handbook of Regulatory Impact Assessment*, Edward Elgar, 2016 and Rex Deighton-Smith, Angelo Erbacci and Celine Kauffmann, *Promoting inclusive growth through better regulation: the role of Regulatory Impact Assessment*, OECD Regulatory Policy Working Papers No 3, OECD, Paris, February 2016. All these documents and more show how crude and misleading the process can be; it invariably attempts to give spurious accuracy; for similar ostensibly useful figures see www.tylervigen.com and Tyler Vigen, *Spurious correlations*, Hachette, 2015.

[101] William Mason, *The costs of regulation and how the EEU makes them worse*, The Bruges Group, 2008.

[102] *Winning the global regulation game*, EY, 2015, p3, with a bewildering chart indicating regulatory interactions.

cases however the normal checks and balances are slow to operate to constrain their activities and degree of intervention, their costs are difficult to manage, and the political and cultural drivers are such that it is hard for regulators to limit their activities.

Regulation is often a first resort to solve an apparent problem. Those who work for regulators are hamstrung by lack of specific training and qualification so they do not necessarily appreciate the laws of unintended consequences or of regulatory creep for example. And the management boards of regulators do not have effective control of their operations, and might themselves benefit by having a fully developed code requiring them to intervene more pro-actively rather than concentrate on the minutiae of the organisation, and receive themselves some training on the scope of their duties.

Government of different political persuasions know that they have created monsters which are hard to slay and despite their best endeavours struggle to find the right weapon to control them. Some suggestions for improvement are made in the final chapter.

5

Courts and Judges

Lawyers are getting cases by a ghoulish alertness in studying newspapers for announcements of accidents in factories and streets and sending circulars to injured persons.

The Times, December 1912

Unfortunate patients at hospitals are being persuaded to sign agreements by which solicitors would get 10 per cent of any damages awarded,

Law Society's Gazette, August 1933

Nowadays, if a man chokes over a biscuit he sues the confectioner; it's all rubbish,

Mr Justice Hilbery, 1960 (*Law Notes*, December 1960)

Fewer than 10 per cent of people made ill or injured by their work ever receive any compensation,

A little compensation, *Hazards*, May 2005[1]

5.1 Background

5.1.1 The Role of the Courts Generally

The exigencies of daily court room life are such that reasons for judgment will always be capable of having been better expressed.[2]

However large and detailed a statute may be, and however high a rule-book may tower,[3] there will always be a need to interpret what the text means and how the rules, even if ostensibly clear, apply in a particular

---

[1] All cited by Professor Gary Slapper, *A little something to tickle the memory*, The Times, 18 August 2011.

[2] Lord Hoffman in *Piglowska v Piglowski* [1999] 3 All ER 632 at 643.

[3] The Financial Conduct Authority rulebook has been estimated variously to be 2 metres high and even by its chairman to be ineffective and too big, see John-Griffith Jones, *Regulating in a recovery*, Speech, FCA, 13 November 2014: 'The FCA has eleven principles, and probably eleven thousand rules ... we have made a great many rules already but they don't

case. And where sanctions can involve damage to pocket or reputation imposed by a politically susceptible body, there will need to be the right to appeal to an independent tribunal, especially where sanctions imposed directly by regulators are ever more burdensome, often without evidence of their effectiveness or necessity. Regulators need supervision where they reserve to themselves the interpretation and application of their own rules. So however well drafted the rules, and however well-deserved the penalties for breach, there remains a need for courts, tribunals and determination panels to calibrate the powers of government and regulators, and to offer independent justice to individuals and firms and provide a recourse to appeal.

Historically however it was the courts that imposed sanctions and interpreted or even made the law – and nowadays assume the power to relieve excessive sanctions imposed by regulators or abuse of power by the government. And of course they have wider and more familiar roles. If we want to recover money we have lent to someone who declines to repay it, or claim for the costs and distress of our leg that was broken through someone else's fault, or want to force someone to repair a broken pavement, we can either come to an agreement with the counter-party or tortfeasor, or suggest a mediation process – or sue in a court of law. Suing involves calling on the coercive powers of the state to help us, in order to avoid us having to resort to personal violence to achieve our goal. If we sue in England, the rules about suing, calling in aid the Queen as head of state through her servant the Lord Chancellor, are printed in two volumes, about 3700 pages long, most of them printed in very small type.[4] The public policy underlying the rules, established mostly by the judiciary, does not support the view of Lao Tzu, the father of Taoism, who wrote two and a half thousand years ago 'The more prohibitions you have, the less virtuous people will be.'[5]

---

seem to prevent further problems arising and . . . what starts as an attempt to provide clarity frequently ends up creating complexity.'

[4] Lord Justice Jackson, ed, *Civil Procedure*, Sweet & Maxwell / Thomson Reuters, 2015 ISBN 978-0-41403-917-9 ('The White Book').

[5] Lao Tzu, *Tao Te Ching*, available at www.sacred-texts.com/tao/salt/salt08.htm. He added 'As restrictions and prohibitions are multiplied in the Empire, the people grow poorer and poorer. When the people are subjected to overmuch government, the land is thrown into confusion . . . The greater the number of laws and enactments, the more thieves and robbers there will be. Therefore the Sage says: "So long as I do nothing, the people will work out their own reformation. So long as I love calm, the people will right themselves. If only I keep from meddling, the people will grow rich. If only I am free from desire, the people will come naturally back to simplicity."'

Every legal system which creates laws, rules and regulations, or wishes to support its citizens enforce contracts, or remedy torts and protect the public through punishing crimes, needs courts to interpret the laws or enforce them. The role of the courts in the administration of laws and regulations is critical. But courts also have slightly wider duties here as well. They hold the balance, for example, between the rights of the individual and the power of the state. The UK Freedom of Information Act 2000 allows citizens to see documents in the possession of government, subject to certain limitations. In 2015 the government sought to retain confidentiality of letters written to ministers by the Prince of Wales. After a hearing, the courts ordered disclosure. But then the Attorney General issued a certificate in effect vetoing the court-authorised disclosure. When the case eventually reached the UK Supreme Court, complaining about the behaviour of government circumventing the court order, Lord Neuberger held:[6]

> a statutory provision which entitles a member of the executive to overrule a decision of the judiciary merely because he does not agree with it . . . would cut across two constitutional principles which are also fundamental components of the rules of law . . . the basic principle that a decision of a court is binding as between the parties and cannot be ignored or set aside by anyone, including (indeed it may be fairly said, least of all) the executive [or a higher court of Act of Parliament] . . . it is also fundamental to the rule of law that decisions and actions of the executive are . . . reviewable by the court at the suit of an interested citizen [with some exceptions].

The struggle between the executive and the judiciary on the issue of ultimate authority is explored elsewhere, but the general principle the courts have adopted is that that no one, not even a Minister, is above the law. Simply because a Minister of the Crown wills it does not mean that Parliament has willed it. This view has provoked considerable complaint by government ministers and officials (supported by some think tanks) who consider that it abrogates their democratically appointed sovereignty.

This chapter therefore looks at the role of the courts and the judiciary in

- resolving disputes,
- applying laws and
- imposing sanctions,

---

[6] R (on the application of Evans) v Attorney General [2015] UKSC 21 para 89 et seq.

most of which involve holding the balance between the interests of the individual and the state, and in particular,

- whether the rules and procedures are as simple as they might be.

5.1.2 Access to Courts and to Justice

Ordinary mortals who need to gain, in England, access to the courts need to comply not only with the complicated procedural rules, but also pay a fee to the courts, which in 2016 was set at £10,000 for claims over £200,000, and around 5 per cent of the claim for sums less than that. In addition a litigant is exposed not only to his own legal costs but also the other side's if he fails. So gaining access to civil justice (criminal justice is discussed separately below) can be both complicated and expensive, and in practice is not available to all.

There are of course alternatives to dispute resolution services provided by the state. EBay, for example, handles 60 million disputes a year for virtually nothing and with hardly any rules.[7] And within the European Union there are nominal obligations for producers to offer alternative dispute resolution arrangements to consumers who are aggrieved.[8]

But for most commercial disputes there are few alternatives but to resort to the courts where the question arises why state-run dispute resolution is often so complicated and expensive. Similar, though different, issues apply to the expense and delay of court processes in relation to the management of criminal charges, which are dealt with separately below. For example, Bernard Madoff, guilty of the largest fraud ever, was charged, tried and imprisoned in the US within three months of his crime being discovered; such speed of sanction is inconceivable in England or Italy.[9]

---

[7] www.bbc.co.uk/news/uk-31483099; http://pages.ebay.co.uk/ebay-money-back-guarantee/how-to-help.html.

[8] Alternative Dispute Resolution for Consumer Disputes (Competent Authorities and Information) Regulations 2015 SI 2015 No 0542 and Directive 2013/11/EU of the European Parliament and of the Council of 21 May 2013 on alternative dispute resolution for consumer disputes; for disputes in relation to online purchases see e.g. Regulation (EU) No 524/2013 of the European Parliament and of the Council of 21 May 2013 on online dispute resolution for consumer disputes OJ L 165/1, 16 June 2013, similarly dedicated to out-of-court resolution of disputes. These provisions are still embryonic since they are not yet supported by the enforcement powers of the courts. But they signify dissatisfaction with the conventional court process. In the UK see Department for Business Innovation and Skills, *Alternative Dispute Resolution for Consumers*, November 2014.

[9] See e.g. Rachel Sanderson, *Berlusconi faces another court case*, Financial Times, 7 February 2012. It was not always so slow: the only man to assassinate a Prime Minister committed

One reason for the inefficiency is perhaps that the system involves the provision of court services through a state monopoly or oligopoly. This has not always been the case, and is not a necessary element of state enforcement. For example, at one time in England there were state-backed courts competing with each other for custom; in Salford, a city adjacent to Manchester, the Salford Hundred Court of Record for several hundred years competed with the local Manchester branch of the High Court, charging lower fees, offering a faster and more user-friendly service, and with a two-page rule book (only one copy available).[10]

5.1.3   Experience in the US

Access to justice is easier in some other countries, although there may be individual drawbacks.[11] Litigation costs in much of Europe are much cheaper and hearings before the courts often quicker than in the UK.[12] Litigants in the US enjoy or suffer much easier access to the courts than those of the UK.[13] One reason for the US's addiction to litigation is the fact that the costs can be underwritten by the lawyers in exchange for a share of the proceeds, avoiding the need for legal aid for poorer claimants. John Grisham wrote a simple thriller some years ago about a special form

---

his crime on 11 May 1812, his trial was on 15 May and he was hanged on 18 May (i.e. all within the week), Peter Seddon, *Law's strangest cases*, Pavilion Books, 2016.

[10] The remaining anomalous courts were abolished by the Courts Act 1971.

[11] For India, for example, see Victor Mallet, *India's top judge reduced to tears over caseload*, Financial Times, 26 April 2016 ('vast backload of more than 33m outstanding civil and criminal cases... the longest case is thought to be a land dispute in Varanasi dating back to 1878, in which the Supreme Court has been involved for 40 years... India's Supreme Court, with an official strength of 31 judges, has nearly 60,000 cases outstanding').

[12] Although see e.g. A. A. S. Zuckerman, *Justice in Crisis: Comparative Dimensions of Civil Procedure*, in S. Chiarloni, P. Gottwald and A. A. S. Zuckerman (eds), *Civil Justice in Crisis*, Oxford University Press, 1999, p9–10; Zampia Vernadaki, *Civil procedure harmonization in the EU: unravelling the policy considerations*, [2013] 9(2) Journal of Contemporary European Research 298.

[13] US Chamber, Institute for Legal reform, *International comparisons of litigation costs*, June 2013 expresses costs as a percentage of GDP; there do not appear to be actual comparative cost surveys for individual actions, but an impressionistic report is given in Christopher Hodges and Stefan Vogenauer, *European Civil Justice Systems, Findings of a major comparative study on litigation funding and costs*, The Foundation for Law, Justice and Society, 2010. See also Michael Cross, *UK facing UN censure on costly litigation*, Law Society's Gazette, [2017] (August 7) 1. The Aarhus Convention 1998 requires states to provide procedures that are 'fair, timely and not prohibitively expensive', UNECE Convention on Access to Information, Public Participation in Decision-making and Access to Justice in Environmental Matters, which entered into force on 30 October 2001, and which applies in limited circumstances.

of litigation, class actions,[14] but I never really realised quite how true to life the novel was until in late 2006 a securities class action lawyer from New York came to see me in London about advising on UK securities class actions. Class actions involve organising a group of people all with similar claims and combining them into one law suit. The Grisham thriller was about medical class actions, where it is alleged a drug may have serious side effects which the manufacturer knew about and did not disclose, so that people suffered unnecessarily. My visitor organised similar law suits, but against companies where it was asserted that they had lied about the performance of their business so that investors which relied on their statements bought shares at too high a price and then lost money. Well-known securities class actions involved such famous frauds as WorldCom, Enron and Global Crossing, and there was a substantial industry organised by specialist law firms involving hundreds of similar claims every year.[15]

What shook me slightly was that my guest was working for a relatively small player in the legal world, but had flown in its private jet across the Atlantic. Not even the largest and most successful law firms in the UK acting in the very largest corporate deals run their own plane, even a turboprop. It was clearly a successful law practice, and its jet was paid for by the very large fees (around a third of the sums recovered) involved in the litigation it sponsored. Class action lawyers are less sensitive to complaints about high fees because they take a substantial risk in pursuing a claim if it fails. In the States, the lawyers would lose the time and resources they expended on failed litigation – but are not liable for the other sides' fees, even if they lose, because of the rule in US litigation that each side pays its own costs. There is therefore a certain element of 'blackmail' in US litigation which does not apply to for example European litigation, where the loser pays both sides' costs.[16] It encourages defendants to settle, even if they feel they have nothing to be ashamed of, because it is cheaper than fighting.[17]

Litigation in the US has a well-deserved reputation for excess (there are around 15M cases a year),[18] which seems absent in other jurisdictions such as England. There had been attempts to curb some of the excesses of

---

[14] John Grisham, *King of Torts*, Dell, 2012.

[15] See e.g. *Securities Class Action Settlements: 2015 Review*, Cornerstone Research, 2016.

[16] Clive Wolman, *Securities Class Actions*, [2006] 11(4) Pensions 254.

[17] Not always, see e.g. *City of Providence v Buck Consultants* [2016] 009 PBLR (008) United States: Rhode Island: District Court 2015 November 13 where part of the defence which was accepted was that the plaintiff would incur disproportionate irrecoverable costs even if successful.

[18] *State Court Guide to Statistical Reporting*, 2003, National Center for State Courts. Trial lawyers earned an estimated $40 billion in lawsuit awards that year. CSP DataViewer,

US litigation in the US Tort Law Reform Act in 1999, but they had not had quite the impact intended,[19] and such reform is clearly not needed in the same way in other countries. But there are profound concerns about the inadequacies of the litigation system in some countries (such as England), and there have been several attempts at broader reform in recent years.

5.1.4   Resolving Disputes; Alternative Dispute Resolution

In some, perhaps many, cases it is possible to resolve a dispute by using arrangements other than the courts. Arbitration is a system adopted around the world, often through international conventions, and decisions of arbitrators are enforceable by the courts.[20] It offers (in theory if not always in practice), speed, simplicity, cheapness, progress at the speed of the parties' own timetable – and privacy. In practice an arbitrator is invariably more expensive to hire than a judge, he can be more procedurally pedantic than a judge, and he can take his time. And the fact that the decision is made in private means that developments in the law can take time to emerge.

More recent has been the development of other forms of dispute resolution, collectively known as alternative dispute resolution, of which the most common is mediation. Most peoples' experience of mediation is positive; it involves using maybe half-a-page of procedural requirements, encourages all parties to employ pragmatism rather than pure law, explores looking at a problem in the round rather than as simply a legal issue (which it rarely is), gives the opportunity to continue a business relationship after the conclusion of the case (which is rare in pure litigation) – and requires the parties' joint consent, so reducing contention. It is however in practice usually only available privately, is not always enforceable by the courts once a mediation agreement is arrived at, and is sometimes badly organised when required through the state legal system. In UK 'family mediation' for example the parties absurdly sit in the same room, and have an hour or so to settle, against all the principles of mediation, which is intended to allow a mediator to explore solutions by using the confidences of the parties that they feel unable to share with the other

R. LaFountain, R. Schauffler, S. Strickland, K. Holt and K. Lewis, eds. Last updated 15 March 2016, Court Statistics Project DataViewer, www.courtstatistics.org.

[19] Stephen D. Sugarman, *United States Tort Reform Wars*, University of California, Berkeley, August 2002; *Noneconomic damages reform*, American Tort Reform Association, 2002.

[20] See e.g. International Chamber of Commerce, www.iccwbo.org/products-and-services/arbitration-and-adr/arbitration/icc-arbitration-procedure/ArbitrationAct.

side. Nor does the system grant the time needed to allow the parties during the process to come to terms with their position (usually by 3 pm, if the process starts early in the morning).

5.1.5 Procedural Rules and Their Application

In England, as in other countries, the formal rules of procedure seem, to professionals if not their clients (or judges), reasonably straightforward, and revisions to procedure are frequently proposed to make it even easier, as discussed below. In practice however it is hard though not impossible to manage civil litigation without a lawyer. And the withdrawal or reduction in the availability of legal aid in both civil and criminal matters has resulted in increased numbers of litigants-in-person. In fact, despite predictions that the courts would be clogged with litigants having to be guided by the judges and slowing down the system, there seems to have been a reduction in the application of the formalities – and even the senior judiciary have been pressing for a simplification of the system which they might not otherwise have done.[21] So far, the frequent reviews of procedure have not resulted in material improvements and the reduction of legal aid together with the increase in court costs has made access to justice more difficult. Procedural reform is explored in greater detail below.

5.2 Litigation Policy Issues

5.2.1 Background

Concerns about litigation policy have involved not only that of excessive litigation, but also the costs, delay and complexity of process. Around the world, even where hitherto there have been only modest concerns, there have been increasing comments that businesses and others have

---

[21] See e.g. 'The … Rules of today would be all too familiar in their archaic and sometimes impenetrable language to my distinguished Victorian predecessors … the Rules, like their civil counterparts, are a masterpiece of traditional, if absurdly over-elaborate, drafting. But they are unreadable by litigants-in-person and, truth be told, largely unread by lawyers. They are simply not fit for purpose. The Red Book [family court procedure rules], like the White Book [Civil Procedure Rules], is a remarkable monument of legal publishing, but, I fear, fit only for the bonfire. Rules, to the extent that we still need them, must be short and written in simple, plain English.' Munby LJ, *Address of the President of the Family Division at the annual dinner of the Family Law Bar Association in Middle Temple Hall*, 26 February 2016.

become affected by a compensation culture hitherto absent in the particular jurisdiction.[22]

This chapter therefore looks at whether the concerns about the courts and their adverse impact on day-to-day life and commercial operations are justified – and in particular whether litigation or the threat of litigation, and the enforcement of law and regulations, is a genuine problem. It also separately examines civil and criminal law issues. None of this critique is to decry the astonishingly high quality of judging in many jurisdictions; the question is whether the access to that judging is efficient.[23]

Before looking at the extensive procedural rules which make access to the courts expensive, and involve considerable delay, it might be sensible to examine some policy issues which determine both the creation of the rules, and the way in which they are applied. This involves examining briefly

- how the court structure operates and
- the control of legislation and rules through civil litigation,

and in particular, issues involving

- judicial imperialism,
- the existence or otherwise of a claims or compensation culture and
- the efficiency or otherwise of access to justice.

5.2.2   Judge-Made Law and 'Judicial Imperialism'

The debate, rendered acute in recent years, about the balance of power between those who make the laws, and those who apply them through the courts, has recently received even more attention. It has been evidenced in the US in the refusal of the legislature to appoint a replacement Supreme Court judge pending a presidential election in 2016,[24] because the political flavour of the judge would affect future constitutional decisions; similarly there has been complaint about the appointment of additional European Union judges in 2016 to meet a perceived shortage of

---

[22] See e.g. Tony Blair, *Speech on compensation culture to the Institute for Public Policy Research think tank, setting out plans for a 'common sense culture, not a compensation culture',* full text, Guardian, 26 May 2005.

[23] The deliberations of the English Supreme Court are available in video on its website; watch and admire: www.supremecourt.uk.

[24] Jeffrey Toobin, *The Supreme Court after Scalia,* New Yorker, 3 October 2016.

judicial resource;[25] and in the UK there have been periodic and undignified disconnects between the executive and the judiciary.[26]

Take, for example, a dispute between the government and the judges about whether a terrorist trial should be held in public or private.[27] The dispute continued even after the Court of Appeal ruled it should be held in public and the defendants named. Nonetheless part of it continued to be held in camera and certain evidence was not disclosed, nor where disclosed, was it reported. Understandable though the reasoning was (the protection of witnesses and sources of information) if such a procedure had been adopted in Russia or Libya, there would have been an outcry.

Even Linklaters, a London-based law firm considered to be one of the 'magic circle' and retained by many of the world's largest corporations and several governments, felt the need to issue a warning about the UK executive's encroachment on the independence of the judges.[28] It criticised legislation expressing in broad terms going beyond the scope of the underlying problem it was written to address, and depending on the common sense and reasonableness of the prosecutors not to abuse their powers.[29]

---

[25] Court of Justice of the European Union, *Reform of the EU Court System*, Press Release No 44/15, Luxembourg, 28 April 2015.

[26] See e.g. the dispute over the proper procedure to effect 'Brexit', the leaving of the United Kingdom from the European Union in 2016; see e.g. *Miller v Secretary of State for Exiting the European Union*, [2016] EWHC 2768 (Admin). For an authoritative description and history of the struggle between the executive and the judiciary, see Joshua Rozenberg, *Trial of Strength: the battle between ministers and judges over who makes law*, Richard Cohen Books, 1997. For a balanced view of the Brexit debate, see Joshua Rozenberg, *Brexit in the balance: exactly what is at stake in the Supreme Court?*, Spectator, 3 December 2016. For a less balanced view see Richard Ekins, *A guide to the Supreme Court Justices*, Spectator, 3 December 2016 and for an intemperate view see James Slack, *Enemies of the people: Fury over 'out of touch' judges*, Daily Mail, 3 November 2016, reflecting German Nazi newspapers approaches to the judiciary, https://fullfact.org/law/daily-mail-headine-comparison-to-nazis/.

[27] Sandra Laville, *Major terrorism trial could be held in secret for the first time in UK legal history*, The Guardian, 4 June 2014 (*R v Incedal and Rarmoul-Bouhadjar* per Nicol J, May 2014, reversed on appeal).

[28] *In defence of the rule of law: challenging the erosion of the legal certainty and fairness that business needs*, Linklaters, London, 2015. For a discussion about the attack on the role of proceedings for judicial review, see e.g. Amy Street, *Judicial review and the rule of law: who is in control?*, The Constitution Society, 2013, and Criminal Justice and Courts Act 2015 Part 4, and *Judicial Review and the rule of law*, The Bingham Centre for the Rule of Law, November 2015.

[29] E.g. Proceeds of Crime Act 2002 intended originally to control money laundering but incidentally criminalising for example a teenager who is given what is known to be a pirated copy of music by a friend, by imposing the offence of acquiring criminal property and see e.g. *Sitek v Circuit Court in Swidnica, Poland*, [2011] EWHC 1378 (Admin).

Such legislation allows the issue of European Arrest Warrants using the discretions or otherwise of foreign prosecutors who have not given their assurance to use the principles undertaken in Parliament by Ministers in debate. It also criticised the ever increasing powers of regulatory authorities to impose penalties. For example in November 2014 five banks were ordered to pay £1.1B in fines related to their failure to control business practices in their foreign exchange trading operations. Because there was no understandable scale of penalties that was proportional to the seriousness of offences it was therefore almost impossible to predict the likely level of penalties in any particular case. The Linklater's paper criticised the powers that Parliament grants to ministers to amend primary legislation (Henry VIII clauses).[30] It also criticised situations where the government gives itself the power to regulate business but compels those who are regulated to keep the government intervention secret.[31] The astonishment was not that the paper had been issued; it was that a major law firm felt sufficiently strongly about the issue that it was prepared to prejudice its relations with one of its significant clients, namely the government, to stake the moral high ground.

The courts also are not unaware of the dilemmas and challenges to the rule of law that actions of the executive pose. Lord Neuberger has been cited above; he also referred elsewhere to a famous decision in the *Liversidge* case:[32]

> Unsurprisingly, *Liversidge* was much discussed at the time. The LQR [Law Quarterly Review] published a number of pieces agreeing with the majority. Sir William Holdsworth thought that the majority were 'clearly right'... because the issue was not 'justiciable' or 'within the court's legal competence', as it was an 'administrative or political issue'. Professor Goodhart agreed, even suggesting that Lord Atkin's statement about the majority

---

[30] Banking Act 2009 s75 (passed following the global financial crisis in 2008) gives the UK Treasury power to disapply or modify the effect of *any* past or future enactment or rule of law without Parliamentary approval.

[31] Data Retention and Investigatory Powers Act 2014; Telecommunications Act 1984 s 94 allows the Secretary of State to direct telecommunications operators 'if it appears to the Secretary of State to be necessary' in the interest of national security or international relations. The Secretary of State need not publicise such directions, and the recipients of those directions are prohibited from disclosing their existence. There is therefore no authoritative information in the public domain about when the power has been used, to what extent and with what consequences.

[32] *Liversidge v Anderson* [1941] UKHL 15; it concerned the power of the state to imprison someone without giving a reason in times of national emergency; the case has strong contemporary resonances; see Lord Neuberger, *Reflections on the ICLR's top fifteen cases*, speech, 6 October 2015, para 58 et seq.

being 'more executive-minded than the executive', might amount to contempt of court, as it suggested that his four colleagues had 'consciously or unconsciously, been influenced by their prejudices or political inclinations in reaching their conclusions'. An article in the MLR [Modern Law Review] took rather a different view, suggesting that 'the limited check which Lord Atkin's interpretation involves . . . would impose upon the Executive a reassertion of a principle for which a number of Englishmen in recent years have rather strangely lost enthusiasm' . . . A postscript to the MLR article revealed that Mr Liversidge had been released by July 1943.

Lord Atkin's view has, of course, triumphed in the end. The decision of the majority was described as 'very peculiar' by Lord Reid in 1964 . . . , and in 1979, Lord Diplock said in terms that 'the time ha[d] come' for the Law Lords to acknowledge that the majority were expediently and, at that time, perhaps, excusably, wrong and the dissenting speech of Lord Atkin was right.

Although it was wrongly decided and therefore not even an authority, let alone an important authority, *Liversidge* is rightly included in the list. Lord Atkin's speech is up there with Lord Camden's judgment in *Entick v Carrington*[33] to remind us all of the importance of the rule of law. And the wrongness of four eminent jurists, Viscount Maugham, and Lords Macmillan, Wright and Romer, reminds judges not to forget the rule of law in times of emergency. I leave the last word on *Liversidge* to Lord Atkin:

> 'In this country, amid the clash of arms, the laws are not silent. They may be changed, but they speak the same language in war as in peace. It has always been one of the pillars of freedom, one of the principles of liberty for which on recent authority we are now fighting, that the judges are no respecters of persons and stand between the subject and any attempted encroachments on his liberty by the executive, alert to see that any coercive action is justified in law.'

In practice government has on several occasions failed to appreciate its obligations under the rule of law, with successive Home Secretaries being major offenders. The conventional remedy to deal with an over-mighty state is the use of a judicial process known as judicial review. There has been considerable resort in the last few years to judicial review, with push-back from government. But there is a reason for the growth in the number of cases. Lord Dyson, a former Master of the Rolls, pointed out that the growth of judicial review was in part due to the 'explosion of legislation, much of it rushed through without sufficient consideration'.[34] The

---

[33] (1765) 19 St Tr 1029.
[34] Lord Dyson (Master of the Rolls), *Is judicial review a threat to democracy?* The Sultan Azlan Shah lecture, November 2015.

number of applications had grown from 160 in 1974 to over 11,000 by 2011.[35] The argument by ministers, sometimes frustrated by judicial intervention, is that they are the elected government and it is a political act for a judge to restrict their powers. The long-standing legal authority, Professor Wade, considered:

> If merely because an act says that a minister may 'make such order as he sees fit', or may do something 'if he is satisfied' as to some fact, the court were to allow him to do as he liked, a wide door would be opened to allow him to abuse of power and the rule of law would cease to operate. It is a cardinal axiom, accordingly, that every power has legal limits, however wide the language of the empowering act . . . Although lawyers appearing for government departments often argue that some act confers unfettered discretion, they are guilty of constitutional blasphemy. Unfettered discretion cannot exist where the rule of law reigns.[36]

Over the last decades a stand-off has begun to emerge between politicians and the judiciary. To put it baldly: the politicians (maybe not all of them) assert that they are the democratically elected representatives of the people and that they, through Parliament, are sovereign. Their decisions should not be questioned by largely white men, undemocratically appointed.[37]

The judges have a memory of the battle which King James I eventually conceded about whether the sovereign is above the law. The then Chief Justice, Sir Edward Coke insisted in 1608 to the King that 'The king is not subject to men, but is subject to God and the law'. And, think modern judges, Parliament is like the King: sovereign, but not above the law.

This conflict of constitutional approach is reaching something of an impasse, especially with recent attempts to curtail the procedure of judicial review, through which the organs of government are sometimes held to account.[38]

---

[35] Lord Dyson (Master of the Rolls), *Is judicial review a threat to democracy?* The Sultan Azlan Shah lecture, November 2015, p17.

[36] Wade & Forsyth, *Administrative Law*, 11th edn, 2014, cited from 7th edn, p40.

[37] 'There was a time when it was thought almost indecent to suggest that judges make law – they only declare it. Those with a taste for fairy tales seem to have thought that in some Aladdin's cave there is hidden the Common Law in all its splendour and that on a judge's appointment there descends on him knowledge of the magic words Open Sesame. Bad decisions are given when the judge had muddled the pass word and the wrong door opens. But we do not believe in fairy tales any more.' Lord Reid, 'The Judge as Law Maker' (1972) 12 Journal of the Society of Public Teachers of Law 22, contributed by David Pollard.

[38] See e.g. Lord Thomas of Cwmgiedd, Lord Chief Justice, *The centrality of justice: its contribution to society and its delivery*, The Lord Williams of Mostyn Memorial Lecture, 10 November 2015, and *In defence of the rule of law: challenging the erosion of the legal certainty and fairness that business needs*, Linklaters, November 2015.

There is no doubt that the judges, whilst sensible of the dangers of constitutional challenges to Parliament, are increasingly uncomfortable with
the attempts by the executive to preserve their absolute powers, free of
legal constraint. The reasons include: the reduction in the availability of
legal aid; the impact of such legislation as the Proceeds of Crime Act 2002
which criminalises things other than money laundering which was its
intended purpose;[39] the increase in regulatory penalties without an understandable scale of penalties proportionate to the offence (e.g. FOREX fines
of £1.1B); the introduction of Henry VIII clauses under which ministers
have the power to change the law without reversion to Parliament (e.g.
Banking Act 2009 s75); or situations where the government gives itself
the power to regulate business but compels those who are so regulated
to keep government intervention secret (e.g. Data Retention and Investigatory Powers Act 2014; Telecommunications Act 1984 s94) – and retrospective legislation (Finance Act 2008, s58, Banking Act 2009 s75 again),
where the rule of law becomes the rule of the regulator) and reversals of
the normal burden of proof (e.g. Financial Services and Markets Act 2000;
Bribery Act 2010). Only the judiciary feel they have the power to keep
such excesses under control, especially where even under the democratic
authority, a government may only have gained say a third of the votes cast,
and a smaller percentage of the total electorate.

5.2.3   The Claims Culture

One issue which has caused headlines in the last decade is has been a perception of a growing compensation culture. As discussed above, much of
it has been exaggerated, but some of might have been partly fomented by
regulators, for example in the case of claims for compensation for mis-sold
payment protection insurance by banks in the UK (which anyone with
a smartphone in England would not have been unaware of), with compensation for coalminers afflicted by pneumoconiosis (which became the
subject of legal scandals), and compensation costs for the health service
(where around 30 per cent of the compensation is paid in legal fees). It
is thought that compensation costs around £10B a year (2002), perhaps 1
per cent of GDP. The costs have been increasing at 15 per cent a year and

---

[39] See *Sitek v Circuit Curt in Swidnica, Poland* [2011] EWHC 1378; cf. *Richard O'Dwyer v
Home Secretary* (unreported) on whether a teenage student can be extradited for receiv-
ing pirated music, Adam Gabbatt, *Richard O'Dwyer: living with the threat of extradition*,
Guardian, 6 December 2012.

are estimated to continue to grow at 10 per cent a year. This growth will eventually come to an end, but it is still a considerable sum.[40] An actuaries' research working party suggested it was the outcome of an increasingly litigious society; US costs for example are double, about 2 per cent of GDP. Oddly the virtual withdrawal of legal aid may be seen as a spur to litigation through litigation funders – and plaintiff lawyers argue that much litigation is because insurers and others such as the NHS fight cases rather than settle them.

Whatever the amounts involved, the attempts to calm things down have seemingly not worked; conditional fee agreements and before- and after-the-event insurance are allowing individuals and others who would otherwise have been dissuaded from litigation to try to enforce their civil claims.[41]

The claims culture is easy enough to parody; most people in Britain have had experience of being prompted to claim on their smartphones for PPI losses, or personal accident losses. One report reproduced a joke from the BBC News Online website:

> Life is full of dangers to life, limb and sanity. But lawyers are on hand to make sure victims of life's slings and arrows can claim compensation – a nightmare day in the life of a composite compensation citizen.
>
> **0700: Waking up: Compensation Range £50–£1000 (Supply of Goods Act)**
> Sleeping in the wrong sort of bed can cause back and neck problems and an over-loud alarm clock may cause whiplash injuries. But the 1994 Supply of Goods Act gave consumers the right to demand damages if they are supplied with faulty, dangerous or malfunctioning goods. So if you were injured it might be worth speaking to your lawyer.
>
> **0705: Getting Dresses Compensation Range £50,000–£100,000 (Industrial Tribunal)**
> Much here depends on gender. Women in some occupations can limber up for a day of compensatable victimisation by opting for a pair of trousers. Last year Judy Owen claimed compensation after she was forced to resign from her job with the Professional Golfers' Association because she would not wear a skirt. There is yet to be a case of a man claiming compensation after being sacked for wearing a dress. But doubtless this is just a matter of time.

---

[40] Julian Lowe (Chairman), *The cost of compensation culture*, Institute of Actuaries Working Party, 8 October 2002

[41] E. Lee et al., *Compensation Crazy: do we blame and claim too much?*, Hodder & Stoughton, 2002; Frank Furedi, *Courting mistrust: the hidden growth of a culture of litigation in Britain*, Centre for Policy Studies, 1999

0715: Going Downstairs Compensation Range £50–£5000 (Supply of Goods Act)

Houses are full of hazards and the most common type of accident is a fall on the stairs (or, for the elderly, the danger of falling out of bed). There are about 2.7 million accidents in the home each year which result in a visit to hospital. Falls account for 40% of the non-fatal injuries and 46% of all deaths. Sadly, an injury in the home is likely to be thought of by the legal system as your own fault. So be extra careful. There is not much compensation on offer... at least until you reach the kitchen breakfast table – bristling as it is with negligently designed tin-openers, lethal electric kettles and exploding pop-up toasters – all cause for complaint and potential compensation under the 1994 Act.

0718: Opening the Post Compensation range £1000–£50,000 (Personal Injury, Negligence)

A cheque arrives from your package holiday operator for mishap during a recent winter break – £5000 in respect of a coconut which fell on your head while you were sitting under a palm tree. Your personal injury compensation lawyers have followed the precedent set by Jean Gratton who sued Airtours after a coconut fell on her chest while on holiday in the Caribbean. She got £1700. Travel operators are now so worried about compensation claims that they have established a £1Bn 'fighting fund' to contest cases and make pay outs. There is also a postcard from a distant cousin, a former prison inmate who, following the example of a former IRA terrorist, is suing the Prison Service for injuries sustained during an attempted jail-break.

0720: Breakfast Compensation Range £50–£5000 (Supply of Goods Act, Personal Injury)

The main compensation news here is the danger of injury from badly designed packaging which according to the Department of Trade and Industry results in thousands of compensatable injuries every year. One particular hazard to look out for is the glass milk bottle and, in fact, glass objects in general. The danger arises, the department of Trade and Industry says because: 'Typically milk bottles are left on the doorstep where they can get wet. They are very smooth and slippery and are therefore are frequently dropped.' But there are no known cases of people suing their milkman for supplying overly slippery milk bottles – yet.

0730: Sending the Kids Off to School Compensation Range £500–£500,000 (Human Rights Act, Personal Injury)

Last years' Human Rights Act established a legal claim to a 'good quality education' and there have already been legal threats and demands for compensation from schools said to be failing to deliver a good education to pupils. So as you are sending the kids off to school brief them to take sworn statements providing evidence of sub-standard teaching, overcrowded classes, leaky buildings and smelly changing rooms – all part of a possible compensation goldmine if they later fail their GCSEs or fail to gain entry to Harvard University. At the same time be sure to brief the kids about the personal injury compensation aspects of falling over in the playground, getting a rubber stuck up their noses or getting bruised legs from playing hockey.

0745: Getting to Work Compensation Range £10–£500 (Fare Rebates)

Train companies now routinely pay compensation for inadequate service. But so far only token sums have been involved. It can not be long, surely, until a massive 'class action' featuring the Whole Country v The Entire Rail System leads to a bonanza pay-out.

0830: Work Compensation Range £50,000–£250,000 (Industrial Tribunal, Personal Injury, Human Rights Act)

Stress, bullying, sex discrimination, injuries sustained from overuse or incorrect use of computers, chairs, keyboard, mice, photocopiers and other horrors make the workplace a personal injury hell and, therefore, compensation paradise. Last year bank manager Leslie North was awarded £100,000 after suffering a nervous breakdown when a 'hostile boss' reduced him to tears. He should try explaining reserve deteriorations to a finance director. Working for a local authority or public sector body appears to be a particularly threatening to physical or mental health. Earlier this year local government officer Randy Ingram won £203,000 after his life was 'ruined' by work as a gipsy site manager for Worcester City council. And primary school teacher Jan Howell was last year awarded £254, 362 in compensation after showing that her job had driven her towards a nervous breakdown. The year 2000 saw a total of £320M awarded in compensation as a result of work-related stress.

1300: Lunchtime Compensation Range £50–£5000 (Supply of Goods Act, Personal Injury)

All the dangers of breakfast apply, but in public. Therefore somebody else and not yourself will be liable if there is a problem – opening up much more promising compensation possibilities.

1400: Back at Work Compensation Range £50,000–£1,000,000 (Industrial Tribunal, Personal Injury, Human Rights Act, Defamation Act)

Since your job is damaging your health, you might consider a change of employer. The compensation possibilities here surround the nature of your boss's reference letter. Last year one woman, Belinda Cooke, bagged £195,000 after her employer refused to supply a letter of reference. She might have got even more if her boss wrote an unjustifiably negative reference. This would have counted as libel (defamation in a permanent form) and might have entitled her to 'damages' for loss of reputation.

1700: Mobile Phone Call/Doctor's Appointment Compensation Range £50,000–£1,000,000 (Public Health Liability, Medical Negligence, Personal Injury, Human Rights Act)

You book your place in the impending possible class action against the mobile phone industry by using your mobile to call the GP's surgery.

American lawyer Peter Angelos earned \$4.2B in damages for cigarette addicts from tobacco companies before announcing he was taking on the mobile phone companies over fears that they can cause brain tumours. You arrange an emergency examination with your GP, who is unlikely to give categorical advice because of danger of your suing him for misdiagnosis. GPs are 13 times more likely to face negligence claims than 10 years ago.

2300: Bedtime Compensation Range: Unknown
Sex is full of every unimaginable kind of hazard – though not many attract compensation...yet. Last year a woman attempted to sue Durex for £120,000 when a condom split and she became pregnant. But a judge threw out the case. No jokes about the case not standing up in court.

2400: Sleep Compensation Range Zero
You fall asleep. A Franz Kafka-style nightmare set in a sinister world, of dungeons, castles and law courts where everyone in the whole world is suing everyone else slowly gives way to a heavenly scenario where there are no lawyers at all...but it is only a dream.

That mildly amusing skit on the system only partly reflects reality. Litigation in England for example has been constrained by three rather simple barriers:

- firstly the costs rule, which provided (unlike in the US) that the loser in a court battle pays all (or at least most) of the costs;
- secondly, that it was illegal for a third party to take an interest in legal proceedings, thus discouraging the quantity of litigation because in many cases litigants did not have the resources to fight; and
- thirdly, the court costs. Until recently these were modest, but have been increased by 600% in some cases so that a claim for £200,000, not a great sum in commercial matters, could require court fees alone of £10,000, not to mention legal fees on top.

In the US, by contrast, the costs rules provided for each side to pay their own costs, win or lose. This proved less a disincentive for parties to litigate. And secondly the ancient Magna Carta rules against champerty and maintenance, i.e. the forbidding of third parties to engage in supporting litigation, did not seem to operate in the US – hence the proliferation there of lawyers and litigation. Whether it is cause or effect there is also a distinct cultural difference in the States; litigation is seen as a governance issue, where as in the UK is something of a disgrace for a company or an individual to be involved before the courts. The absence of a litigation culture in England can be seen by the relative infrequency of cases before the higher courts: there were only around 200 cases before the Supreme Court, and around 1250 cases before the Court of Appeal, and few of these cases were about compensation.[42]

There have nonetheless been particular areas of concern: the NHS suffers increasing litigation, and employment litigation has only been curbed by introducing substantial fee penalties. And criminal injuries compensation in the UK exceeds that of most other jurisdictions combined. But the general consensus is that the chatter about a compensation culture in England is overdone. When the House of Commons Constitutional Affairs Committee examined the complaints it concluded that the Compensation Bill then being introduced in the House of Lords was in many respects unnecessary. Nonetheless the reforms did produce some useful minor improvements: it is no longer an admission of liability to apologise for an accident, mesothelioma cases were treated more sympathetically, and claims management companies were regulated. But its first section, the main reason for introducing the Compensation Act in the first place, was considered even by the House of Commons Select Committee itself as mostly a grandstanding piece of legislation. It simply provided that the courts, when considering claims in negligence, and whether the defendant should have taken precautions against a risk (e.g. wearing glasses when playing conkers) should have regard as to whether a requirement to take those steps might prevent a desirable activity from being undertaken at all, to a particular extent or in a particular way or discourage persons from undertaking functions in connection with a desirable activity.[43] But in fact that had been the law for many years; in the well-known case of *Tomlinson*,[44] Mr Tomlinson suffered severe injuries by making a shallow

---

[42] For costs of US litigation see e.g. Tillinghast-Towers Perrin, *US Tort costs 2000: trends and findings on the US Tort system*, 2002. There are only around 80 cases before the US Supreme Court each year, but each state has its own Supreme Court as well.

[43] House of Commons, Constitutional Affairs Committee, *Compensation Culture*, Third Report of Session 2005–06, HC 754–1, 14 February 2006, Compensation Act 2006.

[44] *Tomlinson v Congleton Borough Council* [2004] 1 AC. See also *Miller v Jackson* [1977] QB 966: Cricket had been played at a small cricket ground in Lintz, near Burnopfield, County Durham, since 1905, on land leased to the club by the National Coal Board. The National Coal Board also owned a field adjacent to the ground, which it sold to Stanley Urban District Council. The Council sold the land to Wimpey for development. A line of new semi-detached houses were built next to the ground in 1972, one of which, 20, Brackenridge, was bought by the Millers. The Millers' garden boundary was only 100 feet from the nearest batting crease, and their house only 60 feet further away. Several cricket balls were hit onto their property over the following years, causing minor damage to their house (chipped paintwork, broken roof tiles) and risking personal injury to the Millers.

dive into a lake owned by a council. The House of Lords (Supreme Court) eventually found in favour of the council. It held that although the council had a duty of care to both visitors – and trespassers – to its property, it was

Despite measures taken by the club to minimise recurrences, including the erection of a 8 feet 9 inches high fence in March 1975 on top of a 6 feet boundary wall and asking batsmen to try to hit fours rather than sixes, a few balls continued to be hit out of the ground each season. For example, in 1975, 36 matches were played over 20 weeks in the summer, with 2,221 six-ball overs being bowled. Out of the 13,326 legitimate deliveries (ignoring no-balls and wides) there were 120 sixes, of which six crossed the fence and fell into the housing estate.

The club offered to meet the cost of any property damage (£400), and suggested further countermeasures, such as louvred window shutters, and a net over the Millers' garden. The Millers were not content and sued for damages and an injunction to prevent cricket being played on the ground.

The High Court granted the Millers the injunction they sought, and ordered the club to pay general damages of £150 for negligence and nuisance, for the inconvenience and interference with the use of the Millers' property. The club appealed the injunction.

The Court of Appeal held that there was a foreseeable risk of injury to the plaintiffs and their property from the cricket balls and the club could not prevent accidents from happening. The club was guilty of negligence 'on each occasion when a ball comes over the fence and causes damage to the plaintiffs'. The repeated interference with their property was also held to be an actionable nuisance; the fact that the Millers had 'come to the nuisance' was no defence. The Millers were awarded damages. Lord Denning MR dissented from the finding of negligence and nuisance, and held that 'the public interest should prevail over the private interest'.

Lord Denning by way of dissent held:

In summertime village cricket is the delight of everyone. Nearly every village has its own cricket field where the young men play and the old men watch. In the village of Lintz in County Durham they have their own ground, where they have played these last 70 years. They tend it well. The wicket area is well rolled and mown. The outfield is kept short. It has a good club house for the players and seats for the onlookers. The village team play there on Saturdays and Sundays. They belong to a league, competing with the neighbouring villages. On other evenings after work they practise while the light lasts. Yet now after these 70 years a judge of the High Court has ordered that they must not play there any more. He has issued an injunction to stop them. He has done it at the instance of a newcomer who is no lover of cricket. This newcomer has built, or has had built for him, a house on the edge of the cricket ground which four years ago was a field where cattle grazed. The animals did not mind the cricket. But now this adjoining field has been turned into a housing estate. The newcomer bought one of the houses on the edge of the cricket ground. No doubt the open space was a selling point. Now he complains that when a batsman hits a six the ball has been known to land in his garden or on or near his house. His wife has got so upset about it that they always go out at week-ends. They do not go into the garden when cricket is being played. They say that this is intolerable. So they asked the judge to stop the cricket being played. And the judge, much against his will, has felt that he must order the cricket to be stopped: with the consequence, I suppose, that the Lintz Cricket Club will disappear. The cricket ground will be turned to some other use. I expect for more houses or a factory. The young men will turn to other things instead of cricket. The whole village will be much

not on the facts of the case reasonable to expect the council to protect Mr Tomlinson from his own actions (he ignored prominent warning signs). One might argue that there might not even have needed to be signs if any reasonable person should have thought twice before testing the water. Part of the reason for parliamentary intervention had been a change to the rules on costs so that conditional fee agreements were thought to have encouraged people to claim, but there was no need for a change in the statute.

The House of Commons, and other observers have concluded that, with some minor exceptions, there is not much of a compensation culture in Britain. It is true however that there might be a disproportionate fear of litigation – and there is an increasingly risk-averse culture as a consequence. Attempts by some government agencies such as the Health and Safety Executive to dispel the perception seem to have little impact – and other agencies such as the Financial Services Authority and others have seemed to encourage claims, for example in relation to personal pensions mis-selling or to payment protection insurance. On balance, such culture as does exist seems to be a consequence of regulatory bodies attempting to justify their existence,[45] and according to the then Lord Chancellor, advertising, and maybe the *Daily Mail*.[46]

A magisterial lecture by Lord Dyson, the Master of the Rolls, in October 2015, reached a similar conclusion.[47] He noted that while there had been recent complaints in England and Wales about the compensation

the poorer. And all this because of a newcomer who has just bought a house there next to the cricket ground.

However, on the basis that the club had agreed to pay for any damage, he was 'content that there should be an award of £400 to cover any past or future damage'. Damages were held to be a sufficient remedy, the discretionary equitable remedy of an injunction was not necessary. The court had to 'strike a fair balance between the right of the plaintiffs to have quiet enjoyment of their house and garden without exposure to cricket balls occasionally falling like thunderbolts from the heavens, and the opportunity of the inhabitants of the village in which they live to continue to enjoy the manly sport which constitutes a summer recreation for adults and young persons'. The Millers had bought a house with the benefit of an open space adjacent to their land, and had to accept that the innocent and lawful use of the open land could restrict the enjoyment of their garden.

[45] See also *Barker v Corus UK Ltd* [2006] UKHL 20, which held that a single defendant could only be liable for a fraction of any damages (in relation to mesothelioma) proportional to the exposure for which they were liable. Paradoxically the Compensation Act 2006 increased the opportunity for litigation and compensation, albeit in limited circumstances. Catherine Fairbairn, *Compensation Bill*, House of Commons Library, 19 May 2006. See also Lord Falconer, *Compensation Culture*, speech 22 March 2005.

[46] Lord Falconer, *Risk and Redress*, speech 14 November 2005.

[47] Lord Dyson, *Magna Carta and the compensation culture*, The High Sheriff of Oxfordshire's Annual Law Lecture, 13 October 2015.

culture,[48] with some exceptions (whiplash injury claims in the UK account for a disproportionate number of car accident injury claims – 80 per cent), far in excess of those overseas, the fear was overdone. Compensation claims were often justified; indeed the first English code of law, that of King Æthelbert, King of Kent, in 602, provided that if a freeman were found to have committed adultery he was required to pay the injured party a 'wergeld', the value of the injured party's wife. He would also have to 'provide another wife with his own money, and bring her to the other'.[49] Claims for odd losses are nothing new, but their nature changes over time. And because of the perception that claims are excessive, there have been parliamentary attempts to tone things down.[50] But the overwhelming conclusion is that the compensation culture does not exist in Britain.

5.2.4   Access to Justice

Perversely the counter-complaint is that are to the contrary impediments to accessing justice. Litigation is expensive, the outcome unpredictable and the delay in process inevitable. Court fees are high, and lawyers' fees more so; lawyers are expensive because they are vulnerable to professional negligence claims if they under-engineer their work, so they over-engineer, to avoid criticism. They are also personally liable for costs if they fail to submit court documents in time, so they need expensive project management and information systems. Litigation in England is generally highly professional – but that professionalism comes expensive.

In criminal matters, legal aid may be available but only for the genuinely indigent, so that people may have to sacrifice their homes to defend themselves. There may be scope for criminal defence costs insurance, not available largely for public policy reasons in England. And civil claims are out of bounds for all but the wealthiest of litigants – except curiously

---

[48] See e.g. Frank Furedi, *The compensation culture is poisoning our society*, Daily Telegraph, 9 September 2012; Frank Furedi and J. Bristow, *The social cost of litigation*, Centre for Policy Studies, September 2012,; *Better Regulation Task Force, Better routes to redress*, 2004; Lord Young, *Common Sense, Common Safety*, 2010; *Compensation Culture*, House of Commons, Constitutional Affairs Committee, Third Report of Session 2005–06, HC 754-I; Ministry of Justice, *Reducing the number and costs of whiplash claims – a consultation on arrangements concerning whiplash injuries in England and Wales*, 2012.

[49] *The Laws of Æthelbert*, www.earlyenglishlaws.ac.uk/laws/texts/abt/view/#translation,1/ commentary,1_0_c_7. It provides in certain circumstances for 12-fold compensation, which is a real compensation culture.

[50] See e.g. the Compensation Act 2006; the Social Action, Responsibility and Heroism Act 2015.

where the claims are very large, where after-the-event insurance and litigation funding for, for example, class action lawsuits may be available. By 2017 there was around £1B available for litigation funding, but only for the very best cases. In some ways this is admirable; the costs discourage spurious litigation, unlike the US. But they also discourage meritorious litigation.[51]

5.3 Litigation Practice Issues

5.3.1 Introduction

Three issues amongst others have propelled the issue of how the courts are run to the forefront of policy review. The conflict between the judiciary and the executive is not normally a matter for the man on the street unless he is faced with a major constitutional issue; but costs, delay and complexity certainly are. This marks a return to the theme of the book, namely the inordinate extension of rules which in particular afflict court systems, certainly in England and Wales.

5.3.2 Costs

Costs of litigation have historically involved having to pay lawyers what are regarded by clients as very high fees, and that issue certainly remains. But allied to that these days are the costs levied by the state for access to the courts – and the way in which the courts organise themselves and the parties which can involve lengthy hearings and understanding of complex rules.

5.3.3 Court Fees

Most countries charge something for access to their judicial facilities. Charging for judicial services has mostly been uncontentious, although increases in charges in 2016 for access to English courts provoked discussion, coming as it did soon after the eight-hundredth anniversary of Magna Carta, which mentioned that the Crown would not sell justice to

---

[51] The dilemma is explored at length in *R (on the application of UNISON) v Lord Chancellor* [2017] UKSC 51 where the English Supreme Court held that the level of fees imposed for access to employment tribunals impeded access to justice and were unlawful both under English common law and under international human rights law.

the people.[52] Jeremy Bentham thought it iniquitous to charge for access to justice, calling it a tax on litigation.[53] But in fact for many years probate charges paid for a large part of the justice system in England, and rarely became a matter for political debate, and they eventually fell to relatively trivial levels. More recently pressures on public finances following the financial collapse in 2008 led however to material increases in court fees, certainly in the UK, raising concerns amongst the judiciary about whether that limited access to the courts.[54]

5.3.4 Complexity

The complexity of going to court has been a concern, bordering on a scandal, for hundreds of years, and despite occasional attempts in England to improve access, progress has been sporadic and mostly ineffective. The White Book, the book of procedural rules governing court procedure in England, for example extends over 3000 pages in two volumes, and other courts have similarly expansive rules – and consequently slow and lengthy hearings. There have been attempts in recent times to simplify the system, but mostly to little avail so far.

In more recent times, following the credit crunch, the courts like other public services have had to face the reality that, because of the inability of litigants to afford lawyers' fees, and the reduction in availability of legal aid, more cases are reaching the judges where the litigants are not represented by trained lawyers. In such cases the judges feel it is their obligation to help the litigants-in-person, who are rarely equipped to navigate the rules. This has provoked some of the leading judges themselves to try and simplify the system. Sir James Mumby was the President of the Family Division of the English High Court, which was faced with such pressures, following an acute reduction in the availability of legal aid, and called for such reform:

> In times of austerity, and faced with ever increasing numbers of litigants in person, we must constantly strive to improve, to streamline and to simplify

---

[52] Magna Carta, Clause 40; Ordinance against conspirators, 33 Edward I (1304). Cf Law Commission, *Proposals for the reform of the law relating to maintenance and champerty*, 1966.

[53] Jeremy Bentham, *A protest against law taxes*, 1795, p574.

[54] Lord Thomas of Cwmgiedd, Lord Chief Justice, *The legacy of Magna Carta: justice in the 21st century*, speech to the Legal Research Foundation, 25 September 2015. The UK Supreme Court however found in 2017 that government-imposed charges for access to employment tribunals were so high as to impede access to justice and therefore unlawful, both under international human rights law, and under general principles of English common law, *R (on the application of Unison) v Lord Chancellor* [2017] UKSC 51.

the system. We cannot afford to be complacent or to imagine that there is not much that remains to be done – for otherwise unwelcome changes may be imposed on us from outside. One small, though I believe important, step is the further tightening up of the Bundles Practice Direction by the imposition of pages limits for various types of documents. Consultation is under way: it has already produced mordant comment to the effect that for some unfathomable reasons there is no proposal to impose limits on judgements!...

The Family Procedure Rules, like their civil counterparts, are a masterpiece of traditional, if absurdly over-elaborate, drafting. But they are unreadable by litigants in person and, truth be told, largely unread by lawyers. They are simply not fit for purpose. The Red Book, like the White Book, is a remarkable monument of legal publishing but, I fear, fit only for the bonfire. Rules, to the extent that we still need them, must be short and written in simple plain English. But in reality, much that is currently embodies in rules will in future simply be embedded in the software of the digital court...

The thickets of numberless court forms – I speak literally; no-one knows how many there are, though in the family justice system alone they run into the hundreds – must be subject to drastic pruning... Court orders must be standardised ... with standard templates, self-populating boxes and drop down menus designed to ease and shorten the process of drafting.[55]

The costs, complexity and delay of litigation in England (compared with for example Denmark or the Netherlands, but not Italy) has provoked complaint for many years. And there have been several major attempts at reform. There have been three main ones (*Woolf, Jackson* and *Briggs*) and innumerable minor ones (and of course attempts to reform the criminal system, only briefly the subject of this chapter). While there is universal admiration of the quality of the judiciary – honest, intelligent, learned and experienced – there is less admiration for the fact that they are untrained and have spent several decades as part of a system to which they grown to be accustomed to and comfortable in. The suggestion is that this may make them less conscious of the apprehension that ordinary citizens feel when coming before the courts, the intimidating size of the White Book (the procedural rules) and of course the unpredictable and very high costs. Even US lawyers find English litigation astonishingly expensive.

---

[55] Sir James Munby, President of the Family Division of the High Court, *Speech*, Annual Dinner of the Family Law Bar Association, 26 February 2016.

5.3.5   The Trio of Reforms

In the first of the more recent reforms, Lord Woolf, one of the most highly respected of the judges, with exceptional personal and political skills, and with experience in conducting reviews,[56] was asked in 1996 to conduct a review of the civil procedure system,[57] which led to the eventual enactment of the Civil Procedure Act 1997.[58] It introduced the creation of civil procedure rules (which came into force in 1999) and established the Civil Justice Council, a body composed of members of the judiciary, members of the legal professions and civil servants, and charged with reviewing the civil justice system. Rule 1 of the new rules operated as a mission statement:

1 These Rules are a new procedural code with the overriding objective of enabling the court to deal with cases justly and at proportionate cost.
2 Dealing with a case justly includes, so far as is practicable –
   a ensuring that the parties are on an equal footing;
   b saving expense;
   c dealing with the case in ways which are proportionate –
      i to the amount of money involved;
      ii to the importance of the case;
      iii to the complexity of the issues; and
      iv to the financial position of each party;
   d ensuring that it is dealt with expeditiously and fairly; and
   e allotting to it an appropriate share of the court's resources, while taking into account the need to allot resources to other cases.

The idea was that the court was required to seek to give effect to the overriding objective when it exercised any power given to it by the Rules or interpreted any rule. And the rules were written to be intelligible not just to lawyers but to litigants-in-person.

It streamed claims which were small or large, it set up pre-action protocols, to have a system for sorting things out before the trial, and operated

---

[56] Although his inquiry into the riots at Strangeways prison in Manchester did not in practice lead to long-term material improvements, though slopping-out ended. Nor did similar inquiries into the LSE and Libya, and corruption at arms manufacturer BAe. See e.g. Mark Day et al., *Strangeways 25 years on: achieving fairness and justice in our prisons*, Prison Reform Trust, 2015.
[57] The Woolf Report, *Access to Justice*, 1996.
[58] The Woolf Report, *Access to Justice*, 1996.

a fast track for sensitive cases (like eviction). There are now protocols for all sorts of disputes, such as construction and engineering, defamation, disease and illness claims, disrepair cases, judicial review, personal injury claims, professional negligence and others.

And the new deal introduced penalties in costs (at different rates) and interest if the protocol was breached. Meanwhile the Civil Procedure Rule Committee, which included most of the good and great such as the Head of Civil Justice (i.e. Master of the Rolls), the Deputy Head of Civil Justice (if there was one), two or three judges of the Senior Courts, a Circuit judge, one or two district judges, a Master, three people who have a Supreme Court qualification including at least one with particular experience of practice in county courts, three people who had been authorised by a relevant approved regulator to conduct litigation in relation to all proceedings in the Senior Courts, including at least one with particular experience of practice in county courts, and two people with experience in and knowledge of the lay advice sector or consumer affairs, decided on revisions from time to time.

With the exception of the last two, of course, and even those were mostly quangocrats, there were no representatives of the real users of the courts, i.e. the consumer or commercial complainant.

There had been five specific objectives set by Lord Woolf:

  i to identify the core propositions in the rules and cut down the number of interconnecting provisions which were used
 ii to provide procedures which applied to the broadest possible range of cases and to reduce the number of instances in which a separate regime was provided for a special type of case
iii to reduce the size of the rules and the number of propositions contained in them
 iv to remove verbiage and top adopt a simpler and plainer style of drafting and
  v to give effect to the substantive reforms which he was proposing in the report.

The issue afterwards was whether the reforms had actually made the life of litigants easier. One way of judging their success is to look at the size of the White Book, the manual of court procedure. In 1999, the last edition before the reforms, it was 2400 pages. In 2015, the shorter rules resulted in a publication with around 3200 pages, about a third longer. Lord Justice

Richards, the Deputy Head of Civil Justice and the chairman of the Civil Procedure Rules Committee confessed:

> things have not turned out as Lord Woolf expected them to ... what was intended to be a simplified procedural code has turned out to be substantially larger and more complex than the body of rules it replaced ... the increase in size is not the result of fewer rules and longer commentary; everything has grown. You can go to the online version of the rules to see them without any commentary and you will find it a pretty formidable exercise to run through them. I have to say that without a commentary the rules can seem even more formidable than with a commentary.[59]

Lord Richards concluded that the best hope for simplification was in starting again with a new way of conducting litigation, as with an online court, and trying to make the whole process as well as the related rules, as simple as possible from the outset. But he thought that in fact things were going to become very much more complicated before that might happen. And when a judge says that, it might not be an unreasonable thought that while the will might be there, the mindset might not. English judges are taught in law school the concept of rules for procedure, that the Swiss method (i.e. rules-light) is naïve and unsophisticated and that in practice and theory the glory of the English system depends on sophisticated procedural protocols. As with the reforms described below, the reforms were designed by judges for judges, rather than by litigants for litigants. That brings to the system considerable experience and intellectual clarity, but it is not a natural way to improve a system for consumers. A different mindset might have included in the design committee consumers of the service, taking the views of judges into account, but not being driven by them.

There were subsequent attempts to prune the litigation thicket which the Woolf reforms seemed not to have been able to do. Lord Jackson produced a report in 2009, leading to a change in the system in 2013. The idea was to cut civil litigation costs and take account of the change in public policy which now allowed conditional fee agreements, hitherto banned. It produced complexity of its own, with the introduction of DBAs (damages-based agreements), QOCS (qualified one-way costs shifting) and CFAs (conditional fee agreements).[60]

---

[59] The Rt Hon Lord Justice Stephen Richards, *Civil litigation: should the rules be simpler?*, para 5 et seq., Gresham Lecture, 25 June 2015. He pointed out that the Swiss Civil Procedure Code is 100 pages.

[60] Lord Justice Jackson, *Review of Civil Litigation Costs Review: Final Report*, December 2009, Stationery Office, 2010 (584pp).

Only three years later Lord Briggs tried again.[61] In his Civil Courts Structure Review he suggested better judicial training (to help deal with litigants-in-person), the introduction of online courts for minor claims (under around £25,000 – but with its own rules, thus defeating the objective of simplification), and to cut down on appeals. It suggested unifying the civil justice system and finding more judges and quasi judges. The interim report struggled with how to deal with costs and some of the arcane concerns about the needs of Chancery and Queens Bench divisions and regional centres of specialist excellence. And it similarly failed to involve litigants in the design of the changes. Like its predecessors it did not ask: what do people with a need to get in front of a judge want? And why does it cost so much and take so long when eBay has a system which gives almost immediate results at virtually negligible cost?

5.3.6   Wisdom of the Ancients

In the light of both the suggestions for reform, and the increasingly lengthy court judgments, it might be sensible to refer to a court judgment of 1595; it is reproduced in full below. It is short itself, and does the job ('replication' means 'pleadings', i.e. the statement of complaint) . . .

IN THE HIGH COURT OF JUSTICE
CHANCERY COURT OF ENGLAND

15 February 1595

MYLWARD v WELDON

FORASMUCH as it now appeared to this Court, by a report made by the now Lord Keeper, (being then Master of the Rolls,) upon consideration had of the plaintiff's replication, according to an order of the 7th of May anno 37th Reginæ, *that the said replication doth amount to six score sheets of paper,* and yet all the matter thereof which is pertinent might have been well contrived in sixteen sheets of paper, wherefore the plaintiff was appointed to be examined to find out who drew the same replication, and by whose advice it was done, to the end that the offender might, for example sake, not only be punished, but also be fined to Her Majesty for that offence; and that the defendant might have his charges sustained thereby; the execution of which order was, by a later order made by the late Lord Keeper the 26th of June, Anno 37th Reginæ, suspended, without any express cause shewed thereof in that order, and was never since called upon until the matter came to be heard, on Tuesday lost, before the now Lord Keeper; at which time some mention

[61] Lord Justice Briggs, *Civil Courts Structure Review: Interim Report,* Judiciary of England and Wales, December 2015.

was again made of the same replication; and for that it now appeared to his Lordship, by the confession of Richard Mylward, alias Alexander, the plaintiff's son, that he the said Richard himself, did both draw, devise, and engross the same replication; and because his Lordship is of opinion that such an abuse is not in any sort to be tolerated, proceeding of a malicious purpose to increase the defendant's charge, and being fraught with much impertinent matter not fit for this Court; it is therefore ordered, that the Warden of the Fleet shall take the said Richard Mylward, alias Alexander, into his custody, and shall bring him into Westminster Hall, on Saturday next, about ten of the clock in the forenoon, and then and there shall cut a hole in the *myddest* of the same engrossed replication (which is delivered unto him for that purpose), and put the said Richard's head through the same hole, and so let the same replication hang about his shoulders, with the written side outward; and then, the same so hanging, shall lead the same Richard, bare headed and bare faced, round about Westminster Hall, whilst the Courts are sitting, and shall shew him at the bar of every of the three Courts within the Hall, and shall then take him back again to the Fleet, and keep him prisoner, until he shall have paid 10*l.* to Her Majesty for a fine, and 20 nobles to the defendant, for his costs in respect of the aforesaid abuse, which fine and costs are now adjudged and imposed upon him by this Court, for the abuse aforesaid.[62]

5.3.7   The Leveson Proposals (Criminal) 2015

Similar reforms were proposed by Sir Brian Leveson in relation to at least guilty pleas in criminal cases. It recommended improved integration in computer systems, better management of cases – and in some cases hearings online. This would involve the judge or magistrate sitting in front of one computer using the equivalent of Skype, the accused in front of another, and all the necessary papers from the police and social workers being filed online, and financial penalties being paid by credit card.[63]

The Leveson proposals did not address the dilemma of the intimidatory atmosphere for witnesses in criminal trials, with the delays, cross-examinations and treatment by members of the bar and the judiciary.[64] But it did focus on administrative issues. By the beginning of 2017 the government proposed as an experiment introducing the system for minor

---

[62] *Mylward v Weldon*, BAILII Citation Number: [1595] EWHC Ch 1; 21 ER 136,(1596) Tothill 102, Reg Lib-A 1596, fol.672 (1596); Reprinted in Monroe's Acta Cancellariæ 1545–1625, Vol. 1, p. 692.

[63] *Review of efficiency in criminal proceedings by the Rt Hon Sir Brian Leveson*, Judiciary of England and Wales, January 2015.

[64] *Structured mayhem: personal experiences of the Crown Court*, Criminal Justice Alliance, 2015.

uncontested criminal offences, such as unpaid train and tram fares, and unlicensed rods and lines.[65]

5.3.8   Costs and the Costs Rule

The cost of litigation in Britain is notorious; even the judiciary are aware of the challenge of paying for justice (though they may not be minded to do much about it):[66]

> Legal advice and representation cost significantly more in the UK than in almost any country in Europe. Four caveats should be made at once. First, this is a very broad generalisation indeed, and there are no doubt many exceptions, qualifications and explanation which could and should be made to this statement. Secondly, it is dangerous, and can be unfair, simply to compare the costs of lawyers between different countries. To take an obvious point, in the UK, a judge is largely an impartial umpire, whereas in much of Europe, the judge plays a much more proactive role, and therefore the judicial system in such countries is significantly more expensive than here. Thirdly, there is much to be said for the point that you pay for what you get. UK lawyers have a particularly fine reputation, as their presence and influence internationally demonstrates. Fourthly, any reform should be carried out, bearing in mind the importance of retaining a high quality legal profession, and its importance to the rule of law and to the economy.
>
> Having said that, there is a long-standing and justified concern about the level of cost of litigation . . . I have referred on more than one occasion to the need for 'quick and dirty' justice; it is not perfect, but it is better than no justice.

As will be seen below, reforms have been attempted in the past, and have failed. For example the NHS paid £1.1B in damages for compensation for clinical negligence in 2014 – of which a third went to lawyers. In 2013/14 legal costs paid to claimants amounted to 273 per cent of damages in claims of £1000 to £10,000, 153 per cent in claims of £10,000 to £25,000

---

[65] *Transforming our justice system: assisted digital strategy, automatic online conviction and statutory penalty, and panel composition in tribunals: government response,* Ministry of Justice, February 2017.

[66] Per Lord Neuberger, *The future of the bar,* lecture to the Conference of the Bar Councils of Northern Ireland and Ireland, Belfast, 20 June 2014, para 40, 41. It has proved all but impossible in practice, despite incessant reforms, to cut the costs of going to court, despite frequent attempts at reform, even though public policy has sought it for many years, see e.g. Lord Brougham: 'better something of justice than nothing . . . I should rather even slovenly justice than the absolute, peremptory and inflexible denial of justice' Hansard, (1830) HC Deb XXIV column 259.

and 54 per cent in claims of £100,000 to £250,000.[67] The NHS Litigation Authority when faced with lawyers' views that the costs are high because each case is fought cases when they should simply have paid says that by fighting cases it saves another £1.2B by rejecting claims that have no merit – or reducing the level of claims. It is hard if not impossible to substantiate the figures. By March 2015 the NHS LA had £15.5B of claims on its books; with ongoing care added, the costs are around £29B. That is a lot of negligence, and while the legal costs are clearly grating, they would not have to be paid if the NHS first did not commit negligence and secondly paid when the claim was made, rather than contested. The numbers do not include those who suffer without claiming – or are settled without litigation. And the opaque annual accounts of the NHS Litigation Authority make it hard to see just what was spent in defending claims.[68]

Similarly in family cases, the costs can be seen to be excessive. A distinguished family lawyer, Maggie Rae (a friend of mine) wrote a piece in the *Times* complaining about the fees she was compelled to charge in divorce and family cases.[69] She referred to cases such as those of *KSO v MJO* in 2009 where the family assets were £771,000 and the legal fees £553,000, i.e. 71 per cent of the assets. Or in 2015 *J v J*,[70] where the costs were £920,000 with assets of £2.9M. And in *Seagrove*[71] legal costs of £1.3M were 2.5 times the value of the claim of £500,000. She cited Sir James Munby, the most senior family judge in England and Wales: 'the accusatory finger which in the 19th century was appropriately pointed at the High Court of Chancery is in the modern world more appropriately pointed at the Family Division.' Her analysis concluded that the mischief was in the fact that that lawyers charged by time, and that each case was looked at by the judges on its merits, which takes time. She also noted that clients used lawyers as expensive counsellors, and fought when they should have settled. But the subtext was

---

[67] Frances Gibb, *Lawyers v doctors: counting the cost of clinical negligence*, The Times, 27 August 2015.

[68] *Fair Resolution: NHS LA Annual Review, report and accounts 2014/15*, National Health Service Litigation Authority, 2015.

[69] Maggie Rae, *Why family lawyers must tackle the way we charge for divorce*, The Times, 27 August 2015; *KSO v MJO* [2009] EWHC 2152 (Fam).

[70] *J v J*, unreported.

[71] *Seagrove v Sullivan* [2014] EWHC 4110 (Fam). On the other hand cases are relatively speedy compared with other jurisdictions: see e.g. *Canadian National Railway v Kitchener* [2014] ONSC 4929 regarding pollution, which started in 1989 and was still continuing in 2015. In *Jennens v Jennens* (the origin of Dickens' *Bleak House*), the litigation began in 1798 and was abandoned in 1915 (after 117 years), by which time the estate (£200M in modern money) had been entirely consumed by the legal fees.

that the judges do not take command of the case from the beginning, and are not trained to manage cases and look at proportionality. Nor do they insist as often as they should on the parties exploring mediation – which anyway in family cases is dysfunctional in its implementation.

Libel costs similarly are a perennial topic – largely driven by newspapers and others who often have to bear them. It is argued that libel costs in Britain are around 140 times those of other jurisdictions; such cases are run in the higher courts rather than a cheap-and-cheerful tribunal, although the attraction of such cases has diminished since the Defamation Act 2013 and the reduction in exposure to damages.[72]

The litigation system, with its insistence on form over function, with judges who are prisoners rather than managers of the system, who from their time as practising barristers are trained to enjoy the complexity rather than despair at it, who are often probably too intellectually able for some of the tedious work involved in judging, and who do not always appreciate the needs and financial constraints of the litigants (or 'consumer' in modern regulatory speak) is also at fault. And as we shall see below, it seems that the reforms that have been attempted have predominantly failed to resolve these core issues.

The English costs rules (i.e. that the loser pays both sides costs) made it hard for any but the richest to have recourse to the courts, especially since, until recently, it could be a criminal offence to support litigation.[73] Now there are alternatives.

5.3.9 Champerty, Maintenance, Barretry – and Insurance

Partly because of Magna Carta, third-party support of litigation had become virtually impossible for several hundred years. It and other similar charters outlawed champerty, maintenance and barretry, designed to

---

[72] Programme in comparative media law and policy, *A comparative study of costs in defamation proceedings across Europe*, Centre for socio-legal studies, University of Oxford, December 2008. It was paid for by the *Daily Mail*. It criticised in particular the availability of conditional fee agreements, which allowed law firms to fund cases without legal aid, permitting equality of (financial) arms between persons who felt defamed but could not otherwise afford to pay lawyers, and newspapers with deep pockets who might have defamed them. For an indication of the possible costs involved, see *Denial*, film, 2017, a lightly fictionalised account of defamation in relation to holocaust denial.

[73] Champerty and maintenance were common law offences made legal by the Criminal Law Act 1967 and Bribery Act 2010 (though not professionally acceptable); persons supporting litigation can expose themselves to the other side's costs, Superior Courts Act 1981 s51; *Aiden Shipping Co Ltd v Interbulk Ltd* [1986] AC 965.

avoid knights in armour causing trouble for the King and in later times by analogy to discourage frivolous litigation. 'Maintenance' involved the involvement of a non-interested party to encourage litigation. 'Champerty' involved the same, but in addition taking a share of any winnings in litigation. 'Barratry' was the bringing of vexatious litigation.[74]

In practice it meant that no-win, no-fee arrangements were both civil torts and criminal offences, and would have led to the disbarment of lawyers. These prohibitions were virtually unknown for example in the US, which is one reason why the US litigation rules allows lawyers to take a stake in the action – and provides for each side to pay their own costs, win or lose.

In England however over the last 20 years maintenance and its colleagues have largely become legal,[75] largely prompted by the fact that with heavy legal expenses, and a reduction in the availability of legal aid, litigation was not available to most of the public, and access to the courts was in practice denied. So now in England there are contingent fees, litigation funding and legal expenses insurance available to help mount a case.

5.3.10 After-the-Event Insurance

Legal expenses insurance is intended to provide cover against the potential costs of legal action brought by or against the policyholder; it was invented in the 1910s, following a fatal crash at Le Mans during which some spectators lost their lives and others were severely injured. Almost all such insurance is underwritten by specialist insurers to avoid conflicts of interest suffered by general insurers.

After-the-event insurance covers the possible legal costs involved even though the case involves an event which has already taken place. It can cover a wide range of possible disputes, including employment disputes, general litigation, disciplinary actions, human rights complaints and criminal charges. ATE insurance is taken out after an event, such as an accident which has caused an injury, to insure the policyholder for disbursements, as well as any costs should they lose their case. After-the-event insurance is usually used by people who do not have

---

[74] See Lord Chancellor's Department, Conditional fees: sharing the risks of litigation, 2000.
[75] Although in complicated and restricted ways, see Courts and Legal Services Act 1990 s58; Access to Justice Act 1999 s58A; Conditional Fee Agreements Regulations 2000 SI 2000 No 0692; Conditional Fee Agreements (Revocation) Regulations 2005 SI 2005 No 2305; Damage-Based Agreements Regulations 2013 SI 2013 No 0609.

before-the-event insurance. If the policyholder loses the case, then the insurance company will pay the opponent's legal costs and expenses, as well as the policyholder's own disbursements. Solicitors who take on, for example, personal injury cases on a 'no-win, no-fee' basis, may require their clients (whether defendants or plaintiffs) to take out after-the-event insurance so that costs will be covered if the case is lost. The premium payments, especially in a 'no-win, no-fee' arrangement, may be deferred until the conclusion of the case; thus in most cases the premium itself is self-insured. This insurance is often offered by solicitors and claims management companies. Where the ATE insurance policy was incepted before 1 April 2013, its cost will often be recoverable by the successful party from the losing side as part of an award of costs. ATE insurance policy costs in the UK are no longer recoverable by the successful party from the losing side.

5.3.11   Before-the-Event Insurance

Before-the-event insurance, is taken out by those wishing to protect themselves against potential litigation costs that could be incurred following a usually hypothetical future event. These costs often include fees of solicitors, barristers and expert witnesses, court fines and fees and any legal costs awarded to the other side. Before-the-event insurance is generally paid on an annual basis to an insurance company. It is often sold as part of a home or auto insurance package, and is also sometimes offered as a benefit to members of a trade union or association. The cost of BTE insurance is not recoverable as part of an award of costs.

5.3.12   Litigation Funding

Litigation funding has become a major resource for litigants, following the change in judicial policy. It enables a party to litigate or arbitrate without having to pay for it, whether because they are unable to pay for it or because they do not want to. A third-party professional funder can pay some or all of the costs/expenses associated with a dispute in return for a share of the proceeds of the dispute if it is successful. If the litigation is not successful, the funder bears the costs it has agreed to fund. Whilst it is primarily large cases that receive funding, there is no official minimum requirement for funding; this is decided by each individual funder on a case-by-case basis on what they think the chances are of success. As well as maybe half-a-dozen principal funders, managing very considerable funds, litigation crowdfunding, where hundreds or tens of thousands of individuals can help to pay for a legal dispute, either investing in a case in return for part of a contingent fee, or offering donations to support a legal right that they believe in, may also develop.

These several varieties of litigation support for complainants make for a complex matrix of possible alternatives, and some complainants may use more than one arrangement to allow their case to be mounted. These include therefore conditional fee agreements, damages-based agreements, fixed fees and third-party funding.[76]

5.3.13   Advertising of Legal Services

Similarly contributing to the availability of legal help have been the changes in some jurisdictions increasingly allowing the legality of advertising of legal services. These changes have had mixed consequences, allegedly promoting the frequency of frivolous claims, as well as making legal services unavailable where they would otherwise not have been.

5.3.14   Unavailability of Legal Aid and the Growth of Conditional Fee Agreements/Damages-Based Agreements

Later reforms in the UK following a report by Lord Justice Jackson involved the introduction of damages-based agreements, involving an agreement where lawyer and client shared the risk, and reward, of litigation.[77] Instead of paying fees upfront (by way of a fixed fee, or hourly charges) the lawyers recovers fees only as a percentage of any damages actually recovered. It is a form of success fee; if the claim fails, the lawyer remains unpaid. Because in practice the take-up of the system was modest, further reforms were later proposed, including[78]

- making the regulations clearer;
- increasing the DBA payments on success to make them more attractive to lawyers;

---

[76] Lord Neuberger, *From barretry, maintenance & champerty to litigation funding*, Harbour Litigation Funding, Gray's Inn, 8 May 2013.

[77] See *Callery v Gray* [2002] UKHL 28 on what is reasonable; and *Sarwar v Alam* [2001] EWCA Civ 1401; [2002] 1 WLR 1217, on whether CFA success fees and ATE insurance premiums are recoverable where there is in existence BTE insurance cover; Fairchild (HL 2002).

[78] Civil Justice Council, *The Damages-Based Agreements reform project: drafting and policy issues*, August 2015, 156pp.

- allowing lawyers and clients to agree the trigger point at which the DBA becomes payable and the circumstances under which it could be terminated; and
- that there might be concurrent hybrid damage-based agreements.

Because the risk/reward ratio for lawyers still remained unattractive, such agreements are not commonly used.

5.3.15 Delay

Courts and court systems are well aware that delay is an unattractive feature of a judicial framework. English and Scottish delays are relatively modest, compared with for example Indian delays, but are still slow compared with proceedings in EU jurisdictions or the US. Part of the delay in England and Wales is due to the magisterial procedural requirements which in many ways offer a professional approach to dispute resolution – but are expensive and time consuming. Even what were always supposed to be cheap-and-cheerful dispute arrangements to resolve employment disputes have become over-proceduralised and have themselves become sclerotic, slow and expensive.[79]

5.3.16 Class Actions and the Consumer Rights Act 2015

Class actions are one way in which the costs of litigation might be contained. For one individual with a few shares in Royal Bank of Scotland who might complain that the prospectus underlying the £12B rights issue in 2008 was misleading it is virtually impossible to sue and not cost-effective. The litigation would cost perhaps tens of millions – and the success if achieved would yield only a few pounds. On the other hand, if tens of thousands join together – and maybe obtain costs insurance or litigation funding or a combination of the two – it may well be worth it. Class actions have slowly been gaining traction in England and Wales, and throughout the world, despite the costs concerns in most non-US jurisdictions. And in England and Wales the Consumer Rights Act 2015 gave yet a further

---

[79] Even Magna Carta complained about delay: 'No freeman is to be taken or imprisoned or disseised of his free tenement or of his liberties or free customs, or outlawed or exiled or in any way ruined, nor will we go against such a man or send against him save by lawful judgment of his peers or by the law of the land. To no one will we sell or deny or delay right or justice' 1215, Chapter 29. See Lord Dyson, Master of the Rolls, *Delay too often defeats justice*, Speech at the Law Society Magna Carta Event, 22 April 2015.

encouragement to consumer class actions, for a faulty toaster for example. To claim for a £10 toaster would be absurd. To claim for recovery of the costs for many tens of thousands of toasters is a different proposition and if managed through a trade association (as the legislation requires) may provide a remedy otherwise impossible to achieve.

There are limits to the availability of what are called 'opt-out' class actions (i.e. everyone is in, unless they declare themselves out), the actions are heard by a specialist court, the Competition Appeal Tribunal, there must be a representative appointed by the court – and damages-based agreements are prohibited.

5.3.17   Control of the Court by the Judge

As was pointed out by a former Lord Chief Justice: 'In the Crown Court, time continues to be treated as an unlimited resource'.[80] And, he might have added, in all the other courts too. There are now in the English courts at least, case management conferences when the judges and other court officials have preliminary meetings with the parties to try and plot the eventual trial. But during the trial, judges are remarkably indulgent to the desire of advocates to argue to fill the time available, or mostly not available. By contrast, the US Supreme Court allows advocates 20 minutes apiece to put forward their arguments – as does the European Court of Justice. Criminal trials of course need, in the English system, opportunity for cross examination, and there are witnesses even in civil cases to be examined. But the mindset of the English judiciary is to refrain from hurrying a slow advocate.

5.3.18   Regulation and Compensation

If anything, such compensation culture as there is has been encouraged not so much by the courts, but by regulation. The Financial Ombudsman Service has built a reputation for encouraging claims, so that it has around 1000 ombudsman delivering determinations, i.e. more than the entire number of puisne judges in England, and complaints about PPI, personal pensions mis-selling and other claims have by far exceeded conventional litigation. These issues are dealt with elsewhere, but the encouragement by the regulators of individuals to make claims, coupled with

---

[80] Lord Judge, *The Safest Shield*, Hart, 2015, p101.

press comment, has somewhat changed the claims landscape out of all recognition.[81]

5.4   The Litigation Industry

5.4.1   The Role of the Judiciary

Judges, if anything, have tended to discourage as far as possible the use of litigation. They have promoted mediation and other forms of alternative dispute resolution and although mediation and arbitration remain the little brothers, their costs can be much lower, they are invariably private and they can if properly conducted result in the parties still speaking to each other at the end of the process. Collaborative justice, much debated in family matters, especially divorce, has been profoundly unsuccessful, perhaps because its design is inherently flawed. Commercial mediation for example is conducted normally using shuttle diplomacy, where the mediator shuttles between the parties in different rooms to see if there might be common ground, allowing the parties to divulge confidences without disclosure to the other side. Family mediation is normally conducted in one room with all parties present, to save time and money. It is unsurprising that it only intermittently works.[82]

At the same time judges in England rarely conduct cases with an aim of brevity. Counsel are allowed to expand as long as they wish; US judges run their courts usually with expedition. Counsel in the US Supreme Court are normally allowed 20 minutes – rather like those in the European Court of Justice. By contrast advocates' speeches in the English Supreme Court can last several days – and in one famous case using the English system and an English judge in the Caribbean, around a year.[83] And the judgments of English judges can be long; Nick Warren, a High Court judge specialising in pension disputes, produced a 500-page judgment which only led to further references to the court to tease out complexities in the judgment itself.[84] There are few pressures on judges to engage properly in case management, although they do occasionally complain about the fees involved

---

[81] Virtually all consumer regulators have ombudsman of some description dealing with consumer complaints, e.g. OFT.

[82] See William D. Popkin, *The judicial role: statutory interpretation and the pragmatic judicial partner*, Carolina Academic Press, 2013.

[83] The Thyssen foundation dispute, unreported, 2000; Robert Verkaik, *British lawyers bask in Bermuda heat as feuding family spends £368,000 a week on legal battle*, The Independent, 5 January 2000.

[84] *IBM United Kingdom Holdings v Dalgleish* [2014] 036 PBLR (365); [2014] EWHC 980 (Ch).

for the lawyers, now that they no longer charge them themselves. And even Lord Neuberger, one of the more self-aware judges observed:[85]

> I appreciate that as life gets more complicated, a degree of complexity in legislation is inevitable, but that reinforces, rather than undermines, the need for a self-denying ordinance by the law makers. The same applies to judges, who have the task of interpreting statutes and developing the common law. In the same speech, I referred to the fact that many judgments are much too long, adding this: *'Reading some judgments one rather loses the will to live – and I can say from experience that it is particularly disconcerting when it's your own judgment that you are reading.'* We need to make our judgments leaner and clearer – more accessible. If I ever had a mission statement for the Supreme Court, which I certainly will not, it would [be] to ensure that the law was as simple, as clear and as principled as possible.

5.4.2   The Legal Players: Judges, Barristers, Solicitors and Others (and the Consumers)

There is a slow but steady change in the nature of the players in the legal industry. Lord Neuberger observed that judges are no longer like they used to be: there is a Supreme Court, rather than a House of Lords, court proceedings can be photographed and televised (at least in the Supreme Court) – and there is tweeting and texting from courts (the rules against which are rarely enforced),[86] and judges are more commented upon than they used to be. Curiously judges have only recently enjoyed training, at least in the generally understood meaning of training, following the introduction of a Judicial College. They have experience, and they are selected from a small group of advocates. But they do not take qualifications in judging as do most other judges around the world – and their experience seems to reinforce the status quo.

Meanwhile professional lawyers owe a duty to the court, i.e. to the rule of law, greater than they owe to their clients, which makes them a profession rather than a business; the judges are keen that self-interest for lawyers (if not for judges) should take second place to their obligations to justice.[87] Those obligations were never imposed with the expectation that

---

[85] Lord Neuberger, *The future of the Bar*, lecture to the Conference of the Bar Councils of Northern Ireland and Ireland, Belfast, 20 June 2014, para 28.
[86] Lord Neuberger, *The future of the Bar*, lecture to the Conference of the Bar Councils of Northern Ireland and Ireland, Belfast, 20 June 2014.
[87] Ibid, para 8.

at some time in the future law firms would become publicly quoted companies. And now barristers can form partnership with solicitors and non-lawyers, and some solicitors have rights of audience in the higher courts. At the same time the professions, at least that of the solicitors, remain ever more tightly regulated. As Lord Neuberger observed in relation to financial services:[88]

> ... generally regulation is necessary and important, but it must be kept to a minimum, it must be targeted, and it must be effective. Regulation in the financial world failed to stop the rather obvious abuse of LIBOR fixing and PPI selling by UK banks, and it failed to catch the rather obvious frauds practised by Enron and Madoff in the US. Where regulation fails, a standard response is that we need more of it, whereas the correct response is that we need different regulation not more regulation.
>
> Further, if it is too intrusive and prescriptive, regulation can be positively self-defeating. If a profession is subjected to detailed rules of behaviour with a box-ticking approach and targets, people in the profession will quickly begin to feel that anything which is not forbidden by the rules is permitted. Any sense of what is right and wrong will start to dissipate, or at least to shrink. We therefore are at risk of losing a culture which enforces general standards of honesty, through understanding ... ethics and observing peer group behaviour. And a clear, correct and generally observed culture is very precious; it can do more for the public good, and costs far less, than almost any set of regulations.

There is an observable, though slow, progress towards an effective fusion of the professions, just at a time when specialists, such as legal executives, are breaking away.

5.4.3   Legal Aid

For all practical purposes civil legal aid in England has all but disappeared. But its removal from civil proceedings has identified gaps in the process, inappropriate responses for which are being explored. Instead of simplifying the system and reducing the costs, most remedies proposed have been to expand legal advice (i.e. reinvent civil legal aid). One reason is that the increasing numbers of litigants-in-person, i.e. private individuals without use of lawyers might be clogging the courts (the evidence on which is mixed). Alternatives to lawyers, people who may be paid or unpaid friends (known as McKenzie Friends) are sometimes used to speed the process but such McKenzie Friends are simply unqualified and untrained lawyers,

---

[88] Ibid, para 19.

which hardly solves the problem.[89] As Lord Woolf remarked, litigants-in-person should not be regarded 'as a problem for judges and for the court system rather than the person for whom the system of civil justice exists', and that the 'true problem is the court system and its procedures which are still too often inaccessible and incomprehensible to ordinary people'.[90] Unfortunately the Woolf reforms in practice did little to simplify process or reduce costs; what they could not really deal with was the mindset of judges and the bar, that procedure is important.

5.4.4   Did the Reforms Work?

Not all observers considered the Woolf reforms worked so as to improve access to justice. While the reforms were drafted by a judge, who had had wide experience of the faults of the system, they had failed to take into account the aspirations of the users.[91]

Some considered the changes were a disaster for the civil justice system and sought a radical re-think. Ten years after the reforms a review suggested that they (the Civil Procedure Rules) had failed in their objective. And the complaint, as ever, was that the ordinary member of the public was unable readily to gain access to that system. If that were so it meant that any rights he purported to enjoy were illusory. And access to justice was one of the Magna Carta objectives in 1215, as it was of the European Convention on Human Rights.

To judge by the criteria of access to justice, the revised Civil Procedure Rules seemed to have failed. The number of civil actions begun in the High Court in the year after they came into effect in April 1999 fell considerably. In 1990 and 1991, more than 350,000 actions had been started in the Queen's Bench Division, one of the divisions of the high court, and the one in which most commercial disputes were heard. By 1996 numbers had dropped to 150,000 new claims a year (partly because the jurisdiction of the county courts had been expanded). By 2000 just in excess of 20,000 claims were made. In 2002 and following, new claims dropped below 20,000. The reduction could be seen as achieving the objective; it meant that many cases were dealt with more quickly, cheaply and

---

[89] Monidipa Fouzder, *Give LIPs universal access to legal advice*, Law Society's Gazette, 28 November 2014. Ministry of Justice, *Litigants-in-person in private family law cases*, November 2014.
[90] Lord Woolf, *Access to justice*, 1995, Chapter 17, para 2.
[91] Lawrence West QC, *Have the Woolf reforms worked?*, The Times, 9 April 2009.

simply by more junior courts, or not filed at all. Another way of looking at it however was that fewer complainants could afford the time and money involved of going to court under the new rules. The reason was that the system 'front-loaded' the costs – it was not possible to put in a claim until considerable work had been done. In the past the work was done as the case progressed. The new system meant that the upfront cost of filing a claim had increased markedly and often made it not worthwhile to make a claim. Of course members of the bar and solicitors used to charging high fees for trials were disappointed. One commentator suggested:[92]

> Before the CPR, the corridor outside Court 12 in the Royal Courts of Justice, the Bear Garden and the Master's Corridor heaved with lawyers and their clients waiting hearings. Those places have been wastelands ever since. The experience in the county court has been similar.

The revisions to the CPR were driven by a concentration on those cases that went to trial at the expense of the vast majority of cases that did not, but which were resolved under the pressure of having to respond once the complaint had been filed. The CPR jettisoned the previous practice and procedure in the High Court and in the county court, together with all the law that had developed over more than 100 years following the reforms instituted in Victorian times. It substituted a regime invented by a committee, and involved the wholesale abandonment of years of experiential, incremental development of procedure, with the expected benefit of removing several thousand pages of rules.

Some changes effected by the reforms proved valuable, in particular the harmonisation of procedure between of the civil courts and the elimination of tendentious claims and evasive defences through (principally) the requirement for verification of pleadings by a statement of truth were welcome.

But the general thrust proved to be additional barriers to justice: the front-end loading of the expense of litigation and the paradoxical involvement of the judiciary in managing cases. Cases had to be virtually ready for trial before proceedings could be issued. And pre-action protocols require letters to be written, virtually duplicating pleadings in their detail, full disclosure and exchange of expert reports. In other words, potentially a case had to be fought through twice – once before proceedings were issued and once again afterwards. It ensured that claims that were litigated were

---

[92] Lawrence West QC, *Have the Woolf reforms worked?*, The Times, 9 April 2009.

properly prepared and considered, but it raised significantly increased the costs – and often unnecessarily.

The involvement of judges in case management should have speeded up litigation and reduced costs. But it has resulted in an increase in the cost of all litigation, whether the claim is one of the 90 per cent that would never be tried or not:

> The thought that, after a brief read of the papers, a judge (a former barrister or former solicitor) might be better able to grasp the detail of the case and take sensible decisions on its preparation for trial than are the lawyers with a more intimate knowledge of the case and the issues must always have been a little doubtful. Worse, it was an insult to the professionalism of the legal representatives, couched in mistrust.
>
> The prospects of better decisions being taken by the judiciary than by the lawyers become less and less certain as one moves down through the judicial ranks, given the increasingly variable quality of the personnel. When the variable quality of the office-holder is combined with wide areas of discretion that appeal courts will not review, you have a situation where the due administration of justice becomes liable to distortion and the consequences of becoming involved in litigation are highly unpredictable.
>
> This early involvement in incurring high cost, and the procedural uncertainties of incurring even greater costs, has put the civil justice system beyond the means of most members of the public. The radical changes made by the CPR require radical rethinking to reopen justice. That should begin with the restoration to the parties and their advisers of the right and responsibility to manage cases. Only when parties manage cases and judges decide them will access to justice be restored.[93]

5.4.5   Alternative Dispute Resolution

There have been continual attempts to find alternatives to the ponderous and expensive litigation process. The generic title for non-litigation is 'alternative dispute resolution', which can include negotiation, mediation and arbitration. Arbitration can involve as much expense and technical complexity as litigation; its main benefit is that it is a dispute held in private, and the parties pay for their own 'judge'.[94]

---

[93] Ibid.

[94] *Alternative dispute resolution for consumers: implementing the Alternative Dispute Resolution Directive and Online Dispute Resolution Regulation*, Department for Business Innovation and Skills, March 2014.

5.4.6 How They Fixed It in Ireland

Irish litigation had been seen some years ago as the litigation capital of Europe.[95] The so-called tort tax was alleged to have been rising at twice the rate of the wider economy, but the Irish Government in 2004 established the Personal Injuries Assessment Board, a tribunal system to deal with claims where liability is uncontested. According to the Minister for Enterprise, Trade and Development, Michael Martin, the PIAB was assessing claims three times faster and four times more cheaply than under the old litigation system.[96] The PIAB claimed, perhaps with some justification, that the average cost of processing a claim under the PIAB system was 10 per cent of the award made, while under litigation the cost was 46 per cent. And while around 35,000 writs (claims) had been filed in the Irish High Court in 2004 in respect of personal injury cases, the figure had dropped to 4000 in 2005. Not only that but the adherents of the new system suggest that the compensation is delivered within nine months, rather than the average three years under conventional litigation.

It is not a perfect system. The PIAB is a public service and itself costs the public purse.[97] Its aim as set out in its vision statement is to 'establish a positive claims resolution culture in Ireland through advancing a fair and non-adversarial approach in the assessment of personal injury caused by negligence'. And its mission statement declares it wishes to be 'the independent facilitator in the delivery of compensation entitlements in a fair, prompt and transparent manner for the benefit of society.'

The costs to the country seem low; indeed it seems to be self-financing through fees levied on claimants and respondents (mostly the latter). The role of the state in dispute resolution goes back to invention of society; it was always the duty of the sovereign or chief to sort out disputes rather than allow lynching or the triumph of might over right. The invention of a state system as an alternative to the state's courts is somewhat novel and it seems to have been achieved without heavy resistance by the legal profession.

Its scope is of course limited to personal injury issues, but even there it seems to avoid the problems that afflicted the UK market with claims

---

[95] John Murray Brown, *Lawyers lose out as Ireland bucks trend with crackdown on tort law*, Financial Times, 23 December 2006.

[96] Personal Injuries Assessment Board, *Press Release*, 11 October 2006.

[97] Personal Injuries Assessment Board, *Strategic Plan 2006–2010*, September 2006. www.piab .ie.

farming. There is always a dilemma or tension in policy between involving the state in private matters, where the track record, at least in the UK has been imperfect, and the state's duty to facilitate dispute resolution. The Irish experiment by all accounts has so far been successful, at least in terms of overhead costs and sped of payout, although the jury may still be out in relation to the level of compensation achieved. Not only that, but there is also some (limited) evidence that individuals do like to have their day in court.

5.4.7 How They Fixed It in Italy

Many countries have problems with their judicial systems. The Russian system is corrupted by government influence. But the Italian system has a special place in the study of comparative judicial systems. The slowness of the judicial systems makes it all but impossible for claimants to achieve a remedy, in particular in relation to debt recovery. The president of the main civil court in Turin discovered when appointed in 2002 that the oldest case had been initiated 43 years previously. He succeeded the average length of a civil case was cut from seven years to three. He introduced 'fifo' rather than 'lifo' which had previously been operated. The aim was to cut all trial stages to be completed within 12 months. Italy's system might be on the mend.[98]

That's not quite the case in England.

5.4.8 Judges

There is a considerable shortage of judges in many jurisdictions (the US being a notable exception). They are expensive, and good ones are hard to find.

5.4.9 Judicial Conflicts of Interest

There is no doubt that English (and Scottish) judges are of impeccable integrity. But they, and judges in equally upstanding jurisdictions are human. It is rare in modern times to find instances where judges

---

[98] *Italy's judicial system: justice denied?*, Economist, 19 July 2014, p37; Roger Abravanel, *Meritocrazia*, 2008 (www.meritocrazia.com/). Improvements included shorter judgments, concentration on management rather than jurisprudence and performance indicators for judges.

are corrupt, but it is not unreasonable to find them self-interested. In 1987 the state legislature of Pennsylvania brought into force an act that increased the salaries of judges – and gave legislators (i.e. politicians) an unvouchered allowance of $12,000 a year. The Act provided that if at some stage any part of the act was held to be unconstitutional (and there was a suspicion that the expenses arrangements might have been) then the whole act failed – and of course the increases in judicial salaries. The idea was to persuade the judges if the case ever came before them not to hold the clause unconstitutional because they would themselves suffer.

5.4.10   Judicial Reluctance to Judge

One of the better elements of US television are the legal dramas, *Allie McBeal* etc. of which there used to be a regular quotient. One of the standard scenes was that of the sage figure-wagging judge, who would call the squabbling trial attorneys to 'approach the bench' and instruct them to stop pussyfooting and get on with the case; alternatively he would call them for a meeting in his chambers. This clichéd scene reflected much of reality, and comes as something of an astonishment to English trial lawyers or barristers, who are used not to have their perorations interrupted.

The reason is that while in the States the judge runs his court in England the judge presides over the court, which the barristers all but run. This involves court management rather than case management which is indeed increasingly part of the English system. Even where judges attempt to impose efficiency during oral presentations, the bar may be resistant. Advocates are mostly remunerated on a daily retainer, and efficiency can cut the income, and much of the research they have done, just in case, is not presented. Clients also like their day in court; and many clients also like to see what they have paid for.

This expenditure of court time is very English. The European Court of Justice and the US Supreme Court for example each allow the advocates before them 20 minutes each to present their case. In most cases judgments are usually swiftly delivered thereafter and are predominantly short. English judgments on the other hand can be prolix.[99]

Partly this is because judges are reluctant to use their discretion for fear of being criticised by higher courts for not examining all alternative arguments. Most judges are punctilious in giving advocates every courtesy and

---

[99] See e.g. *IBM United Kingdom Holdings v Dalgleish* [2015] 032 PBLR (173); [2015] EWHC 389 (Ch) (550 A4 typescript pages).

allowing them the opportunity to present arguments without limit. But this courtesy can prove expensive for the parties, and result in high costs and poor justice. When judges do act as judges, i.e. use their discretion and intelligence, it can be instructive:[100]

> Mr Kayes was stopped while driving his trailer full of mobile catering equipment home from a show where he had been trading and was asked for his licence. He explained 'I am green to all this. I have had a lorry purposely built to move my showman's equipment about. That's all I could say. I thought I was doing everything by the book. I classed it as a showman's restricted vehicle. I can only use it for my use'. Since that explanation involves, as a matter of law, the classification of a trailer of catering equipment as a 'vehicle or trailer not constructed primarily to carry a load, but specially designed for the special purposes of engineering operations', it is not perhaps surprising that his explanation was not regarded as entirely satisfactory. In the event, he was prosecuted for unlawful use of a goods vehicle without a license, a test certificate, recording equipment required by EU law; and for having paid the wrong level of vehicle excise duty.
>
> The justices dismissed the charges against Mr Kayes because it was clear to them, as to anybody less concerned with the tedious details of the text of the legislation than with the eternal verities of the law as it has always been 'accepted' to apply, that 'Our findings were based on the persuasive and particular evidence given by Mr Kayes in which we felt that it was self-evident that he was a showman and as such it was self-evident that his vehicle was a showman's goods vehicle within the meaning of the Act'.

The authorities appealed to the Administrative Court and Mr Kayes represented himself. And won. The judge found a reason not strictly law based to excuse him. It was because it was sensible and fair: 'it is not in the public interest and necessary for him to receive convictions.' Judges need to be able to judge – and not be intimidated by the *Daily Mail*, Lord Chancellors or even their superiors. It might be part of their oath; 'I will find a way round strict law if I think it fair and sensible to do so', which was one of the origins of equity. Judges however in recent times where the politicians have been especially irritable about judicial intervention, sometimes exceeding their constitutional brief, have been persuaded to be cautious.[101] There is an uneasy balance between not challenging the

---

[100] Daniel Greenberg, *A refreshing decision, or the rule of law in action: Case note Vehicle & Operator Services Agency, R on the application of v Kayes* [2012] EWHC 1489 (Admin), [2012] 33(3) Statute Law Review 409–411.

[101] Lord Dyson, Master of the Rolls, *Where the Common Law Fears to tread: annual lecture for the Administrative Law Bar Association* [2013] 34(1) Statute Law Review 1–11. See also Lord Bingham, *The judge as lawmaker: an English perspective*, in *The Struggle for Simplicity*

decisions of democratically elected politicians and supporting the rights and freedoms of individual subjects. Parliament sometimes forgets to improve the law, or feels it lacks the time or political capital; in any event it is not reasonable to expect Parliament to foresee every eventually that may occur (which is one of the arguments of this book for less legislation); the most cited example involved a technical legal issue about whether there was a right of recovery to restitution of money paid following an *ultra vires* (beyond its powers) demand by a public authority.[102] And it is not always certain where that boundary is:

> I feel bound however to say that, although I am well aware of the existence of the boundary. I am never quite sure where to find it. Its position seems to vary from case to case. Indeed, if it were to be as firmly and clearly drawn as some of our mentors would wish, I cannot help feeling that a number of leading cases in your Lordships' House would never have been decided the way they were. For example, the minority view would have prevailed in *Donoghue v Stevenson* [1932] AC 562; our modern law of judicial review would never have developed from its old, ineffectual, origins; and *Mareva* injunctions would never have seen the light of day. Much seems to depend upon the circumstances of the particular case.

This common law approach, where the judges take it upon themselves to right a wrong which the law otherwise would not provide for has been under constant challenge by Parliament for many years, but especially in recent years where there have been battles over the extent of the powers of ministers, and the sometimes oppressive decisions of Parliament itself.

In practice there are times when the judges make new law; in consumer protection, this happened many years before Parliament sought fit to intervene.[103] But they will not intervene where it would be excessive to do so; for example they will not intervene to make a health authority

---

in the Law: *Essays for Lord Cooke of Thorndon*, New Zealand, 1997. Lord Thorndon was possibly the most eminent New Zealand judge, and the only one ever to sit in the English House of Lords; he expressed the view that that, in the most exceptional circumstances, an Act of Parliament that egregiously violated fundamental rights might be void at common law. The Chinese are using local courts to make law in difficult circumstances, Chao Xi, *Local courts as legislators? Judicial lawmaking by subnational courts in China* [2012] Statute Law Review 39–57.

[102] See *Woolwich Building Society v Inland Revenue Commissioners* [1992] 3 WLR 366, per Lord Goff; I was a minor beneficiary of this view when I was sued for £30M in respect of tax wrongly paid by a client to the Inland Revenue which they refused to repay. They did repay it, but only after being taken to court, see *Hillsdown Holdings v IRC* 1999 STC 566.

[103] See e.g. *Donoghue v Stevenson* [1932] UKHL 100 (on the duty of a manufacturer to supply decent ginger beer).

decide how to spend its budget,[104] or how discretionary investment management should be exercised.[105]

Such constitutional struggles are now emerging in several areas of law. Delegation of judicial power by the Crown aka Parliament has an ancient history.[106] It has proved effective over the ages. In recent years the battle however has intensified between the government and the judiciary because in particular each have a view (different of course) about who decides what the law means. The government think it should mean what they always wanted it to mean, regardless of the words, or what is fair. The judges think that the law means what the words say it means, and they also use principles of fairness to shade their decisions.

In the past this long-running dispute was usually resolved by a former constitutional anomaly since the Lord Chancellor was at the same time in the cabinet, in the courts and in the House of Lords. In other words he was a member of the legislature, the executive and the judiciary. Despite the breach of the rule of constitutional balance, in practice it used to work well, because if there were a problem, the Lord Chancellor would compromise with himself. Some years ago the system was changed during a Blair administration and a former Lord Chancellor (Chris Grayling) became the first non-lawyer ever to hold the post. His management of the position was not universally admired.

One reason for the then dissonance is that the government sometimes tries to do things that are not exactly in accordance with the words of the law. Governments in the past have been frustrated for example with what the judges have said in relation to its attempts to deport persons such as Abu Hamza, or Somalian murderers. And few politicians take kindly to being held to account by what they regard as unelected officials who do not have to report to an electorate, populist or not.

---

[104] *R v Cambridgeshire Health Authority ex p B* [1995] 1 WLR 898.

[105] *Nestle v National Westminster* [1992] EWCA Civ 12, [1993] 1 WLR 1260.

[106] See e.g. *Exodus*, 18:14–18:

14 And when Moses' father in law saw all that he did to the people, he said, What is this thing that thou doest to the people? why sittest thou thyself alone, and all the people stand by thee from morning unto even?

15 And Moses said unto his father in law, Because the people come unto me to enquire of God:

16 When they have a matter, they come unto me; and I judge between one and another, and I do make them know the statutes of God, and his laws.

17 And Moses' father in law said unto him, The thing that thou doest is not good.

18 Thou wilt surely wear away, both thou, and this people that is with thee: for this thing is too heavy for thee; thou art not able to perform it thyself alone.

This has been most evident recently in the example of two idiosyncratic English politicians on opposite sides of the political spectrum, Margaret Hodge (an MP) and Theresa May (Home Secretary and later Prime Minister). Margaret Hodge, who had a mixed reputation when in local government, was fiercely critical of both companies and HMRC in the Public Accounts Committee when interrogating senior accountants about their tax advice to clients – but failed to comprehend that she was herself responsible for voting for the reliefs and the complexity of the taxation system. She objected when advisers read the legislation which she had voted for; it is entirely probable that she had herself not read or understood the fiscal legislation she had voted for. And she found it hard to come to terms with the fact that taxpayers needed advisers to guide them through the tax reliefs that she and her colleagues had voted for over time. It might have been pointed out to her that there are around 17,000 pages in the tax code and few taxpayers have the resources be able to meet the requirements without external help.[107]

Mrs May wrote a piece[108] in the *Mail on Sunday* castigating judges who allow people that she wants to remove to stay in the country. The reason the judges countermanded her views was that they considered she was operating outside the law. Politicians are uniquely positioned to respond to law they do not like; she and her colleagues can change it, which is more than others can do. This is the reason that courts construe legislation against the government where there is a doubt about the meaning of the law.

Incidentally there is a similar war taking place in relation to the interpretation of tax laws; the judges until recently interpreted the law, if there was an ambiguity, against HMRC – simply because it is HMRC and the government who write the rules, so there is an in-built imbalance against the citizen. Where there is a doubt, the individual should not suffer. The experience in film tax cases in 2015 was particularly unattractive; it was the government that gave special tax reliefs on films, and then pretended outrage when people took advantage of them. Graham Aaronson QC, one

---

[107] See e.g. *Tax avoidance: the role of large accountancy firms (follow up)*, Thirty-eighth report of session 2014–15, House of Commons, Public Accounts Committee, HC 860, 6 February 2015.

[108] Theresa May, '*It's MY job to deport foreigners who commit serious crime – and I'll fight any judge who stands in my way*'. Mail on Sunday, 17 February 2013 and see subsequent similar remarks by the then Lord Chancellor (Chris Grayling) in relation to the Human Rights Act. David Pannick QC, *Home secretary needs to be reminded about separation of powers*, The Times, 28 February 2013.

of the most distinguished and highly remunerated members of the tax bar, devised a system accepted by government involving the use of an independent panel appointed by HMRC, to determine in the case of poorly drafted tax legislation whether it was fair that people take advantage of them, known as the General Anti-Abuse Rule panel.[109] He did not balance that with recommending a similar power for them to judge whether an HMRC which takes advantage of unfair tax laws should also behave reasonably. It is this imbalance of power, and the right to oppress, which reflected adversely on the system.[110]

This rather demeaning conflict between government and judges (this is not a party political issue – similar oppressive tendencies were expressed by former Home Secretaries David Blunkett and Jack Straw on the left of the political spectrum) later emerged in an issue in a pension case. In *Walker* Mr Walker was a member of the Innospec pension scheme, working out of Singapore, and retired in 2003 with a company pension of £85,000 pa. That year he moved with his same-sex partner to London and entered into a civil partnership in 2006. Scheme rules were changed later in 2006 to permit survivor benefits for civil partners, but only in respect of service since December 2005. This meant that the survivor would be entitled to a pension of around £500 pa and not of around £41,000 pa. Mr Walker and his partner thought that amounted to discrimination; if his partner had been female and heterosexually married, she would have been entitled to a full survivor's pension.[111]

The case went before a junior court, an employment tribunal. And the tribunal, not all of whose members were qualified lawyers, concluded that the UK law which gave exemption against the anti-discrimination law to pension schemes in relation to rights earned before 2006, was illegal under EU law. It held that failure to provide survivor's benefits to a civil partner equivalent to those of a married partner amounts to both direct and

---

[109] Graham Aaronson QC, *An Oxymoronic Endeavour? A General Anti-Abuse Rule for taxation to give effect to the will of Parliament by overriding Parliament's statutes*, Statute Law Society, Lecture, February 2013; HM Treasury, www.hm-treasury.gov.uk/tax_avoidance_gaar.htm; House of Commons, Committee of Public Accounts, *Tax avoidance: tackling marketed avoidance schemes*, 29th Report of Session 2012–13, HC 788, 28 January 2013.

[110] *Becket*, film, 1964; Dave Fishwick, *Bank of Dave*, Paperback: 288 pages, Virgin Books (10 May 2012), ISBN-10: 0753540789, ISBN-13: 978-0753540787; Roger McGough, I want to be the leader, www.poemhunter.com/poem/the-leader/; Marc Shoffman, *Pensioner faces £45,000 bill after FAS error*, FT Adviser 27 February 2013; Marc Shoffman, *Sir Hector's trust late filing return*, FT Adviser, 27 February 2013.

[111] *Walker v Innospec* [2013] 036 PBLR (011) (United Kingdom: England and Wales: Employment Tribunal (Manchester)) 2012 November 13.

indirect discrimination, contrary to the provisions of the Equality Act 2010. And the purported exception in the Equality Act for such cases was in contravention of the governing EU Directive. The provisions of the pension scheme were declared to be discriminatory; the decision on the remedy was reserved to a further hearing. It was a brave move for an employment tribunal in Manchester to declare that a UK law is invalid and that Parliament got it wrong.

Some might say that it might be better to trust a decision of an independent, maybe slightly fogeyish, honest, intelligent, incorruptible judge, free of hypocrisy, personal interest and populist pressures to that of a politician who may find it expedient to interpret laws to suit his own interests and those of the *Daily Mail*. Whilst it may be that judges are sometimes be out to lunch, their conclusions seem infinitely preferable to politicians who are sometimes out to lynch.[112]

5.4.11 The Costs

Judges not infrequently inveigh against the costs involved in litigation; and of course there have been several attempts at reform intended to cut the costs, most notably the Woolf and Jackson reforms. They have largely been ineffective because the fault lies not with the parties or even their lawyers, but with the judges themselves, who have always been reluctant to manage trial costs or even take them into account. They call for immense quantities of evidence, only a small quantity of which is ever used in action, and painfully slow giving of evidence.

And proportionality is a concept with which the courts seem to struggle. Mr and Mrs Rawlings made identical wills leaving everything to each other, or if they both died to their adopted son Terry. They did not leave anything to their two natural children. The solicitor who drew the wills forgot to notice that instead of witnessing each other's wills, they witnessed their own (which meant they would have been ineffective; a beneficiary cannot inherit under a will that he has witnessed). When Mrs Rawlings died, the wills were not inspected because everything passed by

---

[112] And the English judiciary do continue to expand the boundaries of the common law to their credit; see e.g. *R (on the application of Unison) v Lord Chancellor* [2017] UKSC 51 on the illegality of high charges for access by employees to employment tribunals, and *Kennedy v The Charity Commission* [2014] UKSC 20 on whether a regulator which used the excuse of an exclusion provision in the Freedom of Information Act 2000 to deny disclosure of information was nevertheless obliged under common law to disclose it. It was.

survivorship. But when Mr Rawlings died later, the mistake was discovered, the natural sons contended his will was invalid, and they should inherit the £70,000 left in the estate. Terry was forced by the solicitors' insurers to bring a formal claim, but of course the costs exhausted the estate. There was a fight about the costs, because an alternative procedure would have been to apply to the court for 'rectification', i.e. for the court to declare that despite the errors the will stood. It should have been no more than an hour or so in court. Eventually the case went to the House of Lords (with two hearings, once on rectification and again on costs).[113]

5.4.12 Solicitors

Solicitors' fees are legion; they have however been largely squeezed out of providing legal aid work by reductions in hourly rates to levels which are unsustainable; and in relation to conventional work the costs of professional indemnity insurance and compliance costs, which indeed protect the public, mean that access to a solicitor can be expensive and in many cases unaffordable for individuals and small companies. Even large companies can find costs intimidating, which is why they sometimes resort to litigation funding. Professional governance costs for solicitors are now high, which is why smaller firms find it harder to survive.[114] But there is also room for improvement in litigation culture adopted by solicitors. Game-playing and gaming the rules is seen by many solicitors as acceptable ways in which to conduct litigation, and attempting to frighten the other side with absurd costs is routine. Changing litigation culture remains a challenge for regulators (who by and large have ignored it) and the judiciary, who offer only mild reproval.[115]

---

[113] Cahal Milmo, *Dispute over 'botched' £70,000 family will signed by the wrong spouses reaches Supreme Court*, Independent, 3 December 2013; *Marley v Rawlings* [2014] UKSC 2, and on costs *Marley v Rawlings & Anor (Rev 2)* [2014] UKSC 51. The dispute involved £70,000, and with two hearings in the Supreme Court, the costs are likely to have been multiple of that. The insurers wanted to make a point, but the judges should have shut the case down.

[114] Michael Woollcombe-Clarke, *The law of legal costs and why the price of justice is so disproportionately expensive*, Legal Cheek, 21 November 2016.

[115] *The RBS Rights Issue Litigation* [2015] EWHC 3422 (Ch), which contained profound criticism of the estimate of defence lawyers' estimate of over £100M defence costs. The case involved substantial sums, around several billion, but the legal issues were relatively simple. The case was not referred however by the judge to the professional regulatory body for review.

5.4.13   Barristers

Barristers are a confection of what US lawyers call trial lawyers, and opinion writers. Their training is again limited to the law, so few have commercial or worldly experience, and most operate in a closed community that is difficult for clients and others to understand. There is a wider than normal disparity between the run-of-the-mill barrister doing divorce and crime on the cheap, barely making a living, and the commercial silk making a very substantial income. But even a cheap barrister can prove expensive for someone on a modest income, which is why there is a resort to either not using solicitors and barristers at all, or using unqualified help.

5.4.14   McKenzie Friends – and the Best Being the Enemy of the Good

Largely because of the reduction in availability of legal aid, there has been a growth of unqualified advice, known in England as McKenzie Friends, where the courts will allow an otherwise unrepresented litigant or defendant to use a friend, who may be remunerated. This has caused minor dissension within the legal profession. On the one hand, what is the point in requiring professionally qualified individuals providing advice and support (and forbidding solicitors from having rights of audience in the higher courts for example) if anyone can stand and speak. On the other hand, it is expensive for the system, and unfair to the individual litigant, not to have support available.[116] But the issue remains whether such support which eliminates the regulatory objective of legal regulators of 'promoting and protecting the public' with indemnity insurance protection, proper training and discipline for wrongdoing. The issue of McKenzie Friends demonstrates the danger of regulating in such a way that makes a service or product too expensive for consumers; in other words allowing the public a five-star service or nothing at all.[117]

5.4.15   Conditional Fee Agreements

The *Rawlings* case mentioned above was dealt with in the Supreme Court under a conditional fee agreement, i.e. the lawyers would be paid out of

---

[116] *Reforming the courts' approach to McKenzie Friends*, Legal Services Board, LSB submission in response to the Judicial Executive Board consultation on the courts' approach to McKenzie Friends, 25 May 2016.

[117] Jonathan Goldsmith, *The LSB and McKenzie Friends*, Law Society Gazette, 1 June 2016.

any winnings. In themselves there have been considerable criticisms of CFA some of whom regard them as malign.[118]

5.5 Conclusions

Despite their best efforts the reformers have struggled to make much headway in making justice accessible. The senior judiciary, at least, are genuinely aware of the challenges in judicial administration, and of delivering judgments that are both compliant with the law, yet do justice to the litigant, not always an easy thing to achieve. There are occasional foolish decisions, but most are reversed on appeal, and the tabloid stereotype of out-of-touch judges seems inaccurate, although they do represent the better-educated and informed section of the population, and may not be the natural readership of the tabloids. The judiciary as a whole is conscious of its lack of diversity, and the problems that poses.[119] They have also by and large dealt with the tendencies to a compensation culture; if anything, regulated products apart, the real problem is that it is hard in most cases to recover damages for genuine harm.

There is clearly room for improvement. The court system, both civil and criminal, is expensive and slow – and procedurally obsessed with the minutiae of the rules, which judges often confuse with better court management and fairness between parties. It lacks input from the users, who might better be consulted about what they seek from a dispute resolution system which has a quasi-monopoly. It may be that there should be competition in dispute resolution provision, more than is offered by private arbitrators, mediators and eBay.

And it may be that there should be more judges, better trained in judicial administration and the commercial realities of life, better recognising that individuals need cheaper if dirtier justice, able to cut to the chase in oral argument and written submissions, adopting where necessary the practice of US and European courts which limit the length of trials.

5.5.1 ADR for Consumers

One reform might be the wider implementation of alternative dispute resolution, a cheaper and quicker alternative to the courts where a consumer

---

[118] Cf *Coventry v Lawrence (No 2)* [2014] UKSC 46. See e.g. Professor Lesley King, *The costs of rectification*, [2014] Law Society's Gazette 6 October 2014.

[119] *Supreme Court selection process launched*, Supreme Court, Press release, 16 February 2017; *Report of the Advisory Panel on Judicial Diversity 2010*, Ministry of Justice, 2010.

is not able to resolve their complaint directly with a business from whom they have made a purchase.[120] In principle ADR aims to help consumers avoid using the courts, but in practice its implementation throughout the EU has been patchy. Following an EU Directive each EU country must appoint an entity to ensure that ADR services function properly (in the UK it is the Trading Standards Institute) – and like ordinary litigation, the system is supposed to be self-funding. There is a similar system for cross-border online disputes.[121] But despite the legislation, and the number of ADR systems available,[122] in practice the system is only lightly used. Now traders, once they fail to resolve a dispute through their own customer service efforts, are required to advise the consumer of an alternative dispute resolution body, relevant to their sector and the nature of the specific complaint. The trader is not compelled to use the ADR body but it was hoped that the requirement to identify an appropriate body, and the potential benefits in customer relations such schemes may offer, would encourage traders to do so. Evidence so far has not been encouraging.

Alternative Dispute Resolution describes a range of processes that offer the parties an easier, quicker and more cost-effective mechanism to resolve complaints when compared to the court process. It is generally accepted that consumers are more willing to use these processes than to use the court process. It is also accepted that these processes are much better at

---

[120] Department for Business Innovation and Skills, *Alternative Dispute Resolution for Consumers*, November 2014.

[121] European Union, *Directive 2013/11/EU of the European parliament and of the Council of 21 may 2013 on alternative dispute resolution for consumer disputes and amending Regulation (EC) No2006/2004 and Directive 2009/22/EC (Directive on consumer ADR)* OJ L 165/63, 18 June 2013. European Union, *Regulation (EU) No 524/2013 of the European parliament and of the Council of 21 May 2013 on online dispute resolution for consumer disputes and amending regulation (EC) No 2006/2004 and Directive 2009/22/EC (regulation on consumer ODR)*, OJ L 165/1, 18 June 2013. Regulation on consumer Online Dispute Resolution. See the EU website webgate.ec.europa.eu/odr/main/index .cfm?event=main.home.show&lng=EN

[122] The Alternative Dispute Resolution for Consumer Disputes (Competent Authorities and Information) Regulations 2015 SI 2015 No 0542: ABTA, ADR Group, Association of Chartered Certified Accountants, British Vehicle Rental and Leasing Association, Centre for Effective Dispute Resolution, incorporating IDRS, Dispute Resolution Ombudsman, Federation of Master Builders, Furniture Ombudsman, Home Improvement Ombudsman, Motor Codes, National Conciliation Services, NetNeutrals EU, Office of the Independent Adjudicator for Higher Education, Ombudsman Services, Pro Mediate, Property Redress Scheme, Renewable Energy Consumer Code, Small Claims Mediation, Skills Funding Agency, The Independent Parking Committee Ltd (The Independent Appeals Service), The Property Ombudsman, The Retail Ombudsman, TrustMark, The Waterways Ombudsman.

maintaining, or recovering, a positive relationship between the consumer and trader. It is clear that ADR is as yet not widely available, and is not yet prevalent enough to help many complainants. And of course, unless both parties agree to a settlement, ADR is unenforceable.[123]

The judiciary are (subject to the normal incidences of human frailty) honest, incorruptible, sensible and understanding of the law – and independent of the state. There are only faint traces of any compensation culture; the courts have been adamant in most cases, certainly in the higher courts, that there is a balance to be struck between risk and fault. While there have been substantial and frequent changes to the procedural systems (judges no longer have to read out the pleadings, or even the judgments) the repeated reforms have failed to deliver the anticipated benefits of lower costs, speedier access to justice – and shrunken rulebooks. There are now better case management conferences to plan the course of an action, but there are nonetheless still expensive procedural impediments. And the judges have yet to adopt a case management mindset in dealing with verbose counsel and confrontational solicitors.

5.5.2 Further Reforms

Despite the quality of the judiciary, and the attempts to improve the system, there remains extensive room for improvement. The rulebooks continually to be absurdly long and complex. The judiciary have been mildly intimidated by politicians into sometimes being reluctant to exercise their powers under common law and the principles of equity to do justice at the expense of black-letter law. And there are clearly insufficient numbers of judges, they are insufficiently well paid, inadequately experienced in matters outside the law, and poorly instructed in case management or the benefits of alternative dispute resolution. Judicial training is formalised but limited, and rudimentary compared for example with similar training in France or Germany, where judging is a separate profession rather than an advancement from advocacy. Anyone who watches US courtroom TV dramas is familiar with the scene where the grizzled judge compels counsel to approach the bench and tells them to stop playing procedural games. Such a scene would be beneficial in English courts where most observers watch with weary despair at the plodding, wordy and interminable advocacy.

---

[123] Legal Ombudsman, *Proposed ADR Scheme Rules*, September 2015; Legal Ombudsman, *Consultation 2016/2017 Draft Strategy*, March 2016.

5.5.3   Competition

As we have seen at one time there was competition amongst courts in England, which was abrogated through rationalisation. Privatisation (even through arbitration or mediation) is regarded somewhat sceptically by the judiciary and the judicial authorities, but has its advantages, one of them being privacy and being subject to the arbitrators' rules rather than judicial procedure. One of the objections is that private judicial proceedings fails to develop common law, that is, making changes to the law to meet changing circumstances, which has been one of the great strengths of the Anglo-Saxon system. Nonetheless there is now international competition in the commercial courts, competing for example with those in England, in Abu Dhabi, the Cayman Islands, Delaware, Dubai, Hong Kong, India, New York, Nigeria, Qatar, Singapore, South Africa, – and even Amsterdam, where the proceedings are conducted in English.[124] Competition would have the advantage of improving procedural rules, leading to cheaper and easier access, at least in commercial disputes.

5.5.4   Private Civil Justice

There has been criticism of the fact that the proceedings and processes of regulators and ombudsmen are not in public, and that an essential facet of justice is that it should be open, unless there is good reason to the contrary.[125] There also need to be proper systems of appeal. Subject to achieving those public policy objectives, the courts have been welcoming of ombudsmen, arbitration, mediation and alternative dispute resolution systems, There are maybe two limitations; private justice is inappropriate in criminal cases, where the state is a party with extensive powers to impose penalties. Only properly constituted state-backed courts will have authority in such cases. And private dispute resolution systems are only indirectly enforceable, through an imperfect contractual arrangement, i.e. using the enforcement of contract powers through the state system. But the courts are now encouraging private resolution, which is private and can be cheaper. The English courts are also intent on introducing online

---

[124] Lord Thomas of Cwmgiedd, Lord Chief Justice, *Developing commercial law through the courts: rebalancing the relationship between the courts and arbitration*, The Bailii Lecture, 9 March 2016.

[125] Lord Thomas of Cwmgiedd, Lord Chief Justice, *The legacy of Magna Carta: justice in the 21st century*, speech to the Legal Research Foundation, 25 September 2015, para 20.

dispute resolution (ODR),[126] which includes facilitation and mediation, and online litigation, with reduced need for representation. So far, online dispute resolution has had minimal take-up. Added to the reforms are suggestions for the use of quasi-judges, called registrars, to operate as facilitators in low-value civil disputes. The judiciary is also keen to see a reduction in the need for legal representation, not on the grounds that they are unnecessary, but because they are too expensive. This reflects similar outcomes in other areas, such as independent financial advisers; IFA's are heavily regulated, with expensive compliance costs, so that they become out of reach for most users. The system has now been changed so that they are not required to advise in many cases, even though that may not be in the best interests of the customer. Judicial remonstrances, which are not uncommon, to solicitors about the costs of litigation, suffer from a slight whiff of hypocrisy, since they are rarely directed at the bar (from which they originally derived) or at their own requirements to file documents in a particular way, and who complain if document are not produced or filed within strict time and expensive limits, and who themselves resile from formal case management within the proceedings. Judicial critics were also not widely known for charging low fees when they themselves practiced at the bar.[127]

5.5.5   Future Reforms

So far the reforms that have been suggested or implemented have been promoted by either the judiciary or the civil service or both. There is however no user group or consultative panel of parties to litigation, or any way for the authorities to examine suggestions for reform by people who really need access to justice. It is of course not always easy to distinguish the

---

[126] *Online dispute resolution for low value civil claims*, Online Dispute Resolution Advisory Group, Civil Justice Council, February 2015.

[127] See e.g. amongst many such observations, Lord Dyson, Lecture, *Magna Carta and Compensation Culture,: the High Sheriff of Oxfordshire's Annual Law Lecture*, 13 October 2015, para 40: 'Most troubling of all is the fact that the cost of litigation is so high. Legal fees are exorbitant. The laws of competition and the market place seem to be helpless in resisting the rising tide of the cost of litigating. Many would-be litigants simply cannot afford to go to court. The obvious solution is to introduce reasonable and proportionate fixed legal costs.' There was no suggestion that judges should be speedier, more involved in case management and take a more practical view in demanding excessive disclosure, or that there should be many more judges more readily available, so that cases could be heard with more expedition. Or any suggestion that judges might return the high fees earned whilst they themselves were at the bar.

vexatious litigants, the inveterate complainers and the grandstanders, but it might be possible for a sensible group to be established to try to reform the system from without rather than within.

5.5.6   A Move towards the Wider Use of Discretion, Common Law and Equity

The experience and training of judges makes them understandably inclined to follow legal rules more than most; they are particularly disinclined to take judicial risk. That very quality however may also contain the seeds of some of the problems. This might be illustrated by the case involving the provision of toilet facilities in cafes in England.[128] Greggs was a well-known chain of bakeries and fast-food outlets. There was a dispute between two local authorities and central government about what was a café (which would normally be required to have washing facilities for customers) and a take-away where there was some occasional seating, which would normally not. The judge involved was distinguished and highly experienced. And there were important legal issues to be decided, namely whether take-aways needed to have washing facilities, whether central government guidance overcame legal obligations and whether declining to impose requirements on one company in one local authority area conferred an unfair commercial advantage.

The dispute in fact became more about which of the warring local authorities was in charge. The licensing law had been changed in 2008[129] in order to help national commercial organisations avoid the need to obtain separate licenses in each local authority area in which they operated; they could choose one local authority to issue a licence, and that would operate as a national licence across England. In other words it was a regulatory simplification exercise. Greggs obtained a licence from Newcastle for their premises throughout the country. Hull objected to the terms of the licence, which contravened their local policy. The question of toilets had become one of jurisdictional power.

In a real world the chief executive of one authority would have called the chief executive of the other (and maybe invited the Minister to join in the call) or even suggested a round of golf, and fixed the dilemma. But

---

[128] *The Queen (on the application of) Kingston upon Hull City Council v Secretary of State for Business Innovation and Skills and the Council of the City of Newcastle upon Tyne and Greggs PLC* [2016] EWHC 1064 (Admin).
[129] Regulatory Enforcement and Sanctions Act 2008, s25.

legal proceedings, at considerable expense to the council taxpayers and central taxpayers, were begun. The judge gave his judgment based on his understanding of the law and gave permission to appeal and contained his presumable irritation at the waste of public funds in coming to his conclusion. Maybe he should have used his judicial powers to dismiss the case as an abuse of process and tell the parties to sit around the table and fix the problem. But judges are reluctant perhaps because of their background to take control of a dispute and adopt a more pro-active role in dispute resolution. Acting in a judicial capacity can be heady[130] and judges have been reluctant to be activists, apprehensive of criticism from the press, the public and politicians.

It seems evident that the courts are party to complexity in their own rules, in interpreting the rules of others, are an expensive route to solve disputes, and are aware of their problems but unable to resolve them. The final chapter explores whether it might improve matters if we were to encourage a change of judicial mindset, adopt a policy to use judges instead of regulators to enforce rules, improve the training of judges in judicial interventionism, appoint more of them, and take lessons from the users of the courts.

---

[130] See e.g. the career of Mr Justice Peter Smith, discussed in an article by Lord Pannick QC, *A case about luggage with a great deal of judicial baggage*, The Times, 15 September 2015.

6

Unregulation

Obsessive law-making simply makes criminals out of ordinary people. So, we'll get rid of the unnecessary laws – and once they're gone, they won't come back.[1]

David Cameron has pledged to cut red tape. The problem is that to do so involves an awful lot more red tape. The government's 'decision map' for its Red Tape Challenge is illustrated by a complex flow chart joined with red lines. Any scrappable regulation must go through seven separate steps – including a ministerial 'star chamber' – before it reaches the Reducing Regulation Committee. Seems like something that Sir Humphrey would have devised to give the illusion of action.[2]

It is no wonder that doctors are shunning general practice – it has become a bureaucratic treadmill.

Sir, Doctors shun general practice because its main attraction, autonomy, has all but disappeared [following discussion in the *Times* of a failure to recruit new GPs, *Times*, 14 August 2014]. The profession, like others, has fallen prey to the law of well-meaning actions having unintended consequences. On the pretext of accountability and patient safety, it has become over-scrutinised, over-regulated and removed from its vocational purpose. GPs have to bureaucratically justify every aspect of their days and comply with an increasing burden of irrelevant regulation that only removes them from caring for their patients. In trying to make an already effective, efficient and safe service safer, we have done the opposite – driving out

---

[1] Nick Clegg, UK Deputy Prime Minister, *Speech*, 10 May 2010 text available on http://news .bbc.co.uk/1/hi/8691753.stm. The paragraph reads: 'And as we tear through the statute book, we'll do something no government ever has: We will ask you which laws you think should go. Because thousands of criminal offences were created under the previous government... Taking people's freedom away didn't make our streets safe. Obsessive lawmaking simply makes criminals out of ordinary people. So, we'll get rid of the unnecessary laws, and once they're gone, they won't come back. We will introduce a mechanism to block pointless new criminal offences. And, we will, of course introduce safeguards to prevent the misuse of anti-terrorism legislation. There have been too many cases of individuals being denied their rights... And whole communities being placed under suspicion.'
[2] Patrick Kidd, *Tangled up in tape*, The Times, 31 January 2014.

excellent doctors, increasing patient list sizes, closing down surgeries and reducing access to clinical care.[3]

This chapter gives a history of failed attempts at unregulation over the last 100 years. Lay readers may prefer to skip this chapter.

6.1   Introduction

Those of us who enjoy chocolate understand that too much can make us sick. And governments, who enjoy regulation like the Aztecs craved criollo, understand that things have probably gone too far in the expansion of legislative and regulatory control. This chapter explores some of the efforts by official bodies and others to slim down the excesses of regulation and discusses why in practice success has been so hard to achieve, despite the throwing of substantial resources at the problem. There have been some successes in unregulation, usually rather minor and cosmetic, and these are also explored. But what is not always clear is why, despite the most noble of efforts, the drive to reduce regulation has been so hard to gain traction.

6.1.1   Terminology

Deregulation can involve one of several meanings. It is commonly used to describe the removal of controls of say an industry, perhaps exercising an oligopoly, like the supply of electricity or water. In some cases it is used to describe removal of rules or the introduction of a lighter-touch regulation of a service formerly highly regulated, such as financial services. In either cases it carries a connotation of a reduction in consumer protection and thus wears somewhat pejorative clothing.

'Unregulation' therefore seemed a better word to use in this chapter and, although inelegant, it so far carries little baggage. It is intended to describe efforts around the globe to remove the burden of regulation as a general policy, and this chapter describes an imperfect history of such attempts.

6.1.2   Recognition of Excess

That history reflects a recognition by government and policymakers that there is indeed an excess of regulation – otherwise they would not have created so many initiatives. It is clear that almost all developed administrations suffer from a schizophrenic approach to regulation: at one and the same time they recognise both the damage that regulation can do but also

---

[3] Dr James Sherifi, *Those GP Blues*, The Times, 16 August 2014 (letter).

believe that a little more would improve the lives of most of us, and maybe them as well.

Whilst under-regulation can indeed prove to be a problem, in many cases the protection of individuals may be undiminished – or even enhanced – by a reduction in regulation. And regulation can lead to undeliverable expectations by the public as to their safety. Following the Great Recession in 2008, much blame was attached to the introduction of a lighter-touch regulation of a formerly higher-regulated financial services industry; others considered however that the collapse was due to regulation giving a false sense of security to the public, which meant they did not take proper care to see what it was they were buying before they bought.[4]

6.1.3   Obsolescence

Obsolescence is a chronic element of much legislation, especially where public morality or culture has changed (e.g. laws against homosexuality or abortion) or where they have become otiose (e.g. the legislation against trading with Japan as the enemy in the 1940s, still extant until 2010) or has become unacceptable (the law enforcing restitution of conjugal rights).[5] And contrary to popular belief, the European Union has occasionally deregulated against the wishes of national member states, so that in the UK, in 2008 bakeries could sell loaves of any size, rather than in either 800g or 400g previously required by laws dating back to the Assize of Bread and Ale 1266. Consumer protection is not always necessary.[6]

6.1.4   Asymmetries of Risk for Regulators

Part of the drive to regulate arises from asymmetries of risk for regulators and their lawmaking colleagues. Regulators feel they need to demonstrate

---

[4] Niall Ferguson, *The Rule of Law and its Enemies*, Reith Lectures, BBC, 2012: Lecture 2 (The Darwinian Economy): 'In my view, the lesson of the 1970s is not that deregulation is bad, but that bad regulation is bad, especially in the context of bad monetary and fiscal policy. And I believe the same can be said of our crisis, too. The financial crisis that began in 2007 had its origins precisely in over-complex regulation.'

[5] See e.g. The Law Commission, *Family law: Restitution of Conjugal Rights*, Working Paper No 22, Second programme Item XIX, 17 February 1969.

[6] The measures were originally in avoirdupois; there remain extensive rules applying to bread generally and packaged bread in particular, see Weights and Measures (Packaged Goods) Regulations 2006 SI 2006 No 0659 and *Labelling for bread and cakes*, Derbyshire County Council Trading Standards Service, 2014.

their purpose in life, and the devil can make work for idle hands. There is also an asymmetry of cost: regulators invariably underestimate the cost of their interventions and most of the cost in any event is borne elsewhere and unnoticed by regulators. Third, they get no credit for reducing regulation. If things go right through diminished rules, the benefits are not accredited to them. If things go wrong, the finger will be pointed at government or regulators for failing the system. And there is always a risk that something will go wrong because of the early release of prisoners, or the reduction of health and safety requirements, and however low the risk, or infrequent the occasion, or proportionate the relaxation, there is little political or other capital to be gained by civil servants and legislators. Indeed many civil servants complain in practice that they are under perpetual pressure from some group or other to introduce new rules or toughen up existing rules when something does indeed go wrong. Finally, the governance of regulators is also asymmetric, and in most cases there are few checks and balances to control regulatory creep. The Pensions Regulator is a case in point. Created in 2005 it had a start-up budget of around £10M pa. By 2017, it was spending around £80M pa, with little evidence of an improvement for consumers, and very probably, though unnoticed, a reduction in their benefit.

Similarly there is an imbalance of political benefit. Politicians feel they gain electoral advantage from the introduction of a law seeming to protect the public, and lose public approval if they participate in its removal, even if it would lead to a societal gain. And it is not always a simple question, witness the dilemma in relation to the rolling back of health and safety legislation discussed below. The prospect of an exhausting and rather fruitless debate with John Humphreys on the Today Programme on BBC Radio 4 about the remote possibility of someone losing some benefit or protection as a consequence of repeal or simplification offers few attractions to politicians. There is always one particular interest group (and a tabloid newspaper) that will object, often rather noisily, to any reduction in regulation.

With the scales so set against unregulation, it is hardly surprising that there is so little enthusiasm for it amongst the political classes; the wonder is that there is any appetite for it at all. The list of initiatives set out later however shows that political pressure from below can have an effect; the complaints about increasing lack of competitiveness compared with jurisdictions that are less well (or less heavily) regulated, and about the disproportionate impact of much of the regulation has began to seep into the consciousness of even the most insistent of martinets.

6.1.5 Measuring Success

Measuring success in unregulation is difficult, since the criteria are hard to define. The number of pages is one measure, but that can be crude. It is harder to determine the financial, social or economic benefit of the repeal or simplification of a rule; in fact, it is all but impossible. There may be advantages gained from repealing one rule – or a series of rules, where the compounding effect is hard to calculate – but the unintended consequences of repeal can be as hard to anticipate as the introduction of the rule in the first place.[7]

6.1.6 Scope of Chapter

This chapter looks first at some of the efforts to unregulate – and then at some of the principles that are beginning to emerge from those efforts. Most of the reforms were devoted to reducing the burdens on business than on the common man, largely because the complaining about over-regulation that business does is more effective. But, as will be seen, virtually all of the efforts have failed; and most of those that have succeeded are cosmetic or trivial in impact.

6.2 Efforts at Unregulation (Central Government)

6.2.1 Historical Background

The current efforts, of which there are many, reflect those going back many years. Henry Thring (Lord Thring) who died in 1907 had been the first head of the Office of Parliamentary Counsel in 1869. He famously possessed an abundance of self-confidence; one cabinet minister was said to have remarked to his colleagues in Cabinet just before Lord Thring was invited to join them that 'I think before he arrives we had better carry a preliminary resolution that we are all damned fools'. But he wrote a much admired textbook, *Practical Legislation*, and a great deal of standard legislation including the Companies Act 1862 and the Merchant Shipping Act 1854, which served for decades as the basic frameworks. Occasionally he exceeded his brief; he was not shy to mention when he thought legislation had gone too far. For example when instructed to prepare a bill to make

---

[7] *Regulatory policy in perspective: a reader's companion to the OECD regulatory policy outlook 2015*, OECD, Paris 2015, p224.

illegal the clandestine conveyance of firearms he responded that creating such an offence was unworkable. One of the civil servants on the bill team then received a minute from the Under-Secretary of State: 'Thring is getting bumptious. Prepare a letter to him for my signature. Just tell him to go and square the circle'.[8] The point is that even then, politicians took little note of the draftsmen. Thring later published a book reflecting his views on the unmanageability of the system.[9] It had little effect.

6.2.2 More Recent Attempts in the UK

Over the last 30 years, however the pressure for reform started to grow, much of it following increasing pressure from trade bodies such as the British Chambers of Commerce and others who were producing studies of the hurt they said their members were feeling. There have been three main approaches to reform:

- reports and inquiries into the issue;
- establishment of departments and offices dedicated to unregulation; and
- promulgation of legislation dedicated to unregulation.

6.2.3 Reports

Henry Thring could have been permitted a wry smile had he survived to see what happened around a century later. The good news was that the authorities now accepted that the position was unsatisfactory. The bad news was that they dealt with it, frequently, in classic Sir Humphrey manner, by commissioning an inquiry, usually under the chairmanship or patronage of a distinguished citizen, and then disregarding the outcomes. In the UK there has been inquiry after inquiry. Setting aside separate inquiries into the standards of legislative drafting, they have included

- the Heseltine Initiative (1986),
- the Haskins Report (1997),

---

[8] T. StJ. N. Bates, *Editorial: Henry Thring – a hundred years on*, [2007] 28(1) Statute Law Review iii.

[9] Henry Thring, *Simplification of the Law: practical suggestions*, R. J. Bush, London 1875. It only looked at legislation in one language, but referred to the problem of Quebec, where there are two equal languages, which can give rise to ambiguities or uncertainties, He might have examined the position in South Africa which has 11 official languages, which puts the Canadian position in the shade, or the European Union where there are even more (24).

- the Sainsbury approach (1999),
- the Hampton Report (2005),
- the Macrory Report (2006),
- the Haythornthwaite Memorandum (2006),
- the John Redwood Report (2007),
- the Arculus Report (2009),
- the Anderson Report (2009),
- the Young Reports (2010, 2011, 2012, 2013),
- the Hodgson Report (2011),
- the Vince Cable Initiative (2010) and
- the Nick Clegg Initiative (2011).

Few, if any, have had much material impact.

6.2.4   The Heseltine Initiative (1986)

Lord Heseltine had at various times been Deputy Prime Minister and President of the Board of Trade. Although there does not seem to have been a formal report, Michael Heseltine having been requested by the government in 2012 to look at how to create wealth in the UK, said:[10]

> My early speeches [in the 1980s] would reveal my support for the simplest of notions of the role of government. Get off our backs, cut the red tape, lower taxes. My laughter would have been loudest at Ronald Reagan's later joke – 'I've come from the government, I'm here to help.'

Disregarding the slight misquotation of Ronald Reagan's punchline, there is a mild element of inconsistency, seeing that Lord Heseltine had earlier famously declared he would intervene between breakfast, lunch and dinner if he thought it would help to achieve reforms, but the trend of thinking was well observed.[11] Apart from privatisation, his career however does not appear to have involved a material rolling back of legislation or regulation during his periods of time in office.

---

[10] The Rt Hon the Lord Heseltine of Thenford, *No Stone Unturned*, Department for Business, October 2012, para 6; cf. Michael Harrison and David Nicholson-Lord, *Heseltine lights flame of change: promised bonfire of red tape aims to widen choice for consumers and help industry by cutting billions of pounds off costs*, Independent, 20 January 1994. It discussed the 1994 Deregulation Act, the effectiveness of which is discussed later.

[11] At the 1992 Conservative Party Conference.

6.2.5   Chris Haskins Report (1997)

As Chairman of the Better Regulation Task Force in 1997, Chris, later
Lord, Haskins produced a set of principles of good regulation.[12] Its principles were subsequently adopted by later reports; they included: proportionality, accountability, consistency, transparency and targeting. Few of
these have ever been achieved in practice. It also suggested alternatives
to regulation including: doing nothing, introducing advertising and education, using the market, employing financial incentives, adopting self-
regulation and codes of practice and enacting prescriptive regulation. He
suggested a series of tests which good regulation should pass including
ensuring balance throughout, avoiding a knee-jerk responses, seeking to
reconcile opposing policy objectives, balancing risks, costs and benefits,
avoiding unintended consequences, being easy to understand, enjoying
broad public support, being enforceable, identifying accountability, and
being relevant to current conditions. Few of his nostrums were in practice
applied, particularly that of accountability.

6.2.6   Tax Law Rewrite Project (1997)

Geoffrey Howe, the former Chancellor of the Exchequer whose 1990
speech famously led to the fall of Margaret Thatcher, recognised in the
1990s that the tax system was too complex; he later initiated a Tax Law
Rewrite project. In 1997 it was introduced by his successor Kenneth
Clarke, with Geoffrey Howe as Chairman and endowed with a £25M
dowry:[13]

> In last year's Budget I announced a project to rewrite Inland Revenue tax
> legislation in plain English. That is a tall order. The project is as ambitious
> as translating the whole of 'War and Peace' into lucid Swahili. In fact, it
> is more ambitious. I am told that 'War and Peace' is only 1,500 pages long.
> Inland Revenue tax law is 6,000 pages long and was not written by a Tolstoy.
> We have consulted extensively on how the project should be carried out
> and I am glad to say that there is wide consensus. The Inland Revenue will
> publish the plans and arrangements shortly after the Budget.
>
> The aim is to prepare a series of rewrite Bills, the first of them to be
> ready for enactment in the 1997–98 session. My noble and learned friend
> Lord Howe of Aberavon has produced a thorough and helpful report on

---

[12] Better Regulation Task Force, *Principles of Good Regulation*, 2003.
[13] Kenneth Clarke, *Hansard*, Commons, 26 November 1996, col 170. The length of the tax
code is now considered to exceed 20,000 pages (2017).

how Parliament might handle those Bills. We endorse his broad proposals, and invite the Procedure Committee to consider how the House is going to handle the Bills in a sensible fashion. I can announce that Lord Howe has agreed to chair the steering committee which will oversee the rewrite project.

The project will bring the benefits of clarity and certainty to businesses and ordinary taxpayers. It has been widely welcomed and deserves the continuing support that it has enjoyed in all parts of the House.

The idea was not so much to change the tax law, but to write it in English. The objective was to write the legislation in a format which was both more consistent and more understandable, and to remove archaic language and impenetrable terminology from tax law and to replace it with modern language and terminology. The team over the years produced five pieces of primary legislation and one piece of secondary legislation, with a sixth and seventh bill going before Parliament. The project focussed purely on primary legislation but special dispensation was given to the re-writing of the regulations governing PAYE by the project.[14]

The Tax Law Rewrite project was disbanded in April 2010.[15] It had produced some useful simplifications of expression, but it was bedevilled by the fact that as fast as they wrote old tax law in modern English, the legislature was producing more, even more complex, law in the old style. And the tax code increased from 6000 pages to 17,000 pages in 2014, which made the task even beyond the skills of Hercules.

6.2.7 David Sainsbury (1999)

David Sainsbury, a member of the famous supermarket family, was a Parliamentary Under-Secretary for Science and Innovation from 1998 until 2006, serving under Tony Blair. He did not produce a report at the time, but in a later book he devoted some space to the deregulatory agenda he had pursued whilst in office.[16] His approach seems on balance to have looked favourably on regulatory intervention on a wider scale, certainly in respect to financial services.

---

[14] Antony Seeley, *The Tax Law Rewrite: the final Bills*, House of Commons Library, SN 5239, 21 April 2010; Geoffrey Howe, *Why we must change the way tax law is made*, Financial Times, 3 July 2008.

[15] http://webarchive.nationalarchives.gov.uk/+/http://www.hmrc.gov.uk/rewrite/index .htm.

[16] David Sainsbury, *Progressive capitalism*, Biteback, 2013.

6.2.8   Better Regulation Task Force Report (2005) (Haskins II)

In 2005 Lord Haskins and the Better Regulation Task Force published *Regulation – Less is More*. It is discussed in more detail below.[17] It made a series of eight major recommendations, many based on Dutch experience, all of which were accepted by the government of the day and few if any of which were implemented. The Task Force was replaced in 2006 by the Better Regulation Commission.

6.2.9   The Hampton Report (2005)

Sir Philip Hampton had a career in merchant banking and as finance director of very large companies until he ended up as Chairman of Sainsbury and Chairman of UKFI, the government body that nationalised the banks in 2008. In 2005 he reported on ways in which the administrative burden of regulation on business, while maintaining or improving regulatory outcomes. He looked at 63 national regulators and 468 local authorities. The regulators he looked at carried out 3 million inspections a year, and sent out 2.6 million forms a year. He also looked at the disproportionate costs for smaller business; it was suggested that businesses with two employees spent six hours per month per employee on government regulation, while larger business could manage with only two hours.[18]

He concluded that the use of risk assessment was patchy, that regulators did not give enough advice to secure compliance, that form-filling was repetitive and overlapping, that regulators needed to be able to apply more sanctions, and to offer more rewards, that the structure of regulators was complex, and there were too many interfaces between businesses and regulators. The fact that additional compliance tools (i.e. punishments) were required seems to suggest that actually many of the regulated were less bothered about the regulations than was generally thought, and it was comforting in some ways to see that a certain degree of Euro-style dismissal of regulation in practice was operating.

The Report itself looked less at whether the regulations were sensible, proportionate or even necessary – but simply at how the regulations that had been introduced were administered. It did lead eventually to a modest reduction in the number of forms (and an improvement in their

---

[17] Better Regulation Task Force, *Regulation – Less is More*, 2005.
[18] Philip Hampton, (Chairman) *Reducing administrative burdens: effective inspection and enforcement*, HM Treasury, March 2005, 140pp.

design) – but its ambition was limited. It mentioned that the Environment Agency over-inspected waste sites, visiting 15 times on average, at least quarterly by law, and a pet cemetery was visited eight times a year. Eventually the number of inspections fell by a third from 125,000 a year to 84,000.[19]

6.2.10   Macrory Review (2006)

Following the Hampton Report it became clear that the imposition of sanctions by regulators had become inconsistent, especially where they were required to implement a risk-based approach to regulation. Professor Richard Macrory was asked to explore the sanctioning powers of 56 regulatory bodies, and came up with a series of penalty principles, using the criminal system, introducing a system of monetary penalties (fines) and restorative justice where appropriate.[20] In due course the Regulatory Enforcement and Sanctions Act 2008 was enacted, designed to provide for more consistent enforcement of regulations across local authority boundaries, better co-ordination between local authorities and central government, and more effective enforcement of regulations. It also required regulators to conform to certain principles. There were four parts to the legislation:

Part 1 re-established the Local Better Regulation Office, already established in May 2007 as a government-owned company, as a statutory corporation with statutory powers.
Part 2 established a Primary Authority scheme, whereby businesses which operate in more than one local authority area can choose to nominate one authority as the primary one for regulatory purposes (see the *Greggs* case below).
Part 3 introduced four new civil penalties that regulatory authorities could impose on businesses.

and, more relevantly here

Part 4 imposed a duty on regulators to keep their regulatory activity under review and remove unnecessary burdens, and to keep their regulatory

---

[19] National Audit Office, *Environment Agency: protecting the public from waste*, National Audit Office, December 2002.

[20] Sir Richard Macrory, Chairman, *Regulatory justice: making sanctions effective*, Final Report, Better Regulation Executive (Cabinet Office), 2006.

activities to a necessary minimum. The duty only applied to a limited number of regulators, and was not a general duty.[21]

6.2.11   The Haythornthwaite Memorandum (2006)

The Better Regulation Commission was established in January 2006 under the chairmanship of Rick Haythornthwaite, a subsequent chairman of Centrica (which owns British Gas). In October 2006 he reported on the role of risk in regulation, calling on regulators to re-think their approach to risk, to encourage more autonomy and self-regulation and co-ordinate the statutes, goals and obligations of the various regulators.[22] The Commission produced a further range of reports, but their impact was minimal.

6.2.12   The John Redwood initiative (2007)

John Redwood was appointed Shadow Deregulation Secretary, the first and last such position, under Michael Howard's period as leader of the opposition in 2005, and repeated his efforts for David Cameron as part of the Economic Policy Review in 2007.[23] There was a small shopping list including easing the data protection rules, rules on employment hours and health and safety regimes, scrapping home information packs and relaxing regulations on herbal remedies, charity bingo and raffles. The package was drawn up by a policy review group headed by John Redwood. Politically it encountered headwinds; the TUC for example complained that 'If these reports are true the Conservative Party will put itself on the side of bad employers and undercut the good who are happy to obey these legal minimum standards.'

6.2.13   David Arculus Report (2009)

From 2002 to 2006 Sir David Arculus a well-known businessman operated as a 'Red Tape Czar' by acting as Chairman of the British Government's Better Regulation Task Force under a Tony Blair administration. He claimed that he helped bring about a number of regulatory initiatives

---

[21] Regulatory Enforcement and Sanctions Act 2008, s72, s73.

[22] Rick Haythornthwaite, *Memorandum*, February 2007.

[23] *Tory plan for red tape 'tax cut'*, BBC News, 13 August 2007. There had been no actual Secretary of State for Deregulation to shadow.

intended to reduce burdens on business which included improved impact assessments; the introduction of common commencement dates and the measurement of administrative burden in the UK economy which led to government imposing a 25 per cent red tape reduction across all departments.

In 2009 the Conservative Party asked him to produce a report on deregulation, which had as its pull-quote: 'If you have 10,000 regulations, you destroy all respect for Law', which is supposed to have been said by Winston Churchill.[24] It quantified the cost of regulation at around 10–12 per cent of GDP, with 18,000 pages of domestic regulation a year, and 11,000 pages of EU regulation. Like previous reports it set out a menu of 'Principles of Good Regulation', including

- proportionality,
- accountability,
- consistency,
- transparency and
- targeting,

coupled with regulatory scrutiny, including the involvement of

- impact assessments,
- simplification plans,
- the Law Commission,
- an administrative cost reduction programme with the aim of reducing the red tape aspect of regulation by 25 per cent,
- consultation,
- alternatives to regulation,
- common commencement dates and
- guidance, by which it meant not 'instead of regulation' but 'as well as'.

If all the reduction targets of the various reports had in fact been achieved, negative regulation would have resulted. The Arculus report also recommended the establishment of an Independent Panel for Regulation and Risk (IPRR), sunset clauses for regulators and proper governance for regulators, with oversight by select committees.

---

[24] David Arculus and Julian Smith, *The Arculus Review: enabling enterprise, encouraging responsibility*, The Conservative Party, May 2009.

6.2.14   The Anderson Report (2009)

The Anderson Report[25] was chaired by Sarah Anderson who had run a specialist catering employment agency for many years and founded Simple Solutions Ltd which made folding toddler's loo seats called 'Toodleloos'. Her group set out eight rules to follow when issuing guidance for businesses and others on how to comply with the law. It led to a code of practice in October 2009 (itself replacing an earlier Code in July 2008) and made three changes, including a requirement that there should be a quick start summary guidance, there should be a removal of legal disclaimers from the guidance, and there should be information in any guidance on how to give feedback. It is possible that it has added to the length of guidance, rather than improved brevity.

6.2.15   The Lord Young Reports (2010, 2011, 2012, 2013)

Lord Young had been a member of Margaret Thatcher's cabinet in the mid to late 1980s. In 2011 he was invited to work on reducing the burden on business from health and safety regulations, working across departments on the implementation of his recommendations. He was also asked to report on removing barriers to growth for small and medium-sized enterprises.[26] They broadly repeated the recommendations of earlier reports, were accepted by the government at the time, but appear to have had little practical impact.

6.2.16   The Hodgson Report (2011)

The Cabinet Office and the Department for Business Innovation and Skills looked for reform of the Big Society and sought to identify regulatory impediments for that initiative. The initiative was chaired by Lord Hodgson who was then the President of NCVO and a former Conservative Minister whose committee produced a report in 2011.[27] The question

---

[25] Better Regulation Executive, *The Good Guidelines Guide: taking the uncertainty out of regulation*, Department for Business Enterprise and Regulatory Reform, January 2009, 20pp (The Anderson Review).

[26] See e.g. Lord Young of Graffham, *Common sense, common safety*, Cabinet Office, October 2010, and *Make business your business: supporting the start-up and development of small business*, Department for Business, Innovation & Skills, 28 May 2012, Lord Young, *Growing your business: a report on growing micro businesses*, May 2013.

[27] Robin Hodgson (Chairman), *Unshackling good neighbours: report of the Task Force established to consider how to cut red tape for small charities, voluntary organisations and social*

it was asked was 'How can we reduce the bureaucratic burden on small organisations, particularly in the charitable, voluntary and social enterprise sectors?'. There was an agenda to the report; the incoming Conservative administration was faced with a major fiscal tightening, and pressure on the provision of public services – as well as a policy determination to try to reduce the role of the state and enhance privately provided social support. It thought that its policy objective would be frustrated by complaints that people who wanted to help provide social services and support, even if they wanted to, were frustrated by bureaucratic impediments, most recently in having to register for criminal checks.

In the end it looked at just three questions:

- what stops people giving time?
- what stops people giving money? and
- what stops CSO's growing?

Its report is replete with anecdotes and it concluded that regulation was only one reason for people declining to take part in the big society as much as they should or ought. It also considered that there were nonetheless impediments:

- people were scared about the risk of litigation, prompted by claims management companies;
- unemployed people were discouraged from assisting by threats from the job centres that they were rendering themselves unavailable for work;
- insurance cover was hard to find;
- repetitive CRB [now DBS] checks were required;
- there was over-cautious implementation of CRB requirements (e.g. requiring school governors who do not have frequent and intensive contact with children and vulnerable adults to be registered);
- low-level and youthful offences were treated as though they were serious crimes when considering employing volunteers;
- licensing for fundraising was intrusive and expensive;
- there was regulatory duplication (e.g. Companies House and the Charity Commission required the same information in different form);
- trustee liability was excessive (and unincorporated trustees were more at risk than incorporated trustees);

enterprises, May 2011, 40pp, Cabinet Office and Department for Business Innovation and Skills.

- there were knee-jerk regulatory pressures (it was recommended that a STORE (speedy treatment of regulatory events), system should be used to slow down regulatory responses);
- planning regulations were excessive and slow;
- the transfer of employment (TUPE) regulations were complex and expensive.

No changes emerged as a consequence of the Report.

6.2.17   The Vince Cable Initiative (2011)

Vince Cable was the Secretary of State for Business in the 2010 UK Coalition Government; in March 2011 he announced a review of 22,000 business regulations as part of his drive to cut red tape – and an exemption of small firms from new domestic laws for three years. He also suggested sunset clauses for regulations after five years, not extending the right to request time off to train for firms with fewer than 250 employees, more transparency into the OIOO (one in one out) rule, by publishing the opinions of the Regulatory Policy Committee where they do not believe the evidence supports a new regulation, and freeing small companies from unnecessary audit fees.[28]

6.2.18   The Nick Clegg Initiative (2011)

Nick Clegg, then Deputy Prime Minister, announced in July 2010 plans to cut red tape for small business, using the medium of a 'Freedom Bill'.[29] The intention was to sweep away meddlesome legislation and free up individuals and business from overbearing rules.[30] A substantial consultation was launched with people invited to submit their ideas for laws which should be scrapped on a website run by his department, the Cabinet Office. The *Daily Telegraph* suggested that three months later, the volume of the information submitted by people had become unmanageable. Around 46,000 people logged on and left their ideas, with each entry generating a stream of comments and debate. It was reported that Mr Clegg concluded that

---

[28] Department for Business Innovation and Skills, *Vince Cable bins business red tape*, Press release, 18 March 2011.

[29] http://webarchive.nationalarchives.gov.uk/20100824180635/http://yourfreedom.hmg.gov.uk/

[30] Melissa Kite, Deputy Political Editor, *Nick Clegg abandons red tape cutting project*, Daily Telegraph, 6 November 2010.

there was simply 'too much detail' and passed the project to the Home Office, where officials were charged with truncating the scheme and turning it into a much smaller civil liberties bill.

Deregulation measures aimed at freeing up business were stripped from the Bill to make it simpler. In a statement at the launch of the Freedom Bill initiative, Mr Clegg had vowed to 'free our society of unnecessary laws and regulations – both for individuals and businesses' and to 'strip away the excessive regulation that stops businesses from innovating.' He urged citizens to get involved and said it was 'a totally new way of putting you in charge'. Launching the Your Freedom consultation site, he said: 'Every suggestion and comment will be read. So please use this site to make yourself heard. Every time you have to fill out three versions of the same form tell us about it. Every time you have felt snooped on by the state, every unnecessary law, every mind-numbing rule, every time your rights are infringed, tell us about it. Be demanding about your liberties, be insistent about your rights.' In a video message left on the website he later concluded that: 'When we launched this site I don't think any of us realised what a success it would be. People aren't shy. The site is full of debates that are honest, forthright and robust.'

As a consequence it was reported that 'Nick felt he was being tied up in knots so he washed his hands of it.' John Redwood, a former government minister, commented, 'We don't need any more consultations. I drew up a set of policies before the 2001 election as Shadow DTI Secretary. I did it again for Michael Howard as his Shadow Deregulation Secretary. I did it again for David Cameron as part of the Economic Policy Review. There are dozens of ideas out there. They need to get on with it. Why don't they just do it?' Mr Redwood said he had sent his latest deregulation report to Mr Clegg for inclusion in his Freedom review but had heard nothing. 'If all are agreed that we have too many rules and regulations, if all accept that many of these rules do not deliver what they promise or even do the opposite, the task ahead is to repeal and amend to cut the burden and improve the effectiveness where regulation is needed.' The Freedom Bill was abandoned.

6.2.19 Red Tape Challenge (2011–2015)

The UK Coalition Government included deregulation as a theme when it came into power in 2010. It had a project to reduce the number of quangos, the success of which was mixed. It also in 2011 introduced a 'Red Tape Challenge'. The intention was to garner complaints about red tape from those who dealt with regulation on a day-to-day basis. It created a website for individuals to submit thoughts on which regulations should stay, which could be merged, and which could be scrapped. Ministers and government officials were then to use this information to help them reduce the incidence of regulation. Every few weeks the department published regulations relating to a specific sector – from retail to transport – and throughout the process it published general regulations that related to all sectors, such as those on equality or health and safety. People commented on the website and the thoughts were collated by government officials to provide a clearer picture of which regulations should stay, which should go and which should change. Ministers had three months to decide which regulations they would scrap, with the presumption that all burdensome regulations would go unless the government departments could justify why they were needed.

The consultation process lasted from April 2011 until April 2013. The programme looked at some of the stock of over 21,000 statutory rules and regulations that were active in the UK, the priority being to focus on regulations that placed the biggest burdens on businesses and society. The exercise did not examine regulations in relation to tax or national security (tax was being looked separately through the Office of Tax Simplification).

Even where it was considered the regulation itself served a useful purpose, it was understood that inconsistent or inappropriate enforcement could cause problems or enforcement could be improved. It implemented a 'Focus on Enforcement' review to gather evidence directly from business to identify where enforcement can be improved, reduced or done differently and to discover and celebrate where it worked well, so others could learn from it. The Focus on Enforcement team also supported an initiative, 'Business Focus on Enforcement', which gave trade associations and representative business groups, instead of civil servants, the dominant role in identifying enforcement issues and driving reform to benefit their industries.

It also reviewed instances of 'gold-plating' of EU-derived regulation – where the UK has gone beyond the minimum required by the EU legislation. It also (in theory at least) introduced a 'one in, one out' rule, meaning Ministers had to identify an existing piece of regulation to be scrapped for every new one proposed, created a strengthened role for the Regulatory Policy Committee to review the costs and benefits of new regulation proposals, and imposed a three-year moratorium on domestic regulation for very small firms and start-ups.

In 2014, the Prime Minister announced that Government had reached its target to identify 3000 regulations to be scrapped or improved, but they were not identified or itemised,[31] nor was there any evidence that they had in fact been repealed.

6.3   Bodies Dedicated to Unregulation

There are (were) several UK government bodies dedicated to deregulation. They have included

- Better Business for All (local authorities regulatory connection with local business),
- Better Regulation Commission (1997–2008),
- Better Regulation Delivery Office (2011–),
- Better Regulation Executive (2007),
- Better Regulation Executive (Department for Business Innovation and Skills) (2008),
- Better Regulation Task Force (1997–2006),
- Bureaucracy Reference Group (in primary and secondary education) (closed 2015),
- Business/Focus on Enforcement,[32]
- Cabinet Sub-Committee on Deregulation (discussed above),
- Cutting Red Tape (from 2015),
- Delegated Powers and Regulatory Reform Committee (House of Lords Select Committee),
- Departmental Better Regulation Unit,
- Law Commission (since 1965),
- Local Better Regulation Delivery Office (until 2012),
- Local Better Regulation Office (2008–2011),
- National Audit Office,
- National Measurement and Regulation Office (until 2016, merged with Regulatory Delivery),
- Natural England Better Regulation,
- Office of Tax Simplification,
- Red Tape Challenge (2011–2015),

---

[31] *Small business, big support*, Department for Business, Innovation and Skills, Press release, 27 January 2014.
[32] Announced to be a permanent office in the UK Government's Autumn Statement 2014, and abolished in 2015.

- Reducing Bureaucracy Programme 2012 (intended to save 4.5 million hours of police time),
- Regulatory Delivery (2016) (formerly Better Regulation Delivery Office),
- Regulatory Excellence Forum (2012),
- Regulatory Impact Unit (Cabinet Office) (2003),
- Regulatory Policy Committee (2009),
- Regulatory Policy Committee of DBIS (2007),
- Regulatory Reform Committee (House of Commons),
- Select Committee on Regulators (House of Lords) and
- Working group on reducing bureaucracy (Scotland, education).

Many of them have produced codes and principles of unregulation. They have almost universally been ignored in practice; a select number of them are discussed below.

6.3.1 Better Regulation Delivery Office (Now Regulatory Delivery)

The BRDO was intended to establish a joined-up system of regulation, especially for business and local government.[33] It is based on recommendations for alternatives to conventional enforcement models, and to encourage a transparent and light-touch system based on real risks.

6.3.2 Better Regulation Executive

The Better Regulation Executive (BRE) is also part of the Department for Business, Energy and Industrial Strategy; its role is intended to lead the regulatory reform agenda across government. Working with and through others, its aim is[34]

- to work with departments to improve the design of new regulations and how they are communicated,
- to work with departments and regulators to simplify and modernise existing regulations and

---

[33] See *Transforming regulatory enforcement: government response to the consultation on transforming regulatory enforcement*, Department for Business Innovation and Skills, December 2011; www.gov.uk/government/organisations/regulatory-delivery.

[34] Better Regulation Executive, *Making it simple*, Annual review 2008, BRE 2009 (www.berr.gov.uk/whatwedo/bre/index.html). Cf Department for Business Innovation and Skills, *Better regulation, better benefits. Getting the balance right*, October 2009, 104pp, DBIS.

- to work with regulators (including local authorities) and departments to change attitudes and approaches to regulation to become more risk-based.

It claims significant progress has been made across all these areas and that the Government's ambitious and wide-ranging regulatory reform agenda was one of the most respected programmes in the world, and which has been confirmed by a number of international surveys. It applies five principles of good regulation, i.e. that any regulation should be

- transparent,
- accountable,
- proportionate,
- consistent and
- targeted only at cases where action is needed.

The big question is how effective it is. One of its own reports looked at six deregulation cases and congratulated itself on meeting another three objectives, clarity, commitment and compliance.[35] It made nonetheless two useful points; first, that 'better regulation has always been about balancing costs and benefits and about making regulation as simple as possible. It means taking effective action where there is a strong case for it. Government should intervene only when regulation is the best, most suitable, approach, and the intended benefits justify costs.' The statement of the objective was made partly in response to a complaint by the chairman of a report in relation to the regulation of education:[36]

> Governors, headteachers, proprietors and inspectors currently have to find their way through a thicket of statutory regulations and standards which carries with it the risk of confusion, mistake and non-compliance.

The chairman seemed to accept that in that particular case regulation was indeed the answer to the problem. And in general terms while the BRE nicely articulated the hidden benefits of regulation, it found it hard if not impossible to conduct anything other than a subjective cost-benefit analysis – and unsurprisingly found few cases where regulation had been counter-productive, other than in some minor areas. The universal self-approbation may lead the more sceptical to conclude that it is hard for the

---

[35] Department for Business Innovation and Skills, *Better regulation, better benefits. Getting the balance right*, October 2009, 104pp, DBIS.

[36] Sir Roger Singleton, *Keeping our schools safe, Review of Safeguarding arrangements in independent schools, non-maintained special schools and boarding schools in England*, 2009.

civil service itself to ever attempt to roll back controls. The cost/benefit analysis for the department (and the minister) and especially the risks are usually too great to overcome the inertia to leave things be or to tinker at the edges. Those subjected to regulation are rarely genuinely asked whether they think it cost-effective, because the regulator would assume that they would automatically disparage it, on the Mandy Rice-Davies principle, which applies equally to the opposite views of a regulator.

The BRE was supposed to target a reduction of £10B in the cost of regulation between 2010 and 2020. Its success or lack of it has been described in a UK government report, which tells the story of saving £1B of the £10B by introducing a mandatory plastic bag charge of 5p.[37] The other £9B savings have not so far been found.

Other attempts to roll back regulation and administration have included efforts to curb data requests by Departments and other regulators. It is understandable that policy makers seek the raw data upon which to base their reforms; after all evidence-based policy is one of the requirements of the reformers. On the other hand, repeated requests for the same or similar information merely adds costs and irritates the questioned. The Better Regulation Executive thought it might be a good idea to try and cut down on the statistical gathering within government itself, but the outcome was limited. The National Audit Office reported[38] on its efforts that

- there was scope to save £1.5B a year in reducing internal requests, but that unless efforts were the same as to reduce statistics gathering in the commercial world, there would be no progress;
- the current strategy was narrow in focus and did not cover all forms of unnecessary bureaucracy;
- the targets were introduced without having a standard measurement methodology to assess their own progress;
- no departments with set targets did actually manage to reduce requests by a quarter [although the methodology was inevitably suspect];
- a light touch to monitoring progress suggested little actual scrutiny of performance and no external validation.

There were several other criticisms; in practice it seems hard within large organisations to cut such requests, and it probably does not help that

---

[37] *Better Regulation*, House of Commons, Committee of Public Accounts, Eighteenth report of Session 2016–17, 12 October 2016, HC 487.

[38] National Audit Office, *Reducing bureaucracy for public sector frontline staff, briefing for the House of Commons Regulatory Reform Committee*, December 2009.

ministers from time to time demand to know (as do MPs) certain information which they deem essential for policy making.[39]

6.3.3   Better Regulation Task Force 2005

British Regulation Task Force published a substantial report in 2005 called 'Regulation – Less is More'; its timing was propitious as the government was about to repeal the Regulatory Reform Act 2001 and replace it with the Legislative and Regulatory Reform Act 2006. The BRTF was in effect an arm of the Prime Minister's Office. The Budget Statement of 2004 announced that Philip Hampton, a former finance director of Lloyds TSB, BT and British Gas, had been appointed to review over-regulation.[40] His report noted that in June 2004 UK companies received forms asking them to itemise the number of different pieces of paperwork (presumably excluding these particular ones) they had to complete. In practice this may have required some effort, since compiling such a register would have involved involving several different departments in most firms – tax, employment, accounts, marketing, health and safety, pensions and payroll – some of which may have had other priorities, and few of which will have been working to the same time frame – and many of which will have outsourced their efforts.

6.3.4   Cabinet: Economy and Industrial Strategy (Reducing Regulation) Sub-Committee (2016)

The sub-Committee is a committee of the Cabinet, originally chaired in on its establishment in 2015 by the then Chancellor of the Duchy of Lancaster, Oliver Letwin. Its terms of reference are: 'To consider issues relating to reducing regulation'. This is a heavy duty beast to deal with what is more of an administrative than a strategic issue, and includes the following in its membership:[41]

- Secretary of State for Business, Energy and Industrial Strategy (Chair);
- Lord Chancellor, Secretary of State for Justice;

---

[39] Source: National Audit Office, *Reducing bureaucracy for public sector frontline staff*, briefing for the House of Commons Regulatory Reform Committee, December 2009, Appendix 1, illustration, p29 (organisations involved in delivering the skills agenda for young people in education, organogram).

[40] Anna Fifield, *Business to have its say on tackling red tape*, Financial Times, 23 June 2004.

[41] Cabinet Office, *Cabinet Committees*, 18 October 2016. See also https://cutting-red-tape .cabientoffioce.gov.uk, which cites some dubious statistics on its achievements in several areas of activity.

- Secretary of State for International Trade;
- Leader of the House of Commons, Lord President of the Council;[42]
- Secretary of State for Environment, Food and Rural Affairs;
- Chief Secretary to the Treasury;
- Minister for Cabinet Office, Paymaster General;
- Minister of State for Employment;
- Minister of State for Exiting the European Union; and
- Minister for Small Business, Consumers and Corporate Responsibility.

Following convention, the Cabinet Office does not disclose the minutes of meetings or even if there have been meetings, and the minutes are not available to any other party if it should assume power at a later date. It is hard to see what might be contentious or politically sensitive in such matters. It is not possible to estimate what the value of the sub-Committee is or has been.

6.3.5 Regulatory Reform Committee (House of Commons)

A select committee of the House of Commons is dedicated to the issue of regulatory reform. The Regulatory Reform Committee is required to examine and report on all draft legislative reform orders proposed by the Government under the Legislative and Regulatory Reform Act 2006 which is intended to allow easier removal of legislative burdens and promote better regulation. The Committee may also examine and report on any and all matters relating to reform of regulation, and examines occasional pieces of legislation that are drawn to its attention. Its role covers

- draft Legislative Reform Orders (LROs), laid before the House under the Legislative and Regulatory Reform Act 2006;
- matters arising from consideration of such LROs; and
- matters relating to regulatory reform.

Legislative Reform Orders (LROs) are a specific type of secondary legislation. An LRO is a statutory instrument laid before Parliament under the Legislative and Regulatory Reform Act 2006; the Committee's role is to judge LROs against specified criteria in the 2006 Act. The work of the

---

[42] In 2015, it was Chris Grayling MP, who had been involved in drafting the otiose Social Action Responsibility and Heroism Bill 2014 (Sarah's Law) (see p 414 below).

Committee is mirrored in the House of Lords by the Delegated Powers
and Regulatory Reform Committee.[43]

6.3.6   Delegated Powers and Regulatory Reform Committee
(House of Lords Select Committee)

The remit of the Committee in relation to delegated powers is to report
whether the provisions of any bill inappropriately delegate legislative
power, or whether they subject the exercise of legislative power to an
inappropriate degree of parliamentary scrutiny. Delegated powers are frequently included in the Bills presented to Parliament by the Government.
These powers allow Ministers to use 'delegated legislation' (usually in the
form of statutory instruments or SIs) to do things which would otherwise
need another Bill. The powers are often practical and sensible: for example, a Bill may set out all the key elements of a policy, but allow a Minister
to make minor modifications to the policy as circumstances change over
time, by making a set of Regulations.

The Committee considers Bills when they are introduced into the Lords
(at present there is no equivalent committee in the Commons). The Government provides a memorandum for each Bill, identifying each of the
delegations, its purpose, the justification for leaving the matter to delegated legislation, and explaining why the proposed level of Parliamentary
control is thought appropriate.

The Committee examines whether the delegations in each Bill are
appropriate. The Committee is careful to restrict its consideration to the
delegation in question, and not the merits of the overall policy. The four
levels of Parliamentary scrutiny are: none; 'negative' instruments, which
are only debated if a Member specifically requests a debate; 'affirmative'
instruments, which must be approved by both Houses of Parliament; and
the rare two-stage 'super-affirmative' instruments. The Committee's recommendations are made in reports to the House, usually before the start
of the Committee stage of the Bill.

The Committee also examines drafts of Legislative Reform Orders
(LROs) laid under the Legislative and Regulatory Reform Act 2006. Again,
the Committee does not examine the merits of the policy in question. The
Committee's role here is to examine whether the tests set out in the 2006
Act appear to have been met (these include, for example, a requirement

---

[43] Cf the Australian model, www.aph.gov.au/parliamentary_business/committees/senate/
red_tape, and in Ontario, Red Tape Commission, 1996–2003.

for thorough consultation), and whether the proposal is appropriate to be delivered by an LRO. The Committee also examines documents and draft orders laid before Parliament under idiosyncratically specific legislation.[44]

6.3.7 Department for Business Energy and Industrial Strategy

The Department publishes a six-monthly review of the efforts at deregulation. Each review has suggested that around £500M is saved by the Department as a consequence of the reduction in regulation, using the OITO (one in, two out) principle. Looking in detail at the report, the conclusions are hard to justify. Amongst many others in the January 2015 review it abolished the Weights and Measures (Knitting Yarns) Order 1988, to deregulate fixed quantities and quantity labelling rules for knitting yarn. It benefitted business by allowing knitting yarns sold in a band rather than pre-packaged to be sold in any size the retailer chooses. The savings were estimated as zero. As was the abolition of the Trading with the Enemy (Custodian) (No 5) Order 1951 which was no longer relevant.[45] It was part of the Red Tape Challenge (later branded Cutting Red Tape) and Focus on Enforcement programmes; it does seem to have achieved some minor reforms, but most of the improvements (if they were such) seemed technical rather than radical or substantive.

6.3.8 Law Commission (Seriatim)

In proposing reforms of the law, the Law Commission does not merely recommend the introduction of new laws; it also proposes the repeal of laws that have become obsolete:

> The purpose of our statute law repeals work is to modernise and simplify the statute book, reduce its size and save the time of lawyers and others who use it. This in turn helps to avoid unnecessary costs. It also stops people being misled by obsolete laws that masquerade as live law. If an Act still features in the statute book and is referred to in text books, people reasonably enough assume that it must mean something. Implementation of our repeal proposals is by means of special Statute Law (Repeals) Bills. 18 such

---

[44] Localism Act 2011 s7(2), s19; Fire and Rescue Services Act 2004 s5E(2); Northern Ireland Act 1998 s85; Local Government Act 1999 s17; Local Government Act 2000 s9; Local Government Act 2003 s98; Local Transport Act 2008 s102.

[45] Department for Business Innovation and Skills, *BIS Ninth Statement of new regulation, regulations covering January–June 2015*, January 2015.

Bills have been enacted since 1965 repealing more than 2000 Acts in their entirety.

It continues to refine the repeal of obsolete law, but considers it a non-trivial task.[46] Its remit covers a number of arcane and much ignored law that troubles few in daily practice. It issues occasional Statute Law Repeals reports, together with draft bills.[47]

6.3.9   Local Better Regulation Office (2008–2012)

The Local Better Regulation Office was established following the publication of the Hampton Report.[48] It later produced the UK Statutory Code of Practice for Regulators. The Hampton Report, together with the later Macrory Review[49] led to the UK Regulatory Enforcement and Sanctions Act 2008, which established the LBRO. It effectively codified the 'Ayres and Braithwaite Compliance Pyramid' into UK law.[50] In practice it attempted to set out standards on how trading standards and other business regulators carried out their work to minimise the impact on business.

The LBRO was dissolved in 2012, its functions being taken over by the Better Regulation Delivery Office, an independent unit within the Department for Business, Innovation and Skills. The 2008 Act continues to apply however, and although its intent was benign, it has not been without its travails. In May 2016 it provoked a dispute about whether some of the Greggs bakery stores, a UK bakery chain with high-street shops, needed to provide sanitary facilities for their customers.[51] The general rule is that

---

[46] *Legal curiosities: fact or fable*, Law Commission, March 2013. It remains illegal to be drunk on licensed premises (Licensing Act 1872 s12) and to carry a plank along a pavement (Metropolitan Police Act 1839 s54).

[47] See *Statute law repeals at the Law Commission: a review of our work 1965 to 2010*, Law Commission, 2010; see also *20th Statute Law (Repeals) Report*, Law Commission, 3 June 2015; it proposes the repeal of more than 200 obsolete statutes covering a wide range of topics from agriculture and churches to trade and industry and taxation. One of the earlier legislative cleansers was Sir Francis Bacon, when Attorney General under James I: 'Repeal all statutes which are sleeping and not of use but yet snaring and in force', *Parliamentary History and Review*, Longmans, London, 1826, p529.

[48] Regulatory Enforcement and Sanctions Act 2008.

[49] *Regulatory Justice – making sanctions effective*, November 2006 (Macrory Report).

[50] Ian Ayres and John Braithwaite, *Responsive Regulation: Transcending the deregulation debate*, Oxford University Press, 1992, p35, which contains an illustration of the regulatory pyramid.

[51] *The Queen (on the application of Kingston upon Hull City Council v Secretary of State for Business Innovation and Skills and the Council of the City of Newcastle upon Tyne and Greggs PLC* [2016] EWHC 1064 (Admin), discussed at p278.

proper cafes need them, but take-away shops do not. Some of the Greggs' places of course fell somewhere in-between. The 2008 Act was intended to avoid complexity in these matters, so that a company could choose one local authority to give guidance on its obligations countrywide, and in Greggs' case it was Newcastle, who said that their two shops in Hull did not need washrooms, even though they had a couple of stools at which shoppers could eat their pasties. Unfortunately, the Hull local authority took a different view, since the Newcastle decision conflicted with its local rules, and put local shops governed by Hull at a disadvantage. It was regarded as a form of regulatory arbitrage. So Hull sued Newcastle and joined in the Department of Business in the judicial review litigation. There was an expensive hearing (with the prospect of an even more expensive appeal). It might of course have been preferable had the two chief executives of the warring local authorities had a coffee in a neutral Costa café and done a deal between them. The experienced and respected judge did not lose his patience, as maybe he should have done, but gave a thoughtful judgment; maybe he should have told them to settle the case privately and avoid a waste of public money. Attempts at legislative simplification can on occasion provoke undue complexity and expense, especially if the mindset of the participants is inappropriate.

6.3.10   Regulatory Impact Unit (Cabinet Office)

One way to assuage public concern about over-zealous regulation is to explain that much of the regulatory impact is marginal, essential or incidental. The Regulatory Impact Unit of the Cabinet Office took this tack in 2003 when it set out what it thought were the consequences of the previous years' statutory instruments.[52] Its background briefing analysed the position as follows:

> Briefing on the 3,849 Statutory Instruments – sometimes described as 'new regulations' – issued in 2002.
>
> - 95 per cent had little or no impact on business.
> - approximately 1,526 (39 per cent of all SIs) implemented temporary, local road speed limits or traffic restrictions to enable road building, repairs and improvement schemes to proceed; or covered air navigation orders

---

[52] Formerly the Deregulation Unit of the Department of Trade and Industry (moved to the Cabinet Office in March 1996); the name changed to the Better Regulation Unit in July 1997, and changed again to the Regulatory Impact Unit in April 1999.

- around 200 SIs issued by the Department of Health in 2002 related to Primary Care and NHS trusts
- social security and social care accounted for 120 SIs
- electoral changes at borough or city level accounted for 83 SIs.

SIs were issued to

- protect the environment;
- prevent terrorism;
- protect disabled persons against discrimination;
- support students attending higher education courses;
- give grants to institutions providing teacher training courses;
- reduce VAT to 5 per cent for grant-funded installation of heating or security equipment;
- provide for payments to those with parental responsibility for disabled children;
- control or eliminate pollution at land fill sites;
- eliminate unlawful racial discrimination and promote equality of opportunity;
- ensure the recognition by the EU of higher education diplomas, qualifications or experience required for the pursuit of professions or other occupations;
- combat late payment in commercial transactions;
- provide allowances to job seekers;
- increase the Sure Start maternity grant;
- increase energy efficiency grants;
- prohibit funding for Al Qa'ida and Taliban;
- introduce regulations under sections of legislation passed in 1989, 1991, 1993, 1994 and 1995;
- tackle bribery and corruption;
- abolish VAT on equipment for lifeboats;
- increase compensation for bereaved families;
- increase pensions;
- increase the capital gains tax allowance;
- increase grants for bus services;
- extend travel concessions for bus passengers;
- stop the supply of arms/funds to Zimbabwe government;
- encourage clean (renewable) energy;
- introduce fines for dog fouling; and
- stop hooligans attending overseas World Cup matches.

The subtext was clearly: 'and what statutory instruments would you advise dispensing with as part of any deregulatory exercise?' Few could argue that terrorism should be thwarted, or dogs and their owners fined for fouling. But whether there were other ways of improving the life of the citizen than by law was not explored; nor did it explore the content of the regulations, nor whether their admirable objectives could have been achieved through simpler or shorter measures. Indeed it is not clear for example whether the Taliban have been rendered short of cash for roadside bombs as a consequence of the statutory instrument controlling money laundering.

The defensive approach is understandable, especially from what was then a highly pro-active government. The government pointed out that the Regulatory Reform Action Plan[53] committed government departments to better regulation – legislating only where necessary, doing so in a light touch and deregulating wherever possible. The Plan benefitted business, charities and public services. The reforms outlined in the plan had to also meet the five principles of good regulation – that they were transparent, accountable, consistent, targeted and proportionate. The measures ranged from simplifying overly complex fire safety legislation to speeding up the planning process system; and freeing up schools to innovate. As the then Prime Minister had said:[54]

> Where regulations or alternative measures are introduced, this should be done in a light touch way, with decisions informed by a full regulatory impact assessment, which includes details of not only the obvious costs and benefits of the proposal but also the wider economic, social and environmental impacts. New regulations should only be introduced when other alternatives have first been considered and rejected, and where the benefits justify the costs.

6.3.11   Regulatory Policy Committee (of the Department of Business, Energy and Industrial Strategy)

Another effort to constrain regulation was launched in 2007 by the Regulatory Policy Committee of the then Department of Business Innovation and Skills. It adopted the principle that policy decisions should be based on strong evidence of costs and benefits, and that regulators operate in line with the Hampton principles.[55]

In 2007, the Government had brought in new arrangements for preparing impact assessments and putting them at the heart of the policy-making process. In January 2009, the National Audit Office reported that the new arrangements had helped improve the standard of impact assessment but that the standards of impact assessments still varied widely, and

---

[53] No longer available on even archived government websites.
[54] Tony Blair, in his foreword to the 2003 edition of 'Better Policy Making: A Guide to Regulatory Impact Assessment', also no longer available.
[55] See www.bis.gov.uk/policies/better-regulation/policy/regulatory-policy-committee.

noted that the prospect of external scrutiny was the most effective motivator for departments to produce high quality impact assessments.

The Hampton Report,[56] published in March 2005, had identified ways in which the administrative burden of regulation on businesses could be reduced while maintaining or improving regulatory outcomes through changes in the way that regulators work with businesses. The government, whilst claiming that it was continuing to embed the Hampton principles in the way that regulators operate, decided to further its commitments to effective and proportionate regulation, by establishing an external Regulatory Policy Committee. It invited the Regulatory Policy Committee:

- to comment on the quality of analysis supporting policy decisions on new regulations, and on whether the policy design will ensure the benefits justify the costs, including
  - the accuracy and robustness of the costs and benefits;
  - whether the range of policy options assessed support minimising costs and maximising benefits; and
  - the degree to which issues of public risk and the practicalities of ensuring compliance are taken into account;
- to review, advise and comment on the performance of regulators against the Hampton principles.

The Committee was prohibited from commenting on the governmental policy objectives, which it regarded as being a matter for ministers, but was intended to focus on the cost-effectiveness of the instruments to deliver them. The Committee was also invited to advise government in areas that it is invited to do so, or areas related to its terms of reference. Amongst other things it requires regulators to impose new regulations or codes only after due process;[57] it also issued a 'Better Regulation Framework Manual'.[58]

The Regulatory Policy Committee (RPC) was then established in 2009 to provide 'independent, wide-ranging and real-time scrutiny of proposed regulatory measures put forward by government'.[59] Its first report

---

[56] Hampton Report, *Reducing administrative burdens: effective inspection and enforcement*, Philip Hampton, March 2005, HM Treasury, ISBN: 1 84532 088 3.

[57] Department for Business Innovation and Skills, *Accountability for Regulator Impact Policy*, 2013.

[58] Department for Business Innovation and Skills, *Better Regulation Framework Manual: Practical guidance for UK government officials*, March 2015.

[59] Regulatory Policy Committee, *Reviewing regulation*, August 2010.

in August 2010 reported bravely that it examined 400 public consultations issued between December 2009 and July 2010 and made some profound observations about the inadequacies of the regulatory regime, and the inability of government departments to meet the normal regulatory objectives.

It set down six principles of its own, later expanded as in Table 6.1.[60]

Its advice can be accepted or rejected by government departments; and in practice its only weapon is publicity (which is limited) to shame departments into reducing the quantity of legislation. Nor does it really examine the quality of legislation. Finally it is itself subject to dequangofication in due course, even though it is probably cheap to run (no accounts were available at time of writing). In practice its influence and effect are marginal.

6.3.12 Office of Tax Simplification

The Office of Tax Simplification is charged with giving independent advice to the UK government on simplifying the UK tax system; it is an independent office of HM Treasury. Its objective involves reducing tax compliance burdens on both businesses and individual taxpayers, and it is responsible for providing the government with independent advice on where there are areas of complexity in the UK tax system that could be simplified, and conducting inquiries into complex areas of the tax system, to collect evidence and advise the government on options for reform. It is broadly ineffective and deals with relatively trivial issues.[61]

6.4 Unregulation Legislation

6.4.1 Introduction

On an irregular basis statutes are produced intended to roll back the activities of the state. It is convenient when analysing them to distinguish several trends in unregulation. Consolidation legislation is in theory at least intended not to simplify the law but to codify it in one place. It is a useful exercise but is not a common exercise because it is expensive – and in

---

[60] *Framework Document*, Regulatory Policy Committee, Department for Business Innovation and Skills, January 2017, p5 See also *Regulatory overview: the regulatory landscape, May 2015 to May 2016*, Regulatory Policy Committee, undated, c2016.

[61] *Simplification review of residual paper stamp duty on shares: progress report and Call for Evidence*, Office of Tax Simplification, March 2017.

Table 6.1 *How the Regulatory Policy Committee will operate*

The RPC will deliver its statutory and non-statutory functions by:
(a) operating an effective, consistent, proportionate and timely system for its
    scrutiny and verification activities, having regard to guidance on prioritisation
    from Ministers;
(b) providing a transparent and public account of its scrutiny work whilst also
    respecting the confidentiality that may be associated with individual
    departmental and regulators' proposals. It will deliver this through the timely
    publication of its opinions, reports, statements of verification made under the
    Business Impact Target and, as appropriate, letters to Ministers;
(c) setting clear quality standards, establishing precedents, and sharing good
    practice; and
In performing its functions, the RPC will also
(d) have regard to the better regulation methodology and other government
    guidance including the Green Book and the Better Regulation Framework
    Manual, and the need for co-ordination of activities to ensure effective and
    efficient operation of the better regulation framework;
(e) engage with stakeholders – including business, business representative bodies,
    voluntary and community bodies, Regulators, Parliament, European
    counterparts and other interested parties – to:
    • share knowledge and experience of independent scrutiny and encourage
      better scrutiny;
    • improve the quality of analysis and evidence in impact assessments; and
    • build and maintain the RPC's understanding of issues affecting different
      business sectors.
In scrutinising the evidence base for legislative proposals or proposals that require
RRC clearance, the RPC will consider
(f) whether an adequate range of options, including non-regulatory approaches,
    have been assessed;
(g) whether the range of options considered supports minimising costs and
    maximising benefits;
(h) where a regulatory option is preferred, the quality, accuracy and robustness of
    the underlying evidence for the preferred option;
(i) the degree to which an assessment of the impact on small and micro
    businesses (SaMBA) has been undertaken and whether consideration has
    been given to the exemption of these businesses or mitigation of the impacts
    on these businesses;
(j) the accuracy and robustness of the cost and benefit calculations, taking into
    account the full range of costs and benefits including those related to the
    enforcement regime; and
(k) the quality of impact assessments, including the evidence and analysis that
    supports Government policy decisions, and the extent to which the reasons
    for the Government's chosen option are set out clearly.

---

any event is it something of a Forth Bridge problem. As fast as the paint is applied at one end, the rust is forming at the other. The legislation could be analysed as follows:

- statute law repeals acts, including
  - Statute Law Repeals Act 2008,
  - Statute Law Repeals Act 2013 and
  - Statute Law (Repeals) Bill 2015 (Law Commission);
- regulatory reform acts, including
  - Regulatory Reform Act 2001,
  - Legislative and Regulatory Reform Act 2006,
  - Regulatory Enforcement and Sanctions Act 2008,
  - Enterprise and Regulatory Reform Act 2013 and
  - Small Business, Enterprise and Employment Act 2015;
- deregulation acts, including
  - Deregulation and Contracting Out Act 1994 and
  - Deregulation Act 2015;
- consolidation acts following Law Commission reports, which included, for example,
  - Wireless Telegraphy Act 2006,
  - Parliamentary Costs Act 2006,
  - National Health Service Act 2006,
  - National Health Service (Wales) Act 2006,
  - National Health Service (Consequential Provisions) Act 2006 and
  - Companies Act 2006.

Some of the initiatives have had merely political purposes; one of the less edifying was proposed followed a suggestion that repealing the Human Rights Act would enhance human rights protections in the UK.[62] Similarly an 'Enforcement concordat'[63] sought to promote consistency and fairness in the application of sanctions in local and central government,

---

[62] *Protecting human rights in the UK: The Conservatives proposals for changing Britain's human rights law*, promoted by Chris Grayling, later Lord Chancellor, (s3.documentcloud .org/documents/1308660/pages/protecting-human-rights-in-the-united-kingdom (2014); cf. Social Action, Responsibility and Heroism Bill parliamentary debates in 2014.

[63] *Enforcement concordat: good practice guide for England and Wales*, Small Business Service, Department of Trade and Industry, June 2003. See e.g. *The Regulatory Reform Bill [HL] Background to red tape issues*, House of Commons Library Research Paper 01/26, 14 March 2001.

especially as they affected small businesses. Both of these failed to gain traction.

6.4.2 Statute Law Repeals Act 2008

The Statute Law Repeals Act 2008 Act, for example, repealed 260 complete Acts and part repealed 68 other Acts, including

- obsolete laws relating to London workhouses including the workhouse at Wapping mentioned by Charles Dickens in The Uncommercial Traveller,
- an Act of 1819 passed following the Peterloo Massacre of that year when 11 people were killed in Manchester,
- obsolete laws on the police including a law of 1839 requiring street musicians to leave the area if required to do so by irritated householders,
- 40 Acts dating from 1700 for building local prisons across 19 counties in England and Wales,
- 12 obsolete Acts relating to the former East India Company and
- obsolete laws on turnpikes dating back to a time when roads were maintained locally, with travellers having to pay a toll to cross a turnpike.

The Law Commission later proposed further repeals, including[64]

- the Statute of Marlborough 1267, the oldest surviving act at the time – it concerned the seizing of goods of debtors,
- an Act of 1947 passed to support the replacement of the League of Nations mandate system by United Nations trusteeships,
- four acts about the Foreign Compensation Commission (which assessed compensation for assets seized by foreign governments),
- a 1964 Act passed to clear away slums and promote house building and
- a 1997 Act passed to authorise the holding of referendums for the Scottish Parliament and Welsh Assembly.

One of the laws intended to be repealed for example was the Guard Dogs Act 1975, which was introduced following a number of fatal killings of children by guard dogs, and which provided for training and licensing of

---

[64] Law Commission, *Statute Law Repeals, Consultation paper: General Repeals*, SLR 03/14, November 2014; cf. Statute Law Repeals Act 2013.

handlers. Only s1 was ever brought into force, and its purpose was broadly overtaken following the expansion of CCTV. It is a prime example of reactionary legislation.

There must be a degree of quiet satisfaction that the statute book is being cleansed, even of laws that are no longer relevant or have long not been enforced. There will also be mild irritation that so much energy went into the promulgation of laws many of which were never brought into force.

6.4.3   Deregulation and Contracting Out Act 1994

One of the earlier deregulatory attempts was the Deregulation and Contracting Out Act 1994. It started bravely, with a Henry VIII power for Ministers to change primary legislation if they thought it offered a deregulatory benefit. The devil was in the details, i.e. the drafting. S1 provides:

1(1) If, with respect to any provision made by an enactment, a Minister of the Crown is of the opinion –
   (a) that the effect of the provision is such as to impose, or authorise or require the imposition of, a burden affecting any person in the carrying on of any trade, business or profession or otherwise, and
   (b) that, by amending or repealing the enactment concerned and, where appropriate, by making such other provision as is referred to in subsection (4)(a) below, it would be possible, without removing any necessary protection, to remove or reduce the burden or, as the case may be, the authorisation or requirement by virtue of which the burden may be imposed he may, subject to the following provisions of this section and sections 2 to 4 below, by order amend or repeal that enactment.

The drafting is brave because it gives astonishing power to the Minister (any Minister) to change primary legislation without reference to Parliament; it is also virtually unworkable because as Sir Humphrey might point out, he has to be satisfied that 'no necessary protection is removed', which is hard to establish. It is not possible to determine how often this regulatory power has been employed, but it is probable that it has been rarely used, if not never.

6.4.4   Regulatory Reform Act 2001

Unusually, the Regulatory Reform Act 2001 Act was a short piece of legislation, intended to widen the scope of deregulation orders made

available by the Deregulatory and Contracting Out Act 1994. It also gave
some statutory support for the 1998 'Enforcement Concordat' which was
adopted for a while by some regulatory authorities, mostly local councils,
and then fell into desuetude. Most of its provisions were later incorporated
into the Legislative and Regulatory Reform Act 2006.[65]

6.4.5   Regulatory Reform Orders

Under the 2001 Act a number of regulatory reform orders were made,
most of them technical or of minor effect; they included, for example,

Regulatory Reform (Special Occasions Licensing) Order 2001 SI
2001/3937

Regulatory Reform (Voluntary Aided Schools Liabilities and Funding)
(England) Order 2002 SI 2002/906

Regulatory Reform (Golden Jubilee Licensing) Order 2002 SI 2002/1062

Regulatory Reform (Carer's Allowance) Order 2002 SI 2002/1457

Regulatory Reform (Vaccine Damage Payments Act 1979) Order 2002 SI
2002/1592

Regulatory Reform (Housing Assistance) (England and Wales) Order
2002 SI 2002/1860

Regulatory Reform (Removal of 20 Member Limit in Partnerships etc.)
Order 2002 SI 2002/3203

Regulatory Reform (Special Occasions Licensing) Order 2002 SI
2002/3205

Regulatory Reform (Credit Unions) Order 2003 SI 2003/256

Regulatory Reform (Assured Periodic Tenancies) (Rent Increases) Order
2003 SI 2003/259

Regulatory Reform (Housing Management Agreements) Order 2003 SI
2003/940

Regulatory Reform (Schemes under Section 129 of the Housing Act 1988)
(England) Order 2003 SI 2003/986

Regulatory Reform (Sugar Beet Research and Education) Order 2003 SI
2003/1281

Regulatory Reform (British Waterways Board) Order 2003 SI 2003/1545

---

[65] The House of Commons Library published a useful note on the background to the red tape
problem in its guide to the Act: *The Regulatory Reform Bill (HL): background to red tape
issues*, Research paper 01/26, 14 March 2001.

Regulatory Reform (Gaming Machines) Order 2003 SI 2003/3275

Regulatory Reform (Sunday Trading) Order 2004 SI 2004/470

Regulatory Reform (Museum of London) (Location of Premises) Order 2004 SI 2004/1939

Regulatory Reform (Patents) Order 2004 SI 2004/2357

Regulatory Reform (Local Commissioner for Wales) Order 2004 SI 2004/2359

Regulatory Reform (Unsolicited Goods and Services Act 1971) (Directory Entries and Demands for Payment) Order 2005 SI 2005/55

Regulatory Reform (Joint Nature Conservation Committee) Order 2005 SI 2005/634

Regulatory Reform (Trading Stamps) Order 2005 SI 2005/871

Regulatory Reform (Prison Officers) (Industrial Action) Order 2005 SI 2005/908

Regulatory Reform (National Health Service Charitable and Non-Charitable Trust Accounts and Audit) Order 2005 SI 2005/1074

Regulatory Reform (Fire Safety) Order 2005 SI 2005/1541

Regulatory Reform (Execution of Deeds and Documents) Order 2005 SI 2005/1906

Regulatory Reform (Fire Safety) Subordinate Provisions Order 2006 SI 2006/484

Regulatory Reform (Forestry) Order 2006 SI 2006/780

Regulatory Reform (Registered Designs) Order 2006 SI 2006/1974

One of them was however of major impact; the 2005 Fire Safety order did not make life simpler for small business, the point of the Act, but it did operate to consolidate over 70 pieces of legislation and two major acts. It also added a layer of bureaucracy, but its effect was generally regarded as beneficial; fire experience has improved considerably over recent years. The order was not however deregulatory.

6.4.6   Legislative and Regulatory Reform Act 2006

There was substantial criticism of the ineffectiveness of the Regulatory Reform Act 2001.[66] So in 2006, a new act was introduced to overcome its bureaucratic impediments (and repeal the Regulatory Reform Act),

---

[66] Cabinet Office, *Review of the Regulatory Reform Act 2001*, July 2005.

and in particular the complexities of a 'Regulatory Reform Order'. But the Legislative and Regulatory Reform Bill 2006 caused a storm when it was published. Its constitutional novelty was to allow acts of parliament to be changed by statutory instrument, and it also allowed governments to cut back on the number of regulations. The change overcame centuries of an understanding that acts of parliament could only be changed by acts of parliament.[67] The Regulatory Reform Committee, a select committee of the House of Commons, which in theory should have welcomed it, was deeply apprehensive.[68] A Liberal Democrat MP, David Howarth, a lawyer and Cambridge academic, said in the Commons:

> I hope that the Leader of the House has had a chance to read a letter in The Times today from six professors of law at Cambridge University, expressing their concern about the extraordinary powers granted to the Government by the Legislative and Regulatory Reform Bill, which is now widely known as the 'Abolition of Parliament Bill'.[69]

The mischief was in s1:

(1) A Minister of the Crown may by order under this section make any provision which he considers would serve the purpose in subsection (2).

(2) That purpose is removing or reducing any burden, or the overall burdens, resulting directly or indirectly for any person from any legislation.

The provision does in principle, even with the safeguards that were later introduced, seem excessive. In practice however it has made virtually no difference. In particular it is hardly ever used, perhaps on average not more than once every couple of years.[70]

---

[67] Richard Kelly and Vincent Keter, *The Legislative and Regulatory Reform Bill*, House of Commons Library, research paper 06/06, 6 February 2006; Richard Kelly, *Legislative and Regulatory Reform Bill – the Bill's progress and further reaction to the Bill*, House of Commons Library, Standard Note SN/PC/3998, 3 November 2006. See also *Gina Miller v Secretary of State R (on the application of Miller and another) (Respondents) v Secretary of State for Exiting the European Union (Appellant)*, 24 January 2017, [2017] UKSC 5.

[68] Regulatory Reform Committee, *Legislative and Regulatory Reform Bill*, 6 February 2006, HC 878 2005–06, p3.

[69] HC Deb 16 February 2006 cc1567–1568.

[70] And for relatively trivial matters: see e.g. *Regulatory Reform (Health and Safety Executive) Order* SI 2004 No 0470; similarly SI 2008 No 0960, SI 2010 No 2452; SI 2013 No 0103; SI 2014 No 0542.

6.4.7   Regulatory Enforcement and Sanctions Act 2008

The Regulatory Enforcement and Sanctions Act 2008 was designed to provide for more consistent enforcement of regulations across local authority boundaries, better co-ordination between local authorities and central government, and more effective enforcement of regulations. It also requires regulators to conform to certain principles. The Act was passed in response to the Hampton report, discussed above. Part 1 re-established Local Better Regulation Office, already established in May 2007 as a government-owned company, as a statutory corporation with statutory powers. Part 2 established a Primary Authority scheme, whereby businesses which operate in more than one local authority area can choose to nominate one authority as the primary one for regulatory purposes. Part 3 introduced four new civil penalties that regulatory authorities are now able to impose on businesses. And Part 4 imposed a duty on regulators to keep their regulatory activity under review and remove unnecessary burdens, and to keep their regulatory activities to a necessary minimum.

6.4.8   Enterprise and Regulatory Reform Act 2013

The Enterprise and Regulatory Reform Act 2013 was a curious portmanteau Act; it covered reforms to bankruptcy procedures; imposed civil liability for breaches of health and safety duties; made changes to the listed building consent regime; established a Green investment bank and many other unconnected matters. It did not meet the standards sought by the Parliamentary Counsel's office in seeking clarity in legislative structure. Its deregulatory impact was minor and mostly trivial. It did not make for a coherent approach to regulatory reform.[71]

6.4.9   Small Business, Enterprise and Employment Act 2015

The Small Business, Enterprise and Employment Act 2015 was intended to simplify company registration – which it did – but at the expense of imposing further obligations including a peculiarly pointless one of reporting annually on who has control of the company. The Act is 275 pages long and comprises a portmanteau of company law revisions, reforming a Payments

---

[71] Enterprise and Regulatory Reform Act 2013; see Edward Scott, *Enterprise and Regulatory Reform Bill HL Bill 45 of 2012–13*, House of Lords Library Note LLN 2012/038.

Systems Regulator, imposing a new system of pubs regulation (with a Pubs Code Adjudicator), revising Childcare regulations, regulating insolvency practice, changing the system of whistleblowing and equal pay in employment law (and dealing with concessionary coal). It is a perfect example of the kind of legislation severely criticised by the Chief Parliamentary Counsel.[72]

6.4.10   Deregulation Act 2015

The Deregulation Act 2015[73] on the surface looked to be a serious attempt at rolling back the tide of legislation. It, like its statutory colleagues, emerged however as yet another portmanteau of minor reforms, lacking a strategic direction. It veered from the driving instructor registration system, to health and safety for the self-employed, to simplifying the process for publishing lists of authorised fuels, to the management of offshore gas unloading facilities and to regulations affecting the sellers of knitting yarn. The outcome was the appearance of regulatory cleansing without any material impact on day-to-day life; it was cleansing something that did not appear dirty to most people. It was also a lesson on the politics of spin; it gave the illusion of reduction of regulation, using measurements which were misleading.[74]

---

[72] See e.g. *Drafting Guidance*, Office of The Parliamentary Counsel, August 2015.

[73] Deregulation Act 2015; Doug Piper et al., *Deregulation Bill*, House of Commons Library, Research Paper 14/06, 20 January 2014; cf. *The Regulatory Reform Bill [HL]: background to red tape issues*, House of Commons research paper, 14 March 2001.

[74] Deregulation legislation is nothing new; see e.g. *A proclamation signifying his Majeties pleasure touching some former Proclamations; and some other things*, Proclamation, Hampton Court, 24 September 1610, reproduced in Larkin and Hughes, *Stuart Royal Proclamations of King James I 1603–1625*, Oxford, 1973 p253: 'As the Princley care and continuall watch, which Wee have over the good of Our loving Subjects, may in part appeare, by the course which Wee have taken, for a review and consideration of many of our Statute Lawes: wherein Wee were desirous, that in stead of the multiplicties of the same, and doubtfulness that may arise in the interpretation of them, (whereof some are worne out with time, some unfit for execution by the change of times, and of others, some branches only standing in force, and the rest repealed) some such new Lawes may be made, as shall be most necessary for the good of Us, and our people, and the same more cleare and plaine to their understanding whom it may concerne, then they have bene or are in some cases; For the better preparation whereof (being a worke of so great labour) we have already caused our Privie Council, to make choice of some discreet persons learned in the Law, not onely to make collections of them as they stand now in force, but to digest them into some such orderly Method.'

6.5   Efforts at Deregulation (Public Bodies)

6.5.1   Introduction

Some attempts at unregulation have had unintended consequences because of the confused mindset of the legislators. Following the death of a UK businessman Robert Maxwell in 1991, the pension schemes operated by his companies were found to have had their investments misapplied, not by the (unregulated) trustees but by an investment management company authorised by a new regulatory body intended to prevent such failures. The irony was overlooked that the unregulated body, the trustees, had been more effective in managing an abusive plan sponsor than a formal regulator. In any event, because of the scandal, a government report was commissioned, which recommended legal changes, including restricting the ability of pension funds under their constitutions to amend their own rules. This was known in the industry as s67,[75] and it eventually posed in practice expensive and administrative impediments to improving pension scheme arrangements. In 2002 the government under pressure from the industry appointed Alan Pickering, a respected industry figure, to review the operation of the legislation. His report recommended amongst other things a drastic simplification of the previous legislation.[76] In the end the troublesome s67 was amended following his proposals – except that the previous 340 odd words of the old s67 were simplified into around 3600 words of the new version of the section.[77] The new rules are slightly more permissive, but very much more complicated; they certainly did not meet the Pickering objective of simplification.

Similarly, the Independent Farming Regulation Task Force in 2011 made 215 recommendations including an overarching recommendation to substitute partnership, responsibility and trust for bureaucracy.[78] The Task Force said:[79]

---

[75] Pensions Act 1995 s67.

[76] *A simpler way to better pensions, An independent report by Alan Pickering*, July 2002 published by the UK Department of Work and Pensions.

[77] Pensions Act 2004 s262.

[78] *Striking a balance: reducing burdens; increasing responsibility; earning recognition. A report on better regulation in farming and food businesses*, Independent Farming Regulation Task Force, May 2011.

[79] *Striking a balance: reducing burdens; increasing responsibility; earning recognition. A report on better regulation in farming and food businesses*, Independent Farming Regulation Task Force, May 2011, p4.

It is difficult and probably wrong to caricature Government thinking on regulation. However, if we did, it would be that successive administrations have been cautious, prescriptive, fearful of EU infraction, and possessive of implementation. As a result, in many instances we have become slaves to the process of regulation and lost sight of the outcomes we have been trying to achieve...

Defra [the Department for farming matters] and its agencies need to establish an entirely new approach to and culture of regulation, otherwise the frustration that we, farmers and food-processing businesses have felt will continue.

A subsequent parliamentary inquiry confirmed:[80]

We agree that a non-regulatory approach should be the starting point for addressing a policy issue. We recommend that Defra enshrines this principle in their policy-making process. Policy-making officials in Defra should be explicitly assessed on how they have given consideration to non-regulatory approaches.

Nothing further appears to have been done following the Report, perhaps because it proved too difficult.

6.5.2   Local Authorities

Local authorities have complained about over-regulation, without much effect, for many years.[81] They have sought the abolition of passports for horses and licences for animal trainers, the removal of the requirement for bicycles to have bells, and the quashing of fines for homeowners who allow their chimneys to catch fire accidentally. They wanted marriages to be allowed to take place in the evening, and to abolish fining shop owners if they allow prostitutes to assemble on their property. These are minor headline-making constraints; but inevitably, given their electorate, local authorities find it hard to focus beyond the trivial to explore how they might decontrol whole areas of activity, such as parking.

---

[80] House of Commons, Environment, Food and Rural Affairs Committee, *The outcome of the Independent Farming Regulation Task Force, Tenth Report of Session 2010–12*, 13 September 2011, HC 1266, para 15.

[81] Christopher Hope, 'Scrap red tape of horse passports and bike bells', Daily Telegraph, 11 August 2010; Local Government Association, *Reducing the burden – allowing councils to get on with their day job*, 2010.

6.5.3 Third Sector

Some of the revolt against regulation goes back some way; the third sector sought simplification of the charities regime in 1994[82] and made another attempt in 2005.[83] But the history of attempts at reform have been unpromising.

6.5.4 Internal Attempts by Regulators

There have been internal efforts by regulators to slim themselves down. The Health and Safety Executive in the UK has tried for some years to tone down some of the more hysterical responses of 'elf 'n' safety' complainants. It published 'health and safety myths', intending to demonstrate that they are simply just that.[84] But rather shamefacedly it has also accepted that the system is over-complicated and for a time in the first decade of the twenty-first century it produced a series of reports intended to show it was indeed simplifying things,[85] and issued a mission statement:

> Good health and safety management in any business/organisation has always been about action not paperwork. HSE's new strategy makes it clear that we want everyone to play their part in preventing death injury and ill health caused by work activities. HSE remains committed to make it easier and simpler for people to take sensible and proportionate measures to protect people and enable their business to succeed.

The HSE argued that it demonstrated that it had saved £500M in bureaucratic savings (including the removal of the need for a licence for business working with textured decorative coatings) but noted 'this figure includes estimated savings that have not been validated and which may be subject to change or revision'. It omitted to mention regulations which had been introduced, such as the need to retain a qualified electrician to fix electrical work in one's own home. On the other hand it had saved the country

---

[82] *Charities and Voluntary Organisations Task Force Report Volume II*, Charities and Voluntary Organisations Task Force, London, 1994.

[83] Better Regulation Task Force, *Better regulation for civil society: making life easier for those who help others*, November 2005, especially Annex D, setting out *Proposals by the Charity Commission for reducing regulatory burdens on trustees*, and cf. for a more combative approach, *Draft monetary penalties policy and revised professional trustee description*, *Consultation Document*, The Pensions Regulator, March 2017.

[84] See e.g. www.hse.gov.uk/myth.

[85] See e.g. *Taking a wider perspective: HSE's fourth simplification plan and progress report*, Health and Safety Executive, December 2009.

£3.6M in removal of a form which required businesses to certify the safety of a boat that takes dock workers to other ships in the harbour to load and unload the cargo. The HSE report shows the complexity of the task when trying to simplify the rules. For example when trying to look at the Sensible Risk Management campaign to help schools reduce the paperwork on risk management, it found itself unable simply to state, as it might have, that teachers should merely think about the risks and use their common sense, or perhaps ignore the need for formal review and rely on the normal laws of negligence and the pressure (if any) from insurers to require controls.

Its efforts were unappreciated, not least by government itself. Several years later, a government minister had clearly not become aware of the change in culture when he introduced an act designed to overcome what he perceived to be the risk-averse HSE culture.[86]

Similarly, Chapter 1 noted that the National Trust managed to cut its own rule book significantly.[87] The National Trust was of course simply a charity; but regulators can with determination cut back their own regulatory framework. In 2017 the Solicitors Regulation Authority cut its handbook from 600 pages to around 50 – and the accounts rules for solicitors were cut from 70 to 10 pages.[88] The code of conduct of 30 pages was cut to 7 pages.[89]

6.5.5 Regulatory Governance

The growth in the number and scope of regulatory interventions has prompted thoughts about whether the governance of regulators is efficient and appropriate. In addition there are signs of a move back to what used to be called 'self-regulation' and now is called 'self-assurance', or as a compromise 'regulated self-assurance' and 'earned recognition'. The conclusion has been reached through experience that there may be

---

[86] Chris Grayling MP (then Minister of Justice and Lord Chancellor), *Our Bill to curb the Elf and Safety Culture*, ConservativeHome.com, June 2 2014, introducing the Social Action Responsibility and Heroism Bill 2014.

[87] Chapter 1.

[88] *Passmore: tell us about red tape*, Law Society Gazette, 2 May 2016 p3. See also https://cutting-red-tape.cabinetoffice.gov.uk/childcare in relation to cutting regulations for registering childcare providers.

[89] Monidipa Fouzder, *SRA unveils slimline handbook and codes*, Law Society Gazette, 6 June 2016; *Consultation: Looking to the future – flexibility and public protection*, Solicitors Regulation Authority, June 2016; *Consultation: looking to the future: SRA Accounts Rules Review*, SRA, June 2016.

alternatives to direct regulation. As yet the move is tentative, but may gain ground.[90]

6.5.6   Unregulation Initiatives in the EU and Internationally

The European Union has been frequently accused of excessive lawmaking, and is conscious of the issue. It set up its own deregulation unit (see Chapter 1), which in some ways goes against the trend, since historically jurisdictions have conventionally sought to increase volume of law, its extent being a symbol of the breadth of its civilisation.[91] The EU's problem in fact may be more talked about than real; in 2001 the total number of pages was estimated at 80,000 pages, compared for example with the 12,000 acts of parliament in the Netherlands with about 140,000 clauses.[92] In addition the Netherlands alone produced in that year about 80,000 pages of legislative instruments.

There is a longish history of simplification initiatives in the EU (and the OECD).[93] In November 2015 the EU appointed Frans Timmermans as Commissioner for Better Regulation,[94] the first, and had in the early 2000s introduced a 'Better Regulation Strategy' intended to improve the regulatory environment.[95] There was an attempt to slim down the extent

---

[90] See e.g. *Regulatory Futures Review*, Cabinet Office, January 2017. The document does not carry the Cabinet Office logo, or address or contact details, suggesting that accountability may have some way to go.

[91] See R. Rustenber, *Regeldruk [Legislative burden]*, Nederland Juristenblad, afl5, p231, cited in Wim Voermans et al., *Codification and consolidation in the European Union: a means to untie red tape* [2008] 29(2) Statute Law Review 65–81 Note 2, which notes that the production of legislation in itself is not an indication of legislative burden, and that during the Renaissance Italian cities like Bologna prided themselves in the volume of their city state legislation as a token of their level of civilisation.

[92] Richard and Cracknell, *Acts and Statutory instruments: volume of UK legislation 1950 to 2006*, 5 February 2007, House of Commons Library.

[93] OECD, *Cutting red tape: national strategies*, January 2007 (www.oecd.org/dataoecd/12/9/308016320.pdf). And see for a comparative analysis of other countries administrative burdens, OECD, *Cutting Red Tape: Comparing administrative burdens across countries*, OECD 20907 ISBN 978-92-64-00821-2; and OECD, *Regulatory policies in OECD Countries: from intervention to regulatory governance*, OECD 2002. In recent years the OECD's interest in excessive governance seems to have waned, although see *Regulatory policy in perspective: a reader's companion to the OECD Regulatory Policy Outlook 2015*, OECD 2015.

[94] *Letter to Frans Timmermans from 27 member states*, European Union, 15 November 2015.

[95] European Union, *A strategic review of better regulation in the European Union*, Communication from the Commission to the Council of the European Parliament, the European Economic and Social Committee and the Committee of the Regions, COM(2006) 690 (Final).

of regulation, using working groups encouragingly called 'Simpler Legislation for the Internal Market – SLIM', who were charged with reducing the volume (though not the content) by 25 per cent. The groups sought codification, consolidation and removal of obsolete legislation but because the law which eventually emerged from the legislative process was the result of hard-fought compromises, consolidating the text for example would have involved renegotiating some elements of the document, but it proved politically too difficult.[96] Despite or perhaps because of the record of failure, every few years there was another initiative (in fact 143 according to one count in 2006).[97]

All these initiatives operated on a mixture of repeal, (disposing of legislation which was unnecessary, irrelevant or obsolete), codification (creating code by putting similar legislation in a single narrative) and recasting, a form of codification; the Commission also tried co-regulation, using standards of independent bodies such as the Financial Accounting Standards Board, the use of regulations rather than directives (which some people considered was simpler than using directives, another form of legislation), screening, reviewing the existing stock of legislation (as happens in France, with some success) and 'inspiring national reform', i.e. campaigning against gold-plating, an endemic British disease, which means using the excuse of having to implement EU legislation in a national form

---

[96] See European Union, *Inter-institutional Agreement of 20 December 1994 on an accelerated working method for official codification of legislative texts*, OJ 102, 04 April 1996 2–3; EU Commission, Staff working paper on 28 February 2000, providing background material to the Commission Communication on the review of the SLIM pilot project; Action Plan, Simplifying and improving the regulatory environment COM (2002) 278 final; *Communication of the Commission, Implementing the Community Lisbon programme: a strategy for the simplification of the regulatory environment*, COM (2005) 535; EU Commission, *Better regulation for growth and jobs in the EU*, October 2005 COM (2005) 97, revised in COM (2006) 690 final.

[97] Previous attempts to reform the system have included the Sutherland Report (*The Internal Market after 1992: meeting the challenge, Report presented to the Commission by the High Level Group on the Functioning of the Internal Market* EC Com (1992); the Brussels Programme (*The Brussels Programme* COM (93) 545; the Molitor Report (*The Molitor Report, the Report of Independent Experts on Legislative and Administrative Simplification*, COM SEC (95) 1379); the Simpler Legislation for the Internal Market project (*Simpler Legislation for the Internal Market*); and the Better Regulation initiative (*Better regulation – Simplification initiative 2006*). The UK had been pressing for reform for several years; on 21 July the Cabinet Office published a *Guide to Better European Regulation*; and the European Council at a special meeting in Lisbon in March 2000 instructed the Commission and Member States to set out a strategy for further co-ordinated action to simplify the regulatory environment at both national and community level. (*Lisbon Conclusions*, Paragraph 17, indent 4).

to introduce some pet rules of the local draftsmen or politician and then blaming the EU or elucidation.

These attempts involved both a reactive strategy, using screening or codification to try and manage the existing legislative base, and a preventative strategy intended to prevent a proliferation of legislation. As anyone who has ventured into the legislative database on the web will know the efforts have signally failed, largely not because of a lack of will of those charged with the challenge, but more because of the mindset of an institution whose very existence depends of using legislation to improve things.

In July 2014 the Stoiber Report[98] suggested that it might be time to introduce what it called 'smart regulation'. This repeated the aspirations of most of the previous reports, with a slightly different pull-quote (*Les lois inutiles affaisblissent les lois nécessaires* – 'useless laws weaken the necessary ones' – by Montesquieu, rather than Winston Churchill's '*If you have 10,000 regulations, you destroy all respect for the law*', cited by David Arculus in his report). It reported that there had been several hundred suggestions on how to reduce administrative burdens, and those it adopted were said to cut the costs to industry by £41B a year. It quoted Aristotle, 'It is not the deeds that move the people, but the words about the deeds'. And it made 12 recommendations, including requiring a political commitment to focus only on those interventions which were indispensable at an EU level. Virtually as the report was published, EIOPA, the European insurance and pensions regulator, announced a sheaf of controls on pension schemes across Europe based on an assumption that pension schemes were badly run for which there was little if any evidence. It is clear that exhortations from one part of government have little effect on other parts where the pressures to act are asymmetrical. EIOPA was charged to do something; they could hardly report back that nothing needed to be done.[99]

6.5.7 The EU REFIT Programme

The European Commission's REFIT programme used to be called Better Regulation and has been operating since about 2004. REFIT stands

---

[98] High Level Group on Administrative Burdens, *Cutting red tape in Europe*, Final Report, Brussels, 24 July 2014.

[99] Gabriel Bernadino, Chairman EIOPA, *EIOPA's vision on private pensions – enhanced sustainability, strong governance and full transparency*, speech to the National Association of Pension Funds, Liverpool, 17 October 2014. It includes a requirement to produce a statement to members of information about the scheme on no more than two pages of A4 in a legible print, including at least six pages of content, an obvious impossibility.

for Regulatory Fitness and Performance Programme, and in essence it amounts to finding regulatory directives (in the acquis communautaire) to abolish, abandon or amend. The suggestions come from the Commission and are then put to the 'legislator' (a portmanteau word for the Parliament and the Council, the collective of member state ministers).

The Commission publishes a 'Scorecard'[100] which reports progress in processing its proposals. In fact the Commission now abandons directives in its pipeline before even putting them to the legislator. Until recently, the member states blocked many suggestions for repeal, perhaps because they preferred to blame the EU for regulations that they see as necessary but unpopular. And of course some member states had been dilatory in implementing the original directives.

The results, as the directives are scrutinised one by one, will depend on the political spectrum of the elected governments in the numerous member states, and the possibly capricious outcomes of the European Parliamentary process. In many cases, removing a restrictive directive will not automatically remove national legislation which had already implemented it; member states would be free to make up their own minds on repeal or retention. The programme also includes measures defined as Regulations rather than Directives, which apply directly without being reinterpreted into national law. Replacing one of these might again require fresh national legislation.

The management of regulations is now an open door for debate, and the Commission continually invites comments on what else should be considered for scrutiny.[101] This is in contrast to the Treaty, where negotiated

---

[100] http://ec.europa.eu/smart-regulation/better_regulation/documents/swd_2015_110_en .pdf; European Commission, *Regulatory Fitness and Performance Programme (REFIT) State of Play and Outlook 'REFIT Scoreboard'*, 19 May 2015 (staff working document SWD(2015)110 final, Strasbourg) and European Commission, *Better regulation for better results – an EU agenda*, 19 May 2015 (Strasbourg, COM(2015) 215 final).

[101] http://ec.europa.eu/smart-regulation/docs/refit_brochure_en.pdf; European Commission, *REFIT: Making EU law lighter, simpler and less costly*, August 2014 (brochure, see http://ec.europa.eu/smart-regulation/refit/consultation). *Better regulation for better results – an EU agenda*, European Commission, 19 May 2015, COM(2015) 215 Final; *Better Regulation Guidelines*, European Commission, Strasbourg, 19 May 2015, SWD(2015) 111 final; *Better Regulation Toolbox*, European Commission, 19 May 2015 (441pp); *Regulatory Fitness and Performance Programme (REFIT): State of play and outlook 'REFIT Scoreboard*, European Commission, 19 May 2015 Strasbourg, SWD(2015) 10 final; *Decision of the President of the European Commission on the establishment of an independent Regulatory Scrutiny Board*, Strasbourg, 19 May 2015, C(2015) 3263 final; *Communication to the Commission: Regulatory Scrutiny Board: Mission, tasks and staff*, Strasbourg, 19 May 2015 C(2015) 3262 final; *Proposal for an interinstitutional agreement on better regulation*, Strasbourg,19 May 2015, COM(2015) 216 final.

agreement on possible changes take time, with further delay for enactment even if the (present) 28 member states can clear domestic hurdles, and yet more for practical application.

The Treaty prescribes the 'competences' subject to reform. Some are policy areas that only the EU itself can exercise – such as trade treaties and running the eurozone; shared competences – where the EU can set the rules by means of directives but does not have to do so; and matters left to member states but where they can ask for EU co-ordination. The second set are clearly eligible for REFIT, but the last area includes Treaty provisions where national policies in general such as health and education are independent but overlap with REFIT items such as rules for procurement.

What this implies for a member government is that the directives it dislikes must first be identified. The Commission can then be encouraged to include them in REFIT. In the UK each of its Whitehall departments (in a 2014 exercise) reported in detail how the EU and national competences affected their responsibilities. This included (it was said) wide consultation with the private sector. Once a directive is targeted and included in REFIT, it is the member states one by one that are supposed to be sounded out, perhaps at official level. This is to be a matter of painstaking detail, rather than of grandstanding. Thus far the outcomes have been modest, especially since in addition to the usual directives, regulations, decisions recommendations and opinion emanating from the EU, there are non-legislative rules, the impact of which is only lightly studied.[102] Finally the costs of implementing regulations is as yet an embryonic science.[103]

6.5.8   The EU Regulatory Scrutiny Board

The Regulatory Scrutiny Board, established in 2015, and which replaced the former Impact Assessment Board, is dedicated to supporting the European Commission's Better Regulation Policy by providing central quality control of impact assessments, ex post evaluations and regulatory fitness checks. It has six full-time members (of whom three are external) and

---

[102] A. Alemanno and A. Meuwese, *Impact assessment of EU non-legislative rulemaking: the missing link in 'new comitology',* [2013] 19(1) *European Law Journal* 76.

[103] See e.g. Renda, *Assessment of the cumulative costs of EU legislation in the steel sector,* study for the European Commission, 2014, ibid, *Assessment of the cumulative costs of EU legislation in the aluminium sector,* study for the European Commission, 2014.

a chairman.[104] The Regulatory Scrutiny Board provides a central quality control and support function for Commission impact assessment and evaluation work. The Board examines and issues opinions on all the Commission's draft impact assessments and of major evaluations and 'fitness checks' of existing legislation. In principle, a positive opinion is needed from the Board for an initiative accompanied by an impact assessment to be tabled for adoption by the Commission. The opinion accompanies the draft initiative together with the impact assessment throughout the Commission's political decision-making. All impact assessments and all related RSB opinions are published once the Commission has adopted the relevant proposal. Evaluation 'fitness check' reports and the related opinions are also published.

The Board is independent of the policy-making departments and is chaired at Director-General level. In addition to the Chair, the Board consists of three high-level Commission officials and three members who are recruited from outside the Commission, selected on the basis of their expertise. All members work for the Board full-time, with no other policy responsibilities.

Apart from the irony of around 1000 pages of guidance devoted to reducing regulation, it is probably too early to determine whether its efforts have been successful, despite some of the limited claims for progress. In 2015 alone, half way through the year, the Commission was reported to have withdrawn 141 proposals for regulation. And some of the other claims for improvements to the legislative system are hard to judge. Compared with the programme of the US (see below) the REFIT programme has no legislative underpinning, the Commission has no obligation to report annually to the Parliament, and the review limits its scope to regulatory burdens on business. But like the US (and the UK) it reports success using arbitrary and unverifiable criteria: in 2014 it reported withdrawal of 53 pension proposals (around 300 since 2006) and a reduction in administrative burdens by 33 per cent (since 2006 in 31 priority areas) leading to savings of €41B.[105]

[104] See *Members of the Regulatory Scrutiny Board*, COM/2015/20009, EU, *Official Journal*, C257A, 6 August 2015; http://ec.europa.eu/smart-regulation/impact/iab/iab_en.htm.

[105] European Commission, *Evaluation*, Better Regulation (ec.europa.eu/smart-regulation/evaluation/index); European Commission, *What is REFIT*, Better Regulation, ec.europa.eu/smart-regulation/refit/index); European Commission, *Regulatory Fitness and Performance Programme (REFIT): State of play and outlook*, COM(2014) 368 final and SWD(2014) 192 final of 18 June 2014; European Commission, *Strengthening the foundations of smart regulation: improving evaluation*, COM(2013) 686 final 2 October

One of the criticisms of the EU has been the quantity of regulation devoted to financial services following the Great Recession in 2008;[106] the EU recognised the complaint and years later called for evidence in a review of the EU regulatory framework for financial services.[107]

6.5.9   Better Regulation Watchdog

The Better Regulation Watchdog is a network of '58 European consumer, environmental, development, citizen and public health organisations advancing social justice' founded in 2015. It claims to represent tens of millions of European citizens; in fact it is a pro-regulation organisation whose objective is to challenge the widely held belief that regulation is a burden for society. It is only organisation or body mentioned in this chapter dedicated to promoting *more* regulation.[108]

Similar scepticism has been expressed by other observers; for example in 2015 the EU Commission's work programme suggested it would engage in 23 initiatives – and withdraw or amend 80 existing proposals for political or technical reasons. It was remarked by one observer:

> The determination of the new Commission to slash much more regulation than the one it would create anew was seen by some commentators as a clear pro-business de-regulatory stance, a return to the 'less is more' rhetoric hardly masked by the publicly stated desire to be 'big on big things, and small on small things'.[109]

2013; European Commission, *Smart regulation in the European Union*, COM(2010) 543 final of 8 October 2010.

[106] Andy Haldane, *The Dog and the Frisbee*, Bank of England, Speech, 31 August 2012; www .bis.org/review/r120905a.pdf.

[107] Jonathan Hill, EU Commissioner, *Speech at the public hearing on the Call for Evidence – a review of the EU regulatory framework for financial services*, Brussels, 17 May 2016: 'This call for evidence is part of a much broader Commission agenda, led by Franz Timmermans, for better regulation. As a Commission, we are committed to legislating 80 per cent less this year compared to the last Commission – and legislating better. We want to work with businesses, supervisors and consumers to develop rules that are evidence-based. And we should have the self-confidence to check that our existing legislation is working as intended – and to be prepared to change it if it is not. That is how we can regulate in a way that commands respect.'

[108] www.betterregwatch.eu; Better Regulation Watchdog, *Founding statement*, 15 May 2015.

[109] Andrea Renda, *Too good to be true? A quick assessment of the European Commission's new Better Regulation Package*, Centre for European Policy Studies, Special Report No 108, April 2015.

6.5.10   Regulation as Deregulation

The EU follows the practice of other regulators in claiming regulatory initiatives as a deregulation achievement. In 2016 the EU required member states to stop requiring 'apostilles' (authenticity stamps) of other member states' identity documents for individuals.[110]

6.5.11   OECD

What is clear about over-regulation is that it is not regarded as simply an Anglo-Saxon problem, a product of over-civilised common law arrangements. The OECD reported that, in 2005, 19 of 22 countries interrogated had a government programme to reduce administrative burdens; 14 had established a system for measuring burdens and 9 had quantitative reduction targets. What is clear is that despite a range of acronyms deployed to help in these enterprises (SCM = standard cost model, ABME = administrative burden measurement exercise, RTA = Red Tape Assessment, RTS = Red Tape Scoreboard) the outcome seemed to be modest. There were efforts (some quite successful, such as motor taxation in the UK, where the licensing of cars has been made very simple electronically), but they are few, and of course still involves a licensing system, although one which is not applicable to bicycles or lawnmowers.[111]

While the measurement of the costs of regulation is imperfect, and in practice pointless, comparison of requirements can be instructive. Road freight is one example. In New Zealand a licence to conduct road freight is granted for a lifetime; it is reviewed only in the case of severe breaches. The European Union requires renewal every five years, Belgium automatically renews the licences, and in Germany the business only has to renew once, and after that the licence is renewed for life. There are rational reasons for the differing requirements but few of them are based on evidence rather than cultural background. No one queries why there should be a licence at all, since there are invariably other laws available to protect the public. But the OECD frequent reports on regulation indicate that while there is

---

[110] European Commission, *Final adoption of new rules to cut red tape on citizens' public documents*, Press release, Brussels, 9 June 2016.
[111] *Cutting red tape: national strategies for administrative simplification*, OECD Publishing, Paris, 2006. The French version seems more immediate: 'Éliminer la paperasserie'; *OECD framework for regulatory policy evaluation*, OECD, Paris, 2014.

considerable deregulatory activity across the globe, little of this effort is effective.[112]

6.5.12   France

The austerity measures demanded of member states as part of the economic governance of the European Union in 2014 involved France, notoriously unwelcoming to deregulation, to have proposed measures in transport, retail, legal profession, the pharmacy trade and dentistry; little was implemented, the then economy minister (later Prime Minister) M Emmanuel Macron remarking that 'Complexity is a French illness – we love laws, decrees and texts.'[113]

6.5.13   US

The Office of Management and Budget in the US has a division called the Office of Information and Regulatory Affairs (OIRA).[114] It is only concerned about major rules, i.e. those with an impact of over $100M. It has operated since 1980, as a clearing house to ensure the legislation meets general principles set out in a presidential executive order, covering the consideration of alternatives to regulation and a proper analysis of both costs and benefits. It was unable however to contain the Dodds-Franks rules (involving about 32,000 pages of regulations for the financial services industry). The Office must by law report annually to Congress on the expected costs and benefits of all new 'significant' regulation passed in the previous year. To the extent possible, OMB commits to provide an estimate of the total annual benefits and costs (including quantifiable

---

[112] See e.g. *OECD Regulatory Policy Outlook 2015*, OECD, Paris, 2015, country by country appendices.

[113] Hugh Carnegy, *France unveils measures for deregulation as it seeks budget approval*, Financial Times, 16 October 2014. The EU inquiry into deregulation quoted another Frenchman Montesquieu: 'Les lois inutiles affaiblissent les lois nécessaires' (useless laws weaken the necessary ones), High Level Group on Administrative Burdens, *Cutting Red Tape in Europe*, Brussels, 24 July 2014.

[114] United States, *Executive Order 12866* (Bill Clinton, 4 October 1993) and *Executive Order 13563* (Barack Obama, 18 January 2011) and *Executive Order 13771* (Presidential Executive Order on Reducing Regulation and Controlling Regulatory Costs) (Donald Trump, 30 January 2017). Its work was described in Carl Sunstein, *Simpler: The Future of Government*, Simon & Schuster, 2013; Carl Sunstein achieved fame as co-author of '*Nudge*', which contains principles later adopted by the UK government. He was the Office's Administrator from 2009 to 2012. See also Administrative Procedure Act 1946 and Regulatory Flexibility Act 1980. These laws and orders seem to demonstrate that it is hard to cut regulation by regulation.

and non-quantifiable effects) of Federal rules and paperwork in the aggregate, by agency and agency programme, and by major law. In 2012 OIRA issued a two-page memorandum requiring agencies to engage in assessing the cumulative impact of their rules.[115] The policy was to simplify requirements on the public and private sectors, especially SMEs, to ensure against unjustified, redundant or excessive requirements and ultimately to increase the net benefits of regulation. The directive called on agencies to take nine steps, including engaging in early consultation, using Requests for Information and Advance Notices of Proposed Rule Making to obtain public inputs, considering in the analysis of costs and benefits the relationship between new regulations and regulations that are already in effect and co-ordinating timing, content and requirements of multiple rulemakings that are contemplated for a particular area or sector. The estimated annual benefits of major federal regulations reviewed by OMB from 1 October 2003 to 30 September 2013 for which agencies estimated and monetised both benefits and costs were in the aggregate between $217 billion and $863 billion, while the estimated annual costs were between $57 billion and $84 billion.[116] A degree of scepticism is in order in relation to these calculations,[117] and meanwhile the political pressures to re-regulate persist.[118]

---

[115] US Government *Improving Regulation and Regulatory Review*, Executive Order 13563, January 18 2011 Federal Register Vol 76/14; *Regulation and Independent Regulatory Agencies*, Executive Order 13579, 14 July 2011, Federal Register 76/135; *Cumulative Effect of Regulations*, OIRA, 20 March 2012; *Identifying and reducing regulatory burdens*, Executive Order 13610, 10 May 2012, Federal Register 77/93; 2014 *Draft Report to Congress on the benefits and costs of Federal Regulation and Unfunded Mandates on State, local and Tribal Entities*, OMB, Washington DC, 2014.

[116] OECD, *Regulatory policy in perspective: a reader's companion to the OECD regulatory policy outlook 2015*, OECD, Paris, 2015, p224.

[117] See Paperwork Reduction Act 1980 and Paperwork Reduction Act 1995. The previous legislation (Federal Reports Act 1942) required agencies to obtain approval of the Bureau of the Budget before imposing information collection burdens on the public – but the Internal Revenue Service and the Government Accountability Office were exempt. The legislation was chronically ineffective, see William F. Funk, *The Paperwork Reduction Act: Paperwork reduction meets administrative law*, [1987] 24(1) Harvard Journal on Legislation 1. See also the Plain Writing Act 2010, which includes no enforcement powers. The Paperwork Reduction Act was the work of Jimmy Carter; a year later Ronald Reagan signed an Executive Order compelling cost-benefit analysis of all major regulations. Bill Clinton issued Executive Order 12866 in 1993 which required every significant regulatory action to be submitted to OIRA for review. George W. Bush issued new requirements for regulatory review in 2007 by Executive Order as did Barack Obama and Donald Trump within a few days of their new governments.

[118] David E. Sanger, *Mr Deregulation's regulations: stuff of politics, mad cows and suspect dietary pills*, New York Times, 31 December 2003. See also papers issued by the AEI-Brookings Joint Center for Regulatory Studies, and Regulatory Studies Center of George

6.5.14   Australia

Australia has published since 2014 an annual deregulation report.[119] In 2014 its report indicated that its previous government had introduced 21,000 new regulations, and that in that year the new government removed over 10,000 unnecessary and counter-productive regulations and redundant acts of parliament; in total it claimed the removal of over 50,000 pages from the law books and reported savings of $2.3B, double its original target. The report is published by the Office of Deregulation, an office within the Department of the Prime Minister and Cabinet and established in 2013, to provide a whole-of-Government focus on the deregulation agenda. The office has a number of oversight roles to facilitate the reduction of red tape across Government, including

• providing deregulation policy advice to the Prime Minister and the Parliamentary Secretary assisting the Prime Minister on Deregulation;
• overseeing and co-ordinating the Government's audit of regulation and the $1 billion annual regulation cost reduction target;
• facilitating the exchange of information on deregulation across the Government, in particular between deregulation units established in each department;
• assisting the Prime Minister to pursue a deregulation agenda with states and territories through COAG; and
• monitoring and provision of reports to the Government on the progress of the deregulation agenda.

The Office of Deregulation coordinates contributions to Repeal Days in parliament. Repeal Days occur twice a year, and allow parliament to debate plans to remove legislation or regulation which the Government considers unnecessary. Repeal Day measures are available on the Australian Government's online deregulation resource at the Cutting Red Tape website. Other useful information, such as the Australian Government Guide to Regulation and the Regulator Performance Framework is also available at

Washington University. There is still profound debate about the impact of deregulation as a factor in the financial collapse in 2008, see Matthew Sherman, *A short history of financial deregulation in the United States*, Centre for Economic and Policy Research, Washington, July 2009.

[119] See Australian Government, *Cutting Red Tape*, cuttingredtape.gov.au, 2015; see also Australian Government, *Annual red tape reduction report 2015*, 2016. Cf Mikayla Novak, *The Red Tape State: Red Tape Research Report No 2*, Institute of Public Affairs, Melbourne, May 2016.

that site. But it is important to put the Australian efforts in perspective; they also struggle to do much more than tinker at the edges. The 70 pages of the Red Tape Reduction Legislation Amendment Act 2016 is devoted mostly to replacing the term 'a statutory declaration' with 'a declaration' in several dozen statutes – and in other clauses actually adding to regulatory burdens.[120]

The success of the efforts has been questioned; it has been argued that the Rudd and Gillard governments in 2007–2013 in fact created over 444 government bodies, of which 198 were involved in the regulatory system. There were at the time around 1100 government bodies in Australia. The later Conservative government reduced the number by 286 from 2013–2015.[121]

6.5.15   Canada

The Canadians in 2015 introduced a short piece of legislation which introduced a one-for-one rule to reduce the administrative burden of regulations. It simply provides:[122]

> 5(1) If a regulation is made that imposes a new administrative burden on a business, one or more regulations must be amended or repealed to offset the cost of that new burden against the cost of an existing administrative burden on a business.

There are procedures laid down to cost any administrative burdens and for an annual report on progress, but the whole act is only 11 sections. Ontario introduced similar legislation in 2014.[123]

6.5.16   Italy

Italy has established, with no sense of irony, the Ministro per la Semplificazione e la Pubblica Amministrazione, the Ministry of

---

[120] Red Tape Reduction Legislation Amendment Act 2016 Schedule 1.

[121] Mikayla Novak, *The Red Tape State: Red Tape Research Report No 2*, Institute of Public Affairs, Melbourne, May 2016; John Roskam, *Red tape ready for Malcolm Turnbull to cut*, Australian Financial Review, 22 September 2016.

[122] Canada, *Loi sur la reduction de la paperasse (Red Tape Reduction Law)*, 27 October 2015.

[123] Ontario, *Burden Reduction Reporting Act 2014*, SO 2014 c12 Sch 1. Ontario, Open for business, *Fewer burdens, greater growth*, 2014; Ontario, Ministry of Economic Development, *Burden Reduction Act 2016*, Press release, 8 June 2016.

Simplification and Public Administration.[124] It does not seem to have had much if any effect; for example Italian tax accountants went on strike in February 2017 following the introduction in the 2017 Italian budget law of eight new requirements for the communication of VAT data, perhaps the first recorded instance of an accountants' strike. It followed repeated demands for simplification of the VAT system.[125]

6.5.17   Denmark

Denmark runs a 'Burden Hunters project', supported by a Business Forum for Better regulation established in 2012. It operates a comply or explain protocol, so that the government is obliged to pursue its proposed initiatives or explain why not – and sets concrete simplification targets.[126]

6.5.18   Switzerland

In Switzerland a regulatory impact assessment must be carried out for all regulations. Consultations are required under the Swiss Constitution as is the subsequent evaluation of legislation. The parliamentary Control of the Administration and the evaluation unit of the Swiss Federal Audit Office undertake around 15 per cent ex post evaluations of government policies each year. Even the Swiss have concluded that the system is ineffective.[127]

6.5.19   World Bank

The World Bank publishes annually an international survey of business-related regulation across 189 countries. The UK for example can be comforted by its conclusions; it ranks tenth for ease of establishing a new business, but it might be sensible to take an occasional reality check, since it puts China at No 2 after Singapore, in the list. And it puts the US at No 4,

---

[124] See www.italiasemplice.gov.it; devotees of the UK TV series 'Yes, Minister' 30 years ago will recall that Jim Hacker, one of its heroes, was made the Secretary of State for the Department of Administrative Affairs.

[125] Giovanni Parente, Tax lawyers call a strike next month citing more red tape in new rules for VAT payments, Italy Europe 24, 15 December 2016.

[126] Burden Hunter – Hunting Administration Burdens and Red Tape, Danish Business Authority; Danish Forum for Business Activity, Danish Business Authority, both cited in OECD Regulatory Policy Outlook 2015, OECD, Paris, 2015, p84. Cf www.enkleregler.dk.

[127] OECD Regulatory Policy Outlook 2015, OECD, Paris, 2015, p204. The studies contains reviews of most countries in the OECD universe, almost all of whom have some process, and almost all of whom achieve low outcomes.

ignoring other studies that show that regulation in the States is highly burdensome. It points out that on average around the world starting a business takes 7 procedures, 25 days and costs around 32 per cent of income per capita in fees. But the range is wide; it takes 1 procedure, half a day and almost nothing in New Zealand, but 208 days in Suriname, and 144 days in Venezuela.[128]

6.6   Efforts at Deregulation (Private Bodies)

The work of the National Trust has been discussed above; private organisations can move more easily to reform themselves if they suspect excess, and the impact of the rules normally affects the public less than the internal staff. Company rules and codes of practice are rarely deliberately ignored, but equally rarely consulted or applied, and most fall into desuetude, even where backed by sanctions. In practice they are an issue merely for the organisation, and if they are foolish or obsolete or damaging, such as the exclusion of women from a golf club, they will in time be withdrawn. Parenthetically it is probably unnecessary to have rules to control such rules, simply because, in time, the market might normally resolve the issue.[129]

6.7   Principles of Unregulation

Attempts at unregulation have involved a number of techniques, including

- benchmarking,
- cost-implementation review,
- evaluation through triage,
- ex post evaluation,
- impact tracing,
- in-depth reviews,
- OIOO (one in, one out),

[128] *Doing business 2014: understanding regulations for small and medium-size enterprises: comparing business regulations for domestic firms in 189 economics*, 11th edn, World Bank, Washington DC, 2013. The Philippines has an Anti-Red Tape Act 2007, Republic of the Philippines, Civil Service Commission, *Memorandum Circular MC No 12 s2008* and CSC Resolution No 081471, 24 July 2008. One of the penalties for breach is to attend an anti-red tape workshop.

[129] James Corrigan, *No more Open at Muirfield after golf club votes against allowing women to join as members*, Daily Telegraph, 19 May 2016; cf. Alexandra Topping, *Muirfield golf club to allow women to join for the first time*, The Guardian, 14 March 2017.

- OITO (one in, two out),
- OITO No 2 (one in, three out),
- participatory decision-making,
- principles-based review,
- red tape reduction targets,
- regulator-based strategies,
- regulatory impact assessments,
- regulatory reviews and
- stock-flow linkage rules.

In addition attempts at co-ordinating regulation have met headwinds; the European Union's attempts at pan-European regulation have been criticised for following an overarching regime rather than concentrating on mutual recognition of each state's own regulations.[130] One or two of these techniques are discussed below.

6.7.1   One In, Two (Three) Out/One In, One Out (OITO/OIOO)

The UK Coalition Government in September 2010 announced it had adopted a 'one in, one out' rule. It was introduced as part of a comprehensive package of measures to support the Government's drive to tackle unnecessary government interference and red tape.[131] The measures were intended to 'help transform the relationship between people and government by changing how regulations are drawn up, introduced and implemented' by introducing certain tests before they were introduced. Ministers who sought to introduce regulations which imposed costs on business or the third sector were required to identify current regulations with an equivalent value that could be removed. The rule was designed to apply initially to domestic legislation affecting businesses and the third sector, with the intention to expand the system eventually. The Department also planned to

- agree a set of principles of regulation that government departments had to apply when considering new regulations impacting upon business, social enterprises, individuals and community groups;

---

[130] Graeme Leach, *Hung up on red tape*, EA Magazine, Institute of Economic Affairs, 17 July 2013.

[131] Press Release, *New rules to hand over powers to individuals and companies by cutting red tape and bureaucracy*, 5 August 2010, Department for Business, Innovation and Skills.

- ask the independent Regulatory Policy Committee to perform the role of externally scrutinising the evidence and analysis supporting new regulatory proposals, prior to policy decisions being made, and analyse proposals for the implementation of EU legislation; and
- provide the opportunity for the public and businesses to tell the government which onerous regulations they believe should be removed or changed through the dedicated website.[132]

The Department also planned to reduce gold-plating of EU regulations. 'One in, one out' was intended to capture the net cost to business of any given measure; but the system unsurprisingly excluded regulations issued in response to emergencies and to address systemic financial risks. The role of the Regulatory Policy Committee was enhanced in some cosmetic ways and it was asked to work with the Better Regulation Executive, at the then Department for Business, Innovation and Skills.

The 'one in, one out' policy was later expanded to become a 'one in, two out' policy.[133] In March 2016 the Department of Business introduced a revised form of the OITO, the 'one in, three out' principle. The idea was to save £10B, comprising a £2B a year saving. The review (not a law) was intended to save £3 for every £1 of regulation. The review excluded large items such as the National Living Wage, the Apprenticeship Levy, and auto-enrolled pensions (partly offset by a small reduction in corporation tax).[134] These policies have not had any material impact.[135]

6.7.2   'Principles for Good Regulation'

Similarly government departments periodically issue 'principles for good regulation' aimed at regulators, who for the most part find it politically and practically hard to meet the requirements. The principles, which vary from report to report, broadly include the standard notions of proportionality, balance, restraint in the face of public demand, awareness of costs,

---

[132] http://yourfreedom.hmg.gov.uk/.
[133] Department for Business Innovation & Skills, *Policy paper: 2010 to 2015 government policy: business regulation*, updated 8 May 2015.
[134] Philip Aldrick, *'One in, three out' to cut cost of red tape by £10bn*, The Times, 4 March 2016.
[135] House of Commons, Committee of Public Accounts, *Better Regulation*, Eighteenth Report of Session 2016–17, Report, together with formal minutes relating to the report, HC 487, 12 October 2016.

transparency, targeting and accountability.[136] In practice they are hard to apply, difficult to measure and broadly ignored.

6.7.3 Regulatory Impact Assessments

Regulatory Impact Assessments have been applied in several countries for many years. The reported figures struggle to be justifiable under scrutiny and most of the gains appear either trivial, or misleading.[137] The European Union, Canada, the US and many other jurisdictions attempt to either justify or control the regulatory output through various metrics, including attempts at estimating costs to business for example. By 2000 around 20 of the 28 OECD countries had some form of OECD or World Bank approved RIA arrangements. As in other deregulatory measures, the figures are generally treated with some caution and there are few regulations or laws which have either been abandoned or discontinued as a consequence of such testing.[138] Few of the reviews on success or otherwise of RIA's arrangements have been externally validated.

6.7.4 Encouraging the Exercise of Discretion

One principle that appears to be taking hold is that of extending the role of discretion, a role which has been in decline for many years.[139]

---

[136] Better Regulation Task Force, *Principles of good regulation*, 2003. Cf in Scotland, *Five principle of better regulation*, www.gov.scot/Topics/Business-Industry/support/better-regulation/5principlesofBetterRegulation, or Nuclear Regulatory Commission (US), www.nrc.gov/docs/ML1413/ML14135A076.pdf; OECD, *Guiding principles for regulatory quality and performance*, OECD, Paris, 2005; OECD, *Improving the quality of government regulation*, OECD, Paris, 1995.

[137] There is a spurious methodology, see *Business Impact Assessment Calculator*, Cabinet Office, 7 June 2016; *IA Template user manual*, The Stationery Office, March 2016. And cf. Michael Gibbons, *Now is not the time to be relaxing on quality when significant regulatory change is ahead*, speech published 28 March 2017, detailing minor improvements to process. Michael Gibbons was the chair of the Regulatory Policy Committee.

[138] Department of Justice Canada, *Regulatory Impact Analysis Statement*, 4 July 2014; George F. Redling, *Regulatory impact analysis in Canada: successes and challenges*, Regulatory Affairs and Orders in Council Secretariat, privy Council Office, Government of Canada, 25 April 2006. See also articles in Environmental Impact Assessment Review, especially Thomas F. Ruddy and Lorenz Hilty, *Impact assessment policy learning in the European Commission* [2007] 28(2) Environmental Impact Assessment review 90; for the European Union generally see Jacopo Torriti and Ragnar Lofstedt, *The first five years of the EU Impact Assessment system: a risk economics perspective on gaps between rationale and practice* [2012] 15(2) Journal of Risk Research 169. OECD, *Regulatory policies in OECD countries: from interventionism to regulatory governance*, OECD, Paris, 2002.

[139] Onora O'Neill, *The Reith Lectures*, BBC, 2002; Better Regulation Executive, *Reducing regulation made simple*, 2010.

There have been cases when the government has allowed stakeholders to make their own mistakes. For example, in relation to university funding the Department of Education was persuaded in 2003 to reduce its control on university funding. The Better Regulation Review Group, led by Professor David VandeLinde, the then vice chancellor of Warwick University complained that the costs of red tape attached to special funding schemes was disproportionate.[140] Universities feel obliged to bid for special funds and submit to extra monitoring involved; the effect of the process however is that institutions feel micro-managed and constrained in their autonomy. The solution adopted was to absorb the money intended to develop 20 knowledge exchanges into mainstream funding. Golden hellos intended to help recruit university researchers and fellowships to foster their careers were also channelled back into general funds as well as capital funding for leading research institutions. Richard Lambert, a former editor of the *Financial Times*, criticised the links between universities and business as being over-complex (a source of unnecessary costs, uncertainty and inflexibility). As a consequence institutions no longer needed to go through a separate bidding process to get the extra £500,000 that was involved. The Higher Education Minister (Alan Johnson) said that the government was serious about cutting through the paper trail: 'It's about trust; it's about letting go. Universities understood the importance of encouraging talented individuals without the government insisting on for example a separate golden hello scheme.'

Similar proposals have been made in administering the radio spectrum. Ofcom is the UK media and communications regulator; to the surprise of many in the industry it announced in November 2003 a consultation document on the trading of airwave spectrum for mobile phones, radio and television broadcasting, pagers and two-way radios. If introduced it would have made the UK the first country in the world to have introduced tradeable licences in the radio spectrum. The intention, said Stephen Carter, the then Chief Executive of Ofcom, was that 'Spectrum trading will allow innovation and choice to shape the future allocation of spectrum, in place of the centrally planned, top-down approach of the past.' The *Financial Times* noted that 'Not many regulators start their activities by reducing their role in the administration of the sector, but with luck it may demonstrate a trend'.[141]

---

[140] Miranda Green, *University funding to face less red tape*, Financial Times, 20 November 2003.

[141] Tim Burt, *Ofcom considers scheme to trade airwaves*, Financial Times, 20 November 2003.

6.8 Successful Attempts at Unregulation

Not all the unregulation efforts have failed, or had minimal impact. Unregulation can be successful especially where it is driven from below, rather than above. When regulation becomes intolerable the regulated parties may take steps to resolve and improve the position themselves. The position has to be serious enough for the parties to agree to take up such a position – it may mean reduction of responsibility, or sharing of responsibility, or the possibility of fault along the way. Some progress had already been made for example in the public sector. Nine of the principle regulators of the National Health Service in 2004 agreed an 'inspection concordat' aimed at reducing hospital regulation. The review was led by one of the bodies, the Healthcare Commission, an NHS inspectorate, and it was supported by the Audit Commission, the Health and Safety Executive, the medical royal colleges, the social care inspectorate and others. Around 100 organisations inspected, regulated or had the right to demand information from NHS hospitals and other parts of the service.[142]

The case of the NHS is perhaps not one of the best; complaints about its bureaucracy continue. But there are other examples.

6.8.1 Employment: The Dock Labour Scheme

In April 1989 the then Conservative government announced that it was to repeal some employment legislation known as the Dock Labour Scheme. The Scheme ensured that much of the shipping industry was jointly regulated by employers and trade unions (mostly the Transport and General Workers Union). From being a social protection scheme to avoid some of the unpleasant practices formerly involved in hiring dock labour it had degenerated into restrictive practices which seriously affected the working of Britain's ports. In practice it gave dockers a job for life. It became a criminal offence not to be registered as an employer – or to employ a non-registered docker. Even if a docker committed a serious criminal offence it was impossible either to discipline or sack him, and no women were entitled to be employed since the unions barred women from employment. Indeed unless an applicant was related to a docker, no new employees could become dockers, The Scheme came to an end on 6 July 1989. Within

---

[142] Nicholas Timmins, *Principal health service regulators agree 'inspection concordat'*, Financial Times, 23 June 2004.

a short period, after decades of labour unrest the docks became strike-free and competitive. New docks emerged and old ones became competitive and Bristol, Tees, Tilbury and Sheerness were able to compete with non-scheme ports such as Felixstowe. The change needed some political dexterity, since it provoked (and had itself been provoked) by a series of dock strikes. The small act of deregulation created new jobs, allowed new business to be established and shipping lines were more prepared to use British ports.[143]

6.8.2   Health and Safety

The Health and Safety at Work Act 1974 was intended to try and reduce the then annual 650 fatal workplace injuries; it consolidated around 30 acts of parliament and 500 sets of regulations. By 2009 workplace deaths had fallen to 180, with a workforce 12 per cent larger.[144] The general consensus was that around 5000 lives had been saved over the time from the introduction of the Act. It clearly achieved a safer working environment, although the dangers might have reduced in any event as the majority of the workforce moved from manual to cerebral activities. And the number of deaths saved as a percentage of the workforce was even then relatively modest. By 2010 the fatality rate was the second lowest in the EU.

Nonetheless over the following 35 years the application of the Act in practice appeared to have become excessive. There were press stories, some of them accurate, that policemen had stood by whilst children drowned because they did not have the correct certificate under the Act. Hilaire Purbrick was evicted by Brighton and Hove City Council from the seven foot cave he lived in in his allotment in Brighton because it lacked

---

[143] Iain Dale, *The Tories should remember how they revived our docks*, Daily Telegraph, 10 April 2009.

[144] Philip Johnston, *Danger! Daft rules under inspection*, Daily Telegraph, 15 June 2010; see also Philip Johnston, *Bad laws: an explosive analysis of Britain's petty rules, health and safety lunacies and madcap laws*, Constable, London, 2010 ISBN 978-1-8490-1010-8. The Act followed a series of Factories Acts (from 1833), the Factories Act 1961, and the Offices, Shops and Railway Premises Act 1963. The Robens Committee was established by Barbara Castle, the then Secretary of State for Employment in May 1970 and reported in 1972. Its coherent framework was somewhat overtaken by a 'six-pack' of EU legislation from 1992, namely The Management of Health and Safety at Work Regulations 1992; The Workplace (Health, Safety and Welfare) Regulations 1992; The Provision and Use of Work Equipment Regulations 1992; The Manual Handling Operations Regulations 1992; The Display Screen Equipment Regulations 1992; The Personal Protective Equipment at Work Regulations 1992. See also e.g. *May contain nuts [about a ladder training course]*, Panorama, BBC TV, 20 April 2009.

a fire exit.[145] There are innumerable other examples of excessive application of the Act reported by the press, some of them true. But it is also
hard not to sympathise with the enforcers; if the troglodytic Mr Purbrick
had improbably burned himself to death, there was a substantial chance
that the City Council would have been prosecuted by the authorities and
vilified by the same press.

The question as ever was one of balance and proportionality. The
health and safety legislation is a piece of law that does not impose absolute liabilities; when introduced it attempted to apply what has been rare
in English legislation, namely principle-based law. It repeatedly employs
terms such as 'so far as is reasonably practicable' and 'as may be appropriate' to its provisions[146] in order to introduce the sense of proportionality
and balance.

Whether English bureaucracy and maybe the judiciary find such prin-
cipled legal provisions difficult to apply is not clear from the evidence;
what is clear, however, is that officials who are in the front line if there
is a breach, and find themselves faced with possible civil and criminal
penalties for breach (and loss of advancement) unsurprisingly take a cautious approach to implementation. They have everything to gain and
nothing to lose by excessive caution. The inevitable press attacks, and
possible court response, (and no gain for a relaxed approach) for people who are by nature risk-averse in risk-averse occupations, lead to the
inevitable excess application of the Roman law principle 'ex abundante
cautela'.

Press reports over the years began to bring the legislation into disrepute. In 2010 a former Conservative Party trade and industry secretary
of state was invited by the government to review health and safety legislation, with a view to injecting 'common sense' into the workplace.[147]
He was asked to investigate concerns over the application and perception
of health and safety legislation, together with the rise of the compensation culture over the previous decade. In announcing the review David
Cameron, the Prime Minister, said: 'The rise of the compensation culture
over the last ten years is a real concern, as is the way health and safety rules

---

[145] Aislinn Simpson, *Eco-warrior evicted from cave dwelling without fire exit*, Daily Telegraph,
17 June 2010. The provision was originally a response to the tragedy in 1962 when a failure
of a pumping agency at the Hartley Colliery in Northumberland blocked a single mine-
shaft (and thus means of escape and ventilation).

[146] Health and Safety at Work Act 1974 s3(2).

[147] Prime Minister's Office, *Press Release*, 14 June 2010, www.number10.gov.uk/news/latest-
news/2010/06/pm-announces-review-of-health-and-safety-laws-51726.

are sometimes applied. We need a sensible new approach that makes clear these laws are intended to protect people, not overwhelm businesses with red tape. I look forward to receiving Lord Young's recommendations on how we can best achieve that.'

Lord Young said at the same time that Britain needed a system that was 'proportionate and not bureaucratic':

> Health and safety regulation is essential in many industries but may well have been applied too generally and have become an unnecessary burden on firms, but also community organisations and public services. I hope my review will reintroduce an element of common sense and focus the regulation where it is most needed.

The immediate difficulty is that while the legislation called for a balance to be taken by the authorities, the consequences of success or failure for the authorities are imbalanced. The public, and the press, are intolerant of mistakes or accidents, and will seek to blame the appropriate person, or indeed anyone.[148] Similarly a fire tragedy in 2017 was blamed on inadequate regulation, although at the time of writing this remains unclear.[149]

6.8.3 Dequangofication

Removing not only legislation but regulation can, though rarely, be surprisingly easy. The incoming coalition government in 2010 had made significant play of reducing the number of non-departmental bodies as a form of short-cut deregulation, and several removals caused little fuss. Much was done under cover of reducing funding; the abolition of the UK Film Council caused some discussion for example,[150] and raised common issues as to whether such bodies should be arguing for their own survival, if they are simply a creature of statute. Similarly ContactPoint following a commitment in the Coalition Agreement, was abolished in August 2010.[151] ContactPoint (previous working title Information Sharing Index

---

[148] See in a different context the consequences for BP, the oil company, following an accident with a drilling rig in the Gulf of Mexico in June 2010 e.g. amongst a considerable literature www.bp.com/genericarticle.do?categoryId=2012968&contented=7062966.

[149] See e.g. Jamie Doward, *The chronicle of a tragedy foretold: Grenfell Tower: Government and councils were warned repeatedly about fire safety experts' fears over tower blocks as far back as 1999*, Observer, 17 June 2017.

[150] www.culture.gov.uk/news/news_stories/7280.aspx.

[151] www.dcsf.gov.uk/everychildmatters/strategy/deliveringservices1/contactpoint/ contactpoint/.

[or IS Index or ISI] or Children's Index) was a government database that held information on all children under 18 in England, designed by private information management company Capgemini. It was established in response to the abuse and death of eight-year-old Victoria Climbié in 2000 – in which it was found that various agencies involved in her care had failed to prevent her death – to improve child protection by improving the way information about children was shared between services. The database, created under the Children Act 2004, cost £224M to set up and £41M a year to run. It operated in 150 local authorities, and was accessible to at least 330,000 users. It was heavily criticised from a wide range of groups, mainly for privacy, security and child protection reasons. The database was destroyed, but the policy was not itself discontinued. The government continued to consider the feasibility of a new signposting service for professionals to help them to support and protect our most vulnerable children, particularly when these children move areas or access services in more than one area. The argument was not (as it might have been) that certain risks were not worth providing against, but that the database was available too widely since around 300,000 people were given the right to use it. The government looked to a national signposting approach (ContactPoint by another name) intended to focus on helping a strictly limited group of practitioners to find out whether a colleague elsewhere was working, or previously worked, with the same vulnerable child. In the private sector the use of references is normal. The set-up costs were written off (around £¼B) and the annual running costs were saved, although it is not known what the alternative control costs would be, although they would be amortised across the users. Nor is it known what public harm resulted from its abolition.

6.8.4   Department of Transport: Traffic Signs Policy Review 2011

The UK enjoys over 860 traffic signs, with hundreds of permitted variations. Press photographs commonly show that while signs can be useful, they can also be confusing. The Department of Transport suggested in 2011 that local authorities should have more flexibility in the design and application of signs. Getting the balance right has proved something of a challenge. There is probably a public consensus that there should be fewer signs; on the other hand drivers often suffer from inadequate signing. Similarly anyone who has had to pay a parking fine may curse the absence of repeater parking signs within parking zone areas, where there are only perimeter signs.[152]

6.8.5   Institute for Government

The Institute for Government is an independent think tank with cross-party and Whitehall governance, working to increase government effectiveness. It works with all the main political parties at Westminster and with senior civil servants in Whitehall, and tries to provide evidence-based advice that draws on best practice from around the world. It undertakes research, provides development opportunities for senior decision makers and organise events to invigorate and provides fresh thinking on the issues that really matter to government. It is supported by the Sainsbury family trusts which has had considerable experience in government of misdirected government.

6.9   Unregulatory Outcomes

This chapter has described the continual efforts at unregulation. In some ways the proliferation of initiatives suggests that not much of it works, otherwise there would have been no need for further attempts. There have been some successes, such as that of the Solicitors Regulation Authority, also previously described, but the general conclusion is that mostly the efforts have failed.

The reasons are possibly complex. There is no real determination by government, or regulators, to cut back on regulation perhaps because it diminishes their own role. There are few competitive pressures on governments or regulators; indeed there are complaints of 'regulatory arbitrage' where such competition exists, although again the example of the SRA, where solicitors can choose which of several competing regulators they wish to adopt, suggests that competition can have its place.

Secondly, the measurement of unregulation outcomes is notoriously imprecise, The UK government in its 2010–2015 term estimated that it had reduced regulatory overheads by £10B, around £400 for each UK business. But that reduces to £80 for each year, and 90 per cent of the savings related to just 10 changes, with the benefits not always agreed. The changes

---

[152] Department for Transport, Signing the way, *Traffic Signs Policy Paper*, October 2011, p42 (cluttered sign), p40 (uncluttered sign).

included changing the inflation index to increase pension benefits, reducing audit requirements for small companies and streamlining the guidance relating to contaminated land. The reduced audit requirement seems to have been a genuine benefit, but a National Audit Office report suggested that the robustness of the systems to estimate and evaluate the impacts of regulatory decisions may not have been as strong as they might be.[153] And it also pointed out that while there had been some modest progress in for example 2016 by cutting regulation costs by £0.9B, the government had imposed an additional £8.3B of fresh costs. And ignored around 46 per cent of the 951 regulatory decisions made during the previous Parliament were ignored from the count. The government excluded the costs of the National Living Wage, changes to business taxation, involving charges of cherry-picking what it measured.

On the other hand there is criticism of the fact that the system does not measure any wider societal costs and benefits of unregulation (although the NAO did not make the same observation of unregulation, it being itself a regulatory body). There is bureaucracy in unregulation. And there are few measures of continuing costs of regulation. The NAO considered that the processes of calculating costs and benefits is robust, which is not the general conclusion.

There have been generic successes. The UK for example has been considered to be the second least restrictive of the developed economies;[154] and between 2009 and 2014 the proportion of business that saw the level of UK regulation as an obstacle to business success fell from 62 per cent to 51 per cent. But the inevitable conclusion is that unregulation has broadly failed not only in the UK but around the world.

---

[153] National Audit Office, *The Business Impact Target: cutting the cost of regulation, report by the Comptroller and Auditor General*, Department for Business Innovation and Skills and Cabinet Office, HC 236, 29 June 2016.

[154] I. Koseke et al., *The 2013 update of the OECD product market regulation indicators: policy insights for OECD and non-OECD countries*, OECD Economics Department Working Papers, March 2015.

7

Where Next?

I am just recovering from my first attempt at completing the criminal legal aid application forms CDS 14 and 15 on behalf of my client. That these convoluted affairs come with a 22 page guide to their completion, to extract virtually the same information as their predecessors, says it all.

Most of us have now got our heads around the traps in the previous forms (for example, the sneaky little question, buried at the end of the old form 15, enquiring whether our destitute client, residing in a hostel for the homeless, might possibly be the beneficiary of an overseas trust). I can only think therefore that the powers that be need to devise new tricks to justify bouncing them back to us covered in red ink.

One is felt wondering if there is a secret agenda, to make our doing our job so impossible that, in despair, we throw our practicing certificates on the fire and, if financially able to do so, retire to look after our grandchildren.[1]

7.1 Introduction

The consensus of the public, governments and the judiciary seems to be that there is indeed too much law and regulation; even some regulators seem to agree. The evidence also indicates that the excess of law and regulation in most developed economies is doing harm to both economic performance, competition and the quality of life.[2] It is a conclusion that is endorsed even by those whose purpose is the creation of new law and rules, and by the man in the street (perhaps not best qualified to decide).[3]

---

[1] Carol Anthony, Cardiff, *On top form*, letter to Law Society Gazette, 16 February 2012.

[2] The issues of economic impact are discussed elsewhere, see p2.

[3] The law expects different views from different people, cf. 'the man on the Clapham omnibus' (*Tichborne v Lushington*, 1871–72; *Healthcare at Home Limited v The Common Services Agency* [2014] UKSC 49; 'the officious bystander' (*Southern Foundries (1926) Ltd v Shirlaw* [1940] AC 701); and of course 'the moron in a hurry' (*Morning Star Cooperative Society v Express Newspapers Limited*, [1979] FSR 113; *Newsweek Inc v British Broadcasting Corp*

Whilst the conclusion is agreed, the critical question is: what, if anything, can be done about it?

It has been seen that the many attempts to bring balance to the system have struggled to be effective. We have already explored some institutional attempts to cut back the quantity of law, including the Red Tape Challenge in the UK, some initiatives in the European Union and some novel attempts in the rest of the world. They have all, to a greater or lesser degree, faltered if not failed.

There have also been grass-root attempts to improve matters. Some commentators[4] have taken the approach that the solution must come from individual challenges to the system. They suggest that members of the public should complain whenever they have the opportunity, or challenge those who attempt to impose non-existent[5] or excessive rules. This may be a counsel of perfection; in real life few have the time, inclination or persistence to make a difference in this way. It is usually more pragmatic to sigh and carry on.

One solution may be indeed to do nothing and hope that the system will revert to a deregulated norm, in some form of regulatory entropy, or allow it to simply fall over in its own excess, as is it is sometimes said happened to the Roman Empire.[6] We may also hope that others may carry the mantle of reform. We may all develop ways of working round the problem – or simply ignore the more pettifogging rules. Alternatively it may merely be that there are fashions in regulation and at present we are simply in that part of the cycle which is proving temporarily irritating but we will eventually be able to rejoice once the low-regulation cycle resumes.

[1979] RPC 441). There are also varieties of 'prudent man', see e.g. *Harvard College v Amory* (1830) 26 Mass (9 Pick) 446 Massachusetts. And the law also recognises 'men of straw' (distinguished from 'straw men').

[4] See e.g. Tracey Brown and Michael Hanlon, *In the interests of safety: the absurd rules that blight our lives and how we can change them*, Sphere, 2014. See also the efforts of think tanks such as the Institute of Economic Affairs and the Manifesto Club (www.manifestoclub .com). See also Ross Clark, *How to label a goat: the silly rules and regulations that are strangling Britain*, Harriman House, 2006.

[5] E.g. health and safety or data protection rules which rarely actually apply.

[6] Almost certainly an urban legend; there are over 200 theories for the fall of Rome. There is no argument that we need some regulation: 'Most of the time, regulation begins with a noble goal. Laws are typically passed with the intention of addressing or preventing some wrong, and rules are developed to implement those rules. In that way, as Herbert Kaufman noted in his seminal 1977 book, *Red Tape: Its origins, uses and abuses*, "one person's red tape may be another's treasured procedural safeguard." It's when you add up all those rules that you get into trouble at times', Brian O'Keefe, *The Red Tape Conundrum*, Fortune, 20 October 2016.

These are however brave approaches to take. And in the meantime there may be other solutions immediately available; some of those that are currently employed are explored below, followed by some proposed alternatives which may be more effective. We have seen that it is hard for one arm of government to try to rein back another arm (as in the Red Tape Challenge or Cutting Red Tape exercises in the UK), just as it is for a member of the public fruitlessly arguing with immigration officers at hour-long queues at the airport to apply a pragmatic rule on checking for terrorists. In fact the best solution may come instead from the regulators and legislators themselves changing their own way of working and thinking – provided that they have access to the training and incentives to do so.[7]

This approach operates on the basis that those who are responsible for introducing new rules and regulations should become genuinely accountable by accepting increasing responsibility for what they do. In practice some of them do feel responsible. Legislators in particular argue they can be dismissed by the electorate if they fail. In practice however the chain of responsibility seems too long to be effective. Legislators are rather in the position of the bankers before the 2008 financial crisis; they are hard to bring to book because it is difficult (1) to relate the harm caused to (2) the behaviour of a particular individual. Regulatory decisions are usually made in a group or collectively, or at several degrees removed. Trying to pin down responsibility ('accountability' in the current political lexicon) does not seem to have worked in financial services (although it may be early days) nor does it seem to operate well in government.[8]

Imposing responsibility may of course have strong counter-productive consequences; there is evidence that capable individuals (i.e. those that understand the risks) are increasingly unwilling to take positions of

---

[7] Trainee regulators might start with studying the less-than-sceptical studies of the OECD, e.g. *Being an independent regulator: the governance of regulators*, OECD, Paris, July 2016; OECD, *Governance of regulators' practices: accountability, transparency and co-ordination, the Governance of Regulators*, OECD, Paris, 2016. Comparative studies are available in *OECD regulatory policy outlook 2015*, OECD, Paris, 2015.

[8] See e.g. the Senior Managers Regime being introduced into financial services regulation in the UK, and the absurdity of the forms such as www.handbook.fca.org.uk/form/sup/SUP_10C_ann_5D_SOR_20160307.pdf?date=2016-03-07. In Government, David Cameron felt he had to resign as UK Prime Minister following the UK Brexit referendum in June 2016, but his successor, who did not feel she had to resign, had also argued for the losing side. And it is virtually impossible to find e.g. the emails and telephone numbers of individual regulators at the Financial Conduct Authority; nor are they on the website. Neither accountability nor accessibility are expressed as objectives in most regulators' own codes of practice.

responsibility in for example financial services companies. In the private sphere, imposing such responsibilities, and imposing quasi-criminal obligations, where regulators face no such equivalent responsibility, seems likely eventually to bring the system into disrepute because it encourages poor behaviour by regulators.[9] Nonetheless in the public sphere broader and more intelligent solutions, which individually may only have a tangential effect, may collectively encourage a move towards improvement.

This chapter therefore first summarises some of the existing control methods, then examines alternative approaches (not mutually exclusive) to responding to the challenge of implementing reform, in particular looking at

- **changing the attitudes and understanding** of those involved in regulation including changing the mindset of the public, the press, lobbyists and campaigners and – above all – regulators and legislators, so that when they are faced with solving a policy problem, they first consider options other than regulation;
- **changing the mechanisms** of producing law and rules; and
- **introducing professionalisation of, and responsibility for their actions for,** regulators and legislators.

Finally the conclusion suggests professionalisation of rule makers; to achieve that will involve participants accepting at least some if not all of the need for

- training,
- qualification,
- accountability,
- oath taking and
- adherence to a code.

Professionalisation in itself will not necessarily lead to improvements, nor is it enforceable through the application of sanctions. Nor will changing the mechanisms of lawmaking and the introduction of professionalisation by themselves offer a solution. Nor do they have the political attraction of a

---

[9] See e.g. The UK Pensions Regulator policy on fining, which applies fines to trustees who confess minor breaches, yet has no policing of non-confessed breaches, Pensions Act 2014 Schedule 18, para 3(3) and 3(4). See also *Prosecution Policy*, The Pensions Regulator, June 2016; The Occupational Pension Schemes (Charges and Governance) Regulations 2015 2015 No 0879 and *Compliance and enforcement policy for occupational schemes providing money purchase benefits*, The Pensions Regulator, July 2016.

quick fix; they need time and a sympathetic public mood to make progress. But without them there seems little hope of any meaningful change.

7.2   Building on Unregulation

7.2.1   Background

Many of the attempts to roll back regulation have been described in the earlier chapter, and as has been seen their success rate has been modest. The evidence seems to suggests that many of the rules to control rules have been broadly ineffective, for example the attempts to introduce OITO ('one in, two out') principles.[10] Nonetheless there are supporting steps which might be taken which might be more than merely homeopathic.

Some of the existing nostrums may still have modest validity and they might be improved and made more effective. And even though individually each of the remedies seems to have had little impact, cumulatively they might have had some influence, especially if applied as part of a holistic change in approach, rather than as individual policy initiatives. These individual remedies might include the need to articulate policy, improve the process of rule making and then provide for regular review once the rules are in place. They are considered in three sections:

- policy,
- process and
- review.

7.2.2   Policy

It might be helpful for rule makers to commit to basic principles of policy before seeking to introduce new rules, including accepting that

- there is not always a regulatory solution to a problem;
- more is not necessarily better in rule making;
- measurement of the success of deregulation is an imperfect measure;
- alternatives to law may be preferable as a way to solve a policy problem;

---

[10] 'One in, one out' was introduced by a government minister Francis Maude in the UK in the 2010 Coalition Government; it was amended to 'one in, two out' in 2012, and amended again to mean 'one in, three out' in the UK in 2016: *Getting government off your back: our commitment to cutting red tape*, speech by Sajid Javid, Secretary of State, Department for Business, Innovation & Skills, 3 March 2016 at BCC annual conference, QEII Conference Centre, London.

- markets and the internet may be preferable to rules as a way to protect consumers;
- privatisation and competition, with all their drawbacks, may be more efficient than regulation to protect consumers;
- policymakers should adopt a 'better regulation policy' when introducing regulation; and
- 'market failure' should be used sparingly as an excuse for intervention.

7.2.3 Process

The process of lawmaking in many jurisdictions seems superficially efficient and involving adequate governance; the practical reality seems somewhat different. It might be helpful to rationalise the system, so that

- proposals for new rules are accompanied by properly costed regulatory budgets with full and published instructions from government departments, and instructions signed personally by the minister;
- drafting is improved, using Australian standards;
- the parliamentary process is improved, with accountability allocated to individuals;
- there is genuine regulatory impact assessment;
- there is a programme of consolidation of legislation;
- there is a programme of codification of legislation; and
- there is a code of practice for lobbying and campaign groups.

7.2.4 Review

Improved outcomes might result, if once rules are in place, they are reviewed at some stage; this applies to both legislation and regulation, and preferably should be carried out by outside agencies. Such review process could include

- pre-legislative scrutiny;
- post-legislative scrutiny, with responsibility individually allocated;
- default use of sunset clauses;
- increased use of discretion (with allocated personal responsibility) rather than prescription, subject to easier judicial review; and
- improved regulatory audit.

7.2.5   More Policy

Rule makers could, before considering the production of further rules, reflect on some general principles which have been widely accepted as appropriate in past reviews. They include the following:

- there is not always a regulatory solution to a problem.
- alternatives to law may be preferable as a solution.
- measuring the effectiveness of deregulation is not easy.
- more is not necessarily better in rule making.
- solving 100 per cent of a problem can involve unacceptable complexity; an 80 per cent solution might be acceptable.
- the best should not be the enemy of the good.
- voluntary arrangements may be preferable to compulsion.
- using persuasion and discretion may be preferable to black-letter law.
- privatisation and competition should be considered as an option when designing new regulators.
- the internet may be a better solution than regulation when trying to solve market failures or asymmetric information.

7.2.6   There Is Not Always a Regulatory Solution to a Problem

Regulation may not always be the right response to a problem – or there may not actually be a problem, certainly not one that requires a regulation. For example, accountants in practice for many years have complained that standardised accounting rules, designed to help investors make comparative analyses, have had adverse consequences, especially on making companies behave sub-optimally to meet accounting requirements, rather than creating accounting rules that follow the needs of business. The dream of standardisation in accounting has been shown not only to be unachievable, and maybe it should not have been attempted, since it follows a centralised command theory of rule making. While it is easier to compare company performance for the benefit of investors and shareholders if accounting for companies is performed in a standard way, the attempt to introduce standardisation has resulted in perverse outcomes. As the economist John Kay noted:

> You have spent £2 on a lottery ticket. On Saturday evening you may be a millionaire. Or, more likely, not.
>   But meantime, the auditors arrive. They must confirm that your accounts show a true and fair view. An old-fashioned auditor might allow

you to record the lottery ticket at its historic cost of £2. A modern one
would want to assess its fair value.

But there is no market in second-hand lottery tickets. The auditor might
allow you to treat it as a 'level two' asset which can be valued by reference
to the price of other traded items and use a discount to the primary market
price. Or the accountant might encourage you to 'mark to model': multiply
the payouts by their probabilities and compute an expected value, £1.20
say, though good models attach different values to different tickets because
some numbers are more popular than others.

But no-one buys a lottery ticket to trade it... there is no good method
of accounting for transactions whose outcome is binary.[11]

7.2.7 Alternatives to Law May Be Preferable to Solve a Problem

There has already been a discussion of alternatives to law (codes, insurance, peer pressures). There are others which have only infrequently been
adopted, perhaps because they lack the sanctions which seem to be more
fashionable at present. Some alternatives which have proved effective and
more efficient in practice include

- oaths;
- codes of practice, embodying the duties of rule makers;
- voluntary arrangements; and
- wider use of discretion.

The OECD, for example, has proposed that alternatives to regulation be
considered as a standard response to policy objectives.[12] Some of these are
explored in more detail below.

7.2.8 Measurement of the Success of Deregulation Is an Imperfect Science

Most deregulation is as hard to measure as is the cost of regulating in the
first place. And piecemeal deregulation is messy and rather pointless in

---

[11] John Kay, *Why there is never such a thing as a single true and fair view*, Financial Times,
30 July 2014. Unintended consequences are also illustrated by the laws on Snus (a tobacco
product used mostly in Sweden). The European Union has a ban on such products, with
an opt-out for Sweden. In fact Sweden has the lowest smoking rate in Europe (12 per cent
compared with an average rate of 26 per cent), and major forms of cancer are lower, with
the lowest rate of the disease correlating with the highest use of Snus (although mouth
cancer is higher), see Madeline Grant, *It's my party and I'll vape if I want to*, Institute of
Economic Affairs, 31 August 2016.

[12] OECD, *Alternatives to traditional regulation*, Paris 2009.

many cases as has been seen in occasional UK Deregulation Acts or the Canadian Burden Reduction Act 2016. Governments might need to avoid piecemeal deregulation, which is hard to follow, confounds attempts to consolidate and codify, and allows the making of populist announcements whilst not achieving real reduction in regulatory impacts. The policy of specific deregulation measures should probably best be avoided.

Obsolete rules are nowadays commonly dealt with by dedicated repealing legislation, although they can also be dealt with by codification or consolidation of existing laws. Disposing of obsolete regulation can be a useful tidying up process, and offers amusing historical anecdotes, but it should probably not be regarded as a meaningful act of deregulation and offers few day-to-day practical benefits.[13]

7.2.9   More Is Not Necessarily Better in Rule Making

Quantity is a useful measure of outcomes in some cases, but as has been seen following the collapse of the Soviet empire, can be misleading, or lead to too much of the wrong stuff being produced. There is possibly a Soviet-style size problem in regulation; if regulation is good, a regulator can argue, more regulation may be better. Similarly, there is little commendation for a legislator who announces with some pride at the end of his term that he has produced no or very little legislation. It might be useful to develop a system that incentives legislators and regulators for doing nothing, rather like doctors are encouraged to swear to do no harm. It is well known that in practice doctors are pressured by patients to give pills even where letting things sort themselves out would be better. A good doctor will stand firm – or perhaps issue a package of placebos. But a placebo for regulation is hard to imagine.

7.2.10   Voluntary Arrangements

Voluntary arrangements have long been used with some success over many years. Examples include self-regulation of the professions, self-regulation of newspapers (less successful),[14] and regulation of gambling

---

[13] See e.g. 'Sir, the law is as I say it is, and so it has been laid down ever since the law began; and we have several set forms which are held as law, and so held and used for good reason, though we cannot at present remember that reason'. Fortescue CJ, 1458, cited frequently but without a source.

[14] Philip Ward, *Press regulation – the debate*, House of Commons Library, Standard Note: SN/HA/6357, 20 June 2012.

and alcohol. They often lack sanctions, but over time can have the advantage of moral pressure and economy – as well as effectiveness.[15]

7.2.11   Use of Discretion

The use of discretion is often frowned upon by legislators; it can be challenged by those over whom it is exercised, and it can lack rigour – and be unfair. That is why in the UK and the US for example there has been a trend in criminal matters towards prescribing specific sentences for certain criminal behaviour, and withdrawing judicial discretion. The difficulty is that such prescription can sometimes wreak terrible injustice, and loses the point of having judges who are in possession of the evidence and the particular circumstances of a crime if they are not permitted to use their skills and experience. Mandatory life for murder was prescribed by the Homicide Act 1957 as part of deal to abolish the death penalty, and had adverse and unintended consequences.[16]

The law sometimes struggles to cope with questions that require the exercise of a human discretion than the application of a rule. One was discussed in Chapter 1, where the Director of Public Prosecutions announced that despite the rights and maybe the obligation to prosecute individuals in cases of assisted suicide, which some consider murder, he would apply his own guidance and refuse to prosecute where it thought it inequitable to do so:

> As the late Professor Ronald Dworkin observed, discretion, like a hole in a doughnut, does not exist except as an area left open by a surrounding belt of restriction (see R Dworkin, Taking Rights Seriously, Harvard, 1977, p31). It is therefore a relative concept. Like all terms its meaning is sensitive to context.[17]

Similar decisions are made on a daily basis by lawyers working in the Court of Protection (this may not be good example; the Court has a mixed

---

[15] See e.g. the Portman Group, 'the responsibility body for the drinks industry', www.portmangroup.org.uk/.

[16] Frances Gibb, *MPs reopen debate over mandatory life sentences for murder*, The Times, The Brief, 9 September 2016. One of the many unintended consequences includes the overcrowding of prisons, which now need also to provide geriatric care. Similarly, the policy of imprisonment for public protection (IPP) policy the consequences of which have been grotesque (see Georgia Edkins, '*I'm to blame': Blunkett's indefinite prison sentences and the thousands still locked up without hope: Imprisonment for Public Protection (IPP) sentences were ruled a violation of human rights.* New Statesman, 14 August 2017.

[17] Leggatt J, *Brogden v Investec Bank* [2014] EWHC 2785 (Comm); [2014] IRLR 924 at [95].

reputation) where pragmatic but difficult decisions have to be made routinely, rather like medical practitioners deciding whether to resuscitate very ill babies or very old people. Law is not best placed to intervene in such cases, and in practice Parliament often sensibly resiles from becoming involved, and leaves it to individuals to use their discretion. That does not stop the more populist politicians from criticising social workers and others who have to make difficult decisions which they then feel to criticise with the benefit of hindsight. The tragic case of the trafficked children in the Rotherham scandal in 2014,[18] where around 1400 children were sexually exploited in horrific circumstances, and where several individuals eventually served prison terms, showed that in fact there were many efforts to help the children. But the complexity of the system, and the lack of resources, and the dilemma of making decisions where it is not quite black and white what is actually happening on a daily basis, and where advisers have to deal with very troubled people who struggle to give straight answers, means that it is hardly surprising that social workers sometimes get the answers very wrong despite their best endeavours. Society needs politicians and newspapers to try and tone down the witch-hunting and blame-allocating so that individuals will be able to exercise discretions without fear of being blamed with the benefit of hindsight. That is probably a utopian vision.

7.2.12   Extending the Role of the Competition and Markets Authority

Governments have themselves argued that there are perhaps too many quasi-governmental authorities. But one organisation whose role might be enhanced is that of the (in the UK) the Competition and Markets Authority. Within limits, markets can be used to induce good behaviour, and competitors can use reputation as a market force. But capitalism and regulation can combine to produce monopolies or oligopolies; there are only a few high-street banks, or supermarkets or large firms of accountants (and only one Amazon, and in practice only one computer operating system provider); such organisations can offer huge advantages to the consumer, but their dominance can make it hard for competitors to emerge. It is also one of the few genuine example of market failure.

Regulators often invoke market failure as an excuse for them to intervene. But such intervention is often unnecessary; either group litigation

[18] Rotherham Council, *Independent Inquiry into Child Sexual Exploitation in Rotherham (1997–2013)*, 2014.

(for example in the case of mis-sold personal protection insurance) or caveat emptor coupled with TripAdvisor-like customer feedback is usually cheaper and more effective than intervention via a regulator. And such protection or remedy is better for the public protection than after-the-event-regulation; non-intervention neither prevents failure (in fact it might make it more likely), but it is also more honest about the fact that regulators also cannot prevent future corporate or service failure through rule making.[19] Competition authorities may have a role to play as a simpler route to consumer protection – especially as conventional regulators rarely have a remit to enhance competition or where they do, ignore it, and are predisposed to reduce it for their own benefit. And, as the old joke goes, maybe we do in fact need more than one competition regulator.

7.2.13 Privatisation and Competition in Regulation

Private regulation or recourse has received a poor press, some of it from the regulation industry and some from government. But the lack of competition amongst regulators can have adverse consequences for the citizen. In the UK for example judicial recourse, which is a state monopoly, has been made expensive by increases in court costs. Court fees for a claim over £200,000 were increased in 2015 to £10,000, an increase of around 600 per cent. Private courts (such as those operated by eBay) might be cheaper and more efficient, and ironically complaining to a regulator rather than suing in a court can in some cases be cheaper where available.[20] What consumers might prefer could be a state-backed system of enforcement of their rights through an expansion of a cheap-and-cheerful court system.

Private enforcement can apply in both civil and criminal cases. Ketan Somaia a former wealthy Kenyan businessman was privately prosecuted, successfully, when the Crown Prosecution Service had refused to prosecute for a deception of around $19.5M. The Lord Chief Justice noted

---

[19] Jon Cunliffe and Andreas Dombret, *A missing tool against 'too big to fail'*, Wall Street Journal Europe, 2 June 2014; Wolfgang Munchau, *What central banks should do to deal with bubbles*, Financial Times, 14 July 2014: 'Central bankers are fooling themselves if they think macroprudential regulation is a potent independent monetary policy tool'.

[20] Although we could note the absurdity of the UK Financial Ombudsman Service employing around 1000 quasi judges who are broadly untrained in judicial principles and with a budget of around £250M. The whole of the civil justice system for the UK may be only four or five times that.

in 2014 that there had been a rise in private prosecutions 'at a time of retrenchment of state activity in many areas where the state had previously provided sufficient funds to enable state bodies to conduct such prosecutions.'[21] In practice such criminal proceedings are a procedure open only to deep-pocket claimants – but it can be a quicker and cheaper solution for example than organising civil litigation to recover losses. And the threat of prison often persuades reluctant debtors to respond more quickly than the threat of a civil complaint.

Where regulators are less constrained in budget terms than say the Serious Fraud Office or the Crown Prosecution Service or the police, using regulation for recovery seems sensible. But there is also a hidden public cost; there are few constraints on the FCA or tPR budgets for example, and those systems are designed to punish malefactors rather than compensate people who have lost out.

Private recourse is not always attractive – nor is it without disguised cost; litigants-in-person in family law cases for example not only add to public costs by delaying hearings through ignorance of proper procedures, but also because cases take longer, litigants are intimidated, and there are hearing delays. Arbitration can be more expensive than the courts, partly because the parties have to pay for the arbitrator. The hidden or unpublished costs can be significant. On the other hand, the growth in the numbers of litigants-in-person has persuaded the courts for example to reduce reliance on arcane procedural rules.[22] And there are precedents for competition in the civil courts, apart from dispute resolution alternatives such as mediation and arbitration.[23]

Introducing competition in regulation might be more problematic; but it does exist and seems to be working well. The prime example is the ability in the UK for legal practitioners to register with one of several bodies to be able to practice. It has resulted in dramatic reductions in the size of rulebooks and overhead costs.[24] There are also many private quasi-regulators. Most professions until recently governed themselves, and there are bodies which to a greater or lesser extent police their members. A poor example is that of the British Parking Association, which governs through a widely ignored code of practice; a better performing model might be that

---

[21] Jane Croft, *Private prosecutions grow as state bodies retreat in face of dwindling resources*, Financial Times, 28 July 2014.
[22] Lucy Reed, *'Awkward squad' no longer*, Law Society Gazette, 23 June 2014.
[23] See Chapter 5.   [24] See Chapter 4.

of sports bodies or even paradoxically the statutorily approved voluntary labelling of food under EU law.[25]

It is not necessary for all rules to be created by or enforced by the state:[26]

> Contrary to conventional wisdom, the alternative to state regulation is not a regulatory void, but a range of voluntary arrangements. In practice, both types of regulation are to be found in Britain and other democratic societies although, in the clamour for instant solutions which often follows a perceived 'crisis', state regulation may crowd out voluntary solutions because of the widespread assumption, fostered by politicians with short time-horizons, that government always has a remedy which will bring more benefits than costs . . . Experience suggests this assumption is not well founded. Much government regulation has unintended consequences: as one regulation fails to achieve its intended goals, another follows in the hope that it will succeed. Thus, the regulatory state leads to the accumulation of layers of regulation, one effect of which is to reduce the democratic accountability.

7.2.14   Better Regulation Policy

'Better regulation' can mean different things depending on circumstance (see Table 7.1).[27]

One meaning is a reduction in regulation. While licencing requirements in the UK are relatively modest, in other countries they can reach absurd levels. Taxi licences in New York are there less to protect the public than to create some form of limited oligopoly, where badges can trade for several hundred thousand dollars, instead of letting the market find its own level. Meanwhile the drivers are not tested for language or directional skills. In the US, a paradise for licensors, it is estimated that federal regulation (i.e. excluding state regulation) licenses cost the US economy $1.86 trillion in 2013, around $15,000 per household. Most small businesses feel more over-regulated than over-taxed. Around 500 occupations in the various states of the US need a licence, involving around 30 per cent of the

---

[25] EU Regulation No 1169/2011 on Food Information to Consumers introduced in December 2014 sets out requirements for 'voluntary labelling' – including country of origin – stating that any additional voluntary claims must not mislead, be ambiguous or confuse consumers.

[26] John Blundell and Colin Robinson, *Regulation without the state*, IEA, 2000.

[27] OECD, *Regulatory policy in perspective, a reader's companion to the OECD regulatory policy outlook*, OECD, 2015, p15, Table 1.1. Cf. R. Baldwin, *Better regulation: the search and the struggle*, in Baldwin et al., *Oxford Handbook of Regulation*, Oxford University Press, 2010.

Table 7.1 *Overview of different meanings of 'better regulation'*

Reduces perverse effects and unintended effects	Reduce inconsistency, unpredictability and lack of expertise
Regulation will always have side effects and trade-offs, but 'better regulation' might offer one way to reduce the extent/impact of these effects.	Regulation suffers from knee-jerks; 'better regulation' slows down process, enriches information and leads to better expert judgement on costs and benefits of different proposals.
Reduce regulatory 'burden' via de-regulation and 'alternatives to regulation'	**Reduce siloes and lack of professional conversation in regulation**
Regulation is seen as a 'last resort' and needs to be limited; alternatives such as 'benchmarking', market-type mechanisms and naming and shaming offer superior solutions.	Regulation is seen as lacking professional conversation and institutional memory, requiring mechanisms that encourage exchange of knowledge and experiences.

workforce. It is clearly a comfort knowing that an electrician or gas-fitter is trained. But other occupations that require licences include locksmiths, ballroom dance instructors, hair braiders, manicurists, interior designers and upholsterers. Nevada requires anyone wanting to be a travel guide there to conduct 733 days of training and pay $1500 for a licence. And proportionality can be an issue; Michigan requires 1460 days of education and training to be an athletic trainer – but 26 to be a paramedic.[28]

Another meaning of better regulation is increased intervention, sometimes by affixing blame. The blame culture reached one of its apogees when Ed Balls, then Secretary of State for Children Schools and Families, dismissed Sharon Shoesmith, the Head of Haringey Social Services, following the death of a child Baby P who was incidentally in the care of the local authority. Sharon Shoesmith was later exonerated by the

---

[28] Melissa S. Kearney et al., *Nearly 30 percent of workers in the US need a licence to perform their job: it is time to examine occupational licensing practices*, Brookings Institute, January 27 2015. Morris M. Kleiner, *Reforming occupational licensing policies*, The Hamilton project, Discussion paper 2015–10, March 2015 (US). Bounty-hunters, who can legally commit violence, are broadly unregulated throughout the US, (*Delivery men*, The Economist, 3 September 2016); *Taylor v Tainter* [1872] 83 US 366. See also Justin Webb, *Welcome to America, land of the regulated*, Times, 29 August 2017.

court.[29] The Court of Appeal strongly criticised the Minister, who had come to the conclusion that he was entitled to short-circuit the usual checks and balances in employment law because of political pressure arising from a campaign organised by the *Sun*, a populist newspaper. As a consequence of the politically driven ministerial intervention it has now proved hard in some cases to find suitable heads of departments because of the risk of being scapegoated.

The 2008 global financial crisis, in another sphere, also provoked an excess of rule making which is not over yet. Those at the heart of the crisis suggested, vainly, that not everything could or should be reduced to rules. The then Executive Director of the Bank of England charged with ensuring financial stability, Andy Haldane, wrote a frequently cited paper on the crisis which he called 'The dog and the Frisbee'. He pointed out that[30]

> catching a Frisbee is difficult. Doing so successfully requires the catcher to weigh a complex array of physical and atmospheric factors, among them wind speed and Frisbee rotation. Were a physicist to write down Frisbee-catching as an optimal control problem, they would need to understand and apply Newton's law of gravity.
>
> Yet despite this complexity, catching a Frisbee is remarkably common. Casual empiricism reveals that it is not an activity only undertaken by those with a Doctorate in physics. It is a task that an average dog can master. Indeed some, such as border collies, are better at Frisbee-catching than humans.
>
> So what is the secret of the dog's success? The answer, as in many other areas of complex decision-making, is simple. Or rather, it is to keep it simple. For studies have shown that the Frisbee-catching dog follows the simplest rules of thumb: run at a speed so that the angle of gaze to the Frisbee remains roughly constant. Humans follow an identical rule of thumb.

The paper argued for less and simpler regulation; the financial collapse might, he suggested, have been due to too much and too complex regulation rather than too little. Others too have deplored the move from discretion and common sense towards procedural solutions. In some ways adopting formal procedures can save errors and mistakes from occurring,[31] and most of the aviation industry avoids deaths by captains reciting a mantra – as nowadays do surgeons. But box-ticking also carries

---

[29] *The Queen on the application of Sharon Shoesmith v OFSTED* [2011] EWCA Civ 642. For conflicting views, cf Ed Balls, *Speaking Out*, Cornerstone, 2017 and Sharon Shoesmith, *Learning from Baby P*, Jessica Kingsley, 2016.

[30] Andy Haldane, *The dog and the Frisbee*, Bank of England, Speech, 31 August 2012.

[31] Atul Gawande, *The checklist manifesto: how to get things right*, Profile Books, 2011.

a price, less identifiable other than through irritation, and the move from judgment to procedure can impose other, more serious, risks.[32]

7.2.15   Market Failure and the Internet

Market failure is sometimes used by regulators justifying their existence as an argument for regulatory intervention. Such failure is notoriously hard to prove or identify, and can commonly be used by regulators to justify regulation where they have failed in their duties elsewhere. One recent example in the financial services industry is the suggestion by the UK Financial Conduct Authority that investment management fees are too high. The usual argument that the consumer has a poorer bargaining power and poorer access to information is less justifiable following the knowledge available through the internet.[33] Similarly the Pensions Regulator argued that there are too many pension schemes to be efficient, and that there are too many 'master trusts' a particular vehicle for pension provision for the market to bear. That involves making a value judgment of what is the right number of such trusts for the market, akin to soviet planning for the right number of car manufacturers or the right number of computers.[34]

7.2.16   Process: Creating Regulatory Budgets and Improving Instructions

Laws and regulations rarely emerge fully formed from the void. There are invariably consultations (sometimes even genuine), policy papers, internal working documents and drafts. The European Union in 2015 introduced the notion of a regulatory budget, with officials being given a limited number of regulatory initiatives they could pursue in any one period;[35] an alternative method is to impose a limited period of time for legislating, such as shorter parliaments. UK parliamentary draftsmen have long complained that the instructions they receive from departments are confused

---

[32] David Wigton, *Tick the box marked 'personal responsibility'*, The Times, 2 January 2012.

[33] See e.g. Financial Conduct Authority, *FCA publishes terms of reference for asset management market study*, FCA, Press release, 18 November 2016.

[34] Cf 'I think there is a world market for maybe five computers', Thomas Watson, president of IBM, 1943; or 'Television won't be able to hold on to any market it captures after the first six months. People will soon get tired of staring at a plywood box every night.' Darryl Zanuck, executive at 20th Century Fox, 1946.

[35] Jonathan Hill, *Keynote speech on the Call for Evidence on the impact of the EU regulatory framework for financial services*, EU Commission, Bruegel, 12 July 2016. It is a document which should be read and applied by all regulators.

and impractical. The lengthy and complex legislation that emerges is generally as a consequence of confused thinking on policy, made more confused by lack of direction following parliamentary micro-interventions. The Netherlands has adopted a better regulation policy with directives on legislative drafting that provide that new laws shall not be introduced until the need for a regulation has been established and that an investigation is always required to determine whether the objectives of a proposal for new legislation cannot be achieved by entrusting the problem to the self-regulatory capacity in the relevant markets. This constraint does not necessarily work as well as expected in practice, but it has served to modify the mindset of legislators.[36] A resignation speech by an EU Commissioner stated the problem succinctly:[37]

> I joined a Commission which was dedicated to legislating less and legislating better...It is natural that when a micro-prudential regulator or supervisor has to assess risk, they take a highly cautious approach, especially where there has been a crisis caused in part by a lack of regulation or a failure of oversight. No-one wants to be accused of being asleep on the job...the problem comes if a number of different regulators or supervisors are all taking an equally risk-averse approach. Then the cumulative impact of a series of micro-prudential judgments can itself become a source of macro-prudential risk...what lessons have I learned?...legislation is not a science. It is not. It is a series of judgments. Clever people can make it sound as though there is only one answer. But it's not true...Be brave enough not to regulate...As a regulator you cannot expect to win popularity prizes with the businesses you regulate. But you should seek to avoid unnecessary conflict between the regulator and the regulated.

More recently some regulators have been experimenting with 'regulatory sand-boxes' a slightly more sophisticated form of consultation. It is possibly too early to tell whether they are effective, or as anti-competitive and as complex as primary regulation.[38]

---

[36] Rob van Gestel and Marie-Claire Menting, *Ex ante evaluation and alternatives to legislation: going Dutch?*, [2011] 32(3) Statute Law Review 209–226. And have a look at the YouTube video produced by Common Good, the US deregulatory lobby think tank at www.youtube.com/watch?v=fnm7mKp6JTE%feature=youtu.be.

[37] Jonathan Hill, *Keynote speech on the Call for Evidence on The impact of the EU regulatory framework for financial services*, EU Commission, Bruegel, 12 July 2016.

[38] See e.g. Financial Conduct Authority (UK), *Regulatory sandbox*, November 2015, p2: 'A regulatory sandbox is a 'safe space' in which businesses can test innovative products, services, business models and delivery mechanisms without immediately incurring all the normal regulatory consequences of engaging in the activity in question.' The challenge is that it is expensive, and bright ideas from start-ups will struggle to afford a place in the system.

Reformers in the US have also suggested introducing regulatory budgets; this could be in the form of indicating costs (hard if not impossible to calculate with any degree of even approximation) or more practically, a simple page count.[39] The position of the UK in international comparisons by this measure looks not unreasonable compared with other EU countries. While in the US the estimated reduction of GDP through regulatory overheads amounted to around $8.2 trillion, the UK estimates were around $2.4 trillion, lower than Japan, Germany and France.

7.2.17   Process: Improved Drafting

> Any reference in these regulations to a regulation is a reference to a regulation contained in these regulations.[40]

Many countries are guilty of drafting long and complicated legislation. In the US for example Congress refused to vote on a law reforming immigration rules because 'it was a 1,300 page bill that no one had ever read.'[41] In 1948 the average length of a bill that made it through Congress was two and a half pages; by 2015 it was 20. A large number of very short bills helped disguise the fact that there were some very large ones: The US Affordable Care Act 2010 ('Obamacare') was 2400 pages – and was subject to many thousands of pages of subsequent regulations. The No Child Left Behind 2001 bill was 1000 pages.

On the other hand the notorious US pork-barrel arrangements, where individual senators used legislation to insert unrelated pet projects of their own, had diminished by 98 per cent; this improvement took place not because of legislation but following an agreed moratorium, perhaps following peer pressure or personal shame.[42] While the clean-up of American lawmaking has resulted in lawmakers voting a little more with their conscience, the unintended consequence has been a stalemate in US politics, which has made it more difficult for members of one party to support another party's bills. Some have seen that as unacceptable; others that it is a reasonable price to pay. And bills are increasingly portmanteau; they

---

[39] Clyde Wayne Crews Jr, *Ten Thousand Commandments: an annual snapshot of the Federal regulatory state*, Competitive Enterprise Institute, Washington DC (US), 2014, p5.

[40] Banking Act 1979 Appeals Procedure (England and Wales) Regulations 1979 cited in Tom Bingham, *The Rule of Law*, 2010, p 7.

[41] John Boehner, the House Speaker, quoted in *Legislative verbosity: Outrageous Bills*, The Economist, 23 November 2014, p42.

[42] See US think tank Citizens Against Public Waste, www.cagw.org/; *Congressional Pig Book 2016*, CAPW, 2016.

cover a range of unconnected issues, which makes it hard for the regulated to work out what is going on. Meanwhile corruption in lawmaking continues nonetheless by slipping in clauses to bills to benefit certain lobbying groups. Outlawing portmanteau bills, which contain disparate laws, is only one ill that if fixed would result in more readable and understandable law. Drafting in English would also be welcome.

7.2.18   Process: Drafting in Plain Language

The debate about whether law can be written in plain language has been explored earlier; the UK Office of Parliamentary Counsel suggested that in future that it may become more prevalent, especially now that draftsmen in different jurisdictions are learning from each other. Most specialist draftsmen seek to avoid complexity and not use the sophistication of the policy to justify complexity of expression, especially since it does not appear to be necessary.[43] The issue of whether complicated ideas can only be expressed in complicated terms has been widely explored, but modern thinking suggests that simple expression is something worth fighting for. Several countries have long had a 'plain language' policy in their legislative drafting, though application has been mixed, with UK draftsmen in particular having an affectation for the use of the word 'but' at the beginning of a section. There is a long-established 'fog index' test which is used generally to gauge readability; the number used relates to the years of schooling needed to understand a text. Business letters aim for a fog level of 8; Einstein's Theory of Relativity has a fog index level of 12. Ironically the Queensland Parliamentary Counsel's Office reported in its 2007–2008 Annual Report that[44]

> the office adopted a comprehensive plain English drafting policy in 1991. The office continues its commitment to plain English as an attitude or philosophy that is focused on the client and that values simplicity as a way to achieve clear, effective communication. This commitment is an integral part of the office's goal to improve access for all its clients through more effective communication of legislative rights and obligations,

which itself rated a fog level of 16.

---

[43] Anthony Watson-Brown, *In search of plain English – the holy grail or mythical Excalibur of legislative drafting*, [2011] 33(1) Statute Law Review 7–23.
[44] Queensland Parliamentary Counsel's Office, *Annual Report* QPC 2007–9, p14 cited in Anthony Watson-Brown, *In search of plain English – the holy grail of mythical Excalibur of legislative drafting*, [2011] 33(1) Statute Law Review 7–23.

Lord Bingham made it clear that the law 'must be accessible and so far as possible intelligible, clear and predictable'.[45] His argument was manifold. First if anyone is to be imprisoned or otherwise punished they ought to be able without difficulty to find out what they must or must not do on pain of criminal penalty. This is particularly hard nowadays in some regulatory regimes, particularly financial services. Second, he said, if anyone is to claim his rights, he needs to know what the rights and obligations are; for example he needs to know there is a heating allowance before claiming it. This poses a problem particularly in the social security system for example, despite prodigious efforts to simplify it. And the third reason he stated was that the successful conduct of trade, investment and business generally is promoted by a body of accessible legal rules. No one would choose to do business in a country where the parties' rights and obligations were vague or undecided. The obvious breach of that principle is the UK tax code.[46]

Legislation can be so complicated that there are occasions (commonly in the magistrates courts, and not unknown elsewhere) where neither the judiciary, the police nor the prosecution can be confident of the current state of the law. In *R v Chambers* in 2008 the judge said, after Mr Chambers had been fined £60,000, or given 20 months' prison, for evading duty on tobacco products, and who then found that the regulations under which he had been charged had been repealed (which neither the trial judge, the prosecutor, defending counsel, or the judges in the Court of Appeal had realised):

> there is no comprehensive statute law database with hyperlinks which would enable an intelligent person, by using a search engine, to find out all the legislation on a particular topic. This means that the courts are in many cases unable to discover what the law is, or was as the date with which the court is concerned, and are entirely dependent on the parties for being able to inform them what were the relevant statutory provisions which the court

---

[45] Tom Bingham, *The Rule of Law*, 2010, p37.

[46] See e.g. the confusion over tax reliefs for investment into film production (https://stephenfollows.com/film-tax-breaks-by-the-numbers); and see e.g. Finance Act 2004: '(c) in the case of an arrangement to which section 165(3A) never applied but only if the time falls after the member's drawdown pension fund in respect of the arrangement is converted into the member's flexible access drawdown fund in respect of the arrangement of paragraph 8B or 8C of Schedule 28, 80 per cent of the maximum amount that could have been paid in accordance with pension rule 5 in the drawdown pension year in which the conversion occurs had no conversion happened in that year by the operation of either of paragraphs 8B and 8C of Schedule 28.' Finance Act 2014: inserting Schedule 36 paragraph 20(4)(c) of the Finance Act 2004.

has to apply. This lamentable state of affairs has been raised by responsible bodies on many occasions.[47]

The content of company reports for example is much prescribed by law, accounting rules and governance codes. The cost and length of company reports, especially in the quoted sector, has been long a concern. In many ways one of the drivers of excessively lengthy reports (in which it is possible to hide bad news more easily than in a short report) has been a regulator, the Financial Reporting Council, a UK independent regulator 'responsible for promoting high quality corporate governance and reporting to foster investment'. It has made mild efforts to reduce the size of corporate reports, but its efforts have been broadly unsuccessful, largely because the penalties for omitting information are worse than the penalties for inserting it.[48]

7.2.19   Improving the Parliamentary Process

The making of laws in Parliament is generally accepted as being suboptimal; the question is whether there is an appetite for improvement. Whatever solutions are adopted, they will need to take account of the fact that democracy itself contains the seeds of imperfection:

> The great problem of the West is not just that it has overloaded the state with obligations that cannot be fulfilled ... [It] has repeatedly demonstrated the truth of Plato's two great criticisms of democracy: that voters would put short-term satisfaction above long-term prudence and that politicians would try to bribe their way to power – as they have done by promising entitlements that future generations will have to pay for.[49]

And there is fortunately not much equivalent appetite towards adopting another form of rule. As in so many others areas of reform, there unlikely

---

[47] Per Lord Justice Toulson in *R v Chambers* [2008] EWCA Crim 2467, 17 October 2008. An embryonic database using a kind of creative commons is at www.legislation.gov.uk in the UK, but it is unreliable; a private service in the pensions field is as perfect as these things can be but it is expensive and limited to private subscribers only (*Perspective* on www.pendragon.co.uk).

[48] See e.g. *Louder than words: principles and actions for making corporate reports less complex*, FRC, June 2009 and *Cutting clutter: combating clutter in annual reports*, FRC and ASB, 2011. For improvements in drafting, see Office of the Parliamentary Counsel, *Detailed guidance: good law*, 25 November 2015 and House of Commons Political and Constitutional Reform Committee, *Ensuring standards in the quality of legislation*, 25 July 2013, HC 611, session 2013–14 and Cabinet Office, *Guide to making legislation*, 2015.

[49] John Micklethwaite and Adrian Wooldridge, *The Fourth Revolution*, Allen Lane, 2014, p264.

to be any single answer, but there are several elements which could be looked at. Primary lawmaking in particular is widely accepted as being problematic:

- the Parliamentary Draftsman argues that he gets poor instructions from the departments, and he is asked to legislate for things that cannot be done under law.
- the departments commissioning new law argue that their ministers ask them to do things they have advised against based on experience, but that they are constitutionally obliged to follow.
- MPs follow the party line, and vote for laws they have not read, and would not understand if they had read them.
- ministers consider they are obliged to meet manifesto promises, and that they need to meet the demands of the press and the public.

And most MPs they feel that, provided they have followed the processes of the several readings in the two houses, and the voyages through the committees, sufficient due diligence has been performed.

But the outcome indicates that poor legislation is now made too frequently. It might help if MPs were prepared at admit at least a little shame at what they accede to, yet they mostly feel disempowered to do anything about it. The lawmaking process looks effective from the inside, and indeed many parliamentarians commend it, but a major flaw is endemic in all such democratic institutions, namely that there is little obligation on lawmakers to behave with integrity, and there is no accountability for voting tribally. Over time, it might be possible to make such behaviour unacceptable, as has happened partly with pork-barrelling in the US. The downside might mean that a government programme might not be able to be implemented, but it might be a price worth paying. Suggestions for improving the parliamentary process by introducing training and accountability are suggested in the next section.

The legislative process in many jurisdictions is necessarily imperfect. But it could be less imperfect. In the UK for example the theory looks good. Usually the government drafts a bill, perhaps after consultation, and then the draft legislation goes through revision after revision, in practice around four courses, in two houses and in a specialist committee. Reading the transcripts of the proceedings is in some ways impressive; the quality of debate is often outstanding. But in practice what emerges is far from ideal.

The same applies to secondary legislation, with the difference being that it normally enjoys much less scrutiny. In the meantime there are the usual conflicts between the executive and the legislature as to where the power should lie. In 2015 the government objected to the House of Lords refusing to approve legislation passed by the Commons. Since 1911 the Lords had agreed through legislation not to challenge fiscal bills, but in 2015 what the government considered a fiscal measure was implemented not through an act but by a statutory instrument. The Lords refused its passage and claimed it had a constitutional right to do so because the 1911 Parliament Act only applied (1) to taxation measures and (2) primary legislation.[50]

Finally regulation can be used by the state for improper purposes. One example has been the use of RIPA, or the anti-terrorist legislation.[51] Another is the misuse of the tax system in the UK. Tax is used only partly as a means of raising revenue, but also as an instrument of policy. High taxation of wealthier people, and the heavy taxation of alcohol and tobacco, is intended to send a variety of messages to taxpayers, as well as to raise money. Getting it wrong can have expensive behavioural consequences; for example raising tax rates can counter-intuitively result in lower tax takes.[52] In 2013 more than 6B cigarettes were smoked without duty having been paid on them, losing around £2.9B in tax receipts – because the high level of tax rates made it worthwhile for people to cheat.[53]

7.2.20 Reforming Parliament and the Executive

Insiders in particular have concluded that the legislative system is imperfect. A private think tank comprising for the most part aggrieved retired senior civil servants set out a blueprint for reform of the relationship between the government, Parliament and the civil service.[54] Another

---

[50] Parliament Act 1911; *Report of the Committee on Ministers' Powers*, 1932, Cmnd 4060 (The Donoughmore Report); *Secondary legislation and the Primacy of the House of Commons*, HMSO, 2015, Cm 9177, December 2015 (The Strathclyde Review); Daniel Greenberg, *Secondary legislation and the primacy of Parliament*, (editorial), [2016] 37(1) Statute Law Review iii.

[51] See e.g. Anushka Asthana, *Revealed: British councils used RIPA to secretly spy on public: Local authorities used Regulation of Investigatory Powers Act to follow people, including dog walkers*, Guardian, 25 December 2016.

[52] Arthur Laffer, *Disaster looms on HM Roller Coaster*, Sunday Times, 13 July 2014. Arthur Laffer et al., *An inquiry into the nature and causes of the wealth of states*, Wiley, 2014.

[53] KPMG, *Project Sun: a study of the illicit cigarette market in the European Union, Norway and Switzerland, 2014 results*, KPMG, June 2015.

[54] See e.g. *Good Government: reforming parliament and the executive: recommendations from the executive committee of the Better Government Initiative*, January 2010.

insider review concluded that every piece of law (or at least Act of Parliament) should have[55]

- explanatory notes attached to the Bill, which should include a clear explanation of the purpose of the Bill, accompanied by the criteria by which the Bill, once enacted, can be judged to have met its purpose. Today notes are frequently attached – but not the criteria since presumably it would prove a hostage to fortune for most legislators;
- an automatic review (within three years of commencement or six years of enactment) of the effectiveness, using the criteria in the explanatory notes and in consultation with interested parties and appropriate select committee (very rare in practice);
- publication by the Department of the review and its deposit with the appropriate select committee; and
- a budget to enable research by select committees to collect evidence at the discretion of the select committee.

The government later agreed to many of the recommendations,[56] but little was implemented (apart from the Law Commission being asked to carry out further research, i.e. indefinitely deferred). It is unlikely at present that, with financial constraints and an over-active legislative programme, reforms can be anticipated soon.

7.2.21   Genuine Regulatory Impact Assessments

Since 1999 many laws and regulations in the UK have been subjected to a 'Regulatory Impact Assessment' which is intended to judge whether a regulation is worthwhile; it reflects similar arrangements in several other jurisdictions. In principle it is a sensible arrangement, and one intended to weed out pointless or unnecessary regulation;[57] it is supposed to encourage departments and ministers to think twice before regulating or legislating. But it is hard to find a decent example of regulations or legislation being abandoned as a consequence of an adverse conclusion. The difficulty with RIAs, which were thought as a useful moderator for legislative urges, has been that they give little or no attention to the alternatives. Such ideas

---

[55] House of Lords, Constitution Committee, *Parliament and the Legislative Process*, October 2004, HL 173–1, paras 87, 180, 189, 190, 191, 192.

[56] HM Government, *Select Committee on the Constitution, Parliament and the Legislative Process: the government's response*, 2004–05 HL 114.

[57] Comptroller and Auditor General, *Better regulation: making good use of regulatory impact assessments*, Report No HC 329, National Audit Office, 8 November 2001.

as codes of conduct, economic instruments, guidelines or anything else are rarely given serious consideration.[58] Costs imposed by legislation are generally unknown and unknowable, so fingers-in-the-air calculations are adopted. And benefits are equally speculative. There remains no accountability for getting the estimates wrong, nor future re-auditing of outcomes. It is nowadays simply a box-ticking exercise.[59]

At one time regulatory impact assessments were expected to calm down the spate of legislative activity; they were intended to force government departments, before coming up with ideas for legislation, to show the minister and the public what the impact would be, including the costs not only for the department and the government, but also for anyone affected, for example, where it affected business, of the cost to business. Nowadays much legislation has had produced for it some form of RIA, a copy of which is placed in the House of Commons and Lords libraries. The Cabinet Office suggested at some time that RIAs should also include a timetable for post-implementation review as well and include a description of how the policy options would be reviewed. That recommendation was not adopted.[60]

Other countries have been more successful in managing RIA's, albeit to modest degrees, in implementing post-legislative review; there are arrangements in Australia, Canada, New Zealand, Scotland France and Germany – and the European Union.[61]

7.2.22 Sunsetting

Sunsetting, providing a time limit to legislation, or providing it will expire after a certain time, has had limited success. The Cabinet Office noted

---

[58] T. Ambler et al., *The British Regulatory System*, Report for the British Chamber of Commerce, March 2008.

[59] Comptroller and Auditor General, *Evaluation of regulatory impact assessments 2006–7*, Report No HC 606, National Audit Office, 11 July 2007. For comparative US costs of regulation, see Brian O'Keefe, *The Red Tape Conundrum: how the wrong kind of regulation is strangling business – and what to do about it*, Fortune, 20 October 2016, and Susan Dudley and Melinda Warren, *Regulators' budget from Eisenhower to Obama: an analysis of the US Budget for fiscal years 1960 through 2017*, Regulatory Studies Centre, George Washington University, 17 May 2016. The US federal government employed 176,000 regulatory work in 2000, and 279,000 by 2016.

[60] www.cabinetoffice.gov.uk/regulation/ria/ria_guidance/post_implementaion_review.asp.

[61] Law Commission, *Post legislative scrutiny*, 2006, p25; Legislative Instruments Act 2003 (Australia, Cth); Australian Administrative Review Council, *Report on Rule-making by Commonwealth agencies*, ARC 35 1992. In Canada see e.g. Canada, Privy Council, *Guide to making federal acts and regulations*, 2nd edn (Canada, Department of Justice 2001).

there might be limits to sunsetting; their guidance suggested that it should only be used where there is a time-limited problem, where there is scientific uncertainty, where there is uncertainty over the costs and benefits of the legislation; where measures extend the power of the state or reduce civil liberties and where measures are taken in the face of considerable opposition. It is rarely used in practice.

7.2.23   Consolidation

The Law Commission in England and Wales since 1965 has had a statutory obligation to consider consolidation projects.[62] Around 200 consolidation bills have been enacted since that time, but their effort has been overwhelmed by the amount of new legislation that continues to be published.

7.2.24   Codification

Codification is a system which has been adopted by most Continental law systems, and even one or two common law systems. Codification has drawbacks of its own – but it compels lawmakers to consider whether they really need changes to the existing law or can live with applying the law in a different way – and makes it conform to some form of system. It should in practice make the law easier to understand both for laymen and professionals. It is one of the reasons that the practice of Continental law for example is widely regarded as being so much cheaper for consumers.

Codification has never been properly tried in the UK, although there are times when existing legislation has been brought into one act (such as the Equality Act 2010) or when the taxes acts have been rewritten under the Tax Law Rewrite project – but there has never been a formal attempt at codification. The argument against it (if there has ever been an argument) is that it detracts from the power of Parliament and the freedom of ingenuity of the draftsmen. But what it might achieve is a constraint on the excesses of legislation, and the creation of coherent legislation.

7.2.25   Review

Reviews of legislation have long been advocated as a tool for improved governance. Such review could include

---

[62] Law Commissions Act 1965; *The Law Commission and Consolidation*, Law Commission, June 2015.

- pre-legislative scrutiny,
- post-legislative scrutiny and
- primary Parliamentary scrutiny.

7.2.26   Pre-Legislative Scrutiny (Ex Ante Evaluation)

Reviewing whether legislation is really needed is now established in some jurisdictions. The Netherlands has had such a system for some time, and ironically is considering moving to the British system of regulatory impact assessments, on the grounds that the fudging of ex ante evaluations is too prevalent and difficult to manage. The UK has examples of attempts to determine whether legislation is worthwhile, although they are difficult to find.[63]

Many pieces of legislation, especially finance bills, lack sufficient scrutiny because of shortage of parliamentary time. More problematic however is not the detailed line-by-line evaluation which can be helpful in avoiding some of the excesses but the lack of existence of a method of enabling a more general objection to principles. While governments tend to nail their policies to the mast and find it difficult to accept that there may be downsides as well as upsides to their thinking and while, in private, legislators may admit to drawbacks to their schemes, in public they find it hard to admit to flaws in their drafts, seeing it as losing face.[64]

Governments and oppositions in the past have committed to consultation before drafting.[65] In practice relatively few pieces of legislation (although often the larger documents) are currently submitted for evaluation outside Parliament.[66] In practice parliamentarians find such requirements too restricting; they can lead to late publication of draft bills, delays in establishing committees and unreasonable deadlines for reporting.[67] In 2003–2004 around a dozen draft bills were published, and 10 discussed by a committee, out of the 38 that were passed. Pre-legislative scrutiny can be helpful – but commentators are helpless where the government is

---

[63] Rob van Gestel and Marie-Claire Menting, *Ex ante evaluation and alternatives to legislation: going Dutch?*, [2011] 32(3) Statute Law Review 209–226.

[64] See Daniel Greenberg, *Dangerous trends in modern legislation – and how to reverse them*, Centre for Policy Studies, April 2016; Daniel Greenberg, *Dangerous trends in modern legislation* [2015] (1) Public Law 96–110.

[65] Labour Party, *Report of the Joint Committee on constitutional reform*, March 1997.

[66] House of Commons, Library Standard Note, *Pre-legislative scrutiny*, SN/PC/2822, 3 June 2005, p8.

[67] See Richard Kelly and Sarah Priddy, *Pre-legislative scrutiny under the 2015 Conservative governments*, House of Commons Library, Briefing paper 07757, 16 November 2016.

determined on a course of action, and where consultation is reduced to a question of form rather than to genuinely flush out what the policy and its implementation should be.[68]

7.2.27 Post-Legislative Scrutiny/Mandatory Review

Despite the best of intents, in real life there is still gold-plating of European legislation when implemented in the UK, and even purely English legislation may in later years prove to have been excessive.[69] It is as always an issue of resource, but it seems sensible enough that from time to time new legislation should be reviewed with hindsight, perhaps prompted as much by political circumstance as need. There are of course issues – how should such scrutiny be defined, what would be the benchmarks for successful legislation, who should undertake the review, when should it take place, and who in the end would be responsible for making eventual decisions?

Legislators have been talking about post-legislative scrutiny for over 40 years – without making progress. In 1971 the House of Commons Select Committee on Procedure noted:[70]

> Pressure of Government business in each session often reduces the chance of securing a place in the legislative programme for a Bill to amend an Act passed within recent years. For this reason, years may pass before Parliament has an opportunity to consider legislation embodying amendments to a recent Act, the need for which has become imperative following, for

---

[68] Although there are those who are more optimistic, see e.g. Luzius Mader, *Evaluating the effects: a contribution to the quality of legislation* [2001] 22(2) Statute Law Review 119. He recommends a number of administrative steps that do not need implementing legislation to improve the process and concludes: 'No business of any kind would allow its Board and shareholders to take strategic decisions without the inclusion in its end-of-year report of detailed information about its progress and activities in the past year. Parliament, which is in the business of controlling the lives of citizens through a range of legislative activities, should feel the need to ensure that both it and its citizen-shareholders are properly informed'.

[69] Law Commission, *Post-legislative scrutiny: a consultation paper*, Consultation paper No 178, Law Commission, 2006; House of Lords, Select Committee on the Constitution, *Parliament and the legislative process* (2003–04) HL 173-I. See also Hansard Society, *Making the law, The Report of the Hansard Society Commission on the legislative process*, November 1992 (Lord Rippon Report); House of Commons, Select Committee on Modernisation of the House of Commons, *First Report*, July 1997, HC 190; ibid, *A reform programme for consultation, memorandum submitted by the Leader of the House of Commons*, 2001–02 HC 440.

[70] House of Commons, Select Committee on Procedure, *The process of legislation*, (1970–71) HC 538.

example, a judgment in the courts, difficulties in interpretation, impracticability in everyday use, or the nature of the delegated legislation made under its authority.

Legislative scrutiny is more effective if the legislation is designed with this expectation in mind. Such legislation would therefore need to include[71]

- purpose clauses – purpose clauses have been condemned by draftsmen and others,
- explanatory notes,
- policy documents,
- regulatory impact assessments,
- input from a scrutiny committee,
- review clauses in the legislation,
- ministerial undertakings and
- sunset clauses.

In the UK an Act has sometimes been liable to some form of post-legislative review, whether by a Parliamentary Committee or internally within Government. In 2008 an additional and more systematic process was introduced, to act in addition to the other checks and balances.[72] In theory, although not always in practice (actually possibly ever in practice) three to five years (normally) after Royal Assent, the responsible Department is obliged to submit a Memorandum to the relevant Commons departmental Select Committee (unless it has been agreed with the Committee that a Memorandum is not required).

The Memorandum is supposed to include a preliminary assessment of how the Act has worked out in practice, relative to objectives and benchmarks identified during the passage of the Bill. The Select Committee (or potentially another Committee) then decides whether it wishes to conduct a fuller post-legislative inquiry into the Act.

When preparing new legislation, departments are supposed to take into account the commitment that, taken together, the Regulatory Impact Assessment, Explanatory Notes and other statements made during the passage of a Bill should give sufficient indication of the Bill's objectives to allow any post-legislative reviewing body to make an effective assessment as to how an Act is working out in practice.

---

[71] Law Commission, *Post legislative scrutiny*, 2006, p37.
[72] See Cabinet Office Parliamentary Adviser (+44 20 7276 0351), and see *White Paper on Post-Legislative Scrutiny: The Government's Approach* (Cm 7320).

The idea for the system was to improve the preparation of Bills, by focusing attention on likely implementation difficulties:

- helping to identify problems with the implementation of Acts earlier or more systematically and
- allowing lessons (both about what has worked well and what has not worked well) to be learned and disseminated to the benefit of other legislation, and significant achievements to be identified and highlighted.

The intention was to ensure that the scrutiny was proportionate to need. And the policy makes it clear that there was no expectation that there should be a full in-depth review of every Act.[73]

The government of the day committed itself to a full system of review and set out in detailed terms how such reviews should take place. It excluded certain legislation (some of which really should have been reviewed); the excluded legislation included Consolidated Fund and Appropriation Acts, Finance Acts, Tax Law Rewrite Acts, Consolidation Acts, Statute Law Repeal Acts and Private Acts.

But in fact, such scrutiny rarely takes place; it is just too hard. By January 2013, after five years and around 250 major pieces of legislation and maybe 10,000 statutory instruments only 58 memoranda by departments had been prepared (most being formulaic) and only three had been followed by committee scrutiny. As a House of Lords Committee reported:[74]

> Post-legislative scrutiny appears to be similar to motherhood and apple pie in that everyone appears to be in favour of it. However, unlike motherhood and apple pie it is not much in evidence.

In fact therefore to all intents and purposes such scrutiny is rare and ineffective. It could be implemented, but resources are tight, and few have the appetite to rehearse yet again the arguments that were gone through so painfully over many months, especially if perhaps the original experts have moved on to other areas of activity. It is in practice not an effective control mechanism, with some rare exceptions.

---

[73] See Office of the Leader of the House of Commons, *Post-legislative scrutiny – The government's approach*, Cm 7320, March 2008; Richard Kelly and Michael Everett, *Post-legislative scrutiny*, House of Commons Library, Note, SN/PC/05232, 23 May 2013.

[74] House of Lords, Constitution Committee, *Parliament and the legislative process*, 29 October 2004 HL 173-I 2003–4, para 165. Law Commission, *Post legislative scrutiny*, October 2006, Law Com 302, Cm 6945, para 3.19.

Other areas of public activity attract annual audits, some of them inde-pendent, others private. The Hansard Society for example publishes an annual audit of political engagement and both works with and reflects on the work of government bodies.[75]

7.2.28 State Liability for Excess Legislation

In 2006 the National Audit Office explored some of the complexities of the UK benefits system. There is no doubt they are complicated, and the incoming Coalition Government in 2010 appointed a new Secretary of State for Work and Pensions whose previous incarnation as Director of the Centre for Social Justice had seen a publication calling for the sim-plification of the system.[76] The NAO identified one factor that had con-tributed to the complexity, apart from the complexity of the problem, was the scale of the legislation. Between 2000 and 2004 there had been six new acts and 364 new statutory instruments affecting the law on social security.[77] The NAO concluded that the incremental addition of regula-tions and their interaction with current regulations had also added to the complexity; and where legislation is delegated for implementation at local level, the complexity increases yet further.

7.2.29 State Liability for Negligent Legislation

One way of controlling excessive or inappropriate or counter-productive legislation might be to sue the government.[78] Academic studies discuss cases where it has been considered there has not been enough regulation, and indeed the *Francovich*[79] case many years ago in the European Court

---

[75] See e.g. Lord Bew (Chairman of the Committee on Standards in Public Life), *Eleventh Annual Audit of Political Engagement*, Speech, Hansard Society, 30 April 2014. It concluded that 77 per cent of the respondents expected politicians to undertake regular ethics and standards training. It suggested politicians should abide by seven principles: selflessness, integrity, objectivity, accountability, openness, honesty and leadership. It is hard to dis-agree. See also *Strengthening transparency around lobbying*, Committee on Standards in public life, November 2013; House of Lords, *Code of conduct and guidance*, 2014.

[76] Centre for Social Justice, *Dynamic Benefits: Towards Welfare That Works*, A Policy Report by the CSJ Economic Dependency Working Group 16 September 2009.

[77] National Audit Office, *Dealing with the complexity of the benefits system*, 18 November 2005 (2005–06) HC 592.

[78] Leslie Blake, John Pointing and Tim Sinnamon, *Over regulation and suing the state for neg-ligent legislation* [2007] 28(3) Statute Law Review 218–234.

[79] *Francovich and Boniface v Italy* (ECJ Case C-6, C-9/90), [1991] ECR I 5357; see also T. Tridimas, *Liability for Breach of Community Law: growing up and mellowing down?* (2001)

of Justice concluded that national governments that did not introduce legislation as required by the EU would be liable for anything wrong that happened as a consequence. The example given was that of the *Titanic*:

> One of the reasons why so many people died when the RMS Titanic sank in 1912 was because the Board of Trade rules relating to the number (and capacity) of lifeboats that had to be carried on such a ship had not been changed since 1894. Those rules were based upon the tonnage of ships rather than on the number of passengers and crew carried in them. Although Titanic had carried more lifeboats, floats and rafts than Board of Trade rules then required (sufficient to save 1178 lives rather instead of the 'statutory' number of 962) even this capacity would have saved no more than 52 per cent of the 2207 people on board. In fact only 651 people were lowered into the boats.

These reviews generally discuss legislation which is inadequate or where the Minister fails to review the legislation when required to do so. The courts have sometimes, certainly in relation to secondary legislation (statutory instruments rather than Acts of Parliament), considered that such legislation has not received sufficient scrutiny and have amended the law accordingly.[80] But legislative negligence is a brave concept; it involves legislatures accepting responsibility for their failures, which is rare if not unknown, and Ministers or even other ranks being accountable. Since legislation, in the UK at least, is the product of much bargaining and compromise it is always open to a responsible person to say that if it had not been for so-and-so's amendment, the mischief would not have occurred, and counterfactuals are hard to prove, even on a balance of probabilities. On the other hand judges have not hesitated to criticise legislation, even if there was not much they could about it; in some jurisdictions, for example in Australia or New Zealand, they might however be able to declare it unconstitutional for bad drafting. English judges make a similar point:[81]

> It is in the public interest that the criminal law and its procedures, so far as possible, be clear and straightforward so that all those directly affected, in particular, defendants, victims, the police, the probation service, jurors, lawyers for the defence or prosecution, judges and magistrates, professional

---

CML Rev 38, 301; G. Anagnostaras, *The allocation of responsibility in state liability actions for breach of community law* (2001) ELR 26; P. Craig, *Once more unto the Breach: the Community, the State and Damages Liability* (2001) LQR 196.

[80] See e.g. *Porter v Honey* [1988] 1 WLR 1420 where the Town and Country Planning (Control of Advertisement) Regulations 1984 were considered insufficiently scrutinised and the court rewrote the regulations.

[81] Rose LJ in *R v Bradley* [2005] EWCA Crim 20, paras 38 and 39.

and law, should be readily able to understand it. Sadly the provisions of the Criminal Justice Act 2003, which we have had to consider on this appeal, are, as is apparent, conspicuously unclear in circumstances where clarity could easily have been achieved. It is not this Court's function to identify whether the government, Parliament or parliamentary draftsmen are responsible for this perplexing legislation. It is this Court's duty loyally to glean from the statutory language, if it can, Parliament's intention and this we have sought to do in the face of obfuscatory language. The public is entitled to know of the difficulties which such legislation creates for all concerned. The point is graphically highlighted in the present case, because the Crown have advanced to this Court a construction of the statute which is completely contrary to that suggested by the Home Office press release on the day the provisions came into force.

It is more than a decade since the late Lord Taylor of Gosforth CJ called for a reduction in the torrent of legislation affecting criminal justice. Regrettably that call has gone unheeded by successive governments. Indeed, the quantity of such legislation has increased and its quality has, if anything, diminished. The 2003 Act has 339 sections and 38 schedules and runs to 453 pages. It is, in pre-metric terms, an inch thick. The provisions which we have considered have been brought into force prematurely, before appropriate training could be given by the Judicial Studies Board or otherwise to approximately 2,000 Crown Court and Supreme Court judges and 30,000 magistrates. In the meantime, the judiciary and, no doubt, the many criminal justice agencies for which this Court cannot speak, must, in the phrase familiar during the Second World War 'make do and mend'. That is what we have been obliged to do in the present appeal and it has been an unsatisfactory activity, wasteful of scarce resources in public money and judicial time.

As the judge said, there was not much that courts can do to improve the position, although in his modest way he sent a message, rather as legislators themselves often try to do. To be only slightly frivolous he could have imposed a fine on the Prime Minister or the Speaker of the House, two of the Great Offices of State. They would not have paid, and it almost certainly would not have been possible to enforce the judgment, but it would have sent a signal which would have gone down well with the public. The standard defence that 'Parliament is sovereign' would have been limited in the manner that was originally employed to constrain the belief in a monarch's own supreme powers; if they overdid it, there would be a response. Parliament is only sovereign within limits.

But liability for breaches of EU law is one reason why some UK legislators object so strongly to the EU project, even though it is the state that pays rather than the legislators. Oddly under EU law EU institutions seem to be liable for bad drafting, although it seems hard to find a case where the courts have imposed any penalty.[82] It seems improbable at present that such a remedy would be available in English law, and one would need a carapace of iron to suggest it to a parliamentary select committee. One answer might be the award of unenforceable damages, which would bring certain parliamentarians into disrepute, whilst not bankrupting them. One could envisage damages of hundreds of millions or even billions of pounds for some faulty legislation. Some of the sanctimony of certain select committees might be lower in degree as a consequence. But there are respectable suggestions that the courts should establish a tort (a civil wrong) regarding harm that results from negligent legislation, and incorporate a right for the subject or civilian to claim for damage caused by legislation enacted in a way that is so negligent that it caused loss or harm to the claimant.

7.2.30   Sunset Clauses/OIOO/OITO/OITO

In Australia the Legislative Instruments Act 2003 (Cth) provides that legislative instruments are to be kept up to date and only remain in force for so long as they are needed. The basic rule is that such instruments should reach their sunset approximately 10 years after the date that they commence or are required to be lodged for registration. There are exceptions to the rule, and in practice, around the world:

> At the moment all laws are like vampires: Once created they are impossible to kill.[83]

Similarly the policy adopted by Canada, the US and the UK of 'one in, one out', 'one in, two out' and 'one in, three out', in relation to controls on the introduction of new rules, has never been shown to be effective.

7.2.31   Regulation by Market Forces

The need for regulation on behalf of consumers for example is less required now than before, especially that 'market failure' and asymmetry of information is much reduced. The invention of TripAdvisor and similar websites, and such operations as Comparethemarket.com, can offer

---

[82] EC Treaty Article 288(2); J. Wakefield, *What is the nature of the non-contractual liability claim?* in J. Wakefield (ed) *Judicial protection through the use of Article 288(2)*, Kluwer Law International, London 2002, 308.

[83] John Micklethwaite and Adrian Wooldridge, *The Fourth Revolution*, Allen Lane 2014, p266.

the consumer better and cheaper protection than any regulator can produce, largely because of the determined nature of people who have paid money and are prepared to tell others about their experience. The market is imperfect but the imbalance between a powerful producer and an emasculated consumer is now much repaired.[84]

7.2.32   Counterweights to Regulation

US writers with a libertarian bent offer rather angrier responses to excess regulation, and have suggested for example the establishment of a 'Madison Fund' to challenge regulations and regulators on a regular basis, to make life intolerable for them.[85] Understandable as the desire might be, any implementation would tend to confrontation, and it ignores the fact that the regulators themselves can be subject to almost intolerable pressures from the press and the legislators. An unintended side-effect may be the creation of additional expense and the unintended consequence for well-functioning regulation. Libertarianism can find itself as intolerant and fundamentalist as any sect of Al Quaeda or the haredi. But it does offer one form of a market response to excess of regulation.

7.3   Attitudes and Understanding

> There is usually a seductive logic to any new regulation. There is almost always a case that can be made for each specific instrument. The problem is cumulative. All these good intentions can add up to a large expense, with suffocating effects. Sometimes, we need to pause for a moment and think whether we will not do more damage with a hasty response than was done by the problem itself.[86]

The first response of a regulator is to regulate; that is what it does.[87] And it is also the first approach of the press, which demands regulation to

---

[84] Mark J. Perry, *Government regulation vs regulation by market forces and consumer-regulators*, American Enterprise Institute, 16 January 2015; Charles Murray, *Regulation run amok – and how to fight back*, Wall Street Journal, 8 May 2015.

[85] Charles Murray, *By the people: rebuilding liberty without permission*, Crown Forum, 2015 (US).

[86] Tony Blair, former UK Prime Minister, *speech on the compensation culture*, 2005, cited in Harries and Sawyer, *How to run a country: the burden of regulation*, ResPublica, December 2014.

[87] As in the Persian fable of the Scorpion and the Frog. For US studies on regulation see e.g. Sam Batkins, *600 major regulations*, American Action Forum, 6 August 2016; the study suggested that around 94,000 additional employees would be required to complete the forms

remedy some perceived public scandal. A regulator needs substantial strength of character to be able to resist these initial internal impulses and external public pressures.[88] Those responsible for protecting the public are not always equipped with the time or training they deserve to reflect to avoid responding in knee-jerk fashion, nor are they equipped perhaps to manage public expectations.[89] There are however a number of approaches which might make those involved feel more comfortable in resisting the urge to create more rules. First amongst equals includes changing the mindset of both those who are affected (or think they are affected) by lack of regulation and those who feel they are responsible for producing it.

7.3.1   Changing the Mindset

Changing the mindset (from one that considers that to solve a policy problem we need more rules) can have impressive outcomes. In the private sector, for example, individuals who have challenged the previous mindset have achieved success. When Dame Fiona Reynolds was appointed the Director-General of the National Trust, a UK conservation charity, simplification was just one of a number of issues she felt needed to be addressed. During her term of office she reduced the number of board members from 52 to 12, increased turnover from £300M to £400M over 10 years, doubled volunteer numbers and increased visitor numbers from 10M to 17M.

introduced during President Obama's final term. There were similar statistics for other administrations.

[88] The UK's Pension Protection Fund, a pension fund insolvency insurer, paid £600,000 over two years on public relations, Alex Ralph, *Pension fund spent £600,000 on PR*, The Times, 16 November 2016.

[89] Camilla Cavendish, a Times journalist and subsequently ennobled as a Conservative peer, won a Paul Foot award (for investigative journalism) for exposing the problems of the Children Act 1989 (where social workers intervened too often in the South Ronaldsay (Orkney) and Cleveland satanic abuse scandals in 1991, cf. Clyde Inquiry: *Report of the Inquiry into the Removal of Children from Orkney in February 1991*, House of Commons, Edinburgh, 27 October 1992, and see e.g. *It was a routine hospital visit. Baby Maddy wasn't putting on weight ... What happens when the state takes your child away?* Times, 5 January 2013) and later another award for exposing where social workers did not intervene enough, see e.g. *Why focus on meeting targets did not save Baby P*, The Times, 2 December 2008; Sharon Shoesmith. *Learning from Baby P*, Jessica Kingsley, 2016; *Sharon Shoesmith v OFSTED* [2011] EWCA Civ 642, [2011] IRLR 679, [2011] PTSR 1459, [2011] BLGR 649, [2011] ICR 1195, describing the inappropriate behaviour of then Secretary of State (later famous for participating in a TV dance competition). There are now as a consequence around 20,000 more children in care than before, many of whom do not need to be, see e.g. Christopher Booker, *£1 million bill for social workers getting it wrong*, Daily Telegraph, 4 September 2016.

In relation to simplification she discovered that the National Trust applied 980 rules, covering issues relating to the size of vegetable portions sold at its cafes, the contents of a scone, and the management of bats (where there were 18 rules). In the end her team reduced 18 Trust policies and instructions to one. The rulebook was reduced to eight principles, 43 instructions and some guidance that property managers were free to ignore.[90] That was still a lot, but it was a great deal less than it had been.

The private sector, where a single individual can be responsible for the success or otherwise of an organisation, and may have the power to do something about managing change, may find reform easier to implement than government can. Not everyone can be a chief executive with authority to impose change; but it has been suggested, as mentioned, that consumers could use opportunities that present themselves to change the mood. If they are perturbed by excess of regulation they should persistently object in a polite manner. Many people of course do this, but mostly when driven to distraction and not necessarily when in a balanced frame of mind. And of course it is not always easy to object, or to object where it might actually make a point; complaining can be expensive and time consuming, and while as a remedy may be worthy, can be slow and largely ineffective.[91] For example, in practice, it is almost impossible for any of us to read the terms of the hundreds of pages of contracts we sign without looking, the so-called contracts of adhesion and cannot modify them if we do.[92] There is

---

[90] Carly Chynoweth, *The endless list of rules that drove National Trust boss batty*, The Times, 8 October 2010, p83. See also Philip K. Howard, *Democracy for an age of distrust*, The American Interest 16 November 2016: 'Today the FFA [Federal Aviation Authority] certifies new aircraft as "airworthy" based on their expert judgment, not detailed specifications like how many rivets it has. This is not "de-regulation", but an all-too-rare liberation of American common sense inside government... When humans are allowed to take responsibility, law becomes far simpler and more effective. A few legal principles can replace a thousand rules if people are free to take responsibility for implementation. To regulate nursing homes, Australia replaced a thick rulebook with 31 results-oriented principles, such as to have a "home-like setting". Within a short period nursing homes had improved markedly.'

[91] Tracey Brown and Michael Hanlon, *In the interests of safety: The absurd rules that blight our lives and how we can change them*, Sphere, 2014.

[92] We all, however meticulous we are, sign contracts we have not read. This is supposed to be one of the cardinal legal sins, but anyone who buys a rail ticket and does not read the 600 pages of Virgin's conditions of carriage, or ticks a Microsoft or Google or Apple box without scrolling down the several hundred conditions becomes a pernicious defaulter. While Hamlet, Shakespeare's longest play, is 30,000 words long, Paypal's terms of service is 50,000 and Apple's iTunes is 14,500 (just less than Macbeth); see Adam Taylor, *Russian man who got bank to sign homemade credit card contract now suing them for not following terms*, Business Insider, 8 August 2013; Andy Haldane, *The dog and the Frisbee*, speech, Bank of England, 31 August 2012; Edwin W. Patterson, *The Delivery of a Life-Insurance Policy*,

useful legislation in the UK that protects consumers against unfair terms in such private contracts, but it does not protect the consumer against excessive government regulation.[93] And improving the quality of legislation is virtually impossible without a change in mindset:[94]

> We must add that little can be done to improve the quality of legislation unless those concerned in the process are willing to modify some of their most cherished habits. We have particularly in mind the tendancy [*sic*] of all Governments to rush too much weighty legislation through Parliament in too short a time with or without the connivance of parliament, and the inclination of Members of Parliament to press for too much details in Bills. Parliamentarians cannot have it both ways. If they really want legislation to be simple and clear they must accept bills shorn of unnecessary detail and elaboration. We cannot emphasise too strongly that the Government and Parliament have clear responsibility for the condition of the statute book.

7.3.2   Reducing the Belief in Regulation as a Solution to Various Ills

Even those whose living is made through regulation as a provider or enforcer may at times have a degree of scepticism about the effectiveness of regulation. Regulation can help the consumer by setting standards in public health, in supervising weights and measures, and by conducting prison inspections. But much regulation can be ineffective, excessive, counterproductive or disproportionate and the tests of effectiveness, often provided by the relevant regulator are rarely, if ever, double-blind tested.

Pressure groups and the media as well as grandstanding politicians have an appetite for regulation which perhaps might only be curbed over time by diminishing their belief in regulation as a cure for an ill. That belief may take some time to change, but there are steps that can be taken to reduce the belief, and some of them are described below.[95]

[1919] 33 Harv LRev 198; *Terms of Service.* website, https://tosdr.org/about.html; Ian R. Macneil, *Bureaucracy and contracts of adhesion*, [1984] 22(1) Osgoode Hall Law Journal 5. In Mexico insurance related contracts of adhesion must be centrally registered.

[93] Unfair Contract Terms Act 1977. A similar US plea for using a change of mindset as a solution is in Philip K. Howard, *Six presidents have failed to cut red tape. Here's how Trump could succeed*, Washington Post, 13 December 2016.

[94] *The Preparation of Legislation: report of a committee appointed by the Lord President in Council*, May 1975, (the Renton Report) para 1.10. Culture has belatedly been adopted as an issue in financial institutions by the UK regulator, the Financial Conduct Authority, see Andrew Bailey, Chief Executive, *Culture in financial institutions: it's everywhere and nowhere*, Speech to the Hong Kong Monetary Authority, Hong Kong, 16 March 2017.

[95] For grandstanding politicians see e.g. House of Commons Department of Work and Pensions Select Committee, *Inquiry into the sale of BHS and the impact on its pension scheme*,

7.3.3   Regulators and Their Self-Belief

One subset of believers are of course legislators and regulators; their purpose is to create or supervise or enforce rules. It would be curious if they did not have a belief in what they do; and it would be unreasonable for them to call for their own dismemberment. But it might not be unreasonable for there to be a sunset clause in their constitution, and for their existence to have to be periodically justified. In the UK the National Audit Office and similar organisations for example conduct an occasional review, but the process may be sub-optimal, especially where it merely invites a regulator to mark its own book, and simply reproduces its comments. Genuine reviews might lead to improved outcomes were they to include a case for both the prosecution and for the defence.[96]

One alternative might be for the chairman of the regulator to sign a certificate every so often, maybe annually, confirming his belief that the organisation should continue, and that there is no alternative (perhaps after he has retired), or that its purpose and function have become otiose. In 2014, the former UK Financial Conduct Authority reviewed 17 investment managers and 13 brokers and found only 2 were operating at the level the FCA expected.[97] It could be argued be that the firms were such that they should have been closed down, or that the expectations were excessive – either way, either the carrying out of the survey was pointless, or the work of the regulator was ineffective, and the FCA should have felt empowered to say so.

Thus it might also be made inappropriate for regulators to articulate a justification for their own continued existence, especially where they are a creature of statute. Tracey McDermott, an interim chief executive of the former UK financial services regulator, the Financial Services Authority, spoke at the City of London's Lord Mayor's Banquet in 2015 responding to industry complaints about excessive regulation. She argued[98] that

First Report of the Work and Pensions Committee and Fourth Report of the Business, Innovation and Skills Committee of Session 2016–17, HC 54 25 July 2016 under the chairmanship of Frank Field. See also many reports of the Public Accounts Committee of the House of Commons during the 2010–2015 UK government under the chairmanship of Margaret Hodge for grandstanding in action.

96 E.g. National Audit Office, *The Pensions Regulator: progress in establishing its new regulatory approach*, HC 1035, 26 October 2007.

97 Steve Johnson, *Are money changers now welcome?*, Financial Times, 14 July 2014.

98 Tracey McDermott, *The rapidity of change*, Speech to the Lord Mayor's Banquet, 22 October 2015; see also e.g. The Pensions Regulator Press Releases 2016: '*The Pensions Regulator is successful in legal challenge*', Ref: PN16–02, Tuesday 12 January 2016 where it is not possible to discover that the Regulator actually lost its case.

while the car industry objected to the European New Car assessment programme requiring improved emission standards, saying that the four-star
objective in 1997 was so severe that no car would ever be able to achieve
four stars, by 2001 the first five-star car was produced. Her example was
intended to show that regulation resulted in benefits not otherwise available or attainable.

Her views were not universally accepted; one commentator responded
in turn that anyone who wants to buy a new car understands that part of
the price goes to sales and marketing, and that the salesman is not advising
him to buy a car sold by another manufacturer or one which is better for
him and his family than a sports model:

> If you sought someone with wider knowledge – preferably of every car in
> the world you could possibly buy – they would spend a lot of time filling
> in forms to establish that you really would not be happier going by bus
> and then charge you at least £500 for their time . . . and it is the same in
> financial services: the vast majority of people who need advice are unable
> to get it at what seems a reasonable fee. The companies which could provide
> something which would be better than nothing are effectively barred from
> doing so. And the professional advisers only want to deal with people with
> a lot of money – £100,000 or more to invest – because only then do their
> charges seem worth it.[99]

Self-doubt and self-examination might need to be part of the armoury
maintained by regulators in future. It might be sensible for them to argue
against themselves, perhaps through the medium of film, rather in the
manner of a movie which was intended as a paean to the triumphs of lawmaking and which described the passage of the European Union's General Data Protection Regulation.[100] They will need to be cautious; the film
could be seen also as a story of the pointlessness of a very complicated law.
It was never explained for example in the film what was the particular evil

---

[99] Anthony Hilton, *Pension knowledge needs to go up a gear*, Evening Standard, 28 October
2015.

[100] *Democracy: Im rausch der daten*, directed by David Bernet, 2016 (available on DVD); Regulation (EU) 2016/679 of the European Parliament and of the Council of 27 April 2016
on the protection of natural persons with regard to the processing of personal data and
on the free movement of such data and repealing Directive 95/46/EC (General Data Protection Directive), OJ Vol 59 L119/1 4 May 2016. See also Nicola Newson, *Proposal for
government departments to cease devising new legislation for a period of time and concentrate on sound administration*, House of Lords, Library, In Focus, 5 August 2016. It cites
Lord Framlingham (formerly Michael Lord, perhaps a case of nominative determinism)
who noted that during his 27 years as an MP 33 education acts, 35 health acts and 100
criminal justice acts were passed which he described as a 'veritable torrent of legislation
that produced little or no benefit to anyone'.

that the law was intended to counter, nor what the cost of its application would be. In some ways it should be shown to all lawmakers to illustrate when law should not be made, and provided with a more sceptical commentary.

Finally regulators need to be honest about the true cost of regulation. Such costs are hard to evaluate, but they are probably best not evaluated by themselves.

7.3.4 Understanding There Might Be Alternatives to Regulation

It is part of standard guidance to regulators (and in theory to legislators) that they should consider alternatives to regulation,[101] and that legislation or regulation should always be a last resort. So far however there seems little to encourage regulators to adopt alternatives, and they themselves are not always given powers to use their discretion, or are discouraged from using it. For example, a chairman of trustees of a UK defined contribution pension fund is required to sign a statement each year stating that he has amongst other things pursued 'value for money' objectives in the running of the scheme, for breach of which there is a compulsory fine imposed by statutory instrument.[102] The fine is mandatory, although the regulator has discretion in levying the amount between certain limits. But there is no discretion to dispense with levying a fine, even though the Director of Public Prosecutions has discretion not to prosecute for much more serious offences in cases of assisted suicide. A coffee and a chat for an offending chairman might be more sensible and cost-effective – and bring about a difference in attitude by the regulated. Nor is it clear in this example who or what would suffer as a consequence of any breach; the offence is not 'failing to do the best deal for fund members', but for failing to make a tick box declaration.[103]

---

[101] *The Regulators' Code*, Department for Business Innovation and Skills, April 2014; Legislative and Regulatory Reform Act 2006 s21.

[102] The Occupational Pensions Schemes (Charges and Governance) Regulations 2015 SI 2015 No 0879 reg 28.

[103] The Pensions Regulator, *Compliance and enforcement policy for occupational schemes providing money purchase benefits*, July 2016; The Pensions Regulator, *Prosecution Policy*. June 2016; The Pensions Regulator, *Regulatory intervention report issued under s89 of the Pensions Act 2004 in relation to the trustee of Precision Carbide Tools Limited Pension and Life Assurance Scheme, the Comshare Retirement and Death Benefits Plan and the EBC Pension Scheme*, August 2016; The Pensions Regulator, *TPR issues maximum chair's statement fine for professional trustees*, PN16–44, Press release, 17 August 2016; *Compliance and enforcement policy for occupational pension schemes providing money purchase benefits*, The Pensions Regulator, July 2016.

Similarly, the Independent Parliamentary Standards Authority[104] was established following a parliamentary expenses scandal of 2008–2010, where MP's with some official encouragement had incurred additional expenses in lieu of salary increases. The total excess expenditure over five years amounted to £2.5M; the annual cost of running IPSA created to reduce such over-spending was around £6.3M, i.e. around £35M over five years. £35M might have been saved by alternative methods, for example by trusting MPs to do the right thing, removing all rules but one, that rule being a provision that no expenses would be reimbursed unless notified on the MP's website. It would have been self-policing, supervised by officious members of the public, and involving virtually no cost. Transparency could have been a sensible alternative to regulation, would have reduced the civil service headcount and avoided the spending of around £6M a year to monitor around £30M a year of expenses. It is a prime example of creating regulation and a regulator, neither of which would have been needed had there been a modicum of common sense – and modest lateral thinking.[105]

7.3.5   Training in Regulatory Scepticism

Regulators understandably believe that without their presence and intervention, consumers would be prey to white-collar bandits. Such bandits are of course active, but in practice regulators have a poor track record in anticipatory prevention – and it presupposes a jaundiced view of human nature. That supposition may be flawed; as David Hume observed:

> Political writers have established it as a maxim, that in contriving any system of government . . . every man ought to be supposed to be a *knave* and to have no other end, in all his actions, than his private interest. By this interest we must govern him, and, by means of it, make him, notwithstanding is insatiable avarice and ambition, cooperate to public good.
>
>   . . . It is, therefore, a just *political* maxim, that every man must be supposed a knave: Though at the same time, it appears somewhat strange, that a maxim should be true in *politics*, which is false in *fact*.[106]

One of the many objections to regulatory behaviour is the tone they frequently adopt; i.e. that the world is full of perps. In fact, the banking crisis

---

[104] Parliamentarystandards.org.uk; *IPSA Annual Accounts and Report 2013/14*.

[105] See e.g. C. Parker, *The compliance trap: the moral message in responsive regulatory enforcement*, [2006] 49(3) Law & Society Review 591.

[106] David Hume, Essays: *Moral, Political and Literary*, 1742, cited in Samuel Bowles, *The Moral Economy*, Yale, University Press, 2016, on which much of this section is based.

and other financial scandals notwithstanding, the world is mostly full of good people inadequately trying to do their best.[107]

7.3.6   Exploring Alternatives to Regulation

Alternatives to regulation, or using simple regulation coupled with other solutions, have a good track record. Some of them are mentioned below; they include codes, insurance or simply the proper application of existing rules.[108]

7.3.7   Insurance

Private insurance has long been used as an alternative to regulatory insurance; although using regulation to implement it. Its advantage is that it uses competition to manage the costs and complexity of protecting people. In the UK there is for example compulsory motor insurance, and obligatory employers' liability insurance to protect those injured in motor accidents and employment accidents – but it is privately provided, with competition on service and cost. In some cases if insurance is not available, e.g. professional indemnity insurance for small firms of solicitors, or for younger drivers except at very high price, the activity simply cannot take

---

[107] Niall Ferguson suggested in one of his Reith Lectures that the banking crisis was caused by regulation, not in spite of it: 'Once again, however, the difference between the natural world and the financial world is the role of regulation. Regulation is supposed to reduce the number and size of financial forest fires. And yet, as we have seen, it can quite easily have the opposite effect. This is because the political process is itself somewhat complex. Regulatory bodies can be captured by those whom they are supposed to be regulating; not least by the prospect of well-paid jobs should the gamekeepers turn poachers. They can also be captured in other ways – for example, by their reliance on the entities they regulate for the very data they need to do their work... But the regulation we are contemplating today does the very opposite: because of its very complexity – and often self-contradictory objectives – it is pro-fragile... Over-complicated regulation can indeed be the disease of which it purports to be the cure. Just as the planners of the old Soviet system could never hope to direct a modern economy in all its complexity, for reasons long ago explained by Friedrich Hayek and Janos Kornai, so the regulators of the post-crisis world are doomed to fail in their efforts to make the global financial system crisis-free. They can never know enough to manage such a complex system. They will only ever learn from the last crisis how to make the next one. Is there an alternative? I believe there is. But I believe we need to go back to the time of Darwin to find it.' Lecture 2, *The Darwinian Economy*, BBC, 2012:

[108] National Audit Office, *Using alternatives to regulation to achieve policy objectives*, 30 June 2014; see also National Audit Office, *Controls on regulation*, 28 September 2012 and National Audit Office, *Regulatory Reform*, 15 October 2010.

place. It may be unfair to younger drivers, or sole practitioners but public policy accepts that. And the state does not involve itself in rate-setting. For usually political rather than pragmatic reasons some insurance is state-based: national insurance or social security in many countries provides health and pensions through the state; and the Pensions Protection Fund in the UK guarantees to a limited extent the pensions of people in company defined benefit pension schemes. It involves complicated levies, the management of a very large pool of assets, and complex and difficult regulation. Other countries (Sweden and Germany) operate similar forms of insurer (in Sweden run as a mutual at very low cost) which is simpler, easier and very much cheaper. Private insurance can reduce the need for voluminous regulation and an expensive bureaucracy.[109]

7.3.8 Disclosure

Transparency and disclosure can be more attractive than imposing a system of control, since it can improve behaviour through peer pressure rather than policemen. In company law in the UK, for example, directors of companies must within limits disclose their remuneration, rather than have limits on remuneration imposed. The idea is that once shareholders find out about excess remuneration they will impose controls on management. In practice it seems to have been of limited success; curiously it has been argued that public disclosure has forced up remuneration levels, as each company attempts to place its executives in the top quartile (this seems to apply less to junior staff).[110]

One of the arguments for conventional regulation is to improve the balance of information asymmetry between provider and consumer. That argument is slightly less forceful than it used to be. While such asymmetry will rarely be completely eradicated, development of the virtually universally available internet suggests that such asymmetries are no longer so pronounced. Product rating systems with all their imperfections on websites such as Amazon may be more cost-effective and practical than regulation, and can improve the bargaining power and information available to

---

[109] Sole legal practitioners in the UK are unable to practice without insurance; they now find it all but impossible to find cover because they are such high risk (they steal or misapply money more often than lawyers in larger firms); but even solicitors who restrict themselves to low risk work are increasingly unable to find insurance at a sensible price. Atticus Finch would have been unable to represent Tom Robinson had he been subject to UK professional insurance rules.

[110] Companies Act 2006 s420.

consumers. Internet systems may not benefit consumers who are unfamiliar with them, but in many cases it is probably preferable than regulation. It is not itself an unblemished solution; the public might be uncomfortable with knowing that airlines were not inspected but simply had their safety records published on the net.

7.3.9   Improving Atmosphere and Tone

Peer pressure through imposing or encouraging social norms can be effective. Obesity for example, appears to be a growing problem across the world, the abuse of food reflecting in some ways the historic abuse of alcohol. Solutions similar to those applicable to alcohol have been suggested (special taxes on fizzy drinks for example).[111] But it might not be necessary; alcohol consumption amongst students fell around a third in the 2010s, without a need to resort to legislation.[112] It simply became less acceptable to be drunk. Rules requiring Mars Bars to be sold in plain packaging have been proposed in Australia, as have special taxes on sugared carbonated drinks in the USA and UK.[113] But in time sugar consumption might simply be changed by altering public acceptability of sugar-added foods. Similarly legally imposed charges on the use of plastic bags in supermarkets have in fact had a beneficial impact, although it might have been possible to reduce their use without the need for legislation.[114] Similarly,

---

[111] Sarah Neville and Jim Pickard, *UK tax on sugary drinks is 'nannying' and 'impractical'*, Financial Times, 17 March 2016.

[112] Student drinking dropped by a third between 2005 and 2013, Health and Social Care Information Centre, *Statistics on alcohol, England 2015*, National Statistics, 25 June 2015, p5.

[113] Christopher Snowdon, *Plain confectionery packaging a heavy-handed response to health concerns*, Confectionery News, 21 July 2016, www.confectionerynews.com/Regulation-Safety/Comment-Plain-candy-packaging-a-harsh-response-to-health-concerns.

[114] See e.g. Rebecca Smit, *Tesco to end sales of 5p carrier bags*, Guardian, 7 August 2017; cf. *Kenya brings in world's toughest plastic bag ban*, Guardian 28 August 2017; for the Kenyan legislation see Kenya Gazette Notice No 2356 (Feb 28 2017), 119:31 and Kenya Gazette (Special Issue) (Mar 14 2017), at 1077. The ban applies to two categories of bags: the carrier bag, a 'bag constructed with handles, and with or without gussets,' and the flat bag, a 'bag constructed without handles, and with or without gussets.' Any person who contravenes against any provision of this Act or of regulations made thereunder for which no other penalty is specifically provided is liable, upon conviction, to imprisonment for a term of not less than one year but not more than four years, or to a fine of not less than two million shillings [about US$19,417] but not more than four million shillings [about US$38,835], or to both such fine and imprisonment[,] or to both such fine and imprisonment, Environmental Management and Co-ordination Act, No. 8 of 1999, § 144 (Jan 14, 2000).

there has been a significant reduction in under-age mothers in the UK,[115] without regulation (it also having been found that deploying electronic babies ['Virtual Infant Parenting'] can have a counter-intuitive impact).[116] On the other hand legislation can indeed change public behaviour, as has happened with anti-smoking legislation throughout the world, although it is not possible to test whether it would have changed in any event.

7.3.10   Application of Existing Rules

One curiosity of the regulatory framework is the propensity of government to introduce new legislation when there is perfectly adequate existing legislation – or legislation which could simply be tweaked a little. Using existing law may require better administration or enforcement, and may look less dynamic to the press and public, but can be simpler and cheaper. In the 2010s in the UK around seven anti-terrorist laws were passed, each seemingly having little or no impact on the degree of terrorism. What may simply have been needed was some minor reform (or none at all) of laws prohibiting incitement to violence – and a larger intelligence budget.[117] It took many years to imprison Anjem Choudry, a Muslim cleric and former solicitor who preached in favour of a Caliphate in the UK, using laws against promotion of the Islamic State.[118] Whether there is a benefit to society at large by locking up activists simply for expressing their views however generally abhorrent they may be, in the company of troubled and impressionable individuals is unclear. Anti-terrorism laws in the UK and elsewhere are a self-evident example of superfluous legislation, regardless of the uncomfortable undertones of *Minority Report* principles being involved.[119]

Similarly a change in the law relating to 'zombie knives' in the UK seems to have suffered from the same problem that the law against narcotics had; by being prescriptive, it did not make illegitimate the possession or sale of

---

[115] *Under 18 conception rate in England continues to fall*, Public Health England, Press release, 24 February 2015.

[116] Under-age mothers and baby infant simulators: Dr Sally Brinkman et al., *Efficacy of infant simulator programmes to prevent teenage pregnancy: a school-based cluster randomised controlled trial in Western Australia*, The Lancet, 25 August 2016.

[117] Although not too much, see G. K. Chesterton, *The Man Who Was Thursday*, 1908.

[118] Terrorism Act 2000, s12 (inviting support for a proscribed organisation).

[119] *Minority Report* was a film based on a story by Philip K. Dick where the authorities are empowered to imprison those who would otherwise commit a crime. It was intended as a satire rather than a blueprint.

other equally objectionable objects.[120] Home Office officials or politicians did not seem to consider the absurdity of the regulation referring to

> (s) the weapon sometimes known as 'zombie knife', 'zombie killer knife' or zombie slayer knife' being a blade with
>
>> (i) a cutting edge
>> (ii) a serrated edge and
>> (iii) image or words (whether on the blade or handle) that suggests that it is to be used for the purposes of violence,

whilst allowing the sale of a weapon without wording, but just as liable to kill. Maybe it would have been simpler just to outlaw all wording which encourages violence, with the ancillary benefit that there would be no further Steven Seagal or *Terminator* films.

7.3.11 Accepting and Even Encouraging Conflicts of Interest

In recent years there has been a growing effort by regulators against conflicts of interest, with perhaps unintended consequences. Some conflicts of interest are indeed unmanageable; where they are, it may be sensible to make them illegal. But some are actually beneficial and might even be encouraged. For example, having a finance director on the board of a company's pension scheme allows the trustees to see both sides of the argument when it comes to funding the scheme and balancing the interests of members and shareholders. In political life, providing everyone knows about any conflicts of interest in the planning permission (zoning) process, it is useful for councillors to know about their areas or even live in them. Politicians face the same challenges; but transparency is usually regarded as the best fumigant. Any control of conflicts needs to distinguish between the two kinds of conflict. Some conflicts have always been improper, and the courts have managed the issue; it rarely requires a regulator to make the point, and impose several pages of rules – which in some cases paradoxically authorise behaviour which conventional law would have deemed unacceptable.[121]

---

[120] Criminal Justice Act 1988 (Offensive Weapons) (Amendment) Regulations 2016 SI 2016 No 0803 amending SI 1988 No 2019, SI 2002 No 1668, SI 2004 No 1271 and SI 2008 No 0973.

[121] *Armstrong v Jackson* [1917] 2 KB 822 per Sir Henry McCardie; see John Kay, 'Trust me, I am a financial adviser' is not enough, Financial Times, 7 July 2014.

7.3.12   Privatising Regulators and Introducing Competition in Regulation

One option is to privatise regulators, with a time-limited franchise, to avoid in part the bureaucratic behaviour that happens in public regulatory institutions and to diminish moral hazard. It may seem counter-intuitive to have a private body with a licence to regulate, but it might offer advantages, not least paradoxically in improved governance.[122]

Public regulation in some areas seems to have become extreme. In 2011 financial services companies worldwide, for example, were being affected with, on average, 60 regulatory changes every working day, a figure which is probably higher now. In the 12 months to November 2011 there were 14,215 changes.[123] The cost to industry (and thence to the consumer) is immense; one company alone in 2014 hired an additional 3000 compliance officers to cope. The cost is not simply the cost of the hiring; each compliance officer causes the innovative energy of the employer to diminish and adds internal management and compliance expense. Whilst good behaviour in financial services is essential, the question which is not asked by the regulatory community is: is the benefit worth the cost? In other words might it not be preferable to accept there will always be failures in certain areas, and to accept and manage them rather than expend time and treasure in avoiding them.[124]

---

[122] See J. Blundell and C. Robinson, *Regulation without the state: the debate continues*, Readings 52, Institute of Economic Affairs. The UK Pensions Regulator failed to perceive the irony in enforcing its practice of forbidding even minor conflicts of interest (even where a pension fund director was elected by its membership) when its own internal conflicts (to balance the interests of (1) the plan sponsor, (2) plan membership and trustees, and (3) the quasi-state guarantor (the Pension Protection Fund) were profound and more serious.

[123] Brooke Masters, *Financial sector hit by flood of regulation*, Financial Times, 9 December 2011; Thomson Reuters, Governance Risk and Compliance Unit, 2012; Rachel Louise Ensign, *Lenders bolster risk and compliance staff*, Wall Street Journal, 4 May 2014; Jo Mont, *JP Morgan outlines compliance overhaul*, Compliance Week, 22 December 2014: 'JP Morgan will have hired more than 9,500 full-time equivalent employees focussed on financial crime-related matters, a more than 300 per cent increase since 2012'.

[124] See e.g. the pointlessness of the Pensions Regulator and Financial Conduct Authority in trying to prevent individuals making foolish decisions when the courts insist on their freedom to do so, see *Hughes v Royal London*, [2016] 014 PBLR (010); [2016] EWHC 319 (Ch) (United Kingdom: England and Wales: High Court: Chancery Division, 2016 February 19 (Pensions liberation – Transfers – Right to transfer – Whether transfer to occupational pension scheme involves need to be employed by new plan sponsor – Pensions Ombudsman – Appeal.))

Andy Haldane, the Chief Economist of the Bank of England suggested that there have been around 60,000 pages of financial services regulation in the European Union, and around 32,000 expected in the US, and that it is impossible for any human to understand all this or to put it into context.[125] Experience in drafting legislation in the past (e.g. the private drafting of the Sale of Goods Act or the Partnership Act) has been very successful – and resulted in very short and understandable legislation. Privatisation is not a panacea – private consultants can also make simple things more complicated. But private drafting can take away some of the tendency towards prolixity that affects most regulators. And state regulators have had their own failures; France for example 'lacks the moral authority [to regulate] ... Not only did one of its biggest banks egregiously violate international norms by doing business with Sudan and other unsavoury regimes. The government also failed to detect the violation or, worse, did not try'.[126]

Regulators argue that their position should be a monopoly, to avoid a race to the bottom as regulators compete for business. In fact competition seems invariably beneficial, and more rigorous regulators might find they attract business rather than the opposite. There are current examples of competition in the regulation of the legal profession which indicate that there are benefits to competition in regulation.

7.3.13   Emphasise Caveat Emptor/Consumer Responsibility

Caveat emptor has been diminishing as a factor in the relationships between buyer and seller for over a hundred years. It was never a pure concept, and industrialisation made it hard for consumers to inspect the sardine in the tin rather than the cod on the fishmonger's slab. In financial services, for example, it has been argued that the asymmetry of information, where the provider knows much more than the consumer, means that added protection is inevitable, and reverse the usual burden of proof.

The debate has been live for many years: does a consumer have a degree of responsibility so as to avoid the suggestion of financial arbitrage; if the consumer gets it right he reaps the gains; if it goes wrong, he can

---

[125] Andy Haldane, *Turning the Red Tape Tide*, Bank of England, Speech to Financial Law Review Dinner, 10 April 2013.

[126] Barry Eichengreen, *France lacks the moral authority to depose the dollar*, 9 July 2014.

always sue. One much criticised Chairman of a financial services regulator reviewed the position:[127]

> Let me start by explaining why I think we need to make progress in our thinking on these issues. I start with an approach to regulation of any market activity with the belief that the best results – for both customers and providers of goods and services – are obtained by markets which work efficiently, not by regulation; that when markets do not operate efficiently, the first effort should be to improve their efficiency rather than to regulate them; and that regulation should be used only when there is both market failure and the prospect that regulatory intervention will produce benefits which outweigh the costs of that regulation. I would add that it is important to concentrate on the efficiency and effectiveness of any market, not on the existence of that near-myth, 'the perfect market'. There are many effective markets which are clearly not perfect.

For purchasers who only buy a product infrequently, where the outcome is not known for many years, and where the risks involved are imperfectly understood, it is understandable that there may be an imbalance of bargaining power. But the asymmetry of information, or at least experience, is mitigated nowadays by the advent of the internet. Occasionally regulators reflect that customers might need to have 'responsibilities' as well as rights, but shy away from that for obvious reasons. Nonetheless, it is probably time for ombudsmen and others to establish a form of customer obligation, simply to make the system fairer to both parties.

7.3.14 Encouraging Voluntary Standards

> For a regulator, the answer to every regulatory problem is another regulation.[128]

Many professions until recently were self-governing. Such supervision was imperfect in many ways, but it was (relatively) cheap – and no worse than and sometimes very much better than the current arrangements. Recent studies suggest that a return to voluntary standards might be adequate and proportionate, certainly in financial services. A voluntary standards market is a 'commercial system in which actual and potential

---

[127] Callum McCarthy, Chairman of the Financial Services Authority, *What does caveat emptor mean in the retail market for financial services?*, Speech to the Financial Services Forum, 9 February 2006.

[128] Dr Andrew Hilton, Director, Centre for the Study of Financial Innovation, in Stephen Moss, *An outsider's guide to the City of London*, The Guardian, 27 May 2014.

buyers and suppliers of products and services rely on conformity assessments.' Conformity assessments are carried out against standards, and can consist of self-certification, second-party and third-party independent verification and certification. And they can bridge unregulated and regulated markets.[129]

There are tens of thousands of standards in many areas of human activity (around 1000 alone for food in the 20,000 International Standards Organisation list), not to mention individual country and EU lists, and they are enforced as far as they need to be enforced by peer pressure, by commercial pressures, by corporate pride, and by insurance companies who will require compliance with standards before they provide their cover at a sensible price. This does not prevent breaches – but breaches continue even where companies are formally regulated. The difference nowadays is that informal regulation can operate effectively since the internet allows buyers of services to find out more about an organisation than they could before. Cowboys will always exist: regulation can hardly control them. But where everyone in the world can metaphorically chat over the garden fence, it is harder for them to thrive.

7.3.15   Promoting Public Understanding, Management and Measurement of Risk

There has been a chair in the public understanding of risk at Cambridge University since 2007. It is part of its statistical laboratory, but although much of its work is technical, its inaugural professor has devoted much of his time to explaining risk issues to the public. Public understanding is poor in matters of medical risks, for example, and most members of the public find it difficult to estimate whether other risks should be contained by legal prescription. Journalists in particular, especially in what remains of the popular press, might welcome training in such understanding, although it might make for less amusing headlines.[130]

---

[129] *Backing market forces: how to make voluntary standards markets work for financial services regulation*, Chartered Institute for Securities and Investment and Long Finance, November 2013.

[130] The Winton Professorship of the Public Understanding of Risk is a professorship within the Statistical Laboratory of the University of Cambridge. It was funded by a grant of £3.3m from the Winton Charitable Foundation, established on the basis of a fortune derived from asset management. It is the only professorship of its type in the United Kingdom, possibly in the world. It promotes an associated internet-based programme devoted to understanding uncertainty (http://understandinguncertainty.org). See lectures by Professor David

The costs of failure to understand risk have been explored in the context of religious regulation:[131]

> There is no word I know of in the Bible for 'risk'. Modern Hebrew uses the word 'Sakanah', which really means 'danger'. 'Risk' in modern usage can also mean opportunity and healthy ability to go beyond the boundaries in a positive way. The opposite of risk . . . is to play it safe.
>
> When a religion, or any legal system for that matter, plays things safe, it becomes static and inhumane. We can all agree that the humane quality is admired, in theory. At the same time, most conservative religions and legal systems alike claim that they are in no way flexible, changeable, or evolutionary. But I want to extol risk. It is in vogue in economics, social interaction, and of course military tactics . . .
>
> The Biblical (and Hammurabi's) 'an eye for an eye and a tooth for a tooth and a bruise for a bruise, etc' appears to be a very specific standard of retribution. Yet in the text, on either side of its first appearance in the Book of Exodus, we have laws about financial compensation, of different types of assessment of damages that do not follow the principle literally. How would a judge working under a literal interpretation take a tooth from a toothless man who had just knocked out the tooth of someone with a mouthful of teeth? Or, . . . would it be fair and just to take away the eye of a one-eyed man rendering him completely blind as fair compensation for putting out the eye of a man with two?
>
> In other words, even a strict legal system is open to interpretation. Once there are options there are decisions, and once there are decisions there are risks and opportunities to take risks.

This is one of the arguments for supporting a move towards encouraging the judiciary to move more towards applying the principles of equity than the strict rigours of legislation.[132]

Risk management, in this context, is sometimes defined as governmental interference with market or social processes to control potential adverse consequences to health.[133] Governments see it as part of their role to manage such risks for those who cannot manage it for themselves, as in the case of dangerous dogs, or genetically modified foods, or bovine spongiform encephalopathy. Such intervention can lead occasionally to such absurdities as the fact that regulatory systems in Canada permit

---

Spiegelhalter, especially *Communicating risk and uncertainty*, Spring Lecture, Institute of Actuaries, 2016, available on YouTube, which inter alia deals with *Daily Mail* issues.

[131] Jeremy Rosen, *Religious risk*, 25 February 2016, blog.

[132] See Chapter 5, 'Conclusions'.

[133] Christopher Hood et al., *The Government of Risk*, Oxford University Press, 2001, p3.

cyclamates but ban saccharin, while just across the border the US bans cyclamates and permits the use of saccharin.[134]

The table on the next page gives some indication of risk measures; the odds are statistical averages over the entire US population (2013) and do not necessarily reflect the chances of death for a particular person from a particular external cause. Odds of dying are affected by an individual's activities, occupation, and where he or she lives and drives, among other things.

If the odds of dying from all possible causes are 1 in 1, Table 7.2 shows the lifetime odds of death for selected causes, from most likely to least.

It seems possible therefore that as well as a Regulatory Impact Assessment, there should be a comparative risk analysis attached to new legislation. Measuring risk is subject to the same measurement challenges as RIA's but it might encourage legislators and regulators to justify the introduction of new rules on the basis of evidence rather than sentiment. Such a policy might not have dealt with public pressures to legislate in the case of the Soham murders and the establishment of the Disclosure and Barring Service (which went through several incarnations) and the establishment of the post–Harold Shipman requirements applied to doctors, but it might calm the public discourse.[135]

7.3.16   Ethical Conduct by Lobbyists (and Journalists)

Lobbyists are already in some jurisdictions under a statutory obligation to be registered; but neither they, nor campaign groups, seem to have an obligation to present a balanced case when arguing their position. It should perhaps become a badge of pride that whilst presenting the reason for a change in the law (or even no change), their case should also state the (sensibly calculated) cost to the community, and whether it is proportionate. An example might be whether the state health service should provide certain cancer drugs, where any improvement might be in the order of a few months' extra life (of uncertain quality) but where the costs may

---

[134] Kirstin Shrader-Frechette, *Risk and rationality*, Berkeley, University of California Press, 991 p100.

[135] See e.g. the Safeguarding Vulnerable Groups Act 2006, following a procession of similar legislation, and accompanying regulations, reflecting the policy dilemma of protecting children and others with believing in the need to trust, both to reduce costs, and to encourage social participation. It might be said that logicality has been sacrificed to populism. A critique of Basel II, the international bank and financial services regulations developed following the financial crisis of 2008, suggests that risk measurement is virtually impossible, Mark Buchanan, *Risky business as usual*, New Scientist, 6 August 2016; Jon Danielsson and Chen Zhou, *Why is risk so hard to measure?*, June 2016 on www.riskresearch.org.

Table 7.2 *What are the odds of dying from...?*

Cause of death	Odds of dying
Heart disease and cancer	1 in 7
Chronic lower respiratory disease	1 in 27
Intentional self-harm	1 in 97
Unintentional poisoning by and exposure to noxious substances	1 in 103
Motor vehicle crash	1 in 113
Fall	1 in 133
Assault by firearm	1 in 358
Pedestrian incident	1 in 672
Motorcycle rider incident	1 in 948
Unintentional drowning and submersion	1 in 1183
Exposure to fire, flames or smoke	1 in 1454
Choking from inhalation and ingestion of food	1 in 3408
Pedacyclist incident	1 in 4337
Firearms discharge	1 in 7944
Air and space transport incidents	1 in 9737
Exposure to excessive natural heat	1 in 10,784
Exposure to electric current, radiation, temperature and pressure	1 in 14,695
Contact with sharp objects	1 in 30,860
Cataclysmic storm	1 in 63,679
Contact with hornets, wasps and bees	1 in 64,706
Contact with heat and hot substances	1 in 69,169
Legal execution	1 in 111,439
Being bitten or struck by a dog	1 in 114,622
Lightning strike	1 in 174,426

Note: Deaths are classified on the basis of the 10th revision of the World Health Organization's *The International Classification of Diseases*. For additional mortality figures and estimated one-year and lifetime odds, see *Injury Facts* 2016 Edition, pp. 40–43. The table looks slightly odd to UK eyes; for example, there is a higher chance of being legally executed than of being bitten by a dog in the US.

Source: National Safety Council (*Injury Facts 2016*, NSC, Itasca, IL, 2016) estimates based on data from National Center for Health Statistics–Mortality Data for 2013, as compiled from data provided by the 57 vital statistics jurisdictions through the Vital Statistics Cooperative Program.

be in the tens of thousands. In the UK the National Institute for Health and Care Excellence (NICE) is designed to look at the cost-effectiveness of drugs,[136] and ease the political pressure on government to make expensive drugs available to the public. Even with the existence and support of NICE government seem unable to overcome public pressure to arbitrarily provide expensive drugs which take away resources from other healthcare opportunities;[137] in 2013 for example the government felt obliged to find another £200M from taxpayers to meet such pressure. Adherents for more spending in one area should be required to acknowledge that there are finite resources, and indicate the source of funding for their suggestions. In addition, they should be honour bound to present a balanced scorecard, since few changes are without some adverse or unintended or collateral consequences. It would help to control what has been called 'the rise of vetocracy'.[138] Imposing or even developing a code for journalists might however prove a step too far.[139]

7.4   Conclusion: Professionalisation and Mindsets

The governor of California is jogging with his dog along a nature trail. A coyote jumps out and attacks the governor's dog, then bites the governor. The governor starts to intervene, but reflects upon the movie Bambi and then realizes he should stop because the coyote is only doing what is natural.

He calls animal control. Animal control captures the coyote and bills the state $200 for testing it for diseases and $500 for relocating it. He calls a veterinarian. The vet collects the dead dog and bills the state $200 for testing it for diseases. The governor goes to the hospital and spends $3,500 getting checked for diseases from the coyote and getting his bite wound bandaged.

The running trail gets shut down for six months while the California Fish and Game Department conducts a $100,000 survey to make sure the area is now free of dangerous animals. The governor spends $50,000 in state funds implementing a 'coyote awareness program' for residents of the

---

[136] See www.nice.org.uk/guidance.

[137] See e.g. *The Cancer Drugs Fund: Guidance to support operation of the Caner Drugs Fund in 2012–13*, Department of Health, 2012.

[138] Francis Fukuyama, *America in decay: the sources of political dysfunction*, [2014] (09) Foreign Affairs 5. It contains a case study of the emasculation of the Forestry Service in the US by well-meaning lobbyists.

[139] There is a UK National Union of Journalists' *Code of Conduct*, and US Society of Professional Journalists *Code of Ethics*, but not much evidence of sanction for breach or even impact on behaviour, see *Daily Mail* seriatim.

area. The Legislature spends $2 million to study how to better treat rabies and how to permanently eradicate the disease throughout the world.

The governor's security agent is fired for not stopping the attack. The state spends $150,000 to hire and train a new agent with additional special training, re: the nature of coyotes. People for the Ethical Treatment of Animals (PETA) protests the coyote's relocation and files a $5 million suit against the state.

The governor of Texas is jogging with his dog along a nature trail. A coyote jumps out and tries to attack him and his dog. The governor shoots the coyote with his state-issued pistol and keeps jogging.

The governor spent 50 cents on a .380-caliber, hollow-point cartridge. Buzzards ate the dead coyote.

And that, my friends, is why California is broke and Texas is not.[140]

7.4.1   Introduction

A bus-driver needs a public service vehicle licence, because if untested he puts 50 passengers and a hundred pedestrians at risk of death or injury. A doctor needs a licence because he might otherwise harm patients. In some jurisdictions even flower arrangers and cosmeticians require licences. And as well as requirements for training and qualification, many professions and occupations also adopt ethical codes. But an MP or a government minister or a regulator can arrive wet behind the ears, or from a think tank, or from another regulator (having been inculcated with regulatory biases), and vote on or implement legislation without so much as a diploma or reading a book on the principles of regulation or a couple of hours training at night school. He or she can affect the lives of millions and determine the application of billions of pounds, dollars or euros. And the costs to the economy of poor or excess regulation can be substantial and adversely affect the living standards of everyone.[141]

The previous chapter has shown that previous attempts to subdue the regulatory state even with the support of governments themselves have failed. Whilst it would be reasonable to continue some of those efforts, it may be that one or two additional ones would make them more

---

[140] Richard Fisher, President and CEO, Federal Reserve Bank of Dallas, *The United States is not Europe and Texas ain't France: America as the thoroughbred economy*, Speech to the Cato Institute, 10 October 2010.

[141] The costs of regulation have been explored in the United States much more than in other jurisdictions, see e.g. Bentley Coffey, Patrick A. McLaughlin and Pietro Peretto, *The cumulative cost of regulations*, Mercatus Centre, George Mason University, Working Paper, April 2016, Washington, US. It concluded that if regulation had been held steady since 1980, the US economy would have been around 25 per cent greater by 2012.

effective, particularly if they involved attempts to change the mindset of those involved in rule making.

Changing mindsets can take time, but any reform without that will struggle to succeed. Changing mindsets will involve legislators and regulators undergoing training and possibly qualification before being able to enter into the business, profession or vocation of governing – and adhering to codes or principles. Such pre-qualification does not for example need to echo some of the absurdities of the US, where auctioneers and barbers need a licence to work,[142] but it does not seem unreasonable that lawmakers should receive some basic training and adhere to fundamental standards. At the very least it might ensure for example that the UK Financial Conduct Authority would abjure anonymous responses to inquiries, and the use of premium-rate phone numbers to call them – and it might possibly create a consumer culture for its lay and professional clients within the regulator. It would also mitigate the silo mentality seen for example by the UK Pension Protection Fund through which pension scheme members are protected by employers, but which regards itself as the protector. So, to change mindsets, and to introduce the elements of most other professions and crafts, there might need to be

- an adherence to a code;
- the swearing of an oath or declaration as to certain principles;
- training and/or qualification through courses, diplomas and degrees; and
- systems of accountability and transparency.

Such arrangements will not prove a panacea or silver bullet; but taken together they may serve to change the mindset over time, especially if accompanied by public pressure to conform to the principles.

These arrangements would need to be implemented in several areas:

- **Reform of the parliamentary process**, so that legislators take individual rather than collective accountability for their decisions, and become trained in alternatives to legislation, regulatory risk assessment, cost-benefit analysis, legislative instructions and drafting, and the theory and practice of lawmaking – and reform their mindset.

---

[142] See *Occupational licenses: a framework for policymakers*, White House, Washington DC, July 2015 ('A quarter of US workers now require a licence to do their jobs. The share of works licensed at State level has risen five-fold since the 1950's'); Stephen Slivinski. *Bootstraps Tangles in Red Tape: How Occupational Licensing Hinders Low-Income Entrepreneurship* Goldwater Institute, 2015, https://goldwater-media.s3.amazonaws.com/cms_page_media/2015/4/15/OccLicensingKauffman.pdf. And see http://regdata.org/.

- **Reform of regulators**, again so that they are trained in theory and practice of regulation, so that they seek alternatives to regulation; understand the history of government intervention; understand the limits of regulation and understand how to manage the expectations of the press and the public – and reform their mindset.
- **Reform of the judiciary**, judicial systems and professionals in the field, so that they are enfranchised to use discretion, common sense and proportionality, alternative dispute systems and simpler and cheaper access to justice.
- **Establishment of a system of accountability through independent regulatory review** with a power to repeal, and disband laws, regulations and regulators, so that if Parliament wishes to maintain regulation it would need to re-enact it. It would also bring regulators and legislators to account, in the way parliamentary select committees seek to bring government to account other than through the ballot box.

7.4.2   Reform of the Parliamentary Process

To watch Members of Parliament and government ministers trot through the parliamentary buildings to vote on a bill or amendment that they have not read, and probably would not have understood if they had read it, can be dispiriting. There are times when it is sensible for MP's when voting for new law to rely on the advice of whips, government departments, lobbyists and others and the various committees that have examined the texts. But in principle it is not satisfactory, allows the passing of too much, and too complex legislation, and abrogates proper responsibility and accountability. The intervention of select committees can sometimes be valuable, but the absence in such committees of ethical obligations to be fair, to treat witnesses fairly and of any obligation to avoid grandstanding, permits injustice and politically driven law and behaviour that is inappropriate.

It might improve the system immeasurably were MP's to be required to undergo training, perhaps before standing for election, or perhaps once elected but before being allowed to vote on legislation, in order to learn some of the principles of legislation, and of the dangers, ethics and responsibilities that are inherent in the exercise of their powers and duties.

7.4.3   Codes

The advantage of a code is that it is less hard-wired than law; so that it allows for times when it is sensible to break the code and use discretion, without fear of sanction. In some instances codes can have the force of law, witness for example the many codes issued by the UK Pensions Regulator under statute, breach of which may indirectly involve a penalty, or at the least indicate a level of care which if breached could lead to liability.[143] Statutory codes can reverse the burden of proof; most codes, however, are intended not to have legal implications or sanctions for breach – and their advantage is that they can be easily changed from time to time to meet changing circumstances, such as for example a code of practice for victims of crime.[144]

Codes have increasingly been promoted as a form of regulation-light, and over time they can change mindsets. A suitable code might perhaps have changed the mindset of bankers before they fixed LIBOR rates illegally, as one think tank suggested, although they might in some cases best be used in conjunction with the swearing of oaths.[145]

Codes can be helpful – but they can also be ineffective or counterproductive. Their flexibility can also be their weakness. Following some egregious examples of poor boardroom behaviour in the early 1990s a series of corporate governance codes emerged for the better self-management of companies in the UK; they included the Cadbury Code (1992), the Greenbury report (1995), the Hampel Report (1998), the Higgs Review (2003). All these were eventually stitched together into a Combined Code, which went through several editions.[146] The Secretary of State for Business in 2012 suggested an appendix to the governance code so as to provide for 25 per cent of women on FTSE boards by 2016. It is not clear that there has been materially improved decision-making, higher ethics or improved shareholder value as a consequence of this considerable effort.[147]

---

[143] See e.g. The Pensions Regulator's duties set out in Pensions Act 2004, s90 et seq.

[144] *Code of practice for victims of crime*, Ministry of Justice, October 2013, 70pp issued under Domestic Violence, Crime and Victims Act 2004 s32 and EU Directive establishing minimum standards on the rights, support and protection of victims of crime (2012/29/EU) and Directive 2011/92/EU combating the sexual abuse and sexual exploitation of children and Directive 2011/36/EU preventing and combating the trafficking of human beings.

[145] James Ashton, *Bloodlust for bankers won't be sated*, Evening Standard, 29 July 2014; Philip Blond, Elena Antonacopoulou, Adrian Pabst, *In professions we trust*, ResPublica, July 2015; David T. Llewellyn, Roger Steare and Jessica Trevellick, Adam Wildman, *Virtuous Banking: placing ethos and purpose at the heart of finance*, ResPublica, July 2014.

[146] Financial Reporting Council, *UK Corporate Governance Code* and *UK Stewardship Code* (www.frc.org.uk/corporate/ukcgcode.cfm).

[147] Martin Vander Weyer, *All those boardroom codes still can't catch rogues and incompetents*, Spectator 12 September 2015. And see Companies Act 2006 s172 imposing wider

Even without written or official codes, many rules work well using unwritten social codes or norms; as has been pointed out elsewhere there is no rule requiring people to park their cars in a supermarket car park within the white lines – but they do because it is sensible to do so and there is peer pressure. It works without rules.[148]

Public sector codes   Some codes can have the effect of law, even though expressed as codes; it is invariably preferable that these provisions should not be expressed as codes, because while a code can allow wide discretion of the authorities, where appropriate, regulations also constrain the authorities as well as the citizen.[149]

Codes can be used to influence the behaviour not merely of the public or of industry, but also of regulators. Such a model is used by the UK HMRC itself to manage its own conduct,[150] although it struggles in practice to abide by it, and in practice in such cases legislation might be actually preferable.[151]

Codes, especially in the public sphere, can also sometimes miss the point. The code for UK MPs' behaviour focuses almost exclusively on financial behaviour, perhaps inevitably following a parliamentary expenses scandal in 2009. But it only mentions general principles, in broad terms, and then only briefly. And it contains no obligations in relation to the lawmaking role of MPs, such as for example a duty to read the legislation they vote upon, or to understand the legislation before they vote on it, or to owe a greater duty to the country than to their constituents, or

---

social duties on directors. The UK Prime Minister attempted a further reform in November 2016, but it was soon seen that even legislation was impracticable, see *Green Paper: Corporate Governance Reform*, Department for Business, Energy and Industrial Strategy, November 2016.

[148] Rory Sutherland, *How good laws change our ways*, Spectator, 19 July 2014 and see the Smack the Pony parking sketch www.youtube.com/watch?v=nYCRujUspA8.

[149] See e.g. Home Office, *Interception of Communications (pursuant to section 71 of the Regulation of Investigatory Powers Act 2000)*, November 2015; the Pensions Regulator, codes on pensions.

[150] HMRC, *Your Charter*, 12 January 2016, www.gov.uk/government/publications/your-charter/your-charter.

[151] Codes in the private sector can also have merely grandstanding effect; see for a dyspeptic and sceptical approach, Lucy Kellaway, *Codes of conduct are in breach of common sense*, Financial Times, 27 March 2017. A letter in response to the article quoted Albert Camus: 'Integrity has no need of rules' (*The Myth of Sisyphus*, 1942). It followed the resignation of a Bank of England director who had breached the Bank's code, which she had been responsible for writing, *Our Code: our commitment to how we work*, Bank of England, September 2016; Gemma Tetlow, *Bank of England deputy governor admits code of conduct breach*, Financial times, 7 March 2017.

to avoid procedural niceties to make a political point, or to behave with courtesy in the proceedings in the House, or to avoid grandstanding. It is more a code of administration than of principle.[152]

In the UK codes for the public sector include

- code of conduct for MPs,[153]
- code of conduct for members of the House of Lords,[154]
- Regulators' Code,[155]
- HMRC's Your Charter and[156]
- judges' code (Sir Matthew Hale, discussed below).

They are clearly reflective of the different objectives – some are for internal governance, others for external application. Their advantage is that they set a tone, even if unenforceable; their very unenforceability can be their strength. Sometimes a code is not stand-alone; there does not always need to be an authority to promote it or perversely to enforce it. The Regulators' Code for example, has itself no regulator to enforce it, unsurprising where it contains mostly motherhood provisions, involving proportionality, simplicity and commerciality.[157]

7.4.4   Duties of a Legislator

The proclivity of legislators to make law comes as no surprise. It is what they do, so not unnaturally they do it, whether it is a good thing or not.

But in recent years, especially in the UK, more attention has been paid to the issue of their remuneration, rather like debate on the remuneration of

---

[152] House of Commons, *The Code of Conduct: the guide to the rules relating to the conduct of members*, House of Commons, 18 March 2015. The Committee on Standards in Public Life issues *Ethical standards for providers of public services* (June 2014), which is similarly anodyne, focuses on conflicts of interest, and in practice ducks the key issue of 'accountability' (see p29). It recommends training, but there is only slight evidence of ethical training in practice.

[153] *The Code of Conduct together with the rules relating to the conduct of members*, HC 1076, 15 April 2015.

[154] *Code of Conduct for members of the House of Lords*, House of Lords, Fourth edition, 27 May 2015, HL Paper 3.

[155] Better Regulation Delivery Office, *Regulators' Code*, Department for Business Innovation and Skills, April 2014.

[156] HMRC, *Your Charter*, 12 January 2016, www.gov.uk/government/publications/your-charter/your-charter (www.gov.uk/government/uploads/system/uploads/attachment_data/file/91888/charter.pdf).

[157] Better Regulation Delivery Office, *Regulators' Code*, Department for Business Innovation & Skills, April 2014.

bankers, but for different reasons. Some argue they should be better paid, others that they should be less well paid. And for over a year the press ran a campaign against the expenses regime for UK Members of Parliament, that was successful in some respects, with many MP's declining to stand for further election, and the creation of another quango to supervise them.

In fact the sums involved in the excess of expenses was relatively modest, running into the small millions, small in relation to a total budget spent by MPs of around £750B. What seems to have been overlooked in the governance of MPs has been the impact of pork-barrel pressures, which for many years was a blot on the US legislative landscape.

The pork-barrel system does not apply in the same way in the UK, because of the way in which legislation emerges.[158] But there are similar and related concerns. For example, MP's vote on legislation that they cannot possibly understand, but rely on government (or opposition) assurances that the bill or law is satisfactory – and do not check whether there are clauses inserted to benefit one member's constituency or not. In other walks of life, such poor governance would be unacceptable. For example, chief executives often sign take-over documents in corporate transactions that they will not have read – but take responsibility if things go wrong. They normally rely on the advice of their professional advisers – bankers, lawyers, accountants – and hope that matters will be fine. MPs do rather the same, but there are no penalties in their case for poor governance.

7.4.5 A Code for Legislators (and Regulators)

It might be sensible to avoid trying to legislate for better behaviour; legislation has a habit of being counter-productive. Bad guys hide behind it; good guys are constrained by it. It might be preferable therefore to devise a code of conduct for legislators. Such codes themselves have their own drawbacks, but at least they contain an element of flexibility – and it delegates trust to those who need to assume it. A useful code might be along the following lines:

1 **Remuneration.** MPs should maintain their living outside Parliament. Full-time legislators seem to be just that; they spend their time

---

[158] In the UK they are called 'Christmas Tree Bills', i.e. multi-purpose bills, see Nicola Newson, *Proposal for government departments to cease devising new legislation for a period of time and concentrate on sound administration*, House of Lords Library, 5 August 2016. See also Daniel Greenberg, *Dangerous trends in modern legislation . . . and how to reverse them*, Centre for Policy Studies, April 2016.

creating legislation. The need to earn outside the Parliament would more readily align legislators with the consumers of legislation.[159]

2 **Job specification.** The role of an MP is less to be a local constituency rights worker (although in exceptional circumstances that might be appropriate). There is Citizens Advice and there are local councillors who can mostly carry out that function, and lawyers in more difficult cases. But the prime function of an MP is to hold the government to account, and to ensure that the administration of the state is satisfactory. A job specification might set out the details of the function of an MP, and indicate that an MP's role should not be a career choice but incidental. The Civil Service is capable of managing day-to-day governmental affairs; it might be the function of MPs and ministers merely to assess from time to time whether the system is working.

3 **Voting governance.** There could be a sub-code of practice on voting in Parliament. Such voting principles could include not to make being a MP a profession in itself, to retire after two terms (similar to a requirement imposed by them on trustees of charities and housing associations), and to read (and understand) any legislation before voting for it.[160]

4 **Surcharging.** One the most effective controls over poor behaviour in local government is the principle of surcharging. Surcharging applied in the well-known case of Lady Porter when she was held liable for maladministration of the City of Westminster.[161] In practice surcharging MP's would apply more in virtual than actual reality; for example if the Regulatory Impact Assessment suggested a new measure would cost say £100M, and a few years later it transpired its cost was £500M, all those MPs that voted for the measure would be

---

[159] Although moderation might be advised; see the furore when a UK former finance minister having resigned shortly thereafter acquired concurrent multiple employments (including that of banker at $1M a year, public speaking engagements at maybe the same rate, and editorship of a daily London newspaper, whilst retaining his parliamentary seat, see Advisory Committee on Business Appointments, Guidance, 21 December 2016; Vanessa Thorpe, *George Osborne told to choose whether to be MP or Standard editor*, Guardian, 20 March 2017.

[160] See e.g. Commissioner Bill Pincus QC, *Queensland Fuel Subsidy Commission of Inquiry Report*, 21 November 2007: 'Parliaments, State and Federal, produce large quantities of legislation each year. It appears likely that some parliamentarians thoroughly study few of the Bills which come before them. But one would expect that some mechanism within a Parliament would exist to identify the more obvious problems, such as an important obscurity, in Bills being considered. A crucial defect, even in a single sentence, can give rise to serious problems.'

[161] See e.g. *Westminster City Council v Dame Shirley Porter* [2002] EWCA Civ 1591.

surcharged at the amount of the excess. There would be no prospect of it actually being paid; but the deficits would appear on the ballot forms at the next election and on their personal websites. Voters could then see how institutionally spendthrift an MP was. In itself it would not be the most important criteria in deciding whether to vote or not for an MP, but it might add to the understanding of the strength of the MP – and calm any determination to vote for expensive legislation, or legislation which makes a point rather than a rule.

5 **No legislation to make a point or reinforce morality.** Some legislation is introduced 'to make a point'. Policy on equal treatment has been introduced on this basis, and drugs legislation is another example. Discrimination in employment on the grounds for example of gender, disability or sexual orientation is of course unacceptable and foolish, but whether it should be against the law (adultery causes much more grief, but is not illegal) is less certain, especially when it is not generally illegal. Nor do the anti-drug laws make much difference to the consumption of drugs – they are more to send a message that the state disapproves of its citizens being potheads, but their effectiveness is dubious. Grandstanding legislation is a luxury. Ministers, civil servants and MP's should wherever possible avoid creating legislation which is a direct or indirect attempt to change behaviour (or intended to send a message).[162]

6 **Training and qualification.** Legislators can do a great deal of harm, as well as good. In most areas of human activity in complex societies, there is a training requirement. First-aid, the teaching of

---

[162] Stephen Laws, *Giving effect to policy in legislation: how to avoid missing the point*, [2011] 32(1) Statute Law Review 1–16, p5 ('It is the responsibility of the legislative drafter to ascertain whether a proposed legislative proposition is intended to be understood – legally, as well as politically – as an indirect attempt to change behaviour, or is intended to be, something which (for instance by producing better decision-making) is of value in its own right and to be neutral so far as eventual outcomes are concerned.') For an egregious example of pointless law-making, see Chris Grayling, Minister of Justice, who introduced the Social Action, Responsibility and Heroism Bill 2014, intended to direct judges to take a possible tortfeasor's good intentions if subsequently sued for negligence after having attempted to help someone. The good news was that it was short, five clauses on one page. The bad news was that the law was already in force, as the accompanying 5-page explanatory note pointed out. See Chris Grayling MP, *Our bill to curb the Elf and Safety Culture*, ConservativeHome.com, 2 June 2014. See also Bill, *Second Reading*, House of Commons, 21 July 2014; Bill, Explanatory Notes, 12 June 2014; Catherine Fairbairn, and John Woodhouse, *Social Action, Responsibility and Heroism Bill – Commons Library Research Paper*, 8 July 2014, 33pp.

swimming, the practice of brain surgery, even the driving of a bus requires a diploma, a certificate or a degree.[163] But passing laws that affect the lives of all of us at the moment can be done without any such experience or training. The rule should be that MPs would refrain from voting for or against legislation until they had completed a refresher on law making and legislative policy, including issues such as the law of unintended consequences, the principles of legislative drafting, and whether law-making is the best solution to meeting a policy objective. Even a newly minted MP is free to vote on matters of war and of taxation with only the slightest of knowledge of the subject, or of the various universal laws including those of unintended consequences. The training of parliamentary draftsmen is somewhat better in practice, though maybe not ideal; it is carried out with some form of apprenticeship, learning on the job, under the supervision of (not so) grizzled men of experience and wisdom:

> 'Commonwealth countries have recognized for many years that recruiting, training and retaining competent legislative counsel present problems ... [however] the legal community does not yet accept that legal drafting (including legislative drafting) is a foundational discipline of legal and logical analysis that all lawyers should experience. Consequently, there are still too few teachers of legislative drafting.'[164]

There have been courses, mostly in US law schools, dedicated to raising the game of legislative draftsmen. A draft syllabus for the training of legislators and regulators is attached as Appendix I to this book.

Training courses could include exploring a sceptical attitude to regulation; it has been suggested[165] that legislators should be trained in

- encouraging evidence-based regulation;
- exploring alternative solutions – regulation is often more destructive than adopting competence and empathy in administration;

---

[163] See Stephen Leacock, the Canadian humourist and satirist, *Frenzied Fiction, No XVI, Simple stories of success, or how to succeed in life*, 1918.

[164] Dale Dewhurst, Lionel Levert QC and Archie Zariski, *Producing legislative counsel: ways and means*, [2012] 33(3) Statute Law Review 339–353.

[165] Tracey Brown and Michael Hanlon, *In the interests of safety: The absurd rules that blight our lives and how we can change them*, Sphere, 2014.

- managing risk, so as to reduce excessive examples of risk warnings, or using risk warnings that actually bite, and being trained in the understanding of risk;
- avoiding regulatory creep;
- logic and philosophy, so as to avoid being trapped by specious arguments, for example thinking that failing to legislate against an evil means promoting it (in relation e.g. to the misuse of drugs or child molestation);
- training in the understanding of statistics, so as for example to be sceptical of arbitrary periods over which statistics are selected. Child exploitation has hardly changed in frequency since additional rules have been introduced at immense cost since each offender is different and will either circumvent the rules or they will not apply;
- challenging whether the rules actually apply in practice;
- avoiding regulatory 'theatre' such as airport searches;
- avoiding fighting phantoms, e.g. toy guns;
- avoiding confusing the rule from the threat;
- refraining from using the phrases 'something must be done' and 'it must never happen again';
- appreciating the costs of legislation: for example current expensive airport safety measures would have done nothing to have stopped 9/11 and most bombs are actually missed in searches or fortunately fail to work;
- applying a reality check before voting for a new measure; and
- knowledge of advances in artificial intelligence and the impact this has on the design of legislation and regulation.[166]

7 **Ethical conduct in legislating.** It might become unethical for MPs to vote for local causes at the expense of a national benefit. New rail lines and other grand infrastructure projects are harder and more expensive to achieve in the UK because of the propensity to look at parochial matters. The US in the past has suffered badly from pork-barrelling, but the position in the UK is now rather worse.

---

[166] Richard Susskind, *Evidence: the legislative process*, House of Lords, Select Committee on the Constitution, 11 January 2017. Cf House of Lords, Select Committee on the Constitution, *The legislative process*, 2017; House of Lords, Select Committee on the Constitution, *Parliament and the legislative process, Volume I, Report*, 14th report of Session 2003–04, HL Paper 173-I, 29 October 2004.

8 **Consistency and stability in law.** Ministers, civil servants and MP's, should wherever possible maintain consistency in legislation and avoid change unless there are very good reasons.[167] The US legislative system, for all its faults, at least attempts to create a code.

9 **Respect for the rule of law and the judiciary.** Parliamentarians should not call into question a decision of the judiciary, especially where it concerns their own decisions or that of their department. To do so should involve a resignation from office if a minister.

10 **Avoiding meaningless or populist rhetoric.** A politician or regulator should avoid the use of populist phrases; and giving false assurances to the public should be regarded as wrongfully shouting fire in a crowded theatre.[168] Populism can be an insidious corruption of the political and legislative process. One control of it was proposed in the eighteenth century by Edmund Burke:[169]

> I am sorry I cannot conclude without saying a word on a topic touched upon by my worthy colleague. I wish that topic had been passed by at a time when I have so little leisure to discuss it. But since he has thought proper to throw it out, I owe you a clear explanation of my poor sentiments on that subject.
>
> He tells you that 'the topic of instructions has occasioned much altercation and uneasiness in this city;' and he expresses himself (if I understand him rightly) in favour of the coercive authority of such instructions.
>
> Certainly, gentlemen, it ought to be the happiness and glory of a representative to live in the strictest union, the closest correspondence, and the most unreserved communication with his constituents. Their wishes ought to have great weight with him; their opinion, high respect; their business, unremitted attention. It is his duty to sacrifice his repose, his pleasures, his satisfactions, to theirs; and above all, ever,

---

[167] For example, there are virtually annual changes to the levels and structures of business taxes, corporation taxes and carbon taxes: 'The annual investment allowance allows the immediate deduction of expenditure on most machinery from taxable profit. Knowing its level is an important consideration when forming investment decisions. The limit was set at £50,000 between 2008 and 2010 when it increased to £100,000. It was cut to just £25,000 in 2012 but increased to £250,000, supposedly temporarily, in 2013. In the 2014 budget it was raised again to £500,000, but on current plans it will return to £25,000 in 2016. How is that supposed to help businesses that are planning for the future?' Paul Johnson, *A mess and getting worse: we all suffer from Britain's jumbled tax code*, [2014] (July) Prospect 42.

[168] *Schenck v United States* 249 US 47.

[169] Edmund Burke, *Speech to the electors of Bristol*, 3 November 1774 (Works 1:446–8); see also Roger Scruton, *A petition against petitions*, A Point of View, BBC Radio 4, 19 June 2016.

and in all cases, to prefer their interest to his own. But his unbiassed opinion, his mature judgment, his enlightened conscience, he ought not to sacrifice to you, to any man, or to any set of men living. These he does not derive from your pleasure; no, nor from the law and the constitution. They are a trust from Providence, for the abuse of which he is deeply answerable. Your representative owes you, not his industry only, but his judgment; and he betrays, instead of serving you, if he sacrifices it to your opinion.

My worthy colleague says, his will ought to be subservient to yours. If that be all, the thing is innocent. If government were a matter of will upon any side, yours, without question, ought to be superior. But government and legislation are matters of reason and judgment, and not of inclination; and what sort of reason is that, in which the determination precedes the discussion; in which one set of men deliberate, and another decide; and where those who form the conclusion are perhaps three hundred miles distant from those who hear the arguments?

To deliver an opinion, is the right of all men; that of constituents is a weighty and respectable opinion, which a representative ought always to rejoice to hear; and which he ought always most seriously to consider. But authoritative instructions; mandates issued, which the member is bound blindly and implicitly to obey, to vote, and to argue for, though contrary to the clearest conviction of his judgment and conscience – these are things utterly unknown to the laws of this land, and which arise from a fundamental mistake of the whole order and tenor of our constitution.

Parliament is not a congress of ambassadors from different and hostile interests; which interests each must maintain, as an agent and advocate, against other agents and advocates; but parliament is a deliberative assembly of one nation, with one interest, that of the whole; where, not local purposes, not local prejudices, ought to guide, but the general good, resulting from the general reason of the whole. You choose a member indeed; but when you have chosen him, he is not member of Bristol, but he is a Member of Parliament. If the local constituent should have an interest, or should form an hasty opinion, evidently opposite to the real good of the rest of the community, the member for that place ought to be as far, as any other, from any endeavour to give it effect. I beg pardon for saying so much on this subject. I have been unwillingly drawn into it; but I shall ever use a respectful frankness of communication with you. Your faithful friend, your devoted servant, I shall be to the end of my life: a flatterer you do not wish for.

11 **Avoiding misleading titles to legislation.** Legislators and regulators will abjure misleading titles in their legislation or discussion documents. Any legislation which had 'red tape reduction' or 'deregulation' in its title must not contain any disguised additional

obligations (as happens in some UK deregulation acts or the Australian Red Tape Reduction legislation).[170]

12 **Accountability.** All legislation and regulatory reports will be signed by those responsible for them, and will be independently audited after five years. MPs who have voted for legislation and secondary legislation will be held to account after five years.

13 **MPs, ministers and regulators will avoid blame shifting.** The histories of the non-scandals involving Baby P and of Sir Philip Green have been described elsewhere, to the shame of the politicians involved. Blame shifting might be regarded as unethical, despite any political advantage in so doing.

14 **Dealing with lobbying and press comment.** MPs and others will take account of lobbyists and the press to inform themselves of facts and issues, but will follow their conscience and evidence-based policy-making even at the cost of their political capital.

15 **Paying regard to a sanctimony index and the sin of scrupulosity.** MPs, regulators and others might avoid making sanctimonious remarks about their colleagues, opponents or those they are regulating, if only to avoid the possibility of later being accused of personal hypocrisy.

16 **Balance of arguments.** MPs regulators and others will frame their position in setting rules acknowledging that there may be alternatives, or that the facts on which they base their views may eventually prove not to be correct.

17 **Soft law.** MPs, regulators and others will accept that in framing law, less may be more, legislation may not be the answer, and that improved application of existing rules may be sufficient.

18 **Trust, brand and reputation.** The use of trust, and the relevance of brand and reputation should be an increasing element of the design of regulation, so that regulation should not act as factor of moral hazard diminishing the role of reputation as a competitive factor in the provision of goods and services. Ironically legislation can authorise behaviour (because it sets out its own limits) which previously people would have abjured because they would have found distasteful, e.g. employers abandoning pension liabilities.

---

[170] The Deregulation Act 2015 in fact introduced substantial new (and broadly good) law, including protection for tenants against retaliatory eviction and the need for landlords to fit smoke alarms. But it is not deregulation.

7.4.6   Codes of Practice for Lobbying/Campaign Groups

Legislators and others complain with some justification that they can be bounced into regulation because of press comment (as in the Sharon Shoesmith case) or because of effective campaigning. Campaigning can help us all; without campaigning we would not have universal suffrage, anti-discrimination rules, reduced smoking or compulsory seat belts, all of them broadly beneficial.[171] But campaigners, in an understandable efforts to focus their energies on achieving success do not feel that it is part of their remit to put the other side of the argument, or to articulate some of the downsides of their policies; nor do they avoid exaggeration to make their point. They feel that the dice of inertia are loaded against them, and that opponents are best fitted to argue the alternative view and that legislators should be strong enough to resist excess legislation.

But it might benefit society generally if campaigners adopted some form of voluntary code of behaviour to avoid some of the excesses involved in campaigns. There is already a lobbying registration component in many legislators. A lobbying code might be extended to campaigners – and to the press (although that might struggle to gain acceptance).

7.4.7   Oaths

Sometimes linked to codes are oaths; unlike an oath in court, private oaths cannot be enforced through the law of perjury, but they set a tone, and they can make the individual who swears an oath think twice (sometimes) about his duties. The Old Testament imposes some deferred penalties:

> Or if a soul swear, pronouncing with his lips to do evil, or to do good, whatsoever it be that a man shall pronounce with an oath, and it be hid from him; when he knoweth of it, then he shall be guilty in one of these.[172]

Curiously the Old Testament indicates that God was the first to make an oath (following the Flood), but there was no suggestion of a sanction for breach. Today, heavenly penalties are inapplicable, but there can be a sense

---

[171] Although see John Adams, *Risk*, UCL Press, 1995, who famously suggested the best way to reduce road accidents was to place a spike on car steering-wheels to make drivers more cautious. And see Glynis Breakwell, *The psychology of risk*, Cambridge, 2007, which describes how the Chernobyl nuclear reactor exploded in 1986, partly because the rules had not been followed. Although several people died as a consequence, many more would have died if alternative fuel policies had been adopted, but this is not calculated in conventional risk assessments.

[172] Leviticus 5:4.

Table 7.3 *Oaths*

UK MP's current oath	UK MP's proposed oath
I (name of Member) swear by Almighty God that I will be faithful and bear true allegiance to Her Majesty Queen Elizabeth, her heirs and successors, according to law. So help me God.	I (name of Member) swear by Almighty God that I will be faithful and bear true allegiance to Her Majesty Queen Elizabeth, her heirs and successors, according to law.
	I also hereby swear by Almighty God that I will abjure party loyalty where it conflicts with common sense or conscience, refrain from grandstanding to obtain political or personal advantage, abstain from voting on legislation that I have not read and/or understood, commit to taking a diploma on issues of regulation and legislation, and understand my moral obligations not to make statements not supported by evidence, and commit to the interests of the country rather than my constituents where there is a conflict.
	So help me God.

of shame in some individuals were they to break an oath, and making it suggests a wider duty to the obligation. Most oaths at present are expressions of fealty to the state (the Crown in the UK) by judges, public officials and those seeking citizenship. In the UK MPs swear an oath to the Crown, but the terms do not extend to the Crown's subjects or citizens. Set out in Table 7.3 is a short form of a proposed new oath for MPs.

The most famous of the oaths is the Hippocratic oath, sworn by doctors, which in its modern form is as follows:[173]

> I swear to fulfill, to the best of my ability and judgment, this covenant:
>
> I will respect the hard-won scientific gains of those physicians in whose steps I walk, and gladly share such knowledge as is mine with those who are to follow. I will apply, for the benefit of the sick, all measures which are required, avoiding those twin traps of overtreatment and therapeutic nihilism. I will remember that there is art to medicine as well as

---

[173] Written in 1964 by Louis Lasagna, then Academic Dean of the School of Medicine at Tufts University, USA, and in practice commonly used.

science, and that warmth, sympathy, and understanding may outweigh the surgeon's knife or the chemist's drug. I will not be ashamed to say "I know not," nor will I fail to call in my colleagues when the skills of another are needed for a patient's recovery. I will respect the privacy of my patients, for their problems are not disclosed to me that the world may know. Most especially must I tread with care in matters of life and death. If it is given me to save a life, all thanks. But it may also be within my power to take a life; this awesome responsibility must be faced with great humbleness and awareness of my own frailty. Above all, I must not play at God. I will remember that I do not treat a fever chart, a cancerous growth, but a sick human being, whose illness may affect the person's family and economic stability. My responsibility includes these related problems, if I am to care adequately for the sick. I will prevent disease whenever I can, for prevention is preferable to cure. I will remember that I remain a member of society, with special obligations to all my fellow human beings, those sound of mind and body as well as the infirm. If I do not violate this oath, may I enjoy life and art, respected while I live and remembered with affection thereafter. May I always act so as to preserve the finest traditions of my calling and may I long experience the joy of healing those who seek my help.

In practice in the UK at least the oath is not sworn by medical practitioners. Other exemplars of oaths include the Osteopathic Oath, an Oath of Maimonides (also for doctors), an Archimedean Oath (for engineers), a Florence Nightingale Pledge (for nurses), a Helsinki Declaration (for human medical experimentation), the Scout Promise and many others. A modern form of oath is a strapline adopted by commercial organisations, such as Google's 'Don't be evil', a variant of 'do no harm'.

Oaths outside the courtroom have no force of law, but they are intended to set out a form of mission statement, to set boundaries, and to allow the use of discretion – and they set a standard against which other laws may wish to test, for example to determine whether an act was negligent. Harold Shipman, a famous British medical murderer might not have kept to his Hippocratic Oath, if he had sworn it, but nor would the passing of a black-letter law have meant the survival of more of his patients. Oaths set a tone, and give expectations and can have profound value.

In the US, the Civil War led President Lincoln to develop an expanded oath for all federal civilian employees in 1861. When Congress reconvened, members echoed the president's action by enacting legislation requiring employees to take the expanded oath in support of the Union. This oath seems to be one of the earliest direct predecessor of the modern oath; the current oath was enacted in 1884:

> I do solemnly swear (or affirm) that I will support and defend the Constitution of the United States against all enemies, foreign and domestic; that I will bear true faith and allegiance to the same; that I take this obligation freely, without any mental reservation or purpose of evasion; and that I will well and faithfully discharge the duties of the office on which I am about to enter: So help me God.

In the UK the monarch in practice takes an oath, which is coupled with ancient statutory obligations.[174] Members of the House of Commons and House of Lords also take an oath of allegiance[175] as do certain office holders; it has already been noted that it relates more to allegiance than to honour or duty. Judges swear a slightly different, and more purposive, oath: 'I do swear by Almighty God that I will well and truly serve our Sovereign Lady Queen Elizabeth in the office of (office), and I will do right to all manner of people after the laws and usages of this realm without fear or favour, affection or ill will.'

Recruits to the British services must take an oath of allegiance upon joining these armed forces, a process known as 'attestation'. The standard form of the oath is as follows: 'I swear by Almighty God that I will be faithful and bear true allegiance to Her Majesty Queen Elizabeth II, her heirs and successors and that I will as in duty bound honestly and faithfully defend Her Majesty, her heirs and successors in person, crown and dignity against all enemies and will observe and obey all orders of Her Majesty, her heirs and successors and of the generals and officers set over me.'

Privy Counsellors take office on being 'sworn of the Privy Council'. It was formerly regarded as criminal to disclose the form of Privy Council oath, which includes an undertaking of secrecy as to the proceedings in Council (where the Oath is taken). On 28 July 1964 it was published by the President of the Council in answer to a written parliamentary question:

> You do swear by Almighty God to be a true and faithful Servant unto the Queen's Majesty, as one of Her Majesty's Privy Council. You will not know or understand of any manner of thing to be attempted, done, or spoken against Her Majesty's Person, Honour, Crown, or Dignity Royal, but you will lett and withstand the same to the uttermost of your Power, and either cause it to be revealed to Her Majesty Herself, or to such of Her Privy Council as shall advertise Her Majesty of the same. You will, in all things to be moved, treated, and debated in Council, faithfully and truly declare your Mind and Opinion, according to your Heart and Conscience; and will keep secret all Matters committed and revealed unto you, or that shall be treated of secretly in Council. And if any of the said Treaties or Counsels

---

[174] See Coronation Oath Act 1688.   [175] Promissory Oaths Act 1868.

shall touch any of the Counsellors, you will not reveal it unto him, but will keep the same until such time as, by the Consent of Her Majesty, or of the Council, Publication shall be made thereof. You will to your uttermost bear Faith and Allegiance unto the Queen's Majesty; and will assist and defend all Jurisdictions, Pre-eminences, and Authorities, granted to Her Majesty, and annexed to the Crown by Acts of Parliament, or otherwise, against all Foreign Princes, Persons, Prelates, States, or Potentates. And generally in all things you will do as a faithful and true Servant ought to do to Her Majesty.

A possible oath, less pompous or antique than that of the Privy Council, for individual regulators and legislators might be in long form something along the lines of:

I Janet Smith, attest that in the performance of my duties as a Member of Parliament / member of the board of the regulator / officer or senior manager of the regulator I will [delete as appropriate]

- Act without regard to
  - tribal or party affiliations
  - thought of personal gain
- Act with regard to
  - the interests of the country [rather than the interests of my party]
  - the possible unintended consequences of my actions [and votes]
- Take into account when implementing or voting on legislation or regulation my duty to
  - constrain costs for government and affected parties
  - employ alternatives to regulation, including peer pressure, codes and guide, wherever possible
  - employ the use of mercy and proportionality in imposing sanctions
  - acknowledge that there is a balance of costs and benefits in legislation and regulation and confirm them at the outset
  - ignore populist and tabloid pressures
  - decline to vote in favour of legislation I have not read
  - decline to vote to introduce legislation I do not understand
- when dealing with my colleagues and others
  - speak with dignity and in measured terms
  - decline to speak on matters in which I have no knowledge, or have not properly investigated
  - will treat witnesses who are before me in a select committee with dignity, respect and on the assumption that they are competent and experienced in matters with which I am not familiar
- act with the transparency I expect in others
- speak with courtesy, humility and decency – and brevity

- when introducing legislation or regulation have regard to the intended users and subjects, including the requirements of readability and comprehension
- be aware of the possible sins of sanctimony and scrupulosity
- be aware that in legislation less might be more
- be aware than in legislation the best may be the enemy of the good
- take responsibility for my acts, rather than hide in committee form, and be accountable for signing my name to legislation
- review within five years whether my actions were in the event appropriate or correct.

The terms of the oath or declaration may involve motherhood and apple pie – and be unenforceable; but they may also set a tone and expectation amongst both rulers and the ruled.

7.4.8 Judicial Oath

An oath without knowing what the rules might be is helpful but probably not sufficient. Most professions themselves also have a rulebook of some description; even Adam Smith considered there was a need for rules. Rulebooks, or codes, have an ancient history. They do not have the force of law, but they have the force of conscience, and a standard against which others may judge. One such code was that of Sir Matthew Hale's resolutions for judges in the 1650s:[176]

1 That in the administration of justice I am entrusted for God, the King and Country; and therefore
2 That it be done (1) Uprightly (2) Deliberately (3) Resolutely
3 That I rest not upon my own understanding or strength but implore and rest upon the direction and strength of God.
4 That in the execution of justice, I carefully lay aside my own passions, and not give way to them however provoked.
5 That I be wholly intent upon the business I am about, remitting all other cares and thoughts as unseasonable and interruptions.
6 That I suffer not myself to be prepossessed with any judgment at all, till the whole business and both parties be heard.
7 That I never engage myself in the beginning of any cause, but reserve myself unprejudiced till the whole be heard.

---

[176] T. Thirlwall, *The works, moral and religious, of Sir Matthew Hale, Knt*, Vol I, 1805, p23, *Things necessary to be had in remembrance*, c1665, reproduced in Tom Bingham, *The Rule of Law*, 2010, p20.

8 That is business capital, though my nature prompts me to pity, yet to consider that there is also pity due to the country.

9 That I be not too rigid in matters purely conscientious, where all the harm is diversity of judgment.

10 That I be not biased with compassion to the poor, or favour to the rich in point of justice.

11 That popular or court applause or distaste, have no influence into anything I do in point of distribution of justice.

12 Not to be solicitous what men will say or think, so long as I keep myself exactly according to the rule of justice.

13 If in criminals it be a measuring cast, to incline to mercy and acquittal.

14 In criminals that consist merely in words when no more harm ensues, moderation is no injustice.

15 In criminals of blood, if the fact be evident, severity in justice.

16 To abhor all private solicitations of whatever kind soever and by whomsoever in matters depending

17 To charge my servants (1) Not to interpose in any business whatsoever (2) Not to take more than their known fee (3) not to give undue preference to causes (4) Not to recommend counsel.

18 To be short and sparing at meals that I may be fitter for business.

Like oaths, there are similar codes and oaths for doctors, for Google, for pension fund trustees, and some have been proposed elsewhere for newspapers. Newspapers is a particular example where breach of the code is in practice self-policed and where many newspapers glory in its non-observance. Nonetheless breach of it brings the newspaper into disrepute over time, and it can be seen with the News of the World, and may be seen in future with the *Daily Mail*, breach of the principles of integrity, even with a scandal sheet, can be mortal.[177]

7.4.9 Courts, Litigation, the Judges and Legal Professionals

The judges, at least the senior judiciary, seem deeply conscious of the need for reform, and have attempted several exercises in response. The urban myths about judicial excess, and encroaching on the will of Parliament

---

[177] Health services in the UK are subject to a 'duty of candour', and the body (though not the officers) must act in 'an open and transparent manner', and have regard to codes and guidance issued by the government, see The Health and Social Care Act 2008 (Regulated Activities) Regulations 2014 SI 2014 No 2936 regulations 20 and 21. See also Elkan Abrahamson, *Call by families for a 'Hillsborough law' to criminalise cover-ups'*, The Times, 8 September 2016 which argued for a law criminalising public officers who fail to disclose wrongs, and requiring public bodies to adopt a code of ethics.

seem simply to be myths. And it clear that there is not a compensation culture (in Britain), despite some occasional horror stories. The judiciary are accepted in most jurisdictions as being incorrupt, honest, hard-working and intellectually proficient.

But there are impediments to access to justice for most of us. There need to be changes in procedure, the establishment of competing jurisdictions, and easier access to judges, which high fees, complex procedures and Ministry of Justice budgetary constraints on the number of judges make difficult. There needs to be more input by court users, so far excluded from the process of reform. A change in judicial mindset, professionalisation of judges and their training, and acceptance of a policy that alternative methods of dispute resolution may be better cheaper and easier (and that imperfect resolution of a dispute is better than no resolution) could add to the improvements. Allowing judges to use their judgment rather than being constrained by black-letter law would also help.[178]

Judges, in jurisdictions such as the UK where they are brought in from the practice of law, rather than being trained from the beginning of their career as judges, might benefit from improved formal training in judicial issues and awareness of the challenges faced by parties to litigation, (although anyone wanting to train a Law Lord, especially a Law Lord who translated direct from the bar such as Lord Sumption in the UK, would be a brave man or woman).[179] The judiciary are experienced in law and the procedures; but in the UK they are not formally trained as judges, as they are in many other jurisdictions; they mostly pick it up as they go along. That training might need to inculcate a sense of case management, of the importance of time and brevity, and a willingness to interfere in the propensity of the parties to spend incontinently. They need to call for less evidence and be satisfied with less impressive documentation – and not criticise or hold liable in costs lawyers who take short cuts for the benefits of all. It may be the mindset, not the rules, that needs changing, which might encourage a more interventionist, more commercially aware, and

---

[178] As in e.g. *Yemshaw v London Borough of Hounslow* [2011] UKSC 3, where Lady Hale, one of the Supreme Court justices of the UK, extended the meaning of 'domestic violence' to some criticism, Donald L. Drakeman, *What Yenshaw could have said*, Statute Law Society, lecture, 12 October 2015.

[179] In England and Wales, the Judicial College (formerly Judicial Studies Board) treads on eggshells when dealing with barristers and sole solicitors who feel they are already familiar with the system, see *Strategy of the Judicial College 2015–2017*, Judicial College, January 2015. It concerns itself, for example, with value for money of the judiciary – but barely of the system or of the policy and only lightly on case management (see e.g. Judicial College *Prospectus*, April 2014–March 2015).

more consumer aware, judiciary. The move towards online justice[180] suggests that that should not be difficult to achieve.[181]

7.4.10   Legislation

It is probably more sensible to consider a mixed programme of reforms in primary lawmaking which deals with the issue in an indirect rather than a direct way – in other words, not by producing yet more protocols, but by a programme of attempting to change the mindset. This could include

- training MPs and legislators according to a syllabus along the lines set out in Appendix I, to include the understanding of risk, the cost of regulation, cost-benefit analysis, and management of public expectations;
- requiring legislators and regulators to swear an oath along the lines set out above, and follow codes; or
- improving accountability, by requiring legislators and regulators to be supervised by a select committee which will impose notional surcharges where rules and regulations cost more than stated.

Little of this will work on its own; but it should stand a better chance that the varied catalogue of failed responses detailed in Chapter 6. And if we do manage to produce a more risk-accepting society, a reduction in the nanny state, and a reduction in the volume and application of regulation, we might enjoy better and cheaper products and services, lower degrees of frustration, and a more relaxed and accepting approach to failure (provided of course it is not my plane that crashes or my money that is defrauded).

7.4.11   Regulation and Penalties

In August 2010 the Financial Services Authority fined Zurich Insurance UK £2,275,000 when it lost the personal details of 46,000 policy holders. The regulator imposed the fine on Zurich UK for failing to have adequate systems and controls in place to prevent the loss of customers' confidential

---

[180] See Prisons and Courts Bill 2017, which offers a tentative dip into cyber justice, being limited to fines on trains, trams and unlicensed fishing rods. The 77-page Judicial College prospectus sets out training for judges on technical areas of the law – but there are no seminars on soft skills or policy issues or of judging skills – and most seminars are only a day or so long.

[181] See e.g. the recommendation on reform of criminal procedures by Sir Brian Leveson, 2015.

information; it was the highest fine levied at that date on a single firm for data security failings. The failings came to light following the loss of 46,000 customers' personal details, including identity details, and in some cases bank account and credit card information, details about insured assets and security arrangements. There was no evidence to suggest the personal data was compromised or misused but the FSA said the loss 'could have led to serious financial detriment for customers and even exposed them to the risk of burglary'. Zurich UK had outsourced the processing of some of its general insurance customer data to Zurich in South Africa, which in August 2008 lost an unencrypted back-up tape during a routine transfer to a data storage centre. Zurich UK did not learn of the incident until a year later. Zurich UK agreed to settle at an early stage of the investigation so the firm qualified for a 30 per cent discount; without this discount the firm would have been fined £3.25 million. Margaret Cole, director of enforcement and financial crime at the FSA, said Zurich UK had let its customers down badly: 'It failed to oversee the outsourcing arrangement effectively and did not have full control over the data being processed by Zurich SA. To make matters worse, Zurich UK was oblivious to the data loss incident until a year later. Firms across the financial sector would do well to look at the details of this case and learn from the mistakes that Zurich UK made.'

The proceeds of the fine went to subsidise the overheads, salaries and bonuses of the FSA (now the Treasury) and seemed to be arbitrarily calculated. There have been similar data losses in the past, and there will continue to be such losses in the future, and the level of the fine may induce increased care at the company and other companies, but will not guarantee that such failure will never occur again. It is hard to see what the fine achieved compared with for example making the company publish the failure in the press, i.e. making the failure transparent. That would do more damage to the business than a fine which is simply taken as part of the cost of losing the tape, which in fact the UK end of the business could do little to prevent. Mistakes happen. More creative approaches could be adopted to try and improve procedures where mistakes happen; it is by no means certain that the cost of fines (borne by the shareholders) is proportionate to the mistake. Regulatory breaches may not need to involve accidental mistakes unless there is evidence of gross negligence. If fines would have had any effect, a fine on the FSA itself might have led to the avoidance of the credit crunch in the UK or the Equitable Life affair for example. At some stage the fining and shaming, with the added legal and other expenses involved might prove not to be necessary where the commercial pressures would have the same impact without the needs for heads to roll.

7.4.12   Fair Regulation of Regulators

Regulatory penalties can be heavy; the FCA fined Deutsche Bank £163M for poor money laundering controls in 2017. But the FCA had committed errors of its own in the past, for which the penalties were rather different, i.e. nil. Similarly the Information Commissioner's Office fined 11 charities for breaching the Data Protection Act, having already fined the British Heart Foundation and the RSPCA. Charities of course do not have shareholders or make profits; they have beneficiaries, so that the ultimate payers of the penalties can be ill-treated dogs and patients with heart failure – and in this case 11 other kinds of charitable beneficiaries. The ICO itself self-reported 14 breaches, some of them serious by its own standards, committed by itself, but with unsurprisingly no fines being imposed – and with no damning press releases being issued. Instead, without telling anyone, it ordered itself to take action to prevent further breaches.[182] Its breaches were only discovered after a Freedom of Information Act request.

Similarly in 2007 two discs containing a full copy of HMRC's entire data in relation to the payment of child benefit were lost en route to the National Audit Office. The discs covered 25 million individuals, about half the country's population, including names, addresses and dates of birth of the children and the national insurance and bank details of their parents. The discs contained very light password protection. Eventually the Chairman of HMRC, a civil servant of unusual ability and one who had no responsibility for the mistake, was persuaded to take responsibility and resign following press comment; none of the penalties conventionally imposed by the ICO otherwise applied.[183]

7.4.13   Zealousness Control / Putting a Fence around the Law

Binge drinking has been a worry for policy makers (and parents) for many years. One way of trying to control this is a legal prohibition on sales of alcohol to minors by supermarkets, off-licences and pubs; a minor in the

---

[182] Joe Murphy, *Data watchdog finds itself guilty of 14 breaches of confidentiality laws*, Evening Standard, 3 January 2017.

[183] Deborah Summers, *Personal details of every child in UK lost by Revenue and Customs*, Guardian, 20 November 2007.

UK is considered to be under 18. (There are similar rules for knives.) The Coalition Government in 2010 in the UK proposed to raise the penalty for shopkeepers and others who sold alcohol to under 18s to £20,000. In the meantime many local police forces ran sting operations especially to catch smaller shopkeepers who did not take enough care.

So it is hardly surprising that the larger supermarkets and others sought to avoid any trouble; the penalties could be (and were) draconian, and the press publicity uncomfortable. So they fired check-out people who didn't take sufficient care at the cashpoint; and they introduced a 'Challenge 25' code. Anyone who looked under 25 was requested to show identity. The intention was to filter out young-looking people, and give a margin for error for hard pressed cashiers, so as to reduce the risk of an illegal sale to a minimum. While the law in fact did prohibit sales to persons under 18, it looked reasonable, because the defence includes an exclusion for anyone who reasonably believed the individual was over 18 and had taken all reasonable steps to establish the individual's age – or, alternatively that nobody could have reasonably have suspected from the individual's appearance that he was aged under 18, a broad defence.[184] But because of the problems with the application of the law, the supermarkets (and more particularly their staff) became excessively cautious. They imposed a higher age limit of 21 or more often 25 (and sometimes 30 [Tesco in Yorkshire]) by way of appearance.[185] And cashiers imposed rules of their own. First, most of them imposed their own limit of 25 (not 18) because they misunderstood their own shop's rules. The fact that cashiers would challenge 30-year-olds to prove their age sometimes seemed faltering, but it became increasingly irritating. And when 60- and 70-year olds were asked to provide evidence of age it became more than irritating. Cases were reported of alcohol sales being refused where parents were accompanied by their minor children (for example a 17-year-old girl was not allowed to help her grandmother carry her shopping because there was alcohol in the bag). Identity checks were imposed for the sale of UHU glue, matches, a gentleman's manicure case, paracetamol, Christmas crackers, bleach, chocolate cherry liqueurs, Rizlas and cough drops.

Perversity is endemic in regulatory systems. For example in the US, where similar restrictions apply to the sale of alcohol, it is easier for teenagers to buy cannabis than alcohol. And in any event the controls

---

[184] Licensing Act 2003 s146.
[185] Dolan Cummings, 28¾ – *How constant age checks are infantilising adults*, Manifesto Club, September 2010.

seem disproportionate; excess drinking has been rife at UK universities, and what has reduced it has been a combination of increased tuition fees and a change in the drinking culture. To add to the Looking Glass story, a change in the law in 2010 made a breach of a shops' own policy (i.e. where it had a challenge-25 policy) also a criminal offence, which seems excessive to put it mildly.[186] The regime seems to have the effect of infantilising adults and the overpolicing seems to have had little practical effect. A cashier knows that a 15-year-old jailbait who looks 20 years old will have removed her mascara when the case comes to court. The issue is the over-zealousness in application (seen also in relation to money laundering regulations) where more effort is devoted to policing the rules than to the mischief itself. The solution to zealousness may be a combination of introducing common sense defences to such charges, to imposing proportionate rather than draconian fines for breach, and (in the immediate case) to removing on-the-spot fines. Such reform again may need to be one involving a change of culture: asking cashiers and others to use their common sense, rather than policing by extremes to make a point.

7.4.14   Same Rules for All

The principle of the rule of law that it should apply to all has been discussed a page or two back above in relation to regulators. Were legislators similarly subject to the same laws as the ordinary subject, there might be increased pressure for proportionality and good management in the drafting and application of law. There are innumerable minor and irritating examples; one is that the travel expenses rules for MPs and the general population are different. Tax relief for the use of late-night taxis was abolished in 2011; this has caused great hardship to certain classes of late-night workers, especially nurses and cleaners who are low paid and yet taxed on taxis laid on when public transport is not readily available. MPs on the other hand have specific statutory rights to untaxed use of late-night taxis.[187]

---

[186] Licensing Act 2003 (Mandatory Licensing Conditions) Order 2010 SI 2010 No 0860 para 4.
[187] See e.g. Income Tax (Earnings and Pensions Act) 2003 s248 (for ordinary subjects) and s293A(1)(a) for MPs; HMRC Employment Income Manual EIM21813; 'Hodgy', *Late night taxis*, [2011] (July 21) Taxation which pointed out that while HMRC impose limits of taxi journeys to home for employees, MPs are exempt from the restrictions as to the number of journeys, and there is no requirement for them to show irregularity or to working after 9 pm.

7.5   The End

It is clear that we need rules; every civilised country requires a rule of law. We probably need even a few more rules here and there; it was argued soon after an appalling tragedy which cost 80 lives in a fire in a block of flats in London in 2017 that the building regulations which permitted cladding to be affixed to a high-rise were inadequate.[188] We might even need some regulators.

But it is also evident that we have too many rules, inadequately briefed rule makers, over-zealous regulators and under-trained and too few judges. It is also clear that the over-government evident in many countries causes irritation, substantial cost, and unintended and adverse consequences for all of us.

The good news is that there are workable, though largely untried, remedies to deal with the plague of excess rules; those remedies include a simple mixture of proper training and qualification for legislators, regulators and judges, coupled with the adoption of codes, oaths, and changes in procedure leading eventually to changes in the mindset of legislators, regulators and judges. Such changes could improve the lives of all of us and even of rulemakers themselves.[189]

Whether there is an appetite for reform within the rule-making community is of course another matter. Meanwhile, although Latin has been outlawed for lawyers for several years in England, it is not unreasonable to quote Ovid's remark that *Cui peccare licet peccat minus*.[190]

---

[188] The cause or causes of the fire awaits the outcome of an official inquiry at the time of writing.

[189] For the astonishing incompetence inherent in the system, see e.g. Nicola Hughes, *How to be an effective minister*, Institute for Government, March 2017. Similarly see Emma Norris and Robert Adam, *All change: why Britain is so prone to policy reinvention, and what can be done about it*, Institute for Government, March 2017: 'In the FE [further education] sector, since the 1980s there have been 28 major pieces of legislation, 48 secretaries of state with relevant responsibilities, and no organisation has survived longer than a decade. In the industrial strategy space, there have been at least two industrial strategies in the last decade alone – and we are now moving into a third.'

[190] One who is allowed to sin, sins less, *Amores*, Elegy IV.

Appendix I

Diploma in Lawmaking and Regulation

Set out below is a draft syllabus designed as a discussion or training basis for legislators and regulators. It reflects a UK-centric approach, but could be adapted to suit local circumstances. It is not designed to meet any specific training requirements of particular regulators to meet the requirements of their own office, such as that provided for example to the Financial Conduct Authority by the Henley Business School MSc in regulation of financial services.

1.0   Introduction

1.1 One of the fastest growing areas of governmental activity in recent years is lawmaking and regulation (especially in financial services, partly accelerated by the financial crisis of 2008). The rulebook emerging from the European Union Market in Financial Instruments Directive for example contains over 1.4 million paragraphs, and other pieces of legislation exceed 60,000 pages.

1.2 In many areas regulation has supplanted the previous vector of the management of rights and obligation, namely primary and secondary law. Regulation involves the use of quasi-legislators with sometimes immense powers, where the effective checks and balances are under-developed compared with for example those involved with purely legal rights and obligations.

1.3 Whilst lawyers (and most other trades and professions) are trained both academically and professionally, and many of those who exercise powers over others (i.e. judges and other judicial officials e.g. magistrates) are required to either have many years of experience or practice before they become involved in exercising jurisdiction, legislators and regulators conventionally lack specialised training or enjoy it only incidentally. Lawmakers and regulators conventionally often have enjoyed experience in other areas of activity, and some may have professional qualifications, but few are trained in principles of lawmaking and regulation.

1.4 Regulators' powers are now very substantial, and legislative powers are in practice virtually limitless. Regulatory powers can be used to remove an individual's livelihood, impose substantial fines and penalties sometimes in excess of those awarded by the courts. In an increasing number of cases, the normal checks and balances of primary sanctioning systems do not apply, and those that do are lacking or deficient or unfair. In due course it can be expected that regulatory excess will precipitate a scandal. One of the factors involved in such a regulatory failure is likely to be lack of governance of regulators, in particular a lack of appropriate training. Similarly lawmakers have the power to provide for substantial sanctions for breach (or even suspected breach) and affect the lives of millions of citizens and involving costs of billions of pounds, but are often unfamiliar with such concepts as the rule of law, or of cost-benefit analysis in lawmaking, or of achieving policy objectives by routes other than lawmaking.

1.5 This course is designed to enable officials and others at both senior strategic and tactical levels to be aware of some of the issues involved, some of the pitfalls and some of the challenges in lawmaking and regulation. It provides participants the opportunity to explore substantive regulation and wider issues of balances, the purpose of regulation, the duties and responsibilities of lawmakers and regulators, dilemmas of regulation, costs and benefits for regulators and the regulated, dangers of regulation and alternatives to regulation, behavioural concerns, risk analysis in lawmaking, practicalities of regulation and the unintended consequences of lawmaking and regulation.

1.6 The course is designed to provide participants with resources to enable them to respond to deregulatory initiatives by central governments around the world (including in the UK the Red Tape Challenge), and explore

- disconnects between policy objectives of senior regulators and the way these are expressed and applied by junior management
- central government policy on regulation and deregulation, deregulatory initiatives, and deregulatory outcomes
- the impact of the international organisations (including the EU) on lawmaking and regulation, and issues of domestic implementation
- the balancing the need to remedy a wrong, with unintended and unanticipated consequences
- protecting regulators against claims and personal liability
- the challenges of communication with the public, the regulated persons and the government

- principles of regulation including behavioural regulation, the use and abuse of consultation, proportionality, understanding of risk, and communication of policy, understanding of conflicts of interest in others
- managing the balance of risks to regulators, risks for the public and risks for the regulated and adverse outcomes of asymmetry of risks for regulators
- the application of soft and hard regulation, and principles of better regulation
- the development of policy on penalties and sanctions and their counter effectiveness
- limits to regulation, alternatives to regulation and the danger of regulatory creep
- responding to calls for regulation by press, politicians and lobbyists
- ethical issues for regulators, including conflicts of interest
- the application of regulators' codes and government policy
- principles of drafting of laws, rules and guidance

It is a multi-disciplinary course, with teaching by lawyers, legislators, behavioural scientists, philosophers, civil servants, judges and regulators, local government officials and councillors, agencies, compliance officers and directors.

The course is designed to encourage regulators and legislators (as well as in-house counsel and compliance officers) to be able to respond to both external and internal pressures. It does not cover management, HR, or financial management, or broader policy management issues.

The cost of such a course is around [£XX,000] per head assuming the involvement of [YY] students.

2.0   Market

2.1 The market is substantial, and is expanding following the expansion of primary and secondary regulators in both consumer and commercial and economic regulation including the public utilities, and increasing concerns by legislators. Secondary regulators in the UK include:
- Adult Learning Inspectorate
- Appointments Commission
- Arts and Humanities Research Council (AHRC)
- Arts Council
- Bank of England
- Biotechnology and Biological Sciences Research Council (BBSRC)

- Boundary Commission
- British Council
- British Educational Communications and Technology Agency (Becta)
- British Library
- CAFCASS
- Care Quality Commission (CQC)
- Central Police Training and Development Authority
- Charity Commissioners
- Children's Workforce Development Council
- Civil Nuclear Police Authority – Civil Nuclear Constabulary
- Commission for Patient and Public Involvement in Health
- Commission for Racial Equality
- Commission for Rural Communities
- Commission for Social Care Inspection
- Committee on Climate Change (CCC)
- Competition Commission
- Competition Service
- Council for Healthcare Regulatory Excellence
- Countryside Agency
- Economic and Social Research Council (ESRC)
- English Heritage
- English Nature
- Environment Agency
- Equality and Human Rights Commission
- FSA/FCA/PRA
- Gangmasters Licensing Authority
- General Social Care Council
- General Teaching Council for England
- Healthcare Commission
- Homes and Communities Agency
- Human Fertilisation Embryology Authority
- Human Tissue Authority
- Independent Safeguarding Authority (ISA)
- Information Commissioner's Office
- Infrastructure Planning Commission
- Legal Services Commission
- Local Better Regulation Office
- Medical Research Council
- Museums, Libraries and Archives Council

- National Audit Office
- National Institute for Health and Clinical Excellence Special Health Authority
- National Policing Improvement Agency (NPIA)
- National Treatment Agency
- Natural England
- Natural Environment Research Council (NERC)
- OFCOM
- OFWAT
- Particle Physics and Astronomy Research Council
- Pensions Protection Fund
- Qualifications and Curriculum Authority
- Serious Organised Crime Agency (SOCA)
- Sport England
- Tenant Services Authority
- The Parole Board
- The Pensions Ombudsman
- The Pensions Regulator

and around 800 other bodies, not all of whom have regulatory powers. They operate in many areas of activity including:

- Advertising regulation
- Bank regulation
- Consumer protection
- Cyber-security regulation
- Financial regulation
- Food safety and food security
- Noise regulation
- Nuclear safety
- Minerals
- Occupational safety and health
- Public health
- Regulation and monitoring of pollution
- Regulation of acupuncture
- Regulation of nanotechnology
- Regulation of sport
- Regulation of therapeutic goods
- Regulation through litigation
- Telecommunication
- Vehicle regulation
- Regulation of ship pollution in the US
- Regulation and prevalence of homeopathy

- Regulation of science
- Wage regulation
  The Diploma is also expected to be of interest to those operating as advisers, lawyers and consultants, as well as civil servants and those working in the judicial field.

2.2 It does not cover

- issues posed by economic regulation, in reaction to such issues as monopolies, oligopolies, competition etc. These are widely covered elsewhere (although one module covers these in broad outline)
- legal issues posed by tribunals and determination panels; they are usually aware of their responsibilities and operate with lawyers involved.

2.3 It does discuss issues such as externalities including free riders, external costs, monopolies and collusive oligopolies, use of taxation, and the use of the market as an alternative to regulation.

2.4 *Finances*
  [TBA]

3.0 Course Programme

A series of 15 × 3 hour evening lectures, each consisting of 2 × 90 minute presentations, as follows:

1 **Introduction**	The module provides an introduction to the course, explores the growth of regulation as an alternative to law, sets out the nature and objectives of the course, and considers general principles of regulation, the pros and cons of regulation and issues involved in being a regulator.	

Resources:
Charles Murray, *By the people: rebuilding liberty without permission*, Crown Forum, New York, 2015; David Graeber, *The Utopia of Rules: on technology, stupidity and the secret joys of bureaucracy*, Melville House Publishing, Brooklyn, 2015; Simon Hills, *Strictly No!*, Mainstream Publishing, 2006
Speakers:
(1) Course leader
(2) Guest: academic/think tank

(*continued*)

2	**The function of legislation and regulation**	Why law, why regulation, alternatives to law and regulation, principles of lawmaking and regulation; litigation as regulation
		Resources:
		Cass R Sunstein, *The cost benefit state: The future of regulatory protection*, 2002
		Cass R Sunstein, *Behavioural law and economics*, 2000
		Cass R Sunstein, *Risk and reason*, 2004
		Howard Davies, *Can financial markets be controlled?*, Polity Press, Cambridge, 2015
		Speakers:
		(1) Course leader
		(2) Academic/regulator
3	**Ethics and tone in legislation and regulation**	Ethical obligations of lawmakers and regulators; management of disagreement with strategy or manner of regulation; use of sanctions, fines and penalties; destination of financial proceeds of penalties; relationships with regulated persons; regulatory behaviour
		Resources:
		Anthony Ogus, *Regulation: Legal form and economic theory*, Hart Publishing, Oxford, 2004; Robert Baldwin, Martin Cave and Martin Lodge, *The Oxford Handbook of Regulation*, Oxford University Press, 2010; Tom Bingham, *The rule of law*, Allen Lane, 2010
		Speakers:
		(1) Course leader
		(2) Think tank/regulator
4	**Legal principles of legislation and regulation**	The judge over your shoulder; equality of arms, constitutional rights; the role of judicial review; constitutional limits to legislation
		Resources:
		Helen Xanthaki, *Drafting legislation: art and technology of rules for regulation*, Hart Publishing, Oxford, 2014; Anthony King and Ivor Crewe, *The blunders of our governments*, Oneworld, 2013; Lord Justice Sedley, *Freedom, law and justice*, Hamlyn Lectures, Sweet and Maxwell, 1999.
		Speakers:
		(1) Course leader
		(2) Judge (High Court+)

| 5 | Cost-benefit in regulation | Cost-benefit analysis; regulatory impact assessments; measurement issues |

5 **Cost-benefit in regulation**

Cost-benefit analysis; regulatory impact assessments; measurement issues

Resources:

Philip Booth, *Sharper axes, lower taxes: big steps to a smaller state*, IEA, 2011; Stephen Law, *Believing bullshit: How not to get sucked into an intellectual black hole*, Prometheus Books, New York, 2011; Al Gore, *Common Sense Government*, Random House, New York, 1995

Speakers:

(1) Course leader

(2) Accountancy firm

6 **Checks and balances in regulation**

Governing bodies, user-groups; regulation of corporate persons and private persons; legal proceedings and disputes; use of lawyers and legal advice; the Wednesbury principle; governance; appointing members

Resources:

Charity Commission, *Governance framework*, online

Commissioner for Public Appointments, *Code of Practice for Ministerial Appointments to Public Bodies*

Cabinet Office, *Making and managing public appointments;* J A Farmer, *Tribunals and government*, Weidenfeld and Nicolson, London, 1974

Speakers:

(1) Course leader

(2) Parliamentary counsel

7 **Economics of regulation**

Regulation and economics; control of monopolies and oligopolies; remuneration of regulators; consumer issues

Resources:

http://regulation2point0.org/; Kenneth A Armstrong, *Regulation, Deregulation, Re-regulation*, Kogan Page, 2000; Dan Gardner, *Risk: the science and politics of fear*, Virgin Books, 2009

Speakers:

(1) Course leader

(2) Economic regulator (e.g. Ofcom)

(continued)

8 **Effectiveness of legislation and regulation, and the role of the courts**	Direct regulation, the use of nudge, court reform, access to courts, the courts and the executive, training of the judiciary, management of litigation, litigants-in-person *Resources:* Alternative Dispute Resolution for Consumer Disputes (Competenet Authorities and Information) Regulations 2015 No 0542; *In defence of the rule of law: challenging the erosion of the legal certainty and fairness that business needs*, Linklaters, London, 2015. Amy Street, *Judicial review and the rule of law: who is in control?*, The Constitution Society, 2013; Criminal Justice and Courts Act 2015 Part 4; *Judicial Review and the rule of law*, The Bingham Centre for the Rule of Law, November 2015. *Speakers:* (1) Course leader (2) Judge
9 **Regulatory capture**	Interactions between regulators and the regulated; imbalance of reward; influence, bribery and corruption, lobbying, delay in transfer of employment, secondments *Resources:* Jonathan R Macey, *The death of corporate reputation: how integrity has been destroyed on Wall Street*, Yale University Press, 2013, Chapter 11; Thomas Winslow Hazlett, *The political spectrum: the tumultuous liberation of wireless technology from Herbert Hoover to the smartphone*, Yale University Press, 2017; Stephen Glover, *We have never been closer to state control of the press*, Spectator, 10 January 2004. *Speakers:* (1) Course leader (2) Lawmaker

10	**Behavioural issues in imposing regulation**	Assymetry in regulatory outcomes; the best being the enemy of the good; political influences; payment of fines and fine-farming; *Resources:* Raymond Snoddy, *Media mergers face red-tape hurdle*, The Times, 6 January 2004; www.radioauthority.org.uk; *Ofcom guidance for the public interest test for media mergers*, January 2004, www.ofcom.org.uk/codes_guidelines/ofcom_ codes_guidancve/pi_test. Andrew Child, *Tackling a business burden: red tape remains a serious challenge, especially for small and mid-sized companies, Financial Times*, 10 May 2011. David Currie and John Cubbin, *Regulatory creep and regulatory withdrawal: why regulatory withdrawal is feasible and necessary*, City University, March 2002. *Speakers:* (1) Course leader (2) Behavioural economist
11	**Duties, and responsibilities of lawmakers**	Following strategic objectives; relationship with authorising body; maintaining or relinquishing independence; developing policy; ethical obligations; lawmakers oaths; regulators codes; duties and responsibilities *Resources:* *Speakers:* (1) Course leader (2) Judge
12	**Legislative and regulatory failures, responses and the never again syndrome**	This module explores a number of higher-profile regulatory failures (mostly financial failures) and enables participants to discuss possible reasons for failure and whether there are lessons to be learned for current regulators (examples discussed include Equitable Life, Financial Services Authority, credit crunch); Dickens coverage of scandals in *Little Dorrit* and *Nicholas Nickleby; Anthony Trollope in The Way We Live Now*, the South Sea Bubble, railway shares, bonds in newly independent countries (Kingdom of Poyais), IOS, Saavundra, Rolls Razor, Bank of Gibraltar, BCCI, endowment mortgages, Barlow Clowes, Equitable Life, Maxwell, Lloyd's names, Lehman Brothers, payment protection insurance, *(continued)*

	Resources:
	FSA report on Northern Rock
	FSA Report on Equitable Life
	Equitable Life academic report
	OECD regulatory reform papers;
	Speakers:
	(1) Course leader
	(2) Senior journalist
13 Efforts at unregulation	This module explores efforts by a multiplicity of agencies over the last 20 years to reduce the incidence of regulation, following several government initiatives. The module discusses in particular the 'Bonfire of the quangos' and the Red Tape Challenge, and why it seems so difficult to make progress.
	International efforts at deregulation (Advisory Board on Regulatory Burden (ACTAL, Netherlands)), Nationaler Normenkontrollrat (NKR, Germany); Swedish Better regulation Council (Regelradet); Regulatory Impact Assessment Board (RIAB, Czech Republic); High Level Group of Independent Stakeholders on Administrative Burdens (HLG) (EU Committee on Smart Regulation); European Union
	Resources:
	Regulatory Policy Committee, *Assessing regulation*, 2012 (Regulatory Policy Committee, UGV1, 1 Victoria Street, London, SW1H 0ET +44 (0)20 7215 1460 www.independent.gov.uk/ regulatorypolicycommittee)
	Speakers:
	(1) Course leader
	(2) Cabinet Office civil servant
14 Legislative and regulatory design	This module gives participants the opportunity to rehearse the common debate on whether regulation is better rules based or principles based; what can be done to improve regulatory design; the politics of regulation; the process of lawmaking and regulatory design

Resources:

Lawrence A Cunningham, *A Prescription to Retire the Rhetoric of 'Principles-Based Systems' in Corporate Law, Securities Regulation and Accounting,* George Washington University Law School, Boston College Law School Research Paper No. 127, Vanderbilt Law Review, Vol. 60, October–November 2007

Speakers:

(1) Course leader

(2) Judge

| 15 | **Being a legislator and regulator** | Ethical issues; conflicts of interest; duties of regulatory boards; duties of front-line staff; relationships between board and staff; oaths; codes of conduct; training and qualification; training; experience; remuneration; relations with politicians and the press; moral obligations; self-reviewing; external reviewing |

Resources:

Being an independent regulator: the governance of regulators, OECD, Paris, July 2016; OECD, *Governance of regulators' practices: accountability, transparency and co-ordination, the Governance of Regulators,* OECD, Paris, 2016. *OECD regulatory policy outlook* 2015, OECD, Paris, 2015; *Getting government off your back: our commitment to cutting red tape,* speech by Sajid Javid, Secretary of State, Department for Business, Innovation & Skills, 3 March 2016 at BCC annual conference, QEII Conference Centre, London; OECD, *Regulatory policy in perspective, a reader's companion to the OECD regulatory policy outlook,* OECD, 2015; R Baldwin, *Better regulation: the search and the struggle,* in Baldwin et al., Oxford Handbook of Regulation, Oxford University Press, 2010.

Speakers:

(1) Course leader

(2) Regulator

***

Alternatively, each session may comprise a 90 minute lecture, a 60 minute interactive workshop plus a 30 minute discussion of a 5000 word essay written by a participant on a topic chosen by them.

4.0   Outcomes

Participants should emerge with an improved understand of the roles of lawmakers and regulators, the dilemmas of and limits to lawmaking and regulation, the politics and drivers involved, issues of communication and relationships with politicians, the public and the regulated community, costs-benefits, alternatives to lawmaking to achieve policy objectives, the role and limits of sanctions, different modes of regulation

In due course, it will become as unacceptable to practice as a lawmaker or regulator without a diploma as it is to drive a bus without a PSV or practice as a brain surgeon without a certificate from the appropriate college.

5.0   Alternatives

The **Institute for Government**, a Sainsbury-funded think tank explores public policy issues in government; it is less concerned with the practicalities of regulation. It conducts 'training' for government ministers.

The **Henley Business School** offers an MSc in financial services regulation designed as an in-house non-critical training system for FCA officials.

The London School of Economics offers a Short Course on Regulation as part of its LSE Executive Training Programme, designed for economic regulators.

6.0   Resources (Periodicals)

- Yale Journal on Regulation
- Regulation and Governance (Wiley)
- International Journal of Regulation and Governance

7.0   Faculty

- Judge
- Regulator

- Parliamentary draftsman
- Lawmaker (MP)
- Academic
- Economic regulator
- Local government lawmaker/official
- Behavioral economist
- Journalist
- Central government civil servant/cabinet office

Appendix II

Executive Order 13563 (US) (2011), Executive Order 13771 (US) (2017), Executive Order 13777 (US) (2017)

THE WHITE HOUSE
OFFICE OF THE PRESS SECRETARY
FOR IMMEDIATE RELEASE

January 18 2011

Executive Order 13563

Improving Regulation and Regulatory Review

By the authority vested in me as President by the Constitution and the laws of the United States of America, and in order to improve regulation and regulatory review, it is hereby ordered as follows:

S1 General Principles of Regulation

(a) Our regulatory system must protect public health, welfare, safety, and our environment while promoting economic growth, innovation, competitiveness, and job creation. It must be based on the best available science. It must allow for public participation and an open exchange of ideas. It must promote predictability and reduce uncertainty. It must identify and use the best, most innovative, and least burdensome tools for achieving regulatory ends. It must take into account benefits and costs, both quantitative and qualitative. It must ensure that regulations are accessible, consistent, written in plain language, and easy to understand. It must measure, and seek to improve, the actual results of regulatory requirements.

(b) This order is supplemental to and reaffirms the principles, structures, and definitions governing contemporary regulatory review that were established in Executive Order 12866 of September 30, 1993. As stated in that Executive Order and to the extent permitted by law, each agency must, among other things: (1) propose or adopt a regulation only upon a reasoned determination that its benefits justify its costs (recognizing that some benefits and costs are difficult to quantify); (2) tailor its regulations to impose the least burden on society, consistent with obtaining regulatory objectives, taking into account, among other things, and to the extent practicable, the costs of cumulative regulations; (3) select, in choosing among alternative regulatory approaches, those approaches that maximize net benefits (including potential economic, environmental, public health and safety, and other advantages; distributive impacts; and equity); (4) to the extent feasible, specify performance objectives, rather than specifying the behavior or manner of compliance that regulated entities must adopt; and (5) identify and assess available alternatives to direct regulation, including providing economic incentives to encourage the desired behavior, such as user fees or marketable permits, or providing information upon which choices can be made by the public.

(c) In applying these principles, each agency is directed to use the best available techniques to quantify anticipated present and future benefits and costs as accurately as possible. Where appropriate and permitted by law, each agency may consider (and discuss qualitatively) values that are difficult or impossible to quantify, including equity, human dignity, fairness, and distributive impacts.

S2 Public Participation

(a) Regulations shall be adopted through a process that involves public participation. To that end, regulations shall be based, to the extent feasible and consistent with law, on the open exchange of information and perspectives among State, local, and tribal officials, experts in relevant disciplines, affected stakeholders in the private sector, and the public as a whole.

(b) To promote that open exchange, each agency, consistent with Executive Order 12866 and other applicable legal requirements, shall endeavor to provide the public with an opportunity to participate in the regulatory process. To the extent feasible and permitted by law, each agency shall afford the public a meaningful opportunity to comment through the Internet on any proposed regulation, with a comment period that should generally be at least 60 days. To the extent feasible and permitted by law, each agency shall also provide, for both proposed and final rules, timely online access to the rulemaking docket on regulations.gov, including relevant scientific and technical findings, in an open format that can be easily searched and downloaded. For proposed rules, such access shall include, to the extent feasible and permitted by law, an opportunity for public comment on all pertinent parts of the rulemaking docket, including relevant scientific and technical findings.

(c) Before issuing a notice of proposed rulemaking, each agency, where feasible and appropriate, shall seek the views of those who are likely to be affected, including those who are likely to benefit from and those who are potentially subject to such rulemaking.

S3 Integration and Innovation

Some sectors and industries face a significant number of regulatory requirements, some of which may be redundant, inconsistent, or overlapping. Greater coordination across agencies could reduce these requirements, thus reducing costs and simplifying and harmonizing rules. In developing regulatory actions and identifying appropriate approaches, each agency shall attempt to promote such coordination, simplification, and harmonization. Each agency shall also seek to identify, as appropriate, means to achieve regulatory goals that are designed to promote innovation.

S4 Flexible Approaches

Where relevant, feasible, and consistent with regulatory objectives, and to the extent permitted by law, each agency shall identify and consider regulatory approaches that reduce burdens and maintain flexibility and freedom of choice for the public. These approaches include warnings, appropriate default rules, and disclosure requirements as well as provision of information to the public in a form that is clear and intelligible.

S5 Science

Consistent with the President's Memorandum for the Heads of Executive Departments and Agencies, "Scientific Integrity" (March 9, 2009), and its implementing guidance, each agency shall ensure the objectivity of any scientific and technological information and processes used to support the agency's regulatory actions.

S6 Retrospective Analyses of Existing Rules

(a) To facilitate the periodic review of existing significant regulations, agencies shall consider how best to promote retrospective analysis of rules that may be outmoded, ineffective, insufficient, or excessively burdensome, and to modify, streamline, expand, or repeal them in accordance with what has been learned. Such retrospective analyses, including supporting data, should be released online whenever possible.

(b) Within 120 days of the date of this order, each agency shall develop and submit to the Office of Information and Regulatory Affairs a preliminary plan, consistent with law and its resources and regulatory priorities, under which the agency will periodically review its existing significant regulations to determine whether any such regulations should be modified, streamlined, expanded, or repealed so as to make the agency's regulatory program more effective or less burdensome in achieving the regulatory objectives.

S7 General Provisions

(a) For purposes of this order, 'agency' shall have the meaning set forth in section 3(b) of Executive Order 12866.

(b) Nothing in this order shall be construed to impair or otherwise affect:
   (i) authority granted by law to a department or agency, or the head thereof; or
   (ii) functions of the Director of the Office of Management and Budget relating to budgetary, administrative, or legislative proposals.

(c) This order shall be implemented consistent with applicable law and subject to the availability of appropriations.

(d) This order is not intended to, and does not, create any right or benefit, substantive or procedural, enforceable at law or in equity by any party against the United States, its departments, agencies, or entities, its officers, employees, or agents, or any other person.

BARACK OBAMA
THE WHITE HOUSE,

January 18, 2011

FOR IMMEDIATE RELEASE

January 30, 2017

Presidential Executive Order on Reducing Regulation and Controlling Regulatory Costs

EXECUTIVE ORDER

- - - - - - -

REDUCING REGULATION AND CONTROLLING REGULATORY COSTS

By the authority vested in me as President by the Constitution and the laws of the United States of America, including the Budget and Accounting Act of 1921, as amended (31 USC 1101 et seq.), section 1105 of title 31, United States Code, and section 301 of title 3, United States Code, it is hereby ordered as follows:

S1 Purpose

It is the policy of the executive branch to be prudent and financially responsible in the expenditure of funds, from both public and private sources. In addition to the management of the direct expenditure of taxpayer dollars through the budgeting process, it is essential to manage the costs associated with the governmental imposition of private expenditures required to comply with Federal regulations. Toward that end, it is important that for every one new regulation issued, at least two prior regulations be identified for elimination, and that the cost of planned regulations be prudently managed and controlled through a budgeting process.

S2 Regulatory Cap for Fiscal Year 2017

(a) Unless prohibited by law, whenever an executive department or agency (agency) publicly proposes for notice and comment or otherwise promulgates a new regulation, it shall identify at least two existing regulations to be repealed.

(b) For fiscal year 2017, which is in progress, the heads of all agencies are directed that the total incremental cost of all new regulations, including repealed regulations, to be finalized this year shall be no greater than zero, unless otherwise required by law or consistent with advice provided in writing by the Director of the Office of Management and Budget (Director).

(c) In furtherance of the requirement of subsection (a) of this section, any new incremental costs associated with new regulations shall, to the extent permitted by law, be offset by the elimination of existing costs associated with at least two prior regulations. Any agency eliminating existing costs associated with prior regulations under this subsection shall do so in accordance with the Administrative Procedure Act and other applicable law.

(d) The Director shall provide the heads of agencies with guidance on the implementation of this section. Such guidance shall address, among other things, processes for standardizing the measurement and estimation of regulatory costs; standards for determining what qualifies as new and offsetting regulations; standards for determining the costs of existing regulations that are considered for elimination; processes for accounting for costs in different fiscal years; methods to oversee the issuance of rules with costs offset by savings at different times or different agencies; and emergencies and other circumstances that might justify individual waivers of the requirements of this section. The Director shall consider phasing in and updating these requirements.

S3 Annual Regulatory Cost Submissions to the Office of Management and Budget

(a) Beginning with the Regulatory Plans (required under Executive Order 12866 of September 30, 1993, as amended, or any successor order) for fiscal year 2018, and for each fiscal year thereafter, the head of each agency shall identify, for each regulation that increases incremental cost, the offsetting regulations described in section 2(c) of this order, and provide the agency's best approximation of the total costs or savings associated with each new regulation or repealed regulation.

(b) Each regulation approved by the Director during the Presidential budget process shall be included in the Unified Regulatory Agenda required under Executive Order 12866, as amended, or any successor order.

(c) Unless otherwise required by law, no regulation shall be issued by an agency if it was not included on the most recent version or update of the published Unified Regulatory Agenda as required under Executive Order 12866, as amended, or any successor order, unless the issuance of such regulation was approved in advance in writing by the Director.

(d) During the Presidential budget process, the Director shall identify to agencies a total amount of incremental costs that will be allowed for each agency in issuing new regulations and repealing regulations for the next fiscal year. No regulations exceeding the agency's total incremental cost allowance will be permitted in that fiscal year, unless required by law or approved in writing by the Director. The total incremental cost allowance may allow an increase or require a reduction in total regulatory cost.

(e) The Director shall provide the heads of agencies with guidance on the implementation of the requirements in this section.

S4 Definition.

For purposes of this order the term "regulation" or "rule" means an agency statement of general or particular applicability and future effect designed to implement, interpret, or prescribe law or policy or to describe the procedure or practice requirements of an agency, but does not include:

(a) regulations issued with respect to a military, national security, or foreign affairs function of the United States;

(b) regulations related to agency organization, management, or personnel; or

(c) any other category of regulations exempted by the Director.

S5 General Provisions

(a) Nothing in this order shall be construed to impair or otherwise affect:

(i) the authority granted by law to an executive department or agency, or the head thereof; or

(ii) the functions of the Director relating to budgetary, administrative, or legislative proposals.

(b) This order shall be implemented consistent with applicable law and subject to the availability of appropriations.

(c) This order is not intended to, and does not, create any right or benefit, substantive or procedural, enforceable at law or in equity by any party against the United States, its departments, agencies, or entities, its officers, employees, or agents, or any other person.

DONALD J. TRUMP
THE WHITE HOUSE,

January 30, 2017

THE WHITE HOUSE
OFFICE OF THE PRESS SECRETARY
FOR IMMEDIATE RELEASE

February 24, 2017

Presidential Executive Order on Enforcing the Regulatory Reform Agenda

EXECUTIVE ORDER

ENFORCING THE REGULATORY REFORM AGENDA

By the authority vested in me as President by the Constitution and the laws of the United States of America, and in order to lower regulatory burdens on the American people by implementing and enforcing regulatory reform, it is hereby ordered as follows:

Section 1. Policy.

It is the policy of the United States to alleviate unnecessary regulatory burdens placed on the American people.

Sec. 2. Regulatory Reform Officers.

(a) Within 60 days of the date of this order, the head of each agency, except the heads of agencies receiving waivers under section 5 of this order, shall designate an agency official as its Regulatory Reform Officer (RRO). Each RRO shall oversee the implementation of regulatory reform initiatives and policies to ensure that agencies effectively carry out regulatory reforms, consistent with applicable law. These initiatives and policies include:

(i) Executive Order 13771 of January 30, 2017 (Reducing Regulation and Controlling Regulatory Costs), regarding offsetting the number and cost of new regulations;

(ii) Executive Order 12866 of September 30, 1993 (Regulatory Planning and Review), as amended, regarding regulatory planning and review;

(iii) section 6 of Executive Order 13563 of January 18, 2011 (Improving Regulation and Regulatory Review), regarding retrospective review; and

(iv) the termination, consistent with applicable law, of programs and activities that derive from or implement Executive Orders, guidance documents, policy memoranda, rule interpretations, and similar documents, or relevant portions thereof, that have been rescinded.

(b) Each agency RRO shall periodically report to the agency head and regularly consult with agency leadership.

Sec. 3. Regulatory Reform Task Forces.

(a) Each agency shall establish a Regulatory Reform Task Force composed of:
(i) the agency RRO;
(ii) the agency Regulatory Policy Officer designated under section 6(a)(2) of Executive Order 12866;
(iii) a representative from the agency's central policy office or equivalent central office; and

(iv) for agencies listed in section 901(b)(1) of title 31, United States Code, at least three additional senior agency officials as determined by the agency head.

(b) Unless otherwise designated by the agency head, the agency RRO shall chair the agency's Regulatory Reform Task Force.

(c) Each entity staffed by officials of multiple agencies, such as the Chief Acquisition Officers Council, shall form a joint Regulatory Reform Task Force composed of at least one official described in subsection (a) of this section from each constituent agency's Regulatory Reform Task Force. Joint Regulatory Reform Task Forces shall implement this order in coordination with the Regulatory Reform Task Forces of their members' respective agencies.

(d) Each Regulatory Reform Task Force shall evaluate existing regulations (as defined in section 4 of Executive Order 13771) and make recommendations to the agency head regarding their repeal, replacement, or modification, consistent with applicable law. At a minimum, each Regulatory Reform Task Force shall attempt to identify regulations that:

(i) eliminate jobs, or inhibit job creation;

(ii) are outdated, unnecessary, or ineffective;

(iii) impose costs that exceed benefits;

(iv) create a serious inconsistency or otherwise interfere with regulatory reform initiatives and policies;

(v) are inconsistent with the requirements of section 515 of the Treasury and General Government Appropriations Act, 2001 (44 U.S.C. 3516 note), or the guidance issued pursuant to that provision, in particular those regulations that rely in whole or in part on data, information, or methods that are not publicly available or that are insufficiently transparent to meet the standard for reproducibility; or

(vi) derive from or implement Executive Orders or other Presidential directives that have been subsequently rescinded or substantially modified.

(e) In performing the evaluation described in subsection (d) of this section, each Regulatory Reform Task Force shall seek input and other assistance, as permitted by law, from entities significantly affected by Federal regulations, including State, local, and tribal governments, small businesses, consumers, non-governmental organizations, and trade associations.

(f) When implementing the regulatory offsets required by Executive Order 13771, each agency head should prioritize, to the extent permitted by law, those regulations that the agency's Regulatory Reform Task Force has identified as being outdated, unnecessary, or ineffective pursuant to subsection (d)(ii) of this section.

(g) Within 90 days of the date of this order, and on a schedule determined by the agency head thereafter, each Regulatory Reform Task Force shall provide a report to the agency head detailing the agency's progress toward the following goals:

    (i) improving implementation of regulatory reform initiatives and policies pursuant to section 2 of this order; and

    (ii) identifying regulations for repeal, replacement, or modification.

Sec. 4. Accountability.

Consistent with the policy set forth in section 1 of this order, each agency should measure its progress in performing the tasks outlined in section 3 of this order.

(a) Agencies listed in section 901(b)(1) of title 31, United States Code, shall incorporate in their annual performance plans (required under the Government Performance and Results Act, as amended (see 31 U.S.C. 1115(b))), performance indicators that measure progress toward the two goals listed in section 3(g) of this order. Within 60 days of the date of this order, the Director of the Office of Management and Budget (Director) shall issue guidance regarding the implementation of this subsection. Such guidance may also address how agencies not otherwise covered under this subsection should be held accountable for compliance with this order.

(b) The head of each agency shall consider the progress toward the two goals listed in section 3(g) of this order in assessing the performance of the Regulatory Reform Task Force and, to the extent permitted by law, those individuals responsible for developing and issuing agency regulations.

Sec. 5. Waiver.

Upon the request of an agency head, the Director may waive compliance with this order if the Director determines that the agency generally issues very few or no regulations (as defined in section 4 of Executive Order 13771). The Director may revoke a waiver at any time. The Director shall publish, at least once every 3 months, a list of agencies with current waivers.

Sec. 6. General Provisions.

(a) Nothing in this order shall be construed to impair or otherwise affect:

    (i) the authority granted by law to an executive department or agency, or the head thereof; or

    (ii) the functions of the Director relating to budgetary, administrative, or legislative proposals.

(b) This order shall be implemented consistent with applicable law and subject to the availability of appropriations.

(c) This order is not intended to, and does not, create any right or benefit, substantive or procedural, enforceable at law or in equity by any party against the United States, its departments, agencies, or entities, its officers, employees, or agents, or any other person.

DONALD J TRUMP
THE WHITE HOUSE,

February 24, 2017

GLOSSARY

Accountability for regulator impact: part of a package of measures intended to create greater clarity and fairness for businesses while ensuring regulators focus their resources where they are needed most. Regulators will be asked to follow best practice when engaging with the businesses affected by their policies and practices, assessing and agreeing business impacts with them before making significant changes. They will also be asked to publish those assessments. For more details, see www.gov.uk/government/publications/regulator-impact-accountability-guidance.

Alternative (to regulation):   ways to achieve policy outcomes without 'command and control' regulation, including self-regulation, co-regulation, information and education, economic instruments and better use of current regulation. For more details, see www.gov.uk/government/policies/reducing-the-impact-of-regulation-on-business/supporting-pages/using-alternatives-to-regulation.

Better Regulation Delivery Office (BRDO):   directorate within BIS responsible for promoting the better delivery and enforcement of regulation. BRDO operates Primary Authority. Enquiries can be sent to brdo.enquiries@bis.gsi.gov.uk.

Better Regulation Executive (BRE):   directorate within BIS that leads the regulatory reform agenda across government.

Better Regulation Unit (BRU):   departmental team responsible for promoting the principles of good regulation and advising departmental policy makers.

Business: unless specified otherwise 'business' also refers to civil society organisations.

Business impact target: required by the UK Small Business, Enterprise and Employment Act 2015 to implement deregulatory savings of £10B between 2010 and 2020.

Civil society organisation: a voluntary organisation which is neither a business nor public sector.

Common commencement date (CCD):   refers to the Government commitment that Westminster-based regulation bearing on business will be commenced only on either 6 April or 1 October of any year, subject to limited exceptions.

Department: government departments and agencies.

Deregulate/deregulatory: to have the effect of reducing the scope of government regulation, including the removal of existing regulation, or amendment/recasting that reduces the scope of existing regulation.

Direct impact: an impact that can be identified as resulting directly from the
    implementation or removal/simplification of the regulation.
Domestic: a measure which is neither EU derived nor based on an international
    obligation.
Equivalent annual net cost to business (EANCB): the annualised value of the
    present value of net costs to business, calculated with reference to the
    counterfactual. Details on how to calculate EANCB are provided in 'One in, Two
    out Guidance'.
EU derived (measure): UK measures that implement EU Directives and EU
    Regulations.
EU Directive(s): EU Directives lay down certain end results that must be achieved in
    every member state. National authorities have to adapt their laws to meet these
    goals, but are free to decide how to do so. EU Directives may concern one or more
    member states, or all of them.
EU Regulation(s): EU Regulations have binding legal force throughout every Member
    State, on a par with national laws. National governments do not have to take
    action themselves to implement EU Regulations, but may need to introduce
    legislation to implement or enforce the directly applicable obligations.
Exception: a type or category of measure where a better regulation requirement has
    been disapplied, and that disapplication is set out in the relevant guidance.
Exemption: the disapplication of a regulatory or deregulatory measure in relation to
    certain categories of activity or entity (e.g. small businesses). Most usually this will
    be in the form of an exemption set out in the relevant legislation.
Fast track: a system of light-touch scrutiny for deregulatory and low-cost regulatory
    measures.
Fees and charges: for more details on fees and charges, please refer to HMT guidance
    (Part 6 of Managing Public Money).
Fit for purpose: a 'green' or 'amber' rated opinion from the Regulatory Policy
    Committee (RPC), indicating that the analysis in the policy and calculations of
    the business impact meets an acceptable standard (in the case of amber, this is
    subject to changes specified in the RPC opinion).
Golden Scissors Award: issued for 'leadership and producing meaningful results in
    cutting red tape for small businesses' by the Canadian Federation of Independent
    Business.
Gold-plating: where implementation of an EU regulation, decision or directive goes
    beyond the minimum necessary to comply with the Directive, as defined by the
    EU Transposition Guidance.
Government: government of the UK.
Gross cost to business: the total costs to business from the measure, not taking into
    account any benefits.
Guidance: the treatment of guidance in better regulation depends upon the status of
    the guidance. See statutory guidance and non-statutory guidance for more details.

Guiding principles for EU regulation: guiding principles underlying the Government's approach to EU measures, aimed at maximising the UK's influence in Brussels and ending the gold-plating of EU legislation in the UK.

Impact assessment (IA): Both a continuous process to help the policy maker think through fully and understand the consequences of possible and actual government interventions in the public, private and third sectors; and a tool to enable the Government to weigh and present the relevant evidence on the positive and negative effects of such interventions, including by reviewing the impact of policies after they have been implemented.

IN: a measure (whether regulatory or deregulatory) for which the direct incremental cost to business exceeds the direct incremental economic benefits to business.

Indirect impact: any cost or benefit to a business which is not captured in the definition of a direct impact.

Measure: any primary or secondary legislation, statutory guidance or policy proposal.

Medium-sized business: a business with between 50 and 249 employees.

Micro-business: a business with 10 or fewer employees.

Minister: government minister responsible for the policy, or the chairman or chief executive of non-ministerial departments, non-departmental public bodies and other agencies.

Ministry of Small Business and Red Tape Reduction: British Columbia, Canada.

Net present value (NPV): the difference between the present value of a stream of costs and a stream of benefits.

Non-regulatory: measures which do not involve regulation, such as tax or spending decisions.

Non-statutory guidance: guidance which is issued without a specific power to do so in legislation and where there is no legal obligation to comply with that guidance.

One in, one out (OIOO): a rule which states that no new measure which imposes costs on business or civil society organisations can be brought in without the identification of existing regulatory measures with an equivalent value that can be removed. OIOO applies to all measures that came into force after 1 January 2011; Departments were expected to achieve demonstrate compliance with OIOO measured from January 2011 to the end of the Parliament.

One in, two out (OITO): a rule that any new regulatory measure that is expected to result in a direct net cost to business and civil society organisations must be offset by compensatory deregulatory measures providing savings to business of at least double that amount. OITO applied to all measures coming into force in the UK after 1 January 2013.

OUT: a deregulatory measure whose direct incremental economic benefit to business exceeds its direct incremental economic cost to business. OUTs can be sourced from existing regulations which are removed completely or existing regulations which are recast in order to reduce burdens.

Paperweight Awards: issued by the Canadian Federation of Independent Business to 'highlight outrageous red tape hassles weighing down small business'.

Parliament: Parliament of the UK.

Post-implementation review: a process to establish whether implemented regulations are having the intended effect and whether they are implementing policy objectives efficiently.

Present value (PV): the total value of a policy, over the appraisal period, expressed in present terms by means of discounting.

Primary authority: a scheme established in the Regulatory Enforcement and Sanctions Act 2008 which allows for the creation of legally recognised partnerships between an eligible business and a single local authority in relation to regulatory compliance in order to reduce inconsistency and costs. For more details, see www.gov.uk/government/publications/primary-authority-handbook.

Recast: the consolidation or reformulation of existing legislation or guidance to improve clarity and reduce the administrative cost of compliance, where there is no change the scope of the regulation.

Red Tape Awareness Week: instituted by the Canadian Federation of Independent Business.

Red Tape Challenge: a UK cross-government programme to review the stock of existing regulation. The default is that regulation should go unless it can be well defended.

Red Tape Challenge Measure: a regulatory reform that has been formally reviewed through the RTC process, agreed by the UK Reducing Regulation sub-Committee and announced by departments as part of the outcome of a Red Tape Challenge 'theme'.

Red Tape Reduction Day: statutory provision of British Columbia, Canada, from 2015.

Reducing Regulation Sub-Committee (RRC): a UK cabinet sub-committee established to take strategic oversight of the delivery of the Government's regulatory framework.

Regulate/regulatory: to have the effect of increasing the scope of government regulation or adding government controls to an industry or sector.

Regulation: a rule or guidance with which failure to comply would result in the regulated entity or person coming into conflict with the law or being ineligible for continued funding, grants and other applied for schemes. This can be summarised as all measures with legal force imposed by central government and other schemes operated by central government. Regulation does not include tax and spending decisions.

Regulatory Policy Committee: an advisory committee of independent experts that provides external and independent challenge on the evidence and analysis presented in impact assessments (IAs).

Regulatory Policy Committee confirmation: the decision of the RPC of whether a measure is suitable for the fast track, based on the regulatory triage assessment for that measure and assessed against the eligibility criteria set by RRC.

Regulatory Policy Committee opinion: the decision of the RPC on whether an impact assessment is fit for purpose.

Regulatory Policy Committee validation: the process by which RPC examines and agrees the EANCB figure of fast track measures that are in scope for one in, two out. This would normally be based on the final stage impact assessment prepared by departments, or alternatively the validation stage IA. Validation normally takes place in parallel with final stage policy clearance.

Regulatory Triage Assessment: the form completed by departments for fast track measures that is submitted to RPC in order to obtain RPC confirmation that a measure is suitable for the fast track process.

Secondary legislation: an alternative term for subordinate legislation.

Sensitivity Analysis: analysis of the effects on an appraisal of varying the projected values of important variables.

Small and micro-business assessment (SaMBA): an approach to analysis intended to ensure that all new regulatory proposals are designed and implemented so as to mitigate disproportionate burdens.

Small business: businesses with 11–49 employees.

Standard cost model: provides a framework for measuring the administrative burdens of regulation.

Statement of New Regulation (SNR): a six-monthly publication, setting out measures which will come into force over the coming six months and reporting on progress under one in, one out (OIOO) and one in, two out (OITO).

Statutory guidance: guidance which is produced pursuant to powers or duties in legislation, i.e. where an Act of Parliament explicitly provides for ministers or others to issue guidance and includes a duty to comply with that guidance.

Statutory instrument: the form in which most secondary legislation is made in the UK.

Subordinate legislation: subordinate legislation is defined in s21(1) of the Interpretation Act 1978 as meaning Orders in Council, orders, rules, regulations, schemes, warrants, by-laws and other instruments made or to be made under an Act.

Sunset and review clauses: provisions included in legislation to ensure that regulatory measures with a significant cost to business must face review (and, where applicable, be subject to sunsetting).

Systemic financial risk: the risk that the inability of one institution to meet its obligations when due will cause other institutions to be unable to meet their obligations when due. Such a failure may cause significant liquidity or credit problems and, as a result, could threaten the stability of or confidence in markets.

Tax impact assessment: tailored impact assessment used to understand the wide range of impacts associated with tax policy options to inform decision-making.

Time-limited measure: a measure where the relevant legislation includes a date on which it, or part of it, will cease to have effect.

Transition costs and benefits: transient, or one-off costs or benefits that occur, which normally relate to the implementation of the measure.

Transposition Principles: Principle 5 a) to e) of the Government's Guiding Principles for EU legislation.

Triage: The process of early assessment by departments that determines whether a measure is suitable for the fast track or requires a full impact assessment.

Waiver: a decision to dis-apply a better regulation requirement from any individual measure to which it would otherwise apply. Waivers are agreed by RRC.

Zero net cost: a measure which is scored as zero under one in, two out.

BIBLIOGRAPHY

Aaronson, Graham, *An oxymoronic endeavour? A general anti-abuse rule for taxation to give effect to the will of Parliament by overriding Parliament's statutes,* Statute Law Society, Lecture, February 2013

General anti-abuse rule (GAAR) Advisory Panel, terms of reference, HMRC, May 2013

Abrahamson, Elkan, *Call by families for a 'Hillsborough law' to criminalise cover-ups',* Times, 8 September 2016

Abravanel, Roger, *Meritocrazia,* 2008 (www.meritocrazia.com)

Action on Smoking and Health, *Briefing on Tobacco Vending Machines,* September 2011

Adams, John, *Risk,* University College London Press, 1995

Advisory Committee on Business Appointments, *Guidance,* 21 December 2016

Aldrick, Philip, *'One in, three out' to cut cost of red tape by £10bn,* Times, 4 March 2016

Regular guys?, Times, 25 January 2014

Alemanno, A., and Meuwese, A., *Impact assessment of EU non-legislative rulemaking: the missing link in 'new comitology',* [2013]19(1) *European Law Journal* 76

Ambler, T., et al., *The British Regulatory System,* British Chamber of Commerce, March 2008

Ambler, Tim, and Boyfield, Keith, *Route map to reform: deregulation,* Adam Smith Institute, 2005

Ambler, Tim, Chittenden, Francis, and Obodovski, Mikhail, *How much regulation is gold plate?* British Chamber of Commerce, 2003

American Tort Reform Association, *Noneconomic damages reform,* American Tort Reform Association, 2002

Anagnostaras, G., *The allocation of responsibility in state liability actions for breach of community law,* (2001) European Law Review 26

Andrews, Peter, *Did life and pensions 'disclosure' work as expected?* Financial Services Authority, April 2009

Annan, Kofi, *Essay,* Spiegel Online, 22 February 2016

Anthony, Carol, *On top form*, Letter, Law Society Gazette, 16 February 2012

Appleton, Josie, *Checking up: how the coalition's plans to cut back on criminal records have been defeated*, Civitas, October 2014

    Officious: rise of the busybody state, Zero Books, 2016

    Let's call time in this flow of useless booze rules, Times, 13 August 2010

    PSPOS: a busybodies charter, Manifesto Club, 2016

Archbold, *Criminal pleading, evidence and practice*, Sweet and Maxwell, 1995

Arculus, David, *Better Regulation Task Force*, Press Release, 17 July 2003

Arculus, David, and Smith, Julian, *The Arculus Review: enabling enterprise, encouraging responsibility*, Conservative Party, May 2009

Argument, Stephen, *Legislative scrutiny in Australia: wisdom to export?*, [2011]32(2) Statute Law Review 116–148

Arthur, Terry, and Booth, Philip, *Does Britain need a financial regulator? Statutory regulation, private regulation and financial markets*, Institute of Economic Affairs, 2010

Ashton, James, *Bloodlust for bankers won't be sated*, Evening Standard, 29 July 2014

Asthana, Anushka, *Revealed: British councils used RIPA to secretly spy on public: Local authorities used Regulation of Investigatory Powers Act to follow people, including dog walkers*, Guardian, 25 December 2016

Australian Administrative Review Council, *Report on Rule-making by Commonwealth agencies*, ARC 35 1992

Australian Government, *Annual red tape reduction report 2015*, 2016

    Cutting Red Tape, http://cuttingredtape.gov.au, 2015

Ayres, Ian, and Braithwaite, John, *Responsive regulation: transcending the deregulation debate*, Oxford University Press, 1992, 35

Bailey, Andrew, *Culture in financial institutions: it's everywhere and nowhere*, Speech, Hong Kong Monetary Authority, 16 March 2017

Baker, R., *Harold Shipman: The aftermath, implications of Harold Shipman for general practice*, [2004]80 Postgraduate Medical Journal 303–306

Bakie, John, *DB fined after $10 billion seeps through money laundering controls*, Global Custodian, 31 January 2017

Baksi, Catherine, *Grayling not giving up on regulatory reform*, Law Society Gazette, 9 July 2014

Baldwin, R., *Better regulation: the search and the struggle*, in Baldwin et al., *Oxford Handbook of Regulation*, Oxford University Press, 2010

Ball, James, *Richard O'Dwyer: living with the threat of extradition*, Guardian, 6 December 2012

Bank of England, *Our Code: our commitment to how we work*, Bank of England, September 2016

Barber, Michael, *Instruction to deliver: Tony Blair, the public services and the challenge of delivery*, Politico, 2007

Barber, Sarah, *The Psychoactive Substances Bill 2015–2016: Report on Committee Stage*, House of Commons Library, Briefing Paper Number 7468, 15 January 2016

Bartholomew, James, *Who needs governments? The Spanish seem to be doing better without one*, Spectator, 30 April 2016

Bartlett, Bruce, *How excessive government killed ancient Rome*, [1994]14(2) *Cato Journal* 287

Bartlett, Karen, *Drawing attention to the sex trade*, Times, 20 March 2010

Bates, T. StJ N., *Editorial: Henry Thring – a hundred years on*, [2007]28(1) *Statute Law Review* iii

Batkins, Sam, *600 major regulations*, American Action Forum, 6 August 2016

BBC, *May contain nuts*, Panorama, BBC TV, 20 April 2009

 One foot in the grave, BBC TV, 1990 to 2000

 Tory plan for red tape 'tax cut', BBC News, 13 August 2007

Bennion, Francis, *Statute law obscurity and the drafting parameters*, [1978]5 *British Journal of Law and Society* 235

Bentham, Jeremy, *A protest against law taxes*, 1795

Berlins, Marcel, *A Kafkaesque excuse for ignorance of the law*, Guardian, 3 November 2008

Bernadino, Gabriel, *EIOPA's vision on private pensions – enhanced sustainability, strong governance and full transparency*, Speech, National Association of Pension Funds, Liverpool, 17 October 2014

Better Government Initiative, *Good Government: reforming parliament and the executive: recommendations from the executive committee of the Better Government Initiative*, January 2010

Better Regulation Delivery Office, *Regulators' Code*, Department for Business Innovation and Skills, April 2014

Better Regulation Executive, *A bill for better regulation: consultation document*, July 2005

 Administrative burdens: routes to reduction, September 2006

 Citizens perceptions on regulation, January 2007, Cabinet Office, June 2007

 Making it simple, annual review 2008, 2009

 Reducing regulation made simple, 2010

 The fifth statement of new regulation, December 2012

 The good guidelines guide: taking the uncertainty out of regulation, Department for Business Enterprise and Regulatory Reform, January 2009

 The total benefit/cost ration of new regulations 2008/2009, Department for Business Innovation and Skills, 21 October 2009

Better Regulation Task Force, *Avoiding regulatory creep*, October 2004

 Better regulation for civil society: making life easier for those who help others, November 2005

 Better routes to redress, 2004

Principles of good regulation, 2003

Regulation – less is more: reducing burdens, improving outcomes: a BRTF Report to the Prime Minister, 2005

Better Regulation Watchdog, *Founding statement*, 15 May 2015

Bew, Paul, *Eleventh Annual Audit of Political Engagement, Speech*, Hansard Society, 30 April 2014

Bichard, Michael, *The Bichard inquiry report*, House of Commons, HC653, 22 June 2004

Big Brother Watch, *The grim RIPA*, 28 May 2010

    The Regulation of Investigatory Powers Act (RIPA), briefing note, 4 December 2014

Bindman, Dan, *SRA v Hemmings, SRA Case No 11283–2014, RA v McDonald, SRA Case*, Legal Futures, 6 May 2016

Bingham, John, and Prince, Rosa, *Attorney General Baroness Scotland fined £5,000 over illegal immigrant housekeeper*, Daily Telegraph, 22 September 2009

Bingham, Tom, *The judge as lawmaker: an English perspective, in The Struggle for Simplicity in the Law: Essays for Lord Cooke of Thorndon*, New Zealand, 1997

    The rule of law, Allen Lane, 2010

Bingham Centre for the Rule of Law, *Judicial review and the rule of law*, November 2015

Birch, Hayley, *Do 20 mph speed limits actually work?* Guardian, 29 May 2015

Blair, Tony, *A journey*, Hutchinson, 2010

    Compensation culture, Speech, Institute for Public Policy Research, Guardian, 26 May 2005

    Foreword, *Better policy making: a guide to regulatory impact assessment*, 2003, no longer available

Blake, Leslie, Pointing, John, and Sinnamon, Tim, *Over regulation and suing the state for negligent legislation* [2007]28(3) *Statute Law Review* 218–234

Blaxall, Martin, and Sheldon, Rob, *Out of sight*, Utility Week, 22 February 2008

Blond, Philip, Antonacopoulou, Elena, and Pabst, Adrian, *In professions we trust*, ResPublica, July 2015

Blundell, John, and Robinson, Colin, *Regulation without the state*, IEA, 2000

Booker, Christopher, *£1 million bill for social workers getting it wrong*, Daily Telegraph, 4 September 2016

Bortholomew, James, *The welfare of nations*, Biteback, 2015

Botsford, Polly, *Working to rule*, Law Society Gazette, 23 June 2011

Bowles, Samuel, *The moral economy: why good incentives are no substitute for good citizens*, Yale University Press, 2016

Breakwell, Glynis, *The psychology of risk*, Cambridge, 2007

Briggs, Michael, *Civil courts structure review: interim report*, Judiciary of England and Wales, December 2015

Brinkman, Sally, et al., *Efficacy of infant simulator programmes to prevent teenage pregnancy: a school-based cluster randomised controlled trial in Western Australia*, The Lancet, 25 August 2016

British Chambers of Commerce, *The burdens barometer 2010*, 2010

Broke, Adam, *Simplification of tax, or I wouldn't start from here*, ICAEW Tax Faculty Hardman Lecture, 1999

Brookes, Libby, *Scottish plan for every child to have 'named person' breaches rights*, Guardian, 28 July 2016

Broomer, Charles, *Letter*, Law Society's Gazette, 29 September 2014

Brougham, Lord, *Speech*, Hansard, HC Deb XXIV column 259, [1830]

Brown, John Murray, *Lawyers lose out as Ireland bucks trend with crackdown on tort law*, Financial Times, 23 December 2006

Brown, Tracey and Hanlon, Michael, *In the interests of safety: the absurd rules that blight our lives and how we can change them*, Sphere, 2014

Brunvand, Jan Harold, *Too good to be true*, W. W. Norton, 1999

Buchanan, Mark, *Risky business as usual*, New Scientist, 6 August 2016

Buell, Samuel, *Capital offenses: business crime and punishment in America's corporate age*, W. W. Norton, 2016

Burke, Edmund, *Reflections on the Revolution in France*, Dodsley, 1790
  Speech to the electors of Bristol, [1774]1 *Works* 446–448

Burnet, Gilbert, *The history of the Reformation of the Church of England*, Volume 2, 1680

Burns, Lord, *Final report, committee of inquiry into hunting with dogs*, Home Office, 9 June 2000

Burt, Tim, *Ofcom considers scheme to trade airwaves*, Financial Times, 20 November 2003

Byrne, A., Harrison, D., and Blake, D., *Pyrrhic victory? The unintended consequences of the Pensions Act 2004*, [2006]26(3) *Economic Affairs* 9–16

Cabinet Office, *A better regulation strategy for the public sector*, 2007
  Behavioural Insights Team, *Annual report 2016*, http://38r8om2xjhhl25mw 24492dir.wpengine.netdna-cdn.com/wp-content/uploads/2016/09/BIT_ Update_Report_2015-16-.pdf
  Business impact assessment calculator, 7 June 2016
  Business impact assessment calculator: IA template user manual, March 2016
  Cabinet Committees, 18 October 2016
  Good government: mid term review, November 2012
  Good government: reforming Parliament and Executive, January 2010
  'Good law' initiative: UK government effort to make legislation more effective and accessible, 2013
  Guide to better European regulation, 21 July 2000
  Guide to making legislation, 2015
  Guide to making legislation, June 2012

Next steps in the government's quango programme, Press Release, 28 December 2012

Public bodies 2012, 2012

Public bodies 2016, January 2017

Public bodies reform – proposals for change, 14 October 2010

Regulatory futures review, January 2017

Review of the Regulatory Reform Act 2001, July 2005

Strathclyde review: secondary legislation and the primacy of the House of Commons, Cm 9177, December 2015

UK Ministerial Code, October 2015

When laws become too complex, 16 April 2013

White paper on post-legislative scrutiny: the government's approach, Cm 7320, N.d.

Caddell, Richard, The referee's liability for catastrophic sports injuries – a UK perspective, [2005]15(2) *Marquette Sports Law Review* 415

Cahal, Milmo, *Dispute over 'botched' £70,000 family will signed by the wrong spouses reaches Supreme Court*, Independent, 3 December 2013

Caird, Jack Simson, Hazell, Robert, and Oliver, Dawn, *The constitutional standards of the House of Lords Select Committee on the constitution*, University College London, Constitution Unit, January 2014

Calabresi, Guido, *A common law for the age of statutes*, Harvard University Press, 1982

Caldicott, Fiona, *Report on the review of patient-identifiable information*, Department of Health, December 1997 (the Caldicott Committee)

Caldwell, Miller H., *Authors and children*, Letter, Times, 18 July 2009

Camus, Albert, *The myth of Sisyphus*, 1942

Canada Privy Council, *Guide to making federal acts and regulations*, Department of Justice Canada, 2nd edn, 2001

Cancer Drugs Fund, *Guidance to support operation of the Caner Drugs Fund in 2012–13*, Department of Health, 2012

Carnegy, Hugh, *France unveils measures for deregulation as it seeks budget approval*, Financial Times, 16 October 2014

Carter, Ross, *Statutory interpretation using legislated examples: Bennion on multiple consumer credit agreements*, [2011]32(2) *Statute Law Review* 86–115

Cassini, Martin, and Wellings, Richard, *Seeing Red: traffic controls and the economy*, IEA Discussion paper 68, January 2016

Cavanagh-Pack, Michael, *Letter*, Times, 10 March 2004

Cave, Andrew, *Blame culture 'is road to suicide'*, Daily Telegraph, 3 February 2004

Cavendish, Camilla, *Baby Maddy wasn't putting on weight … What happens when the state takes your child away?* Times, 5 January 2013

Children are safer with their natural families, Times, 8 May 2009

Two men are incarcerated by the State, when they should be the stability in two children's lives, Times, 13 March 2008

We are all suspects in the new inquisition's eyes, Times, 1 May 2009

Why focus on meeting targets did not save Baby P, Times, 2 December 2008

CCH, *Daily Newsletter,* 9 March 2016

Centre for Social Justice, *Dynamic benefits: towards welfare that works,* A Policy Report by the CSJ Economic Dependency Working Group, 16 September 2009

Centre for Socio-Legal Studies, *Programme in comparative media law and policy: a comparative study of costs in defamation proceedings across Europe,* December 2008

Chao, Xi, *Local courts as legislators? Judicial lawmaking by subnational courts in China,* [2012] Statute Law Review 39–57

Charities and Voluntary Organisations Task Force, *Report Volume II,* 1994

Chesterton, G. K., *The man who was Thursday,* 1908

Child, Andrew, *Tackling a business burden: red tape remains a serious challenge, especially for small and mid-sized companies,* Financial Times, 10 May 2011

Chittenden, Francis, Foster, Hilary, and Sloan, Brian, *Taxation and red tape,* Institute of Economic Affairs, 2010

Chynoweth, Carly, *The endless list of rules that drove National Trust boss batty,* Times, 8 October 2010

Citizens against Public Waste, *Congressional pig book 2016,* 2016

Civil Engineer, *The Life of Isambard Kingdom Brunel,* 1870, reprinted in Cambridge Library Collection, 2013

Civil Justice Council, *Online dispute resolution for low value civil claims,* February 2015

The Damages-Based Agreements reform project: drafting and policy issues, August 2015

Clark, Gregory, *The long march of history: Farm wages, population, and economic growth, England 1209–1869,* [2007]60(1) Economic History Review 97–135

Clark, Ross, *How to label a goat: the silly rules and regulations that are strangling Britain,* Harriman House, 2006

Clarke, Kenneth, *Speech,* Hansard, Commons, col 170, 26 November 1996

Clegg, Nick, *DPM announces plans to cut red tape for small business,* Office of the Deputy Prime Minister, 25 October 2011

Speech, Office of the Deputy Prime Minister, 10 May 2010

Clementi, David, *Review of the regulatory framework for legal services in England and Wales,* Department of Constitutional Affairs, December 2004

Coffey, Bentley, McLaughlin, Patrick A., and Peretto, Pietro, *The cumulative cost of regulations,* Mercatus Centre, George Mason University, Working Paper, April 2016

Colander, David, and Kupers, Roland, *Complexity and the art of public policy: solving society's problems from the bottom up*, Princeton University Press, 2014

Coltart, Christopher, *Rip it up and start again*, Law Society Gazette, 30 June 2014

Commissioner Bill Pincus QC, *Queensland Fuel Subsidy Commission of Inquiry Report*, 21 November 2007

Committee on Ministers' Powers, *Report (the Donoughmore Committee)*, Cmd 4060, April 1932

Committee on Standards in Public Life, *Ethical standards for providers of public services*, June 2014

Committee on the Civil Service, *The Report of the Committee on the Civil Service (Fulton Report)*, Cmnd 3638, 1968

Commonwealth Association of Legislative Counsel, *Papers*

Competition Commission, *Safeway plc and ASDA Group Limited (owned by Wal-Mart Stores Inc); Wm Morrison Supermarkets PLC; J Sainsbury plc; and Tesco plc: A report on the mergers in contemplation*, 2003

Comptroller and Auditor General, *Better regulation: making good use of regulatory impact assessments*, Report No HC 329, National Audit Office, 8 November 2001

   Evaluation of regulatory impact assessments 2006–7, Report No HC 606, National Audit Office, 11 July 2007

Corley, Elizabeth, *Investors miss 2.3% of return due to regulatory costs*, Funds Europe, 7 October 2013

Cornerstone Research, *Securities class action settlements: 2015 review*, 2016

Cornford, F. M., *Microcosmographia academica*, 1908

Corrigan, James, *No more Open at Muirfield after golf club votes against allowing women to join as members*, Daily Telegraph, 19 May 2016

Cracknell, Richard, and Clements, Rob, *Acts and statutory instruments: volume of UK legislation 1950 to 2006*, House of Commons Library, 5 February 2007

   Acts and statutory instruments: the volume of UK legislation 1950 to 2014, House of Commons Library, 19 March 2014

Craig, P., *Once more unto the breach: the community, the state and damages liability* [2001] LQR 196

Crews, Clyde Wayne, Jr, *Ten thousand commandments: an annual snapshot of the federal regulatory state*, Competitive Enterprise Institute, 2014

Criminal Injuries Compensation Authority, *Annual report and accounts 2015–2016*, HC 470, July 2016

Criminal Justice Alliance, *Structured mayhem: personal experiences of the Crown Court*, 2015

Croft, Jane, *Private prosecutions grow as state bodies retreat in face of dwindling resources*, Financial Times, 28 July 2014

Cross, Michael, *UK facing UN censure on costly litigation*, Law Society's Gazette, 7 August 2017

Crown Prosecution Service, *Guidance for prosecutors on 'revenge' pornography*, 6 October 2014

Cummings, Dolan, *28¾ – How constant age checks are infantilising adults*, Manifesto Club, September 2010

Cunliffe, Jon, and Dombret, Andreas, A *missing tool against 'too big to fail'*, Wall Street Journal Europe, 2 June 2014

Cunningham, Scott, and Shah, Manisha, *Decriminalizing indoor prostitution: implications for sexual violence and public health*, Working Paper No 20281, National Bureau of Economic Research, 17 July 2014

Currie, David, and Cubbin, John, *Regulatory creep and regulatory withdrawal: why regulatory withdrawal is feasible and necessary*, City University, March 2002

Daintith, Terence, and Page, Alan, *The executive and the constitution*, Oxford University Press, 1999

Dale, Iain, *The Tories should remember how they revived our docks*, Daily Telegraph, 10 April 2009

Dale, William, *The European legislative scene*, [1992]13 *Statute Law Review* 79

Danielsson, Jon, and Zhou, Chen, *Why is risk so hard to measure?* Risk Research, June 2016

Danish Business Authority, *Burden hunter – hunting administration burdens and red tape*, N.d.

Davis, Simon, *Report of the inquiry into the events of 27/28 March 2014 relating to the press briefing of information in the Financial Conduct Authority's 2014/15 Business Plan*, Clifford Chance, 20 November 2014

Dawson, John, and Seater, John, *Federal regulation and aggregate economic growth*, January 2013

Day, Mark, et al., *Strangeways 25 years on: achieving fairness and justice in our prisons*, Prison Reform Trust, 2015

Dear, Geoffrey, *Monitoring of firearms holders needs to be continuous and more effective*, Letter, Times, 17 September 2015

Decker, Christopher, *Modern economic regulation*, Cambridge University Press, 2015

Deighton-Smith, Rex, Erbacci, Angelo, and Kauffmann, Celine, *Promoting inclusive growth through better regulation: the role of regulatory impact assessment*, Regulatory Policy Working Papers No 3, OECD, February 2016

Deloitte, *The cost of regulation study*, Financial Services Authority and Financial Services Practitioner Panel, 2006

Department for Business Energy and Industrial Strategy, *Regulatory impact assessments: a guide for government officials*, 7 June 2016

Department for Business, Enterprise and Regulatory Reform, *25 ideas for simplifying EU law*, 22 July 2008

Department for Business Innovation and Skills, *Policy paper: 2010 to 2015 government policy: business regulation*, updated 8 May 2015

Accountability for regulator impact policy, 2013

Alternative dispute resolution for consumers, November 2014.

Better regulation framework manual: practical guidance for UK government officials, March 2015

Better regulation, better benefits: getting the balance right, October 2009

BIS ninth statement of new regulation, regulations covering January–June 2015, January 2015

Vince Cable bins business red tape, Press Release, 18 March 2011

Alternative dispute resolution for consumers: implementing the Alternative Dispute Resolution Directive and Online Dispute Resolution Regulation, March 2014

Framework document, January 2017

Green paper: corporate governance reform, November 2016

List of regulators, 19 September 2015

Make business your business: supporting the start-up and development of small business, 28 May 2012

New rules to hand over powers to individuals and companies by cutting red tape and bureaucracy, Press Release, 5 August 2010

Regulators' code, April 2014

Regulatory overview: the regulatory landscape, May 2015 to May 2016, [2016]

Small business, big support, Press Release, 27 January 2014

Department for Business Innovation and Skills and Better Regulation Delivery Office, *Regulators' code*, April 2014

Department for Employment, *Discrimination guidance*, undated, www.nidirect .gov.uk/index/information-and-services/employment/discrimination-at-work/sexual-orientation-discrimination.htm

Department for Transport, *Signing the way: traffic signs policy paper*, October 2011

Department of Education, *Guidance on the meaning of supervision*, 2012

Department of Environment, Transport and Regions, *A new deal for transport: better for everyone*, 1988

Department of Health, *Consultation on the future of tobacco control*, 2008

Consultation on the implementation of the revised Tobacco Products Directive (2014/40/EU), July 2015

Guidance on ending tobacco sales from vending machines in England, Local Government Regulatory Support Unit and Department of Health, 25 August 2011

Healthy lives, healthy people: our strategy for public health in England, 2010

Department of Justice Canada, *Regulatory impact analysis statement*, 4 July 2014

Department of Work and Pensions, *Review of employers' liability compulsory insurance, second stage report*, 4 December 2003

Derbyshire County Council, *Labelling for bread and cakes*, Derbyshire County Council Trading Standards Service, 2014

Dewhurst, Dale, Levert, Lionel, and Zariski, Archie, *Producing legislative counsel: ways and means*, [2012]33(3) Statute Law Review 339–353

Dicey, A. V., *Lectures on the relation between the law and public opinion in England during the nineteenth century*, 1914

Dommett, Katherine, Flinders, Matthew, Skelcher, Chris, and Tonkiss, Katherine, *Did they read before burning? The Coalition and quangos*, [2014]85 *Political Quarterly* 133–142

Douglas, Mary, and Wildavsky, Aaron, *Risk and culture*, University of California, 1983

Doward, Jamie, *The chronicle of a tragedy foretold: Grenfell Tower: government and councils were warned repeatedly about fire safety experts' fears over tower blocks as far back as 1999*, Observer, 17 June 2017

Drakeman, Donald L., *What Yenshaw could have said*, Statute Law Society, lecture, 12 October 2015

Dubash, Navroz, and Morgan, Bronwen, *The rise of the regulatory state of the south*, Oxford University Press, 2013

Dudley, Susan, and Warren, Melinda, *Regulators' budget from Eisenhower to Obama: an analysis of the US budget for fiscal years 1960 through 2017*, Regulatory Studies Centre, George Washington University, 17 May 2016

Duff & Phelps, *Global regulatory outlook 2017*, 2017

Duffy, John C., and Snowdon, Christopher, *The minimal evidence for minimal pricing: the fatal flaws in the Sheffield alcohol policy model*, Adam Smith Institute, 2012

Duncan, Gary, *Biting reality of too much regulation*, Times, 27 January 2003

Dunlop, Claire A., and Radaelli, Claudio M., *Handbook of regulatory impact assessment*, Edward Elgar, 2016

Dyson, John, *Delay too often defeats justice*, Speech, Law Society Magna Carta Event, 22 April 2015

    Magna Carta and compensation culture, High Sheriff of Oxfordshire's Annual Law Lecture, 13 October 2015

    Where the common law fears to tread, annual lecture for the Administrative Law Bar Association, [2013]34(1) *Statute Law Review* 1–11

    Is judicial review a threat to democracy? The Sultan Azlan Shah lecture, November 2015

Ebrahami, Helia, *Margaret Hodges's family company pays just 0.01pc tax on £2.1bn of business generated in the UK*, Daily Telegraph, 9 November 2012

Economist, *A toxic mix: risk, regulation and children*, 19 September 2009

    Broken: recollections of a bygone era when the market enforced good behaviour, 13 July 2013

    Delivery men, 3 September 2016

    Hitting at terrorists, hurting business: forcing banks to police the financial system is causing nasty side effects, 14 June 2014

    Italy's judicial system: justice denied?, 19 July 2014

Jail bait: the lock-'em up mentality for white-collar crime is misguided, 29 October 2016

Leader, *A personal choice: the internet is making the buying and selling of sex easier and safer; government should stop trying to ban it*, 9 August 2014

Legislative verbosity: outrageous bills, 23 November 2014

Mens rea: what were you thinking?, 24 January 2015

Over-regulated America: the home of laissez-faire is being suffocated by excessive and badly written regulation, 18 February 2012

Remittances: costly cash: regulation is raising the cost of sending money to the world's poor. reform it, 5 September 2015

The 140,000-code question: how complex are health regulations?, 31 May 2014

Yes, we have no straight bananas, 28 May 2016

Edkins, Georgia, *"I'm to blame": Blunkett's indefinite prison sentences and the thousands still locked up without hope: Imprisonment for Public Protection (IPP) sentences were ruled a violation of human rights*, New Statesman, 14 August 2017

Edmonds, Timothy, *Financial Services: European aspects*, House of Commons Library, Briefing Paper No 07435, 17 December 2015

Edward, Scott, *Enterprise and Regulatory Reform Bill HL Bill 45 of 2012–13*, House of Lords Library Note LLN 2012/038, 2013

Eichengreen, Barry, *France lacks the moral authority to depose the dollar*, 9 July 2014

Ekins, Richard, A guide to the Supreme Court Justices, Spectator, 3 December 2016

Engel, Matthew, *Dispatch*, FT.COM Magazine, 7 November 2009

Ensign, Rachel Louise, *Lenders bolster risk and compliance staff*, Wall Street Journal, 4 May 2014

Erickson, Angela C., *Barriers to Braiding: how job-killing licensing laws tangle natural hair care in needless red tape*, Institute for Justice, July 2016

Essex County Council, *Parking standards: design and good practice*, Consultation Draft, March 2009

Regional Planning Guidance 9 and Planning Policy Guidance 13, March 2001

Etherton, Terence, *Speech*, Ministry of Justice, 25 October 2006

European Commission, *Better regulation for better results – an EU agenda*, COM(2015) 215 final, Strasbourg, 19 May 2015

Better regulation for growth and jobs in the EU, COM (2005) 97, revised in COM (2006) 690 final, October 2005

Better regulation guidelines, SWD(2015) 111 final, Strasbourg, 19 May 2015

Better regulation toolbox, 19 May 2015

Commission communication to the Council and the European parliament, follow up of the Sutherland report, COM(93) 361 final and SEC (92) 2227 fin, December 1993

Communication from the Commission to the Council, the EOP and the ESC, on the handling of urgent situations in the context of implementation of community rules: follow up to the Sutherland report, COM(93)430 fin, December 1993

Communication from the Commission to the European Parliament, the Council, the European Economic and Social Committee and the Committee of the Regions, Regulatory Fitness and Performance (REFIT): results and next steps, COM(2013) 685 final, Brussels, 2 October 2013

Communication from the Commission to the European Parliament, the Council, the European Economic and Social Committee and the Committee of the Regions, EU regulatory fitness, SWD(2012) 422 final, 12 December 2012

Communication from the Commission, follow-up to the Sutherland report: legislative consolidation to enhance the transparency of community law in the area of the internal market, COM (93) 361(fin), 16 December 1993

Communication of the Commission, implementing the Community Lisbon programme: a strategy for the simplification of the regulatory environment, COM (2005) 535, 2005

Communication to the Commission: Regulatory Scrutiny Board: mission, tasks and staff, Strasbourg, C(2015) 3262 final, 19 May 2015

Cutting red tape in Europe, Final Report, High Level Group on Administrative Burdens, Brussels, 24 July 2014

Decision of the President of the European Commission on the establishment of an independent Regulatory Scrutiny Board, Strasbourg, C(2015) 3263 final, 19 May 2015

Deregulation is essential for economic recovery, Press Release EU NEWS 26/98, European Commission, 4 November 1998

European Union Communication from the Commission, European Transparency Initiative, a framework for relations with interest representatives (Register and Code of Conduct), SEC(2008) 1926, (COM(2008)323 final), Brussels, 27 May 2008

Evaluation, better regulation, Brussels, 27 June 2016

Final adoption of new rules to cut red tape on citizens' public documents, Press Release, Brussels, 9 June 2016

Letter to Frans Timmermans from 27 member states, 15 November 2015

Members of the Regulatory Scrutiny Board, COM/2015/20009, EU, *Official Journal*, C257A, 6 August 2015

Opinion of the Economic and Social Committee (ESC) of 5 May 1993 on the Commission communication on the operation of the community's internal market after 1992: follow-up to the Sutherland report, OJ No C 201/59, 26 July 1993

Proposal for a directive of the European Parliament and of the Council on the activities and supervision of institutions for occupational retirement provision, EU 2014/0091 (COD), 2014

Proposal for an interinstitutional agreement on better regulation, COM(2015) 216 final, Strasbourg, 19 May 2015

REFIT: making EU law lighter, simpler and less costly, August 2014

Regulatory Fitness and Performance programme (REFIT), December 2013, European Commission, COM(2012) 746 final, Strasbourg, 12 December 2012

Regulatory Fitness and Performance Programme (REFIT) state of play and outlook 'REFIT Scoreboard', SWD(2015)110 final, Strasbourg 19 May 2015

Regulatory Fitness and Performance Programme (REFIT): state of play and outlook, COM(2014) 368 final and SWD(2014) 192 final, 18 June 2014

Smart regulation in the European Union, COM(2010) 543 final, 8 October 2010

Staff working paper of 28 February 2000, providing background material to the Commission Communication on the review of the SLIM pilot project; action plan, simplifying and improving the regulatory environment, COM (2002) 278 final, 28 February 2000

Strengthening the foundations of smart regulation: improving evaluation, COM (2013) 686 final, 2 October 2013

Subsidiarity and proportionality, 18th annual report on better lawmaking, COM(2011) 344 final, Brussels, 6 October 2011

Supplement to European Report No 1808 of 31 October 1992 ('The Sutherland report'), 31 October 1992

The Brussels Programme, COM(93) 545, 1993

The internal market after 1992: meeting the challenge, report to the EEC Commission by the High Level Group on the operation of the internal market, SEC(92) 2044, 1993

Third annual report on simplifying the regulatory environment, COM(2009) 17 final, Brussels, 28 January 2009

Tobacco Products Directive (Directive 2014/40/EU on the approximation of the laws, regulations and administrative provisions of the Member States concerning the manufacture, presentation and sale of tobacco and related products and repealing Directive 2001/37/EC), OJ L 127 p1, Brussels, 29 April 2014

What is REFIT, Better Regulation, http://ec.europa.eu/smart-regulation/refit/index

European Court of Justice, *Reform of the EU court system*, Press Release No 44/15, 28 April 2015

European Insurance and Occupational Pensions Authority, *Report on issues leading to detriment of occupational pension scheme members and beneficiaries and potential scope of action for EIOPA*, EIOPA-BoS -14/071, 27 June 2014

European Parliament, *Comparative study on the transposition of EC law in the member states*, July 2007

European Union, *A strategic review of better regulation in the European Union, communication from the Commission to the Council of the European*

Parliament, the European Economic and Social Committee and the Committee of the Regions, COM(2006) 690 (Final), N.d.

Directive 2013/11/EU of the European Parliament and of the Council of 21 May 2013 on alternative dispute resolution for consumer disputes and amending Regulation (EC) No 2006/2004

EU Regulation No 1169/2011 on Food Information to Consumers, December 2014

Inter-institutional Agreement of 20 December 1994 on an accelerated working method for official codification of legislative texts, OJ 102, p2–3, 4 April 1996

Report of Independent Experts on Legislative and Administrative Simplification, (Molitor Report) COM SEC (95) 1379, 1995

Simpler Legislation for the Internal Market project (*Simpler Legislation for the Internal Market*), 15 August 2015

Sutherland Report (The Internal Market after 1992: meeting the challenge, Report presented to the Commission by the High Level Group on the Functioning of the Internal Market), EC Com, 1992

EY, *Winning the global regulation game*, 2015

Fairbairn, Catherine, *Compensation bill*, House of Commons Library, 19 May 2006

Fairbairn, Catherine, and Woodhouse, John, *Social action, responsibility and heroism bill*, Commons Library Research Paper, 8 July 2014

Falconer, Charles, *Compensation culture*, Speech, 22 March 2005

Risk and redress, Speech, 14 November 2005

Feldman, David, *Legislation as aspiration: statutory expression of policy goals*, Statute Law Society, lecture, 16 March 2015

Ferguson, Niall, Lecture 2, *the Darwinian economy*, Reith Lectures, BBC, 2012

Fifield, Anna, *Business to have its say on tackling red tape*, Financial Times, 23 June 2004

Fildes, Christopher, *A new bank from a very old stable*, Spectator, 9 May 2009

Financial Conduct Authority, *Consultation paper CP13/10, detailed proposals for the FCA regime for consumer credit*, 3 October 2013

FCA handbook, N.d.

FCA publishes terms of reference for asset management market study, Press Release, 18 November 2016

Regulatory sandbox, November 2015

Financial Reporting Council, *UK Stewardship Code*, 2012

Cutting clutter: combating clutter in annual reports, 2011

Louder than words: principles and actions for making corporate reports less complex, June 2009

UK corporate governance code, 2012

Financial Services Authority, *Business plan 2009/10*, 2009

Report of the Financial Services Authority on the review of the regulation of the Equitable Life Assurance Society from 1 January 1999 to 8 December 2000 which Her Majesty's Government is submitting as evidence to the inquiry conducted by Lord Penrose, 16 October 2001

Fisher, Richard, *The United States is not Europe and Texas ain't France: America as the thoroughbred economy*, Speech, Cato Institute, 10 October 2010

Fishwick, Dave, *Bank of Dave*, Virgin Books, 2012

FitzGibbon, Francis, *Judicial activism*, blog, 6 September 2013

Flinders, Matthew, *MPs and icebergs: Parliament and delegated governance*, [2004]57(4) *Parliamentary Affairs*

Food Standards Agency, *Report from the ad hoc group on raw, rare and low temperature (RRLT) cooked food*, FSA Advisory Committee on the Microbiological Safety of Food, April 2014

   The safe production of beef burgers in catering establishments: advice for food business operators and LA officers, May 2016

Ford, Richard, *Trivial pursuits that turned the town hall snoopers into tyrants*, Times, 17 April 2009

Fouzder, Monidipa, *Give LIPs universal access to legal advice*, Law Society's Gazette, 28 November 2014

   SRA unveils slimline handbook and codes, Law Society Gazette, 6 June 2016

Fowler, Norman, *Ministers decide: a personal memoir of the Thatcher years*, Chapmans, 1992

Frecknall Hughes, Jane, et al., *An empirical analysis of the ethical reasoning process of tax practitioners*, [2013]114(2) *Journal of Business Ethics* 325–339

Freedman, Milton, *Government regulation*, www.youtube.com/watch?v=dZL25NSLhEA

Friel, Martin, *Sants: FSA's tough new stance should be feared*, Insurance Age, April 2009

Fukuyama, Francis, *America in decay: the sources of political dysfunction*, [2014]9 *Foreign Affairs* 5

Funk, William F., *The Paperwork Reduction Act: Paperwork reduction meets administrative law*, [1987]24(1) *Harvard Journal on Legislation* 1

Furedi, Frank, *Courting mistrust: the hidden growth of a culture of litigation in Britain*, Centre for Policy Studies, 1999

   The compensation culture is poisoning our society, Daily Telegraph, 9 September 2012

Furedi, Frank, and Bristow, Jennie, *Licensed to hug*, 2nd edn, Civitas, 2010

   The social cost of litigation, Centre for Policy Studies, September 2012

Gabbatt, Adam, *Richard O'Dwyer: living with the threat of extradition*, Guardian, 6 December 2012

Gaskell, Sarah, and Persson, Mats, *Still out of control? Measuring eleven years of EU regulation*, Open Europe, 2010

Gawande, Atul, *The checklist manifesto: how to get things right*, Profile Books, 2011

Gaziano, Todd F., *The use and abuse of executive orders and other presidential directives*, The Heritage Foundation, 21 February 2001

Gibb, Frances, *Lawyers v doctors: counting the cost of clinical negligence*, Times, 27 August 2015

MPs reopen debate over mandatory life sentences for murder, The Brief, Times, 9 September 2016

Gibbons, Michael, *Now is not the time to be relaxing on quality when significant regulatory change is ahead*, Speech, 28 March 2017

Gigerenzer, Gerd, *Risk savvy*, Allen Lane, 2014

Gill, John, *David Willetts interview: 'what I did was in the interests of young people'*, Times Educational Supplement, 18 June 2015

Gillbe, Ruth, *APFA tells FCA to streamline '8 foot' rule book*, FT Adviser, 2 September 2014

Gilmour, David, *The pursuit of Italy*, Penguin, 2012

Glassner, Barry, *The culture of fear: why Americans are afraid of the wrong things: crime, drugs, minorities, teen moms, killer kids, mutant microbes, plane crashes, roads rages and so much more*, Basic Books, 2009

Global Commission on Drugs Policy, *Advancing drug policy reform: a new approach to decriminalization*, Report, 2016

War on drugs, June 2011

Glover, Stephen, *We have never been closer to state control of the press*, Spectator, 10 January 2004

Goode, Roy, *Pension law reform: report of the Pensions Law Review Committee* (The Goode Committee), HMSO, 1993

Gordon, Richard, *Why Henry VIII clauses should be consigned to the dustbin of history*, Public Law Project, undated

Gould, Nick, *Common sense – the dark matter of business law*, paper given at University College London, Centre for Commercial Law, February 2011

Gower, LCB, *Review of Investor Protection, Report Part I*, Cmnd 9125, HMSO, January 1984

Grant, Madeline, *It's my party and I'll vape if I want to*, Institute of Economic Affairs, 31 August 2016

Grantham Journal, *Horseless vehicles*, 14 November 1896

Grayling, Chris, *Our bill to curb the elf and safety culture*, ConservativeHome.com, 2 June 2014

Protecting human rights in the UK: the Conservatives proposals for changing Britain's human rights law, Conservative Party, 2014

Green, Miranda, *University funding to face less red tape*, Financial Times, 20 November 2003

Greenberg, Daniel, *A refreshing decision, or the rule of law in action: case note Vehicle & Operator Services Agency, R on the application of v Kayes*, [2012]EWHC 1489 (Admin), [2012]33(3) *Statute Law Review* 409–411

Dangerous trends in modern legislation – and how to reverse them, Centre for Policy Studies, April 2016

Dangerous trends in modern legislation, [2015]1 *Public Law* 96–110

Secondary legislation and the primacy of Parliament (editorial), [2016]37(1) *Statute Law Review* iii

Griffith Jones, John, *Regulating in a recovery*, Speech, FCA, 13 November 2014

Griffiths, Brian, *Markets can't be improved by rules. Only by personal example*, Times, 9 April 2009

Grisham, John, *King of Torts*, Dell, 2012

Guardian, *A victim, not a hero: Tony Martin needs protection and help*, 29 July 2003

    Tunnock's sales take the teacake after Commonwealth Games ceremony: confectionery firm 'bowled over' as Waitrose reports 62% sales rise after giant dancing teacakes feature in opening event, 25 July 2014

Hakim, Catherine, *Supply and desire: sexuality and the sex industry in the 21st century*, Institute of Economic Affairs, August 2015

Haldane, Andy, *The dog and the frisbee*, Speech, Bank of England, 31 August 2012

    The Great Divide, Speech, New City Agenda Annual Dinner, 18 May 2016

    Turning the red tape tide, Speech, Bank of England, Financial Law Review Dinner, 10 April 2013

Hampton Report, *Reducing administrative burdens: effective inspection and enforcement*, HM Treasury, March 2005

Handwerker, Lloyd, and Reavill, Gil, *Famous Nathan: a family saga of Coney Island, the American Dream, and the search for the perfect hot dog*, Flatiron Books, 2016

Hanlon, Michael, *Flying scared*, Spectator, 12 July 2014

Hansard Society, *Making the law*, The Report of the Hansard Society Commission on the legislative process (Lord Rippon Report), November 1992

    The devil is in the detail, Parliament and delegated legislation, 2014

Harford, Tim, *How politicians poisoned statistics*, Financial Times Magazine, 16 April 2016

    The great EU Cabbage myth, BBC Radio 4 Programme, April 2016

Hargreaves, Stephen K., *Ashamed of the profession*, Law Society Gazette, Letter, 16 January 2017

Harries and Sawyer, *How to run a country: the burden of regulation*, ResPublica, December 2014

Harries, Richard, *Impact of the Lobbying Act on civil society and democratic engagement*, Commission on Civil Society and Democratic Engagement, September 2014

Harrison, Debbie, et al., *Pyrrhic victory? The unintended consequences of the Pensions Act 2004*, The Pensions Institute, Cass Business School, October 2005

Harrison, Michael, and Nicholson-Lord, David, *Heseltine lights flame of change: promised bonfire of red tape aims to widen choice for consumers and help industry by cutting billions of pounds off costs*, Independent, 20 January 1994

Haythornthwaite, Rick, *Memorandum*, February 2007

Hazeley, Jason, and Morris, Joel, *The Ladybird Book of Red Tape*, Michael Joseph, 2016

Hazell, Tony, *Making contact*, Financial Adviser, 19 May 2011

Hazlett, Thomas Winslow, *The political spectrum: the tumultuous liberation of wireless technology from Herbert Hoover to the smartphone*, Yale University Press, 2017

Health and Safety Executive, *Taking a wider perspective: HSE's fourth simplification plan and progress report*, Health and Safety Executive, December 2009

Health and Social Care Information Centre, *Student drinking dropped by a third between 2005 and 2013*, Health and Social Care Information Centre, Statistics on alcohol, England 2015, National Statistics, 25 June 2015

Heath, Allister, and Smith, David B., *At a price! The true cost of public spending*, Politeia, 2006

Heaton, Richard, *Good law*, Office of Parliamentary Counsel, 7 February 2014

TEDx Houses of Parliament speech, 2014

The Sir William Dale Memorial Lecture on legislation and good law, 14 May 2014

When laws become too complex: a review into the causes of complex legislation, Office of Parliamentary Counsel, 16 April 2013

Henderson, Scott, *Report of the Committee on Cruelty to Wild Animals*, Cmd 8266, 31 December 1951

Henley, John, *Welfare doesn't come into it*, Guardian, 6 January 2009

Heseltine, Michael, *No stone unturned*, Department for Business, October 2012

Hetherington, Tony, *Why are banks allowed to play judge and jury on their customers*, Mail on Sunday, 21 August 2016

Hewart, Lord, *The New Despotism*, Ernest Benn, 1929

Hewitt, Patricia, *Coroner's bill*, Times, 23 March 2009

Hilborne, Nick, *SDT questions prosecution of solicitor with almost 50 years of exemplary service*, Legal Futures, 11 January 2016

Hill, Jonathan, *Keynote speech by Commissioner at Bruegel on the Call for Evidence: 'The impact of the EU regulatory framework for financial services'*, European Commission, Brussels, 12 July 2016

Speech at the public hearing on the Call for Evidence – a review of the EU regulatory framework for financial services, Brussels, 17 May 2016

Hilton, Anthony, *Pension knowledge needs to go up a gear*, Evening Standard, 28 October 2015

Time to end this 'one size fits all' regulation, Evening Standard, 28 October 2015

HM Inspector of Constabulary, *Targeting the risk: an inspection of the efficiency and effectiveness of firearms licensing in police forces in England and Wales*, September 2015

The administration of firearms licencing, 1993

HM Treasury, *Morris review of the actuarial profession*, 16 March 2005

National Insurance Fund Account, 2015–15, HC 485, 6 September 2016

Simplification review of residual paper stamp duty on shares: progress report and call for evidence, Office of Tax Simplification, March 2017

HMRC, *Employment income manual*, undated

Notice 701/14, February 2014

Revenue and customs brief 36 (2014): VAT – liability of snowballs, 13 October 2014

Review of rewritten income tax legislation, Ipsos MORI on behalf of HM Revenue and Customs, Research Report No 104, 2011

VAT Notice 701/14: food, 15 December 2015

Your Charter, 12 January 2016

Hodges, Christopher, and Vogenauer, Stefan, *European Civil Justice Systems: findings of a major comparative study on litigation funding and costs*, Foundation for Law, Justice and Society, 2010

Hodgson, Robin, *Unshackling good neighbours: report of the Task Force established to consider how to cut red tape for small charities, voluntary organisations and social enterprises*, 40pp, Cabinet Office and Department for Business Innovation and Skills, May 2011

Hodgy, *Late night taxis*, Taxation, 20 July 2011

Hogwood, Brian, *The Growth of quangos: evidence and expectations*, in Ridley, F. F., and Wilson, David, *The quango debate*, Oxford University Press, 1995

Home Office, *An evaluation of the use and effectiveness of the Protection from Harassment Act 1997*, Home Office Research Study 203, 2000

Anti-social Behaviour, Crime and Policing Act 2014: reform of anti-social behaviour powers: statutory guidance for frontline professionals, July 2014

Interception of communications (pursuant to section 71 of the Regulation of Investigatory Powers Act 2000), November 2015

Hondius, Ewoud, *Sense and nonsense in the law*, Kluwer Deventer, 2007

Hood, Christopher, et al., *The government of risk*, Oxford University Press, 2001

Hoodless, Dame Elisabeth, *Criminal checks must not discourage volunteers from giving time*, Guardian, 7 February 2009

Hope, Christopher, *Scrap red tape of horse passports and bike bells*, Daily Telegraph, 11 August 2010

House of Commons, *Clyde inquiry: report of the inquiry into the removal of children from Orkney in February 1991*, 27 October 1992

The Code of Conduct together with the rules relating to the conduct of members, HC 1076, 15 April 2015

The Code of Conduct: the guide to the rules relating to the conduct of members, House of Commons, 18 March 2015

Equitable life and the life assurance industry: an interim report, minutes of evidence, HC 449-II, Tenth Report, Volume II – Minutes of Evidence and Appendices, HC 272-II, 30 March 2001

House of Commons Committee of Public Accounts, *Better regulation*, Eighteenth Report of Session 2016–17, HC 487, 12 October 2016

Tax avoidance: tackling marketed avoidance schemes, 29th Report of Session 2012–13, HC 788, 28 January 2013

House of Commons Constitutional Affairs Committee, *Compensation culture*, Third Report of Session 2005–06, HC 754–1, 14 February 2006

House of Commons Department of Work and Pensions Select Committee, *Inquiry into the sale of BHS and the impact on its pension scheme*, First Report of the Work and Pensions Committee and Fourth Report of the Business, Innovation and Skills Committee of Session 2016–17, HC 54 under the chairmanship of Frank Field, 25 July 2016

House of Commons Environment, Food and Rural Affairs Committee, *The outcome of the Independent Farming Regulation Task Force*, Tenth Report of Session 2010–12, HC 1266, 13 September 2011

House of Commons Home Affairs Committee, *Report on the Anti-Terrorism, Crime and Security Bill 2001*, 2001-02, HC 351, 26 February 2003

House of Commons Home Affairs Select Committee, *The work of the UK Border Agency, conclusions and recommendations*, 19 March 2013

House of Commons Information Office, *Parliamentary stages of a government bill*, Factsheet L1, August 2010

House of Commons Library, *Acts and statutory instruments: the volume of UK legislation 1950–2015*, CBP 7438, 12 April 2017

Pre-legislative scrutiny, SN/PC/2822, Standard Note, 3 June 2005

The Regulatory Reform Bill (HL): background to red tape issues, Research Paper No 01/26, 14 March 2001

House of Commons Office of the Leader of the House of Commons, *Post-legislative scrutiny - the government's approach*, Cm 7320, March 2008

House of Commons Political and Constitutional Reform Committee, *Ensuring standards in the quality of legislation*, First Report of Session 2013–14, Volume I: Report, HC 85, 20 May 2013

Ensuring standards in the quality of legislation, HC 611, session 2013–14, 25 July 2013

First Report of Session 2013–2014, HC 85, 9 May 2013

House of Commons Public Accounts Committee, *HM Revenue and Customs, dealing with the tax obligations of older people*, Eleventh Report of Session 2009–2010, HC 141, 25 February 2010

Minutes of evidence, Session 2012–13, HC 716, 12 November 2012

Proceedings under the chairmanship of Margaret Hodge, sessions 2000–2015

House of Commons Public Administration Committee, *Further report on the machinery of government*, Seventh Report of Session 2008–9

Machinery of government changes, HC672, Seventh Report of Session 2006–7

House of Commons Public Administration Select Committee, *Smaller government: shrinking the Quango state*, HC 537, Fifth Report of Session 2010–11

House of Commons Public Administration Select Committee, *Who's accountable? Relationships between Government and arm's length bodies*, First Report HC 110, 10 November 2014

House of Commons Regulatory Reform Committee, *Legislative and Regulatory Reform Bill*, HC 878 2005–6, 6 February 2006

House of Commons Select Committee on Modernisation of the House of Commons, *A reform programme for consultation*, memorandum submitted by the Leader of the House of Commons, 2001–02 HC 440, 5 September 2002

First Report, HC 190, July 1997

House of Commons Select Committee on Procedure, *The process of legislation* (1970–71) HC 538, 1971

House of Lords, *Code of conduct and guidance*, 2014

Code of Conduct for members of the House of Lords, House of Lords, 4th edn, HL Paper No 3, 27 May 2015

Debate on the Financial Services (Banking Reform) Bill 2013, Hansard HL Deb, Col 22, 8 October 2013

House of Lords Committee on Standards in Public Life, *Strengthening transparency around lobbying*, November 2013

House of Lords, Constitution Committee, *Parliament and the legislative process*, HL 173-I 2003–4, 29 October 2004

Public Bodies Bill, 6th report 2010–11, HL51, 2011

The Regulatory State: ensuring its accountability, 6th Report, 2003–4, HL 68, 2004

House of Lords Library, *Volume of legislation*, LLN 2013/008, 10 May 2013

House of Lords Select Committee on Regulators, *UK economic regulators*, 1st Report of Session 2006–7, Paper No 189, 13 November 2007

House of Lords Select Committee on the Constitution, *Delegated legislation and Parliament: a response to the Strathclyde Review*, 9th Report of Session 2015–16, HL Paper No 116, 23 March 2016

Parliament and the legislative process, Volume I, Report, 14th report of Session 2003–4, HL Paper 173-I, 29 October 2004

Parliament and the Legislative Process: the government's response, 2004–5 HL 114, 2005

The legislative process, 2017

Howard, Philip K., *Billions for red tape: focusing on the approval process for the Gateway rail tunnel project*, Common Good, 2016

Democracy for an age of distrust, The American Interest, 16 November 2016

Six presidents have failed to cut red tape. Here's how Trump could succeed, Washington Post, 13 December 2016

Two years not ten years: redesigning infrastructure approvals, Common Good, 2015

Howe, Geoffrey, *Why we must change the way tax law is made*, Financial Times, 3 July 2008

Hudson, Desmond, *Breaking the covenant of trust*, Law Society Gazette, 30 June 2014

Hughes, Nicola, *How to be an effective minister: what ministers do and how to do it well*, Institute for Government, March 2017

Hume, David, *Essays: moral, political and literary*, Fleming and Alison, 1742

Hunt, Crispin, *Speech*, Hansard, Commons, 20 January 2016

Hyde, John, *Mishcon's £1m ID fraud bill sounds alarm bells*, Law Society's Gazette, 30 January 2017

Independent Farming Regulation Task Force, *Striking a balance: reducing burdens; increasing responsibility; earning recognition. A report on better regulation in farming and food businesses*, Independent Farming Regulation Task Force, May 2011

Independent Parliamentary Standards Authority, *Annual report and accounts for 2015–16*, 19 July 2016

Information Commissioner's Office, *ICO issues eleven charities with notices of intent to fine them*, Press Release, 30 January 2017

Inland Revenue, *Letter to Society of Pension Consultants*, 10 October 2002

Inspector Gadget, *Perverting the course of justice*, Monday Books, 2009

Institute for Government, *QPD9, evidence to the Select Committee, smaller government: shrinking the Quango state*, House of Commons, Public Administration Select Committee, HC 537, 2011

Institute of Economic Affairs, *2016 Nanny State Index*, IEA and European Policy Information Centre, 30 March 2016

IPSA, *Annual accounts and report 2013/14*, 2014

Irwin, Wallace, *Owed to Volstead*, 1992, cited in Drowne, Kathleen, *Spirits of Defiance: Jazz age as literature 1920–1933*, Ohio State University Press, 2005

Iscenko, Zanna, et al., *Economics for effective regulation*, FCA Occasional Paper in Financial Regulation No 13, March 2016

Jackson, Lord Justice, ed., *Civil procedure*, Sweet & Maxwell/Thomson Reuters, 2015

Jackson, Rupert, *Review of civil litigation costs review: final report*, Stationery Office, 2010

James I, *A proclamation signifying his Majeties pleasure touching some former Proclamations; and some other things*, Proclamation, Hampton Court, 24 September 1610

Javid, Sajid, *Getting government off your back: our commitment to cutting red tape*, Speech, Department for Business, Innovation & Skills, 3 March 2016

Johnson, Paul, *A mess and getting worse: we all suffer from Britain's jumbled tax code*, [2014]24 *Prospect*

Johnson, Steve, *Are money changers now welcome?*, Financial Times, 14 July 2014

Johnston, Philip, *Bad laws: an explosive analysis of Britain's petty rules, health and safety lunacies and madcap laws*, Constable, 2010

    Danger! Daft rules under inspection, Daily Telegraph, 15 June 2010

    Give us our lives back: a frenzy of unnecessary law-making is seriously damaging our freedom and it's no surprise we're angry, Daily Telegraph, 25 May 2009

Joint Inspectors, *Safeguarding children*, Department of Health, October 2002

Jonathan Goldsmith, *The LSB and McKenzie Friends*, Law Society Gazette, 1 June 2016

Jones, Peter, *Henry III v EU law*, Spectator, 30 April 2016

Jubb, Guy, *Is there no accounting for management?*, Lecture to the Chartered Institute of Management Accountants' President's Conference, 28 October 2015

Judge, Elizabeth, *Small businesses rage at Whitehall*, Times, 6 January 2003

Judge, Igor, *Speech*, Mansion House Lord Mayor's Annual Dinner for Her Majesty's Judges, 13 July 2010

    Statutory oversight, Letter, Times, 7 May 2016

    The safest shield, Hart, 2015

Judicial College, *Judicial College prospectus*, April 2014–March 2015

    Strategy of the Judicial College 2015–2017, January 2015

Justice, *Response to Ministry of Justice Consultation on reforms proposed in the Public Bodies Bill Reforming the public bodies of the Ministry of Justice*, Justice, September 2011

Kaufman, Gerald, *How to be a minister*, Faber and Faber, 1980

Kaufman, Herbert, *Red tape: its origins, uses and abuses*, Brookings Institution Press, 2015

Kay, John, *Absurd roots of modern regulatory practice*, Financial Times, 23 December 2015

    The HBOS collapse offers a lesson on the winner's curse, Financial Times, 25 November 2015

    Lessons for the politicians from the Sage of Omaha, Financial Times, 13 January 2015

    'Trust me, I am a financial adviser' is not enough, Financial Times, 7 July 2014

    Why there is never such a thing as a single true and fair view, Financial Times, 30 July 2014

Kearney, Melissa S., et al., *Nearly 30 percent of workers in the US need a licence to perform their job: it is time to examine occupational licensing practices*, Brookings Institute, 27 January 2015

Kellaway, Lucy, *Codes of conduct are in breach of common sense*, Financial Times, 27 March 2017

Kelly, Jane, *Rules for loneliness: hospitals are putting NHS data-protection policies above simple humanity*, Spectator, 4 February 2017

Kelly, Richard, *Legislative and Regulatory Reform Bill – the Bill's progress and further reaction to the Bill*, House of Commons Library, Standard Note No SN/PC/3998, 3 November 2006

Kelly, Richard, and Everett, Michael, *Post-legislative scrutiny*, House of Commons Library, Note No SN/PC/05232, 23 May 2013

Kelly, Richard, and Keter, Vincent, *The Legislative and Regulatory Reform Bill*, House of Commons Library, Research Paper No 06/06, 6 February 2006

Kelly, Richard, and Priddy, Sarah, *Pre-legislative scrutiny under the 2015 Conservative governments*, House of Commons Library, Briefing Paper No 07757, 16 November 2016

Kenya Gazette, *Notice No 2356 119:31,* 28 February 2017
   Special Issue 1077, 14 March 2017

Kidd, Patrick, *Tangled up in tape*, Times, 31 January 2014

Kimble, Joseph, *Answering the critics of plain language*, [1994]5 *Scribes Journal of Legal Writing* 51–85

King, Anthony, and Crewe, Ivor, *The blunders of our governments*, Oneworld, 2013

King, Lesley, *The costs of rectification*, Law Society's Gazette, 6 October 2014

Kite, Melissa, *Nick Clegg abandons red tape cutting project*, Daily Telegraph, 6 November 2010

Klein, Alice, *Tesla driver dies in first fatal autonomous car crash in US*, New Scientist, 1 July 2016

Kleiner, Morris M., *Reforming occupational licensing policies*, Discussion Paper No 2015–10, The Hamilton Project, Brookings Institute, March 2015

Knight, Ken, *Facing the future: findings from the review of efficiencies and operations in fire and rescue authorities in England*, HMSO, May 2013

Kohn, Marek, *Trust: self-interest and the common good*, Oxford University Press, 2008

Kopel, David, *International perspectives on gun control*, [1995]15 *New York Law School Journal of International and Comparative Law* 247

Koseke, I., et al., *The 2013 update of the OECD product market regulation indicators: policy insights for OECD and non-OECD countries*, OECD Economics Department Working Papers, March 2015

KPMG, *Project Sun: a study of the illicit cigarette market in the European Union, Norway and Switzerland, 2014 results,* June 2015

Kuchler, Hannah, *UK regulator to tighten childcare rules*, Financial Times, 19 April 2013

Labour Party, *Report of the Joint Committee on constitutional reform*, March 1997

Laffer, Arthur, *Disaster looms on HM Roller Coaster,* Sunday Times, 13 July 2014

Laffer, Arthur, et al., *An inquiry into the nature and causes of the wealth of states*, John Wiley, 2014

LaFountain, R., Schauffler, R., Strickland, S., Holt, R., and Lewis, K., eds, *Court Statistics Project DataViewer*, 15 March 2016

Laming, William, *The protection of children in England: a progress report*, HC 330, HMSO, 12 March 2009
   The Victoria Climbie Inquiry (Lord Laming), report, Home Office, CM 5730, January 2003

Lao Tzu, *Tao Te Ching*, c500 BC

Larkin, James F., and Hughes, Paul L, *Stuart royal proclamations of King James I 1603–1625*, Oxford University Press, 1973

Laville, Sandra, *Major terrorism trial could be held in secret for the first time in UK legal history*, Guardian, 4 June 2014

Law Commission, *20th Statute Law (Repeals) report*, 3 June 2015

Annual report 2014/15, 2016

Family law: restitution of conjugal rights, Working Paper No 22, Second programme Item XIX, 17 February 1969

Firearms law: a scoping consultation paper, Law Commission Consultation Paper No 224, July 2015

Law commission consultation paper, 2010

Legal curiosities: fact or fable, March 2013

Post legislative scrutiny, Law Com 302, Cm 6945, October 2006

Post-legislative scrutiny, a consultation paper, No 178, 31 January 2006

Proposals for the reform of the law relating to maintenance and champerty, 1966

Statute law repeals at the Law Commission: a review of our work 1965 to 2010, 2010

Statute law repeals, consultation paper: general repeals, SLR 03/14, November 2014

The law commission and consolidation, June 2015

The need for post-legislative scrutiny, Article No 21, 31 January 2006

Laws, Stephen, *Giving effect to policy in legislation: how to avoid missing the point*, [2011]32(1) *Statute Law Review* 1–16

Leach, Graeme, *Hung up on red tape*, EA Magazine, Institute of Economic Affairs, 17 July 2013

Leacock, Stephen, *Frenzied fiction, No XVI, simple stories of success, or how to succeed in life*, 1918

Leake, Jonathan, *Labour admits tax blunder on deadly diesel*, Sunday Times, 15 January 2015

Lee, E., et al., *Compensation crazy: do we blame and claim too much?*, Hodder & Stoughton, 2002

Legal Ombudsman, *Consultation 2016/2017 Draft Strategy*, March 2016

Proposed ADR Scheme Rules, September 2015

Legal Services Board, *Reforming the courts' approach to McKenzie Friends*, Legal Services Board, LSB submission in response to the Judicial Executive Board consultation on the courts' approach to McKenzie Friends, 25 May 2016

Leith, Prue, *No more steak tartare? Strict food rules won't make you any safer – but they could ruin many small restaurants*, Spectator, 17 August 2013

Leverick, Fiona, and Chalmers, J., *Tracking the creation of criminal offences*, [2013] *Criminal Law Review* 543

Leveson, Brian, *An inquiry into the culture, practices and ethics of the press*, November 2012

Review of efficiency in criminal proceedings, Judiciary of England and Wales, January 2015

Liberty, *Second reading briefing on the Counter-Terrorism and Security Bill in the House of Lords*, Liberty, January 2015

Lilico, Andrew, *We need more risk and less regulation*, Daily Telegraph, 16 March 2009

Linklaters, *In defence of the rule of law: challenging the erosion of the legal certainty and fairness that business needs*, 2015.

Lister, Sam, *How one petty complaint put GP in disciplinary agony for seven years*, Times, 17 April 2009

Llewellyn, David T., Steare, Roger, Trevellick, Jessica, and Wildman, Adam, *Virtuous banking: placing ethos and purpose at the heart of finance*, ResPublica, July 2014

Local Government Association, *Reducing the burden – allowing councils to get on with their day job*, 2010

Lodge, Martin, and Wegrich, Kai, *Managing regulation: regulatory analysis, politics and policy*, Palgrave Macmillan, 2012

Long Finance, *Backing market forces: how to make voluntary standards markets work for financial services regulation*, Chartered Institute for Securities and Investment and Long Finance, November 2013

Lord Chancellor's Department, *Conditional fees: sharing the risks of litigation*, 2000

Lortie, Serge, and Bergeron, Robert C., *Legislative drafting and language in Canada*, [2007]28(2) *Statute Law Review* 83–118

Lott, John, *More guns, less crime*, 3rd edn, University of Chicago Press, 2010

Lowe, Julian, et al., *The cost of compensation culture*, UK Institute of Actuaries, December 2002

Macey, Jonathan R, *The death of corporate reputation: how integrity has been destroyed on Wall Street*, Yale University Press, 2013

Macleod, Iain, *Quoodle*, Spectator, 3 December 1965

Macneil, Ian R., *Bureaucracy and contracts of adhesion*, [1984]22(1) *Osgoode Hall Law Journal* 5

Macrory, Sir Richard, *Regulatory justice: making sanctions effective*, Final Report, Better Regulation Executive (Cabinet Office), 2006

MacShane, Denis, *It is a myth that UK laws emanate from Europe*, Financial Times, 29 November 2014

Mader, Luzius, *Evaluating the effects: a contribution to the quality of legislation*, [2001]22(2) *Statute Law Review* 119

Madison, James, *Federalist Papers 62*, 27 February 1788

Maer, Lucinda, *Quangos*, House of Commons Library, Standard Note No SN/PC/05609, 31 January 2011

Makela, Pia, et al., *Changes in volume of drinking after changes in alcohol taxes and travellers' allowances: results from a panel study,* [2008]103(2) *Addiction* 181–191

Malcolm, John, *The pressing need for mens rea reform*, The Heritage Foundation, 1 September 2015

Mallalieu, J. P. W., *Passed to you please: Britain's red tape machine at war*, Left Book Club, 1942

Mallet, Victor, *India's top judge reduced to tears over caseload,* Financial Times, 26 April 2016

Manifesto Club, *Attention please*, Manifesto Club, 2 July 2009
 Checking the checks: restoring trust, 2016

Marincolo, Sebastian, *High: insights on marijuana*, Dog Ear, 2010

Martin, David, *A new, simple, revenue neutral tax code for business*, Centre for Policy Studies, March 2016

Mason, William, *The costs of regulation and how the EEU makes them worse*, Bruges Group, 2008

Masters, Brooke, *Financial sector hit by flood of regulation,* Financial Times, 9 December 2011

Maxtone Graham, Ysenda, *Imperial ambitions,* Spectator, 9 July 2016

May, Theresa, *Speech,* Conservative Party Conference, 2011
 The shared society, Speech, Charity Commission annual meeting, Royal Society, 9 January 2017

Mayhew, Patrick, *Can legislation ever be simple, clear and certain?* [1990]7 *Statute Law Review*

McBride, Edward, *Cheer up,* Economist, 16 March 2013

McCafferty, Chris, *Speech,* Hansard, Commons, Column 522WH, 21 June 2007

McCarthy, Callum, *What does caveat emptor mean in the retail market for financial services?*, Speech, Financial Services Forum, 9 February 2006.

McCartney, Margaret, *Crossing the guideline,* FT Weekend, 25 April 2009
 Punishing individuals won't prevent mistakes happening, [2017] *British Medical Journal* 441
 Second opinion: screen test, FT.COM magazine, 7 November 2009

McCormick, Roger, *Conduct costs project*, London School of Economics and Political Science, CCP Foundation, 2013

McDermott, Tracey, *The rapidity of change*, Speech, Lord Mayor's Banquet, 22 October 2015

McGough, Roger, *I want to be the leader,* www.poemhunter.com/poem/the-leader

Meadowcroft, John, ed., *Prohibitions*, Institute of Economic Affairs, 2008

Micklethwaite, John, and Wooldridge, Adrian, *The fourth revolution*, Allen Lane, 2014

Miller, Jeffrey, *Where there's life there's lawsuits*, ECW Press, 2003

Miller, Vaughne, *EU obligations: UK implementing legislation since 1993*, House of Commons Library, SN/1A/7092, 29 January 2015

Legislating for Brexit: statutory instruments implementing EU law, House of Common Library, Briefing Paper No 7867, 16 January 2017

Millett, Timothy, *A comparison of British and French legislative drafting* [1986]7(3) *Statute Law Review* 130

Millward, David, *Motorist in parking fine blunder wins £1,000 for stress*, Daily Telegraph, 21 May 2009

Skydiver becomes first to jump 25,000 feet without a parachute, Daily Telegraph, 31 July 2016

Warning: This may be Britain's daftest sign, Daily Telegraph, 22 July 2011

Ministry of Justice, *Code of practice for victims of crime*, October 2013

Litigants-in-person in private family law cases, November 2014

Practice Guidance: McKenzie Friends (Civil and Family Courts), 12 July 2010

Reducing the number and costs of whiplash claims – a consultation on arrangements concerning whiplash injuries in England and Wales, 2012.

Reforming the courts' approach to McKenzie Friends: a consultation, Lord Chief Justice of England and Wales, February 2016

Report of the Advisory Panel on Judicial Diversity 2010, 2010.

Review of efficiency in criminal proceedings by the Rt Hon Sir Brian Leveson, Judiciary of England and Wales, January 2015

Transforming our justice system: assisted digital strategy, automatic online conviction and statutory penalty, and panel composition in tribunals: government response, February 2017.

Transforming regulatory enforcement: government response to the consultation on transforming regulatory enforcement, Department for Business Innovation and Skills, December 2011

Mont, Jo, *JP Morgan outlines compliance overhaul*, Compliance Week, 22 December 2014

Montagu-Smith, Nina, *Nightmare on Benefits Street leaves pensioners humiliated*, Daily Telegraph, 18 June 2004

Moore, David, *SRA and costs*, Letter, Law Society Gazette, 16 January 2017

Moss, Stephen, *An outsider's guide to the City of London*, Guardian, 27 May 2014

Mottram, Richard, *Civil service reform: hidden dangers*, Better Government Initiative, 2013

Mullen, Chris, *A view from the foothills*, Profile Books, 2009

Munby, James, *Address of the President of the Family Division at the annual dinner of the Family Law Bar Association in Middle Temple Hall*, 26 February 2016

Munchau, Wolfgang, *What central banks should do to deal with bubbles*, Financial Times, 14 July 2014

Munro, Elizabeth, *The Munro review of child protection: final report*, Department of Education, Cm 8062, May 2011

Murphy, Hannah, and Marriage, Madison, *Fund managers face $1M bills for research: at least 1.4m paragraphs of rules and more on the way*, Financial Times, 25 July 2017

Murphy, Joe, *Data watchdog finds itself guilty of 14 breaches of confidentiality laws*, Evening Standard, 3 January 2017

Murray, Charles, *By the people: rebuilding liberty without permission*, Crown Forum, 2015

   Regulation run amok – and how to fight back, Wall Street Journal, 8 May 2015

National Audit Office, *Better Regulation: Making good use of regulatory impact assessments, report by the Comptroller and Auditor General*, HC 329, 15 November 2001

   Controls on regulation, 28 September 2012

   Dealing with the complexity of the benefits system, (2005–06) HC 592, 18 November 2005

   Environment agency: protecting the public from waste, December 2002

   HM Revenue and Customs: Effective management of tax reliefs, 20 November 2014

   Progress on public bodies reform, HC (2013–2014), 7 February 2014

   Reducing bureaucracy for public sector frontline staff, briefing for the House of Commons Regulatory Reform Committee, December 2009

   Regulating financial services: the Financial Conduct Authority and the Prudential Regulation Authority, HC 1072, 25 March 2014

   Regulatory reform, 15 October 2010

   The Business Impact Target: cutting the cost of regulation, report by the Comptroller and Auditor General, Department for Business Innovation and Skills and Cabinet Office, HC 236, 29 June 2016

   The Pensions Regulator: progress in establishing its new regulatory approach, HC 1035, 26 October 2007

   Using alternatives to regulation to achieve policy objectives, 30 June 2014

National Center for State Courts, *State court guide to statistical reporting*, 2003

National Health Service Litigation Authority, *Fair resolution: NHS LA annual review, report and accounts 2014/15*, 2015

National Safety Council, *Injury facts 2016*, 2016

Neuberger, David, *From barretry, maintenance & champerty to litigation funding*, Harbour Litigation Funding, Gray's Inn, 8 May 2013

   General, equal and certain: law reform today and tomorrow [2012]33(3) *Statute Law Review* 323–338

   The future of the Bar, Speech, Conference of the Bar Councils of Northern Ireland and Ireland, Belfast, 20 June 2014

Neville, Sarah, and Pickard, Jim, *UK tax on sugary drinks is 'nannying' and 'impractical'*, Financial Times, 17 March 2016

New City Agenda, *Cultural change in the FCA, PRA and Bank of England: practicing what they preach,* 2016

New York Mayor's Office, *Tattooing in New York,* Press Release, 12 March 1997

Newman, Cathy, *Businesses ensnared in Labour red tape, says Howard,* Financial Times, 17 April 2004

Newson, Nicola *Proposal for government departments to cease devising new legislation for a period of time and concentrate on sound administration,* House of Lords Library, 5 August 2016

    Publishing statistics on the time spent on parliamentary proceedings on each part of an act, House of Lords, In Focus, 11 January 2017

Norman, Jesse, *Self-criticism is a habit the Bank of England has to learn,* Financial Times, 26 May 2015

Norris, Emma, and Adam, Robert, *All change: why Britain is so prone to policy reinvention, and what can be done about it,* Institute for Government, March 2017

Novak, Mikayla, *The red tape state: red tape research report No 2,* Institute of Public Affairs, Melbourne, May 2016

Nutt, David, *Drugs – without the hot air: minimising the harms of legal and illegal drugs,* UIT Cambridge, 2012

O'Keefe, Brian, *The red tape conundrum: how the wrong kind of regulation is strangling business – and what to do about it,* Fortune, 20 October 2016

O'Neill, Onora, *A question of trust, BBC Radio 4, Reith lectures 2002,* Cambridge University Press, 2002

OECD, *Alternatives to traditional regulation,* 2009

    Being an independent regulator: the governance of regulators, July 2016

    Better regulation in the United Kingdom, 2010

    Cutting red tape: Comparing administrative burdens across countries, 2007

    Cutting red tape: national strategies for administrative simplification, January 2007

    Éliminer la paperasserie, OECD framework for regulatory policy evaluation, 2014

    Governance of regulators' practices: accountability, transparency and co-ordination, the Governance of Regulators, 2016

    Guiding principles for regulatory quality and performance, 2005

    Improving the quality of government regulation, 1995

    OECD framework for regulatory policy evaluation, 2014.

    OECD regulatory policy outlook 2015, 2015

    Regulatory policies in OECD countries: from intervention to regulatory governance, 2002

    Regulatory policy in perspective, a reader's companion to the OECD regulatory policy outlook, 2015

    Regulatory policy outlook 2015, 2015

Oerton, R. T., *A lament for the Law Commission,* 1987

Ofcom, *Ofcom guidance for the public interest test for media mergers,* January 2004

Office of the Parliamentary Counsel, *Detailed guidance: good law*, 25 November 2015

Drafting guidance, August 2015

Okrent, Daniel, *Last call: the rise and fall of prohibition*, Scribner, 2011

Oliver, Dawn, ed., *The regulatory state: constitutional implications*, Oxford University Press, 2010

Omand, David, Starkey, Ken, and Adebowale, Victor, *Engagement and aspiration: reconnecting policy making with front line professionals*, Cabinet Office, London, 2009

Ontario Ministry of Economic Development, *Burden Reduction Act 2016*, Press Release, 8 June 2016

Ontario Open for Business, *Fewer burdens, greater growth*, 2014

Open University, *Society matters*, No 11, 2008–2009

Ovid, *Amores*, Elegy IV

Oxera Consulting, *The benefits of regulation – what to measure and how*, Financial Services Authority, undated

Pagan, Jill C., *Increasing length and complexity of tax legislation – avoidable or inevitable?* [1993]14(4) *Fiscal Studies* 90–105

Page, Edward, *The civil servant as legislator: law making in British Administration* [2003]81 *Public Administration* 651

Pannick, David, *A case about luggage with a great deal of judicial baggage*, Times, 15 September 2015

Parente, Giovanni, *Tax lawyers call a strike next month citing more red tape in new rules for VAT payments*, ItalyEurope 24, 15 December 2016

Parker, Christine, *The 'compliance' trap: the moral message in responsive regulatory enforcement*, [2006]40(3) *Law & Society Review* 591

Parliamentary Ombudsman, *Equitable Life: a decade of regulatory failure*, 4th Report, Session 2007–8, Presented to Parliament pursuant to Section 10(4) of the Parliamentary Commission Act 1967, HC 815i (Session 2007–2008), 16 July 2008

Fast and Fair?, 9 February 2010

Parris, Matthew, *My week*, Times, 9 April 2009

The Governor's eyebrow should trump the law, Times, 21 March 2009

Patterson, Edwin W., *The delivery of a life-insurance policy*, [1919]33 *Harvard Law Review* 198

Paxman, Jeremy, *The political animal: an anatomy*, Penguin, 2003

Pease, Ken, *Prison, community sentencing and crime*, Civitas, 26 August 2010

Pensions Regulator, *Automatic enrolment: compliance and enforcement*, Quarterly Bulletin, 1 April–30 June 2016

Compliance and enforcement policy for occupational schemes providing money purchase benefits, July 2016

Corporate pensions plan 2016–2019, April 2016

Draft monetary penalties policy and revised professional trustee description: consultation document, March 2017

Prosecution policy, June 2016

Regulatory intervention report issued under s89 of the Pensions Act 2004 in relation to the trustee of Precision Carbide Tools Limited Pension and Life Assurance Scheme, the Comshare Retirement and Death Benefits Plan and the EBC Pension Scheme, August 2016

The Pensions Regulator is successful in legal challenge, Press Release, PN16-02, 12 January 2016

TPR issues maximum chair's statement fine for professional trustees, PN16–44, Press Release, 17 August 2016

Perry, Mark J., *Government regulation vs regulation by market forces and consumer-regulators*, American Enterprise Institute, 16 January 2015

Personal Injuries Assessment Board, Press Release, 11 October 2006

Strategic plan 2006–2010, September 2006

Perspective, *The pensions industry regulatory service*, www.pendragon.co.uk

Persson, Mats, *Out of control? Measuring a decade of EU regulation*, Open Europe, 2009

Philippines Civil Service Commission, *Memorandum Circular MC No 12 s2008 and CSC Resolution No 081471*, 24 July 2008

Pickard, Jim, and Thompson, Barney, *Fierce debate over pros and cons of City's big ban*, Financial Times, 30 December 2014

Pickering, Alan, *A simpler way to better pensions: an independent report by Alan Pickering*, Department of Work and Pensions, July 2002

Piper, Doug, et al., *Deregulation Bill*, House of Commons Library, Research Paper No 14/06, 20 January 2014

Plato, *Laws*, Penguin, 2005

Plender, John, *Financial reforms will make the next failure even messier*, Financial Times, 2 September 2014

Pliatsky, Leo, *Report on non departmental bodies*, Cabinet Office, 2000

Policis, *The future of illegal lending*, Policies, 17 December 2014

Popkin, William D., *The judicial role: statutory interpretation and the pragmatic judicial partner*, Carolina Academic Press, 2013

Porter, Mark, *Pendulum has swung too far after Shipman*, Times, 17 April 2009

Power, Michael, *The audit society: rituals of verification*, Oxford University Press, 1999

Prime Minister's Office, *Review of health and safety laws*, Press Release, 14 June 2010

Prudential Regulatory Authority, *The failure of HBOS plc (HBOS): a report by the Financial Conduct Authority (FCA) and the Prudential Regulation Authority (PRA)*, November 2015

Public Health England, *Under 18 conception rate in England continues to fall*, Press Release, 24 February 2015

Queensland Parliamentary Counsel's Office, *Annual Report QPC 2008–9*, 1 October 2009

Quinn, James, *FCA reforms pay day lending, but loan sharks will still be out there*, Daily Telegraph, 5 January 2015

RadioCentre, *Response to FCA consultation*, December 2013

Rae, Maggie, *Why family lawyers must tackle the way we charge for divorce*, Times, 27 August 2015

Ralph, Alex, *Pension fund spent £600,000 on PR*, Times, 16 November 2016

Ram, Granville, *The law making process*, [1951]NS *Journal of the Society for the Public Teachers of Law* 442

Rank, Brian, *Executive physicals: bad medicine on three counts*, [2008] *New England Journal of Medicine* 1424

Rayner, Jonathan, *Dominic Grieve: Straight talker*, Interview, Law Society Gazette, 12 January 2015

Real Assurance Risk Management, *Estimation of FSA administrative burdens*, Financial Services Authority, undated

Redling, George F., *Regulatory impact analysis in Canada: successes and challenges*, Regulatory Affairs and Orders in Council Secretariat, Privy Council Office, Government of Canada, 25 April 2006

Reed, Lucy, *'Awkward squad' no longer*, Law Society Gazette, 23 June 2014

Regan, Paul, *Enacting legislation – a civil servant's perspective* [2012]34(1) *Statute Law Review* 32–28

Regulatory Policy Committee, *Reviewing regulation*, August 2010

Reid, Robert, *The judge as law maker*, [1972]12 *Journal of the Society of Public Teachers of Law* 22

Reisberg, Arad, *Corporate law in the UK after recent reforms: the good, the bad and the ugly*, in *Current Legal Problems*, Oxford University Press, 2011

Renda, Andrea, *Too good to be true? A quick assessment of the European Commission's new Better Regulation Package*, Centre for European Policy Studies, Special Report No 108, April 2015

    Assessment of the cumulative costs of EU legislation in the steel sector, study for the European Commission, 2014

    Assessment of the cumulative costs of EU legislation in the aluminium sector, study for the European Commission, 2014

Renton, David, *Renton and the need for law reform*, Statute Law Society Annual Lecture, 6 April 1978

    Renton Committee, the preparation of legislation, Cmnd 6053, May 1975

    The evolution of modern statute law and its future, Statute Law Society Lecture, 1 November 1995

Reuters, *Kenya brings in world's toughest plastic bag ban*, Guardian, 28 August 2017

Richards, Stephen, *Civil litigation: should the rules be simpler?*, para 5 et seq., Gresham Lecture, 25 June 2015

Ridley, Matt, *Human intervention ruins wildlife everywhere,* Times, 26 January 2015

  The latest emissions scandal is the draconian and health-threatening regulation being imposed on e-cigarettes, Times, 28 September 2015

Rosen, Jeremy, *Religious risk,* blog, 25 February 2016

Roskam, John, *Red tape ready for Malcolm Turnbull to cut,* Australian Financial Review, 22 September 2016

Ross, Tim, *Ex-MI5 chief [Jonathan Evans] warns spy laws 'not fit for purpose',* Daily Telegraph, 17 January 2015

Rotherham Council, *Independent inquiry into child sexual exploitation in Rotherham (1997–2013),* 2014

Rozenberg, Gabriel, *Whitehall applies EU directives at length,* Times, 19 April 2004

Rozenberg, Joshua, *Brexit in the balance: exactly what is at stake in the Supreme Court?,* Spectator, 3 December 2016

  Trial of strength: the battle between ministers and judges over who makes law, Richard Cohen Books, 1997

Ruddy, Thomas F., and Hilty, Lorenz, *Impact assessment policy learning in the European Commission,* [2007]28(2) *Environmental Impact Assessment Review* 90

Rustenber, R., *Regeldruk [Legislative burden],* Nederland Juristenblad, afl5, p231

Sachs, Jonathan, *Devarim (5772) – prophets and profits,* 23 July 2012

Sainsbury, David, *Progressive capitalism,* Biteback, 2013

Samuels, Simon, *Withering regulations will make for shrivelled banks,* Financial Times, 31 January 2015

Sanderson, Rachel, *Berlusconi faces another court case,* Financial Times, 7 February 2012

Sanger, David E., *Mr Deregulation's regulations: stuff of politics, mad cows and suspect dietary pills,* New York Times, 31 December 2003

Savill, Richard, *Teacher cleared of assaulting 'lying' pupil,* Daily Telegraph, 22 August 2003

Schumer, Charles E., and Bloomberg, Michael R., *Sustaining New York's and the US global financial services leadership,* 2007

Scotland, *Five principle of better regulation,* www.gov.scot/Topics/Business-Industry/support/better-regulation/5principlesofBetterRegulation

Scott, Johnny, *The repeal of the Hunting Act,* The Field, 1 May 2010

Scruton, Roger, *A petition against petitions,* A Point of View, BBC Radio 4, 19 June 2016

Secretary of State for Communities and Local Government, *The Lifting the Burdens Task Force,* July 2006

Seddon, John, *The Whitehall effect,* Triarchy Press, 2014

Seddon, Peter, *Law's strangest cases,* Pavilion Books, 2016

Sedley, Stephen, *Judicial activism,* London Review of Books, 2011

Seeley, Antony, *The Tax Law Rewrite: the final Bills*, House of Commons Library, SN 5239, 21 April 2010

Shaefer, Sarah, and Young, Edward, *Burdened by Brussels or the UK? Improving implementation of EU directives*, Report for the Foreign Policy Centre, August 2006

Shakespeare, William, *Merchant of Venice*, IV.i, 211–214

Sherifi, James, *Those GP blues*, Letter, Times, 16 August 2014

Sherman, Matthew, *A short history of financial deregulation in the United States*, Centre for Economic and Policy Research, July 2009

Shoesmith, Sharon, *Learning from Baby P*, Jessica Kingsley, 2016

Shoffman, Marc, *Pensioner faces £45,000 bill after FAS error*, FT Adviser, 27 February 2013

    Sir Hector's trust late filing return, FT Adviser, 27 February 2013

Shrader-Frechette, Kirstin, *Risk and rationality*, University of California Press, 1991

Silverglate, Harvey, *Three felonies a day*, Encounter Books, 2011

Simpson, Aislinn, *Eco-warrior evicted from cave dwelling without fire exit*, Daily Telegraph, 17 June 2010

Simson Caird, Jack, Hazell, Robert, and Oliver, Dawn, *The constitutional standards of the House of Lords Select Committee on the Constitution*, The Constitution Society, January 2014

Sinclair, Upton, *The jungle*, Doubleday, 1906

Singleton, Roger, *Drawing the line: a report on the Government's vesting and barring scheme*, Home Office, December 2009

    Keeping our schools safe: review of safeguarding arrangements in independent schools, non-maintained special schools and boarding schools in England, 2009

Slack, James, *Enemies of the people: fury over 'out of touch' judges who have 'declared war on democracy' by defying 17.4m Brexit voters and who could trigger constitutional crisis*, Daily Mail, 3 November 2016

Slivinski, Stephen, *Bootstraps tangles in red tape: how occupational licensing hinders low-income entrepreneurship*, Goldwater Institute, 2015

Small Business Service, *Enforcement concordat: good practice guide for England and Wales*, Department of Trade and Industry, June 2003

Smit, Rebecca, *Tesco to end sales of 5p carrier bags*, Guardian, 7 August 2017

Smith, Clarence, *Legislative drafting: English and Continental* [1980] Statute Law Review 14

Smith, Janet, *Shipman: the final report*, Department of Health, 27 January 2005

Smith, Jaqui, *How not to do it*, BBC Radio 4, Analysis, 6 February 2016

Smith, Lizzie, *After 400 years, stepladders are banned from Oxford's library*, Daily Mail, 9 May 2009

Smith, Roy, *Attacking Wall Street with a blunt instrument*, Financial Times, 7 January 2003

Smyth, Michael, *Foreword*, in Dawn Oliver et al., *The regulatory state: constitutional implications*, Oxford University Press, 2010

Snoddy, Raymond, *Media mergers face red-tape hurdle*, Times, 6 January 2004

Snopes, *Of cabbages and kings*, 9 April 2012

Snowdon, Christopher, *Drinking, fast and slow: ten years of the licensing act*, Institute of Economic Affairs, 20 May 2015

    Plain confectionery packaging a heavy-handed response to health concerns, Confectionery News, 21 July 2016

    The art of suppression: pleasure, panic and prohibition since 1800, Little Dice, 2012

    The new ban on 'legal highs' is unworkable: the government doesn't even know what it's banning, Spectator, 27 May 2015

Society of Pension Consultants, *Letter to Inland Revenue*, 5 December 2002

Solicitors Regulation Authority, *Consultation: looking to the future – flexibility and public protection*, June 2016

    Consultation: looking to the future: SRA accounts rules review, June 2016

Soltes, Eugene, *Why they do it: inside the mind of the white collar criminal*, PublicAffairs, 27 October 2016

Spinoza, Baruch, *Theologico-political treatise* (1670), Dover Philosophical Classics, 2013

Stafford, Philip, *Markets break out in sweat as new rules loom*, Financial Times, 5 July 2017

Starmer, Keir, *Policy for prosecutors in respect of cases of encouraging or assisting suicide*, Crown Prosecution Service, 25 February 2010, updated October 2014

Stern, Michael, *Balancing the ledger*, Letter, Economist, 21 January 2012

Stewart, Andrew, *Debate on co-operative housing*, Speech, HC Deb, col 145WH, 11 July 2012

Steyn, Johan, *Dynamic interpretation amidst an orgy of statutes*, Brian Dickson Memorial Lecture, Ottawa, 2 October 2003, [2003]35(2) *Ottawa Law Review* 163

    The intractable problem of the interpretation of legal texts, [2003]25 *Sydney Law Review* 1

Strathclyde, Thomas, *Secondary legislation and the Primacy of the House of Commons*, HMSO, 2015, Cm 9177, December 2015

Street, Amy, *Judicial review and the rule of law: who is in control?*, Constitution Society, 2013

Sugarman, Stephen D., *United States tort reform wars*, University of California, August 2002

Summers, Deborah, *Personal details of every child in UK lost by Revenue and Customs*, Guardian, 20 November 2007

Sumption, Jonathan, *Judicial and political decision-making: the uncertain boundary*, FA Mann Lecture, 2011

Sunstein, Carl, *Financial regulation and cost benefit analysis*, Yale Law Journal Forum, 2015

Simpler: the future of government, Simon & Schuster, 2013

Supreme Court, *Supreme Court selection process launched*, Press Release, Supreme Court, 16 February 2017

Surtees, Joshua, and Churchill, David, *The box junction outside a fire station in East London that rakes in almost £1m each year*, Evening Standard, 19 January 2015

Susskind, Richard, *Evidence: the legislative process*, House of Lords, Select Committee on the Constitution, 11 January 2017

Sutherland, Rory, *How good laws change our ways*, Spectator, 19 July 2014

Swift, Jonathan, *A critical essay upon the faculties of the mind*, 1707

Sylvester, Rachel, *This legal highs law is mind-bendingly useless*, Times, 19 April 2016

Tanner, Michael D., *Too many laws, too much law*, Cato Institute, 2 March 2016

Tate, John, and Clark, Greg, *Reversing the drivers of regulation: the European Union*, Conservative Research Department, Policy Unit, August 2004

Taxpayers Alliance, *ACA to YJB: a guide to the UK's semi-autonomous public bodies 2007–08*, 2010

Taylor, Adam, *Russian man who got bank to sign homemade credit card contract now suing them for not following terms*, Business Insider, 8 August 2013

Taylor, Diane, *No 10 faces legal challenge over ministerial code rewrite*, Guardian, 11 February 2016

Tetlow, Gemma, *Bank of England deputy governor admits code of conduct breach*, Financial Times, 7 March 2017

Tett, Gillian, *Regulatory revenge risks scaring investors away*, Financial Times, 29 August 2014

Thaler, Richard H., and Sunstein, Cass R., *Nudge: improving decisions about health, wealth, and happiness*, 2008

Thirlwall, T., *The works, moral and religious, of Sir Matthew Hale, Knt*, Vol I, 1805

Thomas, John, *The centrality of justice: its contribution to society and its delivery*, Lord Williams of Mostyn Memorial Lecture, 10 November 2015

The legacy of Magna Carta: justice in the 21st century, Speech, Legal Research Foundation, 25 September 2015

Thorpe, Vanessa, *George Osborne told to choose whether to be MP or Standard editor*, Guardian, 20 March 2017

Thring, Henry, *Simplification of the law: practical suggestions*, R. J. Bush, 1875

Tillinghast-Towers Perrin, *US Tort costs 2000: trends and findings on the US Tort system*, 2002

Times, *Say no to state regulation of the press*, 23 October 2016
  We are all suspects in the new inquisition's eyes, 1 May 2009
Timmins, Nicholas, *Contracting-out*, The Independent, 18 December 1990
  Principal health service regulators agree 'inspection concordat', Financial Times, 23 June 2004
Todd, K., *Traffic control: an exercise in self-defeat*, [2004](Fall) *Regulation* 10–12
Tomlinson, Hugh, *Woman given royal pardon for driving may still be flogged*, Times, 15 November 2011
Toobin, Jeffrey, *The Supreme Court after Scalia*, New Yorker, 3 October 2016
Topping, Alexandra, *Muirfield golf club to allow women to join for the first time*, Guardian, 14 March 2017
Torriti, Jacopo, and Lofstedt, Ragnar, *The first five years of the EU Impact Assessment system: a risk economics perspective on gaps between rationale and practice* [2012]15(2) *Journal of Risk Research* 169
Travis, Alan, *Incense in churches safe from new substances bill, say ministers*, Guardian, 2 October 2015
Treanor, Jill, *JP Morgan Chase hires 3,000 new staff in its compliance department*, Guardian, 17 September 2013
Treasury Solicitor, *Judge over your shoulder*, 2006
Tridimas, T., *Liability for breach of community law: growing up and mellowing down?*, [2001]38 *Common Market Law Review* 301
Truss, Elizabeth, *More great childcare*, Speech, Policy Exchange, 29 January 2013
Turnbull-Hall, Caroline, and Thomas, Richard, *Reviewing the length of the UK tax code*, Tax Journal, 1 February 2012
Turner, Ross, *Acts and statutory instruments: the volume of UK legislation 1950 to 2015*, House of Commons Library, Briefing Paper No CBP 7438, 21 December 2015
UK Parliament, *Parliamentary history and review*, Longmans, 1826
University College London, *Code of constitutional standards*, Constitution Unit, 8 January 2014
US Chamber, Institute for Legal Reform, *International comparisons of litigation costs*, June 2013
US Government, *Improving regulation and regulatory review*, Executive Order 13563, Federal Register Vol 76/14, 18 January 2011
  2014 draft report to Congress on the benefits and costs of federal regulation and unfunded mandates on state, local and tribal entities, OMB, 2014
  Cumulative effect of regulations, OIRA, 20 March 2012
  Executive Order 12866, 4 October 1993
  Executive Order 13563, 18 January 2011
  Executive Order 13579, regulation and independent regulatory agencies, Federal Register 76/135, 14 July 2011

Executive Order 13610, identifying and reducing regulatory burdens, Federal Register 77/93, 10 May 2012

Executive Order 13771, presidential executive order on reducing regulation and controlling regulatory costs, 30 January 2017

US Nuclear Regulatory Commission, *NRC at a glance*, 2017

van Gestel, Rob, and Menting, Marie-Claire, *Ex ante evaluation and alternatives to legislation: going Dutch?*, [2011]32(3) *Statute Law Review* 209–226

Vander Weyer, Martin, *All those boardroom codes still can't catch rogues and incompetents*, Spectator, 12 September 2015

Vanderbilt, Tom, *Traffic: why we drive the way we do (and what it says about us)*, Allen Lane, 2008

Verheugen, Guntherm, *The EU has no vision of where we are heading*, Spiegel, 9 February 2010

Verkaik, Robert, *British lawyers bask in Bermuda heat as feuding family spends £368,000 a week on legal battle*, Independent, 5 January 2000

Vernadaki, Zampia, *Civil procedure harmonization in the EU: unravelling the policy considerations*, [2013]9(2) *Journal of Contemporary European Research* 298

Vigen, Tyler, *Spurious correlations*, Hachette, 2015

Vince, Ian, *The little black book of red tape: great British bureaucracy*, Orion, 2008

Voermans, Wim, et al., *Codification and consolidation in the European Union: a means to untie red tape*, [2008]29(2) *Statute Law Review* 65–81

Vollmer, Patrick, and Badger, Lara, *Volume of legislation*, House of Lords Library Note, LLN 2013/008, 10 May 2013

Vowermans, Wim, *Styles of legislation and their effects*, [2011]32(1) *Statute Law Review* 38–53

Wade & Forsyth, *Administrative law*, 11th edn, 2014

Wakefield, J., *What is the nature of the non-contractual liability claim?*, in J. Wakefield (ed), *Judicial protection through the use of Article 288(2)*, Kluwer Law International, 2002

Walker, Clive, *The anti-terrorism legislation*, Oxford University Press, 2002

Walker, Kirsty, *End of the road for signs clutter*, Daily Mail, 14 October 2011

Walsh, Brian W., and Joslyn, Tiffany M., *Without intent: how Congress is eroding the criminal intent requirement in federal law*, Heritage Foundation Special Report No 77, May 5 2010

Ward, Philip, *Press regulation – the debate*, House of Commons Library, Standard Note SN/HA/6357, 20 June 2012

Waters, Cara, *FSA fines Zurich £2.2m for lost customer details*, FT Adviser, 24 August 2010

Watson-Brown, Anthony, *Does it work? Reviewing legislative drafts before others have a chance*, [2008]29(1) *Statute Law Review* 45–52

In search of plain English – the holy grail or mythical Excalibur of legislative drafting, [2011]33(1) *Statute Law Review* 7–23

Webb, Justin, *Welcome to America, land of the regulated,* Times, 29 August 2017

Webber, Alan, *Building regulation in the land of Israel in the Talmudic period,* [1996]27(3) *Journal for the Study of Judaism* 263–288

Webster, Ben, *Limit on garage size reversed to bring drivers back off the streets,* Times, 17 March 2009

West, Lawrence, *Have the Woolf reforms worked?,* Times, 9 April 2009.

White, Matthew, *Climbing accidents – the duty and standard of care,* St John's Chambers, September 2011

White House, *Occupational licensing: a framework for policymakers, a report prepared by the Department of the Treasury Office of Economic Policy, the Council of Economic Advisers and the Department of Labor,* July 2015

Whitehouse, Edward, *The tax treatment of funded pensions,* OECD, 1999

Wigton, David, *Tick the box marked 'personal responsibility',* Times, 2 January 2012

Winnett, Robert, and Rayner, Gordon, *No expenses spared,* Bantam, 2009

Wolfenden, John, *Report of the Departmental Committee on Homosexual Offences and Prostitution,* Committee on Homosexual Offences and Prostitution, HMSO, Cm 247, 1957

Wolman, Clive, *Securities class actions,* [2006]11(4) *Pensions* 254

Wood, Murakami, *A very British tendency must not be ruled by public outcry,* Times, 17 April 2009

Woodcock, Andrew, *Child Support Agency chief quits as criticism mounts,* Independent, 17 November 2004

Woolf, Harry, *The Woolf report: access to justice,* 1996

Woollcombe-Clarke, Michael, *The law of legal costs and why the price of justice is so disproportionately expensive,* Legal Cheek, 21 November 2016

World Bank, *Doing business 2014: understanding regulations for small and medium-size enterprises: comparing business regulations for domestic firms in 189 economics,* 11th edn, 2013

Wright, Tony, *Doing politics differently,* [2009]80(3) *The Political Quarterly* 319

Xanthaki, Helen, *European Union Legislative quality after the Lisbon Treaty: the challenges of smart regulation,* [2014]35(1) *Statute Law Review* 66–80

The problem of quality in EU legislation: what on earth is really wrong?, [2001] *CML Review* 651–676

Young, David, *Common sense, common safety,* Cabinet Office, October 2010

Growing your business: a report on growing micro businesses, May 2013

Zander, Michael, *The law-making process,* 6th edn, Cambridge University Press, 2004

Zieja, Joe, *I love legal disclaimers,* www.youtube.com/watch?v=VSiuxEXV6Nc

Zuckerman, A. A. S., *Justice in crisis: comparative dimensions of civil procedure*, in S. Chiarloni, P. Gottwald, and A. A. S. Zuckerman (eds), *Civil justice in crisis*, Oxford University Press, 1999

Websites

http://cutting-red-tape.cabinetoffice.gov.uk/childcare
http://ec.europa.eu/governance/better_regulation/simplification_en.htm
http://ec.europa.eu/smart-regulation/docs/refit_brochure_en.pdf
http://ec.europa.eu/smart-regulation/impact/iab/iab_en.htm
http://ec.europa.eu/transparencyregister/public/homePage.do
http://nannystateindex.org
http://pressrecognitionpanel.org.uk (Press Recognition Panel)
http://regdata.org
http://stephenfollows.com (film-tax-breaks-by-the-numbers)
http://tosdr.org/about.html
www.bandolier.org.uk (transport risks)
www.betterregwatch.eu
www.bis.gov.uk/policies/better-regulation/policy/regulatory-policy-committee
www.bizzymumsblog.com/2012/03/dear-mr-cameron-open-letter-regarding
.html
www.cabinetoffice.gov.uk/regulation/ria/ria_guidance/post_implementaion_
review.asp
www.commongood.org
www.courtstatistics.org
www.dignitas.ch
www.drugscience.org.uk/ (Independent Scientific Committee on Drugs)
www.enkleregler.dk
www.FrancesBennion.com/2009/011
www.gov.uk/government/consultations/pension-scams/pensions-scams-
consultation
www.handbook.fca.org.uk
www.hse.gov.uk/myth
www.innovatingjustice.com (European Academy for Law and Legislation)
www.int-comp.org
www.ipso.co.uk/ (Independent Press Standards Organisation)
www.italiasemplice.gov.it
www.legislation.gov.uk
www.nannystate.com
www.nice.org.uk/guidance
www.parlament.ch/e/organe-mitglieder/bundesversammlung/Pages/default.aspx
www.Parliamentarystandards.org.uk

www.pedbikeinfo.org/data/factsheet_crash.cfm
www.pendragon.co.uk
www.portmangroup.org.uk
www.thepensionsregulator.gov.uk/pension-scams.aspx
www.tylervigen.com
www.unodc.org (United Nations, Office on Drugs and Crime)
www.youtube.com/watch?v=BkIT7Qy071s
www.youtube.com/watch?v=fnm7mKp6JTE&feature=youtu.be (simplify.gov.uk)
www.youtube.com/watch?v=nYCRujUspA8 (Smack the Pony Woman Driver)
www.z2k.org (Zacchaeus 2000 Trust)
http://yourfreedom.hmg.gov.uk

INDEX

accessibility of law, proposals for
improvement of, 158–163
accountability, in legislation and
regulation, 416–419
Acte for Poysonyng (1530), 146–147
adjudicative procedures, fairness in,
160–161
administrative bodies, growth of,
177n20
administrative discretion, application
of law vs., 160–161
administrative failure, law as solution
to, 127–128
advertising, of legal services, 253
Advisory Council on the Misuse of
Drugs, 112–113
Advisory NDPBs, 180
after the event insurance, 251–252
*Airedale (Lord), 160–161
alcohol
failure of regulation of, 111–112
regulation of, 430–432
solutions to problems with,
113–115
alternative dispute resolution, 224–225
for consumers, 273–275
amendments to legislation
posting of, 145–147
proliferation of, 143
Anderson, Sarah, 293
Anderson Report (2009), 293
Anglo-Saxon rule making
characteristics of, 10–11
tort law and, 81–82
Anti-Social Behaviour, Crime, and
Policing Act 2014, 69–70
application of law

administrative discretion vs.,
160–161
equality in, 160–161
Arculus, David, 52–55, 291–292,
325–327
Aronson, Graham, 268–269
assisted suicide, regulation of, 51
Asylum and Nationality Act 2006,
145–146
Australia, deregulation in, 335–336
Autism Act 2010, 50–51
aviation, regulation of, 183–184

Baby P case, 99–103, 363–366, 416–419
bad law
consequences of, 6–7
solutions for, 147–153
bailiffs, unconstrained behavior of,
12–13
balance of arguments, in legislative
debate, 416–419
Ball, Rita, 195–196
Balls, Ed, 363–366
Banking (Special Provisions) Act 2003,
154–158
banking industry
money-laundering penalties for,
66–68
penalties and absence of law in,
95–97
Bank of England, governance analysis
of, 191–192
Barber, Michael (Sir), 7–8n12, 72n23
Barclays Bank, 43n91
Baroness Scotland, 145–146
Barras, Fred, 91–92
barretry, litigation, 250–251